PSALMS FOR PREACHING
AND WORSHIP

PSALMS FOR PREACHING AND WORSHIP

A Lectionary Commentary

Edited by

Roger E. Van Harn & Brent A. Strawn

WILLIAM B. EERDMANS PUBLISHING COMPANY

GRAND RAPIDS, MICHIGAN / CAMBRIDGE, U.K.

© 2009 William B. Eerdmans Publishing Company
All rights reserved

Published 2009 by
Wm. B. Eerdmans Publishing Co.
2140 Oak Industrial Drive N.E., Grand Rapids, Michigan 49505 /
P.O. Box 163, Cambridge CB3 9PU U.K.

Printed in the United States of America

15 14 13 12 11 10 09   7 6 5 4 3 2 1

Library of Congress Cataloging-in-Publication Data

Psalms for preaching and worship: a lectionary commentary /
    edited by Roger E. Van Harn & Brent A. Strawn.
        p.   cm.
    Includes bibliographical references.
    ISBN 978-0-8028-6321-8 (pbk.: alk. paper)
    1. Bible. O.T. Psalms — Criticism, interpretation, etc.
    2. Common lectionary (1992)
    I. Van Harn, Roger, 1932-   II. Strawn, Brent A.

    BS1430.52.P728 2009
    264'.34 — dc22

                                        2008048958

www.eerdmans.com

Contents

Contents

Contents

Contents

Contents

Contents

Foreword

The book of Psalms constitutes a resource for faith among us that, when we attend to it faithfully, always yields more of grace and truth. It is curious that we regard the Psalter with such familiarity and yet most of it remains unused among us. In the Old Testament itself, it is clear that the Psalter is completely embedded in Israel's larger narrative construal of faith, so that its songs and prayers are connected to the Torah and to the "historical" narratives. It is possible, then, that the Psalter was an initial articulation of Israel's memory, cast from the first as prayer and poem, from which the other narratives subsequently emerged. In any case, the Psalter is a reliable guide for Israel's faith, offered as that faith inescapably must be: in poetic, imaginative form. This is so because the elusiveness of Israel's God requires an elusive, imaginative articulation — a voicing that precludes tight propositional reasoning or thin historical analysis. The Psalter gives us covenantal faith in all its thickness.

For that reason, it is both wonder and scandal that the modern church in the West has largely lost touch with the Psalter. For the most part, appeal has been made to only a half-dozen or so psalms, and even now, in a mode of some recovery, the lectionary still lacks a full presentation. Moreover, even when there is fuller utilization of the Psalter, there is most often "nice" music such that it is difficult to pay attention to the "down and dirty" texture of these prayers. The reason for such neglect, articulated by Claus Westermann, is related to the very reason that they must be recovered among us, namely, that they are *direct speech* about a *realistic faith* that traffics in the *extremities of human life and human experi-*

ence.[1] That is, the Psalms are rhetorically venturesome and theologically dangerous, more so than the established church has been able to entertain. The extremity of the Psalter's rhetoric is, on the one hand, the fullbodied practice of doxology, a *public abandonment* of the selves of faith to the wonder of God. Such abandonment in faith through worship is unwelcome in an established church where controlled theology is reflected in a stable liturgy that yields a controlling morality. On the other hand, the poetry of lament and protest and complaint constitutes a practice of the *public claiming* of self against the reality of God, an insistence on certain rights, expectations, and demands, even in the presence of God. Such claiming in faith through worship is unwelcome in a stable theology where total deference to God is the order of the day. Thus in both praise and prayer, the Psalms practice a dialogic mode of faith that subverts our more settled arrangements. They do so, moreover, in a kind of "realism" that trusts that God can be directly and fully addressed and called to engagement.

The recovery of the Psalter is thus an important enterprise in a society (and in a church) that has reduced human interaction to one-dimensional *techno-speech* or to *narcissistic psychobabble*. This recovery is urgent because such technical and psychological rhetorics are self-contained and lack a reference outside one's self, a reference to another to whom appeal can be made and toward whom love can be expressed. Thus I am inclined to think that the recovery of the Psalter in the public life of the church is an enormously important enterprise, for it offers a public practice that is inherently subversive of the settled world of consumer capitalism and the settled life of much of the church. This means, of course, that it will not do to treat the Psalter simply as "nice" or, worse yet, to pick out a few lines here and there to be set to nice music. Expositors and church musicians must conspire together to work at articulating the Psalms in a way that makes available their compelling subversiveness because that is what is found there. The present volume is a move in this important direction.

It is a truism to say that the Psalms are for *instruction and worship.* The theme of instruction is especially evident in the torah psalms. But in fact, all the Psalms, in a variety of voices, instruct an alternative world. Only . . . rather than "instruct," I prefer to say "construct," as in "the social

---

1. See Claus Westermann, *Praise and Lament in the Psalms,* trans. Keith R. Crim and Richard N. Soulen (Atlanta: John Knox, 1981).

construction of reality." The educational task of the Psalter is to nurture and induct us and our young into a world of faith that stands in deep tension with the practices of our culture.

Beyond instruction, the use of the Psalms in worship and liturgy is for the *performance* of the Psalms, that is, to reenact in contemporary settings the ancient engagements of faith that are possible only in and through text. As Sigmund Mowinckel saw long ago, the Psalms are "effective," and many contemporary worshipers attest to the new reality that is mediated by the regular practice of this rhetoric.[2] As the young are inducted into this "strange new world," so the adult community is invited to practice the dialogue of extreme abandonment and extreme claim, both parts of which the world resists.

I believe, finally, that the texts will not be available for *instruction-construction* and effective *performance* unless they are carefully exposited in preaching. The way to do that, I believe, is indicated by the belated superscriptions that attach several of the psalms to the life of David. That is, the superscriptions make generic speech narratively particular. And that is the wonder of the Psalms: they are *generic* in a way that invites *particularity* in use. They are, in fact, narratives of faith that emerged in particular settings and can be appropriated among us in new particular practices. Thus, narratively the Psalms are about the life and faith of David; alternatively, in the horizon of Dietrich Bonhoeffer (to cite one example), they are about the life and faith and person of Jesus. Or, alternatively, in the practice of preaching, they line out the life and faith of particular congregations and particular individual persons who in their practice must face, with much recurrence, surprising gifts that elate and stunning reversals that debilitate. The language of the Psalter is designed exactly for such elation and debilitation to be taken to God, blessed and broken, and then given back to us as a blessing.

The teacher, the liturgist, and the preacher must insist that this is poetry . . . always poetry! I fear greatly the ideological divisions arising in the church now with such venom. The wonder of the Psalter in this regard is its poetic resilience, so that the truth of praise and prayer in its poetic form undercuts our ideological propensities in a way that tells of the human condition and that pertains to all human selves in all human communities. The Psalter is a place where "Red" and "Blue" Christians

---

2. Sigmund Mowinckel, *The Psalms in Israel's Worship*, 2 vols. in 1 (reprint, Grand Rapids: Eerdmans, 2004).

may stand together without any moral advantage for anyone. As we stand together toward God's holiness without any moral advantage, the tight grip of the closed dominant world begins to lessen, and we are, here and there, set free for a life filled with compassion, wonder, generosity, and buoyancy. The Psalms *in construction* and *performance* do nothing less than make us human and keep us human in a particular way. We may ponder for a long time why the church has feared and avoided this subversive, transformative, revolutionary offer of gospel faith. The present volume, along with others, may be a harbinger that a change is in the air.

WALTER BRUEGGEMANN
Columbia Theological Seminary
Advent 2008

Preface

When *The Lectionary Commentary: Theological Exegesis for Sunday's Texts* was published, it included exegetical essays on the three readings for each Sunday and for Christmas Day, Epiphany, and Ascension Day for Years A, B, and C of the Revised Common Lectionary. The responsorial Psalms and Canticles were not included.

"Why not?" readers asked. As the frequency of that question increased, our initial response to it became less and less convincing: "The Psalms were not included because they are meant to be used as responses to the first readings; therefore, they are more appropriately read, sung, or prayed in the liturgy." For some preachers and liturgists, however, the innocuous "not included" in our response was a euphemism for the harsher reality: the Psalms were *excluded* from consideration as preaching texts.

The need to correct this *exclusion* and *misread intention* can no longer be dodged. As a completion to *The Lectionary Commentary,* this volume includes exegetical essays on all the responsorial Psalms and Canticles in the three-year cycle. Those who are called to preach regularly for gathered congregations know that the stimulus for starting a sermon can come from almost anywhere in life — a news clip, a casual remark, a billboard, seeing children at play, a tragic event, a comical sight, a good book or film. Almost any human experience can "jump-start" the process that sends us to the biblical texts to prepare a faithful sermon for next Sunday. However, it is the conviction behind these essays that exegesis itself can provide the initial stimulus for preaching the good news of God in Jesus Christ.

Part I begins with an introduction by Brent A. Strawn that overviews the types, functions, and poetics for interpreting and preaching the Psalms. Preachers who are new to the task, or to the Psalter, may want to keep this introduction within reach until they are at home in the language and spirit of the Psalms. Following this are the 103 exegetical essays themselves.

The shadow of death fell across the list of contributors with the passing of Gerald H. Wilson on November 11, 2005. His untimely death came after he had submitted exegetical essays on Psalms 15 and 26 and before he could fulfill his purpose to submit two others. He was serving as professor of Old Testament and Biblical Hebrew at Azusa Pacific University in Azusa, California. His exegetical skill served his testimony of trust in the closing words of his essay on Psalm 26, "The center of such blessings [26:12] is the worshiping community of faith where together we look forward with expectant 'hope of sharing the glory of God' (Rom. 5:2)."

The assumption behind excluding the Psalms from consideration as preaching texts was correct but misapplied: *the Psalms are to be read or sung in the liturgy.* Preachers and worship leaders need not choose between preaching from the Psalms and praying the Psalms. Reading, chanting, or singing the psalm for the day need not preclude its use as a preaching text or vice versa. Moreover, exegetical insight into the psalm or canticle may facilitate its proper and optimal use, even and especially if it is not the text chosen for the homily. To encourage liturgical use of the Psalms, John Witvliet's part II, "Worship with the Psalms," will stimulate the imagination. The annotated bibliography of resources for worship will keep worship planners and leaders busy practicing the possibilities. Worship committees, conferences, and classrooms will find ecumenical vision, a biblical insight, and contemporary relevance for their purposes.

The editors and authors offer *Psalms for Preaching and Worship: A Lectionary Commentary* with the prayer that we may be "filled with the Spirit, as you sing psalms and hymns and spiritual songs among yourselves, singing and making melody to the Lord in your hearts, giving thanks to God the Father at all times and for everything in the name of our Lord Jesus Christ" (Eph 5:18b-20).

ROGER E. VAN HARN

Abbreviations

AB	Anchor Bible
ABD	*Anchor Bible Dictionary,* ed. D. N. Freedman, 6 vols. (New York, 1992)
ABRL	Anchor Bible Reference Library
ACW	Ancient Christian Writers
BDB	Brown, Driver, and Briggs, *A Hebrew and English Lexicon of the Old Testament* (Oxford, 1907)
BRev	*Bible Review*
BZAW	Beihefte zur Zeitschrift für die alttestamentliche Wissenschaft
CBQ	*Catholic Biblical Quarterly*
CBQMS	Catholic Biblical Quarterly Monograph Series
ChrLit	*Christianity and Literature*
CTJ	*Calvin Theological Journal*
CurTM	*Currents in Theology and Mission*
ECC	Eerdmans Critical Commentary
ErIsr	*Eretz-Israel*
ESV	English Standard Version
FOTL	Forms of the Old Testament Literature
HALOT	*The Hebrew and Aramaic Lexicon of the Old Testament,* by L. Koehler, W. Baumgartner, and J. J. Stamm (Leiden, 1994-99)
HBC	*Harper's Bible Commentary,* ed. James L. Mays (New York, 1988)
HTR	*Harvard Theological Review*
ICC	International Critical Commentary
Int	*Interpretation*
ITC	International Theological Commentary
JBL	*Journal of Biblical Literature*
JNES	*Journal of Near Eastern Studies*
JPS	Jewish Publication Society Version of the Old Testament (1917)

Abbreviations

JSOT	*Journal for the Study of the Old Testament*
JSOTSup	Journal for the Study of the Old Testament: Supplement Series
KJV	King James Version
LCC	Library of Christian Classics
LXX	Septuagint
MT	Masoretic Text
NAB	New American Bible
NASB	New American Standard Bible
NCB	New Century Bible
NEB	New English Bible
NIB	*New Interpreter's Bible,* ed. L. E. Keck et al. (Nashville, 1998)
NICOT	New International Commentary on the Old Testament
NIDB	*New International Dictionary of the Bible*
NIV	New International Version
NIVAC	NIV Application Commentary
NJPS	New Jewish Publication Society translation (1988)
NRSV	New Revised Standard Version
OBT	Overtures to Biblical Theology
OTL	Old Testament Library
ProEccl	*Pro Ecclesia*
REB	Revised English Bible
RSV	Revised Standard Version
SBLDS	Society of Biblical Literature Dissertation Series
SBLSymS	Society of Biblical Literature Symposium Series
SBT	Studies in Biblical Theology
TDOT	*Theological Dictionary of the Old Testament,* ed. G. J. Botterweck and H. Ringgren, 8 vols. (Grand Rapids, 1974-)
TEV	Today's English Version
ThTo	*Theology Today*
VT	*Vetus Testamentum*
WBC	Word Biblical Commentary
ZAW	*Zeitschrift für die alttestamentliche Wissenschaft*

Illustrations

Psalms and Their Types

Psalm	Type
1	torah (wisdom) psalm
2	royal psalm
3	individual lament
4	individual lament (song of trust?)
5	individual lament
6	individual lament (penitential psalm)
7	individual lament
8	hymn
9–10	individual lament? (acrostic)
11	song of trust
12	community lament
13	individual lament
14 (= Ps 53)	individual lament
15	liturgy for cultic admission
16	song of trust
17	individual lament
18 (= 2 Sam 22)	individual song of thanksgiving (royal)

This list is adapted from Bernhard W. Anderson with Steven Bishop, *Out of the Depths: The Psalms Speak for Us Today,* 3rd ed. (Louisville: Westminster John Knox, 2000), 219-24. Different scholars offer different categories and terminology and often disagree regarding the genre of a psalm; hence, one will want to compare this list with other lists and genre designations in the standard Psalms commentaries. Special note should be taken of Erhard Gerstenberger's volumes (*Psalms, Part I* [Grand Rapids: Eerdmans, 1988] and *Psalms, Part II* [Grand Rapids: Eerdmans, 2001]) and of the two-volume commentary by Hans-Joachim Kraus (*Psalms 1–59* and *Psalms 60–150,* both published in 1993 by Fortress).

19:1-6	hymn
19:7-14	torah (wisdom) psalm
20	royal psalm
21	royal psalm (thanksgiving)
22	individual lament
23	song of trust
24	temple entrance liturgy
25	individual lament (acrostic)
26	individual lament
27:1-6	song of trust
27:7-14	individual lament
28	individual lament
29	hymn
30	individual song of thanksgiving
31	individual lament
32	individual song of thanksgiving
33	hymn
34	individual song of thanksgiving (acrostic)
35	individual lament
36	mixed type
37	wisdom psalm (acrostic)
38	individual lament (penitential)
39	individual lament
40:1-10	individual song of thanksgiving
40:11-17 (vv. 13-17 = Ps 70)	individual lament
41	individual lament
42–43	individual lament
44	community lament
45	royal psalm
46	hymn (song of Zion)
47	hymn (enthronement psalm)
48	hymn (song of Zion)
49	wisdom psalm
50	covenant renewal liturgy
51	individual lament (penitential)
52	individual lament
53 (= Ps 14)	individual lament
54	individual lament
55	individual lament
56	individual lament
57 (vv. 7-11 = Ps 108:1-5)	individual lament
58	community lament

59	individual lament
60 (vv. 5-12 = Ps 108:6-13)	community lament
61	individual lament
62	song of trust
63	song of trust
64	individual lament
65	community song of thanksgiving
66:1-12	hymn
66:13-20	individual song of thanksgiving
67	community song of thanksgiving
68	Zion liturgy?
69	individual lament
70 (= Ps 40:13-17)	individual lament
71	individual lament
72	royal psalm
73	wisdom psalm
74	community lament
75	community song of thanksgiving
76	hymn (song of Zion)
77	individual lament
78	storytelling psalm
79	community lament
80	community lament
81	covenant renewal liturgy
82	liturgy?
83	community lament
84	hymn (song of Zion)
85	community lament
86	individual lament
87	hymn (song of Zion)
88	individual lament
89	royal psalm
90	community lament
91	song of trust
92	individual song of thanksgiving
93	hymn (enthronement psalm)
94	community lament
95	hymn
96	hymn
97	hymn (enthronement psalm)
98	hymn
99	hymn
100	hymn

101	royal psalm
102	individual lament
103	hymn
104	hymn
105	storytelling psalm
106	storytelling psalm
107	community song of thanksgiving
108 (vv. 1-5 = Ps 57:7-11; vv. 6-13 = Ps 60:5-12)	mixed type
109	individual lament
110	royal psalm
111	hymn (acrostic)
112	wisdom psalm (acrostic)
113	hymn
114	hymn
115	liturgy
116	individual song of thanksgiving
117	hymn
118	individual song of thanksgiving (royal)
119	torah (wisdom) psalm (acrostic)
120	individual lament
121	song of trust
122	song of Zion
123	community lament
124	community song of thanksgiving
125	song of trust
126	community lament?
127	wisdom psalm
128	wisdom psalm
129	community lament?
130	individual lament (penitential)
131	song of trust
132	royal psalm
133	wisdom psalm
134	liturgy
135	storytelling psalm
136	storytelling psalm
137	community lament
138	individual song of thanksgiving
139	individual lament
140	individual lament
141	individual lament
142	individual lament
143	individual lament

PART I

Preaching from the Psalms

The Psalms: Types, Functions, and Poetics for Proclamation

BRENT A. STRAWN

> *"Indeed, every Sunday liturgy in many churches has the people sing psalms after the first reading from the Hebrew scriptures, as if we were now gathered in the place of the psalms, in the temple, before God's face."*[1]

The Psalms are arguably the most important part of the Old Testament for Christian faith. On the one hand, they are frequently quoted or alluded to in the New Testament.[2] Indeed, together with Deuteronomy and Isaiah, the Psalms form a triad of "most important" books for the New Testament authors — a factor echoed, interestingly enough, in the community that preserved the Dead Sea Scrolls, which also treasured these three books beyond all others.[3] On the other hand, the Psalms

---

1. Gordon W. Lathrop, *Holy Things: A Liturgical Theology* (Minneapolis: Fortress, 1993), 18-19.

2. In the index of citations of and allusions to the Old Testament in the Nestle-Aland Greek New Testament, the Psalms comprise the most extensive listing. See *Novum Testamentum Graece*, ed. B. Aland, K. Aland, et al., 27th ed. (Stuttgart: Deutsche Bibelgesellschaft, 1993), 783-88. The next closest is Isaiah.

3. For Deuteronomy, Psalms, and Isaiah at Qumran and in the early movement around Jesus, see James H. Charlesworth, "The Dead Sea Scrolls and the Historical Jesus," in *Jesus and the Dead Sea Scrolls*, ed. J. H. Charlesworth, ABRL (New York: Doubleday, 1992), 10; James VanderKam and Peter Flint, *The Meaning of the Dead Sea Scrolls: Their Sig-

---

Thanks to William P. Brown, Walter Brueggemann, Joel M. LeMon, Patrick D. Miller, Brad D. Strawn, and Roger E. Van Harn for reading and commenting on this essay.

3

have played an important role throughout Christian history, especially in devotional and liturgical practices.[4] Indeed, the psalms' nature as devotional and liturgical poetry recommends and even requires such use; so it is that precise usage which has been determinative and is both long established and firmly entrenched. The Psalms are, in short, *deeply loved.*

That said, it is equally true that in many corners of contemporary North American Christianity the Psalms are not well known — or, perhaps better, they are *underknown.* "Deeply loved" does not necessarily translate into "adequately known," let alone "rightly understood" or "correctly utilized." This is a problem because "deeply loved" without "adequately known" can lead to a kind of sterile respect: a dim acknowledgment that, yes, the Psalms are important — so important that they are often the only Old Testament book bound with New-Testament-alone editions of the Bible — but a general lack of clarity regarding *exactly how* they are important, if not a complete opacity on how best to hear them, read them, or pray them. Such a situation, which unfortunately obtains for more books of Scripture than just the Psalms, is highly regrettable because sterile respect will not lead to the transformative potential of hearing, reading, praying, and — the special focus of part I of this volume — *preaching* the Psalms.

This lamentable contemporary situation is exacerbated for the Psalms precisely because so many prior generations of the faithful have found comfort and succor in their poetry. Things are made worse, too, by the fact that to miss the Psalms is to miss a rich resource for *real* faith (precisely what the saints who love the Psalms know firsthand). In our own time — at least in the First World — it seems that one of the most neglected aspects of psalmic faith, which is only recently being rediscovered, is the Psalter's special attention to the dark side of life and faith,

---

nificance for Understanding the Bible, Judaism, Jesus, and Christianity (San Francisco: HarperSanFrancisco, 2002), 150, 173-74; cf. also James L. Crenshaw, "Foreword: The Book of Psalms and Its Interpreters," in Sigmund Mowinckel, *The Psalms in Israel's Worship,* trans. D. R. Ap-Thomas (1962; reprint, Grand Rapids: Eerdmans; Dearborn, Mich.: Dove, 2004), xx-xxi.

4. See, e.g., Harold W. Attridge and Margot E. Fassler, eds., *Psalms in Community: Jewish and Christian Textual, Liturgical, and Artistic Traditions,* SBLSymS 25 (Atlanta: Society of Biblical Literature, 2003); William L. Holladay, *The Psalms through Three Thousand Years: Prayerbook of a Cloud of Witnesses* (Minneapolis: Fortress, 1993); and John D. Witvliet, *The Biblical Psalms in Christian Worship: A Brief Introduction and Guide to Resources* (Grand Rapids: Eerdmans, 2007). The latter work is epitomized in part II of the present volume.

especially via the many laments found in its pages.[5] Perhaps the intense honesty of these poems, which can run as close to blasphemy as one can imagine within the context of prayer, is what has led many Christians to distance themselves from the Psalms, respecting them only in a sterilized and sanitized sort of way.[6] But one of the signal gifts of the Psalms is that they witness *a full-orbed faith.* Perhaps Calvin said it best: "I have been accustomed to call this book, I think not inappropriately, 'An Anatomy of all the Parts of the Soul;' for there is not an emotion of which any one can be conscious that is not here represented as in a mirror. Or rather, the Holy Spirit has here drawn to the life all the griefs, sorrows, fears, doubts, hopes, cares, perplexities, in short, all the distracting emotions with which the minds of men are wont to be agitated."[7] To immerse oneself in the Psalms is thus something like taking an advanced anatomy class — beholding firsthand the astonishing, and at times disgusting, aspects of the body of faith. In contrast, to neglect the Psalms is to neglect

5. In many ways, Walter Brueggemann has led the way in this, and his work has placed special emphasis on the laments. See, e.g., his *The Message of the Psalms: A Theological Commentary* (Minneapolis: Augsburg, 1984), esp. 50-121. Cf. also Kathleen D. Billman and Daniel L. Migliore, *Rachel's Cry: Prayer of Lament and Rebirth of Hope* (Cleveland: United Church Press, 1999), and Sally A. Brown and Patrick D. Miller, eds., *Lament: Reclaiming Practices in Pulpit, Pew, and Public Square* (Louisville: Westminster John Knox, 2005).

6. I think the lack of lament in many First World contexts is not a coincidence but is rooted in the socioeconomic fact that those who have much are not as comfortable with the language of grief, anger, and despair. This is unfortunate because *all* people know of tragedy and sorrow — whether it is socioeconomic or otherwise — and so the Psalms have as much transformative potential in the First World as in any other context. In the Psalms, even the king (David or others) suffers, as does Jesus Christ according to the venerable tradition of reading the Psalms as the prayers of Christ.

7. John Calvin, *Commentary on the Book of Psalms: Volume 1*, trans. J. Anderson (1563; reprint, Grand Rapids: Baker, 1993), xxxvi-xxxvii. The following lines are also noteworthy: "The other parts of Scripture contain the commandments which God enjoined his servants to announce to us. But here the prophets themselves, seeing they are exhibited to us as speaking to God, and laying open all their inmost thoughts and affections, call, or rather draw, each of us to the examination of himself in particulars in order that none of the many infirmities to which we are subject, and of the many vices with which we abound, may remain concealed." For an extended critical study, see Paul A. Riemann, "Dissonant Pieties: John Calvin and the Prayer Psalms of the Psalter," in *Inspired Speech: Prophecy in the Ancient Near East; Essays in Honour of Herbert B. Huffmon,* ed. John Kaltner and Louis Stulman, JSOTSup 378 (London: T. & T. Clark, 2004), 354-400. Note also Holladay, *The Psalms,* 196-98.

the self, to pass up the opportunity to know one's own self, to ignore a mirror onto and into the soul.

This is a very serious situation indeed. Ministers might wring their hands about it, hoping — perhaps even praying! — that their parishioners will start reading the Psalms more. Alternatively, ministers could be more proactive and *preach the psalms,* benefiting both themselves and their flock at the same time. The present volume is intended to assist preachers in exactly this task. The purpose of this introduction is to set the context for the exegetical essays that follow by orienting the preacher to critical aspects in the study and interpretation of the Psalms.[8] From the early twentieth century to the present, no aspect in Psalms study has been more critical than the analysis of the types or forms of the Psalms. It is with this topic, then, that we begin.

1. The Types (Forms) of the Psalms

Similar Psalms: The Work of Hermann Gunkel

While he built on previous work, a major breakthrough in the study of the Psalms must be credited to Hermann Gunkel (1862-1932). He published his famous commentary on the Psalter in 1929; his magisterial *Introduction to Psalms* (coauthored with Joachim Begrich) was published posthumously in 1933.[9] Gunkel's breakthrough pertains to the types or forms of the psalms. Though there are 150 psalms, these can be related to one another with a rather small number of types. Many of the psalms, that is, resemble one another and follow a similar pattern or form — evidently because they were composed using set literary conventions. Gunkel identified two major groupings: the main psalm types, into which some two-thirds of the psalms fall; and the subtypes, to which the

---

8. See part II of this volume for John D. Witvliet's introduction to the use of the Psalms in Christian worship.

9. Hermann Gunkel, *Die Psalmen* (Göttingen: Vandenhoeck & Ruprecht, 1929; 5th ed. 1968; 6th ed. 1986); Gunkel, completed by Joachim Begrich, *Introduction to Psalms: The Genres of the Religious Lyric of Israel,* trans. James D. Nogalski (Macon, Ga.: Mercer University Press, 1998 [German orig. 1933; 4th ed. 1985]). Note also Gunkel, *The Psalms: A Form-Critical Introduction,* trans. Thomas M. Horner (Philadelphia: Fortress, 1967), which is a translation of the article on Psalms that appeared in the German encyclopedia *Die Religion in Geschichte und Gegenwart,* 2nd ed. (Tübingen: J. C. B. Mohr [Paul Siebeck], 1927-31); revised from the 1st ed. of 1909-13.

last third belongs. The five main types, with a few representative examples (according to Gunkel), are as follows:

1. Hymns of Praise (e.g., Pss 8; 67; 98; 145; 150)[10]
2. Individual Songs of Thanksgiving (e.g., Pss 30; 66; 92; 118; 138)
3. Individual Laments (e.g., Pss 3; 54; 88; 102; 109)
4. Communal Laments (e.g., Pss 44; 74; 79; 80; 83)
5. Royal Psalms (e.g., Pss 2; 20; 45; 101; 132)

Subtypes include:

- Songs of Pilgrimage (e.g., Ps 122; cf. Ps 84)
- Communal Songs of Thanksgiving (e.g., Pss 67; 124; 129)
- Wisdom Psalms (e.g., Pss 1; 37; 49; 91; 112)
- Liturgies — Including Torah (e.g., Ps 15) and Prophetic Liturgies (e.g., Ps 75)
- Mixed Types (e.g., Pss 19; 119; 129)

Several observations are in order. (1) It is certainly the case that post-Gunkel research has refined if not challenged both his categories and his categorizations.[11] Not all who study the Psalms would agree on Gunkel's types, would provide the same listing of individual laments as Gunkel, or would even concur that the latter should be called "laments" in the first place.[12] (2) Even so, despite subsequent debates and refinements, Gunkel's typology remains intact and in use. One can hardly pick up a commentary on the Psalms or even a study Bible that does not employ Gunkel's basic categories, even if they have been altered somewhat.

---

10. Gunkel/Begrich related "Songs about YHWH's Enthronement" (e.g., Pss 93; 97; 99) to the hymns (*Introduction to Psalms,* 66).

11. See, e.g., Harry P. Nasuti, *Defining the Sacred Songs: Genre, Tradition, and the Post-Critical Interpretation of the Psalms,* JSOTSup 218 (Sheffield: Sheffield Academic, 1999).

12. Some scholars prefer "prayer for help," "petition," or "complaint song" over "lament." The issues at stake are: What is the ultimate purpose of the prayer and what is the rhetorical purpose of the lament component? Scholars who challenge the term "lament" stress that the ultimate aim of these psalms is petition, plea, and prayer for help; it is not solely or only the articulation of grief or anger. Complaint, that is, is not the center or aim of the poem so much as a preface to the poet's petition. "Lament" retains its usefulness, however, insofar as one could pray for help without articulating the kind of grief, sorrow, even rage that is included in the Psalter. Even so, one must always recall that, in the grammar of the psalms, "lament" includes hope (see below).

(3) Two major insights can be deduced from the above lists: (a) a large distinction may be drawn between those psalms that reflect a singular poetic voice (*individual* psalms utilizing "I" language) and those that reflect a plural one (*communal* psalms; "we" language); and (b) among the ten types listed by Gunkel, three main categories can be discerned — hymns of *praise, laments,* and *thanksgiving* songs — the latter two occurring in both individual and communal forms.[13]

In brief, then, Gunkel's insight relates different psalms to each other by noting their similar structure and form; he looked for what was *typical* among various psalms. Evidently, there was a limited number of such forms and a certain amount of standardization within the forms in ancient Israel so that, for example, *hymns of praise* include: a call to worship ("Praise the LORD" or the like); an invitation to praise; and the body of the hymn, which often begins with "for/because" (Hebrew *kî*) introducing the reasons to praise God.[14]

Anyone who has studied literature knows that literary conventions are nothing new.[15] They existed in the ancient world and still exist today. Think, for example, of the different rules governing the proper composition of a business letter in contrast with a love note. The problem is that our own literary conventions are virtually innate — learned and thus intuited through a lifetime of living within our own culture's language and communicative world. And while many of our literary conventions are prefigured in or developed from ancient ones, we do not have anything quite like a lament psalm or a prophetic lawsuit. The method Gunkel made famous — known as *form criticism* — is thus extremely helpful in gaining insight and understanding on the ancient poems we call psalms. A worked example will help to demonstrate this.

---

13. A fourth category that should not be neglected is the *royal psalm,* especially since it has been important in recent discussions of the overall shape of the Psalms as a book (see below).

14. See Richard J. Clifford, *Psalms 1–72,* Abingdon Old Testament Commentaries (Nashville: Abingdon, 2002), 20-21; more extensively, Gunkel/Begrich, *Introduction to Psalms,* 23-41.

15. See Thomas C. Foster, *How to Read Literature like a Professor: A Lively and Entertaining Guide to Reading between the Lines* (New York: HarperCollins, 2003), and, for the Old Testament proper, John Barton, *Reading the Old Testament: Method in Biblical Study,* rev. ed. (Louisville: Westminster John Knox, 1996), especially 8-19.

Form Criticism in Action: The Lament Psalm(s)

The individual lament psalm is the most frequently occurring type in the Psalter. It is nothing less than the "backbone" of the Psalms.[16] The form includes the following elements: address, complaint, petition, confession of trust, vow of praise.[17] Consider Psalm 13, the quintessential individual lament:

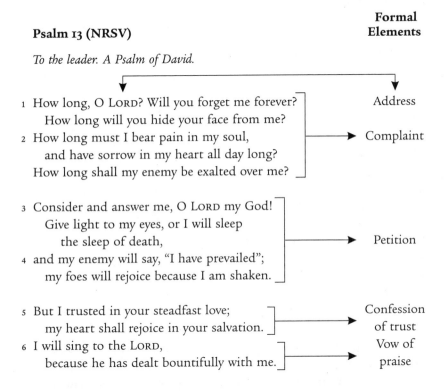

Psalm 13 (NRSV)

Formal Elements

To the leader. A Psalm of David.

1 How long, O LORD? Will you forget me forever?
   How long will you hide your face from me?
2 How long must I bear pain in my soul,
   and have sorrow in my heart all day long?
   How long shall my enemy be exalted over me?

Address

Complaint

3 Consider and answer me, O LORD my God!
   Give light to my eyes, or I will sleep
     the sleep of death,
4 and my enemy will say, "I have prevailed";
   my foes will rejoice because I am shaken.

Petition

5 But I trusted in your steadfast love;
   my heart shall rejoice in your salvation.
6 I will sing to the LORD,
   because he has dealt bountifully with me.

Confession of trust

Vow of praise

One can see in this diagram a perfect correspondence between the formal elements and the specific psalm itself. But this correspondence is somewhat contrived. In reality, the placement of the various elements within lament psalms seems to have been somewhat flexible. Even in

---

16. Crenshaw, "Foreword," xxvi. Gunkel/Begrich, *Introduction to Psalms,* 122: "The individual complaint songs form the *basic material* of the psalter" (emphasis in original).

17. Others use slightly different language. See, e.g., Clifford, *Psalms 1–72,* 22. For a full treatment, see Gunkel/Begrich, *Introduction to Psalms,* 152-86.

Psalm 13, the address does not come first, separately, but is embedded within the complaint itself.

So, while study of a psalm's type or form (today we might even use the term "structure") helps one see what is typical across several psalms, great artists and poets are skilled at upsetting expectations; it is their nature to play with and even break forms. Note, for example, how the formal elements of the individual lament lay out in the following simplified chart of Psalm 22:

Address — v. 1aα
Complaint — vv. 1aβ-18
    Petitionary insert — v. 11
Petition — vv. 19-21a
Confession of trust — v. 21b
Vow of praise — vv. 22-31

All the elements are here, but uniquely so. Note, for instance, that the poet of Psalm 22 introduces *petition* in verse 11, only to return to the *complaint* thereafter. For someone who is as familiar with (ancient) laments as with (modern) business letters, that shift would have been striking. The content of verse 11 would normally mean that the complaint is finished and the petition section of the composition begun, but at just that moment the poet *shifts back to complaint.* This makes the complaint extralong, extrapoignant, even as verse 11 foreshadows the later, fuller petition. The *confession of trust,* on the other hand, is ultrashort — occurring in the space of a half-verse. The *vow of praise* is again extralong, which may serve to balance out the long complaint, but regardless of that, in both form and content, goes much further than other vows in other individual laments.[18]

What this means, of course, is that anyone studying the Psalms must pay attention to *both* what is typical (Gunkel's great insight) *and* what is unique. One must ask, "What *kind of psalm* is this?" but also, "What is contained in *this particular psalm?*" Form criticism puts special accent on the former, but the latter must not be neglected. And while the latter is important, one often recognizes differences between psalms only when one compares their similarities. There are hermeneutical payoffs, that is,

18. See Ellen F. Davis, "Exploding the Limits: Form and Function in Psalm 22," *JSOT* 53 (1992): 93-105.

when one knows the form well enough to trace its presence and to recognize its manipulation.

One brief example: the shift from *petition and complaint* to *confession of trust and vow of praise* in the lament psalms is rather unexpected and astonishing. What can explain this rapid change of mood? How does the psalmist go from "Save me from the mouth of the lion!" (22:21a) to "From the horns of the wild oxen you have rescued me" (22:21b)? Perhaps even more amazingly, since no act of rescue is mentioned, how does Psalm 13 go from "How long will you hide your face from me?" (13:1b) to "I will sing to the LORD / because he has dealt bountifully with me" (13:6)? Various answers have been proposed, with the dominant one holding that those who prayed the psalms did so in the temple. After finishing their complaint, an officiating priest would respond with a word of blessing or oracle of salvation ("The LORD is with you" or the like), which motivated the shift to praise.[19] An example of this sort of dynamic might be found in the interaction of Hannah and Eli (I Sam 1:9-18). Whether or not one must posit an external motive for the shift from lament to praise is uncertain; we lack a clear psalmic example of the kind of transaction depicted in I Samuel I. So the shift to praise may concern other possibilities: the persuasive skill of the poet, composition of the poem after the trouble had been resolved,[20] or even the psychodynamics of grief and lament.[21] What is important, regardless, is that the lament psalms end in this fashion. They all voice petition and complaint and they all end in praise. That is to say that this shift is itself nothing less than *an expected, formulaic element* — one that is deep in theological significance. But, again, one must acknowledge that rules

---

19. See Gunkel/Begrich, *Introduction to Psalms,* 182-84. The classic article on the subject is Joachim Begrich, "Das priesterliche Heilsorakel," *ZAW* 52 (1934): 81-92. See also Ee Kon Kim, *The Rapid Change of Mood in the Lament Psalms: A Matrix for the Establishment of a Psalm Theology* (Seoul: Korea Theological Study Institute, 1985); Patrick D. Miller, *They Cried to the Lord: The Form and Theology of Biblical Prayer* (Minneapolis: Fortress, 1994), 135-77; and, most recently, Federico G. Villanueva, *The 'Uncertainty of a Hearing': A Study of the Sudden Change of Mood in the Psalms of Lament,* Supplements of Vetus Testamentum 121 (Leiden: Brill, 2008).

20. See H. G. M. Williamson, "Reading the Lament Psalms Backwards," in *A God So Near: Essays on Old Testament Theology in Honor of Patrick D. Miller,* ed. Brent A. Strawn and Nancy R. Bowen (Winona Lake, Ind.: Eisenbrauns, 2003).

21. See Erich Fromm, *You Shall Be as Gods: A Radical Interpretation of the Old Testament and Its Tradition* (New York: Holt, 1991 [original 1966]), 207-10; further, Brad D. Strawn and Brent A. Strawn, "From Petition to Praise: An Intrapsychic Phenomenon?" (paper presented in the Psychology and Biblical Studies Section at the national meeting of the Society of Biblical Literature, Denver, Colo., November 2001).

are meant to be broken, and there is one lament, Psalm 88, that breaks the lament form — in pieces! It switches things around a bit, moving from address (v. 1a) to petition (vv. 1b-2) and then to complaint (vv. 3-12). Verse 13 sounds like a confession of trust, but it is followed by one of the deepest and darkest complaints found in the Psalter (vv. 14-18). And that is how the psalm ends. *There is no shift to praise in Psalm 88.* It is no prayer *out of* the depths (cf. Ps 130:1), but one very much still *in* the depths, unable to move out of the depths, perhaps even refusing to be moved. So, even as fundamental and invariable an element as the shift to praise could be (and was) broken if the psalmist and her circumstances so warranted.

Post-Gunkel Developments

As already noted, subsequent scholarship has debated and clarified Gunkel's pioneering work, all the while acknowledging its importance to all subsequent study of the Psalms. An instructive example of this is found in the work of one of Gunkel's most famous followers, Sigmund Mowinckel. For Gunkel, the different forms he had isolated had a particular setting in life (German *Sitz im Leben*). It follows that one could interrogate the form and learn something of that life setting. Consider, again, modern examples: the differences in life setting that can be discerned between a contemporary letter that begins "Dearest Holly" and one that begins "Dear Sir or Madam" or "To Whom It May Concern"; or, how one can instantly tell the difference between these two (written) forms and a similar but quite different (oral) invocation: "Dear Jesus." Gunkel believed that the life setting of the Psalms began in the cult — Israel's worship — but that they were eventually freed from that setting and became more spiritual as a result.[22] Mowinckel took issue with this, and alongside Gunkel's form-critical approach (what Mowinckel preferred to call "type history"), he offered a "cult-functional" approach. Employing this perspective, he was able to relate every single psalm to some aspect of ancient Israelite worship.[23] This meant, among other things, that psalmic

---

22. See Gunkel/Begrich, *Introduction to Psalms*, 331-32; Crenshaw, "Foreword," xxvi.

23. Mowinckel, *Psalms in Israel's Worship*, passim. Among more recent interpreters, Artur Weiser and John H. Hayes have continued to treat the Psalms in a cult-functional manner. See Artur Weiser, *The Psalms: A Commentary*, OTL (Philadelphia: Westminster, 1962), and John H. Hayes, *Understanding the Psalms* (1976; reprint, Eugene, Oreg.: Wipf and Stock, 2003).

themes like praise and worship were not to be related to private experiences of individual pray-ers but stemmed instead from the community and its corporate worship.

Despite the important relationship between the psalms and worship, Mowinckel's totalizing liturgical view has not carried the day. To return to the lament psalms for a moment, if the psalmists were really as sick or as ostracized as they claim to be in many of these poems, it is unlikely that they could have gone to the temple in the first place or would have been allowed to enter if they had. Therefore, in addition to the admittedly important role of cult use of the psalms, one should take seriously the fact that these poems were also used in more private settings such as family worship at home or in personal devotion.[24]

To summarize this section: when considering a psalm for preaching, it pays to know something of its form and typical elements as well as to attend to its specific and particular design. It is also helpful to think about the multiple settings of a psalm: its possible use inside and outside "church," as it were, in both cultic contexts and private devotion. These different settings both correspond to and recommend the continued use of the Psalms in contemporary worship/liturgy and in personal piety. These settings are settings "in life" — the life of the church and the life of the faithful — and the same psalm functions differently in different contexts. Since preachers care deeply about context, timing, and circumstance, it is to further consideration of these points that we now turn.

2. The Functions of the Psalms

Gunkel's categories remain foundational, even though they are constantly being revised and reconsidered. Indeed, since Gunkel, only one typology has been able to gain much traction — namely, that of Walter Brueggemann. Brueggemann's typology is actually not a rival to Gunkel's so much as a complement to it.

24. See the work of Erhard Gerstenberger: *Psalms, Part 1: With an Introduction to Cultic Poetry*, FOTL 14 (Grand Rapids: Eerdmans, 1988) and *Psalms, Part 2, and Lamentations*, FOTL 15 (Grand Rapids: Eerdmans, 2001). Cf. Crenshaw, "Foreword," xxix.

Walter Brueggemann's Functional Typology

Brueggemann first offered his work in an article published in 1980; he then wrote a book-length treatment employing his typology in 1984, which has recently been epitomized in a readily accessible format.[25] Brueggemann noticed the interesting correlation between the main psalmic themes of praise, lament, and thanksgiving and what might be called the seasons of human life. These seasons can be discussed via the sequence of *orientation-disorientation-reorientation*.[26] The dynamic of these seasons can be connected to the three main psalm types such that different psalm types may reflect different *functions* as well as different forms. Certainly the forms are different, as Gunkel and others had shown, but Brueggemann's breakthrough was to ask after what these forms *did* in Israel and also (and especially) what they *do* now for the community of faith that reads, sings, and prays these psalms. He suggests that the different forms function to orient, disorient, or reorient (or newly orient) the one who takes up the psalms.

Hymns of praise are *psalms of orientation*. These are largely static psalms in which there is little dramatic movement.[27] Everything is right in the world, with the poet, and with God. God is reliable, trustworthy, stable — in the words of Martin Luther, "A Mighty Fortress." The problem, of course, is that life also includes seasons of *disorientation* — times of pain and distress that bring the old orientation into serious question. "A Mighty Fortress" — only until the terrible diagnosis, at which point there seem to be cracks in the facade, a weakness in the outer wall, a breachable moat. Of course, it is the *laments* that Brueggemann identifies as *psalms of disorientation*. Movement from orientation to disorientation is painful. Those who are disoriented do not want to be there and much prefer their prior orientation. But they cannot return to what is now an old, defunct

---

25. Walter Brueggemann, "Psalms and the Life of Faith: A Suggested Typology of Function," *JSOT* 17 (1980): 3-32; reprinted in Brueggemann, *The Psalms and the Life of Faith*, ed. Patrick D. Miller (Minneapolis: Fortress, 1995), 3-32; Brueggemann, *The Message of the Psalms: A Theological Commentary* (Minneapolis: Augsburg, 1984); Brueggemann, *Spirituality of the Psalms* (Minneapolis: Fortress, 2002). See also Brueggemann, *Praying the Psalms: Engaging Scripture and the Life of the Spirit*, 2nd ed. (Eugene, Oreg.: Cascade, 2007).

26. Brueggemann draws upon the work of Paul Ricoeur, especially, in articulating this life dynamic.

27. There is some overlap between Brueggemann's orientation psalms and what Fromm called "one-mood psalms" (*You Shall Be*, 203-7).

orientation without sacrificing honesty, integrity, or their own selves. Disorientation is real, painful, and profound. There is no "way home" from it.

But there is a way *beyond* it — not around it, but *through* it. The *psalms of reorientation* or, better, *new orientation* are the *songs of thanksgiving*. These psalms look back on trouble resolved. Indeed, they often have glimpses of orientation and disorientation within them, but the latter has been transcended somehow in an amazing and typically unarticulated way. Consider Psalm 30, for example, a song of thanksgiving and thus a psalm of new orientation, which includes echoes of orientation and disorientation (see p. 16).

This psalm nicely demonstrates the functional dynamic at work in the Psalms and in Brueggemann's typology.[28] Disorientation happens in a heartbeat, in the midst of verse 7. It takes only the hiding of God's face or a phone call in the middle of the night to take one from being a strong mountain (v. 7a) to facing the dust of the Pit (v. 9), physically or emotionally. That is the movement from orientation to disorientation. But Psalm 30 looks back on all that as past history from a point of new orientation and thanksgiving. Somehow — exactly how, the psalmist does not say — they have moved from disorientation in verse 10 to thanksgiving in verse 11. And if the move from orientation to disorientation is full of pain, the move from disorientation to new orientation is dominated by thanksgiving. It is also, according to Brueggemann, an unexpected move, a new thing that cannot be "explained," but for which God must be praised. It is, at one level, the impact of the gospel, where at one moment Jesus is crucified, dead, and buried, and then, suddenly and unexpectedly, is resurrected, or where at one point Israel is enslaved in Egypt, and then is miraculously led out in exodus. The same movement is found in the old hymn "He Touched Me":

He touched me, O he touched me,
And O the joy that floods my soul!
Something happened, and now I know,
He touched me and made me whole.

---

28. In fact, Brueggemann used portions of Ps 30 as the epigraphs to each section of his book-length treatment of the typology: Ps 30:6-7a (orientation), 30:7b-10 (disorientation), 30:11-12 (new orientation). See *Message of the Psalms*, 24, 50, 122, respectively.

Psalm 30 (NRSV)	**Functional Elements/Echoes**

A Psalm. A Song at the dedication of the temple. Of David.

1 I will extol you, O LORD, for you have
      drawn me up,
    and did not let my foes rejoice over me.
2 O LORD my God, I cried to you for help,
    and you have healed me.
3 O LORD, you brought up my soul from Sheol,
    restored me to life from among those gone
      down to the Pit.

Thanksgiving for past rescue and deliverance

4 Sing praises to the LORD, O you his faithful
      ones,
    and give thanks to his holy name.
5 For his anger is but for a moment;
    his favor is for a lifetime.
Weeping may linger for the night,
    but joy comes with the morning.

6 As for me, I said in my prosperity,
    "I shall never be moved."
7 By your favor, O LORD,
    you had established me as a strong
      mountain;
you hid your face;
    I was dismayed.

Recollection of season of *orientation*

Recollection of *painful move* leading to >

8 To you, O LORD, I cried,
    and to the LORD I made supplication:
9 "What profit is there in my death,
    if I go down to the Pit?
Will the dust praise you?
    Will it tell of your faithfulness?
10 Hear, O LORD, and be gracious to me!
    O LORD, be my helper!"

Recollection of season of *disorientation* (lament)

11 You have turned my mourning into dancing;
    you have taken off my sackcloth
    and clothed me with joy,
12 so that my soul may praise you and not be
      silent.
O LORD my God, I will give thanks to
    you forever.

New orientation and *thanksgiving*

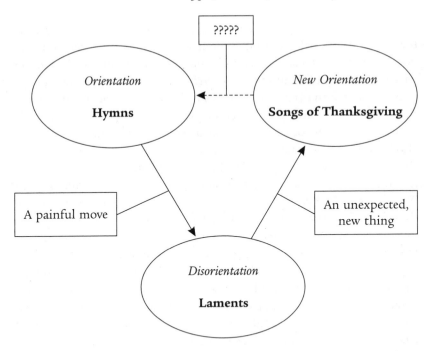

"Something happened." What was it? We do not know because in a real sense the gospel mo(ve)ment cannot be *explained* — certainly not outside the realm and language of faith. But when it is experienced, the faithful must give thanks for it and are newly oriented toward the life-giving, resurrecting, exodus God who gives joy for sackcloth and replaces mourning with dancing (v. 11).

Brueggemann's typology is extremely useful for a number of reasons and bears a strong relationship with the prior work on the Psalms discussed above. As already indicated, his functions can be associated with three of the main categories discerned by Gunkel. Note the diagram above.

Insofar as Brueggemann's typology is one of *function*, however, the seasons of life should *not* be identified *exclusively* with these three genres. It all depends, that is, on *who* uses the psalms, *when* they use them, and *how* they use them.[29] So a hymn of praise could be a psalm of new orientation if it is

29. See John Goldingay, "The Dynamic Cycle of Praise and Prayer," *JSOT* 20 (1981): 85-90, along with Brueggemann's reply: "Response to John Goldingay's 'The Dynamic Cycle of Praise and Prayer,'" *JSOT* 22 (1982): 141-42.

said after lament has been lived through and the psalmist has emerged on the other side of grief and trouble. Similarly — though Brueggemann does not discuss this extensively (hence the question marks in the diagram on page 17) — a song of thanksgiving could become or reflect, in time, a position of orientation from which one is subsequently disorientated.[30] While the lament psalms are closest to a one-to-one correlation with a season of life (disorientation), other psalms, too, depending on circumstance, could also be used during times of disorientation. Elie Wiesel, for example, tells the story of his fellow prisoner Pinhas, who lost his faith while at Auschwitz. When he was selected to go to the gas chamber, Pinhas asked Wiesel to say the Kaddish for him — the liturgical prayer used to mourn the death of a loved one.[31] When Wiesel inquired why, since Pinhas was no longer a believer, he responded: "You do not see the heart of the matter. Here and now, the only way to accuse God is by praising him."[32]

This poignant exchange illustrates how a hymn of praise — typically a psalm of orientation — could be used even in profound times of disorientation. The same is perhaps true for a song of thanksgiving (new orientation): it too could be used as an indictment, reminding God of God's past benevolences and therefore imploring God to be *that* God — that *kind of God* — again, now, when it is needed most.

Brueggemann does not intend his typology to be mechanistic, nor does he mean to suggest that one lives life constantly moving from one season to the others like the proverbial hamster-on-a-wheel. Life is not triangular in this way. Persons could very well inhabit one season for long periods of time. The point is simply that the Psalms are on the move.[33] They do not inhabit just one season, just as they do not exist in only one form. They show that the life of faith, too, is on the move. That means that the season of disorientation and the psalms of lament that most often reflect it are no less faithful than the great hymns of praise

30. See Brueggemann, *Spirituality of the Psalms*, 56-57; Brueggemann, *Message of the Psalms*, 158.

31. One of the main elements of the Kaddish is the response: "May His great name be praised for all eternity" (see Dan 2:20 and Ps 113:2).

32. Elie Wiesel, *Legends of Our Time* (New York: Avon, 1978), 31-38; cited in Rolf A. Jacobson, "The Costly Loss of Praise," *ThTo* 57 (2000): 385.

33. As is David — the putative author or "patron saint" of so many of the psalms. Note Pss 8 and 145; 3-7 and 9; and 30, 34, 40, and 138, for psalms of orientation, disorientation, and new orientation, respectively, that are ascribed, attributed, or dedicated to David.

when all is right and oriented in the world. *Both are equally part of our life with God.*

If the Psalms and the life of faith are on the move, then the faithful are (and must be) as well. But, as already noted, often people find themselves in one season for a long time. What then? How does someone pray a psalm of disorientation when one does not feel disoriented? Or how does one preach on a psalm of disorientation when the congregation is largely oriented?[34] Ellen F. Davis has suggested that praying (or preaching) a psalm that is other than how we feel at the moment is an educative project. Praying a lament psalm helps "keep compassion alive," in part because it tells us how our neighbor might be feeling. "So let the metaphors of the lament psalms help you express your grief. And when you are not yourself in grief, let them instruct your compassion."[35] This wisdom might be reversed for those who find themselves faced with an orientation psalm — whether in morning prayer or in Sunday's lectionary texts — and the felt season of life is that of disorientation. In these moments one prays or preaches the orientation psalm as an act of faith and perhaps as an indictment, that God will do these great things again and be worthy of all our praise even if, for now, God is silent.

So, in these and other ways Brueggemann's functional typology is shown to be quite useful for praying and preaching the Psalms. Moreover, his attention to *psalmic use* finds an interesting resonance with recent work on *psalmic genres* in that scholars are now increasingly aware that genres are not just *given,* they are also *created* — not just *recognized* as literary conventions but *constructed* in the course of reading.[36] So, while a hymn of praise might be inclined toward orientation, in the practice of praying, reading, and preaching, that same psalm could become one of disorientation.[37] The gifted preacher will be able to discern the needs of

34. Though Brueggemann does not discuss it extensively, it is clear from his work that the seasons of life are not to be interpreted solely on an individual level but can also apply to groups of persons, even subcultures.

35. Ellen F. Davis, *Getting Involved with God: Rediscovering the Old Testament* (Cambridge: Cowley, 2001), 20; cf. Davis, *Wondrous Depth: Preaching the Old Testament* (Louisville: Westminster John Knox, 2005), 19, 21.

36. See Nasuti, *Defining the Sacred Songs.*

37. Note, e.g., D. H. Lawrence's dark parody of Psalm 121: "The Hills," in *Complete Poems of D. H. Lawrence,* ed. V. de Sola Pinto and W. Roberts (London: Heinemann, 1972): "I lift up mine eyes to the hills/and there they are, but no strength comes from them to me./Only from darkness/and ceasing to see/strength comes."

the congregation and discover the (function of the) psalmic genre presented in the lectionary — matching the two together in the homiletical moment. Of course, one should always remember that fluidity of function is present within the psalms themselves. Psalm 30, the thanksgiving song and psalm of new orientation considered above, bears a superscription identifying its use in the dedication of the temple — a use not obvious from the content of the psalm itself!

Hence, Brueggemann's typology not only shows how the Psalms *reflect* different functions, it also suggests how one might *utilize* the Psalms *for* different functions. In this fashion the typology casts significant light on the pastoral use of the Psalms: how they ought to be used, both in private devotion and in public proclamation; and how in both cases they ought to be used *pastorally* — a pill of oriented praise not forced down the throat of a disoriented patient, whether the "pastor" present is of the ordained or unordained sort. That much of what passes for the use of Scripture and theology in pastoral care happens between fellow Christians with no ordained minister present shows that the stakes for sensible and informed use of the psalms are rather high.

Finally, Brueggemann's extensive work on the theological importance of disorientation/lament should be underscored.[38] There is a noticeable disconnect between the amount of orientation one hears in many North American mainline and evangelical churches on Sunday morning and the disorientation that dominates life outside church and the lives of those who come to church.[39] Why this disconnect? If pastors are not careful to rectify matters and do a better job acknowledging the reality of (and reflecting on) the disorientation of so much of life, they will be guilty of telling lies in the pulpit — covering over what we know to be true in our lives and true in the Psalms themselves about the dark side of life, even of life with God. Still worse, preachers become what Marx would have called drug-dealers: foisting a narcoticized religion-as-opium on people who are clearly capable of thinking about the world in more

38. In addition to *Message of the Psalms*, 50-121, see Brueggemann's essay, "The Costly Loss of Lament," *JSOT* 36 (1986): 57-71, reprinted in Brueggemann, *The Psalms and the Life of Faith*, 98-111.

39. The disconnect has been verified in a semiempirical manner by W. Sibley Towner in his study of the use of the Psalms in hymnals. See his essay "'Without Our Aid He Did Us Make': Singing the Meaning of the Psalms," in *A God So Near*, 17-34. The same holds true for the place of the laments and imprecations in the lectionary. See Holladay, *The Psalms*, 304-11, 314.

profound and subtle ways as is witnessed by at least some of what they watch on television and in movie theaters, or read in newspapers and books.

This disconnect is real and it is deeply problematic. But the Psalms offer a remedy: the language of lament and disorientation, which in the Psalms is shown to be part and parcel of the life of faith and the life with God. Not only part, but a *major part* — the backbone of the Psalter! Grief, anger, loss, lament — this, too, is what being faithful is all about. And the Psalms show that there is no new life via denial. But new life can — and does! — come through honesty about pain, candor about misery, sincerity about loss — all addressed to the God who hears and who is worthy of praise and receptive of lament. The Psalter, full of laments and songs of thanksgiving, testifies to these truths. Who can claim to know better than it?

The Function of the Psalter as a Book

The preceding comments already indicate that considering the Psalter *as a whole* has something to contribute to the interpretation and use of individual psalms. Alongside consideration of a specific psalm's form and setting in life (Gunkel), whether that is in formal worship (Mowinckel) or outside it (Gerstenberger), study of the Psalms *as a book* suggests that the *immediate literary context* of the psalm may also merit study. Study of the shape and shaping of the Psalter is a relatively recent development in Psalms research.[40] Though such an approach may at first seem strange, given the evidently self-contained nature of individual psalms, several recent works have demonstrated the utility of this perspective.[41]

40. For an introduction and overview, see the essays collected in J. Clinton McCann, ed., *The Shape and Shaping of the Psalter,* JSOTSup 159 (Sheffield: Sheffield Academic, 1993). A groundbreaking study was Gerald H. Wilson's 1981 Yale dissertation, published as *The Editing of the Hebrew Psalter,* SBLDS 76 (Chico, Calif.: Scholars, 1985). See also the earlier chapter on the Psalms in Brevard S. Childs, *Introduction to the Old Testament as Scripture* (Philadelphia: Fortress, 1979), 505-25.

41. In addition to the works cited in the previous note, see the commentaries by Gerald H. Wilson, *Psalms Volume 1,* NIVAC (Grand Rapids: Zondervan, 2002); J. Clinton McCann, Jr., "The Book of Psalms: Introduction, Commentary, and Reflections," in *NIB,* 4:641-1280; and Frank-Lothar Hossfeld and Erich Zenger, *Psalms 2: A Commentary on Psalms 51–100,* ed. Klaus Baltzer, Hermeneia (Minneapolis: Fortress, 2005) — each of which pays particular attention to issues of shape and shaping.

The literary context of the Psalter can influence study of specific psalms in two ways. The *first* is on the *microlevel,* which involves studying individual psalms in relationship to adjacent ones or psalms that occur in smaller complexes, like the Songs of Ascents (Pss 120-134). This sort of work is often very detailed. Brief examples may be found in the way the Psalter begins and ends.

Many scholars are of the opinion that Psalms 1-2 are intended to function together as the editorial introduction to the Psalter.[42] Both psalms lack a superscription (the first occurs in Ps 3) and are united by the repetition of the word "happy" or "blessed" (Hebrew *'ašrê*), which starts Psalm 1:1 and ends Psalm 2:12. Note also the combination of the verb "perish" (√*'bd*) with the word "way" *(derek)* in 1:6 and 2:12. Together, then, these two poems introduce the themes of torah piety and the Lord's rule as the two starting points for the rest of the Psalms.[43]

Somewhat similarly, Psalms 146-150 function as an intentional complex concluding the Psalter. Each poem here begins and ends with "Hallelujah" (Hebrew *halĕlû yāh*), with the exception of Psalm 150, the coup de grâce, which has "Hallelujah" or "Praise him" (Hebrew *halĕlûhû*) in every single verse in addition to the opening and ending "Hallelujah's." Together, these five psalms conclude the Book of Praises (the Hebrew name of the Psalter is *Tĕhillîm,* "Praises"), with unbounded and unrestrained praise.

But how does one move from obedience to torah (Ps 1) to boundless praise (Ps 150)? This question raises the *second* level of literary context for the psalms, which is the *macrolevel.* Given the importance of the opening and ending of any book, a reader might be tempted to think that the themes of torah piety and praise are sufficient indicators — bookends, as it were — of the theology of the Psalms and, correlatively, of life with God. But life with God — and life with God *in the Psalms* — is full of far more than piety and praise. There are, after all, some 143 psalms that live between the Psalter's introduction and conclusion. These psalms include

42. See Patrick D. Miller, "The Beginning of the Psalter," in *The Shape and Shaping of the Psalter,* 83-92; also Childs, *Introduction,* 513-14, 515-17. For what follows, see especially Miller, "The Psalter as a Book of Theology," in *Psalms in Community,* 87-98 (note especially 91 n. 11).

43. As noted above, psalms dealing with the Lord's (or the king's) rule have been deemed particularly important by scholars such as Gerald H. Wilson *(The Editing of the Hebrew Psalter),* James L. Mays *(The Lord Reigns: A Theological Handbook to the Psalms* [Louisville: Westminster John Knox, 1994]), and others.

more of praise, to be sure, and a fair amount about the Lord's reign (e.g., Pss 47; 93; 95-99) and the Lord's law (e.g., Pss 19; 119). But they are also full of laments in dire circumstances and thanksgiving for deliverance experienced or hoped for — what Brueggemann has called "candor about suffering" (see Ps 25) and "gratitude about hope" (Ps 103) via communion with God (Ps 73).[44] The way to move, then, from the Lord's instruction and rule to boundless praise of the Lord is by moving as the Psalter does: through, never around, "in between life" (and "in between psalms") with its ups and downs, sorrows and joys, thanks and laments.

Therefore, the Psalter itself — as a whole — has an important function alongside the functions of its constituent parts. That larger function is in no small way one of *instruction:* instruction about the Lord's law and the Lord's way, but also about the anatomy of the soul, and the nature of life with God along with the piety, praise, and pain that are a part of that life. It is thus no accident that the Psalter is broken into five books, each with a concluding doxology (Pss 1-41 [41:13]; 42-72 [72:18-20]; 73-89 [89:52]; 90-106 [106:48]; 107-150 [150:1-6]). Whatever else these demarcations do, they echo the fivefold pattern of the Pentateuch, the Torah par excellence. One finds in the Psalms, that is, another kind of Torah, matched unto the Torah of Moses.[45] The Psalms, too, are torah: instructing the pray-er in the way of the Lord. This torah is different from the Sinaitic one: it is not primarily legislation given from God via the great mediator Moses. It is, instead, primarily prayer addressed to God by individuals (many anonymous) and by the community of faith. It is a torah of worship and prayer that complements the Pentateuch's torah of law and ethics. But the five-book structure of the Psalter and Psalm 1 as the very first psalm demonstrate that in the Old Testament's perspective the two torahs are not finally distinct, but are profoundly interrelated. The way of prayer is the way of belief *(lex orandi, lex credendi).*

3. The Poetics of the Psalms

To adequately read — let alone preach — the Psalms one must have some sense of their poetry. As Clifford states, "The psalms are, first and fore-

44. See Walter Brueggemann, "Bounded by Obedience to Praise: The Psalms as Canon," in Brueggemann, *The Psalms and the Life of Faith,* 189-213.

45. See the work of J. Clinton McCann: *A Theological Introduction to the Book of Psalms: The Psalms as Torah* (Nashville: Abingdon, 1993).

most, poems and make their statement with poetic means."[46] In fact, it is probably their very nature as poetry that often leads to their neglect in the pulpit. People tend to either love poetry or hate it, and the general decline of poetry, especially high poetry, in secondary education and general cultural purview seems to indicate that there are more who belong to the latter category than to the former. Moreover, for preaching proper, narrative approaches have been the dominant force — at least in North America for the past thirty-some years.[47] While narrative preaching might be thought to be fundamentally opposed to the poetic genres, such a conclusion is not necessary. Whatever the case, recent works have argued for the importance of poetry, poetic conventions, or the Psalms proper for the preaching task.[48]

The minute details of Hebrew poetry need not detain us. Unfortunately, a large number of these are not easily translatable into English anyway, or, said differently, the fine points of Hebrew poetry are no longer recognizable outside the original language. This is, on the one hand, motivation to either learn or brush up on Hebrew! But it is also incentive to avail oneself of the many excellent studies available on the poetry of the Old Testament, including especially the poetry of the Psalms.[49] Inso-

---

46. Clifford, *Psalms 1–72*, 26.

47. A turning point came in Fred B. Craddock, *As One without Authority: Essays on Inductive Preaching* (Enid, Okla.: Phillips University Press, 1971), which has been recently reprinted by Chalice Press (2001).

48. See Davis, *Wondrous Depth*, 17-32; J. Clinton McCann, Jr., and James C. Howell, *Preaching the Psalms* (Nashville: Abingdon, 2001); Cas J. A. Vos, *Theopoetry of the Psalms* (London: T. & T. Clark, 2005); James L. Mays, *Teaching and Preaching the Psalms,* ed. Patrick D. Miller and Gene M. Tucker (Louisville: Westminster John Knox, 2006); cf. also, in a different but not unrelated vein, Brad D. Strawn and Brent A. Strawn, "Preaching and/ as Play: D. W. Winnicott and Homiletics," *Homiletic* 31 (2006): 13-28, and especially Barbara Brown Taylor, *When God Is Silent: The 1997 Lyman Beecher Lectures on Preaching* (Cambridge: Cowley, 1998). Taylor's ultimate metaphor is music, not poetry, but there are close connections between the two — especially via lyric poetry and the many musical connections in the psalms (e.g., reference to instruments, names for tunes and worship functionaries, the presence of refrains [see Ps 136], antiphonal responses [Ps 118], and the like).

49. See, conveniently, Adele Berlin, "Introduction to Hebrew Poetry," in *NIDB,* 4:301-15; and Wilson, *Psalms Volume 1,* 31-56. Useful and accessible book-length studies include: Robert Alter, *The Art of Biblical Poetry* (New York: Basic Books, 1985); J. P. Fokkelmann, *Reading Biblical Poetry: An Introductory Guide* (Louisville: Westminster John Knox, 2001); S. E. Gillingham, *The Poems and the Psalms of the Hebrew Bible* (Oxford: Oxford University Press, 1994); David L. Petersen and Kent Harold Richards, *Interpreting He-*

far as poetry is one of the Old Testament's seminal gifts to Scripture (there is a disturbingly small amount of poetry in the New Testament), preachers ought to become familiar with the main poetic devices and key contributions poetry makes to theological reflection, not to mention homiletical discourse.[50]

Parallelism

Happily, one of the major hallmarks of Hebrew verse *is* translatable and recognizable in English. It is called *parallelism* and is the way Hebrew poets spoke of a subject across two or occasionally three closely related lines. Gerald H. Wilson's definition is worth citing in full:

> It has long been recognized that the most distinctive characteristic of Hebrew poetry is to be found in the frequent linking of successive lines of poetry in a manner that emphasizes grammatical, structural, and thematic similarities between them. This relationship between lines has been traditionally called *parallelism*. The sense of this description is that after the statement of an initial line, a second (and sometimes a third) line is generated that shares some obvious grammatical-structural similarities with the first and yet redirects the focus of the first through alternate words and expression. The close grammatical-

---

brew *Poetry* (Minneapolis: Fortress, 1992); and Luis Alonso Schökel, *A Manual of Hebrew Poetics* (Rome: Pontifical Biblical Institute, 2000). For more specialized studies, see Adele Berlin, *The Dynamics of Biblical Parallelism* (Bloomington: Indiana University Press, 1985; rev. ed. = Grand Rapids: Eerdmans; Dearborn, Mich.: Dove, 2008); James L. Kugel, *The Idea of Biblical Poetry: Parallelism and Its History* (Baltimore: Johns Hopkins University Press, 1981); and Wilfred G. E. Watson, *Classical Hebrew Poetry: A Guide to Its Techniques,* JSOTSup 26 (Sheffield: Sheffield Academic, 2001). An excellent introduction to poetry in general is Mary Kinzie, *A Poet's Guide to Poetry* (Chicago: University of Chicago Press, 1999). See also Edward Hirsch, *How to Read a Poem and Fall in Love with Poetry* (New York: Harvest, 1999). It is surely a truism that one's facility in interpreting poetry is closely correlated with how much poetry one reads.

50. See, e.g., Patrick D. Miller, "The Theological Significance of Biblical Poetry," in Miller, *Israelite Religion and Biblical Theology: Collected Essays,* JSOTSup 267 (Sheffield: Sheffield Academic, 2000), 233-49; as well as the older work by Amos Niven Wilder, *Theopoetic: Theology and the Religious Imagination* (Philadelphia: Fortress, 1976); and, more recently, Brent A. Strawn, "Lyric Poetry," in *Dictionary of the Old Testament: Wisdom, Poetry, and Writings,* ed. Tremper Longman and Peter Enns (Downers Grove, Ill.: IVP Academic, 2008), 437-46.

structural similarity between lines provides continuity that emphasizes the *parallel* character of the two lines, while the distinctive
phraseology of each phase lifts the phenomenon beyond *mere repetition*
and offers the opportunity for expansion or advancement on the original line's meaning.[51]

Note the following example from Psalm 24:1:

	a	b	c
A	The earth is the LORD's		and all that is in it
	a′		c′
B	the world		and those who live in it.

The first line (A) makes a predication of the earth — namely, that it belongs to God. The second line (B) is parallel to the first, seconding that
thought in closely similar language and syntax but with two noticeable
differences: (i) the name of the Lord in line A (element b) is not repeated
in line B, as such slavish repetition is not necessary, given the workings of
parallelism (this kind of omission is typically called ellipsis or gapping);
and (ii) different terms are used in the two lines for the parallel constitu-
ents: "earth" (Hebrew *hā'āreṣ*) versus "world" *(tēbēl)*; "all that is in it"
(*mĕlô'āh*; literally, "its fullness") versus "those who live in it" *(yōšĕbê bāh)*.

Such an example can be found many times over in the Psalms, but a
few important caveats are in order. First, and unfortunately, English
translations are not always reliable guides to the underlying Hebrew text.
In the main, English translations (following standard parlance) often alter their translation equivalents even if the same Hebrew term is used in
both lines. Second, and more significantly, the relationship of the two
(sometimes three) lines is not always as close as it is in Psalm 24:1. Indeed,
parallelism is a highly complicated device, and attempts to describe it adequately are legion.[52] Robert Lowth's *Lectures on the Sacred Poetry of the Hebrews* (1753) is often highlighted as an important breakthrough in research.[53] Lowth discussed three main types of parallelism: what he called
synonymous, antithetical, and synthetic parallelism. More recent work

51. Wilson, *Psalms Volume 1*, 39, emphases in original. For a recent overview, see
Joel M. LeMon and Brent A. Strawn, "Parallelism," in *Dictionary of the Old Testament*, 502-15.

52. See, e.g., the works in notes 49 and 51.

53. Robert Lowth, *Lectures on the Sacred Poetry of the Hebrews*, trans. G. Gregory, 4th
ed. (London: Thomas Tegg, 1839 [Latin original: 1753]).

has shown that the situation is both more complex and more simple than Lowth's categories would permit. It has also challenged the usefulness of his three terms. Wilson, for example, has helpfully offered the following alternatives: affirming (cf. Lowth's synonymous), opposing (cf. antithetical), and advancing (cf. synthetic) parallelism.[54] In *affirming* parallelism, the B line largely reiterates and supports what has been said in line A, as in Psalm 24:1. In *opposing* parallelism, the opposite holds true, with the B line relating to the A line in negative fashion, by challenging and negating it, or by contrasting it with something else. Note, for example, Psalm 1:6:

A   for the LORD watches over the way of the righteous,

B   but the way of the wicked will perish.

In *advancing* parallelism, the B line continues the thought of the A line but in a manner not obviously recognizable as either affirming or opposing, but which is more subtle, supple, and sophisticated than those two rather simple options. Again, from Psalm 1, but this time a three-line (tricolon) verse:

A   They are like trees planted by streams of water,

B   which yield their fruit in its season, and their leaves
        do not wither.

C   In all that they do, they prosper. (v. 3)

The relationship of these lines is not one of simple affirmation or opposition. Instead, the thought is continued but with different nuance, with different imagery, with different sentiment. In a very real sense, however, all three lines are saying the same thing: making a positive predication of the righteous. So most recent work on parallelism has emphasized its seconding or intensifying nature.[55] The B line seconds or intensifies the A line in some important way, though the shape that can take and the range of the lines' content are virtually infinite. Kugel puts it memorably: "Biblical parallelism is of one sort, 'A, and what's more, B,' or a hundred sorts; but it is not three [as in Lowth]."[56]

---

54. Wilson, *Psalms Volume 1*, 40-48. He also discusses climactic parallelism.

55. See especially Alter, *The Art of Biblical Poetry*, and Kugel, *The Idea of Biblical Poetry*. Further, LeMon and Strawn, "Parallelism," esp. 507-10.

56. Kugel, *Idea of Biblical Poetry*, 58.

How this insight might pertain to preaching can be illustrated, once more, by Psalm 1. Consider the very first verse of the Psalter:

A   Happy are those who do not follow the advice of the wicked,
B$_1$ or take the path that sinners tread,
B$_2$ or sit in the seat of scoffers.[57]

These lines could be analyzed as affirming parallelism, and that would be correct. But the seconding and intensifying nature of parallelism also means that together *they are saying one thing.* One practical result of that insight is that the fine nuances among the different terms that are used ("wicked," "sinners," "scoffers") may not be of much significance — poetically or homiletically. Yes, they are different terms (in Hebrew as well), and, yes, the poet chose them instead of other terms (or the same term). But rather than investing precious time in dictionaries or concordances tracking down the niceties of "wicked" versus "scoffer," preachers might be better instructed and informed by the insight "A, and what's more, B," and thus shift their attention from word study to a larger analysis of the lines' overall effect — the one thing they are getting at.[58] In this case, it seems that the lines are stressing that there are "bad" groups out there that one must avoid, even while acknowledging that this is a very hard thing to do since they are *everywhere:* giving advice that might be followed (A), treading the same path (B$_1$), and already occupying the seats that one might like to sit in to get out of these people's way (B$_2$). This understanding of the verse leads nicely and naturally into an interpretation of the rest of the psalm, whereas much sweat over the meaning of "scoffers" (Hebrew *lēṣîm*) will most likely not, since that term is not repeated in the poem.

Imagery

There are other poetic features besides parallelism that preachers should be aware of in the preaching task.[59] Certainly the most important one is

57. There are only two lines here. I have separated line B into two parts to demonstrate the parallel nature of both of these with the latter part of line A.

58. Overall poetic movement, that is, may be more important than specific words. See William P. Brown, *Seeing the Psalms: A Theology of Metaphor* (Louisville: Westminster John Knox, 2002), 215; Berlin, "Introduction to Hebrew Poetry," 314.

59. Berlin, e.g., lists the following figures of speech: allusion, apostrophe, hendi-

that poetry is *affective literature* — it speaks to the heart as much as, if not more than, the head. Bernard of Clairvaux put it this way: "Just as we taste food with the mouth, so we taste the psalm with the heart."[60] Much poetry is also *episodic:* it captures a moment in time. It does not and cannot, in its short space, purport to be the final definitive discourse on a particular subject, even though the most powerful poems are remarkably comprehensive and compelling. The poet writes this poem today and perhaps a very different poem tomorrow. Poetry is also *terse, compressed language.* There are long poems, of course — and long psalms like Psalm 119 — but the language, regardless, is *porous.*[61] Our most concentrated attempt at nonporous language and literature is certainly found in legal discourse, but even here many make their living by successfully identifying the loopholes that lurk therein. And if there are gaps in "legalese," then poetry is more akin to Swiss cheese! It is everywhere open and porous, inviting and requiring interpretation, even as its unusual way of speaking, careful use of language, high diction, and intriguing lineation require interpretation that pays very close attention to what, exactly, is *said* (and not only what is *felt*). As the poet Wendell Berry has said, "a good poem . . . cannot be written or read in distraction." Davis has taken this to mean that one cannot skim a psalm and preach its main idea or gist in some simple fashion: "You have to dwell on the words, and the reward for doing so is a fresh view of the world. The gifted poet uses words to yield a changed perception of what we cavalierly call 'reality.'"[62]

Several of these poetic features are reflected in and facilitated by the extensive use of imagery in the poetry of the Psalms. That is to say that one of the ways that poems are porous, inviting interpretation and application, is by the arresting imagery employed by poets. Imagery (including metaphor, simile, and the like) is ubiquitous in poetry, such that "some

---

adys, hyperbole and litotes, irony, merismus, oxymoron, personification, and rhetorical questions ("Introduction to Hebrew Poetry," 313). Wilson adds word pairs, chiasm, inclusion, repeated refrains, and acrostic structures (*Psalms Volume I,* 48-57). More on these and other features can be found in Alonso Schökel, *A Manual of Hebrew Poetics,* and Watson, *Classical Hebrew Poetry.* See also Kinzie, *A Poet's Guide to Poetry.*

60. From his Sermon 67.2.3 on the Song of Songs; cited in Brown, *Seeing the Psalms,* 207.

61. Note Miller's two hallmarks of the Psalms' poetic language: "open" and "metaphorical" (*Interpreting the Psalms,* 51).

62. Davis, *Wondrous Depth,* 24. The quote from Berry is from his "The Responsibility of the Poet," in Berry, *What Are People For? Essays* (San Francisco: North Point, 1990), 90.

theorists would define poetry in terms of the presence or dominance of metaphor rather than in terms of formal linguistic structures, like meter or parallelism."[63] Good preachers will take special notice of the images and metaphors used in a particular psalm and how they are used throughout the text as well as in the psalm's effect (and affect) on the reader and preacher (and *their* affects). How can it be that the enemies are at one moment strong bulls and the next a ravening and roaring lion (Ps 22:12-13), only to transmogrify into a pack of dogs (22:16, 20) and then, again, a lion (22:21a) and, finally, wild oxen (22:21b)? Or how can the psalmist be "poured out like water" without a bone in joint, with a heart melted like wax, mouth dry as a bone, laid in the dust of death itself (22:14-15), only to be transformed into a preacher who declares the Lord's praise to generations now and not yet (22:22-31)? We might never answer *how*, but exploration of the imagery employed can cast great insight into the meaning and significance of the psalm. Such exploration is absolutely necessary according to William P. Brown, who has pointed out that we have overlooked the Psalter's use of imagery "at great theological cost" and that, in the Psalms, to "read theologically is, in part, to linger over the metaphor."[64] Careful analysis of poetic imagery can also suggest useful homiletical entry points and can begin to teach preachers how to better use open, porous, imagistic language in their own sermons and prayers.[65] It may also reinforce the fact that there is no one "right way" to read a poem or preach a text. Poetic imagery can invite preachers into the play of Scripture, encouraging them to take part in that same "game," even while giving them tools to do the same for their listeners, who will, in turn, be allowed to participate — mind and heart — with the psalm, with the Scripture, with the sermon, rather than sit by passively being beat over the head with discursive point after discursive point.[66]

63. Berlin, "Introduction to Hebrew Poetry," 311.

64. Brown, *Seeing the Psalms,* ix, 13.

65. On the latter, note the instructive remarks of Walter Brueggemann, *Awed to Heaven, Rooted in Earth: Prayers of Walter Brueggemann,* ed. Edwin Searcy (Minneapolis: Fortress, 2003), xvi: "much public prayer in the church is careless and slovenly, and . . . what passes for spontaneity is in fact lack of preparation. Thus, I believe that public prayers must be 'well-said' in an artful way, not to call attention to the artistry itself but to mobilize and sustain the attention of the praying community. Such prayer must be artful enough to be porous, in order to allow the words uttered to be access points for other members of the praying assembly who may take these utterances as their utterances."

66. See Strawn and Strawn, "Preaching and/as Play," and, further, Robert C. Dykstra, *Discovering a Sermon: Personal Pastoral Preaching* (St. Louis: Chalice, 2001).

Much, much more could be said about imagery. One recent development is worth noting: of late, scholars have increasingly taken notice of ancient artistic remains when assessing biblical images and metaphors. The pioneering work in this vein was published by Othmar Keel in 1972.[67] Since then he has published numerous studies, as have his students and others who have followed his lead.[68] Study of the Psalms, in particular, has profited from this new development. Brown's magnificent study of psalmic metaphor, *Seeing the Psalms: A Theology of Metaphor,* for example, makes extensive use of ancient Near Eastern iconography with stunning theological results.[69] Similarly, the massive commentary on the Psalms currently under way by the distinguished German Psalms scholars Frank-Lothar Hossfeld and Erich Zenger has depictions of ancient Near Eastern objects throughout.[70] The present volume follows in this same track, including several images that cast light on some of the psalms and the exegetical essays on these psalms that are included here. It should be stressed that such images are not meant to be simply *illustrative,* but truly *generative* — affording unusual and unexpected insight on the textual image at hand. Preachers may benefit from looking at additional images like these or ones of more recent vintage.[71] Or they may take inspiration on how the word-images they employ in their own sermons should be similarly generative and hermeneutically helpful, not simply used for laughs, human interest, or audience entertainment.

67. Othmar Keel, *Die Welt der altorientalischen Bildsymbolik und das Alte Testament: Am Beispiel der Psalmen* (Neukirchen: Neukirchener Verlag, 1972), translated into English in 1978: *The Symbolism of the Biblical World: Ancient Near Eastern Iconography and the Book of Psalms,* trans. Timothy J. Hallet (New York: Seabury Press, 1978; Winona Lake, Ind.: Eisenbrauns, 1997).

68. A main repository of publications on this front is found in the series Keel coedits: Orbis biblicus et orientalis (Fribourg: Academic Press; Göttingen: Vandenhoeck & Ruprecht).

69. Brown writes that imagery is "fraught with background, both visual and discursive" so that attention to ancient Near Eastern iconography and literature is important. Equally crucial, however, is an image's or metaphor's foreground. Hence, "[d]riving this study is the conviction that literary and iconic form are mutually informative and indelibly wedded" (Brown, *Seeing the Psalms,* 14).

70. Frank-Lothar Hossfeld and Erich Zenger, *Psalms 2: A Commentary on Psalms 51–100,* ed. Klaus Baltzer, Hermeneia (Minneapolis: Fortress, 2005).

71. For two instructive examples of the latter, see Samuel Terrien, *The Iconography of Job through the Centuries: Artists as Biblical Interpreters* (University Park: Pennsylvania State University Press, 1996), and Henri J. M. Nouwen, *The Return of the Prodigal Son: A Meditation on Fathers, Brothers, and Sons* (New York: Doubleday, 1992).

I conclude this section with two of the three characteristics that Davis has recently identified among those who preach the Psalms well. Both pertain directly to the poetics of the Psalms and the ability of preachers to gain full access to those: "First, they have learned *how to think with* the psalm, and even *to feel what the psalmist feels*. . . . A second and closely related point: they *take seriously the poetic character* of the psalm, *dwelling on its particular words and images*, with patience and fascination."[72]

4. In Conclusion: Toward Preaching the (Lectionary) Psalms

Davis's third and final characteristic is that good psalmic preachers "see each psalm not as a freestanding poem but as a structural element of the great cathedral that is the totality of Scripture. Scripture is for these preachers an exquisitely articulated edifice, which for all its complexity evidences also a comprehensive plan and unity. Therefore the primary context of the psalm is for them the Great Story that is the Christian Bible in both Testaments."[73] This characteristic, combined with the other things mentioned above — types, functions, poetics, and the like — provides helpful guidance on how to preach the Psalms, something the exegetical essays that follow in part I also intend to do. Part II of this book then goes further, showcasing the virtually infinite number of ways a psalm can be employed liturgically and how this can facilitate its life among the community of faith so that, to come full circle, the *deeply loved* nature of the Psalms does in fact equate to *adequately known, rightly understood,* and *correctly utilized* (though it may well be that correct usage facilitates deep affection, not the other way around — preachers, take note!).

More specifically, Davis's third characteristic is helpful in its implicit recommendation to actually preach the psalm that is in the lectionary on any given Sunday or, at least, to make use of it as a supportive text for the other lessons that day. In her own words: "What I am suggesting is that the psalms have nearly inexhaustible potential for making connections with the larger biblical story. This relieves the preacher of the anxiety that has become a modern trademark of the profession, namely, the perceived need to 'find an illustration,' on which the success of the ser-

---

72. Davis, *Wondrous Depth*, 20-21, emphasis added.
73. Davis, *Wondrous Depth*, 21.

mon is often supposed to depend. This is a pernicious idea, for very often the illustration proves to be the tail that wags the dog of the sermon (and I use that last phrase advisedly)."[74] The Psalms, that is, can be the primary preached text to which the other lessons are drawn and related. Many of the superscriptions to the Psalms provide examples that are suggestive, though certainly not definitive given the functional fluidity discussed above. Consider, for example, Psalm 3, the first psalm with a superscription, that relates this individual lament to the time when David fled from Absalom (see 2 Sam 15-18); or, even more famously, the superscription of Psalm 51, which relates that beloved penitential psalm to the time when David was confronted by Nathan after the affair with Bathsheba (2 Sam 12:1-15). As Miller notes, "One may be no closer to the actual situation that originally brought forth any one of these laments [by relating them to narrative contexts such as those suggested by some of the superscriptions], but the interpreter is given a wealth of illustrative possibilities for uncovering contexts for these stereotypical expressions [which are used in the psalms]."[75]

Alternatively, even if it is not selected for preaching, the psalm may still provide the "illustration" for the chosen, preached text. The ideal "story" for the sermon may turn out to be a poem! Either way, this kind of intertextual correlation is a good homiletical practice, even if it remains unclear if the crafters of the lectionary intended the lectionary psalms to have the same sort of coherence that often holds true for the other lessons.[76] But, regardless of what the crafters intended, such coherence can be *found* and *created* by good preachers — as Davis herself suggests. Moreover, she is certainly right that the affective nature of the Psalms greatly helps the reading and proclamation of the other texts:

74. Davis, *Wondrous Depth*, 28.

75. Miller *Interpreting the Psalms*, 55; see further, 48-63. Miller's recommendation to relate the psalms to narrative contexts is not limited solely to the data derived from the superscriptions (though that can be part of the process). It is also accomplished by means of intertextual linkages, including the use of certain key words, phrases, and the "stereotypical expressions" mentioned above.

76. See Witvliet, *Biblical Psalms*, 52-55, and the works cited there in n. 10 for insight into the construction of the Revised Common Lectionary and the place of the psalms within it. It seems that the primary function of the lectionary psalms is to serve as a response to the first lesson (Witvliet, 52-55 and 67-68; cf. also Holladay, *The Psalms*, 314). For specific suggestions on the use of the Psalms in different elements of worship and in different seasons of the church year, see *The Worship Sourcebook* (Grand Rapids: Faith Alive/Baker Books, 2004).

"Coming immediately *before* the Scripture lessons or the Gospel, the psalm is meant to do the same thing the sermon should be doing immediately *afterward* — namely, helping us to be personally engaged with the biblical story."[77]

The ways a particular psalm might be correlated with other biblical texts (lectionary or otherwise) are countless — as varied as the texts themselves and the preachers who preach them. Even so, three observations must be made by way of conclusion.

1. This introduction and the other essays in this volume assume and demonstrate that the Psalms are more than important — they are *crucial*. They should not be left aside, neglected, or omitted in worship. Still further: it is surely the case that the Psalms are too important to leave only as communal or choral responsorials. As important as liturgical response may be (and truly is), the Psalms invite and require *preaching*, part of which might include instruction on their proper use both in public worship and in private devotion.[78]

2. As helpful as the lectionary is in the task of preaching the Psalms, it is not foolproof. Simply put, the lectionary omits much that the Psalter deems precious. Fifty-one psalms — more than a third of the Psalter — do not appear in the lectionary.[79] While Holladay is correct that "[t]he range of psalms in this [the common] lectionary is impressive: much of the riches of the Psalter becomes available to the alert listener,"[80] it is nevertheless a real concern that so much of the Psalter is missing. The problem of missing psalms is exacerbated in two ways: *first*, even the ninety-nine psalms that do appear in the lectionary are not all intact; some forty-three of these are *excerpted*.[81] While this excerption is sometimes for reasons of space and (liturgical) time, it must be admitted that at other points it is hard to avoid the conclusion that this excerption reflects *theological censorship*, which is the *second* worsening of the situation.

77. Davis, *Wondrous Depth*, 18, emphases in original.

78. See part II and, further, Witvliet, *Biblical Psalms*.

79. Pss 3; 6–7; 10–12; 18; 21; 28; 35; 38–39; 44; 49; 53–61; 64; 69–70; 73–76; 83; 87–88; 94; 101–102; 108–109; 113; 115; 117; 120; 129; 134–136; 140–144.

80. Holladay, *The Psalms*, 278. At the time Holladay wrote, the Revised Common Lectionary was not yet available.

81. See Pss 5; 9; 17; 22; 25; 31; 33–34; 36–37; 40; 45; 50–51; 62–63; 66; 68; 71–72; 77–81; 86; 89–92; 103–107; 112; 116; 118–119; 132; 139; 145; 147. Four additional psalms that are used more than once appear in both holistic and excerpted fashion: Pss 27; 85; 96; 146.

Holladay's careful study of the Roman Catholic Liturgy of the Hours and the Common Lectionary has demonstrated that the omitted psalms and/or omitted parts of psalms are either laments or imprecations (curses) contained within psalms (especially laments).[82] Certainly, lectionaries are constantly being revised, and Holladay notes a distinct improvement in the Common Lectionary over the Liturgy of the Hours when it comes to the Psalms. That progressive trend is also found in the Revised Common Lectionary. One notes, for example, that Psalm 137:7-9 is omitted in the Liturgy of the Hours but is given in full in the Revised Common Lectionary (though, admittedly, as an optional text). It is clear, regardless, that lament is typically underrepresented in the lectionaries and that lectionaries have a tendency to omit "some, if not all, of the harsh language regarding enemies."[83] As Holladay has ominously put it, there is a "constant tendency" in the church "to bypass material with a negative import."[84] Now it must certainly be admitted that the psalms of divine wrath that often include vicious cursing of the enemies of God (and of the psalmist) are among the Bible's most difficult texts. But even these texts are not without merit, nor are they bereft of spiritual help.[85] Perhaps, again, it is the social location of the pray-er that has rendered these psalms so embarrassing to those well-off and mostly oriented, but that makes them treasured and sacred to those down-and-out and deeply disoriented. Charles H. Spurgeon (1834-92) said it well: "Let those find fault with it [Psalm 137] who have never seen their temple burned, their city ruined, their wives ravished, and their children slain; they might not, perhaps, be so velvet-mouthed if they had suffered after this fashion."[86]

---

82. Holladay, *The Psalms,* 304-15. Note that of the twenty-two psalms that are omitted from the Liturgy of the Hours, no less than eighteen are laments (310)!

83. Holladay, *The Psalms,* 311; see also, again, Towner, "Without Our Aid."

84. Holladay, *The Psalms,* 314.

85. See the excellent study of Erich Zenger, *A God of Vengeance? Understanding the Psalms of Divine Wrath* (Louisville: Westminster John Knox, 1996); also Davis, *Getting Involved with God,* 23-29; Dietrich Bonhoeffer, *Psalms: The Prayer Book of the Bible* (Minneapolis: Augsburg Fortress, 1970), 56-60 (the latter gives a christological reading of the cursing psalms); Miller, *Interpreting the Psalms,* 150-53; Miller, "The Hermeneutics of Imprecation," in *Theology in the Service of the Church: Essays in Honor of Thomas W. Gillespie,* ed. Wallace M. Alston, Jr. (Grand Rapids: Eerdmans, 2000), 153-63, reprinted in Miller, *The Way of the Lord: Essays in Old Testament Theology* (Grand Rapids: Eerdmans, 2007), 193-202. See also the exegetical essay on Ps 137 below.

86. Charles H. Spurgeon, *The Treasury of David: Spurgeon's Classic Work on the Psalms* (Grand Rapids: Kregel, 2004), 627.

The point, made above, is that censorship of lament (or imprecation) simply won't do: the stakes are too high and the results truly deleterious. Such censorship neglects a significant portion of the real life and real faith of the psalmists. And it neglects a significant portion of the real life of those who pray (or *should* be praying) the Psalms now and their real struggle to correlate their lives with something approaching reality and the real faith of the Psalms. In brief, if the Psalms are censored, one will not get the full anatomy of the soul, but something far less, partial, and grotesque — perhaps even hideous, like a skeleton: strangely attractive in its whitewashed articulations but utterly devoid of the parts that make a human being *alive*.[87] An excerpt from Thomas Mann's novel *The Magic Mountain* may say it best (read "lament" for "death" and "faith" for "life"):

> Permit me, permit me, my good engineer, to tell you something, to lay it upon your heart. The only healthy and noble and indeed, let me expressly point out, the only *religious* way in which to regard death [i.e., "lament"] is to perceive and feel it as a constituent part of life [i.e., "faith"], as life's holy prerequisite, and *not* to separate it intellectually, to set it up in opposition to life, or worse, to play it off against life in some disgusting fashion — for that is indeed the antithesis of a healthy, noble, reasonable, and religious view. . . . Death is to be honored as the cradle of life, the womb of renewal. Once separated from life, it becomes grotesque, a wraith — or even worse.[88]

3. Finally, maybe the Psalms should not be thought of as contributing to the "Great Story" of the Bible, so much as the "Great Story" should be thought of as something found already in the Psalter. Luther, for one, called the Psalms "the little Bible," because of the way it contains the full scope of the entirety of Scripture in brief and beautiful form.[89] But if so, in light of the poetic nature of the Psalms, then perhaps the Bible should be likened to a Great Psalm or Great Poem more than a Great Story. That Great Poem, like narrative or dramatic poems,

---

87. And what kind of skeleton would it be, without its backbone — the lament psalms themselves?

88. Thomas Mann, *The Magic Mountain: A Novel,* trans. John E. Woods (New York: Knopf, 1995), 197, emphases in original.

89. See Luther's 1528 "Preface to the Psalter," in *Luther's Works,* vol. 35, ed. E. Theodore Bachman (Philadelphia: Muhlenberg, 1960), 254; cf. Brown, *Seeing the Psalms,* 1, 217-18 n. 3; Witvliet, *Biblical Psalms,* 38.

has moments of plot, characterization, even linearity. But, like lyric poetry, it also has moments that lack those elements but that nevertheless abound with imagery, episodes, metaphors, and terse language that must be read aloud, interpreted, lived into, *felt* — not simply analyzed or dissected.[90]

If Scripture, at the highest level, is more like a great poem than a novel, more like a psalm than a story, then preachers not only will want to but will *need to* dust off their Psalters, brush up on their figures of speech, refine their license in all things poetic, *and preach the Psalms*. Real faith, full knowledge of the soul, robust experience of life with God could very well be the result. That's a possibility that the psalmists would certainly greet with resounding "Hallelujah's" and "Amen's."

Selected Bibliography

The following bibliography is brief and highly selective.[91] It includes a number of English commentaries on the Psalms that are intended as resources for further reading and study of the Psalms along with a few important introductions to and useful monographs on the Psalms.[92]

Allen, Leslie C. *Psalms 101–150*. Rev. ed. WBC 21. Nashville: Nelson, 2002.

Anderson, A. A. *Psalms*. 2 vols. NCB. Grand Rapids: Eerdmans, 1972.

Anderson, Bernhard W., with Steven Bishop. *Out of the Depths: The Psalms Speak for Us Today*. 3rd ed. Louisville: Westminster John Knox, 2000.

Attridge, Harold W., and Margot E. Fassler, eds. *Psalms in Community: Jewish and Christian Textual, Liturgical, and Artistic Traditions*. SBLSymS 25. Atlanta: Society of Biblical Literature, 2003.

Bonhoeffer, Dietrich. *Psalms: The Prayer Book of the Bible*. Minneapolis: Augsburg Fortress, 1970.

Briggs, Charles Augustus, and Emilie Grace Briggs. *A Critical and Exegeti-*

---

90. Cf. Brown, *Seeing the Psalms*, x: "Performative by nature, the psalms find their relevance primarily in what they *evoke* rather than in the countless ways they can be dissected and categorized" (emphasis in original).

91. See also the bibliographies in part II and in Witvliet, *Biblical Psalms*, passim.

92. A number of major commentaries on the Psalms are currently under way but not yet in print. These include works by William P. Brown (OTL); Walter Brueggemann and William H. Bellinger, Jr. (New Cambridge Bible Commentary); and Nancy deClaissé-Walford, Beth LaNeel Tanner, and Rolf A. Jacobson (NICOT).

cal Commentary on the Book of Psalms. 2 vols. ICC. Edinburgh: T. & T. Clark, 1906-7.

Brown, William P. *Seeing the Psalms: A Theology of Metaphor.* Louisville: Westminster John Knox, 2002.

Brueggemann, Walter. *The Message of the Psalms: A Theological Commentary.* Minneapolis: Augsburg, 1984.

———. *The Psalms and the Life of Faith.* Edited by Patrick D. Miller. Minneapolis: Fortress, 1995.

———. *The Spirituality of the Psalms.* Minneapolis: Fortress, 2002.

———. *Praying the Psalms: Engaging Scripture and the Life of the Spirit.* 2nd ed. Eugene, Oreg.: Cascade, 2007.

Clifford, Richard J. *Psalms 1–72.* Abingdon Old Testament Commentaries. Nashville: Abingdon, 2002.

———. *Psalms 73–150.* Abingdon Old Testament Commentaries. Nashville: Abingdon, 2003.

Craigie, Peter C. *Psalms 1–50.* WBC 19. Waco: Word, 1983.

Crenshaw, James L. *The Psalms: An Introduction.* Grand Rapids: Eerdmans, 2001.

Firth, David, and Philip Johnston, eds. *Interpreting the Psalms: Issues and Approaches.* Leicester: Apollos, 2005.

Gerstenberger, Erhard. *Psalms, Part 1: With an Introduction to Cultic Poetry.* FOTL 14. Grand Rapids: Eerdmans, 1988.

———. *Psalms, Part 2, and Lamentations.* FOTL 15. Grand Rapids: Eerdmans, 2001.

Goldingay, John. *Psalms.* 3 vols. Baker Commentary on the Old Testament Wisdom and Psalms. Grand Rapids: Baker Academic, 2006-2008.

Gunkel, Hermann. *Die Psalmen.* Göttingen: Vandenhoeck & Ruprecht, 1929; 5th ed. = 1968; 6th ed. = 1986.

———. *The Psalms: A Form-Critical Introduction.* Translated by Thomas M. Horner. Philadelphia: Fortress, 1967.

Gunkel, Hermann, completed by Joachim Begrich. *Introduction to Psalms: The Genres of the Religious Lyric of Israel.* Translated by James D. Nogalski. Macon, Ga.: Mercer University Press, 1998.

Hayes, John H. *Understanding the Psalms.* 1976. Reprint, Eugene, Oreg.: Wipf and Stock, 2003.

Holladay, William L. *The Psalms through Three Thousand Years: Prayerbook of a Cloud of Witnesses.* Minneapolis: Fortress, 1993.

Hossfeld, Frank-Lothar, and Erich Zenger. *Psalms 2: A Commentary on*

Psalms 51–100. Edited by Klaus Baltzer. Hermeneia. Minneapolis: Fortress, 2005.

Keel, Othmar. *The Symbolism of the Biblical World: Ancient Near Eastern Iconography and the Book of Psalms.* Translated by Timothy J. Hallett. New York: Seabury Press, 1978; Winona Lake: Eisenbrauns, 1997.

Kraus, Hans-Joachim. *Psalms 1–59: A Continental Commentary.* Minneapolis: Fortress, 1993.

———. *Psalms 60–150: A Continental Commentary.* Minneapolis: Fortress, 1993.

———. *Theology of the Psalms.* Minneapolis: Augsburg, 1986.

Lewis, C. S. *Reflections on the Psalms.* San Diego: Harcourt, 1958.

Limburg, James. *Psalms.* Westminster Bible Companion. Louisville: Westminster John Knox, 2000.

Magonet, Jonathan. *A Rabbi Reads the Psalms.* 2nd ed. London: SCM, 2004.

Mays, James L. *The Lord Reigns: A Theological Handbook to the Psalms.* Louisville: Westminster John Knox, 1994.

———. *Psalms.* Interpretation. Louisville: John Knox, 1994.

———. *Teaching and Preaching the Psalms.* Edited by Patrick D. Miller and Gene M. Tucker. Louisville: Westminster John Knox, 2006.

McCann, J. Clinton, Jr. "The Book of Psalms: Introduction, Commentary, and Reflections." In *NIB,* 4:641-1280.

———. *A Theological Introduction to the Book of Psalms: The Psalms as Torah.* Nashville: Abingdon, 1993.

McCann, J. Clinton, Jr., and James C. Howell. *Preaching the Psalms.* Nashville: Abingdon, 2001.

Miller, Patrick D. *Interpreting the Psalms.* Philadelphia: Fortress, 1986.

———. *They Cried to the Lord: The Form and Theology of Biblical Prayer.* Minneapolis: Fortress, 1994.

Mowinckel, Sigmund. *The Psalms in Israel's Worship.* Translated by D. R. Ap-Thomas. Reprint, Grand Rapids: Eerdmans; Dearborn, Mich.: Dove, 2004.

Moyise, Steve, and Maarten J. J. Menken, eds. *The Psalms in the New Testament.* London: T. & T. Clark, 2004.

Reid, Stephen Breck. *Listening In: A Multicultural Reading of the Psalms.* Nashville: Abingdon, 1997.

Tate, Marvin E. *Psalms 51–100.* WBC 20. Dallas: Word, 1990.

Terrien, Samuel L. *The Psalms: Strophic Structure and Theological Commentary.* ECC. Grand Rapids: Eerdmans, 2003.

Vos, Cas J. A. *Theopoetry of the Psalms.* London: T. & T. Clark, 2005.

Weiser, Artur. *The Psalms: A Commentary*. OTL. Philadelphia: Westminster, 1962.

Westermann, Claus. *The Psalms: Structure, Content, and Message*. Minneapolis: Augsburg, 1980.

―――. *Praise and Lament in the Psalms*. Atlanta: John Knox, 1981.

―――. *The Living Psalms*. Grand Rapids: Eerdmans, 1989.

Wieder, Laurance. *Words to God's Music: A New Book of Psalms*. Grand Rapids: Eerdmans, 2003.

―――, ed. *The Poets' Book of Psalms: The Complete Psalter as Rendered by Twenty-five Poets from the Sixteenth to the Twentieth Centuries*. San Francisco: HarperSanFrancisco, 1995.

Wilson, Gerald H. *Psalms Volume 1*. NIVAC. Grand Rapids: Zondervan, 2002.

Zenger, Erich. *A God of Vengeance? Understanding the Psalms of Divine Wrath*. Louisville: Westminster John Knox, 1996.

Exegetical Essays on Common Lectionary Psalms and Canticles

EXODUS 15:1-21

Seventeenth Sunday after Pentecost, Year A
    First Lesson: Exodus 14:19-31
    (Psalm 114 or **Exodus 15:1b-11, 20-21**)
    Second Lesson: Romans 14:1-12
    Gospel Lesson: Matthew 18:21-35

By the Seventeenth Sunday after Pentecost in Year A, the Old Testament selections have led readers from the foundational story of creation (on Trinity Sunday) to the great act of redemption in the exodus event, here remembered in narrative (Exod 14:19-31, the first lesson) and song, with Exodus 15 being one of only five nonpsalmic responses in the lectionary. Psalm 114 is a possible choice for this Sunday (see elsewhere in this volume), providing a shorter treatment of Israel's deliverance at the sea. Depending on the setting for proclamation, however, Exodus 15 offers greater thematic depth and breadth as well as more serious interpretive challenges for the preacher. Some of the important background issues involve selectivity, genre, and history.

  1. *The selectivity of the reading.* The lectionary designates verses 1b-11 and 20-21 as the reading from Exodus 15. The song itself concludes with verse 18, while verse 19 briefly summarizes the defining moment of the crossing, when the Egyptian army is consumed by the waters but the Israelites pass through safely. Verses 20-21 then introduce the role of Miriam and the women, who sing and dance to celebrate Yahweh's victory

(v. 21). Even a quick glance at verses 12-18 reveals that the selectivity is largely based on content, since these verses follow Israel's trek through the wilderness to the holy place Yahweh had chosen for himself (vv. 13, 17). The lectionary's focus is therefore on the exodus event itself, not on the rest of the journey to Palestine, though scholars debate the precise meaning and location of the sanctuary in question (Sinai, Gilgal, Zion). This selectivity notwithstanding, the song's own structure points to the fact that the Hebrews thought of the exodus as part of a larger saga moving inexorably toward possession of a land in which to live and a place at which to worship. Redemption was never disconnected from its context in Israel's story, which provided both the background and the path that carried the story forward.

2. *The genre of ancient Hebrew poetry.* Exodus 15 is widely regarded as the oldest and most consistently archaic piece of literature in the Hebrew Bible. Along with similar poetical treatments of Yahweh's movement from the desert to the Promised Land (e.g., Deut 33; Judg 5; Ps 68), Exodus 15 puts readers in touch with an extremely ancient witness to God's power and salvation. A few detractors have argued that the appearance of antiquity can be accounted for by verbal and thematic parallels in later biblical literature,[1] but this view cannot explain the complete consistency in archaic grammatical forms. Preachers will therefore be able to tap into this historical connection with the ancient community of God's people. It may be the case, as many scholars now argue, that Miriam herself is to be credited with authorship of the whole song instead of just the words in verse 21.[2] Thus, the lectionary's inclusion of verses 20-21 opens the way for a celebration of her contribution to Israel's worship and to ours.

3. *Relationship of song to narrative and theology to history.* A complex history of tradition lies behind both the Exodus narratives themselves and the connection of the song to its narrative context,[3] but for the purposes of proclamation, the canonical shape of the larger exodus drama means that *Israel's worship of* Yahweh is set firmly in *its story with* Yahweh. Terence Fretheim rightly points out that this song, like traditional psalms of thanksgiving, focuses on the exaltation of Yahweh but does so in relation

---

1. See Martin Leon Brenner, *The Song of the Sea: Ex. 15:1-21*, BZAW 195 (Berlin: Walter de Gruyter, 1991).

2. See Gerald Janzen, "Song of Moses, Song of Miriam: Who Is Seconding Whom?" *CBQ* 54 (1992): 211-20.

3. William Propp, *Exodus 1–18*, AB 2 (New York: Doubleday, 1999), 481-85, 550-54.

to "human experience and response."[4] The historicity of the exodus event and the song's description of God's mighty act may be an issue for some congregations. Given the antiquity of the exodus story and the song itself, there can be no doubt that the ancestors of those who settled in the land experienced something amazing in their flight from Egypt that they were compelled to describe as miraculous. Nevertheless, in spite of this clear connection to history, Nahum Sarna is correct in saying that the song is "preoccupied with celebrating the mighty acts of God as He intervenes in human affairs."[5]

With this brief background in mind, preachers can probe some of the powerful themes evoked by the song's form and content.

First, *the victory of God* is surely one of the predominant messages of Exodus 15, proclaimed from the opening line ("triumphed gloriously," v. 1 NRSV; the repetitive form in Hebrew, *gā'ōh gā'â,* implies the decisiveness of the victory) and described in detail in all that follows. To be sure, this victory is not merely over earthly kings and their armies, though that is the immediate message on the surface of the psalm (v. 4, "the chariots of *Pharaoh*"). Rather the very language of the song connotes a level of victory beneath the surface. Yahweh is able to throw the horses and chariots into the sea (v. 1) because Yahweh is victorious over all the chaotic forces in creation. Making no fewer than ten references to water, wind, and storm in verses 4-10 is the singer's way of celebrating Yahweh's power in relation to the created order. We are perhaps not familiar or comfortable with this language of praise, but the references function here as a means both to praise Yahweh and to place him above the deities of the Semitic pantheons. In the Ugaritic myths, for example, Yammu (related to Hebrew *yām,* "sea") is defeated by Ba'lu (Baal), and in the Mesopotamian creation epic *Enuma Elish,* the Babylonian god Marduk conquers Tiamat ("Mother Ocean") and uses her remains to make the structures of the cosmos.[6] It is little wonder, therefore, that following this dance of creation imagery the song erupts in verse 11 with rhetorical questions that exalt Yahweh over all gods. His majesty, splendor, and mighty deeds are unmatched by any power, human or divine.

Having acknowledged the echoes of mythopoetic imagery and the

4. Terence Fretheim, *Exodus,* Interpretation (Louisville: John Knox, 1991), 163-64.

5. Nahum Sarna, *Exodus,* JPS Torah Commentary (Philadelphia: Jewish Publication Society, 1991), 75.

6. See Propp, *Exodus 1–18,* 555-56.

larger canvas on which the portrait of Yahweh's victory is painted, there is still the immediate emphasis on a victory over the Egyptians (14:30-31). Yahweh remains a "mighty warrior" (v. 3; Hebrew *ʾîš milḥāmâ*, literally, "a man of war") whose power overwhelms "the enemy" (vv. 6, 9), clearly referring to the army of Pharaoh. A hymn that commemorated Rameses II's victory over the Hittites suggests that Exodus 15 challenged the Egyptians' praise of their pharaoh: "His [i.e., Pharaoh's] majesty was a youthful lord / Active and without his like / His arms mighty, his heart stout / His strength like [the god] Mont in his hour."[7] Perhaps one finds a deliberate critique of such pharaoh worship in the numerous references to Yahweh's "strength" (v. 2), "right hand" (v. 6), "majesty" (v. 7), and incomparability (v. 11).

A second and related theme is *the judgment of God.* The bulk of the lectionary selection focuses on the act of judgment at the sea (vv. 4-10). Since the rhetoric of the larger song seems to be much more about the exaltation of God over all the nations (see vv. 14-15), this is not merely the celebration of just one nation over another. Indeed, there is very little mention of Israel's role in Yahweh's victory over Egypt or in his movement to his holy abode. The word "Israel" does not even occur in the song, with only a few references to "your people" coming in verses 13-17. Yahweh is indeed Israel's "defender" (*zimrāt,* v. 2),[8] but the complete Old Testament prophetic witness is that Israel, too, may be judged by this Holy One, who is without peer in the divine realm. Perhaps this is why the song begins with such a strong personal note in its opening word *ʾāšîrâ* ("I will sing"; probably a cohortative ["let me sing"]).[9] The first-person forms continue in verse 2 with four pronominal suffixes ("*my* strength," "*my* salvation," "*my* God," "*my* father's"). Thus, the opening lines make the entire song and all its content a call for individual believers to embrace its story, its message, and its God for themselves.

The theme of judgment may also be informed through interaction with the Gospel and Epistle lesson for this Sunday. Romans 14:1-12 is Paul's warning against passing judgment on others in matters of indifference, since all of us belong to the Lord (vv. 7-9). Matthew 18:21-35 is

7. Cited in Gören Larsson, *Bound for Freedom: The Book of Exodus in Jewish and Christian Traditions* (Peabody, Mass.: Hendrickson, 1999), 104.

8. This follows Frank Moore Cross and David Noel Freedman, *Studies in Ancient Yahwistic Poetry,* SBLDS 21 (Missoula: Scholars, 1975), 55.

9. Though see Larsson, *Bound for Freedom,* 107, on the hopeful implications of rendering this in the future tense.

similar in its stress on forgiveness, with the parable of an unforgiving servant who continued to live under a system marked by judgment even after he had been graciously released from it. These words of caution may help the preacher who — in times of international terrorism and war — struggles with the tone of national judgment in the Song of the Sea. The rhetoric of the song is clearly that "Yahweh will see to any fighting that has to be done."[10] But the sense of conflict cannot be eliminated altogether. Walter Brueggemann rightly cautions, "There is in the gospel a model of conflict and a deep struggle for power and authority. To miss this element is to distort biblical faith into a benign, innocent affair."[11] And, just as biblical Israel was not immune to judgment, so also it is only in Christ that we are saved from the judgment of God.

James K. Mead

1 SAMUEL 2:1-10

Twenty-sixth Sunday after Pentecost, Year B
    First Lesson: 1 Samuel 1:4-20
    (1 Samuel 2:1-10)
    Second Lesson: Hebrews 10:11-14, (15-18), 19-25
    Gospel Lesson: Mark 13:1-8

Unlike most of the responsorials in the lectionary, the poem of 1 Samuel 2:1-10 appears within a larger narrative context. The first lesson sets the stage for reading it as "the song of Hannah," the poem's most common title. Heard in the voice of Hannah, a once-barren woman who brings her long-awaited child Samuel to Eli to "lend" him to the Lord (1 Sam 1:28), the song beautifully expresses the depths of Hannah's joy and amazement at the God who reversed her fortunes and brought about the birth of her son.

At the same time, features in the poem and other Old Testament

---

10. Godfrey Ashby, *Exodus: Go Out and Meet God,* ITC (Grand Rapids: Eerdmans, 1998), 67.

11. Walter Brueggemann, "The Book of Exodus: Introduction, Commentary, Reflections," in *NIB,* 1:803.

texts suggest that Hannah's song is also the song of many others. References to princes and kings (vv. 8, 10) as well as enemies (v. 1) and warfare (v. 4) suggest an original use for the poem in royal contexts, perhaps at the birth of a king or the celebration of a king's military victory.[1] And elements of the song resembling archaic Hebrew poetry leave open the possibility that it or parts of it come from still other contexts.[2] Thus Hannah takes up an already existing song and gives voice to it in the light of her own situation. And she is not the only one. The editors of the books of Samuel and Kings use this song to frame an even broader story of Israel's relationship with God, a story that includes the emergence of kingship as a new and triumphant way of living as God's people in the world as well as ironic reversals of fortune experienced by Israel, some positive and others quite tragic (cf. 2 Kings 24-25). Mary the mother of Jesus also adapts this song to celebrate the birth of her own son and to declare the wonders that God would bring through him (Luke 1:46-55). Ultimately, then, the song of 1 Samuel 2:1-10 attests to how the same words of praise have had significance for different individuals or communities uttering them, from victorious kings to grateful mothers to interpreters of history. In so doing, the song offers words that might be taken up by still others who observe or hope for God's world-altering ways, including worshipers today.

It is precisely God's *altering* of the world that stands at the heart of this poem. Far from being a fixed and static realm, the world is the arena for divine activity that brings about dramatic movement and change in human lives. Most often, the poem speaks of people moving upward and downward, being exalted and brought low (vv. 1, 6, 7, 8, 10). In conveying this, the poem itself projects a sense of movement through various literary developments and perspectives. The poem begins on a personal level, with first-person singular language describing the worshiper's experience of God.

> *My* heart exults in the Lord;
>> *my* horn is exalted in the Lord [the LXX reads "my God"].
> *My* mouth is wide over *my* enemies,
>> and *I* rejoice in your salvation. (v. 1, author's translation)

---

1. See David Noel Freedman, "Psalm 113 and the Song of Hannah," *ErIsr* 14 (1978): 56-69.

2. John T. Willis, "The Song of Hannah and Psalm 113," *CBQ* 35 (1973): 139-54.

Put simply, the worshiper's personal exaltation leads to exultation. This quickly leads to wide, sweeping statements about God's action regarding all of humanity. In doing so, the worshiper makes huge claims from a very narrow base of personal experience, demonstrating remarkable audacity.[3] But for someone like Hannah, whose deep longing for a child has been fulfilled in a situation that seemed hopeless, personal experience is convincing enough that broader claims are justifiable. If a barren woman can give birth to a child, then unimagined possibilities for the exaltation of the rest of humanity remain open as well.

In verse 1, two vivid images describe exaltation in ways that bear significantly on the rest of the poem. The raising up of one's "horn" reflects various Old Testament texts in which an animal carrying its head high with a raised horn symbolizes strength (e.g., Ps 92:10) and success (e.g., Ps 89:17) as well as progeny (e.g., 1 Chron 25:5; Ps 132:17; Deut 33:16b-17).[4] Moreover, the exalted horn presents a *conspicuous* sign of strength or success.[5] Hannah epitomizes this by singing of her own strength, success, and progeny in the public space of the Shiloh sanctuary. Patrick D. Miller has proposed that Hannah's prayer is meant to be heard more by others than by God, as is the case with many psalms of thanksgiving that feature more speech *about* God than *to* God.[6] Other humans "are the primary addressees," he writes, "and the Lord listens in" (cf. Pss 40:9a; 66:16). As the poem progresses, God not only exalts the horn of the worshiper but also raises up the poor, the weak, the barren, and the needy. This culminates in God's giving strength to the king and exalting the horn of God's anointed *(māšîaḥ)*. Not only do they have special status, a status that results from God's blessing rather than force or might (v. 9), but they become visible signs of blessing for the community. In keeping with the poem, it follows that the leadership and success of such figures reflect God's provision for the weak and the poor (cf. Pss 47:8-9; 72:2-7, 12-14; Isa 2:2-4; 19:23-25). Through their exalted status, God will exalt the lowly.

Exaltation comes also in relation to a person's enemies (v. 1). The figure of someone stretching his or her mouth wide over enemies refers to opening the mouth wide to swallow and devour them (cf. Pss 81:10; 35:21, 25; Isa 5:14; Prov 1:12; Hab 2:5), not, as most translations have it, simply

---

3. See Patrick Miller, "Praise and Worship," *CTJ* 36 (2001): 53-62.

4. See P. Kyle McCarter, *I Samuel: A New Translation with Introduction, Notes, and Commentary*, AB 8 (New York: Doubleday, 1980), 71.

5. McCarter, *I Samuel*, 71; cf. Pss 75:5-6; 112:9-10.

6. Miller, "Prayer and Worship," 53-62.

gloating over or deriding enemies.[7] While exaltation over enemies reflects
God's own exalted status over enemies (v. 10) and God's judging between
the wicked and the faithful (vv. 9, 10), it may also reflect a polemical edge
in the poem as it describes *reversals* in society rather than *inclusion* in good
fortune. Instead of claiming that the barren will *also* have children, for example, the fertile ones are displaced by those who were barren.[8] Certainly,
this marks the poem's vision with something of a dangerous quality for
those who enjoy power and thus stand to lose much, not to mention the
risk for the one proclaiming such a potentially offensive message.

The worshiper's exaltation and resulting joy come from "*your* deliverance," that is, God's saving action (*yĕšû'â*, v. 1; so NJPS, NIV, NASB, etc.;
NRSV's translation is based on Qumran texts). The string of words with
the possessive pronoun "my" in verse 1 stands in noticeable contrast to
"*your* deliverance." To borrow Brueggemann's language, this highlights
that it is not the worshiper's joy and exaltation but Yahweh's power.[9]
"Not by might does one prevail," the poem makes clear (v. 9), but one
prevails through *God's* power. And it is that power that remains the subject of the rest of the poem, with the poem's language building in intensity to underscore such power. At first the poem speaks of God in negative terms. Three times in verse 2 the same negative phrase ("there is
not . . ."; Hebrew *'ên*) brings across God's incomparability, a point made
similarly in Psalm 86:8 and Deuteronomy 33:26 (cf. Exod 15:11; Deut 4:32-
33; Pss 35:10; 71:19b; 89:8; 113:5, 7-9). This aspect of God's nature leads to a
warning against speaking proudly or in arrogance, a warning that
matches verse 2 in its negative grammar (v. 3; cf. Ps 75:4-5). Speaking arrogantly is foolish because "Yahweh is a mindful God [NRSV: a God of
knowledge] and by [God] actions are balanced" (v. 3).[10]

God's knowledge and balance no doubt reflect a divine ability to
evaluate an arrogant person's actions and speech, but on a much broader
plane they also describe God's work in the world as summed up in the
list of balanced antithetical pairs in verses 4-8. This catalogue of reversals, all of which testify to God's incomparability, reveals the "God of
knowledge" as having a particular mindfulness for the powerless as well
as remarkable intentionality in maintaining a special sense of balance

7. E.g., NRSV, NIV, NASB; see McCarter, *I Samuel*, 72.

8. Walter Brueggemann, *First and Second Samuel*, Interpretation (Louisville: John
Knox, 1990), 18.

9. Brueggemann, *First and Second Samuel*, 17.

10. Translation by McCarter, *I Samuel*, 72.

and symmetry in the world where the low are brought high and the high are brought low. The poem separates these divine actions into two sections, the first of which lists groups that experience a reversal of fortunes (vv. 4-5).[11] The strong (those who are mighty [v. 4], full [v. 5a], and fertile [v. 5b]) lose their power while the weak (those who are feeble [v. 4], hungry [v. 5a], and barren [v. 5b]) gain power. In each case the actions are described in the passive voice without explicitly identifying God as the agent of these actions. Then the second section of actions (vv. 6-8) distinguishes the Lord — whose name is placed emphatically at the beginning of the first sentence — as the one who brings about the astounding reversals. The verses add still more actions to the list, now using the active voice and a number of participles that bring a sense of intensity and immediacy to the divine works.

With this the poem reaches its climax, having subtly built in intensity from negative speech (vv. 2-3) to passive speech (vv. 3b-5) to active speech about God (vv. 6-8, 9-10). Verse 8 provides an extended description of what it would look like for the weak to be exalted — moving from the ash heap to a seat of honor — and grounds this and all other divine activity in God's power as the creator:

> For the pillars of the earth are the LORD's,
>   and on them he [God] has set the world.

As Brueggemann points out, this proclaims not only God's power but also God's complete freedom: "Yahweh need not conform to any legitimated social arrangement. Yahweh is free to reorder the earth and will do so on behalf of the marginal."[12]

The Lord's power and freedom are just what allow humans to hold to the vision of 1 Samuel 2:1-10 when faced with the kinds of crises described in the Gospel lesson (Mark 13:1-8), whether famines or earthquakes or wars or rumors of wars. Jesus makes clear in that text that no mighty buildings or institutions will save people: not religion nor the government nor the military nor the economy. At some point they will all come crashing down. Not by personal or institutional might can a person prevail, but only by God, and this is what gives hope to those who

11. Bruce Birch, "The First and Second Books of Samuel: Introduction, Commentary, and Reflections," in *NIB*, 2:981.

12. Brueggemann, *First and Second Samuel*, 19.

are not protected by the mighty structures of society. It is a hope not only for survival, but also for exaltation and joy.

Jennifer S. Green

PSALM 1

Seventh Sunday of Easter, Year B
>First Lesson: Acts 1:15-17, 21-26
>**(Psalm 1)**
>Second Lesson: 1 John 5:9-13
>Gospel Lesson: John 17:6-19

Eighteenth Sunday after Pentecost, Year B
>First Lesson: Proverbs 31:10-31
>**(Psalm 1)**
>Second Lesson: James 3:13-4:3, 7-8a
>Gospel Lesson: Mark 9:30-37

Sixth Sunday after the Epiphany, Year C
>First Lesson: Jeremiah 17:5-10
>**(Psalm 1)**
>Second Lesson: 1 Corinthians 15:12-20
>Gospel Lesson: Luke 6:17-26

Together with Psalm 2, Psalm 1 serves as the introduction to the book of Psalms. But because it comes at the start of the Psalter, before Psalm 2, readers who lack knowledge of the factors that tie these two poems together (e.g., both lack superscriptions [cf. Ps 3]; "happy" ['ašrê] is used in both 1:1 and 2:12, serving as a literary *inclusio;* and in some manuscripts Acts 13:33 quotes Psalm 2:7 as "the first psalm") will think of Psalm 1 on its own as *the* introduction to the Psalms. This is well and good, but even so, Psalm 1 is something of an odd introduction. Those familiar with the Psalms know that the first psalm, qua introduction, is *hardly representative*. There is no praise of God here, nor is there any hint of lament. Since those two items are the flesh and bones of the Psalter, how can the introductory psalm not sound their notes?

To be sure, Psalm 1's focus on the law *(tôrâ)* of the Lord *is* found else-where, though *not* everywhere, in the Psalms, especially and famously in Psalm 119 (see also Ps 19). But what is significant about Psalm 1 as an in-troduction is not its representative-ness but its *definitional and constitutive power.* That is, Psalm 1 *constructs a world* — a world within the psalm itself, to be sure, but also a world for the Psalms as a whole. Each point deserves some discussion.

1. *The world within Psalm 1.* The world of Psalm 1 is tightly ordered and neatly divided in a dualistic schema that is unforgiving and thoroughgo-ing. There are only *two* types of people, belonging to *two* types or ways of being, with *two* end results. There is no middle ground, "[n]o partly righ-teous, no a-little-bit-wicked."[1] The *first* type is the *wicked,* the *sinners,* the *scoffers* (v. 1), though the predominant descriptor is "wicked," since it is repeated several times (vv. 1, 4, 5, 6). The wicked can be found everywhere, as is evident from the verbs and nouns used in conjunction with them. They give *advice;* they are on the *path* — quite literally, "in the way"; and they have *places of residence* (to sit and scoff together, no doubt!). So it is that one ought not to *walk* with them or *stand* with them or *sit* with them. Their activity and sheer omnipresence, however, surely make such a choice difficult. Regardless of its difficulties, however, the choice is ob-vious given the metaphorical description of the wicked and their ulti-mate future. Metaphorically, they are wasted and wastable chaff, driven away or pursued by the wind *(rûaḥ;* v. 4). As for their future, if not also their present, it is similarly ephemeral: they will not rise up in the judg-ment or in the congregation of the righteous (v. 5). Instead, the wicked way ends in destruction (v. 6b). Given the first part of verse 6, one might well speculate Who is behind that destruction.

The *second* type of person, way of being, and end result is *the righteous,* though that term is held in abeyance until verse 6. Its use at the end of the psalm makes "righteous" and "righteousness" catch terms for what is described earlier in the psalm in fuller and metaphorical ways. The ear-lier descriptions are couched negatively and positively. The righteous are those who do *not* accompany the wicked regardless of their posture or ac-tivity,[2] *but rather (kî 'im;* note the same combination in v. 4: "*but rather* like chaff . . .") are those who delight in the Lord's law *(tôrâ)* and meditate or

1. James L. Mays, *Psalms,* Interpretation (Louisville: John Knox, 1994), 42.
2. Cf. Peter C. Craigie, *Psalms 1–50,* WBC 19 (Waco: Word, 1983), 60: "A person can be happy, from a negative perspective."

muse (even mutter or recite) on it day and night (v. 2). Metaphorically, the righteous one is like a healthy, productive, and fruitful tree (v. 3). It is important to note that the tree is said to be "planted by streams of water" (NRSV). It is stable and firmly rooted in contrast to the varied and frenzied activity of the wicked.[3] To be more precise, the tree is actually said to have been *trans*planted (*šātûl*; cf. Ps 92:12-13; Ezek 17:7-10, 22-23; 19:10-13; contrast √*nṭ*, "to plant"). The tree's prosperity, that is, is not attributable only to itself or the accidental circumstances of its existence, but rather, at least to some degree, to its transplant*or*, as well as the streams of water — a metaphor for God's life-giving torah[4] — that nourish the tree. Given this ideal and nourishing location, it is not surprising that the tree bears fruit as it should, when it should, and that it continues to thrive. And given the careful transplantation that implies a nurturing Gardener — indeed, *primarily* because of that — it is not surprising to find that "in all they do, they prosper" (Ps 1:3). The Lord's agency becomes explicit only in verse 6, which is where this second type of person is finally identified as righteous. By explicitly invoking the Lord's intimate knowledge (√*yd*) of the way of the righteous, the psalmist also reveals Who is ultimately behind the transplantation of the tree and its prosperity. Of course, that prosperity will be challenged, qualified, and redefined at many points in the Psalter,[5] but that is not yet. Psalm 1 is too busy creating a world to be a representative introduction.

For now, then, there are two ways: the way of the righteous and the way of the wicked (v. 6). Standing between them, poised, as it were, at the fork in the road and deciding between them, is "the one" — literally, "the man" *(hā'îš)*, a term often used as an indefinite pronoun ("one," "anyone" — male *or* female) in Hebrew. People can choose, that is, on which way to walk (that of sinners and the wicked, vv. 1, 6; or that of the righteous, v. 6); in which seat to sit (that of scoffers, v. 1; or that of torah-studiers, v. 2); and which plant to be (unusable chaff, v. 4; or the thriving tree, v. 3). The urgency of this decision may be underscored by the use of the singular term in the Hebrew, obscured somewhat by the NRSV's use of the plural (so as to avoid gender specificity). *Each person*, that is, has this choice. And yet, by setting the options as the psalmist does, espe-

---

3. See J. Clinton McCann, Jr., "The Book of Psalms: Introduction, Commentary, and Reflections," in *NIB*, 4:684.

4. See McCann, "The Book of Psalms," 4:685; William P. Brown, *Seeing the Psalms: A Theology of Metaphor* (Louisville: Westminster John Knox, 2002), 58, 131.

5. See Mays, *Psalms*, 44: it is "the claim of faith, not experience."

cially by the rhetoric of verses 1 and 6, the choice is obvious and fore-gone.[6] Already the reader is identified with — *urged* to identify with — that one who chooses rightly and righteously. After all, that is the person who is happy; that person is the tree; that one's way is watched over by the Lord. What other viable choice is there, really?

2. *A world for the Psalms.* This way of putting matters is designed to impact the reader of the Psalms. But, as already noted, the world con-structed in Psalm 1 also creates a context, a world, in which the rest of the Psalms reside. There are at least two important functions that Psalm 1 plays as the introduction to the Psalter. First, Psalm 1 *defines the wicked and the righteous* and their respective ways of life. These two terms (and related synonyms) occur everywhere in the Psalms. The reader who begins with Psalm 1 knows, in every psalm thereafter, how to identify these types, especially the righteous. The righteous are ones that medi-tate on the Lord's law and, because of that, do not accompany the wicked, and because of that, thrive and prosper. This leads directly to the second important function: in Psalm 1 *the righteous are torah-ized.* In doing this, the Psalter prevents and protects against antinomian ten-dencies. (It is perhaps especially important, then, that *tôrâ*, while mean-ing much more than "law" narrowly conceived, nevertheless be trans-lated as "law" or identified, at least in part, with the Lord's law in the Bible, especially the Old Testament.) There is no possibility of bifurca-tion — *torah-folks* (read "legalists" or "fundamentalists") on the one hand and *psalm-folks* (read "mystics" or "spiritual types," even "progres-sives" or "liberals") on the other. *Psalm 1 unites them.* The way of piety, the way of prayer, the way of righteousness, the way of the Psalms *is* the way of torah. Conversely, the way of torah *is* the way of prayer, of piety, of righteousness, and of the Psalms. The structure of the book of Psalms as a whole, broken up into five books in what is probably a con-scious imitation of the five books of the Pentateuch, further stresses the connection. So it is that the Psalms become Torah, instruction from God in the life of faith. The rule of prayer *(lex orandi),* after all, is the rule of belief *(lex credendi).* Prayer and piety, righteousness and justice, law and psalm belong together. That is the way it is if one chooses to

6. See James Limburg, *Psalms,* Westminster Bible Companion (Louisville: Westmin-ster John Knox, 2000), 3; Hans-Joachim Kraus, *Psalms 1–59: A Continental Commentary* (Minneapolis: Fortress, 1993), 121; Walter Brueggemann, *The Message of the Psalms: A Theo-logical Commentary* (Minneapolis: Augsburg, 1984), 39.

walk the way of the righteous. And the reader of Psalm 1 knows the advantages of choosing that way!

Finally, some comments on the place of Psalm 1 in the lectionary. Used as a response to the first lesson in the three different Sundays wherein it appears, the psalm brings its world-constituting power to bear on the other readings in varying ways. As a response to Acts 1:15-17, 21-26, Psalm 1 reads as *explanation* — more specifically, as *warning after the fact*. How could Judas have failed so terribly? Psalm 1's answer is that he must have walked in the counsel of the wicked, stood in the way of sinners, sat in the seat of scoffers. Other perspectives on Judas exist, of course (see esp. Matt 27:3-10), and ought not to be neglected, but the preceding judgment is at least one of the results created by the juxtaposition of Acts 1 and Psalm 1. That juxtaposition also raises questions about Matthias. Will he be Judas's heir or will he be like a tree planted by streams of water? The choice, in Acts 1 (and Ps 1), is up to him. Unfortunately, the New Testament does not tell us what he chose, speaking no more of Matthias.

Psalm 1's reply to Proverbs 31:10-31 is also *explanatory,* but the mirror opposite of Acts 1: it is *commendation after the fact.* Here, in this famous ode to the valorous wife, Psalm 1 lends further clarity to what is only hinted at until verse 30: "a woman who fears the LORD is to be praised." Fearing the Lord is often connected with keeping the Lord's commands (e.g., Eccles 12:13) — that is, obeying torah (cf. Prov 31:20 with Deut 15:7-8). As a response to Proverbs 31, Psalm 1 explains how everyone, including and especially women, can be numbered among the happy ones (not just "the man" [so KJV, NIV, NJPS]!) of Psalm 1:1. It is altogether noteworthy that the valorous woman's children call her "happy" or "blessed" (Prov 31:28) — the same root used in Psalm 1:1 and 2:12.

Jeremiah 17:5-10 is a hybrid of the preceding. It echoes Psalm 1's world in its description of those who turn from the Lord and trust only in themselves. They are not happy, but cursed (v. 5); they may not be chaff, but they are equally destitute: a shrub in the desert (v. 6). But those who "trust in the LORD" (note the straightforward description) are blessed (*bārûk;* v. 7), and the prophet proceeds to describe them with the tree metaphor. Verses 9-10 also echo Psalm 1 in attributing the discernment of ways to the Lord, but verse 9 is more poignant than the psalm as it raises the issue of human responsibility and deviousness by discussing the human heart (*lēb;* see also vv. 6 and 10 [NRSV's "mind" is literally "heart" (*lēb),* whereas "heart" is literally "kidneys"]).

The heart is devious above all else;
    it is perverse —
    who can understand it?

Jeremiah's voice thus indicates that the matter of the two ways is, at some level — perhaps at the *ultimate* level — a *matter of the heart.*

Brent A. Strawn

PSALM 2

Last Sunday after the Epiphany, Transfiguration, Year A
    First Lesson: Exodus 24:12, 15-18
    (Psalm 2)
    Second Lesson: 2 Peter 1:16-21
    Gospel Lesson: Matthew 17:1-9

Together with Psalm 1, Psalm 2 forms a two-part introduction to the Psalter (see the essay on Ps 1). In terms of genre, Psalm 2 is a *royal liturgy* (see the introductory essay); it was most likely used originally in Jerusalem as part of a ceremony involving the Judean king. When it was placed at the start of the Psalter, of course, the Judean monarchy had been reduced to a distant memory — yet it was also a lingering hope. And that is one of the points that Psalm 2 makes as a co-introduction to the Psalter: hope in God's promise to act once again through David's seed! As J. Clinton McCann has noted, "Psalm 2 is really more about the reign of God than about the Davidic monarchy." According to McCann, in the final form of the Psalter the royal psalms function eschatologically. They affirm "that God's rule is effective *now* and will ultimately be manifest."[1] The psalm's reference to God's "anointed" (Hebrew *māšîaḥ*) may also be evidence of an early brand of messianic hope. For its part, the New Testament certainly interpreted the psalm in a messianic way (cf. Heb 1:5).

The psalm consists of four stanzas, which have an *abb'a'* structure:

1. J. Clinton McCann, *A Theological Introduction to the Book of Psalms: The Psalms as Torah* (Nashville: Abingdon, 1993), 42, 45.

Psalm 2

Stanza 1	*a*	The "kings of the earth" speak rebelliously.
Stanza 2	*b*	The divine King enthroned in heaven laughs.
Stanza 3	*b'*	The Davidic king enthroned in Zion reports God's speech.
Stanza 4	*a'*	The "kings" are warned to serve God.

Each of the first three stanzas ends with a quotation, in which a different voice speaks from a different location. One main theme of the psalm is kingship. A second theme is the idea of "speech," as the many references to discourse suggest: "rage" (Hebrew √*rgš* implies speaking), "murmur," "laugh," "mock," "speak," "tell," "say," and "ask." All the action of the psalm takes place in the act of speaking — the kings of the earth rebel by speaking, God responds by speaking, God's anointed king announces God's speech, and in the end, the kings of the earth are warned to be speechless and serve God.

Stanza 1. The psalm opens with a rhetorical question that indicates amazement and puzzlement that the nations would seek to rebel. Then follows a lengthy indicative "answer" (vv. 2-9) to this "question," which provides the reason why rebellion against God is a fruitless and hazardous undertaking. It is worth repeating that the action in the first stanza — as in the rest of the poem — occurs solely in the act of the characters *speaking.* Here the kings and officials of the nations speak words of rebellion against the Lord. The poem deftly sets up the conflict between the "kings" and "rulers" (both plural) and "the LORD and his anointed" (both singular). If the struggle were merely a matter of numerical superiority, there would be little hope for those who trust in the Lord.

Stanza 2. The second stanza shifts the scene to heaven, and the speaker is now the heavenly king ("He who sits" in v. 4 is a technical term for "the one who is enthroned" — a phrase denoting God's kingship). The Lord responds to the rebellious speech of the nations' kings with a countering speech: "I have set my king on Zion, my holy hill." God's response to the rebellion of the nations is *to act in and through the Davidic king.* As noted above, the ancient editorial decision to make this "royal" response to evil part of the introduction to the Psalter most likely demands an eschatological interpretation to this verse.

Stanza 3. The speaker and location again shift in the third stanza. The last words of the second stanza indicate that the "I" who speaks in the third stanza is the Davidic king enthroned on Zion in Jerusalem. This king announces God's promise to him:

You are my son;
> today I have begotten you.
Ask of me, and I will make the nations your heritage,
> and the ends of the earth your possession.

The Judean king was considered God's "son" (cf. 2 Sam 7:1-17). In terms of the psalm's plot of a rebellion of the "nations" and "kings of the earth," the surprise here is that the fate of the nations and the ends of the earth has already been determined: these entities have been promised to the Davidic king.

Stanza 4. The last stanza of the poem breaks the pattern to which the hearer/reader has grown accustomed. As expected, there is a new speaker, this time the same narrator who voiced the first stanza. But rather than the stanza ending with a quotation as did the first three stanzas, this one ends with a warning and with the rebellious nations remaining silent in renewed obedience to God. The Hebrew text of Psalm 2 is difficult (compare the translations of the NIV and NRSV), but the general sense is clear. Rather than continuing to speak words of rebellion, the leaders of the nations are to remain silent and to "kiss" either God's feet (so NRSV and others) or God's son (so NIV and others).[2] Note also that the closing admonition in verses 10-12 rounds off the rhetorical structure of the psalm: verse 1: question; verses 2-9: answer; verses 10-12: admonition.

The Lord's response in Psalm 2 to human rebellion is noteworthy in two ways. On the one hand, it is a response of "derision," "wrath," and "fury." Modern readers often stumble over the concept of God's wrath. But God's wrath is merely the flip side of God's love. God, who loves the creation, sees sin and evil being done and responds in anger. A God who cannot get angry at sin and evil is an uncompassionate and distant God — not the sort of God who risks all to become incarnate in a human being. In a world in which the reign of God is disputed by many forces bent on rebellion, with those forces inevitably bringing about evil due to that rebellion, there is good news in the announcement that God does not greet the suffering caused by such rebellion with indifference. Psalm 2 confesses that while God's reign is contested, the ultimate outcome is beyond doubt.

On the other hand, God's response is not to take vengeance via an

---

2. For a discussion of the textual problem, see Peter C. Craigie, *Psalms 1–50*, WBC 19 (Waco: Word, 1983), 64.

"act of God" — God is not in the fire, the wind, or the earthquake (cf. I Kings 19:11-12) — rather, God responds through the Davidic king. As noted above, Psalm 2 is a royal psalm, one of those psalms that originally had to do with Jerusalem's kings. A historical explanation for this psalm must reckon with the reality that the psalm originally had to do with God's actions in and through the Davidic king. But in its canonical setting the psalm demands a theological explanation. According to the theological vision of the Old Testament, one factor that contributed to the failure of the monarchy was that Israel's kings never lived up to God's ideals. Yet Israel's prophets had consistently promised the advent of a Davidic king who would fulfill those ideals and reign as the ideal Davidic king (cf., e.g., Isa 11). Psalm 2 is assigned by the lectionary for use on Transfiguration Sunday, immediately before Lent. At the transfiguration, as well as in the rest of the New Testament, Jesus is identified as that promised ideal king. In the context of the end of Epiphany and the start of Lent, Psalm 2 announces that a rebellion that seeks to achieve independence from God is not a "way" that will find genuine freedom. Instead, such a rebellion is the "way" to bondage. Genuine freedom is found in a living relationship with the Lord who has promised to act through Israel's king, the Lord who became a human being and walked the lonely valley to the cross. In the words of the Fourth Gospel, "If the son makes you free, you will be free indeed" (John 8:36).

Rolf A. Jacobson

PSALM 4

Third Sunday of Easter, Year B
   First Lesson: Acts 3:12-19
   (Psalm 4)
   Second Lesson: 1 John 3:1-7
   Gospel Lesson: Luke 24:36b-48

Psalm 4 appears only once in the Revised Common Lectionary, as a response to Acts 3:12-19, a speech given by Peter to unbelievers who were astonished that he and John had just healed a lame man. "The God of Abraham, the God of Isaac, and the God of Jacob . . . has glorified his servant Jesus, whom you handed over and rejected," he told them (v. 13). It was "his name," Peter insisted, "[that] has made this man strong" (v. 16).

Psalm 4, sung or said as a response, reiterates Paul's exhortation that we put our trust for healing, peace, and security in the Lord. According to many commentaries,[1] the psalm is a prayer for rain (cf. vv. 6-7) uttered by a faithful believer in God (v. 3) who is chastising those who have resorted to beseeching idols in their desperation (v. 2). Its implications, of course, extend to all the faithful who refuse to compromise on their allegiance to God in times of crisis. The prayer, then, is simultaneously a prayer of trust (v. 8) and one of supplication (v. 1).

As John Eaton notes, a "striking feature" of the psalm is that a little over half of it is addressed not to God but to "you people" (v. 2). The psalmist "links . . . [his] cause with that of the Lord," issuing five imperatives he urges them to follow: "know that the LORD has set apart the faithful for himself" (v. 3); "when you are disturbed, do not sin" (v. 4); "ponder it on your beds, and be silent" (v. 4); "offer right sacrifices" (v. 5); and "put your trust in the LORD" (v. 5). Eaton notes that "it is as though the supplicant, through converse with God, gains strength to address words of inspired power to the hostile people."[2] Presumably, this strength is gathered as the psalmist himself lies in bed, pondering the affairs of the day even as he says his evening prayers (cf. v. 8). It might be helpful, along these lines, for pastors and worship leaders preparing this text to contemplate the context in which we formulate the "righteous words" we plan to deliver to our adversaries. Are they chosen as we lie in silence, in a posture of prayer, as those who trust in the Lord?

Also striking is the psalmist's certainty that his prayers will be heard. Clearly, his confidence is founded in his history of relationship with God, who "gave [him] room when [he] was in distress" (v. 1). The psalmist trusts that the One who saved him before will save him again. Though he has not yet received an answer to this particular prayer, he believes that the Lord hears him (v. 3). The psalmist's uncompromising trust in God functions in several ways. First, it propels the offering of the prayer itself. Because the psalmist has absolute trust in God, he does not hesitate to ask God for help. Second, it fuels a warning to the people who have dishonored the psalmist. God will answer, the psalmist insists, and they will be proven wrong. Third, it gives way to a feeling of utter security — the

1. See, e.g., Mitchell Dahood, *Psalms I: 1-50*, AB 16 (New York: Doubleday, 1965), 23.
2. John Eaton, *The Psalms* (London: T. & T. Clark, 2003), 71.

psalmist will sleep well because he trusts God to protect him. Finally, it inspires a desire for inclusion. The psalmist is so certain that God is reliably gracious that he invites the very ones to whom he is issuing a warning into the circle of the faithful. "Offer right sacrifices," he tells them, "and put your trust in the LORD" (v. 5). God will come through not only for him, the psalmist believes, but also for all who enter into faithfulness.

In our era of much discussion about nurturing spirituality, Psalm 4 offers an intimate glimpse into how a faithful follower of God should pray in times of crisis and conflict. John Calvin explains that there are four "rules" for the prayer of the faithful, all of which are reflected in the psalmist's prayer.[3] First, Calvin argues for the "devout detachment" that the psalmist exemplifies in being "set apart" and in recommending that the people "ponder . . . on [their] beds, and be silent" (v. 4). Second, Calvin insists that we should "pray from a sincere sense of want, and with penitence." Certainly, the psalmist's desire for vindication and security is apparent (vv. 2, 8); his penitence is seen in his vulnerable plea for God's graciousness (v. 1). Third, Calvin recommends that "we yield all confidence in ourselves and humbly plead for pardon." The psalmist's confidence is clearly not in himself but firmly set in God; the pardon he is asking for in this prayer is not forgiveness for his own sin but liberation from the sin of those who dishonor him (v. 2). Fourth, Calvin holds that we should "pray with confident hope." Surely, there is nothing more hopeful than the psalmist's testimony that God has put "gladness in [his] heart" even before his prayer has been answered (v. 7). Where, in today's weary society, do we see manifest such hope that one can "lie down and sleep in peace," trusting God for protection even in the midst of a crisis (v. 8)?

The psalm also offers challenging guidance for how we, as faithful believers in God, should think of our adversaries. The psalmist does not excuse their sinful behavior. He is quite explicit about what it would look like for them to turn away from idolatry and trust in the Lord. And yet the imperatives he issues are not only accusatory but also full of yearning. The psalmist clearly hopes that those who have dishonored him will not simply be proven wrong, but that they will be reconciled to the fellowship of the faithful. Samuel Terrien goes so far as to argue that the "us" on which the psalmist desires "the light of [the LORD's] face" to shine includes those the psalmist hopes will someday stand at his side (v. 6). In requesting

---

3. John Calvin, *Institutes of the Christian Religion*, ed. John T. McNeill, 2 vols. (Philadelphia: Westminster, 1960), 2:853-74 (3.20.4-16).

God's blessing on "us," Terrien insists, the psalmist "thereby invites his detractors to enter the circle of his intimates."[4] So, in the final analysis, the minister or church leader who shares in this reading of the psalm might well ask her or his congregation: How often do we ask God's blessing on our enemies, yearning for them to enter into fellowship with us?

Cynthia L. Rigby

PSALM 5

Fourth Sunday after Pentecost, Year C
> First Lesson: 1 Kings 21:1-10, (11-14), 15-21a
> **(Psalm 5:1-8)**
> Second Lesson: Galatians 2:15-21
> Gospel Lesson: Luke 7:36–8:3

Psalm 5 may be categorized as an *individual lament* or a *prayer for protection* (see the introductory essay). It consists of five stanzas that alternate between two themes: the petitioner before the Lord (vv. 1-3, 7-8, 11-12) and the threat of the wicked (vv. 4-6, 9-10). The structural and theological center is at verses 7-8, where the psalmist requests safe passage to the house of God. The psalm thus moves from anguished prayer to confident expectation that those who fear and love the Lord will surely find refuge in him. An important trope in the psalm is the power of human speech and its ability to destroy life, or — when that speech is constituted as prayer/praise in accordance with the reign of God — to safeguard it.

The psalm begins plaintively and insistently with a threefold plea: "give ear to my words," "consider my sighing," "heed the sound of my cry" (vv. 1-2). The 3 + 2 meter typical of laments, in conjunction with the characterization of the prayer as a "sigh" too deep for words (cf. Rom 8:26) and a "cry" for help, conveys a tone of anguish. Yet, here at the outset, no elaboration of the crisis provokes the prayer. What is underscored, instead, is speech *addressed to God*. The language is highly personal and relational. In addition to the pronoun "you" (twice in vv. 2-3), God is addressed four

---

4. Samuel L. Terrien, *The Psalms: Strophic Structure and Theological Commentary*, ECC (Grand Rapids: Eerdmans, 2003), 102.

times in the vocative: twice as Yahweh, "the LORD" (vv. 1, 3), and for the first time in the Psalms, as "my King" and "my God" (v. 2). The image of God as king is a root metaphor that occurs frequently in the Psalter (see Pss 24; 29; 47; 93-99). God reigns in the world, upholding creation, working salvation (cf. Pss 44:4; 74:12), and judging all the inhabitants of the earth in righteousness. In addressing God as King, then, the psalmist appeals to the final arbiter of justice who graciously attends to the pleas of his servants. Hans-Joachim Kraus captures the marvel of this dynamic: "Yahweh in the power of his dominion can be addressed by me; he is there for me."[1]

So the psalmist is bold to pray and plead his case (v. 3). There is some ambiguity in the Hebrew expression that the NRSV renders "I plead my case." The Hebrew text simply reads "I prepare" (Hebrew √'rk), without an explicit direct object. The verb may refer to preparing one's words in a legal case (cf. Job 13:18; 23:4; 32:14; 33:5; 37:19; Ps 50:12). It may also be used with respect to formal arrangements for a sacrifice (cf. Lev 1:8-9, 12), hence the rendering "I set out my morning sacrifice" in some translations (e.g., NEB, ESV). Additionally, the verb may refer to the act of praying itself, that is, the setting forth of one's requests (so KJV, NIV). Prayer, in turn, is what prepares the supplicant to enter the divine presence.[2] However the verb is understood, the psalmist presents his plea before God and *watches* expectantly, as in Habakkuk 2:1: "I will stand at my watchpost . . . I will keep watch to see . . . what [God] will answer concerning my complaint." The psalmist does this at daybreak — the anticipated time of divine deliverance (cf. Pss 46:5; 130:6-7; Job 38:12-13). Hence, *the tone of anguish* is accompanied by *eager expectation*.

The basis for the psalmist's plea is given in the next stanza (vv. 4-6), introduced by the conjunction "for" (Hebrew *kî*). It praises God as the one who does not tolerate wickedness and brings an end to those who do evil. At the same time, however, the hymnic element serves to remind God that the psalmist's "enemies" (v. 8) belong to the company of the wicked and should be destroyed.[3] The portrayal of the wicked in these verses is elaborated via traditional categories: the boastful, evildoers, liars, those who shed blood and deceive. It is intensified later in the psalm with imag-

---

1. Hans-Joachim Kraus, *Psalms 1–59: A Continental Commentary* (Minneapolis: Fortress, 1993), 154.

2. Peter C. Craigie, *Psalms 1–50*, WBC 19 (Waco: Word, 1983), 88; Artur Weiser, *The Psalms: A Commentary*, OTL (Philadelphia: Westminster, 1962), 124.

3. Richard J. Clifford, *Psalms 1–72*, Abingdon Old Testament Commentaries (Nashville: Abingdon, 2002), 56.

ery that evokes the destructive potential of human speech (vv. 9-10). These evildoers are unscrupulous, bloodthirsty people, whose lies endanger the lives of the innocent and the weak.[4] The tragic end of Naboth at the hand of lying scoundrels, and their false accusations, in the first lesson (1 Kings 21) is a potent illustration of the murderous power of the lie.

The psalmist finds solace in recalling that such evildoers cannot "sojourn" or "dwell" with God (v. 5). According to Psalm 15:1-3, that privilege is reserved for those who "do what is right" and "speak the truth," who "do not slander . . . or take up a reproach against their neighbors." Moreover, the three negative statements concerning God's intolerance of the wicked (Ps 5:4a, 4b, 5a) are matched by three statements that declare positively that God "hates," "destroys," and "abhors" those who do evil (vv. 5b, 6a, 6b). God's opposition is stated in the strongest possible terms.

In contrast to the wicked, the psalmist identifies himself as one who may enter the house of God (v. 7). In the sacred place the righteous find protection from danger (vv. 11-12; cf. 1 Kings 1:51-53; 2:28-29). Yet the emphasis in verse 7 is on "the abundance of God's steadfast love *(ḥesed)*." It is only by the Lord's sovereign grace that the supplicant has access to the divine presence. So, unlike those who boast and rebel against the Lord (vv. 5, 10), the psalmist vows to bow in fear of God, the posture befitting a loyal servant. The life of the faithful, however, is not without opposition. The psalmist is ever aware of the malice of "enemies" (v. 8) and therefore requests:

> Lead me, O LORD, in your righteousness . . . ;
>   make your way straight before me.

Divine guidance is necessitated not only because of the reality of hostile enemies, but also because the psalmist knows that he himself must take care to avoid the way of the wicked.

As one commentator puts it: "The prayer for protection is not only for protection *from* wicked persons, but also a prayer for protection from becoming *like them.*"[5] This prayer for protection, then, may also — and ultimately — be a "prayer for self-examination."

Eunny P. Lee

---

4. See James L. Mays, *Psalms,* Interpretation (Louisville: John Knox, 1994), 58; J. Clinton McCann, Jr., "The Book of Psalms: Introduction, Commentary, and Reflections," in *NIB,* 4:702.

5. Craigie, *Psalms 1–50,* 89.

PSALM 8

Trinity Sunday, Year A
  First Lesson: Genesis 1:1–2:4a
  (Psalm 8)
  Second Lesson: 2 Corinthians 13:11-13
  Gospel Lesson: Matthew 28:16-20

Trinity Sunday, Year C
  First Lesson: Proverbs 8:1-4, 22-31
  (Psalm 8)
  Second Lesson: Romans 5:1-5
  Gospel Lesson: John 16:12-15

When measured according to its form, Psalm 8 is usually described as *a hymn* (see introductory essay). In fact, it is the first hymn in the Psalter, although it is a slightly odd hymn. Most hymns open with a characteristic *call to praise* such as "Praise the Lord!" or "Bless the Lord!" (often repeated at the end of the psalm), followed by *reasons for praise,* usually introduced by "for" (Hebrew *kî*). Psalm 8, however, begins and ends not with a call to praise but with an exclamation of praise. That is, rather than speaking to other humans, summoning them to the praise of God, this psalm starts by speaking words of praise *directly to God.* In fact, the characteristic call to praise is entirely missing from Psalm 8; it is doxology rather than exhortation. Thus, Psalm 8 is in many ways the counterpart to Psalm 150, a praise psalm that is pure exhortation (see the essay on Ps 150).

When measured according to its content, Psalm 8 is usually described as a creation psalm[1] because it praises the Lord for the work of creation: the earth, heavens, moon, stars, sheep, oxen, birds, fish, and of course, humanity. Like other creation texts, this psalm is a theological witness to *the faithfulness of God.* God is praised not primarily for the aesthetic beauty of the world, but for the fidelity God shows in creating and continuing to maintain creation.

The psalm has a concentric structure that is built around the question of verse 4:

---

1. See Claus Westermann, *The Psalms: Structure, Content, and Message* (Minneapolis: Augsburg, 1980), 93-96; see also Pss 19; 104; 139; and 148.

v. 1a Praise Sentence ("How majestic . . .").

   vv. 1b-3 The splendor of God's "glory" in creation.

     v. 4 Question: What is humanity that you care for it?

   vv. 5-8 Answer: God has crowned humanity with responsibility.

v. 9 Praise Sentence ("How majestic . . .").

James Limburg has called this a psalm for "stargazers."[2] This is an apt characterization, for the psalm is not a portrait of God or humanity but a landscape that portrays God, humanity, and nature — painting all three in a vast panoramic sweep. The psalmist, the modern reader may imagine, has wandered into nature on a starry, starry night and come face-to-face with God's "glory" in nature (vv. 1b-3). (Many of us have had a similar experience, realizing how small and insignificant we are when measured against the scale of time and nature.) And having come face-to-face with God's glory, the psalmist has further wandered into a question: "What are human beings that you are mindful of them, mortals that you care for them?" This essentially existential question is the spine of the psalm. The NRSV's decision to pluralize the Hebrew terms *'ĕnôš* (literally, "a man") and *ben 'ādām* (literally, "a son of man") for the sake of inclusive language is legitimate, because the psalmist is not asking only about his or her own purpose, but about the worth and purpose of the entire human race.

But if the question of verse 4 is the spine of the psalm, the theological answer provided in verses 5-8 is the *beating heart* of the psalm. The answer is as profoundly *theological* as the question is *existential* (there is no gap between the two categories here!). And the answer is surprising. Within the whole witness of Scripture, there are many answers to the questions, "What are we that God cares for us?" and "How do we know God cares for us?" In the Gospel of John, for example, we know that God cares for us because the only Son died for us (John 3:16). In the book of Deuteronomy, we know that God cares for us because God has given us just laws (Deut 4:7-8). In Psalm 139, we know that God cares for us because we are so lovingly created (Ps 139:13-18). But here in Psalm 8, we know that God cares for us and that we have worth *because God has given us responsibility for other parts of God's creation!*

The psalm says, literally, "You made him [us] to rule over the work of

2. James Limburg, *Psalms*, Westminster Bible Companion (Louisville: Westminster John Knox, 2000), 24.

Fig. 1. Psalm 8 speaks of the dominion of humans over the animal world (vv. 6-8). This image shows that such dominion should not be interpreted in reckless, cavalier fashion. Instead, as the conjunction of Genesis 2 with Genesis 1 reveals, human rule over the animal world (Gen 1:26, 28) is to be marked by protection (√*šmr*) and service (√*'bd*) of the earth (Gen 2:15; cf. v. 5). This image shows an anthropomorphic figure (probably a deity) "ruling" the deer (the foot placement signifies subjugation; see figs. 11-12), but in order to protect it from the leonine monster (probably a demon of some sort).

---

your hands, all things you have set under his [our] feet" (v. 6). The concept of "rule" or "dominion" (the causative [hiphil] verb form of √*mšl*) is borrowed by the psalmist from the realm of royalty. Kings were given responsibility and authority to go with that responsibility, but the authority (or dominion) was not to be misused or abused. It was to be used *for the care* of those governed (see Pss 72 and 74). Psalm 8 pictures all of humanity as the kings and queens of creation, bestowed with special divinely given gifts, which we are to use for the care and keeping of creation (cf. Gen 1:26-28; 2:15; see also fig. 1).

This is both a surprising and remarkable answer to the question, "What are we that God should care about us?" The answer, in effect, says that God not only cares about us, but also has a job for us to do — one befitting a king, no less! Every child in the process of growing up can relate to this answer. Children want to help their parents; they do not want to be taken care of forever. Children grow in part through responsibility; they do not grow if they are forever the objects of parental sheltering. I think of the special joy my own daughter takes when she brings her mother a piece of cake and says, "I helped Daddy make it!" In that moment, you can feel the self-worth dripping off her proud words. That is the message of Psalm 8: God not only knows who I am, God has given me a part in baking the cake that is God's kingdom.

A few words about how Psalm 8 fits in the lectionary. Psalm 8 is the assigned psalm twice, with both occasions falling on Trinity Sunday. The context in Year A is especially apt for the preaching of Psalm 8, since the Gospel that day is the Great Commission from Matthew 28. The two texts fit well together, since both speak of the responsibility bestowed upon believers by the Father, Son, and Holy Spirit. Redeemed free of charge by the love of Christ, we are called to serve as evangelists, teachers, and caretakers of God's creation.

Rolf A. Jacobson

PSALM 9

Fifth Sunday after Pentecost, Year B
First Lesson: 1 Samuel 17:(1a, 4-11, 19-23), 32-49
(Psalm 9:9-20)
Second Lesson: 2 Corinthians 6:1-13
Gospel Lesson: Mark 4:35-41

For a number of reasons, it appears that Psalms 9 and 10 were originally one psalm and should therefore be considered together. First, there is no heading for Psalm 10; note the heading for Psalm 9, "To the leader . . ." That Psalm 10 would lack a superscription is unusual, since, after the introductory Psalms 1-2, every psalm in Book I (Pss 1-41) except for Psalm 33 begins with a heading. Second, the two psalms appear as one in early Greek and Latin translations. Third, certain expressions occur only in these two psalms (for example, "times of trouble" in 9:9 and 10:1). Fourth and most important, the two psalms taken together are built on an acrostic pattern, with every other line beginning with a successive letter of the Hebrew alphabet (though a few letters are left out or out of order). A number of psalms exhibit this acrostic pattern, which serves, among other things, as a structuring device (see Pss 25; 34; 111; 112; 119; 145; cf. Prov 31:10-31).

Whatever the case, the heading at the beginning of Psalm 9 dedicates the psalm to the choir director; "according to Muth-labben" (NRSV) is probably a reference to a tune, and the psalm is to be associated in some way with David.

The fact that the lectionary reading begins with verse 9 highlights that the Lord will be "a stronghold in times of trouble." Indeed, this is the key interpretive phrase in the psalm. Even so, the piece does not follow an easily discernible progression of thought because the author is constrained by the alphabetical pattern. For this reason, the psalm jumps back and forth among various typical psalm themes.

It opens by speaking about the Lord with a call to praise, announcing that the psalmist is going to give thanks because of the "wonderful deeds" the Lord has done (v. 1). The opening continues by shifting into "you" language, addressing the Lord directly (vv. 1b-2). Verses 3-6 indicate what some of these "wonderful deeds" have been. The segment is framed by reference to "enemies" (vv. 3, 6) who have been crushed in military victories. The psalmist is saying, "God was at work in these victories, and for that I give thanks!"

With verses 7-10 the focus shifts from the "wonderful deeds" of the past to the concerns of the present and the future. In verses 7-9 the psalm speaks about the Lord, giving instruction to those listening. The focus is universal: the Lord is portrayed as a king on a throne, ruling and judging all the nations of the world. Verses 9 and 10 express the central teaching point of the entire psalm. First, an affirmation of trust is expressed in a third-person statement about the Lord:

> The LORD is a stronghold for the oppressed,
> a stronghold in times of trouble.

Then a declaration of trust is addressed directly to the Lord in second-person "you" language:

> And those who know your name put their trust in you,
> for you, O LORD, have not forsaken those who seek you.

The preacher dealing with this psalm will want to focus on these two verses as a sturdy, repeatable, applicable affirmation of confidence in the Lord's care and power.

From this point on the psalm moves back and forth among various psalmic themes. The psalmist calls the congregation to *praise* (v. 11) and gives a reason for that praise: God does not forget those who are suffering (v. 12). Next, the writer focuses on his own *suffering* with a call for help asking that the Lord who took him from the "gates of death" bring him safely to the "gates of Zion," that is, to Jerusalem (vv. 13-14).

Verses 15 and 16 look back at what has happened to those *nations* who had been plotting evil: they have fallen into their own trap! The same notion is expressed in Psalm 7:15-16. Verses 17 and 18 are an articulation of the *psalmist's trust* in the Lord, offering a hopeful view of the future when the wicked will be gone and the poor and needy will be restored to normal sorts of lives. Finally, verses 19 and 20 express another *call for help*, asking that the Lord remind these enemies who they are ("mortals . . . only human") and who the Lord is (the one who "executes judgment").

The preacher who wishes to tie the psalm to other lectionary readings for the day will need to sense the links among them. The lesson from Paul's second letter to the church at Corinth indicates that the apostle, too, experienced the Lord's help and salvation at times when he underwent a great variety of "afflictions, hardships, calamities" (2 Cor 6:1-13; note especially vv. 1-2). A powerful illustration of the Lord's help in a time of trouble is found in the Gospel story of the stilling of the storm. It also concludes with a reminder of who the Lord is: "Who then is this, that even the wind and the sea obey him?" (Mark 4:35-41).

James Limburg

PSALM 13

Sixth Sunday after Pentecost, Year A
First Lesson: Genesis 22:1-14
(Psalm 13)
Second Lesson: Romans 6:12-23
Gospel Lesson: Matthew 10:40-42

Psalm 13 is the quintessential *lament psalm* (see the introductory essay). All elements of the lament form are present, in order, even though the psalm is only six verses long. The brevity of the poem does not detract from its content, however. It is short, yes, but in this case the concision underscores the pain and power, not to mention the promise, of the lament.

If the psalm is brief, the *address* is ultrashort. It comprises only one word: "Yahweh" (NRSV: "O LORD"; v. 1ab) — which is embedded already in the *complaint* (vv. 1-2). It is a terse and urgent beginning.[1] The complaint, a third of the entire poem, is punctuated by the repetition of "How long?" This phrase, not uncommon to laments (cf., e.g., Pss 6:3; 35:17; 74:10; 79:5; 80:4; 89:46; 90:13; 94:3; 119:84), evokes the terrible circumstances of the psalmist and asks for immediate reprieve. It is also found in Babylonian laments,[2] so the cry is not specifically biblical or Israelite but "entirely human."[3] It is with this painful and human cry that the poet *starts* ("*How long,* O LORD?"). After this plaintive beginning, Psalm 13 repeats the phrase three more times. Four times "how long" equals far too long! The psalmist is insistent, right from the start: the Lord must act soon.

The need for immediate attention is underscored in other ways as well. The situations described by the psalmist are not only no longer endurable, they are also attributed to the Lord's direct (active) or indirect (passive) actions. The Lord has *forgotten* (inadvertently?) the psalmist — *forever,* no less! And God has *hidden God's face* (advertently?) from the psalmist (v. 1). Like the phrase "how long," both of these complaints are often found in the lament psalms (see, e.g., Pss 42:9; 77:9; and 10:1; 27:9; 88:14, respectively). The claim reflects the poet's perspective: the cause (or blame, as it were) lies at the Lord's door; it is the Lord's doing.

The following situations are also punctuated by the "how long" refrain and might be independent statements, but by beginning with two "how long's" directed toward the deity, the poet gives the impression that the following two are *the result* of the first two. If so, God's forgetfulness and hidden face lead directly to the psalmist's soul-pain and heart-sorrow (v. 2a), as well as to the triumph of the psalmist's enemy (v. 2b; cf. v. 4). The NRSV's "pain in my soul" (v. 2a) is actually taken from the Syri-

1. Cf. Walter Brueggemann, *The Message of the Psalms: A Theological Commentary* (Minneapolis: Augsburg, 1984), 59: "It is as though the pain is so acute that there is no time for convention or nicety."

2. See, e.g., Hans-Joachim Kraus, *Psalms 1–59: A Continental Commentary* (Minneapolis: Fortress, 1993), 214.

3. See Claus Westermann, *The Psalms: Structure, Content, and Message* (Minneapolis: Augsburg, 1980), 55; James Limburg, *Psalms,* Westminster Bible Companion (Louisville: Westminster John Knox, 2000), 38.

ac version of the Old Testament and does fit the poetic parallelism nicely. Some other translations are closer to the Hebrew (and Greek) text, however. Note, e.g., KJV: "How long shall I take counsel in my soul?"; NJPS: "have cares on my mind"; NIV: "wrestle with my thoughts." While less poetically synonymous, the Hebrew text is nevertheless quite evocative: the Lord's absence leaves the psalmist to his or her own devices. The psalmist has nowhere else to turn: with God gone, whether by accident or design, the psalmist sits alone wondering what has happened. Heartsickness "all day long" (v. 2b) is the understandable and altogether expected outcome.

So, although brief, the complaint is quite poignant and powerful. The precise circumstances behind the psalmist's distress are unclear and probably unrecoverable, but they are ultimately of little import. What is significant, rather, is the psalmist's urgency and the mention in the complaint of all three standard entities that are typically part of lament scenarios: God, the self, and the enemy, or, to use other language, theology (God), psychology (psyche), and sociology (society). These three are also involved in the *petition* proper (vv. 3-4), which constitutes the second third of the poem. Here too the psalmist begins with God, addressing imperatives to the throne: "Consider [literally, 'look!']! Answer me, Yahweh my God!" The personalized addition to the divine name — "Yahweh *my* God" — supports the rhetorical move to petition. Even if God has forgotten the psalmist (v. 1), the psalmist has *not* forgotten. So, now, the poem indicates that divine consideration and answering would undo the divine forgetfulness and hiding of verse 1. The psalmist's third imperative, "Give light to my eyes," speaks to the distress in verse 2, but the poet elaborates the point with two arguments: *first,* that without such light the sleep of death is imminent (v. 3b); and *second,* that without such light the psalmist's enemies will claim victory and rejoice (v. 4). The latter point obviously reflects verse 2, but what is elaborated is that the singular enemy of that verse has become the *plural* enemies of verse 4 and they have been worsened. They are no longer "my enemy" (vv. 2b, 4a). They are now "my enemy . . . and my foes" (literally, "my distressors"). And they are no longer simply exalted over the psalmist (v. 2b); they are now able to claim that they have *overcome* the psalmist (v. 4a) and will rejoice (a term often used of *religious* affect and action; cf. v. 6; Pss 2:11; 9:14; 14:7; etc.) when they see the psalmist shaken (*'mwt,* a possible wordplay with "death," *hmwt,* in v. 3).

The petition gives way, finally, to the *confession of trust* (v. 5) and the *vow of praise* (v. 6), which together constitute the final third of the psalm. Complaint and petition remain dominant, two-thirds of the poem, but Psalm 13 ends — like almost every other lament — not in complaint and petition but in trust and praise. As stated in the introductory essay, a definitive explanation for this move is not forthcoming. In Psalm 13, as in others, it could perhaps be a final rhetorical device of a gifted poet. Verse 5 begins with a focus on the psalmist by use of a redundant and emphatic first-person pronoun: "(But) *as for me,* I trusted in your steadfast love" *(ḥesed).* Again, the psalmist has not forgotten (cf. v. 3), but this is not a bootstrap, triumph-of-the-individual sort of mentality. The psalmist trusts, not in his or her own self, but in *God's faithfulness,* God's *ḥesed,* a rich term representing, in McCann's words, "the most important theological concept in the book of Psalms."[4] And the psalmist is not yet done, asserting that his or her heart will rejoice in God's *salvation (yěšû'â),* another deep pool (see Pss 3:2, 7, 8; 12:1, 5 [translated variously in the NRSV by "help," "safety," "deliverance," etc.]). This latter statement certainly answers the foes' rejoicing (v. 4) since it is the same verb (√*gyl*); the fact that the psalmist indicates that it is his or her *heart* that will rejoice certainly responds to the daily *heart*sickness of verse 2. The psalmist concludes, finally, with the strong expectation and intention (if it is not in fact already enacted in the statement itself) to sing to the Lord, because "he has dealt bountifully with me" (v. 6b).

The last clause is difficult to reconcile with earlier portions of the psalm and again raises the question of the relationship between lament and praise. Is the latter voiced only later, after the lamentable circumstances are resolved? Or is it the rhetorical coup de grâce, whereby the poet seeks to move (or even guilt) God into action? Or is it that somehow the lament enables and facilitates, permits, even causes the shift to praise? We do not know for certain, but again, perhaps such information is unnecessary — maybe it is too wonderful for us. What we do know and do have is the testimony of this faithful poet: faithful in pain and problem, faithful in prayer and petition, faithful in praise and song. All three parts, equally faithful! And the final testimony of the psalmist is that his or her own faithfulness pales in the face of Yahweh's — the One who deals bountifully, despite pain, problems, sickness, and despair. As Kraus states, "the center of attention is not the change of fortune but the sav-

4. J. Clinton McCann, Jr., "The Book of Psalms: Introduction, Commentary, and Reflections," in *NIB,* 4:670; see Pss 5:7; 21:7; 107:1; 118:1; 136; etc.

ing God alone, who rescues from the realm of death, enlightens the eyes
. . . and does good things."[5]

The other readings of the day contribute to this discussion. In the
first, the near sacrifice of Isaac (Gen 22:1-14), one could easily imagine
Abraham praying the words of Psalm 13. When the test (see Gen 22:1)
comes — to sacrifice his only, beloved son — it is not hard to envision
Abraham praying, "How long, O Lord? Have you forgotten the promise
of this child — that this child was your doing, your gift? Consider that!
Answer me!" But we do not hear any of that in Genesis 22, learning only
of Abraham's silent obedience (v. 3). Reading Genesis 22 with Psalm 13
helps us realize that more vocal, lamenting, painful speech can also be
faithful and may in fact be what the faithful say, even if they say it under
their breath, so no one else hears, or through clenched teeth. But Genesis
22 also narrates what the poet of Psalm 13 testifies to in the end: that God
is faithful, that God will see to it — whether that is the lamb for the
burnt offering (Gen 22:8, 14), or the less specific but still poignant circumstances of the psalmist.

Genesis 22 thus provides a parade example of God as problem but
also of God as provider — as the One who ultimately deals bountifully.
The other two lessons can also be read in this light: Romans 6:12-23,
which tells of the God who has brought us from death to life, is further
evidence of God's gracious dealings with us in Christ. Matthew 10:40-42
shows that those who deal bountifully with others (by welcoming them)
do the same for Christ. Indeed, it can be said that Christ *expects* such behavior from those who have first experienced God's bountiful welcome
(cf. Mark 9:37, 41; John 13:20) and that such bounty can be experienced in
even the smallest of gestures: a cup of cold water. When a cup of cold water can reflect the extraordinary dealings of God with us, then we certainly have much reason — like the psalmist — to end our poems, our
songs, and all our days in praise.

Brent A. Strawn

5. Kraus, *Psalms 1–59*, 217.

PSALM 14

Tenth Sunday after Pentecost, Year B
First Lesson: 2 Samuel 11:1-15
(Psalm 14)
Second Lesson: Ephesians 3:14-21
Gospel Lesson: John 6:1-21

Seventeenth Sunday after Pentecost, Year C
First Lesson: Jeremiah 4:11-12, 22-28
(Psalm 14)
Second Lesson: 1 Timothy 1:12-17
Gospel Lesson: Luke 15:1-10

Psalm 14 paints a picture of humanity that could hardly be more dismal. Whereas most psalms open by acknowledging God in heartfelt praise or supplication, this one begins with a fool *(nābāl)* declaring in his or her heart, "There is no God." The fool, moreover, proves to be quite wicked, revealing a corrupt nature and carrying out abominable deeds (v. 1). The wicked character of the fool illustrates one of the psalm's most salient points, that foolishness and wickedness are closely linked. In a most basic sense, a fool is one who holds mistaken ideas about reality and then acts incorrectly or wickedly on the basis of those wrong assumptions.[1] The character Nabal (note: *nābāl*) in 1 Samuel 25, for example, typifies such foolishness in the way that his mistaken assumptions about David lead him to act selfishly and inhospitably.[2] In other Old Testament texts the term *nābāl* describes fools with even more perverse behavior: they scoff at and revile the name of the Lord (Ps 74:18, 22), scorn righteous people (Ps 39:8), and unjustly gain wealth only to lose it all (Jer 17:11). In 2 Samuel 13:13 Tamar calls her brother Amnon one of Israel's "fools" or "scoundrels" (√*nbl*) just before he rapes her. The moral decency that people like these lack reflects their basic lack in understanding, or wisdom, about reality (Deut 32:6). Psalm 14 traces this deficiency to a fundamental mistakenness about the reality of God. The foolish belief that "there is no God" results in the situation that "there is no one who does good."

Broadening the depiction to all humanity, the psalm heaps on more

1. James L. Mays, *Psalms,* Interpretation (Louisville: John Knox, 1994), 81.
2. Mays, *Psalms,* 81.

allegations of moral corruption stemming from people's failure to have discernment and seek the reality of God (v. 2). People go astray and are perverse (v. 3). Put simply, they do not do good (vv. 1, 3). More specifically, people, now deemed "evildoers" (v. 4), act improperly in their treatment of other people, especially the poor and the righteous (v. 6). God, or one speaking on God's behalf, declares that they "eat up my people as they eat bread" (v. 4). These words, used also in Micah 3:1-4, likely refer to economic or social oppression by an upper-class element of society.[3] According to the NRSV and other translations, the evildoers who engage in that activity have no knowledge ($\sqrt{yd}$) and do not call upon ($\sqrt{qr}$) the Lord (v. 4). Translating these two verbs differently, however, Stuart Lasine has proposed an alternative understanding of verse 4 that may better fit the context of this psalm: "Do they not reason [$\sqrt{yd}$; cf. Isa 9:9; 44:19; Judg 18:14; 2 Sam 24:13], all the evildoers who eat up my people as they eat bread, that they do not encounter [$\sqrt{qr}$] Yahweh?"[4] This use of the verb qr corresponds to the way it refers to divine judgment in Amos 4:12: "Prepare to meet [qr] your God, O Israel!" Read this way, verse 4 asks a rhetorical question that points out how evildoers assume they can abuse people and not worry about divine retribution.[5] As far as the wicked are concerned, "there is no God" with regard to their evil actions, and they do not look for or seek God to see if this assumption is true (v. 2). In their foolish minds, God remains detached from human wickedness, a belief shared by the wicked ones in Psalm 10, who also declare, "There is no God," as they persecute the poor (Ps 10:4; cf. Pss 10:11-12; 12:4; 73:11; 94:4-7; Jer 5:12; 12:4; Zeph 1:12). The lectionary text of 2 Samuel 11:1-15 (first lesson, Tenth Sunday after Pentecost, Year B) offers another example of this attitude. Though David does not utter the words, he carries out his reprehensible plan to cause Uriah's death and steal Uriah's wife as if there is no God and no consequences for those actions.

In fact, however, the evildoers *do* meet God in their actions. As it turns out, God is in the midst of the very people they "eat up," serving as a refuge for the poor and being present among the righteous (Ps 14:5-6; cf. Pss 9:17-18; 10:17-18; 12:4-7). The evildoers' oppression of the poor and righteous thus brings them into the presence of God and reveals their ul-

---

3. J. Clinton McCann, Jr., "The Book of Psalms: Introduction, Commentary, and Reflections," in *NIB*, 4:730.

4. Stuart Lasine, "A Note on Psalm 14:4," *JBL* 114 (1995): 465.

5. Lasine, "A Note," 465.

timate foolishness in thinking that God is absent. How this occurs precisely is not made clear. Perhaps the wicked ones, in a rare moment of insight, would see God by recognizing their victims' trust in divine protection even as they are being traumatized. Or the oppressors might glimpse the divine by seeing the oppressed community band together in times of trouble, sharing with each other out of their poverty and lifting each other up as they themselves are beaten down. The terrifying realization of the oppressors' complicity in persecuting others and in rejecting God may reflect the "terror" coming over them in verse 5. Psalm 53, an expanded version of Psalm 14, offers another interpretive possibility with its description of the evildoers' encounter with God as a horrifying experience in which God rejects the evildoers and scatters their bones (Ps 53:5). However the evildoers meet God — whether through some dramatic demonstration of divine justice or through God made visible in the lives of those clinging to God's protection — it is exactly *there* (*šām*, v. 5), in the evildoers' terrorizing oppression of others, that *they* now feel terror in the stunning experience of meeting God.[6]

The reference to the righteous in verse 5, of course, creates an obvious tension in the text that merits some discussion. Earlier the psalm emphatically states twice that "there is no one who does good" (vv. 1, 3), echoed by the phrase "there is not even one" (v. 3). Even from a perfect vantage point in heaven, the Lord cannot find one discerning person (*maśkîl*) who seeks God. Instead, "all" *(kōl)* have turned aside and are "all alike" *(yaḥad)* in perversion (v. 3). Likely, these phrases describe society as a whole, a corrupt entity that oppresses individuals and groups within it; as Mays puts it, the psalmist likely speaks more as "the prophet doing social analysis than the theologian discussing anthropology."[7] These words may portray countless groups throughout history that have taken advantage of the powerless (e.g., Isa 1:21-23; Amos 2:6-8; 4:1; 5:11-12; Mic 2:1-2; 3:1-3; Ezek 34:1-10), demonstrating that it seems there is "not even one" among them who does good. Still, one might take these statements at face value as a reflection on the human condition and the tendency of all people to act as if there is no God, to exploit those who have less power.

6. See Mays, *Psalms*, 83; Lasine, "A Note," 465; McCann, "The Book of Psalms," 4:730; Hans-Joachim Kraus, *Psalms 1–59: A Continental Commentary* (Minneapolis: Fortress, 1993), 219; Artur Weiser, *The Psalms: A Commentary*, OTL (Philadelphia: Westminster, 1962), 164-66; Mitchell Dahood, *Psalms I: 1–50*, AB 16 (Garden City, N.Y.: Doubleday, 1965), 80-81.

7. Mays, *Psalms*, 82.

No one, including the reader, can escape accusations of wrongdoing, as the second-person ending on the verb in verse 6 makes clear: *you* are at fault. Even the people of God, "my people," may be foolish and fail to know the reality of God, as the lectionary text (first lesson, Seventeenth Sunday after Pentecost, Year C) from Jeremiah 4:22 charges:

> For my people are foolish,
> they do not know me;
> they are stupid children,
> they have no understanding.
> They are skilled in doing evil,
> but do not know how to do good. (NRSV)

Paul quotes the opening lines of this psalm (vv. 1-3) in the book of Romans to demonstrate that all people "are under the power of sin" (Rom 3:9 NRSV; cf. 3:23) and thus depend on God's grace for deliverance from that sin (Rom 3:24). So too Psalm 14 ends with a call to God for deliverance (v. 7). Many read the final lines as a postexilic addition to the psalm, signaled by the phrase "restore the fortunes" — one that often refers to return from exile (cf. Deut 30:3; Jer 29:14; 30:3, 18; 31:23; 32:44; 33:7, 11; Pss 85:1; 126:1). As such, the psalm may call for Israel's deliverance from nations that dominated it, or, more generally, deliverance of the oppressed from their oppressors.[8] Such an event certainly would bring about the kind of rejoicing described in the psalm's last verse. At the same time, one might read this as a call for deliverance for the oppressors, that is, all humans who engage in some forms of exploitation — who also stand in need of being rescued from their foolishness and resulting terror (v. 5). Only when deliverance comes and restoration occurs can this group also hope to rejoice and be glad (v. 7).

Jennifer S. Green

8. McCann, "The Book of Psalms," 4:730.

PSALM 15

Fourth Sunday after the Epiphany, Year A
  First Lesson: Micah 6:1-8
  (Psalm 15)
  Second Lesson: 1 Corinthians 1:18-21
  Gospel Lesson: Matthew 5:1-12

This group of lectionary readings circles around the twin topics of true worship and true discipleship. Together these readings suggest that true worship of God can be accomplished only when worshipers arrive with hearts and lives truly committed — what we call discipleship. The Micah passage makes this connection most clearly by reducing worship to its essence: "Do justice . . . love kindness . . . walk humbly with your God" (6:8). Matthew's Beatitudes drive home the awareness that those who would follow Christ into the kingdom will demonstrate characteristics that set them apart from the world in which they live. And in 1 Corinthians 1, we learn that participation in the salvation of God requires a foolish wisdom at odds with the wisdom of the world.

In Psalm 15 we encounter what is known as *an entrance liturgy* (see introductory essay). These words most likely were spoken by priests who confronted worshipers entering the Temple Mount to join in the worship of God in the temple. Archaeologically, we are informed of numerous ritual baths (or *mikvaot*) carved into the limestone steps at the southern end of the Temple Mount. Obviously, one of the most important preparations for entering the holy presence of God was first to remove all ritual impurities by immersing oneself in one of these ritual baths; the unclean emerges clean. Fresh from their cleansing bath, the worshipers would be confronted anew by the words of Psalm 15. It is not enough to wash the outside. True worship requires a life of commitment that continues both on and off the Temple Mount, inside and outside the temple precincts, inside and outside the worshiper.

The psalm begins with a pair of theme-setting questions that address Yahweh and create the context for the remainder of the psalm. The questions regarding who may hope to "abide" or "dwell" in God's "tent" or "holy hill" invoke an ethos of divine presence and nearness that is at once attractive and unsettling. In Psalm 5:4 we learn that "evil will not sojourn" with God; the same Hebrew word used there is behind "abide" in Psalm 15. The kind of dwelling envisioned here is tentative and temporary in nature, drawing on terms that describe the residence of aliens who own no fixed property or of nomads who can strike their tents and move on to another location. Evil, it seems, cannot take up even temporary residence with God! The "tent" of God is an allusion to the tabernacle that traveled with Israel in the wilderness as the place where God's presence could be met. Here, coupled with the "holy hill," it likely intends the temple in Jerusalem. Elsewhere we note that the presence of the holy God threatens unholy humans who must take precautions to prevent destruction (Gen 28:10-17; Exod 33:17-23; Judg 13:15-23).

If the divine presence represents such threat to humans, the question "who may abide in [God's] tent" is of particular importance to those who desire to draw near in worship and not be rejected as the "evil" in Psalm 5:4. Those who approach unwisely or inappropriately risk death, as Nadab and Abihu discovered firsthand when they worshiped Yahweh with "unholy fire" (Lev 10:1-3).

Following these opening questions, the remainder of the psalm is composed of eleven answers arranged for the most part in couplets with a concluding exhortation and promise (Ps 15:5b). These eleven answers offer a comprehensive though not exhaustive response to the thematic concern: What kind of life prepares one for life with God? The first couplet of answers describes the foundational characteristic of the one who would dwell with Yahweh. To walk "blamelessly" is no claim of absolute sinless perfection, but describes a life that is "whole" and "complete" in its consistent devotion to Yahweh's way. The one who does "what is right" fulfills the expectations of God and takes advantage of the mechanism of repentance, forgiveness, and restoration in maintaining relationship with God and fellow humans.

The third answer combines with the first two to provide a picture of a person of integrity whose heart, speech, and deeds are transparently aligned with the purpose of God. The heart is the seat of moral deliberation and decision making and reflects the innermost, truest character of the individual unobservable by others. The person who dwells with God speaks clearly and without deception in ways that reveal a true heart fully grounded in a continued and consistent relationship with God. This idea of restrained, truthful speech is carried on into the fourth answer, which denies hurtful slander directed toward others. This is a great image in the Hebrew text, which describes the slanderous speaker "roaming about on his tongue" — an indication of how rumor and innuendo have a way of traveling quickly. Thus the one who wishes to experience the hospitality of God does not misrepresent herself or others.

The third set of questions extends the concern for others even further. Moving from general to more specific, the blameless guest is said not to "do evil" to a neighbor or to "take up a reproach" against a friend. Integrity and truthfulness have consequences not only for personal character but also for how one treats others — even one's closest associates.

Answers seven and eight stand in instructive opposition to one another. As in Psalm 1, the person who desires to remain in God's presence adopts a response to evil that mirrors God's own attitude. The "wicked" whom the individual "despises" here in Psalm 15 are those who "are rejected" by God himself. On the other hand, those who assume the appropriate attitude of reliance on God alone (this is what "fear of Yahweh" means in the Old Testament) are honored, both by God and by his true disciple.

The last three answers — an extended single saying (Ps 15:4c) and a parallel couplet (15:5ab) — call the true disciple to self-restraint and sacrifice. There is a giving up at work here. First, one is expected to keep an oath made even when it turns out to be inconvenient or even detrimental to the oath-taker. A commitment to care for an elderly parent or a debilitated child may lead to great personal heartbreak and even lead to the edge of financial ruin. But self-interest is clearly not the hallmark of those who would dwell with God. As Christ emptied himself (Phil 2) and took on death because of his commitment to humanity, so true disciples are called to die to self — considering others before themselves.

The final couplet describes two practices that were evidently commonly known although prohibited in the law. The first of these, lending money at interest to a fellow Israelite, was prohibited repeatedly in the legal codes (Exod 22:25; Lev 25:36, 37; Deut 23:19, 20). Taking interest for the loan of money and goods was widespread in the ancient world and was carefully regulated in the law code of Hammurabi (ca. 1792-1750 B.C.). Such transactions are a means of acquiring wealth, but they can also become a way to gain power and control over others. Those unable to repay the interest demanded of them were often forced into slavery for the creditor (Lev 25:39; Neh 5:5). The one who hopes to dwell with God avoids building up financial wealth and power on the backs of the poor and unfortunate. Finally, the answers turn to bribery as a means of perverting justice for personal gain at the expense of the poor and innocent. One is reminded of the trumped-up charges arranged by Queen Jezebel (1 Kings 21) to gain the conviction and death of Naboth so that King Ahab could possess the vineyard Naboth refused to sell. Such legal bribery is condemned in biblical law (Exod 23:8; Deut 27:25), although Proverbs (17:8; 21:14) recognizes the pragmatic efficiency of a bribe to clear the way for the giver. Both interest taking and bribery center in placing self-concern above the legitimate interests of others. Again, we are grateful that Jesus did not follow the path of self-interest, and we are called instead to follow his path of self-giving.

The psalm concludes (15:5c) with the confident summation that "Those who do these things shall never be moved." By "moved" the Hebrew means "shaken" by earthquake or caused to stumble on rough, treacherous ground. Such characteristics as described in this psalm depict persons who have given up trust in their ability to control and shape their own world. Instead, the one who hopes to share the hospitality of God finds the source of trust in God alone. This final statement is not just a promise that those who follow this example will find their ultimate security in heaven. We trust that is the case, but this psalm is offering access to the hospitality of God in our here and now. Even today — in the midst of the swirling insecurities of family, job, nation, and natural disaster — we can sit at the divinely prepared table of abundant blessing. From this table we can rise and go forth in confidence to meet what enemies of body or spirit as might appear in our day. And we can trust that we "will never be shaken."

†Gerald H. Wilson

PSALM 16

Second Sunday of Easter, Year A
> First Lesson: Acts 2:14a, 22-32
> **(Psalm 16)**
> Second Lesson: 1 Peter 1:3-9
> Gospel Lesson: John 20:19-31

Psalm 16 has been difficult to categorize perhaps because, as James Luther Mays notes, it "is a prayer of unusual proportions."[1] But while

---

1. James L. Mays, *Psalms,* Interpretation (Louisville: John Knox, 1994), 86.

Psalm 16's proportions may seem somewhat skewed, this does not detract from the overwhelming sense of trust that is clearly and repeatedly expressed. Psalm 16 may best be described, then, as similar to Psalm 23 — a psalm of almost unparalleled trust — but with a more biting theological agenda.

Our psalm begins with a simple yet forceful plea from reality:

> Protect me, O God, for in you I take refuge.
> I say to the LORD, "You are my Lord;
>   I have no good apart from you."

Here in the first verses an important theological statement is made — out of trouble, the psalmist prays to *the* Lord *(yhwh)*, as *her* lord *('dny,* "my lord"). This construction unites the divine name with a title often given to earthly masters (and perhaps to other gods), making clear the psalmist's commitment to and reliance upon *the* Lord. What follows this beginning is an expression of the trust of the person who prays this psalm, and a contrast or argument against idolatry and apostasy.

1. *You, Lord, are my Lord.* Right from the start, Psalm 16 addresses a significant theological issue, that of turning to other gods or agencies for refuge. At many points in Israel's history this seems to have been a not uncommon, perhaps even acceptable, practice. But the author of this psalm takes a much more restricted and pointed view of the religious landscape. His claim is that those who are holy (the "holy ones" [*qdwšym*] of v. 3), those who like the psalmist take refuge in the Lord alone, are seen to be mighty, or noble (NRSV) or perhaps well-to-do. The Hebrew adjective usually means "majestic" in the Psalter (see Pss 8:2, 10; 76:5; 93:4; 136:18); when read with "holy ones" (v. 3) and "your faithful one" (*ḥsdyk;* v. 10), it describes the beneficent or blessed life of God's faithful ones. This is in contrast to those who turn to other gods and call upon their names (v. 4). For Psalm 16, the theological axe is ground to a fine edge — those who remain faithful to God and turn to the Lord for help are holy, majestic, and a delight; those who pour out blood offerings to other gods are left only with sorrows multiplied.

2. *I have no good apart from you.* With these definitions in place, the psalmist takes the next logical theological step. She enumerates the blessings and benefits that the majestic holy ones of the Lord enjoy. Theirs are a portion, a cup, and a lot made secure (literally, held in God's hand, v. 5). Theirs are boundary lines laid out in pleasant places, and a

goodly heritage or inheritance (v. 6). Theirs is sure and unmovable footing (v. 8) upon the path of life (v. 11), eternal pleasures realized through the good counsel and instruction of the Lord (v. 7), and ensured by God's own presence with them (v. 11).

The theological case that the psalm makes is simple, and is intended to be compelling. There is one God to be trusted, one God who can show the path of life and give one a heart that is glad and a soul that rejoices (v. 9). This theological case is couched in confident trust, and invites the hearer or reader to join in this trust, and so share in the benefits of God's presence and counsel.

3. *The psalm and the apostle.* For many hearers and readers, the most provocative verse of this psalm is the last (v. 11). Read as a summary of the good that the Lord brings and provides, and with the earlier confidence that there will be no journey to Sheol or the Pit as background (v. 10), it is a simple and seemingly seamless move to an eschatological Christian reading of this verse and the entire psalm with it. The Lord — in the case of Christian reading: the Christ — as the goal and guarantor of eternal life may well seem the obvious and only reading for the Christian.

While it may be important for Christians not to jump too quickly to reading this prayer through the lens of Christ, those who do so will not be alone. The apostle Peter makes just this move in his Pentecost sermon in Acts 2, the first lesson. In Acts 2 the move is made clearly and deliberately: first, verses 25-28 quote Psalm 16:8-11 quite closely, but then in verse 31 Peter makes a key interpretive move: "Foreseeing this, David spoke of the resurrection of the Messiah, saying, 'He was not abandoned to Hades, / nor did his flesh experience corruption.'" The move is not subtle and marks another important theological agenda, parallel to that of Psalm 16: that the path of life is found in Christ Jesus, and in his presence and at his right hand are pleasures forevermore for those who believe.

Psalm 16 is a psalm of trust, perhaps disproportionately so, but making an important and moving theological case for fidelity to the Lord, who alone is God, and who alone has good things to offer a faithful, faith-filled people.

Karl N. Jacobson

PSALM 17

Eleventh Sunday after Pentecost, Year A
First Lesson: Genesis 32:22-31
(Psalm 17:1-7, 15)
Second Lesson: Romans 9:1-5
Gospel Lesson: Matthew 14:13-21

Psalm 17 is the prayer of an individual who has been persecuted by some oppressors. Some scholars have concluded that the oppressors made false accusations against the petitioner, based on language in verse 1 that the psalmist has a "just cause" and in verse 10 that may indicate that the psalmist has been the target of false witnesses ("with their mouths they speak arrogantly"). This life setting for the psalm must remain hypothetical, however, because the language is stereotypical in the Psalms and may simply indicate a more general situation of oppression.

The psalm's structure and logic are straightforward, containing three stanzas, each opening with a request or requests followed by a passage that supports them in some way.

vv. 1-5　　First stanza
　　vv. 1-2　　Opening petition to be heard
　　vv. 3-5　　Supporting assertion of innocence
vv. 6-12　　Second stanza
　　vv. 6-8　　Petition to be heard and protected
　　vv. 9-12　　Supporting description of the oppressors
vv. 13-15　　Third stanza
　　vv. 13-14　　Petition to be saved and have oppressors defeated
　　v. 15　　Supporting statement of trust

The first stanza focuses almost entirely on the psalmist, who asks for the prayer to be heard and asserts innocence. The second stanza focuses almost entirely on the oppressors, emphasizing their violence. The third stanza brings these two foci together, as the psalmist asks for both deliverance for himself and judgment on his enemies. This psalmic logic has been cleanly summarized by Richard J. Clifford: "The psalmist is portrayed as utterly faithful to God, the mirror image of the lawless enemies.

It behooves God to act."[1] One should also note that Psalm 17 may have been placed after Psalms 15-16 because the psalmist's claim of righteousness echoes the concern in Psalm 15 that only the blameless may abide with God; likewise, the closing vow in Psalm 17 echoes Psalm 16's praise of the protection that is found in God's presence.

In the first section of the psalm, the pray-er asks for God to hear. There is a textual problem in verse 1. The Hebrew text reads simply "righteous" *(sedeq)*, which makes no sense. In context, especially in the light of verses 3-5 in which the psalmist asserts blamelessness, verse 1 likely should be understood as "hear my just cause." The key to the psalmist's opening plea is this: the psalmist begs God to hear her prayerful words because those words come from "lips free of deceit" and because "my mouth does not transgress." One need not assert that the psalmist is claiming complete blamelessness about all of her life. Rather, the psalmist is asserting that in *this particular matter* for which she is being persecuted, she is blameless. As Clinton McCann has noted, "The psalmist's certainty of the rightness of his or her cause (vv. 1-2) and the protestation of innocence (vv. 3-5) seem problematic; they may suggest that the psalmist is proud or self-righteous. But . . . the psalmist asserts not sinlessness in general but rightness in a particular case involving false accusation by opponents. In this sense, Psalm 17, like Psalm 7, is reminiscent of the book of Job."[2]

In the second stanza the psalmist turns from personal innocence to the oppressors' guilt and violence. Again, the psalm may seem problematic because of the psalmist's plea that God "overthrow them" and his prayer to be delivered "by your sword" (v. 13). Especially problematic is the wish of verse 14b:

> May their bellies be filled with what you have stored up for them
> [i.e., the retribution];
> may their children have more than enough;
> may they leave something over to their little ones.

This so-called "double wish" in the Psalms — that God save the psalmist *and* punish the wicked — is difficult for us, particularly in the light of Christ's commands both to love our enemies and to pray for those who

---

1. Richard J. Clifford, *Psalms 1-72,* Abingdon Old Testament Commentaries (Nashville: Abingdon, 2002), 101.

2. J. Clinton McCann, Jr., "The Book of Psalms: Introduction, Commentary, and Reflections," in *NIB,* 4:742.

persecute us. But, as Claus Westermann has noted, if "a righteous person dies in misery and a godless person triumphs . . . then that could not have been understood in those days in *any other way* than as a decision of God against the righteous and for the evildoer, and with that the foundation of Old Testament faith in God would have been really shattered." Therefore, "if God intervened for the righteous, this was at the same time an intervention against the enemies."[3] Today, there is still truth to such an insight. There are indeed innocent people who suffer at the hands of evildoers, and sometimes in these cases the only way to rescue the oppressed is to overthrow the wicked. But here is the catch: we need to remember that we are just as likely to be the guilty oppressors as we are the innocent sufferers. We do well to read this psalm as the psalm of someone who has suffered because of our sin, rather than identifying ourselves only and always with or as the innocent sufferer. Since so few of the wealthy in America suffer at another's hands, this may be the most faithful way for affluent North Americans to read Psalm 17 — as a psalm prayed against us.

The psalm ends with a declaration of faith. In this confession the psalmist reverses the vocabulary that had begun the psalm in verse 1. "Hear my *righteous* plea" and "may your eyes *see* what is right" have become "in *righteousness* I will *see* your face." Thus, the psalm ends with the pray-er expressing confidence and trust in the grace of God. Rather than enemies dominating the psalmist's vision, the psalmist closes with an image of her eyes fixed firmly on God.[4] The language of verse 15 suggests that the psalmist may have spent the night in the temple awaiting God's response. For the modern reader, the ending of the psalm promises that those who lay themselves down to sleep can trust in the care of the Savior.

The psalm is assigned for the Eleventh Sunday after Pentecost, Year A. The text's relevance for this day lies in two things. First, the psalm reminds us of the age-old problem of oppression and wickedness. The psalm insists that God is not distant from the suffering of the innocent and indeed that the covenantal God of Abraham, Isaac, and Jacob has something intimately at stake when people suffer. The psalm can be prayed today especially on behalf of those who suffer oppression at the hands of the wicked. The psalm reminds us that while there is no sinless-

3. Claus Westermann, *The Psalms: Structure, Content, and Message* (Minneapolis: Augsburg, 1980), 66.

4. See Peter C. Craigie, *Psalms 1–50,* WBC 19 (Waco: Word, 1983), 164-65.

ness in the world, there are those who suffer wrongly. Second, almost everyone has had trouble going to sleep or staying asleep when burdened by great troubles. Some verses in Scripture we recite not because they express what we already feel, but because in the act of reciting them, we come to feel what they express and be what they say. Psalm 17 closes with such a word of hope.

> As for me, I shall behold your face in righteousness;
> when I awake I shall be satisfied, beholding your likeness. (v. 15)

Rolf A. Jacobson

PSALM 19

Third Sunday in Lent, Year B
First Lesson: Exodus 20:1-7
(Psalm 19)
Second Lesson: 1 Corinthians 1:18-25
Gospel Lesson: John 2:13-22

Third Sunday after the Epiphany, Year C
First Lesson: Nehemiah 8:1-3, 5-6, 8-10
(Psalm 19)
Second Lesson: 1 Corinthians 12:12-31a
Gospel Lesson: Luke 4:14-21

Twentieth Sunday after Pentecost, Year A
First Lesson: Exodus 20:1-4, 7-9, 12-20
(Psalm 19)
Second Lesson: Philippians 3:4b-14
Gospel Lesson: Matthew 21:33-46

Seventeenth Sunday after Pentecost, Year B
First Lesson: Esther 7:1-6, 9-10; 9:20-22
(Psalm 19:7-14)
Second Lesson: James 5:13-20
Gospel Lesson: Mark 9:38-50

James Luther Mays has referred to Psalm 19 as one of the "problem children" of the Psalter. He has noted that Psalms 1, 19, and 119 are "leftovers" in most introductory books on the Psalms. These three psalms, in which the torah or "instruction" of the Lord plays a central role, "do not fit into any of the established genres or into any of the proposed orders for cultic procedures in ancient Israel."[1] Among these three psalms, Psalm 19 also has the special problem of being a "mixed-type psalm." That is, it seems to be a composite poem, cobbled together from two originally separate parts: a nature hymn (vv. 1-6) and a torah poem (vv. 7-14). In fact, Artur Weiser wrote separate entries on what he called "Psalm 19A" and "Psalm 19B" and concluded that the reasons for joining these "dissimilar psalms . . . cannot any longer be established with any degree of certainty."[2]

Psalm 19 in its final form, however, is neither a haphazard accident nor the result of some imagined clumsy editor. Rather, it is an intentional composition, an example of a composite poem that has been thoughtfully constructed from segments of earlier poems. The gravitational center around which Psalm 19 orbits is the concept of "word" or "speech." This poetic motif unifies the otherwise divergent segments of the psalm. The psalm can be divided into three sections:

vv. 1-6   Nature's inaudible words praising God
vv. 7-10   Torah's tangible words instructing humanity
vv. 11-14 The psalmist's faithful words of prayer

Each section is developed poetically around the concept of word/speech. The second section interprets and builds upon the first section, and the third section interprets and builds upon the second section.

1. *Nature's inaudible words praising God (vv. 1-6).* Verses 1-4 describe the inaudible speech that creation employs to praise its Creator: "recount," "declare," "pour forth" (the root *nb'* means "to gush forth" but normally refers to speaking; cf. Pss 78:2; 119:171; 145:7; Prov 10:31), "speech," "declare," "knowledge," "words," and "voice" (assuming that *qawwām* in v. 4 should be emended to *qōllām*, "their voice" — see the text note in NRSV). The point — if such a prosaic word can describe such dense poetry — of this part of the psalm is twofold. On the one hand, *creation praises its Cre-*

---

1. James L. Mays, *The Lord Reigns: A Theological Handbook to the Psalms* (Louisville: Westminster John Knox, 1994), 128.

2. Artur Weiser, *The Psalms: A Commentary,* OTL (Philadelphia: Westminster, 1962), 197.

ator — each day, each night, the very heavens and sky, all praise the Lord. On the other hand, *this praise is inaudible to humanity:*

> There is no speech, nor are there words;
>> their voice is not heard. (v. 3)

The poem here explores the mysterious relationship between nature, God, and humanity. We discern in nature a magnificent testimony and witness to God's glory. And yet we cannot fully or completely distill our experience of that testimony down to intelligible formulae. The message is not merely that we can experience something of God in nature. Rather, the message is that what we learn of God in nature is mysterious, elusive, oblique. It is worth pointing out that in this part of the psalm the Lord is referred to by the generic term for "God" *('ēl)*. From this, some have concluded that the first part of the psalm originated as a Canaanite hymn to the Canaanite god by the same name (El). While this cannot be ruled out, there is far more at stake here than the question of where this part of the psalm originated.

2. *Torah's tangible words instructing humanity (vv. 7-10).* In the second movement of the psalm, the tone, style, name for God, and focus shift. The focus is now on the "law of the LORD" *(tôrat yhwh)*. Note the use of the personal name for God (Yahweh, usually translated as "The LORD"). The free-flowing language of the first movement gives way to poetry with a crisp and measured meter. Six phrases in verses 7-8 are constructed similarly. The pattern is: a synonym for "the law of the LORD" + an adjective (such as "perfect") + an action the law affects (such as "reviving the soul"). The climax of this part of the poem is: "More to be desired are they than gold . . . sweeter also than honey" (v. 10).

As mentioned above, the second stanza builds upon and develops the first. The inaudible speech of nature has morphed into the concrete and particular word of God that we find in the Torah — which here means both the abstract concept of God's instruction and the canonical Scripture (especially, of course, the Pentateuch). Whereas the first stanza describes nature, the second describes God's word as "more to be desired" than two of nature's finer products: gold and honey. And whereas the generic God ("El") is praised by nature, the personal Yahweh is encountered in Torah.

3. *The psalmist's faithful words of prayer (vv. 11-14).* The psalm ends with more speech — this time the personal prayer of the psalmist to the Lord.

Moved by the abstract praise of creation and made wise (v. 7) and "warned" (v. 11) by the instruction of the Lord, the psalmist now asks to be found "blameless" before God. The psalmist knows that the law, for all its perfection, cannot make the sinner perfect, because we all have "errors" and "hidden faults." So the psalm ends with a prayer that the poet and the poet's words might find a gracious reception in heaven. In the rhetoric of the psalm, it is not the law that makes the psalmist blameless, but the Lawgiver.

When the psalm is assigned in its entirety by the lectionary, it is paired either with the giving of the Ten Commandments in Exodus 20 (Third Sunday in Lent, Year B; Twentieth Sunday after Pentecost, Year A) or with Ezra's reading of the "book of the law of Moses" (Neh 8:1; Third Sunday after the Epiphany, Year C). In these settings the ending of the psalm is particularly important, since it helps place the law in its proper theological context: the law is God's good gift, but it is not designed as a means to eternal salvation; rather, it is designed as a guide for the earthly pilgrimage. The psalm also has an important witness regarding what has been called "natural theology" and the argument that we can find God in nature. Martin Luther distinguished between the hidden God and the revealed God. According to verses 1-6, the God a human can find in nature per se is the hidden "God" (El!), about whom we know little because we cannot discern the words. Nature is, after all, red in tooth and claw. But God also has chosen to be revealed to us in God's word. Here we find not an impersonal "God" but the personal "Lord" (Yahweh!). This Lord meets us as a rescuing kinsman (Hebrew *gō'ēl*, often translated "redeemer," the final word of the psalm), as one who is related to us and who acts to deliver us.

Rolf A. Jacobson

Psalm 20

Fourth Sunday after Pentecost, Year B
>   First Lesson: 1 Samuel 15:34–16:13
>   **(Psalm 20)**
>   Second Lesson: 2 Corinthians 5:6-10, (11-13), 14-17
>   Gospel Lesson: Mark 4:26-34

In the first three books of the Psalms (Pss 3-89), psalms of need, thanksgiving, and confidence predominate.[1] Psalm 20 demonstrates these themes with its obvious emphasis on *need* (vv. 1-5, 9) and *confidence* (vv. 6-8). This psalm is a *royal psalm* (see the introductory essay; cf. Pss 2; 18; 20; etc.), as revealed at two different points in the passage. First, the "anointed" *(māšîaḥ)* in verse 6 refers to God's designated king who represents divine rule and the kingdom of heaven on earth (see the first lesson for the anointing of David as king). Second, the psalmist explicitly uses the term "king" *(melek;* v. 9), further underscoring that the anointed king is critical for this psalm. In fact, the king is the main person in *need,* as indicated by the final plea to "give victory to the king, O LORD" (v. 9).

This psalm seeks God's help for the ruling king. His trouble may be in the present or in the future, so he needs divine intervention. The speaker opens the psalm with

> The LORD answer you in the day of trouble!
> The name of the God of Jacob protect you! (v. 1)

There is imminent trouble, so the king needs protection, "help" (v. 2), "support" (v. 2), divine answers (vv. 1, 6, 9), and ultimately "victory" from God (vv. 5, 6, 9). Traditionally the king's trouble has been thought to be an impending war, so the psalm functions as a prayer before the king and army go out to war; or, alternatively, perhaps it is a prayer at his enthronement, in anticipation of future wars. War imagery is present in this psalm in its reference to the military force of "chariots" and "horses" (v. 7), in the setting up of "banners" (v. 5; cf. Num 10:13-28) that represent a military unit, and in the cries for victory (vv. 5, 6, 9) in the battle. Because of this apparent historical setting of the psalm in a battle and the specific sequence of verses, some scholars have connected this psalm to a ceremony or service related to the king as military officer and defender of the nation, calling it a liturgical service before battle.[2]

The liturgical character of this psalm is evident by the mentioning of the "sanctuary," "offerings," "burnt sacrifices," and "petitions." The king is possibly in the temple to pray while offering ritual sacrifices as the first voice declares (vv. 2-5). Then there is a priestly assurance of victory in a second, antiphonal voice (vv. 6-8), which is followed by a closing prayer

---

1. James L. Mays, *Psalms,* Interpretation (Louisville: John Knox, 1994), 16.
2. See Carroll Stuhlmueller, "Psalms," in *HBC,* 443; cf. 2 Chron 20:1-19.

(v. 9) that summarizes all that has been articulated. The faithful people of God are interceding for the praying king because they know their destiny is wrapped up in his. His loss is their loss and his victory is their victory. This is why they hope to "shout for joy" over his "victory" (v. 5) and declare that "we shall rise and stand upright" while the adversaries "collapse and fall" (v. 8). God's people, including the king, pray because they are in great need. They exude a great *confidence* in God by turning to the Lord in prayer.

The king is important in this royal psalm, but even more important is the "primary actor" in this liturgy — God.[3] From the outset the psalmist is full of faith in God, turning to the "Lord" and "the God of Jacob" for an answer and protection (v. 1). This turning — just turning — to God requires faith. The psalmist would not even pray if there were not an initial trust in God. This trustworthy God is the God of the covenant of whom Jacob said, "God answered me in the day of my distress and has been with me wherever I have gone" (Gen 35:3). Thus the psalmist recalls such divine answers in verse 1 and knows that his God (the God of Jacob) will answer the king in the day of trouble just as the Lord did for Jacob. The Lord who is a "rock" (a metaphor of God's trustworthiness) and "redeemer" in Psalm 19:14, and strong to save the king in Psalm 21, is shown to be the same type of God in Psalm 20. Despite trouble, God is definitely present to help and deliver. The psalmist demonstrates this with the threefold emphasis on the "name" of God (vv. 1, 5, 7). In the Hebraic tradition the "name" signifies God's presence, power, and character, suggesting that the Lord is present on earth even though God is in the heavens (see 1 Kings 8:15-30; Pss 44:5; 54:6; 118:10-12). The "name" is representative of the Lord (see Pss 54:1; 124:8), and God is not only present and powerful through the divine name but also is highly active by means of it.

The speaker of this psalm is consumed with the action of God who has a history of helping (e.g., the exodus from Egypt). Through most of the psalm God is the subject of the verbs. God is called upon to answer (vv. 1, 6, 9), protect (v. 1), send help (v. 2), give support (v. 2), remember offerings (v. 3), regard sacrifices (v. 3), grant desires (v. 4), fulfill plans and petitions (vv. 4, 5), and help his anointed (v. 6). This God is active and powerful enough to give victory to the king (v. 9). The action and nature of God are amplified to magnify the One who truly brings victory to the

3. J. Clinton McCann, Jr., "The Book of Psalms: Introduction, Commentary, and Reflections," in *NIB*, 4:755.

people of God. God needs to act to bring a resolution to the problem — this is why the king and the people pray. In addition to the emphasis on the "name" of God, the psalmist stresses the verb "answer" (vv. 1, 6, 9) three times in relation to God, for God is the One who must answer for help to come to the king. Furthermore, the writer stresses that God will "answer" with "victory" (the Hebrew word for "salvation" is the same as "victory"; "help" in NRSV at v. 6 is from the same root, *yšʿ*; see vv. 5, 6, 9). "Victory/help" is thus mentioned four times in relation to God's work, suggesting that it is the Lord who will bring ultimate victory in the battle.

Only God can give victory because victory is dependent on the heavenly King, not the earthly one. "The king is not the savior but the saved. The saving victory will be God's work."[4] In Hebrew verse 9 suggests that the real king is the Lord, for the verse may be read: "give victory, O LORD; let the king answer us when we call," the "king" being, in fact, none other than the Lord. Human power is not the basis of trust for victory or salvation; but rather, only the ruling power of God constitutes that basis. The psalmist makes sure the hearers know that Israel's "pride is in the name of the LORD our God," though "some take pride in chariots, and some in horses" (v. 7). "In Israel's world, horse and chariot were the supreme weapons of royal military might. Egyptian and Mesopotamian rulers had themselves portrayed in chariots and on horses to glorify their power in war," but "the psalms reiterate that trust in weapons is a contradiction to faith in the Lord (33:16-19; 44:3, 6-7; 147:10-11)."[5] Human resources, power, and prestige cannot save; God alone saves (cf. Ps 33:16-17). Even the most powerful on earth — namely, monarchs! — must rely on God for deliverance because battles belong to God (Deut 20:1; 2 Kings 6:17; Isa 31:3; 37:23-36).

This message of the psalm is thus "a voice of the gospel, God's good word addressed to God's faithful people."[6] That "good word" is indeed that "the LORD reigns" (Pss 47; 93; 95-99), which some believe to be the overarching theology of the Psalter.[7] This gospel word is timeless and is at the same time a timely word *for us* because the Psalms are not "time-bound" by history or content.[8] The Lord's reign is evident when God

4. Mays, *Psalms,* 101.

5. Mays, *Psalms,* 102.

6. Walter Brueggemann, *The Message of the Psalms: A Theological Commentary* (Minneapolis: Augsburg, 1984), 15.

7. Cf. Mays, *Psalms,* 30-31.

8. See Patrick D. Miller, *Interpreting the Psalms* (Philadelphia: Fortress, 1986), 22-23.

brings large growth from little seeds as in the Gospel lesson for this Sunday (Mark 4:26-34). God does not need human power and technological resources to make God's kingdom grow and flourish. People may "not know how" (Mark 4:27) "the smallest of all the seeds on earth" "grows up and becomes the greatest of all shrubs" (Mark 4:31-32), but God runs this divine farm. "Chariots" and "horses" are not needed to succeed; only the power of God is necessary to bring growth, salvation, and victory. Because the Lord reigns, we can have "confidence" (2 Cor 5:6, 8) and be "convinced" (2 Cor 5:14) that the anointed King of kings, Jesus Christ, the one who has "died for all" and been "raised," has defeated the powers of death so that we may live in a "new creation" where "everything has become new!" (see the second lesson, 2 Cor 5:6-10, 14-17). God has given the ultimate victory to Jesus Christ, our king, causing us to say in the words of the psalmist, not that salvation belongs to us, but "Salvation belongs to the LORD" (Ps 3:8).

Luke A. Powery

PSALM 22

Twenty-first Sunday after Pentecost, Year B
First Lesson: Job 23:1-9, 16-17
(Psalm 22:1-15)
Second Lesson: Hebrews 4:12-16
Gospel Lesson: Mark 10:17-31

Second Sunday in Lent, Year B
First Lesson: Genesis 17:1-7, 15-16
(Psalm 22:23-31)
Second Lesson: Romans 4:13-25
Gospel Lesson: Mark 8:31-38

Fifth Sunday of Easter, Year B
First Lesson: Acts 8:26-40
(Psalm 22:25-31)
Second Lesson: 1 John 4:7-21
Gospel Lesson: John 15:1-8

In the Christian tradition, Psalm 22 is easily the most familiar of the *lament psalms* (see the introductory essay), primarily because its first verse is famously quoted by Jesus on the cross: "My God, my God, why have you forsaken me?" (Ps 22:1; see Matt 27:46; Mark 15:34). The psalm's popularity is reflected in its use in the lectionary, where it appears on three different Sundays in three different liturgical seasons with no less than nine different lessons. There is much more to this psalm, however, than its first verse or the other portions evoked or echoed in the passion narratives (cf. Ps 22:7-8, 18 with Matt 27:39-44; Mark 15:29-32; Luke 23:34-37).[1] This point, too, is noted by the lectionary, which suggests *three* different excerpts of the psalm for liturgical use. Two of these overlap, including verses 25-31. A brief section of the psalm (vv. 16-22) is omitted from the lectionary, which is signally unfortunate, given the poem's content and form (see below). Indeed, the piecemeal approach of the lectionary to Psalm 22 destroys the formal unity of the poem, and preachers and worship leaders, if they choose to follow suit, should at least be aware of the omitted portions and how they impact the overall composition and the meaning of the psalm. Whatever the case, the richness of Psalm 22 in content and later significance for the New Testament and Christian theology means that it is a gold mine to come back to, again and again and again — in Lent, Easter, Pentecost, and beyond.

I. *Verses 1-15 (Twenty-first Sunday after Pentecost, Year B)*. The first lectionary cutting covers the standard elements of *invocation/address* (v. 1aα) and *complaint* (vv. 1aβ-15), though the latter element actually continues through verse 18. At the same time, the element of *petition*, which is especially prominent in verses 19-21a, is also found in verse 11, which functions, then, as a kind of foreshadowing of the later, fuller petition. Or, perhaps better, here is evidence of this poet's skill: the psalmist introduces the petition in verse 11, only to upset our expectations by returning to complaint in verses 12-18. Besides being unexpected, this move makes the complaint *extralong*, underscoring its severity. The seriousness of the situation is also accomplished by the short introduction that, like some other lament psalms (e.g., Ps 13:1), is embedded within the complaint: "My God, my God, why . . . ?" (Ps 22:1).

The content of the complaint also emphasizes the gravity of the

---

1. See Raymond E. Brown, *The Death of the Messiah: From Gethsemane to the Grave; A Commentary on the Passion Narratives in the Four Gospels*, 2 vols., ABRL (New York: Doubleday, 1993), 2:1455-65.

Fig. 2. This image vividly depicts language used in Psalm 22 — especially that of being surrounded by bulls (v. 12), as well as the psalmist's need to be saved from the horns of the wild oxen (v. 21). Note the prominent horns that impact the man's head as well as the placement of three of the hooves on the man's body, indicating trampling and domination.

---

psalmist's plight. God has forsaken the poet and is *distant* ($\sqrt{r\d{h}q}$) — a repeated and key term, as the psalmist first accuses God of being distant (v. 1), then implores the Lord to not be distant in the face of present trouble and helplessness (v. 11), repeating this same request again in verse 19 (painful distance is also at work in the first lesson from Job 23:1-9, 16-17). God's distance flies in the face of the psalmist's constant prayers (v. 2) and remembrance of the Lord (vv. 1-2: "*my* God"; also v. 10), not to mention God's beneficent treatment of the ancestors (for examples, see the texts from the first and second lessons in the Second Sunday in Lent, Year B: Gen 17:1-7, 15-16; Rom 4:13-25). Those saints trusted ($\sqrt{b\d{t}\d{h}}$) in God and were delivered, they cried ($\sqrt{z^{\cdot}q}$) and were saved, they trusted ($\sqrt{b\d{t}\d{h}}$) and were not ashamed ($\sqrt{bw\check{s}}$; vv. 4-5). The psalmist, too, is trusting (cf. v. 9's use of $\sqrt{b\d{t}\d{h}}$,

NRSV: "kept me safe") and crying out. Right now, however, the psalmist can see only the disparity between himself and the ancestors and can only imagine that it is a difference not just of degree but also of kind: the poet is subhuman, subject only to mockery and reproach by others (vv. 6-7). These voyeurs of the psalmist's suffering make a critical mistake, however, when they implicate the Lord in their cruel remarks (v. 8).[2] But mention of the Lord leads the poet to recount the Lord's past beneficence to him: God served as midwife, delivering him unto the safe care of his mother (vv. 9-10). How much more is God's help needed now, since enemies are near (v. 11) and God far off! These enemies are animalistic, perhaps even demonic,[3] strong as bulls, ferocious as lions (vv. 12-13; see fig. 2). The effects of all this on the psalmist are social, physical, and visible — and they are not just the enemies' fault: "You [God] lay me in the dust of death" (v. 15).

2. It is unfortunate that *verses 16-22* are omitted by the lectionary since this unit is integral to the structure and movement of the lament. First, this section continues and completes the complaint by returning to the enemies in both mammalian and human form. These enemies treat the psalmist as if she were already dead, dividing up her clothes and casting lots for her garments (vv. 16-18). Here too the debilitating bodily state of the psalmist is underscored (v. 17), connecting the enemies and their effects with Yahweh and his effects (vv. 14-15). Once again the complex interrelationship of self, enemy, and God in the lament psalms is underscored,[4] though hardly explained to our satisfaction.

Second, the *petition*, prefigured in verse 11, comes into full view in verses 19-21a. Given God's distance earlier in the psalm (v. 1; cf. v. 11), it is not surprising to find the poet begging for God to overcome that distance (v. 19a). Nor is it surprising, given the litany of terrors in verses 1-18, to find the psalmist praying for God to come *quickly*, to deliver from sword and dog, and to save from the mouth of the lion — symbols and

2. Cf. A. A. Anderson, *Psalms*, 2 vols., NCB (Grand Rapids: Eerdmans, 1972), 1:188. The pronominal referents in this verse are not fully clear; see Jonathan Magonet, *A Rabbi Reads the Psalms*, 2nd ed. (London: SCM, 2004), 95.

3. See J. Clinton McCann, Jr., "The Book of Psalms: Introduction, Commentary, and Reflections," in *NIB*, 4:763; Hans-Joachim Kraus, *Psalms 1–59: A Continental Commentary* (Minneapolis: Fortress, 1993), 297; contrast Artur Weiser, *The Psalms: A Commentary*, OTL (Philadelphia: Westminster, 1962), 223 n. 1.

4. See the introductory essay; also James L. Mays, *Psalms*, Interpretation (Louisville: John Knox, 1994), 106; and Patrick D. Miller, *Interpreting the Psalms* (Philadelphia: Fortress, 1986), 101.

synecdoches, no doubt, for the enemies and for the psalmist's distressing circumstances. It is also not surprising to find the psalmist where she began: directly appealing to her God, calling the Lord "my aid" (v. 19b) as she earlier called Yahweh "my God" (vv. 1-2, 10).

And, just like that, it is over. In the middle of verse 21, if the NRSV and others are correct,[5] the ordeal is over. The psalmist cannot even catch his breath, cannot even complete the parallel line because things have changed. "From the horns of the wild oxen you have rescued me" — this is the *confession of trust:* the rescue is accomplished (see fig. 2). How it occurred we do not know and cannot say because the psalmist does not say. Perhaps the psalmist does not know. Perhaps the shift in mood is due to an oracle of salvation (see the introductory essay), and one should note in this regard that the verb translated "rescued" in NRSV is literally "answered" (√'*nh,* the same verb used in v. 2 about God's *lack* of answer). But we have no clear script available to us, so that here, as in the other laments, we are faced with the mysterious shift to praise, to thanksgiving, to new orientation — all of which are predicated on a theological *novum,* something profoundly mysterious, unexpected, and inexplicable . . . something profoundly divine: in a word, the gospel has taken place between verse 21a and verse 21b. Somehow, "in the midst of and in some way from the terrible situation itself," the psalmist has heard God's response.[6]

This is, then, a third reason why it is unfortunate that the lectionary leaves out verses 16-22. Even if one delays the shift to praise until verse 22,[7] that delay is at most only half a verse. Either way, *the vow to praise* begins in verse 22. So, if preachers choose to follow the lectionary, they should be advised of the important — better: irreplaceable and evangelical! — material that goes missing in the loss of verses 16-22.

3. *Verses 23-31 (Second Sunday in Lent, Year B; vv. 25-31 in Fifth Sunday of Easter, Year B).* There are at least three striking things to note about the vow to praise, which was begun in verse 22 and runs to the end of the psalm. First is its *length:* it is formally complete in verse 24; but the fact that it continues for another seven verses, that this vow is extralong, may be a way the poet balances out the extralong complaint (vv. 1-18).[8] Per-

5. KJV; Kraus, *Psalms 1–59,* 298.

6. Miller, *Interpreting the Psalms,* 107.

7. Note the translations in NIV and, e.g., NJPS; cf. Richard J. Clifford, *Psalms 1–72,* Abingdon Old Testament Commentaries (Nashville: Abingdon, 2002), 127.

8. So also Ellen F. Davis, "Exploding the Limits: Form and Function in Psalm 22," *JSOT* 53 (1992): 97.

haps this poetic match even mirrors life in some way: life is dominated mostly by two seasons — that of trouble, pain, complaint and that of praise. Seasons of petition (vv. 11, 19-21b) and deliverance (v. 21a) are relatively brief, punctuating these larger periods. And yet they are crucial, serving as the fulcrum that shifts one from complaint to praise, the latter being the end point of the psalm and our lives.

Second, the vow to praise is *expansive*. It is common for praise to be public and to address the worshiping community (note "offspring of Jacob/Israel" in v. 23). But Psalm 22 explodes the limits of the standard form,[9] returning to address and praise God directly (v. 25) and extending the praise to everyone, everywhere, at every time — the poor (v. 26), the ends of the earth, the families of the nations (v. 27), the nations themselves (v. 28), even the dead ("who sleep in the earth . . . who go down to the dust," v. 29) and the unborn (vv. 30-31: "Posterity . . . future generations . . . a people yet unborn"). It must be admitted that the Hebrew of verses 29-31 is quite confused and difficult. Even so, it is clear that the deliverance wrought by the Lord in the space of a half-verse has nothing less than cosmic ramifications for all people everywhere. Such is the audacious unrestrained testimony of the delivered!

Finally, *the specific content* of verse 24 is shocking, especially in how it matches the complaints of God's distance (vv. 1-2) and people's mockery (vv. 6-8). In the final analysis — ultimately — Yahweh was *not* far off, did *not* despise or abhor, did *not* hide his face, but heard the psalmist's cry. How one gets from "no answer" (v. 2) to "heard my cry" (v. 24) is, again, a mystery. Verse 24 is worth pondering, regardless, in the light of the possibility that Jesus quoted Psalm 22 from the cross,[10] whether in full or by means of citing the first line (a common practice in antiquity, perhaps supported by the use of portions of Ps 22 elsewhere in the passion accounts). If Jesus (or the Gospel writers) intended for us to hear all of Psalm 22 in his mouth on the cross, the cry of dereliction becomes terribly misnamed. "Cry of trust" or "affirmation of faith"[11] would be much better. If so, one must no longer think of *divine abandonment*, because "he did not despise . . . abhor . . . hide his face," but of *divine deliverance* because "he heard" (v. 24). The subsequent explosion of good news to the poor, the ends of the earth, the na-

---

9. See Davis, "Exploding the Limits," 93-105; Claus Westermann, *The Living Psalms* (Grand Rapids: Eerdmans, 1989), 299; McCann, "The Book of Psalms," 4:762; Mays, *Psalms*, 106-7.

10. Westermann, *The Living Psalms*, 298; cf. Brown, *Death of the Messiah*, 2:1050.

11. So McCann, "The Book of Psalms," 4:766.

tions, the dead, and the yet-to-be-born is a drama that still plays out following the Crucified's life and his praying of Psalm 22.[12] His praying shows that even our Lord found occasion to lament; that God can be present in lament and suffering (note especially the connection of suffering and divine things in Mark 8:31-38); and that lament can be answered, distance overcome, complaints matched with deliverance in an instant, in the space of a half-verse or the space of three days.

Brent A. Strawn

PSALM 23

Fourth Sunday of Easter, Year A
First Lesson: Acts 2:42-47
(Psalm 23)
Second Lesson: 1 Peter 2:19-25
Gospel Lesson: John 10:1-10

Fourth Sunday of Easter, Year B
First Lesson: Acts 4:5-12
(Psalm 23)
Second Lesson: 1 John 3:16-24
Gospel Lesson: John 10:11-18

Fourth Sunday of Easter, Year C
First Lesson: Acts 9:36-43
(Psalm 23)
Second Lesson: Revelation 7:9-17
Gospel Lesson: John 10:22-30

Fourth Sunday in Lent, Year A
First Lesson: 1 Samuel 16:1-13
(Psalm 23)
Second Lesson: Ephesians 5:8-14
Gospel Lesson: John 9:1-41

12. Cf. McCann, "The Book of Psalms," 4:765-66; Miller, *Interpreting the Psalms,* 108, 110.

Psalm 23 is probably the most well known and well loved of all the psalms. It is the classic *psalm of trust* (see introductory essay). The poem has become so woven into the fabric of American culture that it can appear in any genre of literature or any walk of life. In John Wayne's movie *Rooster Cogburn (... and the Lady),* Katharine Hepburn bravely recites it in the face of danger. In Clint Eastwood's *Pale Rider,* a young girl weeps it as a lament over her dead puppy. The hip-hop artist Coolio samples the psalm in his famous song "Gangsta's Paradise." The psalm was carved into the waiting room of the hospital where this commentator was born. It is read at more funerals and gravesides than perhaps any other text. Deep familiarity with any text — including and perhaps especially this one — can insulate us from being touched by its eloquent message. To preach on such a foundational text is to run the risk of either trivializing the sublime, of turning the sermon into an autopsy on a beloved passage, or of trying to do too much to wring some new profundity from the text. But to preach on the psalm is also to give life to the dead, to put people in touch with the beating heart of the gospel, and to proclaim once again the very basis of the faith.

The rhetoric of the psalms of trust assumes that the psalmist has passed through a time of crisis or is perhaps in the midst of or about to enter such a crisis. But whether the crisis is past, present, or future, the crisis is not incidental to these psalms. Rather, *it is the crisis that generates the words of trust* (compare Pss 27:1-3; 46:1-7; 62:1-7; etc.). Thus, the genre teaches us that danger, evil, and crisis are *part of the life of faith.* In and through crises, faith is tempered and trust matures. These crises come in many forms — physical, emotional, financial, spiritual, social (this is especially true for the psalms), professional. Psalm 23 does not specify the exact crisis its author faced; rather, its metaphorical language can adapt to and speak to as wide a range of crises as there are people to pray the psalm.

The psalm mixes two metaphors for God's guidance in the midst of crisis: the shepherd (vv. 1-4) and the banquet host (vv. 5-6). Each metaphor is deeply rooted in the ancient context in which the Scriptures were incarnated. Each metaphor still speaks powerfully today to those of more recent times. The two images of God do not so much teach about the faithfulness of God as they do *bear* God's faithfulness to the one who prays the psalm. For those who pray the psalm still, it is not that we pray the psalm because it says what we mean; instead, we pray the psalm because *through saying it we come to mean and be what it says.*

Verses 1-4. The psalm launches immediately with its powerful, primary metaphor and promise: "The LORD is my shepherd." In the ancient Near East, the shepherd was a central image for the king (see Jer 23:1-4). Throughout the Old Testament this royal metaphor is used to portray God's protective and guiding grace. During the exile the great prophet drew on this metaphor to promise deliverance to a people in whom the flame of faith had just about died:

> He will feed his flock like a shepherd;
>> he will gather the lambs in this arms,
> and carry them in his bosom,
>> and gently lead the mother sheep. (Isa 40:11)

After the introduction the psalm continues to develop the shepherd metaphor, poetically portraying the caring and nurturing actions of God. Notice that immediately following the opening declaration the psalm begins with one phrase in which the psalmist is the subject of the verb followed by four phrases in which God is the subject of the verb and the psalmist is the object. The psalmist trusts that "I shall not want." A better translation would be "need" or "lack." The sense of the verb *ḥāsēr* in this case is that the psalmist will not lack for any basic need (cf. Neh 9:21: "Forty years you sustained them in the wilderness so that they *lacked nothing*"). The reason the psalmist can confess such trust is that God is the author of his or her life, just as God is the subject of the verbs that follow: "He makes me lie down . . . he leads . . . he restores . . . he guides." All these actions describe things that the shepherd does for the sheep *because they cannot do them for themselves* — so it is with God and us! It should be noted that the phrase traditionally translated "paths of righteousness" is ambiguous — it can mean either that God leads in "safe paths" or that God leads in "moral paths" (see fig. 3). Both are possible, and the phrase is probably best interpreted as a double entendre — both meanings are present (this is poetry, one need not limit the sense of the language). All these actions God does "for his name's sake." The point is that God's actions are consistent with God's nature, especially as God has revealed that in the covenant with Israel, in which God's name plays a crucial role (see Exod 3:13-22; 20:2, 7).

The confession in verse 4 that "you are with me" is the linguistic center of the psalm,[1] and more importantly its theological center. As Pat-

---

1. See James Limburg, *Psalms*, Westminster Bible Companion (Louisville: Westminster John Knox, 2000), 74.

Fig. 3. The language used in Psalm 23:3 for "right paths" *(mā'ğĕlê-ṣedeq)* may be related to the word for "calf" *('ēgel)*, "heifer" *('eglāh)*, and, similarly, "cart" *('ăgālāh)*, as drawn by animals of various sorts, especially oxen (2 Sam 6:3-6) — all of which are derived from the root *'gl* (see *HALOT*, 2:609, 784; BDB, 723). In this light, perhaps it is not going too far to suggest that the right paths are tracks beat down by the animals, wagons, and travelers that have gone before (cf. Ps 65:11). The image presented here suggests that such tracks would be well worn indeed, further underscoring the point that the way of the righteous is well traveled and clearly marked out (see Ps 1), not to mention led by a shepherd (Ps 23:1; see Keel, *The Symbolism of the Biblical World*, 229-30).

---

rick D. Miller has aptly written, "The fourth verse of the psalm is the gospel kernel of the Old Testament, that good news that turns tears of anguish and fear into shouts of joy. . . . The psalmist has heard that word, probably in the midst of threat and danger, and life is now controlled by it."[2] In the poetry of the psalm, verse 4 is where the psalmist stops talking *about God* (as a third-person subject) and starts talking *to God* (as a second-person object). According to the psalm, the place where God turns from an "it" about which we memorize creedal statements into a "you" with whom we have a relationship and in whom we trust is "in the darkest valley." (It should be noted that the Hebrew word normally translated "shadow of death" is *ṣalmāwet*, which actually means "darkness"; Hebrew does not have any compound words, which was the understanding behind the traditional translation "shadow" [*ṣēl*] of "death" [*māwet*].)

Verses 5-6. The "you" language that suddenly appeared in verse 4 continues into the last part of the psalm. But the metaphor switches to God as banquet host: "You prepare a table before me in the presence of my enemies." Throughout the Psalms, the psalmists insist that social relation-

2. Patrick D. Miller, *Interpreting the Psalms* (Philadelphia: Fortress, 1986), 115.

ships — with the poor, with the powerful, with persecutors and enemies — are a matter in which God is intimately involved. The table host as a metaphor for God's redeeming actions is important throughout Scripture (see Luke 14:7-14). The metaphor's power depends in part upon the cultural values of honor and shame (see Luke 14:8). In the context of Psalm 23, the image portrays the Lord as the one who honors the psalmist in front of those who wish him or her ill. Again, the point is that God does this for the psalmist, who cannot do it for herself. In the psalms, it is usually the enemies who "pursue" the psalmist to do harm or cause shame. Here God's "goodness and mercy" literally "pursue" the psalmist (the traditional translation "follow" is too weak a rendering for the Hebrew verb *rādap*). We do not merely receive or seek God's grace; at times it chases us down with the vigor and doggedness of a bloodhound.

In the context of the church year, Psalm 23 is heard each year on the Fourth Sunday of Easter, often called "Good Shepherd Sunday." In this context the psalm is an echo of the alleluias of Easter Sunday. In each of the three lectionary years, the psalm is paired with a passage from John 10. In such a context the shepherd of the psalm is likely to be identified with Jesus, a fitting association. But the image of the banquet host can also be emphasized. The image still retains its power — for youth, for example, there are few times during the school day as threatening or as defined by the peer group as the lunch period. Young people can resonate with the promise of the Lord who offers them a place at the table. Any adult who has been similarly left alone or ostracized at the table can also sense the power of the promise.

The psalm is also assigned during Lent in Year A. The Gospel lesson for that Sunday is the lengthy narrative in John 9 of the man born blind. That story, like Psalm 23, is at least partially concerned with the work of God to welcome and honor those who have been shut out by the insiders. Similarly, in the context of the somber, penitential season of Lent, a verse that may be highlighted is verse 4:

> Even though I walk through the darkest valley,
>   I fear no evil;
> for you are with me;
>   your rod and your staff — they comfort me.

Again, the connection with the story of Jesus is powerful. The promise of Immanuel, God with us, will ring out all the more clearly against the backdrop of the narrative of Jesus moving toward his death in Jerusalem. The promise that God is with us precisely in the darkest valley is no different from the promise that God is with us in the dying Savior, tortured to death on the cross.

Rolf A. Jacobson

PSALM 24

Eighth Sunday after Pentecost, Year B
> First Lesson: 2 Samuel 6:1-5, 12b-19
> **(Psalm 24)**
> Second Lesson: Ephesians 1:3-14
> Gospel Lesson: Mark 6:14-29

One message pervades Psalm 24: Yahweh conquers chaos. According to ancient Near Eastern mythology, the forces of chaos — often personified as the sea — constantly threaten the divinely established order. This psalm claims that Yahweh alone, the warrior-God of Israel, subdued the sea in the primordial battle at creation (vv. 1-2). This victory guaranteed God's continuing dominance whenever the forces of chaos threatened to overtake Israel. As the Lord repeatedly intervenes to reestablish order throughout Israel's history, Israel responds by worshiping him as the ruler of the world, the reigning King of Glory (vv. 7-10). Israel also participates in Yahweh's conquest. By committing themselves to the Lord's law (vv. 3-6), Israel helps maintain the order Yahweh founded.

The three clear sections of Psalm 24 constitute a liturgy for the procession of the ark of the covenant into Israel's central shrine, celebrating the Lord as the victorious heavenly king. The first section (vv. 1-2) describes Yahweh as creator and owner of the world. The second section (vv. 3-6) contains prescriptions for purity for those going up to worship God on Mount Zion. The third section (vv. 7-10) records an antiphonal liturgy accompanying the installation of the ark.

Since the power of God was centralized in the ark, the Israelites carried it on military campaigns to muster Yahweh's strength against their enemies (cf. 1 Sam 4:3). After a successful battle the ark was carried in a procession back to the temple in Jerusalem. God sat invisibly on the ark's cherubim, enthroned as the victorious king (1 Sam 4:4; 2 Sam 6:2; 1 Chron 13:6). As the ark neared Jerusalem, trumpets blared and choirs shouted. Led by the king, all the people exulted in the victory that Yahweh had given (cf. 2 Sam 5:17-25). 2 Samuel 6, the first lesson for this Sunday, describes such a joyful procession after David's battle against the Philistines. Psalm 24 may have been sung in a procession like this, as well as in symbolic, ritualized celebrations of Yahweh's kingship as part of an annual enthronement festival.

1. Structure and message of Psalm 24. The first lines of this entrance liturgy recount God's primordial victory over chaos — the source of all subsequent victories (vv. 1-2). Israel's testimony that *Yahweh* created order from chaos stood in direct opposition to myths of other ancient Near Eastern peoples. In Syro-Palestine and Mesopotamia, other warrior-gods, such as Baal or Marduk, were credited with creating the world by conquering the waters of chaos. In these myths, and likewise in Israel's story, a warrior-god's victory establishes him as the king of heaven, the sovereign over the entire cosmos.[1] The psalmist argues against these traditions, that *the Lord,* not Baal or Marduk, is the creator and lord of the world, the one who overpowers the chaos waters ("seas" and "rivers") and, in so doing, founds the earth.

Since God created it, the world is his possession (v. 1). The standard word order for indicating ownership in Hebrew requires that the property be placed before the proprietor.[2] Yet, in verse 1 the psalmist reverses this normal word order (*lĕyhwh hā'āres*, literally, "to Yahweh, the earth"), drawing attention to the uniqueness of the theological claim that "the earth is *the Lord's.*"[3] Only God — no other god or human — can claim sovereignty over anything or anyone.

The psalm describes the Lord as a God of order. Those who worship the Lord participate in his ordering work by acting faithfully toward God and one another. In the liturgy, as the procession nears the temple, some people (perhaps the priests) utter a double question: "Who can ascend? . . . Who can stand?" (v. 3); that is, *what kind of person* can come up to the temple to worship this divine king? The response to these questions is a

1. See Frank Moore Cross, *Canaanite Myth and Hebrew Epic* (Cambridge: Harvard University Press, 1973), 93.

2. Bruce Waltke and M. O'Connor, *An Introduction to Biblical Hebrew Syntax* (Winona Lake, Ind.: Eisenbrauns, 1990), 209-10.

3. Erhard Gerstenberger, *Psalms: Part 1 with an Introduction to Cultic Poetry,* FOTL 14 (Grand Rapids: Eerdmans, 1988), 117.

list of stipulations for community living in right relationship (for similar lists of righteous behavior, see Ps 15 and Isa 33:14-16).

The stipulations fall into the (modern) categories of ethics and piety: Those coming to worship must have "clean hands" (v. 4); they cannot carry the guilt of having shed innocent blood. Also, they do not "swear deceitfully"; they do not give false witness and thus compromise the order of the community by spreading falsehood (cf. Deut 5:20). These ethical norms, however, cannot be separated from the demands of true piety. Having a "pure heart" and not lifting up one's soul to "what is false" refer to worship of and fidelity to the Lord alone (v. 4). To worship idols ("what is false," v. 4) is to give assent to a view of the cosmos that denies Yahweh's role as creator and divine king. The section ends with the affirmation that contributing to God's order in these ways ensures Yahweh's blessing and keeps one in right relationship with God (vv. 5-6).

The final portion of this psalm (vv. 7-10) may be an antiphonal liturgy spoken between the watchmen of the gates and the company processing with the ark.[4] If so, the company summons the gatekeepers to attention: "Lift up your heads . . . that the King of Glory may come in" (v. 7). The gatekeepers respond by asking for a liturgical password, "Who is this King of Glory [*mî zeh melek hakkābôd*]?" In response, the company employs epithets for the Lord that indicate his victory in the battle against the enemies of order (v. 8).

In verses 9-10 the call and response pattern repeats with only slight variation. In verse 10 the gatekeepers' question is more emphatic: "*Who, then,* is this King of Glory [*mî hû' zeh melek hakkābôd*]?" The company responds by evoking Yahweh's aspect as commander of the hosts of heaven: *Yhwh ṣĕbā'ôt* — "the LORD of Hosts." This martial title for Yahweh was closely associated with the ark and was the name by which David blessed the people at the end of the triumphal procession in 2 Samuel 6:18. These final verses complete the image of a God who conquers chaos: by his power, Yahweh creates the world upon the chaotic waters (vv. 1-2), authors order within the community (vv. 3-6), and protects the community from the forces of chaos (vv. 7-10), perhaps, as suggested by Samuel, in the midst of international conflicts (see above).

2. Psalm 24 and Christian theology. Like Psalm 24, the Apostles' Creed begins with the confession of God's creative activity: "I believe in God the Father Almighty, Maker of heaven and earth." Psalm 24 works out some of

4. Peter C. Craigie, *Psalms 1-50*, WBC 19 (Waco: Word, 1983), 214.

the implications of this fundamental claim. Several implications seem obvious. First, our society invests heavily in concepts of personal ownership such that we often ignore *God's ultimate ownership* of all things. As the Creator, God supersedes all other claims made on creation, which is, after all, the Lord's to begin with (v. 1; cf. Exod 19:5). God's creation is also an act of ordering, and it is incumbent upon God's people to promote the order God establishes. We do this by creating and preserving right relationships — that is, *righteousness* — among all members of the *world* community.

The Lord has subdued chaos at the foundation of the world. But, for whatever reasons, chaos persists, so Yahweh continues to act in history to reestablish order. Christians affirm that Jesus' life, death, and resurrection are the ultimate expression of God's victory over the forces of chaos, sin, and death. The Israelites sang this psalm to celebrate the creating and saving acts of the Lord of Hosts, the King of Glory. When Christians sing Psalm 24, we recall those same mighty saving acts — and find them also and especially in the person and work of Jesus Christ. Our song celebrates the victory we have been given through him, the King of kings and Lord of lords (Rev 19:16).

Joel M. LeMon

PSALM 25

First Sunday in Lent, Year B
    First Lesson: Genesis 9:8-17
    (Psalm 25:1-10)
    Second Lesson: 1 Peter 3:18-22
    Gospel Lesson: Mark 1:9-15

First Sunday of Advent, Year C
    First Lesson: Jeremiah 33:14-16
    (Psalm 25:1-10)
    Second Lesson: 1 Thessalonians 3:9-13
    Gospel Lesson: Luke 21:25-36

Psalm 25:1-10 is the aleph through kaph (or *A* through *K*) section of *an acrostic psalm* (see introductory essay) about the instruction of God that is needful for the sinner. The first ten verses of the psalm, which make up the present lection, constitute, at root, a theological reflection and heartfelt plea rising out of that reflection. The second half of the psalm, not included in the lectionary reading, contains the classical elements of *lament* or *prayer for help* in a time of trouble (see introductory essay). One might then categorize the opening verses of the psalm as an introit to lament, and as the element of trust that is so integral to any complaint to God.

The opening verses request instruction in avoiding shame and disgrace, and offer instruction for those who await the Lord. The case is made step by step, from *A* to *K,* regarding the benefits of living in (and remaining in) relationship with God (cf. "those who keep" in v. 10) and the benefits of waiting for the God of salvation.

1. *The mechanics of the psalm.* Psalm 25 is widely considered something of an ugly duckling among the Psalms. The acrostic psalms in general are often considered overly rigid and mechanistic. They are often dismissed as lacking cohesion or logical progression outside the formal imposition of the alphabetic lockstep of *A* through *Z* (aleph through taw). In Psalm 25 the cola of the individual verses are uneven, and in all but a few manuscripts the sixth letter of the alphabet (waw) is missing at the beginning of verse 5. Even when it is present, that unit forms an abnormally short colon.

Structurally, Samuel Terrien has located a series of parallel verses in Psalm 25 that together serve to form a chiasm:[1]

    a   vv. 1-3   contrast: the righteous/the enemy
       b   vv. 4-7   request for instruction
          c vv. 8-14   covenant relationship
       b′ vv. 15-18   request for deliverance
    a′   vv. 19-21   contrast: the righteous/the enemy

The point of all this is simply that Psalm 25 is not overly enslaved to the rhythm and form of acrostic poetics — and neither should be one's analysis of this psalm. The chiastic structure seeks to guide the reader from (or perhaps through) the stark contrasts of reality — the righteous and the enemy — and the fearsome threats of shame and treachery. The two-

---

1. Samuel L. Terrien, *The Psalms: Strophic Structure and Theological Commentary,* ECC (Grand Rapids: Eerdmans, 2003), 253; adapted.

fold structure of the psalm, chiastic and acrostic, deftly guides the reader/hearer/pray-er to the promise of the covenant relationship cradled at its center.

2. *The makeup of the psalm.* The psalm has two stanzas: verses 1-10 and verses 11-21 (v. 22 is an addition to the acrostic structure). The primary themes and vocabulary are shared by both stanzas: teach (vv. 4, 14), covenant (vv. 10, 14), foes/enemies (vv. 2, 19), deliverance/salvation (vv. 5, 20), shame (vv. 2, 20), and waiting (vv. 3, 21). Even though the lectionary includes only the first stanza of the psalm, the first half of the psalm's "alphabet," there is nevertheless a certain logic to the break between verses 10 and 11.

Verses 1-10 make the case for trust in the Lord. Faced with waiting, amidst enemies who ridicule and gloat and deal treacherously, fearing shame and the wages of sin, the one who prays this psalm maintains trust in the good and upright Lord whose ways are steadfast love and truth. Ending as the lection does, the greater chiasm of the psalm as a whole is lost. But the crescendo of the opening verses remains, building to the climactic theological assertion of verses 8-10.

The psalm begins with a striking phrase: "To you, O LORD, I lift up my soul." This phrase is an idiomatic expression of trust, a metaphor of supplication and the need for help. Interestingly, this phrase is always connected at least loosely to the need for instruction or guidance when used in the Psalms (cf. Ps 24, an exercise in rhetorical instruction, and Pss 86:4, 11; 143:8, 10). This attitude of the soul lifted up to the Lord for help and instruction is in contrast to the way the phrase is used outside the Psalms. In Deuteronomy 24:15 the laborer is said to be dependent on his wages, literally to have his soul "lifted up" to them. And in Hosea 4:8 the priests are said to have their souls "lifted up" to the sins and iniquity of the people — that is, they relish them and indulge in them. But in the Psalms, and in Psalm 25 specifically, the soul is set squarely on the Lord, the Lord's teaching, the Lord's saving power and efficacy, and the Lord's everlasting covenant.

What comes next is a threefold exhortation to remembrance. What is remarkable is that it is the Lord, the one who instructs and guides and teaches, who is called to remembrance: remember "your mercy" (v. 6), do *not* remember "my sins/rebellion," remember "me (because of your goodness)" (v. 7). Another striking contrast in this psalm may be seen between the mercy and goodness of the Lord that are from of old and everlasting, and the sins of one's youth that are in the past, and to be forgotten. The

Lord is asked to remember selectively, while teaching an old sinner new ways.

Finally comes a simple but powerful theological assertion that serves as the basis for the psalmist's trust and confident waiting for the Lord: "Good and upright is the LORD" (v. 8). As Robert Culley has observed, this language is formulaic, following a set pattern of adjective–conjunction–adjective–divine name (cf. Pss 103:8; 111:4; 145:8), and in each case it points to the fundamental understanding of the Lord as compassionate and merciful.[2] "Good and upright is the LORD." This formulaic expression is indicative of the core theological vision of the nature of the Lord. It is this core belief that marks the climax of the first portion of Psalm 25, an empowering trust that the Lord directs sinners in the way precisely because the Lord is good, and that all the ways of the Lord are steadfast and true, precisely because the Lord is upright.

3. *A-K at large.* Psalm 25 is the appointed psalm for two very different sets of texts. For the First Sunday in Lent, Psalm 25 accompanies texts related to baptism. Genesis 9:8-17 resounds with the Lord's promise to "remember" the covenant made with Noah following the great flood. 1 Peter 3 clearly reflects on that event and its import for the baptized. And Mark 1:9-15 is the story of the baptism of Jesus. With its attention to instruction and guidance, and the confidence in the Lord who provides such direction, Psalm 25 addresses both the benefit and the importance of the covenant relationship that is sealed in baptism — the Lord guides the humble in the right, and teaches the humble in the way (v. 9), and does not let those who wait come to shame (v. 3). Regardless of one's religious tradition, whether baptism is understood as the beginning promise of such instruction or the culmination of it, Psalm 25 models the soul's attitude and approach to the life of faith that is marked physically by baptism.

For the First Sunday of Advent the connection is less clear, and less uniform. Jeremiah 33:14-16 contains the promise of the "righteous branch," whose very name will be "the LORD is our righteousness" (v. 16). This righteous branch comes to "execute justice and righteousness." As Artur Weiser has observed, the sure justice for which the righteous wait is "the foundation on which his [the poet's] life is unshakably established by saying God is 'good' and 'upright.' In that statement the two

---

2. Robert Culley, *Oral Formulaic Language in the Biblical Psalms* (Toronto: University of Toronto Press, 1967), 62.

aspects of God's nature and rule are interwoven."[3] It is God's "inflexible will" to show good to the people. What accompanies that inflexible willing of good for us is the expectation of and the demand for justice on our part. 1 Thessalonians 3:9-13 brings together the love and holiness that may be instilled in the faithful who are guided in what is right by their Lord. Finally, in Luke 21:25-36, which is something of an apocalyptic teaching, we see the faithful, trust-filled waiting that the psalm models as the way to proceed in life. This waiting is what will stand the believer in good stead in turbulent times, amidst persecution of whatever flavor or ferocity, and perhaps even empower her to stand in the presence of the "Son of Man" when heaven and earth pass away — and the gloating and treacherous dealings of enemies along with them — and the Lord's Word, guidance, teaching, instruction, and Way alone remain.

Karl N. Jacobson

PSALM 26

Twentieth Sunday after Pentecost, Year B
    First Lesson: Job 1:1; 2:1-10
    (Psalm 26)
    Second Lesson: Hebrews 1:1-4; 2:5-12
    Gospel Lesson: Mark 10:1-16

The four passages in this Sunday's readings explore the twin issues of human obedience and who may enter the kingdom of God. The Job passages illustrate the life of one who, although declared righteous by God, suffers horribly, leading others to question his essential righteousness. Job nevertheless perseveres in holding on to God regardless. In Hebrews we learn that we are siblings along with Christ, not because we reach a critical level of Torah obedience, but because we have been sanctified by trust in him and by sharing his suffering. The question of divorce in the Mark passage leads us to the question of how one is justified before God. Jesus' opponents use the law of divorce to excuse their lack of commit-

---

3. Artur Weiser, *The Psalms: A Commentary*, OTL (Philadelphia: Westminster, 1962), 240.

ment and fidelity. In calling the little children to him, however, Jesus claims that entry into God's kingdom is founded on childlike trust rather than self-justification. Into this mixture Psalm 26 enfolds the voice of one who claims to walk "in integrity" and who desires not to be "swept away with sinners." This is quite similar to the movement that takes place in the heart of the book of Job, where the suffering righteous man seeks divine confirmation and public vindication.

Psalm 26 begins with a plea for divine vindication based on a claim of righteous integrity and openness to divine scrutiny and examination (vv. 1-2). The imperative cry for God to "vindicate" ($\sqrt{špt}$) the psalmist pictures a legal setting in which a judge renders a public judgment (Hebrew *mišpāṭ*) of "righteous" to exonerate the psalmist. This is only just, the psalmist claims, since he has "walked in . . . integrity." It is striking, however, how this act of integrity is defined in the remainder of this verse. Integrity is not — according to this psalm — a matter of scrupulous attention to the details of the law. It is rather a consequence of *unwavering trust* in God! Here we see an echo of the passage in Mark. Of course, this claim of integrity and unwavering trust does not suppose a sinless life. Instead, as in Job, it means a life of committed relationship of dependence on God alone and full participation in all the accepted means of restoration God offers: repentance, confession, acceptance of divine grace, and testimony to its restorative effect.

The psalmist closes the opening plea with an invitation to close scrutiny and examination by God. Like Job, the psalmist is confident that God — who already knows all — will respond with an affirmation of innocence. God is invited to examine and test the psalmist's innermost secret parts (literally, "kidneys") and the seat of moral decision making (literally, "heart"). As a person of integrity, the psalmist claims that outward deeds and words are consistent with the most secret, inner reflections. It is for this reason that Jesus takes issue with the Pharisees' interpretation of divorce, because their inner motivation was not in accord with their outer scrupulosity. How fearful — but how necessary — to open our hidden inner world to the clear gaze of our redeeming Lord!

Following this opening invocation of God's grace and the invitation to examination, we encounter the psalmist's protestation of innocence (vv. 3-6). It is as if the law court has been convened, the judge seated, and now the evidence must be presented. This section begins and ends with balanced couplets containing claims of innocence in response to the divine presence in worship. In the first set (v. 3), the psalmist claims that

God's "steadfast love is before my eyes," meaning the poet's constant focus on and attention to God's defining grace. The term "steadfast love" here is the Hebrew word *ḥesed* that describes loyal commitment to covenant obligations. This is, however, more than committed love — which it is — since it describes loyalty to covenant obligations one faithfully performs. This sort of commitment is not just *emotion,* but involves a divine decision to *remain faithful come what may.* In response to God's faithfulness, the psalmist claims a position of faithfulness in return: "I walk in faithfulness to you" (v. 3).

The second couplet at the end of this section reverses the order of claims of innocence and depiction of divine presence. Here the psalmist describes washing the "hands in innocence" (v. 6) — a ritual expressing the freedom of the participant from any violent evil perpetrated on the innocent. The verse calls to mind Pilate washing his hands following the decision to allow the crucifixion of Jesus to continue unhindered (Matt 27:24). The innocence proclaimed by this act of ritual washing makes it possible for the psalmist to enter the presence of God in the temple: "I . . . go around your altar, O LORD" (v. 6).

Between these two related couplets stand two more couplets offering additional evidence of the psalmist's innocence on the basis of disassociation from persons of evil (vv. 4-5). Walking faithfully with God and entering his presence means more than ritual correctness. Here the psalmist claims to exercise daily care in the choice of relationships. The four lines of the two inner couplets are arranged in *chiastic* form with references to "sitting" in the outermost lines (vv. 4a, 5b) and mentions of consorting with evil in the innermost lines (vv. 4b, 5a). The verb for sitting here (Hebrew *yāšab*) means long-term, settled residence — the kind of dwelling in which one becomes a citizen and adopts the customs and language of the land. We are not talking about casual or even redemptive relationships with the sinful here. Even Jesus associated with the darker elements of society as a way of calling them to the light. Neither is there any justification for a self-protective withdrawal from society. In contrast, we are called to be a light to the nations rather than allowing our illumination to be snuffed out by becoming indistinguishable from the broader culture in which we live (see Isa 49:6; Matt 5:14-16).

Those with whom the psalmist denies association are examples of willful deception and evil. The first are described as "worthless" (Hebrew *mĕtê-šāw'*) and represent men who consistently prevaricate, building their lives on a web of lies. The "hypocrites" so hide themselves from others that their true thoughts and motivations can never be known, while the last two categories move from those whose deeds are evil to those whose essential selves are thoroughly saturated with wickedness. In the Hebrew, this passage employs alternating past and future verbs ("I *have not* sat . . . I *will not* consort . . . I *have* hated . . . I *will not* sit") to express past, present, and future commitment to avoid evil influences. There are many ways in our modern culture that we need to acknowledge evil for what it is and not turn a blind eye or become complicit by maintaining a studied indifference or tolerance. God is "not a God who delights in wickedness; / evil will not sojourn with [him]" (Ps 5:4).

At the center of this psalm stands an experience of heartfelt worship and thanksgiving. The final couplet of the preceding section prepares the way with its reference to going around the altar after having prepared ritually by the washing of the hands. The preparation of heart and hands has been intended just for this — entering into the presence of God. The purpose of the disciplined life described in this psalm has been to lead to this very point of worshipful communion with God. And so the psalmist envisions breaking out in hymns of thanksgiving and testimonies to the great works of God in the psalmist's behalf.

Caught up in the spirit of worship, the psalmist acknowledges the importance of the divine presence in the life of the faithful. Love for the "house in which you dwell . . . the place where your glory abides" (Ps 26:8) is more than a reference to the temple. The psalmist here captures the overwhelming emotion that washes over the pilgrim who enters the Jerusalem temple after a long journey and joins with the worshiping throng. This is the heart of the faith: knowing God and living in his presence. It is this experience that makes possible continued faithful living in exile amidst the evil of a broken world.

The psalm now turns to its final movement. Fresh from this experience of the presence of God, the psalmist is reminded of the distance that separates sinful humans from holy God. The world in which the psalmist daily lives is a far different place than the temple of God bathed in the glory of God's presence. And so the psalmist pleads not to be carried away (a reference to divine judgment) with the "sinners" and the "bloodthirsty" among whom he dwells (v. 9). These evil persons come to worship insincerely with their hands filled with manipulative "devices" or "plans," and they bring "bribes" rather than true sacrifices of contrition and thanksgiving (v. 10). They seek to control their lives by controlling God.

Our psalmist has already described a disciplined life, careful to avoid the corrupting influence of such persons (vv. 1-6a), and now builds on this life of integrity as the basis for the concluding plea for redemption. The words "I walk in my integrity" (v. 11a) restate the psalm's opening words (v. 1) and recall a life spent in unwavering trust in God. This is the foundation of hope for divine grace and redemption. The feet of the one who so trusts in God will find themselves firmly planted on level ground, providing a motivation for the desire to "bless the LORD" (v. 12) — a desire to return to him the goodness and grace that have been received. The center of such blessing is the worshiping community of faith where together we look forward with expectant "hope of sharing the glory of God" (Rom 5:2).

†Gerald H. Wilson

PSALM 27

Second Sunday in Lent, Year C
 First Lesson: Genesis 15:1-12, 17-18
 (Psalm 27)
 Second Lesson: Philippians 3:17–4:1
 Gospel Lesson: Luke 13:31-35 or Luke 9:28-36

Third Sunday after the Epiphany, Year A
 First Lesson: Isaiah 9:1-4
 (Psalm 27:1, 4-9)
 Second Lesson: 1 Corinthians 1:10-18
 Gospel Lesson: Matthew 4:12-23

Psalm 27 issues compelling statements of trust, faithfulness, and hope. The psalm begins with a confession of trust (vv. 1-3) and a meditation on the sanctuary (vv. 4-6) that together form a song of confidence. However, a lament commences in verse 7, signaling a stark change in mood. The intrepid tone of the first six verses gives way to a plea for Yahweh to deliver the psalmist from encircling enemies (vv. 7-12). A strain of renewed confidence and encouragement concludes the psalm (vv. 13-14).

 1. *A song of confidence.* The psalm's opening verses convey the psalm-

ist's confidence in the face of the most daunting threats (vv. 1-3). The confidence stems from Yahweh's character: God illumines, protects, saves, and dispels fear. The psalmist also characterizes his enemies in these verses, largely through military images (v. 3). The enemies pictured as devouring the psalmist's flesh (v. 2) may be an idiom for slander[1] or a portrayal of them as ravenous animals (for similar images, see Ps 22:12-13, 19-21). Yet, despite these threats, the psalmist adamantly proclaims confidence in Yahweh.

This vivid imagery clearly evokes emotions of security and comfort, as does the psalm's repetitive poetic construction. In general, statements with steady tempo and clear structure inspire confidence. Rambling, disconnected phrases do not. The regular rhythm in verses 1-3 conveys the message that Yahweh's strength is unyielding. Repetition undergirds the message of steadfastness: *"whom shall* I fear . . . *of whom shall* I be afraid" (v. 1); *"though* an army encamp *against me* . . . *though* war rise up *against me"* (v. 3).

The second section of this song (vv. 4-6) further develops the theme of confidence through a meditation on the temple — a place of refuge, secure because of God's very presence there. The phrase "to behold the beauty of the LORD" (v. 4) — especially given the opening characterization of Yahweh as *light* — may refer to the experience of a solar theophany at the temple, in which the sun's beaming rays manifest Yahweh's presence and creative power.[2]

In Yahweh's temple — that is, "his shelter" and "his tent" (v. 5) — the divine presence envelops the psalmist, ensuring his protection. As Yahweh causes the psalmist's enemies to fall down (v. 2), Yahweh lifts up the psalmist and secures him on a rock (v. 5). The psalmist's head is not bowed in defeat. Rather, Yahweh has lifted his head in victory (v. 6; cf. Pss 3:3; 110:7). The psalmist responds by offering up sacrifices and lifting his voice in song (v. 6).

2. *A cry for help.* At the midpoint of the psalm, the psalmist begins to address God directly. His tone changes drastically as his lament commences (vv. 7-14), yet many of the same themes and images echo from the opening song.[3] The psalmist's three petitions in verse 7 ("hear," "be gra-

---

1. Peter C. Craigie, *Psalms 1-50,* WBC 19 (Waco: Word, 1983), 232.

2. See William P. Brown, *Seeing the Psalms: A Theology of Metaphor* (Louisville: Westminster John Knox, 2002), 84; cf. Pss 27:1; 43:3; 104:1-2.

3. Craigie, *Psalms 1-50,* 231.

cious," "answer") constitute a plea to see Yahweh's *face*, a metonym for his presence. This presence of God — *Deus praesens* — was the very thing the psalmist celebrated in the preceding song. Yet in the lament, the psalmist experiences *Deus absconditus* — the hiddenness of God. The psalmist described his unbending will to *seek* (√*bqš*) the presence of God in the song of confidence (v. 4), and he reiterates this desire here during his lament in the context of trouble (v. 8).

The psalmist's use of images from the preceding section continues in verse 9 of the lament. In verse 5 the psalmist proclaimed: "He will *hide* me [√*str*] in the *shelter* [√*str*] of his tent." In the lament he pleads: "do not *hide* [√*str*] your face from me." The interplay of images between the song of confidence and the lament testifies to the psalm's organic unity, but more importantly, it shows how intricately *trust* and *need* are interwoven. As Mays writes, "the voice of neediness speaking urgent pleas for help arises from trust, which transforms mere anxiety to prayer."[4]

Indeed, a brief statement of trust arises even in the midst of the lament, though its tone differs from the earlier confessions framed with military images (v. 3). By contrast, verse 10 draws from the personal realm. Evoking familial imagery, the psalmist imagines the deepest interpersonal pain: abandonment by one's parents. As an answer to this pain, the psalmist employs an image of divine adoption; as a child of God, he has nothing to fear. The wisdom literature, especially the book of Proverbs, attests to the vital role parents play in the instruction of children (e.g., Prov 4:1-9). Following his brief statement of trust, the psalmist's request — *teach me* — seems to assume that Yahweh has in fact become his parent, instructing him in practices leading him to security in the face of his enemies (v. 11).

Verse 12 contains the first declaration of the source of the psalmist's anxiety. His enemies are those who bear false witness, the ones to whom the psalmist alluded in verse 2. In ancient Israel, as today, words could be dangerous. A lying witness threatened one's standing within the community, since false testimony could lead to one's internment, banishment, and even death.

In yet another stark change of mood, the psalm concludes with a reaffirmation of the psalmist's confidence in God. The credo of verse 13 clearly belongs on the lips of the psalmist, yet some argue that the exhortation in the following verse (v. 14) is actually made *by* a priest *to* the

---

4. James L. Mays, *Psalms,* Interpretation (Louisville: John Knox, 1994), 132.

psalmist — that is, it is a priestly oracle of salvation.[5] This is not, however, a necessary assumption. The final words of the psalm may very well be the testimony of the psalmist to others who find themselves in similarly desperate situations. Even with her salvation not fully realized, the psalmist calls on other individuals in the community to be courageous and join her in hope. So it is in all communities of faith: the conviction of the suffering offers encouragement to others. Bound and strengthened by our shared experiences of suffering and salvation, we trust God together.

3. *The "openness" of Psalm 27.* As with most psalms, we cannot be certain of the particular historical context of Psalm 27. We do know, however, that in ancient Israel psalms like this were uttered in times of trouble. Likewise, in desperate situations today, faithful communities and individuals employ the phrases of the Psalms as they cry out to God. Patrick D. Miller has called this the "openness" of the Psalms. Precisely because their emotions and images cannot be bound to any one individual or historical situation, the Psalms have invited centuries of readers to understand their own stories as closely tied to those of the psalmists.[6] In Psalm 27 the trouble caused by enemies is captured in a variety of diverse images spanning the battlefield, the courtroom, and the family. Miller maintains that the enemies in the Psalms are "an *especially* open category, and the content of the category is filled by the predicament and plight not only of the psalmist but also the *contemporary singer* of the psalm."[7]

One such "contemporary singer" is the Namibian pastor-theologian Zephania Kameeta. In the early 1980s, southern Africa was struggling mightily to shake the grip of apartheid. In response to this crisis, Kameeta published a collection of sermons and psalm paraphrases, with the double goal of alerting the world to the crisis of apartheid and encouraging Christians in the midst of the struggle.[8] His treatment of Psalm 27 is bold and particularizing, and clearly illustrates the powerful "openness" of this psalm.

> The Lord is my light and my liberation;
> I will fear no so-called world powers.

5. See Hans-Joachim Kraus, *Psalms 1–59: A Continental Commentary* (Minneapolis: Fortress, 1993), 337.

6. See Patrick D. Miller, *Interpreting the Psalms* (Philadelphia: Fortress, 1986), 23.

7. Miller, *Interpreting the Psalms,* 51, emphasis added.

8. Zephania Kameeta, *Why, O Lord? Psalms and Sermons from Namibia* (Philadelphia: Fortress, 1986).

The Lord protects me from all danger;
I will never be afraid.

When their "security forces" attack me
and try to kill me,
They stumble and fall.
Even if the whole imperialist armies surround me,
I will not be afraid;
I will still trust in God my liberator. (vv. 1-3)

Teach me, Lord, what you want me to do,
And lead me along in this difficult situation.
Do not abandon me to the worshippers of apartheid
        and their collaborators
Who attack me with lies and threats.

I know that I will live to see in this present life
The Lord's victory over the enemies of the oppressed people
        in Southern Africa.
Trust in the Lord: have faith, do not despair.
Trust in the Lord. (vv. 11-14)[9]

It is worth noting that in the twenty years since Kameeta penned this paraphrase, Namibia gained its independence and Kameeta served for ten years as deputy speaker of its parliament before becoming the bishop of the Evangelical Lutheran Church in Namibia. Taking advantage of the psalm's "openness," Kameeta adopted the psalmist's final call that he and his fellow sufferers should trust in God and not be afraid. Their trust, like that of the psalmist, was proven true.

Joel M. LeMon

---

9. Kameeta, *Why, O Lord?* 30-31.

PSALM 29

Baptism of the Lord, First Sunday after the Epiphany, Year A
    First Lesson: Isaiah 42:1-9
    (Psalm 29)
    Second Lesson: Acts 10:34-43
    Gospel Lesson: Matthew 3:13-17

Baptism of the Lord, First Sunday after the Epiphany, Year B
    First Lesson: Genesis 1:1-5
    (Psalm 29)
    Second Lesson: Acts 19:1-7
    Gospel Lesson: Mark 1:4-11

Baptism of the Lord, First Sunday after the Epiphany, Year C
    First Lesson: Isaiah 43:1-7
    (Psalm 29)
    Second Lesson: Acts 8:14-17
    Gospel Lesson: Luke 3:15-17, 21-22

Trinity Sunday, Year B
    First Lesson: Isaiah 6:1-8
    (Psalm 29)
    Second Lesson: Romans 8:12-17
    Gospel Lesson: John 3:1-17

Psalm 29 is especially important for our time because of what it says about two issues: (1) God and the religions of the world (ecumenical concerns); and (2) God and nature (an attitude of awe and wonder; environmental issues). This psalm displays the structure typical of a *hymn of praise* (see the introductory essay and, e.g., Ps 113), with an opening call to praise (vv. 1-2), a major section providing reasons for praising (vv. 3-9), and a conclusion bringing everything to a peaceful ending (vv. 10-11; the last word of the psalm in Hebrew is *shalom*).

At the heart of the psalm in verses 3-9 is a description of an encounter with a powerful storm. We may bring it up to date. Imagine standing on the shore of a great lake, watching a storm develop. At first there is an eerie calm. Then the western sky darkens. In the distance you can see jagged flashes of lightning and hear the dull roar of thunder. Clouds race across the sky. The wind comes, first as a gentle breeze, then as a more powerful force, throwing the lake into whitecaps. There is a flash of lightning, followed by a loud clap of thunder, and a branch on a great pine tree breaks and hits the ground with a thump (v. 3)! Finally, a massive gray curtain of rain moves across the water, coming toward you, and you run into the cabin for shelter. As you look out the window and see this display of nature's power, the words of William Cowper's hymn come to mind:

> God moves in a mysterious way,
> His wonders to perform:
> He plants his footsteps in the sea
> And rides upon the storm.[1]

The poet got it just right: God as Storm Rider! See also Psalm 104:3.

Alternatively, the experience of the storm may call to mind another hymn:

> O Lord my God, when I in awesome wonder
> Consider all the worlds thy hands have made,
> I see the stars, I hear the rolling thunder,
> Thy power throughout the universe displayed;
> Then sings my soul, my Savior God to thee;
> How great thou art! How great thou art![2]

Once again, the hymn writer got it just right. The wind, the rain, the lightning, and the rolling thunder call forth an attitude of *wonder* that then erupts into an expression of praise: "How great thou art!"

The opening call to praise is not directed at worshipers gathered in a temple. Here a cosmic dimension is introduced, directing the calls to certain "heavenly beings" surrounding God's throne. We might call them angels. The Bible assumes the presence of these heavenly creatures, elsewhere calling them "gods" (Ps 82:1, 6) or "angels" (Ps 148:1-2) or "seraphs" (Isa 6:2).

One of the key notions in this psalm is "glory" (Hebrew *kābôd*), occurring in verses 1, 2, and 9. The basic sense of the word is "heaviness, abundance." For example, a cloud may be described as "thick" *(kābôd)*

---

1. See *Lutheran Book of Worship*, #483.
2. See *The United Methodist Hymnal*, #77.

with rain (Exod 19:16), or one may speak of "heavy" *(kābôd)* hail (Exod 9:24). The word may also denote splendor, like the splendor of a great banquet (Esther 1:4; see also 1:5-9 and 5:11). When used of the Lord, *kābôd* denotes weightiness, splendor, majesty, magnificence. How should these heavenly beings "ascribe *kābôd*" to the Lord? Since they are capable of singing (see Isa 6:3), it appears that they join both supernatural and natural creatures in singing or shouting the word "glory" *(kābôd;* v. 9).

Commentators have long pointed out the similarities between this psalm and the hymns of Israel's neighbors, especially Canaanite hymns that speak of Baal as the storm god. For example, a Canaanite text says of Baal: "And now Baal will appoint the time of his rain. And he will make his voice ring out in the clouds, by flashing his lightning to the earth."[3] Here an *ecumenical* point might be made. We know that the writers of the Hebrew Bible often appropriated materials from their neighbors and adapted them for use in their own Scriptures. We know that Christian writers have long set their words to the best in tunes picked up from their environment. Claus Westermann says in regard to the religion of the Canaanites and the Israelite faith:

> [I]t became perfectly possible to accept what the two religious systems had in common, awe in the presence of the Creator and His word of power, recognition of God as king and homage paid to Him in worship. It cannot be denied that, in later stages of religious development, where the rational element came to assume a dominant role, especially in the area of doctrine, awe before God's majesty and its effects in creation largely receded into the background or even entirely disappeared. It is this awe before God's majesty which Psalm 29 can still mediate to us today.[4]

Most of us have well learned that the biblical God acts through the *events of history* (see Deut 26:4-14; Pss 105–106; Acts 13:13-41). Psalm 29, as well as texts like Psalms 19, 104, 148, can remind us that God is also active in the *events of nature.* Moreover, texts like Genesis 1-2 and Psalm 8 can remind humans of their *responsibility* for the care of their natural environment.

3. Walter Beyerlin, ed., *Near Eastern Religious Texts Relating to the Old Testament,* OTL (Philadelphia: Westminster, 1978), 209; see also 220-21, etc.

4. Claus Westermann, *The Living Psalms* (Grand Rapids: Eerdmans, 1989), 236.

The lectionary suggests a variety of ways in which Psalm 29 can complement and point to other texts in four different contexts. Matthew's account of the baptism of Jesus (Year A) reports how the voice of the Lord was heard over the waters in a quite different way from that reported in Psalm 29 (see Matt 3:17). The psalm text exemplifies through water the Lord's work in nature; the Matthew text shows God working through water at the beginning of the story of God's saving work through Jesus. The Year B text provides Mark's account of Jesus' baptism. On this Sunday, the first lesson, Genesis 1:1-5, speaks of the Spirit of God (NRSV: "wind from God") hovering over the waters. The Lukan text for Year C connects with Psalm 29:3; Isaiah 43:2 refers to the Lord's act of deliverance when Israel "passed through the waters" in the event of the exodus. The connection with the Isaiah 6 text for Trinity Sunday has been mentioned above.

James Limburg

PSALM 30

Sixth Sunday after the Epiphany, Year B
First Lesson: 2 Kings 5:1-14
(Psalm 30)
Second Lesson: 1 Corinthians 9:24-27
Gospel Lesson: Mark 1:40-45

Third Sunday of Easter, Year C
First Lesson: Acts 9:1-6, (7-20)
(Psalm 30)
Second Lesson: Revelation 5:11-14
Gospel Lesson: John 21:1-19

Seventh Sunday after Pentecost, Year C
First Lesson: 2 Kings 5:1-14 or Isaiah 66:10-14
(Psalm 30)
Second Lesson: Galatians 6:(1-6), 7-16
Gospel Lesson: Luke 10:1-11, 16-20

Psalm 30 is remarkable in that it has not one superscription, nor two, but *three:* this is "a Psalm," "a song of dedication of the temple," and "of David." The psalm itself, aside from its titles and despite its relative brevity, is a many-splendored thing. Psalm 30 is an exercise in praise, it tells a story, and it models a reality — the reality of one who is humbled, delivered, and sustained by the Lord.

1. *What's in a name?* It is generally agreed that the superscriptions are later additions to the psalms (see the introductory essay). Still, it is interesting to note that at some point this psalm came to be understood in terms of and used in remembrance of the dedication (Hanukkah) of the temple. Read in that light, the psalm's call for praise and its basic understanding of the relationship between Creator and creature define the critical exchange that is central to worship and the temple. This song of dedication, used as a part of corporate worship or in individual devotion, may play an important role in the life of faith.

2. *How the psalm works.* Psalm 30 is generally read and interpreted in terms of the classical definition of a *psalm of thanksgiving* (see the introductory essay). To be sure, the issue of praise and the issuing of praise in thanks by one who has been delivered by the Lord (vv. 2-3) are critical to the psalm. The opening declaration of the poem is clearly one of praise: "I will extol you." And the fourth verse includes the imperative invitation to join in the psalmist's praise: "*Sing* [zmrw] to the LORD . . . *and praise* [whwdw] his holy name." Much is made of the dialectic of praise and silence that dominates the well-known and theologically weighty question of verse 9. Without question this is a psalm of thanksgiving — hence, an occasion of thanksgiving provides a meaningful context for understanding this psalm. But, as William P. Brown has noted, the language of this psalm is both intense and emotive, and "such language invites appropriation across a wide range of contexts, reaching beyond generic divisions."[1]

What is often overlooked or underemphasized under the rubric of the individual psalm of thanksgiving is the *series of contrasts* that serves as the skeletal framework of the psalm and defines the movement and being of the poem — the *way* the psalm *means* for those who read it.

---

1. William P. Brown, *Seeing the Psalms: A Theology of Metaphor* (Louisville: Westminster John Knox, 2002), 16; see also the important work of Harry P. Nasuti, *Defining the Sacred Songs: Genre, Tradition, and the Post-Critical Interpretation of the Psalms,* JSOTSup 218 (Sheffield: Sheffield Academic, 1999).

The opposition of praise to silence is set in the critical question of verse 9:

> What profit is there in my death,
>> if I go down to the Pit?
> Will the dust praise you?
>> Will it tell of your faithfulness?

With the psalmist's death and descent to Sheol, the land of the dead, there is little possibility of praise from still, silenced lips (see, similarly, Ps 6:5). Silence is the polar opposite of praise, and this is the ultimate contrast in the psalm. But there are many other contrasts, some explicit, some implied: "my" extolling versus my enemies' *not* rejoicing (v. 1); healing versus illness (v. 2); anger that is momentary versus favor that is lasting (v. 5); weeping that lingers for a night versus joy that comes with dawn (v. 5); prosperity versus dismay (v. 6); by your favor versus hid your face (v. 6); (like a) strong mountain versus dismayed and brought low (v. 7); mourning versus dancing (v. 11); off with sackcloth versus on with joy (v. 11). It is between these many oppositions that the meaning of the psalm lies — both for the psalmist as he tells his story and for the reader or listener who is invited into this poem, into — it should be stressed — the possibility of a redeemed reality.

One further word about the critical question of verse 9. Pleading with the Lord for help, the psalmist puts the Lord on the spot:

> What profit is there in my death,
>> if I go down to the Pit?

The key word is "profit" *(bṣ')*. Generally speaking, this word has negative connotations in the Bible (cf. Isa 33:15; 56:11). In Psalms 10:3 and 119:36, "profit" is about greedy or selfish *gain*. In Genesis 37 Judah suggests that there is greater *profit* in selling off his little brother than in killing him. In Judges 5:19 Deborah sings of *spoils* sought in war. It is quite striking that the psalmist hangs her argument with God on such a negative word. The implication is troubling: the Lord is dealing, if not unfairly, then at least unprofitably, with the psalmist. But if the psalmist's praise is silenced, the greedy Lord will get no paycheck.

In contrast to such a scenario stands the poem of the author. The psalmist recounts her own experience, the ups and downs (and ups again) in her life, in full honesty and humility. She does so by two "past tense" statements:

Verses 6-7. First, the psalmist admits to overconfidence, to self-confidence, to hubris. Out of prosperity, the psalmist makes an outrageous claim that "I shall never be moved." But at that moment the Lord's favor is removed, and fortune turns to folly. The Lord's face is hidden, and the psalmist is dismayed.

Verses 8-9. Second, the psalmist recognizes his mistake, his need for mercy and help, and turns to the Lord in supplication.

> Hear, O LORD, and be gracious to me!
>   O LORD, be my helper!

In each case it is the speech of the psalmist that is definitive of the moment.[2]

These turning points, recalled from the past, now make up the present-tense praise of verses 11-12, which express a new reality, or perhaps better, a return to reality that is rightly understood in honesty and humility and reliance on God's blessing and favor — in short, a return to a reality that is a "Godly orientation" to life. We who read this prayer are called to recognize this reality and to embrace it as it has been modeled for us.

3. *Psalm 30 in the lectionary.* The most compelling connection between Psalm 30 and its lectionary companions may be with the conversion of Saul and the recommissioning of Peter, both on the Third Sunday of Easter, Year C. For Saul there is his fall from what he perceived as grace — his blindness, healing, and conversion from a persecutor of the gospel to a proclaimer of it. For Peter there is a threefold turnaround from denial to tending Christ's sheep. In each of these texts there is a changing of reality, an altering of state and situation, that is effected by God. This reality alteration is the same new or renewed reality modeled by the psalmist, and presented to the present reader as both promise and motivation to give thanks and praise to the Lord whose "favor is for a lifetime."

Karl N. Jacobson

2. See further Rolf A. Jacobson, *Many Are Saying: The Function of Direct Discourse in the Hebrew Psalter*, JSOTSup 397 (London: T. & T. Clark, 2004).

PSALM 31

Passion Sunday, Years A, B, C
    First Lesson: Isaiah 50:4-9a
    (Psalm 118:1-2, 19-29 or **Psalm 31:9-16**)
    Second Lesson: Philippians 2:5-11
    Gospel Lesson: Matthew 21:1-11 (A); Mark 11:1-11 (B); Luke 19:28-40 (C)

Fifth Sunday of Easter, Year A
    First Lesson: Acts 7:55-60
    (Psalm 31:1-5, 15-16)
    Second Lesson: 1 Peter 2:2-10
    Gospel Lesson: John 14:1-14

Ninth Sunday after the Epiphany, Year A
    First Lesson: Deuteronomy 11:18-21, 26-28
    (Psalm 31:1-5, 19-24)
    Second Lesson: Romans 1:16-17; 3:22b-28, (29-31)
    Gospel Lesson: Matthew 7:21-29

This psalm, beginning as a *prayer to God for help* from distress (vv. 1-18) and ending as a *song of thanksgiving* for deliverance (vv. 19-24; see the introductory essay), portrays an individual in great suffering who pleads with God for release from enemies. Central to the prayer is a plea for God's protection, specifically that God remove the psalmist from the sphere of the enemy's power into the shelter of divine refuge.

    The text is full of images of God as a *protective stronghold*. Following the assertion "I seek refuge in you" and the plea "rescue me" in the first verse, the text continues envisioning God as a protecting enclosure: "a rock of refuge," "a strong fortress" (v. 2; cf. vv. 3-4), and "shelter" (v. 20). Curiously, the situation that the psalmist is pleading to be saved from is also portrayed in terms of enclosed spaces. Using imagery derived from hunting and the treatment of war prisoners, she prays that God "take me out of the net that is hidden for me" (v. 4; see fig. 4), and while giving thanks for God's deliverance, she says her past struggle made her like "a city under siege" (v. 21). The psalmist wants to be rescued from enclosed spaces controlled by the enemy (a net, a besieged city), to the *enclosed space of God's protection* (a fortress, a shelter). It may be that the background for this imagery of refuge and protection comes from the ancient

Fig. 4. This Egyptian painting illustrates one kind of net employed by ancient hunters, who first hid the net and then suddenly drew it closed around their quarry. The psalmist employs this image of confinement when praying "take me out of the net that is hidden for me" (Ps 31:4) or when complaining of being hunted with a net (see, e.g., Pss 10:9; 35:7).

---

custom of seeking sanctuary from foes at holy places.[1] As such, the psalm indicates the desire not for freedom per se (if that is understood as total lack of connection or boundary), but for deliverance out of the power of the enemy into God's protecting domain. Salvation in Psalm 31 entails being enclosed by the divine.

A similar pattern is in play with the text's use of the term "hand," another symbol of power and protection. After committing his spirit "into your [i.e., God's] hand" in verse 5, the psalmist later gives thanks to God for not delivering him "into the hand of the enemy" (v. 8). In verse 15 the psalmist asserts to God, "My times are in your hands," and also pleads, "Deliver me from the hand of my enemies and persecutors." With the imagery of hand and stronghold, the psalmist represents the enemy and God similarly and also indicates her comparative weakness. In a situation where the psalmist feels at the mercy of the enemy, she begs to be taken up by the protective mercy of God.

Within this petition for rescue are many expressions of praise —

---

1. James L. Mays, *Psalms,* Interpretation (Louisville: John Knox, 1994), 144.

praise that seems both to *express* and, at the same time, to *encourage trust in God.* Because acclamations to God such as "you are indeed my rock and my fortress" (v. 3) and "you are my refuge" (v. 4) are said by someone who seeks refuge and deliverance (vv. 2-3), such praise might function to remind the psalmist what she knows to be true on the ultimate level but is not currently experiencing. Praise in a time of distress can sometimes refresh those memories of divine intervention that sustain endurance. In addition, the text ends with a thanksgiving to God for "hearing my supplications" (v. 22) and asserts that "the LORD preserves the faithful" (v. 23; this praise might be the result of a cultic oracle originally inserted between vv. 18 and 19; see the introductory essay and the entry on Ps 13). The full text can thus be construed as a witness to those currently suffering, testifying to God's gracious help to those in similar situations and encouraging them to maintain their hope in the Lord.

To be considered alongside these aspects of praise is the sense in which praise also *motivates God to act.* That is, in addition to working in the human sphere to generate trust in God, it also works in the divine sphere to prompt God to alleviate the suffering of the psalmist. For example, God's character and reputation are called upon as the motivating agent for liberation and direction: "in your righteousness deliver me" (v. 1) and "for your name's sake lead me and guide me" (v. 3). In these verses the supplicant is imploring God to act according to God's own nature. In addition, part of the purpose for the detailed and lengthy enumeration of the psalmist's physical and social suffering in verses 9b-13 (failing strength, wasting bones, being the object of scorn, dread, and murderous plots) might be to generate a sense of pity in the heart of God, a pity that will move God to alleviate such suffering. Indeed, the affirmation that God is moved with such compassion is assumed by two lines that precede the detailed description of suffering in verses 9b-13: "I will exult . . . because you have seen my affliction" (v. 7) and "Be gracious to me . . . for I am in distress" (v. 9a). Underlying both utterances is the firm trust that, once God is aware of the psalmist's affliction, God will act to alleviate such distress. As a prayer addressed to God, the author presents a case, sensitively and strategically motivating the Lord to act according to God's nature and out of God's compassion.

The church reads this text every Passion Sunday, directed there, at least partially, by Luke's presentation of verse 5 as Jesus' dying words (Luke 23:46: "Into your hands I commit my spirit"). With these words the Gospel writer expresses both Jesus' suffering and Jesus' faith. If we hear in Jesus' quotation of verse 5 an invoking of the whole psalm, he telegraphs his great distress. The use of this text also manifests Jesus' faith, for in the time of his greatest powerlessness he uses his last breath to commit himself to God. His language of commitment stems from the world of commercial transactions — the verse pledges a valuable object in the sure hope that it will be kept secure and redeemed.[2] As such, his statement should be understood not as passive resignation in the face of death but as sure faith in God's ultimate power, power that can take him out of the "net" of the enemy and put him into God's own protection (cf. the essay on Ps 22). Though the psalmist asks to be spared from death, Jesus will be taken by God through death, after which his resurrection promises deliverance from all forces that threaten to undo humanity.

Following Jesus' example as presented in Luke, Christians through the ages (including such notables as Polycarp, Bernard, and Luther) have said as their last words "Into your hand I commit my spirit."[3] The psalm thus not only witnesses to God's help for those suffering, it is also a model to teach us how to die in the faith.

Melody D. Knowles

PSALM 32

First Sunday in Lent, Year A
> First Lesson: Genesis 2:15-17
> **(Psalm 32)**
> Second Lesson: Romans 5:12-19
> Gospel Lesson: Matthew 4:1-11

Fourth Sunday in Lent, Year C
> First Lesson: Joshua 5:9-12
> **(Psalm 32)**
> Second Lesson: 2 Corinthians 5:16-21
> Gospel Lesson: Luke 15:1-3, 11b-32

2. See Adele Berlin and Marc Zvi Brettler, eds., *The Jewish Study Bible* (Oxford: Oxford University Press, 2004), 1315.

3. A. F. Kirkpatrick, *The Book of Psalms* (Cambridge: Cambridge University Press, 1939), 127.

In the time of confession and truth telling that Lent entails, Psalm 32 reminds us of our sin, our need for confession, and the speed and power of God's mercy. As an *individual thanksgiving* that includes a personal testimony and wisdom elements (see the introductory essay), the text encourages the community to confess their sins and receive divine forgiveness.

The text begins with two aphorisms and, with "happy" as the opening word, calls to mind Psalm 1, which begins the same way. Both Psalm 32 and Psalm 1 also present a dichotomy of humanity, but in the latter the contrast is between the righteous and the wicked, whereas in the former the contrast is between those who are forgiven and those who are not. That is, Psalm 32 assumes that sin is an inexorable part of the righteous life: those who are "happy" incur guilt, and the three separate terms for their sin in verses 1-2 speak to the full gamut of the transgression of the righteous. Furthermore, the commonality between the wicked and the righteous is not only their misdeeds, it is also the agony they undergo — Psalm 32 does not draw a clear line of demarcation between the outward effects of the many "torments of the wicked" (v. 10) and the agonies of the righteous one with unconfessed sin (vv. 3-4, 6b, 7a). Yet even though sinful acts and distress may be common to all humanity, the experience of God's forgiveness distinguishes the righteous from the wicked. Although this perspective is expanded later in the text, it is telegraphed in the first two verses by the order of words: the three terms for sin are always preceded by a term for forgiveness (literally, "is forgiven transgression," "is covered over sin," and "not held by the LORD his guilt," vv. 1-2). For the author of Psalm 32, the "happy" one is someone whose sin cannot be spoken of before divine forgiveness is named.

The following verses are a personal testimony to the effects of unacknowledged sin and the swiftness of God's forgiveness following confession. For the psalmist, the consequences of unconfessed sin are borne by the body: limbs "waste away" and strength "dries up" (vv. 3-4). The immediate cause of such physical torment is not the sin itself but the silence of the transgressor (v. 3: "As long as I said nothing . . ."). The physical maladies caused by silence are remedied by confession (v. 5: "I said, 'I will confess . . .'"). The presentation of events in verse 5 emphasizes not only the need to articulate transgressions but also God's immediate response of forgiveness: the clause expressing an intent to confess is followed by the report of God's absolution: "*You* [emphatic] forgave . . ." (v. 5). Curiously, the confession itself is lacking, a situation possibly explained by the deliberate nonspecificity of the Psalms in general or the inappropriateness of a personal confession in a testimony to the community (which would perhaps be "more than anyone else wants to hear," according to Brueggemann).[1] Yet it can also be said that the absence of the confession poetically exhibits the rapidity of God's forgiveness. Without the confession, God's pardon follows immediately upon the intent to confess ("I said, 'I will confess . . .'" [v. 5]), and the text instantly emphasizes God's haste to forgive.

Following the testimony of the effects of sin and confession, the psalmist encourages others to follow her example: "Therefore . . ." (v. 6). The recitation of past events functions thus to teach the larger community. Besides serving as a reason to praise God (v. 11), the psalmist's personal history is here a witness for others so that "the rush of mighty waters" might not reach them (v. 6). Although the lines are addressed to God, the text "comes very close to being a homily on penitence,"[2] in which the psalmist's personal experience witnesses to the need for confession and God's forgiveness.

The homily also gestures beyond the immediate rectification of sin through confession to an entire way of life. Verses 8-9 seem to be an address from God[3] (perhaps delivered by a priest), in which God offers "instruction" and "counsel." The effect of such divine enlightenment is to change the believer from a senseless beast whose desires are curbed only by the brute physical force of bit and bridle. In these verses the God who provides the confessing sinner an immediate shelter from distress (v. 7) also offers to teach "a way" in which to travel through life.

With its acknowledgment of the inevitability of sin, the force of confession, and God's swiftness to forgive, Psalm 32 is an instructive text for Lent. In the larger community of faith, the passage instructs us in the knowledge of God and humanity through a personal witness. Yet the text has a larger arch than this one liturgical season — according to tradition, Augustine had this text written on the wall by his sickbed before his death so he could be reminded of his sins and, at the same time, comforted by the reality of God's forgiveness.[4] In addition, when choirs in the Eastern

1. Walter Brueggemann, *The Message of the Psalms: A Theological Commentary* (Minneapolis: Augsburg, 1984), 97.

2. Erhard S. Gerstenberger, *Psalms, Part 1* (Grand Rapids: Eerdmans, 1987), 143.

3. Hans-Joachim Kraus, *Psalms 1–59: A Continental Commentary* (Minneapolis: Fortress, 1993), 371.

4. A. F. Kirkpatrick, *The Book of Psalms* (Cambridge: Cambridge University Press, 1939), 161.

Orthodox Church sing this psalm after a child has been baptized,[5] they too witness to a lifelong experience of human sin that, through confession, is met, again and again, by God's swift forgiving grace.

Melody D. Knowles

PSALM 33

Third Sunday after Pentecost, Year A
    First Lesson: Genesis 12:1-9
    (Psalm 33:1-12)
    Second Lesson: Romans 4:13-25
    Gospel Lesson: Matthew 9:9-13, 18-26

Psalm 33 begins by instructing the "righteous ones" (v. 1) to "rejoice in the LORD" with a variety of instruments (vv. 2-3) on account of the "uprightness" of God's word and the "faithfulness" of God's works (v. 4). The example the text gives of God's moral word and work is creation. Verse 5 declares that "the earth is full of the steadfast love [*ḥesed*] of the LORD," and this is explicated with a description of God's involvement in the creation of the sky and seas (vv. 6-7). As in Genesis 1, God creates the heavens via speech, and as in both Genesis 1 and Genesis 2, the "breath" or "spirit" of God is also involved in the creative process. The psalm moves from the sky to the seas in verse 7, and the language used here ("gathers" and "puts") denotes a marshaling of bodies of water (sometimes understood to represent the forces of chaos), also similar to Genesis 1 where God created an expanse to divide the waters.

Verse 8 begins the second major part of the psalm, and like the first section, an imperative is followed by a motivating clause. In this section, however, the imperative is not "praise God" but rather "fear" and "stand in awe" of the Lord; and those to whom the imperative is addressed are not the righteous but rather the whole earth and its inhabitants. The content of the second motivating clause, however, is the same as in the first section, namely, God's work in creation:

---

5. See William L. Holladay, *The Psalms through Three Thousand Years: Prayerbook of a Cloud of Witnesses* (Minneapolis: Fortress, 1993), 181.

For he spoke, and it came to be;
> he commanded, and it stood firm. (v. 9)

Again, and also as in Genesis 1, God's creative word is the agent for the beginning of the world.

The text emphasizes that God's work in creation is an expression of moral import, and as such, the text reworks and reinterprets the traditions now present in the Genesis narratives. According to verse 4, God's word (which, according to vv. 6 and 9, is the divine agent for the creation of the world) is "upright," and God's work is done in "faithfulness." These moral categories continue in verse 5 with the claim that the earth is "full of the LORD's steadfast love [ḥesed]." The Genesis narratives are not as explicit about the moral import of God's deeds in creation, and the temptation is to locate God's primary ethical deeds in the later act of liberating the enslaved Israelites (although note that vv. 7-8 may obliquely refer to the exodus). Yet Psalm 37 locates God's moral agency further back, at the very beginning of the world. According to Patrick D. Miller, the text asserts that "[t]he beginning of the faithful love of God and the justice of God is not an act of deliverance from oppression. . . . It is the beginning of everything."[1]

The text also emphasizes the work of God in creation as an act that is ongoing. Even as God uttered the world into being in the past (vv. 6 and 9), God also continues to "fashion" the hearts of humanity and keep watch upon them (vv. 13-15). God's involvement in these verses is emphasized through no fewer than four verbs that tell of God's visual connection with the inhabitants of the earth: "looks down," "sees," "watches," and "observes." God's ongoing commitment to creation is also seen in the context of war, since the assertions of verses 16-18 imply that the Lord alone brings victory in battle.

It may be that this text speaks most appropriately in a context of military threat. The reference to death and famine (v. 19), the assertions of the inadequacies of armies, warriors, and horses (vv. 16-17), together with the designation of the Lord as "our helper and shield" (v. 20) seem to find clearest resonance in a time of war and insecurity. In such a context, part of the force of remembering God's work in creation has to do with the claims it makes for the scope of God's power. This is the God who spoke skies into being and continues to watch over all humanity, in-

1. Patrick D. Miller, *Interpreting the Psalms* (Philadelphia: Fortress, 1986), 75-76.

cluding those involved in battle. The scope of this power also has a destructive force: the God who created the world can "bring the counsel of the nations to nothing," and the one whose designs endure "frustrates the plans of the people" (v. 10). According to William P. Brown, "God's watchful, omniscient gaze renders all earthly affairs contingent and unpredictable, including military engagements."[2]

The startling aspect of the creation motif in this text is not only the explicit attribution of moral agency but also its use in the probable context of military threat. In such a situation, it might seem more appropriate to retell the story of the exodus when God vanquished the foes of the nation. Yet this psalm goes back before the Lord became Israel's God to when the Lord created the entire universe and filled it with "steadfast love [ḥesed]." The psalmist explicitly points to the import of this moment for the whole world: it forms the basis of the motivating clause for the praise of the righteous (vv. 1-7) and the fear of "the inhabitants of the world" (vv. 8-9). This praise and fear stem from God's claim over creation as initiating agent and continuing sustainer, and the moral category out of which this claim was worked. In its reformulation and reuse of the narratives that underlie the Genesis stories, Psalm 32 tells a "new song" in a time of danger.

The final verse, technically the only passage of the psalm addressed to God, is both a request and an assertion:

> May your unfailing love [ḥesed] rest upon us, O LORD,
>   even as we put our hope in you.

In a context of threat, the psalm's request is remarkably terse. It asks neither for victory nor even for strength, but only for God's unfailing love *(ḥesed),* which, according to verse 5, already fills the earth! Such an uncomplicated request flows out of the preceding assertions about God: because God is the moral creator and ongoing sustainer of creation, no specific request is necessary for the community, even a community in dire circumstances. In this context the final assertion ("even as we put our hope in you") is less a stance of passivity than an active refusal to hope in other options (such as horses, armies, etc.), and a bold choosing not to fear. It is a courageous proclamation of "God's reign amid persons

2. William P. Brown, *Seeing the Psalms: A Theology of Metaphor* (Louisville: Westminster John Knox, 2002), 172.

and circumstances that deny it."[3] This stance of hoping in God also calls the reader back to the imperative in verse 3 ("Sing to him a new song"), for now the reader knows that such skillful and loud singing is called forth as a concrete expression of hope in God in a threatening time.

The other lectionary texts also speak of hope and faith in God in the context of anxiety and weakness. Abram and Sarai's obedience to a God who asked them to leave all that was familiar (Gen 12:1-9, and the interpretation in Rom 4:13-25); Matthew's obedience to Jesus' call to follow him (Matt 9:9); the ruler who requested that Jesus raise his dead daughter; and the woman who reached out to touch Jesus' garment (Matt 9:18-26) all witness to a radical hope. Such a hope is not unduly tethered to past expectations of God, but is open to a new presentation of God's ongoing care for creation.

Melody D. Knowles

PSALM 34

Twenty-third Sunday after Pentecost, Year B
    First Lesson: Job 42:1-6
    (Psalm 34:1-8, [19-22])
    Second Lesson: Hebrews 7:23-28
    Gospel Lesson: Mark 10:46-52

"Give it a try!" says the most well-known verse in this psalm. "Look at it. Taste it. Try living it for thirty days. Try prayer and try praise. Let me teach you something about our faith. See for yourself that this religion that we practice is good!" This is the sense of verse 8: "O taste and see that the LORD is good."

The heading for the psalm refers to a time when David "feigned madness before Abimelech," an incident not known from the Bible. 1 Samuel 21:10-15 tells of a time when David pretended to be insane in order to save his life before King Achish of Gath, and it is possible that the names got mixed up. Or the reference could be to an event not recorded

---

3. J. Clinton McCann, Jr., "The Book of Psalms: Introduction, Commentary, and Reflections," in *NIB*, 4:811.

in the books of Samuel. These headings were supplied by the editors who put the book of Psalms together and represent an early example of the reapplication of these psalms to new situations (see the introductory essay). The editors searched for likely events in the lives of biblical people that fit the situations assumed by certain psalms (see also, for example, the heading for Ps 51). The headings thus encourage us to make our own new applications of the psalms.[1]

The psalm may be classified as a *song of thanksgiving* (see the introductory essay; cf. Ps 30 for a classic example) with a good deal of *instructional* material. Recent study of the Psalms is pointing out that in addition to psalms of *praise* and psalms of *lament,* psalms of *instruction* are an important grouping.[2] Thus the book of Psalms has functioned as a hymnbook, a prayer book, and an instruction book. Another mark of the instructional nature of this psalm is its acrostic structure, each line beginning with a successive letter of the Hebrew alphabet (a feature that can be observed, of course, only in the original Hebrew, but see NJPS). A number of psalms exhibit this acrostic pattern: 9-10 together; 25; 111; 112; 145; and 119; interestingly, the sixth letter of the Hebrew alphabet is missing in Psalm 34.

The psalm begins with a *call to worship* in verses 1-3. While the word "bless" usually refers to something God does, it is used in verse 1 with a human subject and with the sense of "praise," as the balancing word shows (see also Ps 26:12 for this sense of "bless"). Verse 2 identifies the congregation being addressed. They are called "the humble," later the "righteous" (vv. 15, 17, 19, 21), and the psalmist counts himself among them (v. 6).

Verses 4-10 are framed by the expression "sought/seek the LORD." The psalmist's story of answered prayers is told twice (vv. 4 and 6). The imperative verb ("look") identifies verse 5 as instructional material, as do the verbs "taste," "see," and "fear" of the further instructional material in verses 8 and 9. These *short summaries of an experience of rescue* as answer to prayer are typical of the songs of thanksgiving; see also the short summary in Psalm 30:1-3 and the longer account in verses 6-12 there.

Verses 11-22 are another *instructional* section. Central to this instruc-

---

1. See James L. Mays, *Psalms,* Interpretation (Louisville: John Knox, 1994), 53-54, for helpful comments along these lines.

2. See Mays, *Psalms,* 6-7 and throughout, and, most extensively and conveniently, J. Clinton McCann, Jr., *A Theological Introduction to the Book of Psalms: The Psalms as Torah* (Nashville: Abingdon, 1993).

tion is the notion of the "fear of the LORD," "an all-encompassing term for worship and obedience, [designating] the proper relationship to God."[3] This fear "is at the heart of the teacher's curriculum, indicating that 'fear of the LORD' is something that can be taught (v. 11). To fear the Lord means to enjoy the Lord's protection (v. 7) and provision (v. 9). The book of Proverbs indicates that it is the starting point for becoming an educated person (Prov. 1:7)."[4] Psalm 34:15-22 offers intensive instruction about the Lord, or, as we would put it, theological instruction. Note that the Lord is the subject of every sentence except for verse 21. The references to the Lord's "eyes," "ears," and "face" indicate that the Lord is viewed as a *Person* with whom one can relate (vv. 15-16). But apparently all are not instantly rescued. The psalm refers to the "brokenhearted" and "crushed in spirit," recognizing that God's people, too, experience suffering (vv. 18-19). The reference to "evil" in verse 21 links up with the same word in verse 13, doubling the warning against doing evil.

These recommendations to "try it out for yourself" come in response to what the first lesson has reported about Job. After experiencing suffering, loss of health, and loss of family and friends, Job has been listening to a lengthy speech from the Lord. Question after question has left Job speechless (Job 38–41). Finally Job makes a confession of faith to the Lord, saying,

> I had heard of you by the hearing of the ear,
> but now my eye sees you. (42:5)

"Seeing is believing" goes the old saying. Somehow, through all this wrestling with God, Job can now say that he has not only "heard about" the Lord but he sees for himself. Like Thomas, who finally saw for himself and believed in Jesus (John 20:24-29), Job has finally seen for himself. This psalm invites all who hear to see for themselves that the Lord is good. Or, in other words, to try out the biblical faith.

The Gospel for this Sunday tells about a blind man who cried out, asking Jesus to have mercy on him and let him see. Jesus healed him from his blindness. This formerly blind man would have an especially deep un-

---

3. Patrick D. Miller, in *The HarperCollins Study Bible,* ed. W. A. Meeks (New York: HarperCollins, 1993), 829; see also vv. 7, 9, 11.

4. James Limburg, *Psalms,* Westminster Bible Companion (Louisville: Westminster John Knox, 2000), 111.

derstanding of the psalm's language about *seeing* that the Lord is good, and of the *happiness* that it promises (v. 8).

James Limburg

PSALM 36

Second Sunday after the Epiphany, Year C
First Lesson: Isaiah 62:1-5
(Psalm 36:5-10)
Second Lesson: 1 Corinthians 12:1-11
Gospel Lesson: John 2:1-11

The apparent discontinuity between Psalm 36:1-4, 11-12 and verses 5-10 is so sharp that commentators have sometimes concluded that Psalm 36 actually consists of two separate psalms. The "edition" of Psalm 36 in the lectionary seems to reinforce this conclusion, since the reading consists of only verses 5-10; however, the final form of the whole psalm is important and instructive. When the entire psalm is in view, the words and witness of the faithful psalmist are surrounded by the attention given to "the wicked" (vv. 1, 11). This literary structure suggests a biblical and existential truth: that the faithful *always* seem to be surrounded by opposition. It was true of the ancient psalmists (see Ps 3:1); it was true of the prophets; and it was true of Jesus! God, God's ways, and God's faithful people are regularly opposed (see also Pss 1-2, which introduce those who oppose God's *torah* [1:2] and God's own self [2:2]).

The very first word of Psalm 36 ordinarily introduces something that God "speaks" (√*n'm*), but here it is "transgression" or "rebellion" that speaks to "the wicked." This striking reversal of typical usage effectively indicates what the remainder of verse 1 makes explicit — the wicked have no inclination to worship or obey God. Instead, "their eyes" (v. 1b; see also v. 2a) are focused squarely upon themselves and their own desires. Such arrogant autonomy, such utter self-assertion, is the antithesis of what the Psalms (and the rest of Scripture) consider wisdom (v. 3; see Ps 2:10). So consumed are the wicked by their own selves and schemes that they do not even sleep at night (v. 4a; see Mic 2:1). Perceiving no accountability to anyone but themselves (see Pss 10:4, 6, 11, 13; 14:1; 73:11), the wicked are driven to oppose the "good" that God wills (vv. 3-4). As verses 2-4 suggest, they oppose God and God's purposes in every possible way: in thought (vv. 2, 4a), word (v. 3a), and deed (vv. 3b, 4bc).

The opposition is real; but amid the presence of the enemy, the psalmist perceives a deeper, more fundamental, and more enduring reality — God, and God's all-pervasive and all-providing "steadfast love" (vv. 5-9; note the repetition of "steadfast love" in vv. 5, 7, 10). The two attributes of God in verse 5, "steadfast love" and "faithfulness," often occur together as a word pair (see Exod 34:6; Pss 89:24; 92:2; 98:3); together they serve as an admirable summary of God's character. The two attributes of God in verse 6, "righteousness" and "justice" (NRSV "judgments," but the Hebrew is singular), also occur frequently as a word pair (see Pss 89:14; 97:2; 99:4; Amos 5:24); together they serve effectively to summarize God's will for the world. The artistic arrangement of verses 5-6, which move in descending order from "the heavens" to "the great deep," communicates the psalmist's affirmation that God's character and God's will permeate the universe. The fortunate result is that *life* — biblically speaking, "salvation" means life — is possible for "humans and animals alike" (v. 6).

Just as the psalmist dared amid opposition to proclaim the good news of God's all-pervasive love, so Psalm 36 invites us to do likewise. Our reality is that "the heavens" are full of spy satellites, and that "the clouds" bear acid rain that is slowly eroding "the mighty mountains," and that "the great deep" is threatened with pollution as well — all because we humans "do not reject evil" (v. 4). Nevertheless, we people of faith refuse to simply acquiesce to human arrogance and self-assertion. We cannot deny it, and we must not ignore it. It is real, but like the psalmist, we perceive a deeper, more fundamental, and more enduring reality — God, and God's all-pervasive and all-providing love. So, amid destructive and deadly human inclinations and actions (including our own!), we stake our lives and the life of the world on the reality of God's never-failing love, and such trust draws us into the struggle on the side of life against the forces of destruction and death.

Verses 7-9 are a celebration of God's love for and provision for the world. Precisely because arrogant self-assertion is real and produces destructive effects, it is good news that God offers a safe alternative — we "may take refuge in the shadow of your wings" (v. 7; see Pss 17:8; 57:1; 63:7; see fig. 5). In short, we can live in dependence upon God rather than self. Precisely because the temptation is to be driven to accumulate or "suc-

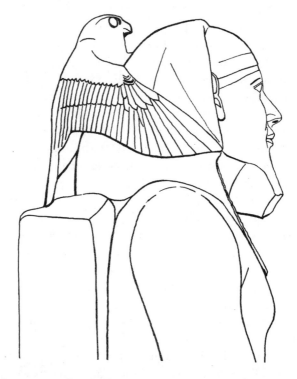

Fig. 5. Psalm 36:7 speaks of taking refuge in the shadow of the Lord's wings. While the metaphor of God's wings appears a number of times in the Psalms (e.g., Pss 17:8; 57:1; 61:4; 63:7; 91:4) and elsewhere (e.g., Exod 19:4; Ruth 2:12; Mal 4:2), and each passage must be interpreted carefully, one aspect of the wing imagery is protection. In this image, the god Horus extends his wings around the head of Pharaoh Khafra (responsible for one of the great pyramids at Giza). The fact that this sculpture is carved of one single piece further underscores the protection of the king by his patron deity.

---

ceed" (and this is perhaps especially true in contemporary North America), the good news is that life is God's gift to "all people" (v. 7), for whom there are food and drink in abundance (v. 8). Life's source and destiny are God (v. 9), an affirmation that disperses the darkness produced by destructive, deadly self-assertion (see John 1:3-5).

Because arrogant self-assertion was and is real, the psalmist (and we ourselves) must continue to pray for the manifestation of God's love and for the life that God wills (v. 10). Verse 11 continues the prayer. The psalmist asks God to oppose evil and oppression, not as a matter of revenge but rather as a step toward establishing the justice and righteousness that God wills for all people. The lection does not include verses 11-12, probably because they are judged to be too violent. But verse 12 suggests that God's purposes for the world will ultimately prevail. By implication at least, while "the evildoers . . . are . . . unable to rise," God's love, faithfulness, justice, and righteousness will be manifest. Or, to borrow the words of hymn writer Shirley Erena Murray, who is in turn borrowing from Martin Luther King, Jr., "Truth pressed to the earth will rise again . . . justice trampled down will rise again. . . . And through these resurrections we have hope."[1] Psalm 36 is finally a song of hope for the world, a hope grounded in God's unfailing love for God's whole creation.

In a North American culture enamored with autonomy and saturated with self-assertion, Psalm 36 is particularly timely. Our motto tends to be that of the U.S. Marines, a motto boldly plastered on the sides of tractor-trailers for all to see: "Earned. Never Given." The psalmist's (and gospel's) motto, or perhaps better, *credo*, is just the opposite: "Given. Never Earned." Life is God's good gift to the world and all its people. Perhaps, if we could hear and act upon this good news, the current form of what we call "globalization" would be transformed. "Globalization," as it is being practiced, is a set of economic arrangements that is making the rich richer and the poor poorer, thus breeding global despair and discontent.[2] Psalm 36 suggests that God has a different plan for "globalization," one grounded in an all-pervasive and all-providing love, which invites all people to the table and to "the fountain of life" (v. 9). Quite appropriately, then, Psalm 36:5-9 was the text chosen as the Scripture theme for the 2002 Week of Prayer for Christian Unity, which happened during the season of Epiphany. While the mention of "light" in verse 9 may explain the choice of Psalm 36 for the season of Epiphany (see Pss 4:6; 27:1; 44:3; 97:11; 118:27; Isa 9:2; and note "shine" in Num 6:25; Pss 4:6; 31:16; 67:1; 80:3, 7, 19), it is crucial to realize and affirm that as this light shines throughout the universe, it is manifest as God's steadfast love, faithfulness, righteousness, and justice.

J. Clinton McCann, Jr.

1. "Truth Pressed to the Earth Shall Rise Again," a hymn sung at the 2005 Montreat Conferences on Worship and Music (Carol Stream, Ill.: Hope Publishing, 2004).

2. See Walter Brueggemann, ed., *Hope for the World: Mission in a Global Context* (Louisville: Westminster John Knox, 2001); Joseph E. Stiglitz, *Globalization and Its Discontents* (New York: Norton, 2002).

PSALM 37

Seventh Sunday after the Epiphany, Year C
First Lesson: Genesis 45:3-11, 15
(Psalm 37:1-11, 39-40)
Second Lesson: 1 Corinthians 15:35-38, 39-40
Gospel Lesson: Luke 6:27-38

According to the lectionary, this text is read at the end of winter and very beginning of spring. The church together hears Psalm 37 during the season in which nature holds out the promise of possibility. In spring's promise, we are tempted to solidify the relationship between work and reward, to expect that what we plant in the spring we shall reap in the fall.

Psalm 37 can be read as a spiritual version of this hoped-for agricultural relationship between work and reward: the righteous will succeed and thrive, and although the unrighteous may temporarily flourish, ultimately they will be cut off. In the first couple of verses the text asserts that the wicked "will soon fade like the grass," but the ones who trust in God "will live in the land and enjoy security" (vv. 1-3). A similar sentiment is repeated throughout the work:

> For the wicked shall be cut off,
>> but those who wait for the LORD shall inherit the land. (v. 9)

> Yet a little while, and the wicked will be no more. . . .
> But the meek shall inherit the land,
>> and delight themselves in abundant prosperity. (vv. 10-11)

Even the form of the psalm seems to affirm the predictability of this secure and just vision of ultimate vindication for all. As an *acrostic,* the first term in every second verse begins with the next letter of the alphabet (see the introductory essay). In this form, the text proceeds in a secure and predictable, perhaps even plodding, pattern, with no surprises.

But for all the security of this vision, the psalm also indicates that it has not yet been realized. Most of the assertions that the righteous will be rewarded and the wicked punished are in the imperfective Hebrew verbal formation — an aspect that allows for a future sense. According to the text, the wicked *"will* wither," they *"will* fade" (v. 2), they *"shall be* cut off" (v. 9), and their bows *"shall be* broken" (v. 15). But now, apparently, they are in the prime of health, possessing the land and sharp bows, flourishing like trees in full leaf. The righteous ones are being plotted against, and teeth are being gnashed against them (v. 12). The imperatives directed to the righteous are noteworthy in this regard: "do not be envious of the wrongdoers" (v. 1), "refrain from anger, and forsake wrath" (v. 8). In the course of the first eight verses, the reader has been issued the command "do not fret" no fewer than three times (vv. 1, 7, 8). The audience for whom this text is written is thus the righteous, but the righteous are in a time of distress, currently fretting, envious, angry, and wrathful. Security is not yet.

In such a context, Psalm 37 can be understood to be *a statement of faith*, written to those who seem to be on the verge of losing it all. In addition to all the imperatives not to fret, be angry, or be envious, the text presents a vision of the future:

> There is posterity for the peaceable. . . .
> [But] the posterity of the wicked shall be cut off. (vv. 37-38)

The end of the text names the ultimate end of human striving, and for a community in crisis this is a vision of reassurance in a time of chaos. This reassurance is also intimated through the use of the acrostic — by ordering the verses alphabetically, the author intimates that, although present circumstances might seem unpredictable, the end is clear. After A will come B, then will come C, D, E, and so on. And at the very end of the psalm, even after the various "ends" of the peaceable and the wicked are named, the final verses and the final letter of the alphabet speak of the Lord's salvation:

> The salvation of the righteous is from the LORD; . . .
> he rescues them from the wicked, and saves them,
> because they take refuge in him. (vv. 39-40)

The surety of this end is such that the psalm doesn't even include a petition — here God's salvation needs no invitation because it will surely come; it is as predictable as the end of the alphabet.

Reading this text in the spring, along with the other lectionary texts, the community is presented with both a warning and a promise. The warning is that the wicked will thrive and flourish, and hope for the righteous will seem lost. In the Genesis text we are reminded of Joseph's betrayal, enslavement, and imprisonment. 1 Corinthians 15 speaks of the inevitability of death. But, just as Psalm 37, these texts also speak of the hope of God's ultimate salvation: Joseph tells his brothers that his difficult journey was part of God's plan to save his family: "do not be distressed, for God sent me before you to preserve life" (Gen 45:5). Paul speaks of death as the necessary precursor to life: "what you sow does not come to life unless it dies" (1 Cor 15:36). And when Jesus instructs his disciples to love their enemies and do good to those that hate them (Luke 6:27-38), he is not simply urging them to trust in a simple social reciprocity but is showing them how to act as children of the Most High, children of the God who will ultimately measure out mercy, judgment, and forgiveness.

Melody D. Knowles

PSALM 40

Second Sunday after the Epiphany, Year A
First Lesson: Isaiah 49:1-7
(Psalm 40:1-11)
Second Lesson: 1 Corinthians 1:1-9
Gospel Lesson: John 1:29-42

Psalm 40 contains a *song of thanksgiving* (vv. 1-10) and *an individual lament* (vv. 11-17; see the introductory essay). The song of thanksgiving tells a story of radical transformation. The psalmist recounts a dramatic rescue (vv. 1-4), praises Yahweh for this saving act (vv. 5-7), and explores the repercussions of Yahweh's acts, both for himself and for the larger community (vv. 8-10), before concluding the psalm with a prayer for help (vv. 11-17).

1. *Structure and movement of Psalm 40:1-11.* The text begins with the image of the psalmist trapped in a deep, muddy pit (v. 2), an allusion to the ancient practice of internment in exhausted cisterns.[1] The picture conveys shame, isolation, and above all, dread, for the mire at the bottom of the pit evokes the dangerous waters of chaos threatening to swallow up one's life. In short, to be stuck in a pit was to experience Sheol on earth.

Yahweh, however, transforms this situation. Yahweh brings the

---

1. See Othmar Keel, *The Symbolism of the Biblical World: Ancient Near Eastern Iconography and the Book of Psalms,* trans. Timothy J. Hallett (New York: Seabury Press, 1978; Winona Lake, Ind.: Eisenbrauns, 1997), 69-72; cf. Jer 38:1-13.

trapped psalmist up, out, and onto a high rock inaccessible to his foes (v. 2). The feet of the psalmist, once stuck in the sludge, now walk steadily (v. 2). At the psalmist's rescue, the cry of pain (v. 1) becomes a song of praise (v. 3). Yahweh's salvation has changed the psalmist's life completely, and this section ends with a blessing on those who, like the psalmist, wait on and trust in God (v. 3). As the psalmist's story attests, trust in Yahweh is well founded. Trust in any other is vain (v. 4).

Having recounted Yahweh's acts, the psalmist responds with praise (vv. 5-7). Verse 5 proclaims God's incomparable character, God's innumerable saving acts, and God's care for the community. This community is a primary concern for the psalmist, for his rescue from the lonely pit signals his move from total isolation to complete reintegration with the community. The psalmist also characterizes his salvation as one among the ever-multiplying, wondrous deeds that Yahweh has worked within the community (v. 5). United with others through Yahweh's salvation, the psalmist joins their chorus. He sings praise to "our God" (v. 3) and affirms Yahweh's gracious activities "toward us" (v. 5).

In the third section (vv. 8-10), the poet details the many implications of her salvation. The psalmist is obedient to Yahweh (v. 8) and continually announces God's gracious acts toward her (vv. 9-10). The psalmist's use of contrast and repetition continues here as she describes her testimony before the "great congregation." Though the psalmist keeps Yahweh's law *within her inmost parts* (*bĕtôk mēʿāy*, v. 8), she claims not to hide the good news of her salvation *within her heart* (*bĕtôk libbî*, v. 10). The section includes a series of repeated claims emphasizing the persistence and constancy of the psalmist's testimony: "I have told" (v. 9), "I have spoken" (v. 10); "I have not restrained my lips, . . . I have not hidden" (vv. 9-10), "I have not concealed" (v. 10).

Repetition and contrast link the end of the song of thanksgiving with the first line of the lament (v. 11), demonstrating the fundamental unity of these larger sections of the psalm. Since the psalmist has not *closed up* his lips (*klʾ*, v. 9), he begs that God not *close off* compassion (√*klʾ*, v. 11). Further, since the psalmist does not conceal Yahweh's *steadfast love and faithfulness* (v. 10), he asks God to share continually this *steadfast love and faithfulness* in his latest hardship (v. 11).

In most laments of the individual, the tone of the prayer moves from lament to praise (see the introductory essay). In Psalm 40, however, that structure is reversed: the song of thanksgiving (vv. 1-10) precedes the complaint (vv. 11-17). In fact, the belated lament thoroughly recasts the preceding song of thanksgiving. With this new horizon in mind, the psalmist's narration of salvation, her proclamations of faithfulness, and her expressions of praise become the background for her current crisis. The psalmist characterizes this crisis as another opportunity for Yahweh to act decisively, adding to the Lord's growing list of wonderful deeds (v. 5). Placing the thanksgiving before lament, the psalmist pleads: *since you saved me in the past,* "Do not, O LORD, withhold / your mercy from me" (v. 11).

2. *Psalm 40 as testimony.* We find clear modern analogues to Psalm 40 in *testimony,* a well-established — though most often unscripted — (low) liturgical feature in certain Christian traditions (usually of the free church type) in which an individual from the congregation tells a story of salvation. As in Psalm 40, the narrative is usually an intensely personal one, recounting dramatic events such as recovery from illness, protection in dangerous situations, deliverance from addiction, sin, and so on. Like Psalm 40, a moving testimony deals handily in *contrasts.* According to the logic of such testimonies, the more desperate the situation, the more amazing God's deliverance. Similar to the psalmist, those offering a testimony frequently trade in the emotions of isolation, shame, and dread. In the midst of these, God's action brings wholeness, safety, and integration into a community. The community plays a vital supportive role in such testimonies, just as in Psalm 40, often punctuating an individual's narrative with "Amen's" and "Alleluia's."

Testimonies can, however, be dangerous for the community. Churches echoing with such testimonies may tend to believe that God's work is most clearly seen (or *only* seen) in emotionally charged personal experiences of salvation. Testimonies may also suggest that God's work in one's life is complete once an individual has had an intense (but momentary) encounter with God's saving grace. On the contrary, individuals and communities *constantly* need God's saving and sanctifying activity. The two distinct parts of Psalm 40 bear out this lesson, for after the psalmist's rousing testimony of salvation (vv. 1-10), the ensuing lament (vv. 11-17) shows that new dangers have emerged that require the psalmist to again cry out, trust, and hope for Yahweh's ongoing saving acts. The psalm encourages pastors to create and foster environments where individuals can utter testimony and the community can receive it. Though this is a sensitive task, it is essential for every community of faith to see, hear, and celebrate God's continual saving activity within its midst.

3. *Hope in the Pit.* The first verses of the psalm paint the picture of a lone figure crying out in the darkness, waiting on Yahweh. This lightless

scene is a place of hope. While English connotations of *hope* and *wait* are very different, in Hebrew these notions are often expressed with a single verbal root — √*qwh* — which appears twice in the psalmist's opening statement: "I waited patiently for the LORD" (v. 1). The repetition of the root *qwh* as an infinitive followed by the perfect verb *(qawwō[h] qiwwîtî)* is a particular construction that intensifies the action of the verb.[2] In the pit, the psalmist waits — that is, hopes *intensely* — for Yahweh's salvation. For the psalmist, the image of √*qwh*, the image of hope, is one crying out to God from the bottom of a deep, muddy hole, pleading that God would lift her out. To hope is to wait, and as the psalmist would attest, hope is a messy, important, and public business.

Joel M. LeMon

PSALM 41

Seventh Sunday after the Epiphany, Year B
   First Lesson: Isaiah 43:18-25
   (Psalm 41)
   Second Lesson: 2 Corinthians 1:18-22
   Gospel Lesson: Mark 2:1-12

This psalm offers *instruction* about the way to happiness, as the first three verses indicate.[1] The psalm closes Book I of the Psalter (Pss 1–41) and gives evidence of that closing function. The beginning of the psalm is a reminder of the beginning of Psalm 1; only these two psalms begin with "Happy are those . . ." The concluding doxology (v. 13) is the work of the editor who put the collection of psalms together; each of the five "books" of the Psalter ends with such a word of praise (Pss 72:18-20; 89:52; 106:48; 150, which concludes Book V and the entire Psalter).

The psalm consists of a *"happiness" saying*, or beatitude, in verses 1-3 (see also 112:1; 119:1-2; 127:5; 128:1; Matt 5:1-12; etc.); a *prayer* containing ele-

---

2. See Bruce K. Waltke and M. O'Connor, *An Introduction to Biblical Hebrew Syntax* (Winona Lake, Ind.: Eisenbrauns, 1990), 584-89.

1. See James L. Mays, *Psalms,* Interpretation (Louisville: John Knox, 1994), 6-7, and J. Clinton McCann, Jr., *A Theological Introduction to the Book of Psalms: The Psalms as Torah* (Nashville: Abingdon, 1993).

ments typical of a lament (cf. Ps 13 for a classic example) in verses 4-10; an expression of thanks for answered prayer and of *trust* in the Lord's continuing help in verses 11-12; and the *doxology* in verse 13 (see the introductory essay).

Psalm 1 speaks of the happiness that comes from being absorbed in the study of the teachings of the Lord ("teachings" may be a more helpful translation of Hebrew *torah* than NRSV's "law"). Psalm 41 speaks of two sources of happiness. First is the happiness that comes with *being healed from illness* (v. 3). Apparently the one praying this psalm had been sick and in need of healing (v. 4, "heal me," and v. 10, "raise me up"). The Lord had healed the psalmist, and the writer formulated that experience into a general statement about what the Lord does all the time:

> The LORD sustains them on their sickbed;
> in their illness you heal all their infirmities. (v. 3)

The second source of happiness celebrated in this psalm is the joy that comes from *helping the poor* (vv. 1-2). Those who have helped victims of a flood or a fire or a tsunami can testify to the happiness that results from such caring deeds. Consideration and concern for the widow, the orphan, the poor, the aged have always been marks of the lifestyle of God's people, according to the Bible. I recall working on a doctoral dissertation in the 1960s that involved tracing the theme of care for the widow, orphan, and poor as it ran through the Bible. During those days I was also helping with the "poor people's campaign," when we fed and housed a group of poor and often homeless people who were marching across the Union Seminary campus in Richmond, Virginia, on their way to a demonstration in Washington, D.C. The biblical study impressed me with the centrality of care for the poor and the powerless, and the work with these needy and often discouraged people made it all very real. Running through the Bible is a passionate concern for the powerless. These include the widow who has no power because she has no husband, the orphan who has no parent, and the poor who has no money (see Isa 10:1-4). To this listing add the stranger or alien who has no friends and the aged who is losing strength (Lev 19:32). Here is a sampling of the theme of care for the powerless as it runs through the Bible:

- in legal materials: Exodus 22:21-24; Leviticus 19:33-34; Deuteronomy 14:28-29; 24:19-22

- in the Prophets: Isaiah 1:10-17, 21-26; 5:1-7; 10:1-4; Amos 2:6-8; 4:1-3; 5:11-12; 8:4-8; Micah 2:1-5; 6:6-8
- in the Gospels: Matthew 25:31-46
- in the letters: James 1:26–2:7

Many others could be added to this list.[2] According to this psalm, the way to happiness for God's people involves not only considering the Scriptures (Ps 1) but also considering and caring for the poor.

Having stated that the Lord helps and sustains the Lord's people (vv. 1-3), the psalmist provides an example of that help with a story of his own experience of healing. Here are the typical elements of a *lament* or prayer in a time of trouble.[3] Verses 4 and 10 express a *call for help* rooted in the conviction of God's amazing grace: "Be gracious to me." The cry is doubled for the sake of emphasis and frames the prayer for help. The one praying asks for healing (vv. 4, 10b) and also for forgiveness (v. 4); in some way the psalmist sees sin and sickness as connected. Verses 5-9 are a *complaint* about enemies who have turned against the psalmist. They are "miserable comforters" like those who made a pastoral call on Job (v. 6; see Job 16:2). Even an old trusted friend has turned against the psalmist (v. 9). The writer of the Fourth Gospel saw in the actions of Judas a similar kind of betrayal of friendship and cited this verse from Psalm 41 (John 13:18).

Verses 11 and 12 acknowledge the Lord's help and express the writer's *trust* that the Lord will support him forever. Verse 13 ends the psalm and the first book in the Psalter on a note of praise.

The story of the healing of the paralytic in the Gospel text for this Sunday invites the use of this psalm to speak about sin and sickness and healing (see also Ps 103:3). The first lesson, from Isaiah 43:18-25, speaks of Israel's sins, iniquities, and transgressions, and then declares that the Lord will blot them all out and forget them (vv. 24-25). The 2 Corinthians lesson does not have a direct connection with the themes of the psalm, but of interest is the acknowledgment of the Trinity (God, Christ, Holy Spirit) in verses 21-22.

James Limburg

---

2. On this theme, see further James Limburg, *The Prophets and the Powerless* (Atlanta: John Knox, 1977; reprint, Lima: Academic Renewal Press, 2001).

3. See further Limburg, *Psalms,* Westminster Bible Companion (Louisville: Westminster John Knox, 2000), 37-40.

PSALMS 42 AND 43

Fifth Sunday after Pentecost, Year C
   First Lesson: 1 Kings 19:1-4, (5-7), 8-15a
   (Psalms 42 and 43)
   Second Lesson: Galatians 3:23-29
   Gospel Lesson: Luke 8:26-39

As the lectionary correctly recognizes, Psalms 42 and 43 form a single psalmic unit. Similar rhetoric and, most decisively, the concluding refrain (43:5; see 42:5, 11) indicate that the canonical division is artificial.

Psalms 42-43 (hereafter "the psalm") chart the rugged journey of "faith-seeking communion" with God. Breaking the mold of a typical individual lament, the psalm leads the reader into a series of laments or complaints, coupled with occasional affirmations of trust or vows to praise. The psalm concludes with an extended petition (43:1-4), including a lament (v. 2b), and the refrain (v. 5). Given its repetitious structure, the psalm evinces a more cyclical than linear "progression," as if to suggest that the search for God's saving presence is never fully fulfilled. Rather than ending on a resounding note of praise, the psalm concludes with a self-directed admonition of hope that, at best, *anticipates* praise in the future. The speaker remains in a state of lament.

The psalm opens with the striking imagery of a deer (more accurately a "doe" in the light of a plausible textual emendation) searching desperately for flowing wadis in the desert. The image is powerful and poignant. Indeed, archaeologists have discovered at least a half-dozen name seals and bullae in southern Palestine (biblical Judah) dating from the eighth and seventh centuries B.C.E. that bear the image of a grazing doe. Such an image was a popular mode of self-depiction, perhaps as a model of piety.[1]

The psalm presents the image within a situation of distress: the thirsty doe cannot find water in the desiccated land (for similar imagery, see Ps 63:1). The image of flowing channels connotes God's sustaining presence, for which the psalmist yearns. Faith's journey, the psalmist affirms, is itself a pilgrimage of deep desire, sometimes frustrated, sometimes fulfilled, but never fully. With this poignant image the psalmist makes a bold claim: the object of our deepest desire, of our most fervent

---

1. See Othmar Keel and Christoph Uehlinger, *Gods, Goddesses, and Images of God* (Minneapolis: Fortress, 1998), 185-86.

yearning, is (or should be) God (see also Ps 73:25). The picture of the thirsty doe says more than Augustine's inspired reflections on desire, more than Schleiermacher's sense of absolute dependence, more than Tillich's ultimate concern. In their place, as it were, the psalmist offers a simple image that is far more profound. God is the object of our thirst, and that thirst can drive us to despair as well as to joy.

The water imagery in this psalm takes on various shapes in the first four verses. As the image of flowing streams morphs into shed tears, thirst turns into grief (v. 3). The speaker is beset internally and externally: she asks herself when she will see God (v. 2b) as she is taunted with "Where is your God?" (vv. 3b, 10b). Her adversaries project her greatest fear: being cut off from God's saving presence. But to sustain her hope she recalls two vivid memories: of Israel at worship in the temple (42:4) and of nature at "worship" (vv. 6-7). The first scene revels in the reverberations of a "multitude keeping festival" (v. 4b), an experience she yearns to relive (43:4). The second memory is more ambiguous but just as powerful. Far removed from the temple setting, God's presence is encountered at the headwaters of the Jordan River, which gush out from the foot of Hermon in northern Palestine (Mount Mizar is, presumably, one of the three peaks of Hermon). Towering above the Biqaʻ valley at 9,232 feet above sea level, Hermon is snow-capped most of the year (one of its Arabic names is Jabal al-Thalj, "the snow mountain"). Like a sponge, this large convex block of limestone soaks up the melting snow, thereby providing water for the Jordan at its foot in the form of spectacular waterfalls (at et-Tannur, for example). There the speaker hears the roar of cascading, turbulent waters, and is figuratively swept away. She finds the voice of the deep powerfully liturgical (42:7a). For this thirsty "doe" the floodgates were once opened. God is no mere "babbling brook." No cool, still waters are depicted here. Rather, the psalmist recalls a time when she was on the verge of drowning in God's presence.

The pairing of these two memories highlights their mutual resonance: the surround sound of worship in the temple and the enveloping roar of mighty waters in the wilderness. Both share in the divine *mysterium tremendum,* an awe-filled presence. It is with these two memories that the psalmist can celebrate God's ḥesed (NRSV: "steadfast love") in 42:8. Though she cannot find God now, she insists that the object of her quest is for the *"living* God" (42:2). The God she seeks is not dead, but in fact is alive and, more so, life-giving! Yet this God is also elusive.

Memory provides the basis of hope, even as the quest plunges the speaker into despair. The expression of walking about in the dark (42:9b; 43:2b) borrows from the ancient language of depression.[2] More pointed is the discourse of the divided self: the psalmist addresses her "soul" three times in the refrain. In each case she begins with a self-rebuke ("Why so downcast . . . ?") and follows with an admonition ("Hope in God . . . !"). The psalm, thus, is an intensely self-reflective prayer. Rather than a disembodied spirit imprisoned within the body, the "soul" here denotes the individual's most personal identity, what could also be called the "heart": the place of deep emotions and dispositions. In this psalm the speaking self is intensely dialogical, and such self-deliberation embodies the never-resolved conversation between hope and despair.

As a whole, the psalm charts the extremes of joy and despair, of God's presence and absence, of flood and drought, which seem to alternate in ever-repeatable succession within the narrated life of the psalmist. One extreme, the psalmist affirms, does not level out the other to bring about a comfortable equilibrium. The psalmist gives searing testimony that the journey of faith is not happy trails; rather, it is a pilgrimage that oscillates between the poles of lament and praise. In short, this psalm acknowledges, perhaps more than any other, that the life of faith is itself bipolar.

William P. Brown

PSALM 45

Seventh Sunday after Pentecost, Year A
First Lesson: Genesis 24:34-38, 42-49, 58-67
(**Psalm 45:10-17** or Song of Solomon 2:8-13)
Second Lesson: Romans 7:15-25a
Gospel Lesson: Matthew 11:16-19, 25-30

---

2. See Michael L. Barré, "'Wandering About' as a *Topos* of Depression in Ancient Near Eastern Literature and in the Bible," *JNES* 60 (2001): 171-87.

Fifteenth Sunday after Pentecost, Year B
  First Lesson: Song of Solomon 2:8-13
  (Psalm 45:1-2, 6-9)
  Second Lesson: James 1:17-27
  Gospel Lesson: Mark 7:1-8, 14-15, 21-23

Psalm 45 is classified as a *royal psalm,* along with Psalms 2, 18, 20, 21, 72, 89, 101, 110, 132, and 144 (see the introductory essay). It most likely was composed as a wedding song for the marriage of a king of Judah or Israel. The words of verse 12, "a princess of Tyre," suggest to some that the psalm may date to the time of Solomon, who married an Egyptian bride (1 Kings 3:1); some connect it to the union of Jehoram and Athaliah (2 Kings 8:18). But the marriage of Ahab to the Sidonian princess Jezebel (1 Kings 16:31) is the most common association for Psalm 45.[1]

A vexing problem for modern readers of Psalm 45 is how to understand and appropriate the poem in a modern context. Isn't the psalm, after all, indisputably about the marriage of a Hebrew king? What possible relevance can it have for our modern situations? Early interpreters struggled with the same questions. The Aramaic Targum of Psalm 45 understands the psalm messianically. Its comment on verse 2 reads, "Thy beauty, O King Messiah, is greater than that of the children of humanity." The writer of the book of Hebrews quotes verses 6 and 7 of the psalm in the book's opening words about the Son God sent to reveal God's self to humanity (Heb 1:8-9).

The words of Psalm 45, addressed to a royal groom and bride, may also be understood as words addressed to the church as the bride of Christ. The Bible certainly provides many analogies of the relationship between God and the Israelites as that of husband and wife (see Hos 1–3; Jer 2; Ezek 16 and 23; and Isa 62:1-5). In the New Testament, the analogy is continued (see Matt 9:15; John 3:29; Eph 5:22-33; Rev 19:7-9).

The two interpretations of Psalm 45 discussed here — messianic and allegorical (concerning the church and Christ) — are what C. S. Lewis called "second meaning in the psalms."[2] But is this the only way the modern reader may understand and appropriate the words of Psalm 45? Two other options are available. First, the words of Psalm 45 convey to the reader the power and majesty of the earthly ruler, but an earthly ruler

---

1. Peter C. Craigie, *Psalms 1–50,* WBC 19 (Waco: Word, 1983), 338.
2. C. S. Lewis, *Reflections on the Psalms* (San Diego: Harcourt, 1958), 101-15.

whom God alone has chosen as a representative of God on the earth. Thus the psalm can be read as a reflection of God's powerful reign over this world we inhabit. Second, the words of Psalm 45 may simply reflect, as does the Song of Songs, the sensuous joy of sexuality, a God-given gift to humankind.

However one may interpret it, Psalm 45 in its basic form contains words addressed to a royal groom and bride as they prepare for a celebration of marriage. The psalm begins with the words of a poet, the composer of the psalm (v. 1); moves on to praise the royal groom and the bride (vv. 2-8 and 9-15); and closes with the words of the poet once again (vv. 16-17).

The poet speaks introductory words in the opening verse of the psalm —

> I address my verses to the king;
> my tongue is like the pen of a ready scribe.

Psalm 45 provides the only instance in the Psalter of a poet being self-consciously present in a composition.[3] The words remind the reader of the originally oral nature of psalm composition.

In verses 2-8 the poet offers words of praise to the groom, who is most likely a king or king-to-be of Israel. Descriptive words dominate in these verses, eulogizing the ideal king. The king is just and honorable (vv. 2, 6, 7), mighty in battle (vv. 3-5), and sensually pleasing (vv. 8-9). In verse 6 the psalmist sings, "Your throne, O God [*Elohim*], endures forever and ever," apparently in reference to the groom-king. Since Psalm 45 is unique in using such language to refer to the human king, one might question whether we should understand the words as addressed to the human king or to the Lord, the ultimate keeper of the throne of ancient Israel. While the latter option is tempting, divinization of human kings was a pervasive concept in some cultures of the ancient Near East. In Israel these ideas were adapted into a concept of the king being the "son of God," an earthly representative of the Lord, chosen by the Lord to rule over the people Israel.[4] In Psalm 2:7, for example, the psalmist declares:

---

3. James L. Mays, *Psalms,* Interpretation (Louisville: John Knox, 1994), 181.

4. J. Clinton McCann, Jr., "The Book of Psalms: Introduction, Commentary, and Reflections," in *NIB,* 4:862.

I will tell of the decree of the LORD:
He said to me, "You are my son;
    today I have begotten you."

In the highly poetic language of Psalm 45, the psalm singer addresses the groom-king with a hyperbolic appellation that reflects the ancient Near Eastern culture of which Israel was indisputably a part.

In verses 9-15 the poet turns attention to the bride-queen, first giving words of advice to the future wife of the monarch (vv. 10-12) and then offering an eloquent description of how she will look as she is led to the chamber of the groom-king, outfitted in woven gold and fine embroidery (vv. 13-15).

The first-person voice of the poet returns in verses 16-17, stating confidently that the royal couple will have progeny through whom their rule will be extended in all the earth through many generations:

In the place of ancestors you, O king, shall have sons;
    you will make them princes in all the earth. (v. 16)

The psalm ends in verse 17 with a vow from the psalmist: "I will cause your name to be celebrated in all generations." But how? As it *was* recited over and over as a part of the fabric of wedding ceremonies in ancient Judah, and as it *is* recited over and over as part of the Psalter, the psalm becomes the living witness to the groom-king and bride-queen and fulfills the vow of the psalmist as each new generation hears the words of praise for the royal couple. Psalm 45 is a joyous celebration of new life and human sexuality. The psalm is also a celebration of God's intimate involvement in our lives. It invites us, as modern worshipers, to wonder at the God who rules over us and yet is so invested in, aware of, and supportive of our humanness.

In Year A, the first lesson associated with Psalm 45 comes from Genesis 24, the story of the marriage of Isaac and Rebekah. In Year B, the lectionary reading is from Song of Songs 2. As with Psalm 45, scholars debate the purpose and thrust of the book of Song of Songs. Is it a sensual love poem or an allegorical story of the love of God for Israel, or of Christ for the church? In Song 2 the maiden sings the praises of her beloved, using images from nature — mountains and hills, gazelles and stags, flowers and turtledoves, fig trees and vines. The God who has created the wondrous world in which we live gives us the eye, the touch, the sensations to enjoy that world and revel in it as human beings. The maiden's song is echoed in the psalm:

> My heart overflows with a goodly theme. . . .
> You are the most handsome of men. . . .
> The princess is decked in her chamber with gold-woven robes.

(Ps 45:1, 2, 12)

Nancy L. deClaissé-Walford

PSALM 46

Second Sunday after Pentecost, Year A
    First Lesson: Genesis 6:9-22; 7:24; 8:14-19
    (Psalm 46)
    Second Lesson: Romans 1:16-17; 3:22b-28, (29-31)
    Gospel Lesson: Matthew 7:21-29

Psalm 46 is a *confession of trust* in Yahweh's protecting presence (see the introductory essay). The three sections of the psalm describe Yahweh's defense of the people against threats posed by cosmic and geopolitical forces (vv. 1-3, 4-7, 8-11). In the face of all these dangers, the community reiterates its fundamental claim: Yahweh is with us (vv. 1, 7, 11).

  1. *Structure and movement of Psalm 46.* The first section of the psalm (vv. 1-3) testifies to the people's confidence in Yahweh in the midst of cosmic turmoil. First-person plural pronouns appear in the opening verses: "God is *our* refuge . . . therefore *we* will not fear" (vv. 1-2). The image of Yahweh as refuge occurs frequently throughout the Psalms, but usually within psalms of the *individual*.[1] In Psalm 46, however, the scope of Yahweh's protection encompasses *the entire community*, for the collapse of the cosmic order threatens everyone. Verses 2-3 depict creation in total disarray — the earth is changing, mountains are tottering and shaking, waters are roaring and foaming. Though modern seismology might classify this phenomenon as a tsunami caused by an earthquake, ancient cosmology understood the image as a herald of the watery forces of

---

1. James L. Mays, *Psalms*, Interpretation (Louisville: John Knox, 1994), 183.

chaos violently overthrowing the order God established over them at creation (cf. Pss 24:1-2; 104:5-9).

Water — a multivalent motif — links the first section of the psalm to the second (vv. 4-7). While verses 2-3 describe the power of the surging, chaotic sea, verse 4 paints a picture of the watery forces of chaos tamed: a river nourishing the holy city (cf. Ezek 47:1-12 for further development of this trope). Because of God's presence in that city, order reigns.

If the first section of the psalm (vv. 1-3) focuses on God's protection of the people from *cosmic threats,* the second section confidently proclaims Yahweh's protection against *political threats* (vv. 5-7). Both represent the encroachment of chaos on God's order, but neither can match Yahweh's power. As the waters roar (√*hmh,* v. 3), so "the nations are in an uproar (√*hmh*)" (v. 6), and as the mountains totter (√*mwṭ,* v. 2), so "the kingdoms totter" (√*mwṭ,* v. 6) when they encounter the voice of God. Through all this tumult the holy city *will not totter* (√*mwṭ,* v. 5), for Yahweh is in her midst.

The refrains in verses 7 and 11 echo the psalm's opening line (v. 1) and confirm the central theme of God's protecting presence. The divine titles in the refrains reveal the character and activity of God. The first title, *Yahweh of Hosts,* signifies his aspect as divine warrior, the commander of the heavenly armies who sits enthroned between the cherubim on the ark (cf. 1 Sam 4:4; 2 Sam 6:2; Isa 37:16). The second title, *God of Jacob,* indicates that this divine warrior inhabiting Zion is the same God to whom the ancient traditions bear witness: the God of the patriarchs.

Mitigating the tendency to have confidence in the strength of Jerusalem on the basis of its military strength, the two divine titles proclaim that it is *Yahweh alone* who provides refuge. Especially in its refrain, Psalm 46 asserts that the city stands only because Yahweh is in her midst. Indeed, as if to guard against the notion that "*Jerusalem* is our refuge," the psalm never directly identifies the holy city as Zion or Jerusalem, an anomaly among the psalms commonly classified as *songs of Zion.*[2]

The final section of the psalm (vv. 8-11) exalts Yahweh and declares his dominion. A pair of imperative verbs, "come" and "behold" (v. 8), introduce the community's testimony, possibly addressed to the nations.[3]

---

2. On this category see Hans-Joachim Kraus, *Psalms 1–59: A Continental Commentary* (Minneapolis: Fortress, 1993), 459; and Erhard Gerstenberger, *Psalms, Part 1: With an Introduction to Cultic Poetry,* FOTL 14 (Grand Rapids: Eerdmans, 1988), 190-94.

3. Mays, *Psalms,* 184.

Yahweh exercises his unquestioned power over both cosmic (v. 8) and political (v. 9) forces, to such an extent that he obliterates war itself and unbuilds the technology of combat (v. 9). The program of disarmament is universal, for in verse 10 another pair of imperative verbs appear: "be still" and "know." The double command issues from Yahweh's mouth to the entire world; this is the end of all hostilities. In the acknowledgment of the Lord's power, nations cease their struggling and join together in praise (v. 11).

2. *Psalm 46 and the message of Pentecost.* Despite numerous proposals, scholars have failed to reach a consensus regarding a particular historical context for this psalm, for the tropes of war and disorder — so pervasive in this psalm — cannot be limited to any single period in Israel's history. Like the psalm's ancient singers, we, too, are familiar with these tropes, for our young twenty-first century has already seen the devastation wrought by natural and geopolitical powers. Through wars, terrorist attacks, earthquakes with ensuing tsunamis, and hurricanes, the modern church longs to see an expression of God's sovereignty over the forces of chaos, and experience the quiet confidence that comes from knowing God is with us.

The season of Pentecost, wherein Psalm 46 falls, offers just such a promise — the very presence of God availed to us all through the saving work of Jesus Christ. With the Israelite community who first sang this psalm, we recall Yahweh's overcoming the powers of chaos at creation. As Christians, we recall Jesus' victory over sin and death, giving us new life in him. Finally, we realize that we have become a community baptized in the Holy Spirit; God abides within us. Like the ancient Israelites, we claim that God is present, so we need not fear.

3. *A psalm of confidence in an age of fear.* With its vivid imagery, clear poetic structure, and confident tone, Psalm 46 has been an anthem of the faithful in difficult times throughout history. In the turmoil of the Reformation, as Martin Luther sought the comfort and confidence of God's presence, he turned to Psalm 46. His robust melody and stirring lyrics became the definitive hymn of the Reformed tradition, "A Mighty Fortress Is Our God" (*Ein' feste Burg*, ca. 1529).

Today, as Christians sing Psalm 46 and Luther's paraphrase, we do well to remember the central message of both compositions. Especially during the unsettling times of war and terror, we are tempted to place our trust in earthly powers. These institutions — the military, political parties, the academy, our professions, even ecclesiastical hierarchies —

cannot remedy fear, for they are unable to match the power of God. In the age of fear, we make the clear and unyielding claim: "A mighty fortress is *our God.*"

Joel M. LeMon

PSALM 47

Ascension of the Lord, Years A and B
    First Lesson: Acts 1:1-11
    (**Psalm 47** or Psalm 93)
    Second Lesson: Ephesians 1:15-23
    Gospel Lesson: Luke 24:44-53

Ascension of the Lord, Year C
    First Lesson: Acts 1:1-11
    (**Psalm 47** or Psalm 110)
    Second Lesson: Ephesians 1:15-23
    Gospel Lesson: Luke 24:44-53

Psalm 47 is classified as an *enthronement psalm,* a psalm that celebrates the enthronement of the Lord as king in the midst of the people (see the introductory essay). It is the first enthronement psalm that readers of the Psalter encounter; the remainder are found in Book IV (see Pss 93 and 95-99). Sigmund Mowinckel maintains that this type of psalm was used in preexilic Israel during the annual New Year's festival (Rosh Hashanah), which is celebrated just prior to the Feast of Tabernacles (Booths or Sukkoth), the fall harvest festival.[1] He writes: "The enthronement psalms salute Yahweh as the king, who has just ascended his royal throne to wield his royal power. The situation envisaged in the poet's imagination, is Yahweh's ascent to the throne and the acclamation of Yahweh as king; the psalm is meant as a song of praise which is to meet Yahweh on his 'epiphany,' his appearance as the new, victorious king."[2]

---

1. Sigmund Mowinckel, *The Psalms in Israel's Worship,* trans. D. R. Ap-Thomas (reprint, Grand Rapids: Eerdmans; Dearborn, Mich.: Dove, 2004), 1:106-92.
2. Mowinckel, *Psalms in Israel's Worship,* 106.

Ceremonies celebrating the annual enthronement of the gods over the peoples were common throughout the ancient Near East. The epic story known as *Enuma Elish* celebrates the enthronement of the god Marduk over the Babylonians.[3] We have no clear evidence in the biblical text of the celebration of such a festival, though some have cited the story of David bringing the ark of the covenant into Jerusalem as a possible example: "David and all the house of Israel brought up the ark of the LORD with shouting, and with the sound of the trumpet. . . . They brought in the ark of the LORD, and set it in its place, inside the tent that David had pitched for it; and David offered burnt offerings and offerings of well-being before the LORD. When David had finished . . . , he blessed the people in the name of the LORD of hosts, and distributed food among all the people" (2 Sam 6:15-19).

Psalm 47 is a simple hymn with two well-defined stanzas (vv. 1-5, 6-9a), each beginning with a call to revere the Lord, followed by a rationale for giving reverence, which is introduced with the Hebrew causal particle *kî*, which means "for" or "because." The first stanza (vv. 1-5) begins with a call to the people to "clap hands . . . shout to God" (v. 1) and concludes with the rationale for such action in verses 2-5, introduced by "For [*kî*] the LORD, the Most High, is awesome." The second stanza continues to exhort the people — "sing praises to God" (v. 6) — and again provides the rationale: "For [*kî*] God is the king of all the earth" (v. 7). The psalm ends in verse 9b with a concluding rationale for revering the Lord, again introduced by *kî*: "For the shields of the earth belong to God."

God is mentioned eleven times in the nine short verses of Psalm 47, beginning with the "call to worship" in verse 1. The call is given, not just to the people of Israel, but to "all people." In verses 2-5 the worshipers are told why they should shout: "Because the LORD, the Most High, is . . . a great king over all the earth" (v. 2). The appellation "Most High" is a term often used to describe the God of Israel when people other than the Israelites alone are being addressed (see, e.g., Gen 14:18-20; Num 24:16; Isa 14:14). Thus, from the outset the psalm celebrates the enthronement of the Lord Most High as a "great king" over "all peoples."

And yet the center of the first stanza declares that God will choose

---

3. See the text in Bill T. Arnold and Bryan E. Beyer, eds., *Readings from the Ancient Near East: Primary Sources for Old Testament Study* (Grand Rapids: Baker Academic, 2002), 31-50; James B. Pritchard, ed., *Ancient Near Eastern Texts Relating to the Old Testament*, 3rd ed. (Princeton: Princeton University Press, 1969), 60-72, 501-3.

"for us" "our possession," "the splendor of Jacob," "whom he has loved" (v. 4). God is king over all the earth, and all peoples are to reverence God, but God has chosen a special people for a possession, "the splendor of Jacob."

Verses 1 and 5 use the same words to admonish the people to acclaim God as king — "shout" and "sound" — although the repetition of words is obscured in many English translations. The word translated "loud songs" in the second half of verse 1 is actually the Hebrew word *qôl,* which is also used in the second half of verse 5. The repeated use of the words forms an *inclusio* around the first stanza of Psalm 47. Verse 1's "sound of rejoicing" is complemented in verse 5 with the "sound of a shofar," the trumpet blown repeatedly at the New Year's festival. In modern Jewish life, the sound of the shofar at the New Year's festival serves to remind the faithful of many things, including acclaiming God as king and the giving of the Torah at Mount Sinai. "On the morning of the third day, there was thunder and lightning, with a thick cloud over the mountain, and a very loud trumpet (shofar) blast. Everyone in the camp trembled. . . . Mount Sinai was covered with smoke, because the LORD descended on it in fire. The smoke billowed up from it like smoke from a furnace, the whole mountain trembled violently, and the sound of the trumpet grew louder and louder. Then Moses spoke and the voice of God answered" (Exod 19:16-19). The acoustic component of the theophany at Mount Sinai is reenacted annually as a reminder to the people of the powerful presence of their God as king over all the earth.

The opening verse of the second stanza of Psalm 47 admonishes the people to "sing praises" by repeating the phrase four times. As already stated, verses 7-9a are introduced by the word *kî* so that these verses provide the rationale for why worshipers should "sing praises." Sing praises because

> God is king of all the earth; . . .
> God rules over nations;
> God sits upon his holy throne;
> princes of many peoples have gathered at the throne
> along with the people of Abraham.

In verse 9b the psalmist uses *kî* for the third time. Ultimately, when all is said and done, the reason all peoples should clap hands, shout to God, and sing praises is that God rules the earth. The shields of the earth and the weapons and symbols of power and rule belong to God; God alone is exalted above the earth.

Nancy L. deClaissé-Walford

Psalm 48

Day of Pentecost, Year B
First Lesson: 2 Samuel 5:1-5, 9-10
(Psalm 48)
Second Lesson: 2 Corinthians 12:2-10
Gospel Lesson: Mark 6:1-13

Psalm 48 is the last of a group of three poems celebrating the Lord on Zion. Zion is a designation for Jerusalem that emphasizes its holiness and beauty. Psalms 46 and 48 focus on the city where God dwells, and Psalm 47 on his enthronement and reign over the nations. Like several other *songs of Zion* (Pss 46; 76; 84; 87; 122; see the introductory essay), the poem narrates the foundation story of the city (Ps 48:4-7); in Psalm 48 the Lord's great victory over rebellious kings, his triumphal return to the city, and his building of a palace (the temple) to enshrine that victory are recounted. That primordial victory makes the city and its temple grand symbols of peace and justice. A possible setting of the poem was in ceremonies connected to the three pilgrimage feasts of the year. To pilgrims arriving from villages and small towns, the splendid city on the hill would have made an unforgettable impression and reminded them afresh of God's steadfast love for them and power over their enemies.

The foundation story in verses 4-8 — rebellious kings attacking Zion and then fleeing in terror from the powerful Lord — was a version of the combat myth, well known in the ancient Near East as an explanatory myth (cf. Ps 76). The plot of the combat myth begins with a massive threat to the stability and peace of the universe by a chaos monster or, in some versions, by the monster's human instruments, evil kings. In response to the crisis, the Lord enters the fray, defeats the forces of chaos, and then returns triumphant to his mountain home, Zion. There God is acclaimed king and builds a palace to celebrate and symbolize the newly won peace.

Psalm 48 is framed by two panels (vv. 1-3 and 12-14, each with twenty-four Hebrew words) that tell of the grandeur of the city and its palace. Within these frames, two other panels describe the Lord's victory (vv. 4-8) and the joyous reaction to it (vv. 9-11). The structure of the poem is therefore *abb'a'* — a "sandwich" or chiastic pattern.

> *a* vv. 1-3: The grandeur of Mount Zion
> *b* vv. 4-8: The foundation story: God's victory over rebellious kings
> *b'* vv. 9-11: Joyous reactions to the victory
> *a'* vv. 12-14: Invitation to view and tell of the grandeur of Mount Zion

The first section *(a)* applies seven epithets to Zion in two clusters, each with three epithets of Zion and each beginning with the Hebrew word for mountain (NRSV uses both "mountain" and "mount"). Verses 1c-2b are the first of the clusters, and verses 2c and 2d the second. Each cluster moves from "local" to "universal" dominion: the first begins with "his holy mountain" and ends with "all the earth," and the second begins with "Mount Zion" and ends with "the great King." Hence, the very arrangement of the epithets underlines *the increasing power and dominion of the Lord.* "The great King" is a political term in the ancient Near East, used of suzerains in the Hittite kingdom, Mesopotamia, and Egypt. NRSV's "in the far north" should be rendered "the Heights of Zaphon," which is the storm god's mountain in Canaanite texts.

The second unit *(b)* depicts the battle and its virtually instantaneous conclusion. The "east wind" (v. 7a) is a weapon of the Lord, who is depicted here as the powerful storm god. Panic was always a factor in holy wars, and in this case the kings panicked at the very sight of the Lord and fled. Verse 8 can mean either that worshipers have actually witnessed the battle and victory (NRSV "so have we seen") and concluded that the ancient traditions have been fulfilled ("as we have heard"), or that the beauty and size of the temple symbolize the grandeur of the God dwelling there.

The third section *(b')* is the community's reaction to the victory: the people remember the Lord's "steadfast love" (*ḥesed*) manifested in the divine victory. What better place to remember than in the temple, the very symbol of the victory! God's victory changes the course of history, inviting worldwide acclaim ("your praise" means "the praise of you"). Lest modern readers conclude that the Lord's victory glorifies violence, one should note that the Lord's fighting is a means to justice and peace. Threats to justice must be beaten back.

The last unit *(a')*, harking back to verses 1-3, invites people to walk through the holy city and appreciate the hidden meaning of the buildings: they symbolize God's victory. The very buildings partake of the holiness of the One who dwells in them. God is pleased to dwell in the midst of the people. The Jewish scholar Michael Wyschogrod comments: "There is a place where [God] dwells and that place is Jerusalem. He dwells in Number One Har Habayit [= Mount of the House/Temple] Street. It is a real dwelling and for every Jew, the sanctity of the land of Israel derives from the sanctity of Jerusalem, and the sanctity of Jerusalem derives from the sanctity of the temple, and the sanctity of the temple derives from the sanctity of the holy of holies where God dwells."[1]

The great buildings are virtually sacraments of God's powerful presence and love for his people.

How does this psalmic celebration help a modern congregation to respond to the lectionary readings of 2 Samuel 5:1-5, 9-10 and Mark 6:1-13? It shows that David's conquest of Jerusalem was not merely military strategy, but the means for the Lord to dwell in the midst of the people. In Mark, Jesus' hometown rejects him, foreshadowing his own people's rejection. The Lord's presence among the people will need to take a new form.

Richard J. Clifford

PSALM 50

Last Sunday after Epiphany, Transfiguration, Year B
First Lesson: 2 Kings 2:1-12
(Psalm 50:1-6)
Second Lesson: 2 Corinthians 4:3-6
Gospel Lesson: Mark 9:2-9

1. Michael Wyschogrod, "Incarnation," *ProEccl* 2 (1993): 208-25.

Twelfth Sunday after Pentecost, Year C
    First Lesson: Isaiah 1:1, 10-20
    (Psalm 50:1-8, 22-23)
    Second Lesson: Hebrews 11:1-3, 8-16
    Gospel Lesson: Luke 12:32-40

In this *covenant renewal liturgy* (cf. Pss 81 and 95; and see the introductory essay), a speaker charges the people with breach of the covenant and invokes the witnesses of the original covenant — heaven and earth — to testify to the people's failure. Similar charges are found in Deuteronomy 32 (see v. 1), Isaiah 1:1-9 (see v. 2), and Micah 6:1-8. Psalm 50 is the first of the twelve Asaph psalms (the others are 73-83). These psalms contain prophetic echoes and allude to the great exodus song (Exod 15), which may account for the reference to the Ten Commandments in Psalm 50. Though our psalm seems fiercely accusatory, it has a positive goal — to invite the people to acknowledge the Lord's sovereignty and to renew their commitment to his commands. The psalm may reflect a ceremony in which a cultic prophet spoke in God's name to the people gathered in the courtyard of the temple at one of the three annual pilgrimage feasts — Passover, Pentecost, and Booths. All these feasts commemorated the Lord's great deeds for the people and would have been appropriate occasions for this psalm.

The voice of God thundering forth in a storm (spoken by a human officiant) was familiar from Israel's origins at Mount Sinai: "There was thunder and lightning, as well as a thick cloud on the mountain, and a blast of a trumpet so loud that all the people who were in the camp trembled. Moses brought the people out of the camp to meet God. . . . As the blast of the trumpet grew louder and louder, Moses would speak and God would answer him in thunder" (Exod 19:16-19). Liturgical enactment collapses the distance between the present and the past and enables people of a later time to respond to that original event. The theophany at Mount Sinai is transposed to another holy mountain, Zion, in Jerusalem.

At Sinai, God's direct proclamation of the Ten Commandments so terrified the people that they authorized Moses to mediate all future divine-human encounters (Exod 20:18-21; Deut 5:22-31). We can presume that an officiant took on the role of Moses and spoke the Ten Commandments in the case of Psalm 50.

How did the Ten Commandments function in the life of the people? In the words of the Israeli scholar Moshe Weinfeld, "The Decalogue was solemnly uttered by every faithful Israelite as the God of Israel's fundamental claim on the congregation of Israel, and it became the epitome of Israelite moral and religious heritage."[1] Adherence to the Ten Commandments and engaging in right worship made Israel the Lord's people.

Psalm 50 has three parts: (1) the self-manifestation of the Lord in a storm and summons to Israel (vv. 1-6); (2) teaching on proper sacrifices and attitudes toward God (vv. 7-15); and (3) rebuke of the people for violations of the Decalogue along with positive exhortations (vv. 16-23). In part 2, verses 7-13 echo Isaiah 1:10-20 in castigating thoughtless sin offerings as the equivalent of reducing the Lord to just another deity needing care and feeding. Animal sacrifice itself is not condemned, for the thanksgivings demanded in verse 14 involve animal sacrifices. These latter, however, differ from sin offerings in that they are performed with rejoicing, sharing of food, and giving thanks for God's gifts. It seems that, unlike sin sacrifices, they were not a substitute for genuine conversion.

In part 3 (not in the lectionary excerpt), the sins in verses 17-20 are violations of the Ten Commandments (theft, adultery, bearing false witness). Violators reject ("hate") instruction (v. 17), steal, commit adultery (v. 18), and join up with slanderers (v. 20).

Certain words require comment. "The mighty one, God the LORD" is better rendered "Yahweh, the God of gods" (so NAB), meaning that Israel's God, as the Most High of all heavenly beings, has the right to summon the whole earth. "Heavens" and "earth" are witnesses of the original covenant. In comparable lists of witnesses in treaties, Heaven and Earth (and other cosmic pairs such as Abyss and the Springs, Day and Night) were listed (cf. Deut 4:26; 30:19; 31:28; Mic 6:1-2). In verse 5, NRSV's "faithful ones" is better rendered "consecrated ones" (NIV) or "devotees" (NJPS). One should not be surprised at the harsh tone. Brutal rebukes and questions were evidently typical of covenant renewal ceremonies (see Ps 81; Deut 32; Josh 24; 1 Sam 12). Joshua 24 shows that the purpose of such rebukes was to spur the people to self-examination and repentance: "You cannot serve the LORD, for he is a holy God. He is a jealous God; he will not forgive your transgressions or your sins. If you forsake the LORD and serve foreign gods, then he will turn and do you harm, and consume you" (Josh 24:19-20; cf. 1 Sam 12:10).

How does Psalm 50 enable a modern congregation to respond to the

---

1. Moshe Weinfeld, "What Makes the Ten Commandments Different?" *BRev* 6 (1991): 35-41.

lectionary readings? For Transfiguration Sunday, Year B, it serves as the response to the ascension of the righteous Elijah in "a chariot of fire and horses of fire" in which he "ascended in a whirlwind into heaven" (2 Kings 2:11), evidently a storm theophany. Only verses 1-6 of Psalm 50 are read, however, which describe the Lord's manifestation in a storm while saying:

> Gather my faithful ones to me,
> who made a covenant with me by sacrifice. (v. 5)

The psalm is therefore a perfect response to the scene of Elijah's ascension.

In the lectionary for the Twelfth Sunday after Pentecost, Year C, Isaiah rebukes the people for their sacrifices without conversion of heart, and Psalm 50:1-8, 22-23, with its rebuke of the people, fits this theme nicely.

Richard J. Clifford

PSALM 51

Eleventh Sunday after Pentecost, Year B
> First Lesson: 2 Samuel 11:26–12:13a
> **(Psalm 51:1-12)**
> Second Lesson: Ephesians 4:1-16
> Gospel Lesson: John 6:24-35

Fifth Sunday in Lent, Year B
> First Lesson: Jeremiah 31:31-34
> **(Psalm 51:1-12** or Psalm 119:9-16)
> Second Lesson: Hebrews 5:5-10
> Gospel Lesson: John 12:20-33

Psalm 51 is one of the thirteen psalms associated with a particular episode in David's life, in this case David's taking of Bathsheba and the prophetic response (2 Sam 11–12). Almost certainly the association of Psalm 51 with David is a late editorial arrangement by the editors of the Psalter;

however, 2 Samuel 11-12 provides an instructive narrative context for reading and interpreting Psalm 51 (see the pairing of Ps 51:1-12 with 2 Sam 11:26–12:13a for the Eleventh Sunday after Pentecost, Year B). In short, if David did not pray Psalm 51, he certainly could have, and indeed, *should* have!

Although David had sinned grievously, breaking at least half of the Ten Commandments during the Bathsheba affair, and although verses 1-5 are dominated by the vocabulary of sin, it is striking that Psalm 51 actually begins by featuring the vocabulary of grace in verse 1: "Have mercy" (usually translated "Be gracious"), "steadfast love," and "abundant mercy" (a word derived from the same Hebrew root as "womb" and thus seeming to have the nuance of maternal compassion). This beginning is a significant clue for the interpretation and proclamation of the psalm — that is, it is not only about the reality of human sinfulness, but it is also about the reality of God's amazing grace. The vocabulary of grace in verse 1 is reminiscent of Exodus 34:6-7, where, following Israel's grievous sin during the golden calf episode, God reveals the divine self to be essentially gracious, merciful, and steadfastly loving. The verbal connections between Psalm 51 and the culmination of the golden calf debacle suggest that Exodus 32-34 is another appropriate narrative context for hearing and proclaiming Psalm 51. It is fitting, therefore, that the alternate Old Testament lections for the Seventeenth Sunday after Pentecost, Year C, pair Psalm 51:1-10 with Exodus 32:7-14, the beginning of the golden calf episode, where God "changed his mind about the disaster that he planned to bring on his people" (Exod 32:14). The point is not that God is whimsical or capricious, but rather, that God cannot help but be gracious, merciful, and forgiving. At this point in the exodus narrative, Israel is saved by grace.

So also is the psalmist saved by grace. He or she admits that God is "justified in your sentence, and blameless when you pass judgment" (v. 4). But a guilty verdict and subsequent sentence are not the final words. If we have David in mind as we read the psalm, we realize that several of the multiple sins that he committed were capital offenses. David deserved to die, but God allowed him to live. David too was saved by grace.

Verse 4 does not mean to say that David's sin or the psalmist's sin had no human repercussions. After all, Uriah died as a result of David's misdeeds. Rather, the intent is to affirm that sin and its destructive consequences derive ultimately from failing to honor God and God's claim on our lives. Verse 5 is also subject to misunderstanding. The intent is not to say that sin is transmitted biologically, as Augustine and others concluded, and that hence sex is "dirty" or wrong. Rather, verse 5 communicates the reality that every one of us is born into a situation where sin already exists; and hence, none of us will be able to escape sin and its consequences.

This is the bad news about the human situation; but, as suggested above, Psalm 51 is finally about the good news of God's mercy, grace, and love. Human sin does not have the final word in Psalm 51, and it will not have the final word in the human situation. So, after verses 1-5, the vocabulary of sin no longer dominates the psalm. Verses 6-12 consist primarily of requests for cleansing and forgiveness. Verses 10-12 are particularly noteworthy. The verb "create" is used in the Old Testament only of divine action. The word "spirit" occurs in verses 10, 11, and 12, including the rare phrase "holy spirit" in verse 11 where the reference is clearly to God. As Shirley C. Guthrie suggests, the work of God's spirit both in Scripture and beyond is best "summarized with the word *new*."[1] The word "new" occurs in verse 10; and in effect, verses 10-12 are the psalmist's request to be made into a new person.

And the request is granted! God can do new things, and verses 13-17 describe the remarkably new situation. Once a prime exemplar of sin, the psalmist is now a teacher of sinners and transgressors. The word "bloodshed" in verse 14 could refer to the psalmist's former guilt, or it could suggest the persecution the psalmist may now incur for daring to represent God and God's purposes. In either case, the psalmist demonstrates the appropriate response to God's amazing grace — grateful praise (v. 15) and the humble offering of the whole self to God (v. 17). Verses 18-19, perhaps added later to the original verses 1-17, suggest that transformed individuals may even breathe new life into old traditions and practices.

The echoes of Psalm 51 in the New Testament offer one additional context for interpreting and proclaiming the psalm. The apostle Paul knew Psalm 51. He quotes it in Romans 3:4 to support his case that all have sinned. Paul is leading up, of course, to the good news that all have also been justified by God's grace. And Paul's own life is a striking example, as he moved from killing Christians to proclaiming God's ways (cf. Ps 51:13). Psalm 51 also anticipates 2 Corinthians 5:17-20, which proclaims

1. Shirley C. Guthrie, *Always Being Reformed: Faith for a Fragmented World* (Louisville: Westminster John Knox, 1996), 83.

that as a result of God's reconciling work, "everything has become new!" (2 Cor 5:17). And, as in Psalm 51, reconciled persons are entrusted with God's reconciling work. Very appropriately, the Epistle lesson for Ash Wednesday, accompanying Psalm 51, is 2 Corinthians 5:20b-6:10.

One of the church's seven penitential psalms, Psalm 51 is clearly appropriate for Ash Wednesday and the season of Lent; but its use should not be restricted only to these times. Psalm 51 offers the opportunity to do what psychiatrist Karl Menninger recommended for contemporary persons — that is, "to study sin," not to wallow in our guilt, but rather to rejoice in and join in God's reconciling work in the world.[2] Or, to put it slightly differently, if we do not "study" or talk about sin, neither will we "study" or talk about grace. And if we do not talk about grace, we fail to appreciate who God is and how God operates in the world. To hear, interpret, and proclaim Psalm 51 is to put ourselves in touch with the heart of the good news!

J. Clinton McCann, Jr.

PSALM 52

Ninth Sunday after Pentecost, Year C
First Lesson: Amos 8:1-12
(Psalm 52)
Second Lesson: Colossians 1:15-28
Gospel Lesson: Luke 10:38-42

At first glance, most preachers would pass over this psalm on the way to something less dangerous for a summer Sunday morning. The overall message is abrasive in a world where Christians come in hundreds of different denominations and there remain dangerous tensions between Christians and Muslims. The message of this psalm is clear: you are either righteous or you are not. Thematically, this psalm has much in common with Psalm 1, where the same clear division of God's kingdom is made — either you are for God or against God. There is no middle ground. How can we preach this in modern-day North America?

2. Karl Menninger, *Whatever Became of Sin?* (New York: Hawthorn Books, 1973), 192.

The first thing any preacher of these polarized texts must remember is Israel's theology. The writers of these prayers knew nothing of denominations. Their basic formula was simple and was stated as the prologue of the Decalogue: "I am the LORD your God who brought you out of the land of Egypt, out of the house of slavery, (so) there are no other gods for you except me" (Exod 20:2-3, my translation). The formula for the original readers and hearers of these texts is simple: either you are God's or you are not (see also Josh 24:14-16). It is from this (exclusivist) perspective that one must begin to look at this psalm.

The first four verses are unusual in that they address not God, but a human. The human is called "the mighty one" *(haggibbōr)* in verse 1. A mighty one is usually a hero or great leader, one who has a place of honor in the Israelite community. Yet as the psalm unfolds, this one is far from honorable. He may be a warrior, but here the weapon is not one of iron, but one of words (v. 2: "tongue like a razor"; v. 4: "words that devour"). Yet it is more than just words, for verse 3 claims this one "loves evil more than good" and "lying more than righteousness" (NRSV uses "truth" for *ṣedeq*). The heart is to love God above all else (Deut 6:5), but the love of this particular individual's heart is elsewhere. It is clear from the first four verses that this "mighty one" is not really part of God's kingdom, even if he is an Israelite. This honorific title represents "bitter sarcasm" according to Limburg.[1]

The question posed at the beginning of the psalm is not really one for "the mighty one" to answer. Indeed, he would be incapable of comprehending an answer. The question is like the one I pose every morning as I read the *New York Times:* Why have a worldwide war of words about politics and trade agreements when people are starving and dying all over the world? Or why is war the only way to settle disagreements between nations and peoples? Just like the psalmist, I don't expect an answer from "the mighty ones" of my age either.

The next stanza focuses on the psalmist's sure belief in the integrity of God and God's kingdom. Other texts may ask, "Why do the wicked prosper?" But there is no such doubt here as to the fate of the one addressed in verses 1-4. God will "pull you down," "snatch you," "tear you," and "uproot you" (v. 5). All the verbs indicate a removal from a perceived place of safety. Verse 7 intensifies this understanding by demonstrating

---

1. James Limburg, *Psalms,* Westminster Bible Companion (Louisville: Westminster John Knox, 2000), 175.

that the mighty one's safety came from riches and wealth instead of God. This way of life has only one end: removal. Interestingly, God's action serves not only as an end for the mighty one. Indeed, verse 6 shows that the ultimate failure of this one is a lesson for the righteous: "[they] will see and fear and laugh." The laughter may seem harsh or triumphant in today's world, but here it is aimed at the foolishness of placing trust somewhere other than in God. The laughter of God in Psalms 2:4, 37:13, and 59:8, as well as of personified Wisdom in Proverbs 1:26, reflects a similar reaction to the foolishness of perceived human power.

Verses 8-9 present the other way of life and also parallel Psalm 1. The mighty one may be "uprooted" by God (cf. Ps 1:4), but the righteous one is "like a flourishing olive tree in the house of God" (cf. Ps 1:3). Moreover, instead of trusting in wealth, this one "trusts in the steadfast love of God forever and ever." By the end of the psalm, the correct way is abundantly clear. Like other psalms, especially the Torah psalms, Psalm 52 is one of teaching and persuasion (see the introductory essay).

All the texts for this Lord's Day speak of choice. In the Amos text, the day for choosing is over. God has had it with the injustices of the people. The passage clearly lays out the way of "the mighty ones" that, as in the psalm, should cause all of us to choose a different path. In the Colossians text, Paul presents a confession about Jesus; to accept this confession is one reason for his letter (1:21-23). To agree with Paul is to accept the life-changing message of the gospel. Finally, the Gospel text is well known and often preached: Jesus visits Mary and Martha. Martha is busy with all the preparations for this visitor while Mary sits with Jesus. Martha looks to Jesus to justify herself, but Jesus suggests that it is Mary who has "chosen the better part" (10:42). The Gospel shows that caring for Jesus is not the same as listening. Jesus makes the choice clear.

The truth is that even in our complex world today, we still have a choice. We are still part of the kingdom or, perhaps, we are not. We love making war with words or we love God. We build our security on our own wealth and perceived abilities or on the steadfast love of God. We can risk being uprooted from our security or grow deep roots while flourishing in the house of the Lord. The kingdom brings abundant life; outside the kingdom are destruction and alienation. These texts are not about which denomination is correct, nor do any of these texts declare that a choice for the (Christian) God necessarily, automatically, or simplistically translates into a holy war against Muslims or Hindus. Instead, these texts ask a much more personal question: Where is your heart and what do you value above all else? This is as apt a question for a summer Sunday morning in our day as it was at the time of the psalmist.

Beth LaNeel Tanner

PSALM 62

Third Sunday after the Epiphany, Year B
    First Lesson: Jonah 3:1-5, 10
    (Psalm 62:5-12)
    Second Lesson: 1 Corinthians 7:29-31
    Gospel Lesson: Mark 1:14-20

Just a week before sitting down to write these comments on Psalm 62, I had the good fortune of spending a few days in Wittenberg, Germany, officially known as Lutherstadt (Luthertown) Wittenberg. Among the many reminders of the reformer's presence in this city is the tower of the Castle Church. Near the top of the tower in large letters, one can read the words "EIN' FESTE BURG IST UNSER GOTT," the first line of Luther's hymn translated into English as "A mighty fortress is our God." God as "eine feste Burg," or "a mighty fortress," is imagery that recurs in the refrain of Psalm 62: "my fortress; I shall never / not be shaken" (vv. 2, 6), and is thus central to the psalm's meaning.

While the lectionary suggests considering only verses 5-12, the psalm's careful structure recommends that we do well to consider it as a whole. The heading dedicates the psalm to the music director and associates it with King David. "Jeduthun" in the superscription may refer to a tune of the day, though the matter is not certain.

This is a psalm with a refrain (vv. 1-2, 5-6) with slight differences in the second occurrence of the refrain (the second lines of vv. 1 and 5). Since the substance of the refrain is stated twice, it should be considered carefully. The psalm is made up of the standard elements of the *lament* but with some variations (see the introductory essay). Verses 1-2 and 5-7 are *affirmations of trust,* speaking *about* God. Since the element of trust dominates the refrain, this psalm is often classified as a *psalm of trust* (along with Pss 11; 16; 23; 27; 63; 131). Verses 3-4 are *complaints,* first *to* the enemy in "you" form, and then *about* the enemy in "they" form. Verses 8-10 are framed by imperative verbs, offering *instruction* ("trust," "pour out," "put," "set"). Verse 9 makes an observation about humanity as a whole. The psalm concludes with the writer reporting a message twice received from God (v. 11) and then addressing God for the first time, with words of *trust.*

The first part of the psalm (vv. 1-7) portrays God as *solid as a rock.* Psalm 61 had offered the prayer,

> Lead me to the rock
> that is higher than I;
> for you are my refuge,
> a strong tower against the enemy. (61:2b-3)

Psalm 62:3-4 provides a clue to the psalmist's situation. The psalmist pictures himself as a wall about to fall over and these opponents in the community as a wrecking crew, hammering, banging, battering, ramming, until the wall topples! Even (or perhaps one could say "especially"!) members of churches can understand these sorts of conflicts that take place in a community. Just what was going on? A hint is provided in verse 4: while these people are smiling and gracious on the outside, they are vicious slanderers and gossips in their secret groups!

The *affirmations of trust* in verses 1-2 and 5-7 should be read against the background of the hurt caused by these reputation-wreckers. How is the psalm writer handling all these barbs being thrown at her? Not by retaliating or fighting back. The psalmist responds to these attacks by silence (vv. 1, 5). But this is not just an empty, void silence. This is a silence that is expectant (v. 1), pregnant with *hope* that God will soon act and right the situation (v. 5). The Hebrew word translated as "silence" also occurs in Psalm 131, there translated as "quieted." Psalm 131 pictures God as a mother and the believer as a baby having finished nursing and lying peacefully at its mother's breast.

One other word in the refrain deserves comment. "Salvation" (vv. 2, 6) translates the Hebrew *yĕšûʿâ,* "save" or "rescue," which comes over into the New Testament as "Jesus," the one who will save his people from their sins (Matt 1:21).

The second part of the psalm (vv. 8-10) changes from complaint and affirmation of faith to *instruction.* The listening congregation is advised to "trust in the Lord." Two reasons for this trust are provided. These enemies, whether low or high ranking, are about as significant as a puff of smoke or a breath of air (*hebel;* v. 9; this is the Hebrew word usually translated "vanity" throughout Ecclesiastes). And riches will not buy security and happiness (v. 10). Finally, verse 12 addresses God for the first time on a note of *praise,* declaring that the Lord is the source of steadfast love.

A sermon on this Sunday could focus on the rock imagery in this psalm, balancing it with the story Jesus told about the wisdom of building on a rock (Matt 7:24-27). The hymn for the day could, of course, be "Built on a Rock" (see *Psalter Hymnal* [Grand Rapids: CRC Publications, 1987], #503). The Gospel and the Jonah texts for the day suggest a different sermonic tack, centering on repentance. The Jonah story tells of the repentance of Nineveh; in a remarkable anticipation of our own ecological concern, even the animals repent.[1] The focus of the Gospel is on John's call to repent.

James Limburg

PSALM 63

Third Sunday in Lent, Year C
    First Lesson: Isaiah 55:1-9
    (Psalm 63:1-8)
    Second Lesson: 1 Corinthians 10:1-13
    Gospel Lesson: Luke 13:1-9

Psalm 63, like Psalms 27, 42–43, 61, and 84, expresses an ardent longing for the Jerusalem temple — to dwell safely in its precincts and joyously celebrate the liturgy with fellow worshipers. Temples traditionally provided sanctuary for people pursued by enemies (e.g., 1 Kings 2:28). The superscription situates the poem at a time in David's life when he was fleeing from Saul in the Wilderness of Judah (see 1 Sam 23:14-15 and 24:1). Our psalmist, however, desires not only protection from enemies (Ps 63:9-10) but also communion with God, which is expressed metaphorically as seeing (v. 2; cf. Pss 11:7; 17:15), singing praise (vv. 3-4; cf. Ps 43:4), and eating (v. 5; cf. Ps 23:5).

Two uncertainties in the poem must be cleared up. First, is the

---

1. See James Limburg, *Jonah: A Commentary,* OTL (Louisville: Westminster John Knox, 1993).

psalmist already in the sanctuary and delighting in its protection, or is she absent from it and desirous of going there to escape the dangers of exile? NRSV seems to presume the psalmist is already in the sanctuary (v. 2: "So I have looked upon you in the sanctuary"). The psalms of longing mentioned above, however, suggest that looking upon the Lord in the sanctuary is here a *future hope,* and that the Hebrew verb (perfect tense) should be rendered either as a precative (prayer) perfect, "O that I might look upon," or a perfect of certainty expressing so firm a hope that it can be expressed as something already experienced (e.g., REB: "With such longing I see you in the sanctuary"). In either case, "I shall behold you" fits the context best. Supporting a future meaning are the imperfect (future) verbs in the neighboring verses 3-5: "will praise," "will bless," "will lift up," "will be satisfied."

The second uncertainty is the meaning of the phrase "when I think of you on my bed" (v. 6), which in Psalms 4:4, 36:4, 149:5, and Hosea 7:14 designates a private attitude *in contrast to* public performance of ritual. Though NRSV is not alone in taking verse 6 as a subordinate clause in a sentence that begins in verse 5, two factors suggest that the verse begins a new section: (1) verses 1-5 and 6-7 display an acrostic mechanism of aleph-kaph (the first and last letters of the first half of the Hebrew alphabet), the repetition signaling a fresh beginning; (2) "thinking of [better: remembering] you upon my bed" expresses spontaneous private conviction in contrast to commanded ritual performance as in Psalms 4:4 and 149:5. Verse 6 thus marks a fresh start:

> I call you to mind on my bed
> and meditate on you in the night watches. (REB)

Verses 6-8 describe a private sentiment like that of verse 1. Both parts of the poem thus have the same starting point — private resolve (vv. 1 and 6) — but each part develops it differently. The first part expresses the hope of dwelling safely in the temple; the second part acknowledges God's saving presence now. Longing for the temple enables the psalmist to appreciate in a new way God's protective care even of people far from the temple and its worshiping community.

The poem thus has two parts:

- Part I. Hope of "seeing" God in the sanctuary (vv. 1-5).
- Part II. Awareness that God is with me wherever I am (vv. 6-11).

Formal features like those already noted above support this division. Note also that "God" occurs in the first and last verses of the poem; and "my soul/life" occurs twice in the first part (vv. 1, 5) and twice in the second part (vv. 8, 9).

Several phrases in the psalm require comment. "My soul" (*nepeš*, v. 1) basically refers to the throat area where the vital signs of a person (moisture, breathing, warmth) are especially palpable. Experiencing the absence of God is expressed as the pain of thirst, and experiencing the presence of God as seeing the face of God (cf. Pss 27:4 and 42:2). Both metaphors are rooted in the facial and throat area of the body ("my soul"). "Better than life" in verse 3a is a unique phrase, suggesting perhaps that God's steadfast love is more precious than life itself. The verbs "think" and "meditate" are better rendered as "recite" or "remember," for they mean recalling, even reciting audibly, what God has done, as in Psalm 77:11. The psalmist characterizes God in verses 7-8: you have been my saving God and I have been your loyal and responsive friend — which is to say, we are in a mutual relationship.

In summary, the poet is driven by a thirst for seeing God in the temple, and of joining with others in worship and feasting. The desire acts like a powerful magnet, ever drawing the psalmist forward.

The lectionary excerpt does not include verses 9-11, perhaps because the verses pray that the psalmist's enemies die suddenly and prematurely. Their "unnatural" death will show they were slain by God. It is crucial to note that, to the psalmists, evil was concrete and embodied in particular people. Moreover, note that the timetable and mode of destruction are left entirely in the hands of God. The poem closes by mentioning the king. Possibly the king was the speaker, or considered by the psalmist the symbol of triumphant divine justice.

Psalm 63 is a fine response to Isaiah 55:1-9 (the first lesson), which invites the hungry and thirsty to come to the banquet of the Lord. It suggests to Christian congregants that the Lord feeds them with his word and, in the Eucharist, with his body and blood.

Richard J. Clifford

PSALM 65

Twenty-third Sunday after Pentecost, Year C
    First Lesson: Joel 2:23-32
    (Psalm 65)
    Second Lesson: 2 Timothy 4:6-8, 16-18
    Gospel Lesson: Luke 18:9-14

In opening, Psalm 65 declares that "Praise is *fitting* [so the ancient versions; the Hebrew text is uncertain in meaning] for you, / O God, in Zion; / to you shall vows be paid." (Bach's Cantata 120, available on Harmonia Mundi with Philippe Herreweghe conducting, provides a magnificent embodiment of this verse in its alternate translation: "God, one praises Thee in the *stillness* of Zion.") The rest of the psalm describes *why* praise is fitting to God "who hears prayers" (present) and to whom "all flesh will come" (future). The psalm also *portrays* some of that praise (vv. 8, 12-13; cf. Pss 96; 98; 148). Before all else, Israel's God forgives the sins that overwhelm individuals (v. 3a, the alternative and more difficult Hebrew reading, "overwhelm *me*," is to be preferred over the easier "overwhelms *us*") and communities (v. 3b). In this remarkable verse, individual and group are distinguished but not separated. The person speaking is likely the king who represents the community, but even in our individualistic society communal and individual sin and guilt are inseparable realities.[1] This interplay of I/we language continues in verse 4, with blessing for the *one* (the verb is singular) chosen to live in the courts of God's "house," while the *"we"* is more than "satisfied" (our English term is weaker than Hebrew √*śb*ʿ) with the goodness and holiness of God's temple. Thus, this first section of the psalm (vv. 1-4) moves from fitting praise and paid vows (word *and* deed, "talk *and* walk"!), through confession and forgiveness of sin, and finally to the result: the blessing of life in God's holy presence, in God's "house," where his people are "filled with good things."

It is the movement from confession to living in God's "house" that connects our psalm to the Gospel reading (the Pharisee's and the publican's prayers), and to entrance liturgy psalms like Psalms 15 and 24 (who may enter God's temple?). In the Epistle lesson we find the aged Paul ready to depart his difficult life and enter into the life to come, where God's "heavenly kingdom" will be fully realized only when heaven and

---

1. See Dietrich Bonhoeffer, *Ethics* (New York: Macmillan, 1965), 67, 240-41.

earth are one (cf. Rev 21–22; Matt 6:10). Paul, the Apostle to the Gentiles, spread the good news of Jesus to all nations. In Jesus, God's righteousness was displayed (Rom 1:17; 3:21-26), showing his "awesome deeds" to the world, so that Christ became "the hope of all the ends of the earth" (cf. Ps 65:5).

The I/we movement of Psalm 65 has an important parallel in the psalm as a whole. Praise begins "in Zion" but moves from Israel "to the ends of the earth," to all nations and creatures, for the valleys themselves, clothed with grain, "raise a shout" and "break into song" (v. 13; cf. vv. 8b, 12b; Pss 96; 98; 148; Isa 55:12).

But how did the psalmist connect the first part of the psalm (vv. 1-4), which focuses on praise and confession in Zion's temple, to the second (vv. 5-8) and third (vv. 9-13) parts with their focus on the "ends of the earth" and on the glorious fertility and music of creation itself? The key to this psalmic move is found in the complex and rich meaning of God's "house" or temple in biblical thought.[2] God's house was on Mount Zion in Jerusalem, in the "most holy place." Here the God of all creation was intensely, locally present as king of his people, a God of holiness who atoned for sin but also judged it (Isa 6:1-8). Yet, this local "house" of God was a microcosm of the whole earth, God's true house and dwelling place (Isa 66:1-2). By its design and symbolic art the temple represented the plants, the seas, and the fields and fruits of the whole earth. This basic assumption, that the world is God's "house," filled with his glory (Isa 6:3), is what makes possible the move from particular, local talk of God in verses 1-4 to the rule of God over all nations and creatures in verses 5-8, 9-13. In this way the psalm reveals the intricate dialectic of universal and particular, of cosmos and history, of Israel and the nations, and of humans and all creatures — a dialectic that easily permeates this psalm and the Psalter as a whole.

In the second and third parts of the psalm (vv. 5-8, 9-13), the ultimate issue for Israel and the world is revealed: Who is the savior-king and provider of Israel, the nations, and the cosmos itself? Who provides the earth with bounty — a duty of gods and kings throughout the ancient Near East?[3] The answer: none other than Israel's God, worshiped as king

2. Cf. G. K. Beale, *The Temple and the Church's Mission: A Biblical Theology of the Dwelling Place of God* (Downers Grove, Ill.: InterVarsity, 2004).

3. See, e.g., the prologue to Hammurabi's law code; James B. Pritchard, *Ancient Near Eastern Texts Relating to the Old Testament,* 3rd ed. (Princeton: Princeton University Press, 1969), 164-65.

in the Jerusalem temple.[4] Thus the move outward in the psalm is not just geographical, political (all nations), and cosmic (all creatures); it is ultimately eschatological, pointing toward a time not yet fully come, because in our world even God's folk sin, and the nations, like the seas, still rage destructively (v. 7; cf. Ps 2; Acts 4:25-26). The kingdom of God *has begun* in the temple, God's house. But it *has not yet come* to all nations, to all creatures. That still requires the return of the King, Jesus, in whom the people of God have already become God's local house and fruitful field, the church (cf. 1 Cor 3:5-17; 6:19-20). It also requires the eschatological coming of the Messiah to fulfill the work of death and resurrection he accomplished two thousand years ago. For much of the world, this work and the life it entails still remain "hidden" (Col 3:1-17).

In the concluding sections of the psalm, what astonishes is not the eschatological perspective, that it sees the future restoration and flourishing of all creation. It is rather that the psalmist sees these things, even in a rebellious, wicked world, already happening in this present world around him. He sees the "I," the "we," Israel, the nations, and the fruitful earth itself, already now giving praise and "paying vows" to God, who like a royal farmer blesses the fruitful earth with his "waterworks," so that the hills and fields are clothed with grain and flocks, but most of all with joy and music. To this God praise is due in Zion.

Raymond C. Van Leeuwen

PSALM 66

Twenty-first Sunday after Pentecost, Year C
First Lesson: Jeremiah 29:1, 4-7
(Psalm 66:1-12)
Second Lesson: 2 Timothy 2:8-15
Gospel Lesson: Luke 17:11-19

4. Cf. Pss 2; 93-99; and James L. Mays, *The Lord Reigns: A Theological Handbook to the Psalms* (Louisville: Westminster John Knox, 1994).

    First Lesson: Acts 16:9-15
    (Psalm 66:8-20)
    Second Lesson: 1 Peter 3:13-22
    Gospel Lesson: John 14:15-21

This psalm confesses that God's reign extends far beyond the bounds of Israel. God's particularity is for the chosen ones, but the end purpose is for all to "bless our God" (v. 8). The psalm is thus one of praise, first in global terms (vv. 1-12) and then in terms of praise offered by the individual (vv. 13-20).

The psalm opens with the same line as Psalm 100:1, except here the praise is to "God" (Elohim) instead of Psalm 100's "the LORD" (Yahweh). The first stanza begins with a series of imperative verbs: "make a joyful noise," "sing," "give," "say." The opening calls on the whole earth to act. The fourth imperative statement (v. 3) moves from praise to the reason for praise. The earth is to express how awesome are God's deeds: "because of your great power, your enemies cringe before you." God's might here is expressed in terms of subduing the enemy. This may seem like an extreme statement in modern terms and one that could encourage ideas of "my God is bigger than your God," but one should notice that other nations are mentioned only in verse 7. The real enemy in the first half of this psalm is Israel itself (vv. 10-12). In other words, a preacher should not shy away from verse 3. It is not necessarily a statement against others (or, if it is, the "others" may well be "us"), but is indeed a clear statement of who rules the world. Other nations will not control God, but then again, neither will Israel.

Verse 5 serves as an introduction to verses 6-12. Here all are invited to come and see "what God has done." The verse continues tersely, even awkwardly: "awesome deeds among humankind" (my translation). The preposition "among" (*'al*) is crucial here, for it declares something about this God. God's work is done *among* humans, or, said another way, God enters human history and acts. Kraus notes that "it is obvious that he is the Lord of history and that all nations live before his eyes."[1]

Indeed, the next six verses deal with God's great acts in history. Verse 6 reflects the great act of God in the exodus. Some commentators have

---

1. Hans-Joachim Kraus, *Psalms 60–150: A Continental Commentary* (Minneapolis: Fortress, 1993), 37.

argued that this verse represents the crossing of the Jordan (Josh 3:14-17).[2] However, since "sea" and "river" are both used in verse 6, it is possible that these two lines mark the beginning and end of the exodus/wilderness period. In any case, what is clear is that a particular event, or events, in Israel's history is cause for the whole world to marvel and give praise. The particularity of this event of salvation will have worldwide ramifications and will also transcend time (v. 6). The "they" who crossed the river becomes the "we" who rejoiced there. This is not just "your" ancestors' salvation, but is also salvation for the "we" who rejoice in the very act (for similar declarations see Deut 5:3; 6:21).

Verses 8-12 move from the event of salvation to the relationship between God and Israel. All was not perfect after God's great act, indeed the people were barely across the waters before doubt set in (Exod 15:22). The poetry here does not reveal specifics about the incident to which the psalmist is referring. It could be anytime from the wilderness through the close of the Old Testament period. What is clear is that God's teaching of Israel, even by correction and judgment, is cause for praise by all peoples (v. 8). This section reminds all that the postsalvation road is not an easy one. Israel had to learn very hard lessons. This is not, nor will it ever be, "cheap grace."

In verses 13-20 the subject changes from the world and Israel to an individual worshiper. First, the worshiper acts, giving sacrifices (vv. 13-15), then tells of God's great steadfast love. This individual is joining the chorus that began in verse 1. The reasons given are that God heard and "gave heed to my prayer" (v. 19). God hears the psalmist in the same way that God heard the cries of the oppressed in Egypt (Exod 3:7). God's acts in human history are for the community, but also for the individual, as many of the prayers for help in the Psalms testify. The psalmist's praise is part of the praise that is to be given by all peoples. The whole world must stand in awe of God's power and offer praise; this particular individual, however, praises the personal: God's listening ear (v. 19) and God's steadfast love (v. 20).

The lection for the Twenty-first Sunday after Pentecost focuses on the first part of the psalm and can be preached with the Jeremiah text where the "testing" is the advice to the exiles to settle in because their punishment will be seventy years (Jer 29:10). They are even to pray for the

---

2. See, e.g., Kraus, *Psalms 60–150,* 36; Erhard Gerstenberger, *Psalms, Part 2, and Lamentations,* FOTL 15 (Grand Rapids: Eerdmans, 2001), 26.

welfare *(shalom)* of the conqueror's city. A difficult test, indeed, from God (cf. Ps 66:10). The Luke passage tells of ten lepers, yet only one, the outsider, returns to Jesus. As noted in verses 8-12, Israel is often the enemy of God. Both texts remind us of the ways God's people often act. The psalm teaches us to praise God, not only for the great acts of salvation, but also for the acts of testing and correction (cf. James 1:2-4).

The second lection calls for verses 8-20, which focus exclusively on Israel, first in its testing by God and second as the praise given to God by a worshiper in the temple. When seen as the focus text with the background of verses 1-9, Israel's particular relationship with God is the point stressed. The psalm teaches that we must learn to praise God for both the good and the difficult lessons we learn when we choose our own way. That lesson can be a hard one to preach, but the psalm presents it in such a way that it is not scolding but in fact is praise. It offers a new way to look at our lives and a new opportunity to see God as something other than the punishing ruler. God does rule the world, yet God is forever a teacher of humans, offering salvation in the exodus and creating a people from a group of slaves through the testing and training of the wilderness era. God continues to this day, saving and creating us. God should be constantly praised for both acts of salvation and constant creation of a kingdom people of God!

Beth LaNeel Tanner

PSALM 67

Sixth Sunday of Easter, Year C
> First Lesson: Acts 16:9-15
> **(Psalm 67)**
> Second Lesson: Revelation 21:10; 21:22–22:5
> Gospel Lesson: John 14:23-29 or John 5:1-9

Psalm 67 is a *communal prayer for blessing* (see the introductory essay). Because of the reference to the earth yielding its increase in verse 6, some commentators connect the psalm to a harvest festival. That association is possible but hardly necessary. The harvest is not the dominant theme. What *is* dominant is the significance of Yahweh's blessing Israel for the peoples of the world. Readers of the Old Testament are inescapably confronted with the tension between the claim that Israel is the unique and privileged people of God and the claim that God is Lord of *all* creation. Old Testament traditions variously acknowledge and negotiate that tension. Here in this psalm, it is the central theme. Indeed, the dynamics of blessing and praise provide an ideal framework in which to explore the dialectic theologically.

The psalm is structured according to a chiastic *(abcb'a')* pattern. The prayer for blessing at the beginning and end (vv. 1-2, 6-7) forms a frame around the psalm. Moving inward, a refrain that summons all peoples to praise God is repeated twice, with the two occurrences perfectly mirroring each other (vv. 3, 5). At the heart of the psalm (v. 4, the only verse with three lines) is the theological basis of Israel's blessing and the praise of the nations: God judges the nations with equity and guides them. How does the Israel-centered blessing relate to the praise that springs up from all the earth? For answers to that question, we must consider the rhetorical movement of the psalm.

The initial blessing closely echoes the Aaronic benediction (Num 6:24-26):

> May God be gracious to us and bless us
>> and make his face to shine upon us. (v. 1)

The syntax of the Hebrew emphasizes that it is *God* alone who blesses. The blessing of God — the bestowal of gifts that enhance life — cannot be realized apart from the gracious presence of the deity. So the psalm asks that God's shining countenance, a symbol of divine presence, be directed toward "us." In these verses a *particular* community prays: favor *us,* bless *us,* shine upon *us.* There is no doubt that this "us" refers to Israel as it gathers for worship. But the worshiping community is not content to claim and reserve that blessing for itself. Immediately the psalm goes on to state the purpose and desired consequence of the blessing upon Israel:

> that your way may be known *upon earth,*
>> your saving power *among all nations.* (v. 2)

The *universal horizon* of this prayer is evident in the dense cluster of words that look beyond Israel: various words for "nations" (Hebrew *gôyîm,* *'ammîm, lĕ'ūmmîm*) occur eight times; "earth" four times; and "all/every" four times. The farthest ends of the earth are in view (cf. v. 7); *all* nations come to acknowledge the sovereignty of the God who graciously blesses and does marvelous deeds (summarized by the expressions "your way" and "your saving power") in and through Israel.

Hence, the central portion of the psalm rings with praise, gladness, and exultation among the nations. It calls forth:

> Let the peoples praise you, O God;
>> let all the peoples praise you. (v. 3)

And yet again:

> Let the peoples praise you, O God;
>> let all the peoples praise you. (v. 5)

This chorus surrounds the theological centerpiece of the psalm:

> Let the nations be glad and sing for joy,
>> for you judge the peoples with equity
>> and guide the nations upon earth. (v. 4)

Indeed, this is the profession that represents the theological heart of the Psalter: God reigns over all the earth.[1] This universal, missional dimension is fundamental to the praise of God in the Psalms. The proclamation is also *invitation;* it expresses as well as *evokes* praise. It ever seeks to draw others into the circle of those who worship this God.[2]

But it is not entirely self-evident how the Israel-centered blessing of verse 1 is related to the universal praise of the nations. As noted above, the logic of verses 1-2 suggests that the knowledge of God is mediated through Israel's life. In verse 4, however, the nations are called to praise God because of God's actions *on behalf of all creation.* The ground for praise is God's just governance and guidance of *all* who inhabit the earth. And yet, the language used here is that which characteristically describes God's actions in, with, and for Israel. It is primarily in Israel that God "judges with equity." Similarly, whenever the deity is the subject of the

---

1. See James L. Mays, *The Lord Reigns: A Theological Handbook to the Psalms* (Louisville: Westminster John Knox, 1994).

2. See Patrick D. Miller, *Interpreting the Psalms* (Philadelphia: Fortress, 1986), 68-72.

verb "to guide," it refers to God's providential guidance of his covenant people, most notably during their formative journey through the wilderness (see Exod 15:13, 18; Pss 77:20; 78:14, 53, 72). Remarkably, this language is now extended and applied inclusively to all nations.

Finally, the psalm is rounded out with another blessing (vv. 6-7). First, there is thanksgiving for the gift of the earth's increase. Every bountiful harvest is a fulfillment of the Lord's promise (Lev 26:4) and a visible pledge that God is with God's people. So the psalmist declares that "God, our God, has blessed," and prays, "May God continue to bless us." But the "us" in these final verses cannot but be transformed by the expansive vision of verses 3-5. Walter Brueggemann suggests that the pronoun no longer refers only to the congregation of Israel, but also the peoples of the world who stand alongside Israel in worship of God.[3] The ancient blessing of Israel — to be uttered by the Levitical priest over the congregation — is now taken up by the congregation as a communal prayer that embraces the broadest possible circle of humanity. As one interpreter puts it, "Israel is the world's high priest . . . if Israel has the light of God's face, the world cannot remain in darkness."[4] Similarly, in the New Jerusalem envisioned in Revelation 21:23-24, "the city has no need of sun or moon, for the glory of God will be its light, and its lamp is the Lamb. The nations will walk by its light" (see the first lesson). Our psalm therefore ends appropriately with the hope that "all the ends of the earth will revere him," that is, they will gladly obey and walk in the "way" of the Lord (v. 3).

Eunny P. Lee

3. Walter Brueggemann, "The 'Us' of Psalm 67," in *Palabra, Prodigio, Poesía: In Memoriam P. Luis Alonso Schökel, S.J.* (Rome: Editrice Pontificio Instituto Biblico, 2003), 233-42.

4. I. Abrahams, cited by Marvin E. Tate, *Psalms 51–100*, WBC 20 (Dallas: Word, 1990), 159.

PSALM 68

Seventh Sunday of Easter, Year A
First Lesson: Acts 1:6-14
(Psalm 68)
Second Lesson: 1 Peter 4:12-14; 5:6-11
Gospel Lesson: John 17:1-11

"Let God rise up," Psalm 68 begins, echoing the ritual battle call that signaled the presence of the ark on the field of Israel's early battles. "Whenever the ark set out, Moses would say, 'Arise, O LORD, let your enemies be scattered, / and your foes flee before you.' And whenever it came to rest, he would say, 'Return, O LORD of the ten thousand thousands of Israel'" (Num 10:35-36). The ark was Israel's war palladium and "Rise up, O God" was its rallying cry.

> Let God rise up, let God's enemies be scattered;
> let those who hate him flee before him. (Ps 68:1)

At least until it took up residence in Solomon's temple, the ark was the visible evidence of God's presence and protection (see Josh 3–8; 1 Sam 4:1-22; further 1 Sam 4–7; 11; 14; 2 Sam 6; 11; 15). Solomon uses this same invocation in his dedicatory prayer during the ark's installation in the temple:

> Now rise up, O LORD God, and go to your resting place,
> you and the ark of your might.
> Let your priests, O LORD God, be clothed with salvation,
> and let your faithful rejoice in your goodness.
> O LORD God, do not reject your anointed one.
> Remember your steadfast love for your servant David.
>> (2 Chron 6:41-42; cf. Ps 132:8-10)

Psalm 68 is a *psalm of thanksgiving* and praise for God's deliverance (see the introductory essay). Its identification is complicated by its frequent use of quotations from other Israelite poetry, such as was noted above. In the past some commentators have even suggested that the psalm is actually a catalogue of incipits — that is, the first lines of hymns and poetry. This suggestion is unnecessary, however, because Psalm 68 displays an internal coherence that argues for its unity in its final form.

The deliverance celebrated in Psalm 68 is from historical enemies, armies, and kings.

> Sing to God, sing praises to his name;
> lift up a song to him who rides upon the clouds —
> his name is the LORD —
> be exultant before him. . . .
> "The kings of the armies, they flee, they flee!"
> The women at home divide the spoil,
> though they stay among the sheepfolds —
> the wings of a dove covered with silver,
> its pinions with green gold.
> When the Almighty scattered kings there,
> snow fell on Zalmon. (vv. 4, 12-14)

The language of conquest celebrates God's military prowess.

> Ascribe power to God,
> whose majesty is over Israel;
> and whose power is in the skies.
> Awesome is God in his sanctuary,
> the God of Israel;
> he gives power and strength to his people.
> Blessed be God! (vv. 34-35)

The psalm's use of military imagery should be reason for pause for the interpreter. In the past, Christians and the church have too easily appropriated these kinds of military metaphors of God's power and might for selfish and oppressive motives. The challenge to the preacher today would be to take the theological claims of God's salvific acts seriously, while at the same time resisting the urge to transfer the military solutions wholesale into the contemporary context. This appropriation of military metaphors has the danger of baptizing our causes with "God's sanction."

In Psalm 68, as happens frequently in Old Testament poetry, God's and Israel's enemies are not only military or political. The forces against which God fights are also of a cosmic nature.

> Father of orphans and protector of widows
> is God in his holy habitation.

God gives the desolate a home to live in;
>   he leads out the prisoners to prosperity,
>   but the rebellious live in a parched land. (vv. 5-6)

Like the ideal ruler, God's concerns extend far beyond geopolitical borders and claims. God's goals are justice and righteousness, and these are to be visited first upon the least in any society. The fates of the "widow, the orphan, and the stranger" provide the litmus tests under God's sovereign rule. "You shall not wrong or oppress a resident alien, for you were aliens in the land of Egypt. You shall not abuse any widow or orphan. If you do abuse them, when they cry out to me, I will surely heed their cry; my wrath will burn, and I will kill you with the sword, and your wives shall become widows and your children orphans" (Exod 22:21-24). God's power is arrayed against forces that enslave the powerless.

The forces of chaos are no match for the strength of God. Israel's God is the one who restores order and puts down the powers of evil that rule the natural and cosmic worlds.

>   Rebuke the wild animals that live among the reeds,
>   the herd of bulls with the calves of the peoples.
>   Trample under foot those who lust after tribute;
>   scatter the peoples who delight in war. (v. 30)

All nature is in tune with the reign of God.

>   O God, when you went out before your people,
>   when you marched through the wilderness, . . .
>   the earth quaked, the heavens poured down rain
>   at the presence of God, the God of Sinai,
>   at the presence of God, the God of Israel.
>   Rain in abundance, O God, you showered abroad;
>   you restored your heritage when it languished;
>   your flock found a dwelling in it;
>   in your goodness, O God, you provided for the needy. (vv. 7-9)

The final enemy is death.

>   Our God is a God of salvation,
>   and to GOD, the Lord, belongs escape from death. (v. 20)

191

The lectionary recommends reading only Psalm 68:1-10, 32-35, thus eliminating some of the thornier issues raised by the remainder of the psalm. The recommended reading also brackets out important imagery and sometimes tough theological assertions that must be grappled with for the full person of God to be encountered. In a time when violence is too quickly and slickly the answer, it would behoove the church to lean in to the difficulties Scripture often tells us about God, rather than editing them out.

Kathryn L. Roberts

PSALM 71

Fourth Sunday after the Epiphany, Year C
    First Lesson: Jeremiah 1:4-10
    (Psalm 71:1-6)
    Second Lesson: 1 Corinthians 13:1-13
    Gospel Lesson: Luke 4:21-30

Fourteenth Sunday after Pentecost, Year C
    First Lesson: Jeremiah 1:4-10
    (Psalm 71:1-6)
    Second Lesson: Hebrews 12:18-29
    Gospel Lesson: Luke 13:10-17

Psalm 71 is the petition of an alienated, elderly person who, despite desperate circumstances, cleaves to the God he has known for so long. The psalm's diffuse character and mixed moods make defining its structure difficult, but one can discern two large sections: verses 1-13, containing cries of distress interspersed with confessions of trust, and verses 14-24, a variegated vow of praise for God's imminent salvation.

The first four verses move between two aspects of God's care: God's hiding the psalmist (vv. 1, 3) and God's delivering her (vv. 2, 4). The psalm employs the classic "rock of refuge" metaphor to describe Yahweh's protection (cf. 2 Sam 22:3; Pss 18:2; 31:2; 94:22). The metaphor evokes the image of one fleeing for her life from enemies in hot pursuit. When she comes to a cliff or boulder promising shelter, she wedges herself into one of its shady crags, pressing against the cool, hard surface (cf. Exod 32:22). In this scene *Yahweh* is the rock — solid, steadfast protection. Further, the images of hiding in verses 1 and 3 suggest that Yahweh is close, that his very near presence can ward off any enemy threatening to advance. By contrast, the pleas for deliverance in verses 2 and 4 suggest that Yahweh is far-off. In verse 4 the psalmist describes herself as in "the hand of the wicked . . . the grasp of the unjust and cruel." In response to this predicament, the psalmist asks that Yahweh "deliver" (√*nṣl*, v. 2) or, according to another translation, "snatch away." Thus, in these two verses the poet prays that Yahweh would hear, come near, and extricate her from the enemy's grip. The interwoven images of protection and deliverance raise the question: Where is Yahweh anyway? Is God *near*, as verse 1 suggests ("In you, O LORD, I take refuge"), or *far-off*, as verse 4 would indicate? The ambiguity of the divine presence in the psalm resonates with modern readers who, in the midst of difficult situations, also struggle with the question, "where is God?"

Wherever God is, however, the psalmist knows he can cry out to God because of their long personal history together. They *go way back* — all the way back to the womb. For, like a midwife, Yahweh assisted with this petitioner's birth, after which the psalmist "leaned" on him (v. 6). The verb NRSV translates "leaned" (√*smk*) could also be translated "brace oneself for support," capturing images of a child resting on a mother's breast or grasping his father's hand to steady himself in his first steps. This tender imagery no doubt prompted the lectionary's binding of this psalm to Jeremiah 1:4-10. In the call to the prophet, God proclaims,

> Before I formed you in the womb I knew you,
> and before you were born I consecrated you. (Jer 1:5)

1. *A song of the aged.* The imagery of infancy and childhood in verses 5-6 (also v. 17) provides a fitting counterpoint for further characterizations of the psalmist as an old man, frail and gray (vv. 9, 18). By juxtaposing these images, the psalmist establishes the broad scope of his relationship with God — a long history of faithfulness to which the psalmist now clings.

Descriptions of the passage of time pervade the text. The word *tāmîd*, translated "continually" or "every day," occurs frequently, as, for example, in verse 6: "my praise is *continually* of you" (see also vv. 3, 14). Likewise, "all day" or "every day" *(kol hayyôm)* regularly appears: for instance, the psalmist cries,

Fig. 6. A processional celebration, replete with singers and instrumentalists, moves toward a royal figure sitting on a cherubim throne (cf. fig. 9). The images of celebration through music making are not unlike those captured in Psalm 71.

> My mouth is filled with your praise,
> and with your glory *all day long.* (v. 8; see also vv. 15, 24)

The psalm beautifully portrays the continuity of Yahweh's actions through time in the repetition of verses 20-21: "You will revive me *again* . . . you will bring me up *again* . . . [you will] comfort me once *again*" (NRSV). The psalm's central theme emerges through each of these examples. From youth to old age the psalmist has trusted and praised Yahweh, and Yahweh has proven faithful again and again.

Though its theme is clear, the overall form and structure of the psalm has perplexed interpreters. Erhard Gerstenberger notes that "the designation of form elements and division of units can be tentative only, because this psalm is rather diffuse in character," and proceeds to call

Fig. 7. Like figure 6, this image also bears comparison with Psalm 71 (especially vv. 22-23), with the difference that here the singer is depicted as directly addressing the deity (in this case, the Egyptian god Ra-Horakhty-Atum). Other psalms, too, speak of singing to please the Lord (see, e.g., Ps 104:33-34).

the psalm's middle section (vv. 14-21) "a loose, heterogeneous discourse."[1] So, as Richard J. Clifford observes, the opaque structure of the psalm has prompted a wide variety of strophic divisions.[2] Indeed, the text seems to move erratically between desperate pleas and sublime statements of trust. The psalm begins with a series of petitions intermingled with justifications for hope (vv. 1-6). Confessions of trust (vv. 7-8) come before a frightening description of the enemies (vv. 9-11), followed by pleas for sal-

1. Erhard Gerstenberger, *Psalms, Part 2, and Lamentations,* FOTL 15 (Grand Rapids: Eerdmans, 2001), 58.

2. Richard J. Clifford, *Psalms 1–72,* Abingdon Old Testament Commentaries (Nashville: Abingdon, 2002), 327.

vation (vv. 12-13). Next, confident vows of praise appear again, mottled however with further petitions for help (vv. 14-18), before a final conclusion with an extended, exuberant vow of praise (vv. 20-24).

The tangled form of this psalm is not the mark of elderly dementia. Rather, it shows a mature understanding of the nature of prayer. Through years of faithfulness, the psalmist has learned how to hold together and simultaneously the frightening reality of a desperate situation and a firm conviction that Yahweh will indeed deliver. In alternating lines, this prayer expresses sure trust, profound anxiety, and in the end, overarching praise: a reasonable — and laudable — end to the golden years.

2. *A song for the ages.* The final verses of the psalm detail the music devoted to the adoration of God (vv. 22-24). The aged psalmist is a skilled instrumentalist, familiar with the sensation of the harp and lyre resonating against her chest (v. 22; see figs. 6-7). The psalmist also sings, and depicts *herself* as an instrument of praise. Her lips shout (v. 23), her tongue declares (v. 24), and her soul — like a sounding box — reverberates with praise for Yahweh, her hope and her salvation (v. 23). In sum, this *psalm of the aged* is a *song for the ages* — a liturgy of petition, hope, and praise. Throughout history and across the world, countless lives resonate with its themes, for the psalm gives voice to the suffering of the elderly, and for all the faithful — regardless of age — it provides a model for honest, integrated prayer.

Joel M. LeMon

Psalm 72

Epiphany of the Lord, Years A, B, C
    First Lesson: Isaiah 60:1-6
    (Psalm 72:1-7, 10-14)
    Second Lesson: Ephesians 3:1-12
    Gospel Lesson: Matthew 2:1-12

Second Sunday of Advent, Year A
    First Lesson: Isaiah 11:1-10
    (Psalm 72:1-7, 18-19)
    Second Lesson: Romans 15:4-13
    Gospel Lesson: Matthew 3:1-12

This psalm is well suited for both Epiphany and Advent. It is a *royal psalm* (see the introductory essay), and several scholars describe it as a coronation hymn.[1] Its major theme is to praise Israel's king, not for his great power, but for his justice and righteousness (v. 1). The psalm presents in poetic form the job description of Israel's king, the one who is to be the quintessential human representative of God's kingdom. The psalm sets forth how the kingdom of God is to be governed.

The psalm opens with a series of wishes for the king offered to God in prayer (vv. 1-11). These petitions are simple but profound. God is petitioned to give the king *God's* ("your") justice and righteousness (v. 1). From the beginning, then, there is an understanding that these great gifts come not from human ability, but are bestowed by God. Verses 2-7 continue with specific wishes that are based on God's gifts petitioned for in verse 1.

Verse 2 focuses on the court system and how the king is to act as a judge of the peoples. Again the wish or petition is for "justice" and "righteousness," but in this verse the "poor" or "afflicted" are specifically mentioned. This term *ʿānî* (NRSV: "poor") has a wide range of meanings in Hebrew that no one English term can convey. It certainly means those who are economically disadvantaged, but it can also mean those who are falsely accused or falsely attacked by others in the community.[2] The king, then, is to be especially concerned for those in the community who are marginalized for any reason.

Verse 3 changes the focus from the king to the creation. It wishes that the mountains would bring forth well-being *(shalom)* and the hills, righteousness. The common English translation of *shalom* as "prosperity" could easily mislead in our contemporary context. This term certainly does not reflect an abundance of "worldly riches," but rather a wealth of well-being and contentment. Why the change in subject here? It was commonly understood in the ancient Near East that a king's rule could also impact nature,[3] but a close reading here shows that the understanding of the Israelites is a bit different. The change of subject in this verse indicates, not that the human king has control over nature, but that the king and the creation work in different ways for the good of the world. Both do the work of God as God has ordained it.

---

1. Hans-Joachim Kraus, *Psalms 60–150: A Continental Commentary* (Minneapolis: Fortress, 1993), 76; Marvin E. Tate, *Psalms 51–100*, WBC 20 (Dallas: Word, 1990), 222.

2. Hans-Joachim Kraus, *Theology of the Psalms* (Minneapolis: Augsburg, 1986), 150-54.

3. Kraus, *Psalms 60–150*, 37.

The final three verses of this section turn from the *work* of the king to the *person* of the king. He is wished long life (v. 5), akin to the long life thought to be part of God's kingdom (Isa 65:17-25). Verses 6-7 liken the king to gentle rain that falls on the earth so that righteousness and *shalom* can flourish. Here, too, Israel's theology shows that the king is to be like the rain *so that* (reading back to v. 1) God's righteousness and *shalom* can flourish "until the moon is no more."

Verses 8-14 move from how the people of Israel are to be blessed to how this king, who follows God's rule, will have worldwide impact. The king will, in essence, be king of the world (vv. 8-9). The other rulers will come to him and *voluntarily* offer tribute and bow down before him. Verse 11 summarizes the section: all kings fall down before him and all nations *serve* him. Verses 12-14 give the reasons for the acts in verse 11. Israel's king will be worshiped by all because of his care for the poor, the oppressed, and the marginalized. What a difference from the reasons most kings are showered with praise! Israel's king will be known far and wide for his care and justice for the least of his kingdom (cf. Matt 25:40, 45).

The next section, verses 15-17, is a summary of the attributes praised in verses 1-14. These petitions call for the king to be a focus of prayer (v. 15), for the creation to be "fruitful and multiply" (v. 16), and for all the nations to be blessed through the king (v. 17). Verses 16-17 wish for the king the same blessings given by God to the first Israelites (Gen 1:28 and 12:3).

The last section (vv. 18-19), like verse 1, makes it clear that the king is not doing any of these things through human power. The wishes for the king's reign are offered to God as prayer. The king is simply to be a conduit for God's kingdom.

There is no doubt that the focus of this prayer is Israel's king. And yet the account is clearly idealized, for Israel's history demonstrates that no king lived up to this job description. As with much of human community, power is a powerful master. So, in a sense, this prayer is eschatological. It becomes the hope, the "not-yet," the goal of living in the kingdom.

The New Testament, with all its words about the kingdom of God, never offers a definition of that kingdom because the kingdom had already been defined in the images of the blessing of God in Genesis, in the laws of the Torah, and in the images offered in the Psalms and the Prophets (e.g., Isa 65:17-25). Here, in the beautiful words of Psalm 72, is one such text, this one treating how God's kingdom ought to be governed. It is a new definition of power, because here power is not might but justice. Power is not special treatment for the rich and powerful but special treatment for the least of the world. It is human power turned upside down.

As already stated, this is a very appropriate psalm for Epiphany and Advent, for it describes the very kingdom that Jesus came to show to the world. The wise men brought their gifts and pay tribute to a baby — one with no apparent power or status in the world. This act declares that God's reign is fundamentally different from Herod's.

Christian preachers, however, should be careful not to limit the power of this psalm only to prediction of the Messiah, if only because if this psalm is solely or ultimately about Jesus and his life, then these words of the kingdom remain exclusively the purview of Christology — that is, about *Christ* and *his* life and ministry. To be sure, the kingdom is what Jesus came to preach, just as the Old Testament shows us what the kingdom ought to be. But the king was not the only one responsible for just rule. That job description was not only for the kings of Israel, or the Messiah for that matter, but for all of us who claim to serve in God's kingdom. "The one who believes in me will also do the works that I do and, in fact, will do greater works than these, because I am going to the Father" (John 14:12). Psalm 72 shows us the way we should structure our lives and our relationships. The royal and messianic job description belongs now to all who confess God as Lord.

Beth LaNeel Tanner

Psalm 77

Sixth Sunday after Pentecost, Year C
First Lesson: 2 Kings 2:1-2, 6-14
(Psalm 77:1-2, 11-20)
Second Lesson: Galatians 5:1, 13-25
Gospel Lesson: Luke 9:51-62

This psalm is prayed by a person in distress. It does not easily fit into traditional genres of psalms. Every commentator describes it somewhat differently. This lack of agreement on the psalm's form indicates what most of us know intuitively and experientially: distress is not uniform.

The cause of the distress is not identified. The distress or "trouble" (v. 2) is a Hebrew noun meaning "need, distress, anxiety." The verbal root means "to be cramped, restricted, hampered, constricted." The psalmist faces a situation of "dire straits," a feeling of being trapped with no way out. The use of exodus language and imagery in the second half of the psalm makes it clear that this psalmist nevertheless seeks deliverance — a way out ("ex-odus").

Most of us, in distress, become very self-centered, which is reflected in the dominance of "I" and "my" in the psalm. This self-centeredness is not a problem to be fixed but a recognition that pain is individual. But the psalmist recognizes that there is a "Thou" besides her troubled "I" and lifts her voice and cries out in the hope that God will hear (v. 1). When "horizons close," only God can somehow make a difference and open a new way.

Verses 2-4 describe the physical expression of such distress. The psalmist prays 24/7. She would hold her hands up in supplication forever if necessary. She remembers God and "meditates" to the point of fainting. The level of energy expended is present in repetition. The verbs "remember," "meditate," "consider," "muse," and "seek" appear a total of ten times between verses 3 and 12. Yet no matter how fervent or persistent the psalmist's prayer, her soul finds no comfort. Nights are the worst. Insomnia is imaged with God literally seizing the psalmist's eyelids to prevent them from closing. She is so troubled that she "cannot speak." She has reached the point of "sighs too deep for words" (cf. Rom 8:26).

Instead of trying to formulate the words of a petition, the psalmist remembers the past (v. 5). The first stich of verse 6 is difficult. It might be rendered:

> I remember my music played on strings at night.
> I commune with my heart,
> and it searched out my spirit. (author's translation)

The problem some translations (e.g., NRSV) avoid is how to interpret the reference to "music played on strings." Perhaps the psalmist remembers previous psalms of praise sung in the past, which contrast starkly with the present. In any event, in biblical idiom the "heart" is the place of thought, decision, and will. In the Hebrew text it is not "I" who search the spirit (cf. NRSV), it is the heart. It is as if the psalmist's whole being is trying to sort out the theological puzzle her situation has created. That puzzle is expressed in questions that wonder why everything normally expected of God seems to be the opposite:

We are supposed to be *accepted* by God, not *rejected*.

God is supposed to *delight* in us and show us *favor*.

God's steadfast love is supposed to be . . . well, *steadfast*. How do you explain the contradiction of the cessation of something steadfast?

God is supposed to *keep promises*.

Verse 9 employs female imagery. Unlike a woman who may forget her child, God is not supposed to forget us (Isa 49:15). The seemingly odd expression that compassion is "shut up" makes sense when we recall that the word for compassion *(rḥmym)* is derived from the Hebrew word for womb *(rḥm)*. The womb, the bond between mother and child, is the source of compassion. And just as God opens and shuts physical wombs in the Bible (e.g., Gen 29:31; 1 Sam 1:5; Isa 66:9), God has apparently shut her own womb, as if God no longer considered this pray-er to be her child.

It is bad enough to be in a situation where you feel trapped. It is even worse when the One whose acceptance, favor, steadfast love, promises, graciousness, and compassion would make it all bearable, is absent. Clearly, it is as if God has changed sides (v. 10).

The psalm shifts at this point. The psalmist decides to take four actions: "call to mind," "remember," "muse," and "meditate." The objects of these verbs are: "deeds of the LORD," "wonders of old," "all your work," and "mighty deeds" — all of which refer to the exodus. The psalmist turns her attention from her own distress and God's current absence to the past when God was present. What prompts her to do this? How will this help?

She begins by praising God in verses 13-15. What God did in the past stands in stark contrast to her current experience of God (vv. 7-9). The psalmist describes the experience of deliverance in the mythic language of the warrior god who defeats the forces of chaos (cf. Exod 15:1-18; Ps 114). The language of "waters" and "deep" (v. 16) also evokes the primeval chaos of Genesis 1:2. Verses 17-18 vividly portray the biggest, baddest thunderstorm imaginable, which is Yahweh unleashing his full arsenal (wind, lightning, thunder, rain) against the chaos. Israel is freed from its grip as the Lord makes a path for them to cross over. With hindsight the psalmist knows that it was God who shepherded the people through that chaos, yet at the sea "your footprints were unseen."

It is not surprising that the psalmist recalls the exodus. In Hebrew the name Egypt is itself related to the same root as "troubles." Traditionally, Egypt has also been understood as a spiritual state, the narrow place of confusion, fragmentation, and spiritual disconnection — the same place in which the psalmist now finds herself. If God, in the midst of that greater chaos, could redeem the people, surely God can redeem this psalmist. It is a biblical tenet that God can work from the greater to the lesser. The God who brings forth a people from slavery or a nation from their graves (cf. Ezek 37), can bring forth one man from a tomb, and therefore one psalmist from distress.

The psalm is unfinished. Did this help? Did the psalmist's life change? Did the distress go away? Was she delivered? There is no way to know. Perhaps the point of this psalm is not that through prayer you will be miraculously delivered from distress. Instead, perhaps the point is that when there is no way out, when all that you think God is seems turned on its head, what remains for you to do is to remember God's past wonders. A pastor wrote how conflicted he felt in a time of great crisis when he felt abandoned by God, yet was preaching the love of God to his congregations: "I felt a great deal of grief for my feeling and the untruths (as I saw them during the time) that God was always standing by us. Yet I could not reveal how I felt for fear of leading the people astray." The lection omits the central section, which poses the theological dilemma of divine rejection. Without it there is no conflict in the psalm. But the power of this psalm is the determination to recall God's past mighty acts *in spite of* the current experience of divine absence. The dilemma of the pastor was that it seemed blasphemous to admit to feeling God's rejection. Yet this psalmist *publicly proclaims* feeling the very same thing. In hindsight, the pastor now knows that God was standing nearby: "His love was there all the time; I just could not see it. God is near even when we can't see his presence. We must continue to trust in his faithfulness." The message of this psalm is that *both* God's absence and God's presence are truth.

Nancy R. Bowen

PSALM 78

Nineteenth Sunday after Pentecost, Year A
    First Lesson: Exodus 17:1-7
    (Psalm 78:1-4, 12-16)
    Second Lesson: Philippians 2:1-13
    Gospel Lesson: Matthew 21:23-32

Twenty-fifth Sunday after Pentecost, Year A
    First Lesson: Joshua 24:1-3a, 14-25
    (Psalm 78:1-7)
    Second Lesson: 1 Thessalonians 4:13-18
    Gospel Lesson: Matthew 25:1-13

Several psalms in the Hebrew Psalter deal extensively with historical matters. Often for an explicitly stated purpose, these psalms employ historical references to communicate and to make their point. Psalm 78 is the first of them (the others are 105; 106; 135; and 136; while many other psalms make historical references, none are as comprehensive as these five). History in this psalm might be characterized as a vehicle for theological education. Psalm 78 describes itself as "a parable" and as "dark sayings" (a pairing that also appears in Ezek 17:2: "riddle" and "allegory" in NRSV), and states its goal quite clearly: to teach and call to mind the wonders that the Lord has done (v. 4),

> so that [coming generations] should set their hope in God,
> and not forget the works of God,
> > but keep his commandments. (v. 7)

Psalm 78 is a historical teaching, a recollection of past events distilled through wisdom's craft for the edification of God's people.

    1. *Open mouths and parables.* The bulk of Psalm 78 is an attempt to obey the decree, law, and command that the Lord has established for the people of Israel (v. 5). The language of the psalm seems consistent with Deuteronomy.[1] As such, this essay at instruction may be fruitfully read under the rubric of Deuteronomy 6:7: "Recite them to your children and

---

1. Cf. Richard J. Clifford, *Psalms 73-150*, Abingdon Old Testament Commentaries (Nashville: Abingdon, 2003), 43, 44.

talk about them when you are at home and when you are away." The opening verses set the tone for all that follows in the psalm. Perhaps written as early as 722 B.C.E., following the destruction of the shrine to the Lord at Shiloh (see Ps 78:60-64), this psalm is an attempt to prevent further destruction and devastation in Israel. This instruction is meant to counter the testing and rebellion and faithlessness that caused the downfall of the northern kingdom.

2. *Verses 1-7.* Taken alone, verses 1-7 are crafted around this "open mouth" and the parables and dark sayings that are forthcoming. At the heart of this short reading we find the key to the teaching of the greater psalm — the "glorious deeds," the "might," and the "wonders" that the Lord has done on Israel's behalf (v. 4). God's actions, "the works of God," are not to be forgotten (v. 7).

In these seven verses are several sets of three that are noteworthy: teaching *(torah),* parable, and dark sayings (vv. 1-2); a decree in Jacob, a law in Israel, and a command for the ancestors (v. 5); their children, children yet unborn, and these children's children (v. 6); glorious deeds of the Lord, wonders God has done, and works of God (vv. 4, 7). These triplets line up to describe the purpose and commitment of the psalm:

teaching	their children	decree in Jacob	glorious deeds of the Lord
parable	unborn children	law in Israel	wonders God has done
dark saying	children's children	command	works of God

The psalm establishes a national or cultural religious pattern of remembrance and instruction. This pattern is woven subtly and repeatedly throughout its opening section. These triplets also lead into the sharp contrast that the lectionary division of the psalm stops short of. A final triplet in verse 8, not included in the lectionary, describes the faithlessness of the people: a rebellious generation, not steadfast of heart, not faithful in spirit. This climactic criticism need not be ignored as harsh condemnation, but may be held up as the key contrast or comparison between a generation that remembers the Lord and one that does not — the former being the kind of generation that the psalm seeks to help mold and maintain.

Verses 1-7 encourage keeping the commands of the Lord and remaining in relationship with the God who has done glorious deeds on the people's behalf even as they instruct present and future generations in the memory of Israel and its God.

3. *Verses 12-16.* These five verses serve the purpose that the psalm sets out in verses 1-7: they recollect and reiterate the historical memory of the wonders the Lord has done for the people in the past. Taken as an introduction to verses 12-16, the first four verses of Psalm 78 in particular point directly and specifically to the foundational and defining action of God on behalf of the chosen people. Verse 12 picks up on the "wonders" that the Lord has done (cf. v. 4), citing the "marvels" worked in Egypt. So, in Psalm 78:12-16 we have a relatively swift summary of the exodus and wilderness years, a summary fleshed out in verses 17-55. Poetically, these verses fall into the familiar pattern of Hebrew parallelism, beginning in verse 12 with the hendiadys of Egypt and Zoan (see Exod 1:11 on Zoan; here it balances "Egypt"), the sea being divided and the waters heaped up (v. 13), the Lord leading the people in the day by a cloud and in the night by "fiery light" (v. 14), and so on.

This unit moves the reader *beyond* the commitment to instruction and remembrance to *the act itself* — recalling for them the wonders in Egypt, at the Red Sea, and during the wilderness wandering.

4. *Reading the psalm on Sundays.* Psalm 78 is well suited as a response to the first readings in the lectionary. As a companion to Exodus 17:1-7 (Nineteenth Sunday after Pentecost, Year A), which tells the story of Massah and Meribah, where the Israelites complained of thirst and where, at the Lord's command, Moses "split rocks open . . . and gave them drink abundantly as from the deep" (Ps 78:15), the exercise of memory enjoined by the psalm is fitting. And paired with Joshua 24 (Twenty-fifth Sunday after Pentecost, Year A), where Joshua challenges the people of Israel, the psalm matches the people's response well: "Far be it from us that we should forsake the LORD . . . for it is the LORD our God who brought us and our ancestors up from the land . . . who did those great signs . . . [and who] protected us along all the way" (Josh 24:16-17). But the psalm stands equally well on its own. It is a fitting exercise and invitation to teach and remember the deeds of the Lord our God, so that we might set our hope in God, not forget our God's works and God's commandments, and so live.

Karl N. Jacobson

PSALM 79

Eighteenth Sunday after Pentecost, Year C
> First Lesson: Jeremiah 8:18–9:1
> **(Psalm 79:1-9)**
> Second Lesson: 1 Timothy 2:1-7
> Gospel Lesson: Luke 16:1-13

This psalm is a *communal lament* (see the introductory essay) and exhibits typical elements of that form: *complaint* (vv. 1-5, 8c), *request* (vv. 6-8ab, 9-12), *affirmation of trust* (v. 13a), and *vow to praise* (v. 13bc). The original occasion of this psalm was likely the destruction of Jerusalem and the temple in 587 B.C.E. But the lack of specific references to that event allows the psalm to easily become a paradigm for any and all other invasions and oppressions. For Americans this psalm, and other communal laments, can be used to reflect theologically on the events of 9/11. Palestinian Christians might use this psalm to reflect upon the events of 1948 and 1967.

1. The opening stanza (vv. 1-4) describes the national trauma. The scene is grotesque and not dissimilar from what we see on the nightly news. Jerusalem has been invaded. The temple has been defiled. Bodies lie everywhere, unburied, carrion for the birds and wild animals. The streets run with blood. Everyone spits on Jerusalem's name and uses it as a swear word.

Two issues arise from this opening. First, it is important to voice what has happened. Whether it is the Holocaust, Rwanda, Sudan, or 9/11, victims must be allowed their voice, to speak the truth of their experience. To deny or minimize the horror revictimizes the survivors. Second, more than a building was destroyed. The core, meaning, and structure of Israel's life were also undone in 587. Humans develop mental "models of the world" that contain assumptions and expectations about future events. Psychologists speak about "shattered assumptions" as the essence of trauma. Trauma destroys our core assumptions about ourselves and our world. For this reason it is appropriate to describe the mood of such psalms as "disorientation."[1]

2. Two issues are intertwined in verses 5-12. The first is the plea that

---

1. See Walter Brueggemann, *The Message of the Psalms: A Theological Commentary* (Minneapolis: Augsburg, 1984), 51-121.

divine anger be turned against the perpetrators. Verses 5-7, 10b, and 12 raise the issue of vengeance and revenge. Shame, or the loss of honor, creates the need for revenge. When people are humiliated, they feel that they have to lash back. "Getting even" expresses how one satisfies the need for revenge (cf. Gen 4:15; Judg 16:28; Esther 8:13). Revenge means seeking a kind of cosmic, primal balance, restoring equilibrium to one's sense of dignity and honor. It is an issue of justice. Injury should not go unanswered.[2] The argument of this psalm reflects this dynamic: the slaughter of God's saints and the defilement of God's temple shamed God (cf. Deut 32:43; Jer 50:28; 51:36). The petition that God do to the perpetrators as they have done to others is a way to restore balance. It is a kind of justice for the victims.

It is important that we acknowledge our feelings of revenge because as long as there are injuries, there will be desire for vengeance. Certainly after 9/11 many advocated "bombing Afghanistan back to the Stone Age." Americans felt a loss of honor, which needed to be restored. There needed to be justice for the victims. The question is, what do we do with these feelings? Can we respond to pain without inflicting further pain? Is the "eye for an eye" style of justice the only option (see the essay on Ps 137)? This psalm does not answer those questions beyond telling us to take it to the Lord in prayer. The request is made to God. It is now up to *God* to act. How God will do this is unknown. But this psalm prays that it happen "before their eyes." Israel wants to know that balance has been restored. But in the end all we can do is pray; but even then there is no guarantee of God's response.

The second issue at work in verses 5-12 is deliverance and forgiveness for the victims (vv. 8-10a, 11). The thought in these verses follows the traditional prophetic viewpoint that Jerusalem's destruction is divine punishment for Israel's sins. Deliverance is therefore linked with forgiveness. The people make two petitions of Yahweh. The first is "do not remember." In Psalm 77:9 the psalmist bewails that God has forgotten to be gracious and wants God's memory restored. And yet, at the same time that we want God to remember us in our distress, we want God not to remember the sins that may have led to that distress in the first place. "Forgive our sins" finds echoes in the Lord's Prayer. The Hebrew word means "to cover over." We joke about "it's not the crime, it's

2. See Laura Blumenfeld, *Revenge: A Story of Hope* (New York: Simon and Schuster, 2002).

the cover-up." But that is the essence of this petition. We want God to reclaim the garbage dump by covering it over and restoring its original condition.

In forgiveness, Israel then seeks deliverance "speedily." When we are in desperate need we ask God to be our help. The Helper is one who has the resources and ability to provide what is needed. The second petition, "deliver us," evokes the exodus (see Exod 3:8; 6:6; 18:8, 10). The word has connotations of being snatched up from one place and put in another, to be taken from a place of danger to one of safety (cf. Zech 3:2). The motivation for these petitions is God's honor. If Israel is not delivered, the nations will question the Lord's existence.

These twin themes of vengeance and compassion in verses 5-12 result in a theology that claims that God is the God of *our* salvation and *their* destruction, which is reinforced in verses 11-12. It is assumed that those who are imprisoned and doomed to die (cf. Ps 102:20) are God's people, the flock of God's pasture. They can rely on the biblical tradition that God releases those imprisoned (Pss 68:6; 107:10-16; 142:7; Isa 42:7; 49:9; 61:1; cf. Luke 4:18) but judges their enemies sevenfold.

The proclamation of this message requires great care. On the one hand, victims of human-inflicted trauma need to hear that God will right things. Those imprisoned need to hear the hope of release, and those whose blood has been poured out need to hear the hope that their injury will not go unanswered. On the other hand, the message might easily become the justification for intolerance. For example, it is possible to imagine both the religious right and the religious left claiming that the other side is the equivalent of the nations, laying the country in ruins. Each side sees itself as the faithful who have given their entire lives to public service and whose good works have been defiled by the others' lying. And each side claims the other has made the term "Christian" a term of derision because of the beliefs they cling to. And so each side petitions God for its deliverance and prays for sevenfold vengeance upon the other. So in addition to praying this song as hope when we have been victims, we should pray that God forgives those times when we ourselves have been the enemy of God's people.

The selection of verses in the lectionary stops at verse 9, which deletes the worst of the vengeance verses. A serious pastoral question is whether this editing lessens feelings of vengeance or only conceals them.

Nancy R. Bowen

PSALM 80

Fourth Sunday of Advent, Year A
First Lesson: Isaiah 7:10-16
(Psalm 80:1-7, 17-19)
Second Lesson: Romans 1:1-7
Gospel Lesson: Matthew 1:18-25

First Sunday of Advent, Year B
First Lesson: Isaiah 64:1-9
(Psalm 80:1-7, 17-19)
Second Lesson: 1 Corinthians 1:3-9
Gospel Lesson: Mark 13:24-37

Fourth Sunday of Advent, Year C
First Lesson: Micah 5:2-5a
(Luke 1:47-55 or **Psalm 80:1-7**)
Second Lesson: Hebrews 10:5-10
Gospel Lesson: Luke 1:39-45, (46-55)

Thirteenth Sunday after Pentecost, Year C
First Lesson: Isaiah 5:1-7
(Psalm 80:1-2, 8-19)
Second Lesson: Hebrews 11:29–12:2
Gospel Lesson: Luke 12:49-56

This psalm is a *communal lament* (see the introductory essay). References to Israel, Joseph, Ephraim, Benjamin, and Manasseh have led commentators to view this psalm as a response to the destruction of the northern kingdom, which would make it a companion piece to Psalm 79. But, unlike Psalm 79, the focus is not on one occasion of disaster. Instead, the psalm encompasses ongoing oppression. The people of Psalm 80 are chronically downcast and suffer constant aggression from hostile forces. A contemporary parallel might be the "war on terror" and how we pray in the midst of protracted conflict.

The psalm opens immediately with petitions. The first stanza (vv. 1-2) consists of four petitions. The situation is not yet described, but clearly there is trouble. The imperatives imply their opposites. God is deaf — unable to hear their plea — and dark and weak — unable to help. Yahweh needs to pay attention and do something.

The second stanza (vv. 4-6) outlines the trouble: God is angry with his people. As a result, God's people exist on a diet of tears instead of God's satisfying provisions (v. 5). The question that troubles the psalmist is "how long" must the intolerable be tolerated.

The third stanza (vv. 8-18) expands on the trouble. A parable of a vine is the poetic device for making the complaint (cf. Isa 5:1-7). The imagery of Israel as a vine is well known in the Bible (Gen 49:22; Isa 27:2-6; Jer 2:21; 12:10; Ezek 15:1-8; 19:10-14; Hos 10:1; cf. John 15:1-6). The parable states the complaint in the before/after structure that is typical of lament. *Before,* the vine was great and magnificent — there was a great nation. *After,* the vine is reduced to forage for wild beasts — the nation is plundered by enemies (vv. 8-13). In another petition (v. 14) the demands made of God are arranged chiastically.

> "turn again"
>> "look down"
>> "see"
> "have regard"

The point is that God needs to give to this vine the attention it sorely needs (cf. Isa 63:15).

Verse 16 is difficult. The first clause describes the situation — the vine is destroyed. The second clause may be an imprecation against the enemies (so NRSV). But the "they" is ambiguous and could also refer to Israel ("they [i.e., Israel] perish at the rebuke of your countenance"), which would indicate that the devastation of the vineyard is ultimately at Yahweh's hand. This latter option actually fits the pattern of alternating petition and description of situation in this psalm better than the former. This would mean that both verse 4 and verse 16 argue that Israel's real problem is Yahweh's anger. Verse 6 and the parable blame human enemies for Israel's trouble. But the problem is one and the same since divine judgment is mediated through human enemies.

The petitions focus on different aspects of the divine-human relationship as motivation for God to act. Verses 1-2 appeal to the shepherd's care for the sheep. Verses 14-15 appeal to the vinedresser to tend the vine. The final petition (v. 17) makes appeal to the obligations of a sovereign for a vassal. The petition is for God's "hand" (or power) to be on the one "at your right hand." The phrase evokes Ephraim, who was blessed by Jacob's right hand (Gen 48:14, 17, 18). Likewise, Benjamin is literally "son of the right hand." This is the place of honor next to the king (cf. 1 Kings 2:19). The phrase "you made strong for yourself" echoes the choosing of Joshua, whose name means "Yahweh saves" and which is the Hebrew equivalent of Jesus (Deut 31:23; Josh 1:6-7). Later Jewish tradition interpreted verses 17-19 in a messianic sense, and verse 17 can be understood as referring to a future condition. This final petition can be interpreted as an appeal for God to strengthen the king (note the association of the king with the vine in Ezek 19:10-14). However, the psalm as a whole focuses, not on the king, but on "your people." Therefore the psalm is not an abstract plea for empowering the nation's leader. That empowerment is for the sake and well-being of the nation as a whole.

The psalm closes with a vow presented in parallel "if/then" clauses: (1) if you let your hand (an idiom of power) be upon Ephraim, then we will not backslide; (2) if you bring us back to life, then we will call on your name.

There is no mention of repentance in this psalm. Instead, it is a bold promise of obedience — but one that is conditional on survival.

The petition "Restore us, O (LORD) God (of hosts); / let your face shine, that we may be saved" (vv. 3, 7, 19) functions as the refrain and main point of this psalm. "Restore" (literally, "cause to turn") can range in meaning from the physical return from exile to spiritual rebirth. God's shining face is a sign of favor and blessing (see Ps 4:6 and especially Num 6:24-26), while in a time of anger God's face will be hidden (e.g., Pss 10:11; 13:1; 30:7). Together, these two things constitute salvation.

Throughout the psalm appeal is made to God's power and ability to save. It is the shepherd who leads the flock from danger to safety (see Exod 15:13; Ps 23). The phrase "enthroned upon the cherubim" evokes the image of God as King (cf. Ps 99:1; 1 Sam 4:4; 2 Sam 6:2; Ezek 10:1-20; see also fig. 9), as does the imagery of the power of God's right hand. "God of hosts [ṣĕbā'ōt]" (vv. 4, 7, 14, 19) is literally "God of armies" and reflects the power of God to direct battles (see 1 Sam 17:45; 2 Sam 5:10; Ps 59:5; Isa 2:12). If Israel is to survive this conflict, it will be through God's power and not its own.

The psalmist's question of "how long" is never answered. But regardless of how long, survival is clearly contingent upon affirmation of God as both Judge and Redeemer (cf. Exod 34:6-7).

The lections in different seasons use different portions of this psalm.

In Advent (Year A, B, C) the psalm selections, along with the other lections, focus on the petition of God to save. In the time after Pentecost (Year C), the focus is on disobedience that leads to judgment.

Nancy R. Bowen

PSALM 81

Ninth Sunday after the Epiphany, Year B
> First Lesson: Deuteronomy 5:12-15
> **(Psalm 81:1-10)**
> Second Lesson: 2 Corinthians 4:5-12
> Gospel Lesson: Mark 2:23–3:6

Fifteenth Sunday after Pentecost, Year C
> First Lesson: Jeremiah 2:4-13
> **(Psalm 81:1, 10-16)**
> Second Lesson: Hebrews 13:1-8, 15-16
> Gospel Lesson: Luke 14:1, 7-14

This psalm is often classified as a *liturgical sermon* comparable to Psalms 50, 75, 78, and 95.[1] The liturgical aspect is immediately evident in the opening call to worship (vv. 1-4a). This call has four aspects, which appear in sets of three. First, those assembled are *commanded to sing* to God ("sing aloud," "shout for joy," "raise a song"). Second, *instruments* are to accompany the song ("tambourine" [literally, hand drum], "sweet lyre with the harp," "trumpet" [literally, *shofar*]; see figs. 6-7).

(Note that "tambourine" is an inaccurate and anachronistic translation. The tambourine was not a musical instrument until the medieval period. The instrument in question, the hand drum, was primarily played by women in the context of celebrations of victory in battle [see Exod 15:20; Judg 11:34; 1 Sam 18:6]. By extension, then, the appearance of this word indicates the presence of women in texts like Genesis 31:27; 1 Samuel 10:5; 2 Samuel 6:5; Isaiah 5:12; 24:8; 30:32; Jeremiah 31:4; Psalms 149:3; 150:4;

---

1. Erhard Gerstenberger, *Psalms, Part 2, and Lamentations*, FOTL 15 (Grand Rapids: Eerdmans, 2001), 109-11; Marvin E. Tate, *Psalms 51–100*, WBC 20 (Dallas: Word, 1990), 321.

and Job 21:12. This in turn suggests that at times the act of worship was inclusive of women who played key roles in the leadership of the service.)

Third is the *occasion* for this call ("new moon," "full moon," "festal day"). The fourth aspect of the call concerns its *reason* ("a statute," "an ordinance," "a decree"). This last item raises the issue at the center of this psalm: obedience. These three terms appear together in Deuteronomy 4:45 and 6:20. The implication is that worship is not just something nice to do or to fill the time on Sunday morning. Worship is essential to covenant obedience.

The preacher in this psalm is God, whose "sermon" appears in verses 6-16. God is introduced by a worship leader who speaks of hearing "a voice I had not known" (v. 5c), probably in the sense of not previously understanding its full meaning. What follows is a historical recital of God's wonders and mighty works in the exodus and wilderness (cf. Ps 77:11-12). The sermon emphasizes what God did for Israel.

- "I relieved" — The imagery of the "yoke" and carrying baskets of bricks and straw evokes the oppression in Egypt, from which God gives relief.
- "I rescued" — This condenses Israel's experiences in the wilderness and their complaining against the lack of food and water (Exod 15:22-26; 16:2-15; 17:2-7; Num 11:4-6, 31-32; 20:13). God's response underlies the theology of complaint psalms. The need for complaint arises when the pray-er cries out and God *does not* rescue (e.g., Pss 22:1-2; 69:3; 88:13-14)!
- "I answered" — The imagery of the "secret place of thunder" evokes the giving of the torah at Sinai (Exod 19:16, 18; 20:18).
- "I tested" — Exodus claims that Israel tested Yahweh at Meribah by doubting whether God could quench their thirst in the wilderness (Exod 17:1-16; Num 20:2-13). This psalm claims that it was really Yahweh who tested Israel, to discern if they would be obedient or not (cf. Exod 16:4; 20:20).

In the light of all that God has done, God calls the people to hear (v. 8). The Hebrew root for "hear" is repeated five times in the psalm: verses 5 ("I hear"), 8 ("hear," "listen to"), 11 ("did not listen"), 13 ("would listen"). The imperative in verse 8, "Hear, O my people," is reminiscent of Deuteronomy 6:4, "Hear, O Israel." Hearing is an important theme in Deuteronomy and is integrally related to obedience. If one hears, *really* hears, God's word, then one *does* God's word. The failure to hear/listen leads to disobedience. Therefore the prophets pronounce judgment against those who "have ears but do not hear" (Isa 42:20; Jer 5:21; Ezek 12:2; cf. Mark 8:18). That this might be a problem in this psalm is reflected in God's admonishment and plaintive longing for the people to listen. In response to God's acts of salvation, God calls us to live life on divine terms. Yet instead of the joyful song of obedience, we turn a deaf ear. Why is listening so difficult?

Verses 9-10 echo, but do not repeat verbatim, the demand of the first commandment (Exod 20:2-3). The "testing" between God and Israel in the wilderness was over whether God would provide Israel with sustenance and whether Israel would follow Yahweh alone. The essence of that conflict is summed up in these verses. The God who frees calls Israel to worship. Israel's obedience brings forth the God who feeds.

Yet God's people did not listen to God's voice and as a result they "would not submit." This is an unfortunate translation. The Hebrew is, literally, "Israel did not love me." How poignant, when Israel has been called to love God with their whole being (Deut 6:5)! "Love" in Hebrew is much more than warm, sentimental feelings. It is covenant language. It implies commitment to the other. And since Israel will not listen to God's counsel, God permits them to follow (literally, "walk") their own counsel — with undoubtedly disastrous results. If only they would walk (or follow) in God's ways, how different things would be. Instead of distress, Israel would find its enemies subdued and its foes turned away.

The theme of sustenance closes the psalm. The wilderness story ends when the people enter the Promised Land, the land of "milk and honey." And that is how this psalm ends. To love God and walk in God's ways will take us to that promised place where we are fed with the finest wheat and that sweet "honey in the rock."

It might be easy for worshipers today to distance themselves from Psalm 81 by claiming their obedience in contrast to Israel's disobedience. However, the point of this psalm is to remind *the congregation* that *they* are Israel. For ancient and modern congregations the enemies and foes of verse 14 might be actual, physical enemies. But there are also (and always) the enemies within ourselves such as sexism and racism. If we were obedient, how much more quickly God might defeat those ancient foes and we might feed on the sweet honey of equality and justice.

The lectionary's selection of verses, along with the other lections in Year B, reinforces the association between God's act of liberation, worship, and obedience. The first lesson is the Deuteronomic version of the commandment to "observe the Sabbath," which invokes the exodus as motivation. The God who *frees* calls us to *worship*. The Gospel lesson raises the issue of the proper interpretation of obedience. The Pharisees claimed that Jesus was disobedient in what he did on the Sabbath. How do we determine what it means to observe the Sabbath?

The lectionary's selection of verses and the other lections for Year C echo the themes of disobedience and feeding. The first lesson is also a divine sermon that questions why the people have forsaken the God who freed them. The Gospel lesson suggests that all are eligible to feed (whether on God's word or on literal food). Those on the margins are most in need of hearing God's liberating word and having their open mouths filled.

Nancy R. Bowen

Psalm 82

Eighth Sunday after Pentecost, Year C
    First Lesson: Amos 7:7-17
    (Psalm 82)
    Second Lesson: Colossians 1:1-14
    Gospel Lesson: Luke 10:25-37

Psalm 82 is rife with ancient mythopoeic imagery and thought. As such, it will need some explication and interpretation if it is to be used to maximum benefit (and minimum damage) in contemporary communities of faith.

The first important concept that must be understood is "the divine council" (v. 1). This notion is not uncommon in the OT but is somewhat odd in the contemporary context. The divine council is elaborated perhaps most fully in 1 Kings 22, where the prophet Micaiah ben Imlah recounts being taken into the Lord's heavenly council, where "all the host of heaven" stood around the throne (1 Kings 22:19). But the notion is also present elsewhere, for example in Isaiah 6, where Isaiah's call is invited by the Lord's question: "Whom shall I send, and who will go *for us?*" (Isa 6:8). Almost proverbially the prophets enjoyed access to this council, so that Amos 3:7 can state:

Surely the Lord GOD does nothing,
without revealing his secret to his servants the prophets.

Traces of the heavenly assembly are found elsewhere as well (e.g., Jer 23:18, 22; Job 1:6-12; 2:1-6), even in the Psalms (see 89:7; cf. 95:3; 96:4). It lies behind the "we" language famous in the opening chapters of Genesis (1:26; 3:22; 11:7) and may be reflected in the divine title Yahweh Sebaoth, "LORD of Hosts" — those hosts probably being the heavenly armies created by the Lord.

The image is thus of a pantheon, a kind of divine bureaucracy or primitive democracy. God stands as head of the pantheon, president of the assembly in Psalm 82:1a. The council members are also portrayed as divine, called here "gods" (*'ĕlōhîm;* vv. 1, 6) and "sons of the Most High" (*bĕnê 'elyôn,* v. 6). It is clear from the rest of the psalm that these "lesser gods" bear responsibility for various duties and tasks, perhaps even nation groups (see v. 8). The psalm stands close in conception, therefore, to Deuteronomy 32:8, a piece of old and obscure poetry that indicates that "the Most High" (*'elyôn;* note the same term in Ps 82:6) apportioned (the same verbal root is used in Ps 82:8 [NRSV: "belong"]) the nations and divided humankind, fixing the boundaries of the peoples "according to the number of the gods" (so LXX and Qumran; see the textual notes in NRSV). The next verse indicates that the Lord chose Israel ("Jacob"; Deut 32:9). Other brief and tantalizing (but equally opaque) passages in Deuteronomy indicate that the same did not hold true for other nations, however. These other nations were evidently thought to have been apportioned by Yahweh to other deities (see Deut 4:19; 29:26). Be that as it may, the emphasis in passages such as these is not on these other deities, whoever they may be. Instead, the point is quite the opposite: Israel is not to have anything to do with any other than the Lord. Even if God does have "other stories,"[1] Israel is not to play a role in those, but instead must remain loyal — and exclusively so, as Deuteronomy loves to point out — to the Lord.

If this is an adequate reconstruction and if it is operative in the background of Psalm 82, the psalmist is about to turn the scenario on its head. God has called this special session of the divine council, but it is hardly a run-of-the-mill, business-as-usual meeting. Far from it! The

---

1. See Patrick D. Miller, *Israelite Religion and Biblical Theology: Collected Essays,* JSOTSup 267 (Sheffield: Sheffield Academic, 2000), 593-602.

opening verse makes it clear that this meeting is for judgment (√*špṭ*; v. 1b). In verses 2-4 God issues the indictment. The gods have failed to judge (√*špṭ*) justly, but have shown partiality to the wicked (literally, "lifted the face of the wicked" — a sign of approval; see Gen 4:7). This is a troubling, even *lamentable*, situation. The "how long" language is often used in lament contexts (see Pss 6:3; 74:10; 80:4; 90:13; 94:3). Surely the gods should know better! God proceeds to command them to do what they should have been doing all along. First, to "judge [√*špṭ*] the weak and the orphan" (v. 3a). The NRSV's "give justice" hides the fact that the same verbal root is used here as in the previous two verses. Since the gods have failed to do (v. 2) what they should have done and must in fact do (v. 3) — namely, *judge* rightly — God must stand in *judgment* upon them (v. 1; cf. 58:1-2).

The gods have also failed to "maintain the right of the lowly and the destitute" (v. 3b); God commands that this deficiency be set right. God's imperatives continue in verse 4 — the weak and needy must be delivered and rescued — but the commands just further the case, continuing the indictment against the gods and their failures. This is all the more apparent when it is realized that protection of the weak and needy was something widely held to be a sign of legitimate authorities in ancient Israel (e.g., Exod 22:22; Lev 19:15; Deut 1:16; 24:17; 27:19) and the broader ancient Near East.[2] The gods, in short, are "wicked powers."[3]

The scene painted is thus clear and emphatic: the Bible's long-standing concern with the poor, needy, and oppressed is again on display here, with God yet again taking the side of the downtrodden and standing in judgment against the most powerful (here the gods), who have taken their stand on the other side: with big business, power politics, money-market tycoons, shady judges. By its use of repetition and synonymous terminology, the psalm is unambiguous about who is in the right and who is in the wrong. The gods' doom is imminent.

(Note that the issue of which side one is on and which side has ultimate authority is also very much at issue in the first lesson, Amos 7:7-17, which recounts the standoff between Amos and Amaziah, the high priest of Bethel. Amaziah is resolutely an insider, the king's crony [see vv. 10, 13].

---

2. See Hans-Joachim Kraus, *Psalms 60–150: A Continental Commentary* (Minneapolis: Fortress, 1993), 156; further Moshe Weinfeld, *Social Justice in Ancient Israel and in the Ancient Near East* (Minneapolis: Fortress, 1995).

3. Kraus, *Psalms 60–150,* 157.

Amos, by contrast, cannot claim sacerdotal or prophetic lineage [v. 14], but he nevertheless has the call of God and the divine word with him [v. 15; cf. vv. 7-9, 16-17]. Needless to say, it is Amos's [i.e., Yahweh's] authority that is finally and ultimately decisive [v. 17]!)

Despite the psalm's earlier clarity, verse 5 *is* somewhat ambiguous. The first line could refer to the weak and needy, to the wicked (the nearest antecedent), or to the failed and failing gods. All are possible depending on the precise valence of "not having knowledge or understanding" and "walking around in darkness" — a point that is not altogether certain (cf., e.g., Isa 44:18; 50:10; Jon 4:11). Given the direct address to the gods in verses 2-4 and 6-7, they may be the least likely referent, since verse 5 speaks in the third person. If the poor are referenced, then it is all the more obvious that they need help given their pitiful condition. Whatever the case, the second line (v. 5b) makes it clear that the despicable situation described in verses 2-4 (and 5a?) is not a matter of local politicking. Instead it is fraught with cosmic significance. Let it not be forgotten that the presiding judge is God and the defendants are the gods, God's own sons (v. 6)! It is not surprising, then, to hear that "all the foundations of the earth are shaken" (v. 5b). Injustice is a *cosmic* sin with ramifications *both* in heaven and on earth.[4]

In verse 6 God issues the judgment. Though God had invested the council with their divine powers, that status is now gone, revoked in one word by God's "nevertheless." In a kind of bizarre twist on the Eden fiasco (see Gen 3), the lesser gods are now made to die like mortals (literally, "like *'ādām*") and to fall (a euphemism for death, especially in battle) like any prince (v. 7; see NRSV text note). The Lord himself will have no other gods before him (cf. Exod 20:3); these pseudogods must go, as they have proven unfit and unsuitable for the job. This meeting of the divine council is, as it were, "permanently adjourned."[5] The gods are dead — literally and figuratively.

The psalmist's voice returns in the final verse. The psalmist no longer describes God's heavenly judgment (v. 1); instead, the psalmist begs (better: commands) that God do the same *on earth* (v. 8). "Rise up," an imperative, may imply that God has been sitting (contrast God's standing

4. Cf. J. Clinton McCann, Jr., "The Book of Psalms: Introduction, Commentary, and Reflections," in *NIB*, 4:1007: "Where injustice exists, the world — at least the world as God intends it — falls apart."

5. McCann, "The Book of Psalms," 4:1006; cf. James L. Mays, *Psalms,* Interpretation (Louisville: John Knox, 1994), 270.

[NRSV: "taken his place"] in v. 1, which "indicates that a very important matter is being decided"),[6] or at the very least, that God has been in repose. "Judge" (√*špṭ*), another imperative, is the same verb used repeatedly in the beginning of the psalm. Its use here echoes that earlier situation, perhaps indicating that the psalmist is facing the same situation: one of injustice, neglect, and oppression. The psalmist, that is, may be one of the weak and needy overlooked by the gods. The focus of verse 8, however, is resolutely on "the earth" *(hā'āreṣ)* and "all the nations" *(kol-haggôyim)* — terms rich with geopolitical significance. God's rule is in process, not yet fully accomplished. But the psalmist prays for it with the equivalent of "Your kingdom come."[7]

Given the first seven verses, it would seem that the psalmist believes the cosmos to work in this way: injustice on earth is due, at least in part, to unjust cosmic rule, attributable to negligent members of the divine council. At the very least, this is how the psalm images matters. Whatever the case, God can set such matters right, with just one meeting and just one word, and the psalmist implores God to do so. Even if the psalmist's picture remains somewhat foreign in the modern context, the close connections drawn throughout the psalm between heaven and earth must not go unnoticed. God is the judge and the gods are the accused, but the victims are altogether earthly — salt of the earth, to be precise. Moreover, elsewhere Scripture knows of the problems posed by rival gods or, at the very least, other interests that parade as divine, threatening Israel's sole allegiance to the Lord. There is, in fact, a long-standing tradition that interprets the "gods" of Psalm 82 as human judges or officials.[8] Today, the CEO's boardroom or the judge's chambers may not typically be thought of as a meeting place of the gods, but they are no less powerful, and often oppressively so, especially when the interests of the poor and needy are at issue. Psalm 82 images an alternative universe: the powerful, the "gods" of the earth and of nations, are granted their authority from the Lord. If and when (!) they misuse such power and do not do what gods are supposed to do — seeing to the rights of the weak and destitute, defending the orphan and the lowly — our Lord stands ready to indict, to judge, to revoke all power and status, to deliver death in a word. All the nations of the earth belong to the

---

6. Marvin E. Tate, *Psalms 51–100*, WBC 20 (Dallas: Word, 1990), 335.
7. See Matt 6:10; Mays, *Psalms*, 269-71; McCann, "The Book of Psalms," 4:1008.
8. See Tate, *Psalms 51–100*, 340-41; Kraus, *Psalms 60–150*, 155.

Lord (v. 8), and all concerned — both the "gods" and the nations presently in power as well as poor pray-ers like the psalmist and us readers — would do well to remember it.

Brent A. Strawn

PSALM 84

Fourteenth Sunday after Pentecost, Year B
  First Lesson: 1 Kings 8:(1, 6, 10-11), 22-30, 41-43
  (Psalm 84)
  Second Lesson: Ephesians 6:10-20
  Gospel Lesson: John 6:56-69

Both Old Testament readings for this Sunday depict the temple on Mount Zion as the locus of cult and piety in ancient Israel. In 1 Kings 8, pilgrims from across Israel have traveled to Jerusalem to witness the consecration of the sanctuary. In an address before the congregation, Solomon proclaims that Yahweh's name dwells there (1 Kings 8:1-2, 22-53). Since Yahweh uniquely inhabits the temple, he will listen and respond to prayers offered there (8:27-30, 42-43). This theology of divine presence spurred pilgrimages to Mount Zion and is reflected in several psalms — often called the Songs of Zion (Pss 46; 48; 76; 84; 87; 122; 132; cf. 137).

Psalm 84 conveys a deep desire to visit Yahweh's abode in Jerusalem. Likely composed as a hymn to accompany a pilgrimage at the autumn Festival of Tabernacles,[1] the text describes the beauty of the temple (vv. 1-4) and recounts the pilgrims' difficult but rewarding journey, culminating in an experience of God (vv. 5-7). At Mount Zion, the longing for God's presence finds fulfillment as the pilgrims pray to and extol the king of heaven, Yahweh of Hosts (vv. 8-12).

  1. *"How lovely."* In the opening verses the psalmist employs the language of *love* to describe the temple: "How *lovely* [*yĕdîdôt*] is your dwelling place" (v. 1). The use of this adjective to modify an inanimate object is

---

1. See Lev 23:33-44; Erhard Gerstenberger, *Psalms, Part 2, and Lamentations,* FOTL 15 (Grand Rapids: Eerdmans, 2001), 125-26.

unique in the Old Testament. Elsewhere the adjective describes people, and translators consistently render it "beloved," according to its root √*ydd*, "to love" (see Deut 33:12; Pss 60:5; 108:6; 127:2; Isa 5:1; Jer 11:15). Love motivates this pilgrimage, and the psalmist's yearning for God encompasses soul, heart, and flesh (v. 2). Like the experience of love between people, the longing for Yahweh's presence exasperates and exhilarates; the psalmist's emotions are so charged that he alternately faints and sings for joy (v. 2).

Envisioning the beloved temple, the psalmist describes the birds that populate its courts (vv. 3-4). With a striking juxtaposition of images, he recalls delicate swallows finding shelter for their chicks near the altars of Yahweh, where the very fire of God consumes sacrifices. Even these tiny creatures receive Yahweh's protection and blessing. Following the description of the birds, we should understand the benediction on "those dwelling in Yahweh's house" to include both human and avian worshipers (v. 4), for at the temple continuous birdsongs play counterpoint to the pilgrims' hymns (see Ps 148:7-13).

2. *"From strength to strength."* The second stanza, introduced by another benediction, recounts the pilgrims' progress through the difficult valley of Baca (v. 6). Scholars disagree about the location (and existence) of such a valley along a pilgrim route to Jerusalem. Regardless, the textual references suggest that Baca — whatever its location — was an exceedingly dry place, sharing its name with the trees that grew there.[2] "Baca" (Hebrew *bākā'*) may also be a wordplay on the Hebrew root *bkh*, meaning "to weep." Thus, the dry valley of Baca may have evoked an image of a valley of tears.

As a pilgrim's strength flags in these difficult environs, Yahweh provides and sustains. Springs bubble up at the feet of the pilgrims and autumn rains drench the thirsty valley from above (v. 6). The transformation shows that Yahweh's reach extends beyond the temple confines, drawing in pilgrims with the "highways to Zion" in their hearts (v. 5). Yahweh brings them ever closer and their courage gathers: "they go from strength to strength" (v. 7).

3. *"Better is one day in your courts."* The psalm's final stanza focuses on the heavenly king and his earthly representative. Commissioned by Yahweh to protect the people, the Jerusalemite sovereign is called God's "anointed" and the people's "shield" (v. 9). The prayer fits naturally within this song of Zion given the central role the king would have

---

2. Marvin E. Tate, *Psalms 51–100*, WBC 20 (Dallas: Word, 1990), 353 n. 7.

played in the temple cult (see 1 Kings 8). Indeed, he likely participated in the pilgrimage the psalm describes.[3]

The concluding verses of the psalm glorify Yahweh, the divine king, and proclaim the immeasurable value of even the briefest moment in his presence. The psalmist employs a common trope from wisdom traditions — the "better than" formula — to convey that God's nearness transforms the value of time and status.[4] One day with Yahweh, the psalmist claims, is better than a thousand days away from him. Likewise, low status in the presence of God, namely, standing at the *edge* of God's house, is better than high status apart from him, living *inside* the cozy domiciles of the wicked.[5]

Throughout the psalm the pilgrim employs royal epithets to establish the kingship of Yahweh as a central theme. In addition to the outright attribution of the title "king" to Yahweh in verse 3, the appellation "LORD of Hosts" (*yhwh ṣĕbā'ôt*) appears four times in the psalm's twelve verses (vv. 1, 3, 8, 12), more frequently than in any other biblical text. Among those who first sang this psalm, this divine name would have conjured images of God as the commander of the armies of heaven and the divine king, seated upon the cherubim throne in the temple (see fig. 9).[6] The further descriptions of Yahweh as "sun" and "shield" in verse 11 express Yahweh's heavenly dominion and sovereign protection.

Reflection on this characterization of God reveals surprising contrasts. Yahweh, the *heavenly* king, nevertheless chooses to dwell among the people in a particular, *physical* structure. Further, Yahweh's protection extends not just to the king, but also to those who journey toward him and call on his name (cf. 1 Kings 8:41-43), and even to the tiny creatures inhabiting his earthly abode. Yahweh's terrific power and willingness to protect compel the pilgrim ultimately to declare:

O LORD of Hosts,
blessed is the one who trusts in you. (v. 12)

4. *Psalm 84 and Christian worship.* In both church and concert hall, one of the most popular musical settings of Psalm 84 is Johannes Brahms's

---

3. Tate, *Psalms 51–100*, 360.
4. On the formulaic language, see Gerstenberger, *Psalms, Part 2*, 125.
5. James L. Mays, *Psalms*, Interpretation (Louisville: John Knox, 1994), 274.
6. See 1 Sam 4:4; 2 Sam 6:2; and T. N. D. Mettinger, "YHWH Sabaoth — the Heavenly King on the Cherubim Throne," in *Studies in the Period of David and Solomon*, ed. T. Ishida (Winona Lake, Ind.: Eisenbrauns, 1982), 135-36; cf. also 1 Kings 6:27.

treatment of the text within his choral masterpiece, *Ein deutsches Requiem* (1868). Brahms's richly harmonized melody swells and surges, augmenting the power of the text to convey the pilgrim's desire for God's presence. By setting Psalm 84 within a requiem — a mass for the dead — Brahms has recast the pilgrimage to the temple as the individual's journey from life into death. Thus the "dwelling place" of God (v. 1) becomes *heaven* where God communes with the saints, instead of an earthly locale where living pilgrims meet in worship. Understandably, many sermons on Psalm 84 adopt this spiritualized reading, since the Jerusalem temple was destroyed in antiquity and pilgrimages are relatively infrequent in modern Protestant Christianity.

Yet this reading should not be the primary one, since it tends to undercut the plain sense of the psalm. Above all else, Psalm 84 proclaims the supreme good of experiencing God's presence through corporate worship. Today, because of the indwelling Spirit of Jesus, God abides with us. We have witnessed God's salvation, and like the ancient pilgrims, God's presence draws us together and into praise.

Joel M. LeMon

PSALM 85

Second Sunday of Advent, Year B
First Lesson: Isaiah 40:1-11
(Psalm 85:1-2, 8-13)
Second Lesson: 2 Peter 3:8-15a
Gospel Lesson: Mark 1:1-8

Tenth Sunday after Pentecost, Year C
First Lesson: Hosea 1:2-10
(Psalm 85)
Second Lesson: Colossians 2:6-15, (16-19)
Gospel Lesson: Luke 11:1-13

The lectionary makes double use of Psalm 85. Year B links verses 1-2, 8-13 with the Advent prophecy from Isaiah 40 (used by John the Baptist in Mark 1 to proclaim his identity and mission: to prepare the way and to ready a holy people for the coming of God in the Messiah), and with the eschatological passage in 2 Peter 3, which prepares God's people for a final coming, when God fulfills the hope of every godly heart: "a new heavens and a new earth in which righteousness dwells" (2 Pet 3:13; cf. Ps 85:10-13).

Year C uses the psalm for Pentecost season, where the coming of God as Holy Spirit is proclaimed, prayed for, and praised. Its interaction with the three lessons is more complicated than in Year B. The Hosea lesson is both grim and hopeful. A sinful people, which had received mercy time and again, is finally rejected, and the people of Yahweh are no longer his "son[s]" (cf. Exod 4:22; Hos 11:1 = Matt 2:15c [of Jesus!]). Instead, their names are a reversal of Yahweh's covenantal attributes (vv. 6, 8-9; cf. Exod 6:7; 34:6-7), so that he is no longer their Yahweh (*lō' 'ehyeh* in Hos 1:9b is a negative pun on God's name in Exod 3:15). But in the end, "Not My People" will be "'Sons' of the Living God" (Hos 1:10) — a work that Paul attributes to the Holy Spirit (cf. Rom 8:9-17, where "sons," including women, are heirs).

Luke 11 reminds us that the great issue in all this is the coming of God's kingdom, for which Christ teaches us to pray. At the lesson's end, the prayer for the Holy Spirit — a request God will not refuse (Luke 11:13; cf. Matt 7:11) — is actually a prayer for the kingdom. For in Luke's theology all the promises and purposes of God are fulfilled in the Holy Spirit, who makes Christ and his kingdom present to us.[1]

Psalm 85 probably comes from the early postexilic period, when the hard realities of life after the return to Judea did not match the glorious promises of restoration made by exilic prophecies such as Isaiah 40–55. The first part of the psalm (vv. 1-3) apparently looks back at the initial joy of that period (see Ps 126) and the forgiveness that went with it (cf. Isa 40:1-2). God's judgment was accomplished, his anger withdrawn. (An alternate reading, as in NJPS, takes the verbs in verses 1-3 as "prophetic perfects," referring to future joy.)

But in the psalm's second part (vv. 4-7), the present difficulties of life lead the psalmist to question whether God is again angry with his people. This is a natural human move: when things go wrong, we ask an almighty God (who could make things right), "Why? Are you displeased with us?" Even the innocent faithful do this, for trouble drives them to question God (note Ps 44). Because humanity's relationship with God is personal

---

1. See Oliver O'Donovan, *Resurrection and Moral Order: An Outline for Evangelical Ethics,* 2nd ed. (Grand Rapids: Eerdmans, 1994).

and cosmic, human suffering always involves God personally. The verbs in verses 4-7 are patterned as a chiasm (imperative, question, question, imperative), and they repeat a key word from verse 1b (*šûb*, "return, restore, do again"), as if to say, "Do again, O Lord, what you did for your people in the past. Will you be angry forever? Will you not make your people live again (v. 6a; cf. Col 2:13), so that people can rejoice in their God? Let us experience (literally, 'see') your covenant love *(ḥesed)* and salvation."

God's wrath and judgment are problems for all humans.[2] Modern people find them especially difficult, perhaps because we think of anger in emotional terms, as the opposite of love. In the Bible generally, though God's anger is mysterious, it is not irrational but measured and righteous, in keeping with the Lord's loving-kindness. In fact, justice is the flip side of God's love, and the two are inseparable. God's righteous anger is an appropriate response to genuine evil, which destroys the people and planet that God loves. What parent would not be properly angry at the violation and brutalization of a child he or she loves? Moreover, God's anger and judgment are for restoration of good at the end.[3]

The last part of the psalm (vv. 8-13) is a prophetic answer to the people's prayers in the first two parts. It declares God's ultimate purposes for his "faithful" people and for those who "fear the Lord." The "faithful" are the *ḥāsîdîm,* those who manifest the same steadfast, covenant-keeping "loving-kindness" *(ḥesed)* that is basic to God's character (see v. 10; cf. Exod 34:6). They remain faithful in spite of experiences that seem to contradict God's promises of blessing. In biblical shorthand, those who "fear the Lord" live the totality of their ordinary lives in service of God.[4] Verse 8c is difficult: NRSV follows the Septuagint, but the Hebrew text may be read, "But let them not return to folly" (so NIV). That is, as in times past, future sinful foolishness may for a time thwart God's ultimately unstoppable blessing.

The prophetic blessing in verses 8-13 is one of the loveliest in Scripture. It promises the people what they pray for (v. 8)! Its scope is as deep and wide as creation itself, or, to use NT language, the "all things" of God's kingdom (see Matt 7:11 and Luke 11:13). The psalmist describes this

2. See Erich Zenger, *A God of Vengeance? Understanding the Psalms of Divine Wrath* (Louisville: Westminster John Knox, 1996).

3. See Hos 1; see further Abraham Heschel's classic discussion of the pathos of God in *The Prophets,* 2 vols. (New York: Harper and Row, 1975).

4. See Al Wolters, "Nature and Grace in the Interpretation of Proverbs 31:10-31," *CTJ* 19 (1984): 153-56.

blessing by using basic, all-inclusive, biblical concepts: *šālôm,* "peace/well-being"; *yĕšû'â,* "salvation"; *kābôd,* "glory"; *ḥesed* and *'emet,* "steadfast love and faithfulness/truth"; *ṣedeq,* "righteousness"; and *ḥaṭṭôb,* "the good" (cf. Gen 1). These words are so basic to biblical thought (and so often mangled in modern usage) that pastor and congregation should get to know their biblical sense well over time.

But what makes this blessing so beautiful is its splendid metaphors. They make these key concepts personal, they show their cosmic scope, and they relate them to God's royal character. As in Jesus' day, "salvation" is "near" (v. 9), so that God's glory will "tent" (√*škn;* cf. John 1:14) in Israel's land (*'ereṣ,* v. 9) — which is a microcosm of God's glory filling the entire earth (*'ereṣ;* see Isa 6:3). "Steadfast love and faithfulness will meet" (v. 10), not just in God's character (Exod 34:6) but also in the experience and character of God's people — even government officials (see Prov 20:28), who, by God's grace, become like him! "Righteousness" and its fruit, *šālôm,* will "kiss" (v. 10a). Here the language of love ("kiss") reshapes our understanding of righteousness, which so often opposes it to love instead of seeing it as love's instrument for a peaceful and fruitful world. Inner "love" without righteous action is useless (Prov 27:5-6), as faith without works is dead. Faithfulness springs up from the fruitful earth, righteousness looks down from the heavens, and the earth returns to the primal "good-ness" that God made in the beginning. This will happen, finally, someday, when God himself steps into the path of our reality with righteousness as his herald before him.

Raymond C. Van Leeuwen

PSALM 86

Fifth Sunday after Pentecost, Year A
First Lesson: Genesis 21:8-21
(Psalm 86:1-10, 16-17)
Second Lesson: Romans 6:1b-11
Gospel Lesson: Matthew 10:24-39

Psalm 86, an *individual lament* (see the introductory essay), moves between urgent pleas and confident proclamations of salvation. The psalmist petitions Yahweh to hear and answer, while reaffirming their relationship through time-tested doxologies (vv. 5, 10, 15). By professing fidelity and reliance on Yahweh alone, the psalmist hopes to motivate God to reciprocate faithfulness and bring decisive action against his foes.

1. *"I am poor and needy."* The psalm begins with an extended petition marked by brief affirmations of God's certain response (vv. 1-7). The seven imperative verbs in the first six verses underscore the intensity of the psalmist's plea: hear (literally, "bend your ear"), answer (v. 1), preserve/save (v. 2), be gracious (v. 3), gladden (v. 4), give ear, attend (v. 6). Taken together, these petitions characterize Yahweh as one capable of saving, but currently unresponsive. Peppered among these pleas are short confessions of trust (vv. 5, 7) describing God's reliability. The psalmist's faith is evident not only in these confessions of trust, but also in her petitions. That the psalmist utters her cries aloud demonstrates that she has not lost faith in God, nor in the relationship between them. A bold claim concludes this section and summarizes the previous verses:

> In the day of my distress I call to you,
>   for you will answer me. (v. 7)

2. *"You are great and do extraordinary things."* Spurred by this affirmation of Yahweh's faithfulness, the psalmist praises Yahweh outright and pledges fealty to him alone in the next section (vv. 8-13). The psalmist adores Yahweh as the sole god (vv. 8, 10), whose creative power (v. 9) and extraordinary acts (v. 10) are preeminent throughout the universe. The psalmist counts himself one among the multitude honoring Yahweh (v. 9), but also claims a personal relationship with this Creator God, as he repeatedly addresses Yahweh as *"my* God" and *"my* Lord," both here (v. 12) and throughout the psalm (vv. 2, 3, 5, 8, 9, 15).

Verses 11-13 provide a fuller picture of the relationship between Yahweh and the psalmist, for unlike the string of petitions in verses 1-6, promises follow each appeal. In verse 11 the psalmist pleads for Yahweh's instruction and pledges faithfulness in return. The imperative verb "teach me" comes from the same root, *yrh,* from which comes the noun *tôrā(h),* meaning "teaching or instruction." The psalmist demonstrates her faithfulness by promising to "walk" (√*hlk*), that is, *live,* according to Yahweh's clearly established path, Yahweh's *tôrâ.*

The psalmist also pleads for a "united heart" (v. 11) — a will completely devoted to Yahweh.[1] The psalm witnesses the individual's internal struggle to hold fast to his relationship with Yahweh when it seems that God has turned from him, remaining unresponsive in this difficult time. The trouble has left the psalmist with a divided — even *broken* — heart that only Yahweh can repair.

The "day of distress" threatens to shake the psalmist's confidence, not in Yahweh's existence nor in his ability to save, but in the status of the relationship between them. To remind Yahweh of his obligations and motivate him to action, the psalmist repeatedly employs language of lordship and servitude. The psalmist addresses Yahweh as "Lord" (*'ădōnāy*) more often than any other title. The term occurs seven times (vv. 3, 4, 5, 8, 9, 12, 15) — more frequently than *'ĕlōhîm*, "God" (vv. 2, 10, 12, 14, 15), or the name "Yahweh" itself (rendered by most English translations as "the LORD," vv. 1, 6, 11, 17). Nowhere in the Psalter, in fact, does *'ădōnāy* occur with such frequency. Accordingly, the psalmist portrays himself as totally reliant on Yahweh by using the terms "your servant" (*'abděkā;* vv. 4, 16), "the son of your maidservant" (*ben 'ămātekā;* v. 16), "a devoted one" (*ḥāsîd;* v. 2), and "poor and needy" (*'ānî wĕ'ebyôn;* v. 1). The psalmist clings to Yahweh, waiting for Yahweh to confirm their relationship by saving him. That salvation will prompt full-throated, *wholehearted* praise:

> I will thank you, my Lord, my God, with *all my heart,*
> And I will glorify your name forever. (v. 12)

Most English versions translate verse 13 in the past tense, since the psalmist uses the perfect aspect of the verb to describe the saving activity of Yahweh: "*You have delivered* [√*nṣl*] my soul from the depths of Sheol" (v. 13 NRSV). This change of tense is remarkable. The following verse (v. 14) makes clear that trouble is *present*, yet the psalmist treats Yahweh's salvation as a *completed* event. The psalmist is so convinced of the future activity of Yahweh that he pronounces salvation as if it has already happened. This confidence, juxtaposed with desperate cries, is not as incongruous as it may initially appear. This back-and-forth is the rhythm of the life of faith.

3. *"Save the son of your maidservant."* On the heels of the psalmist's proclamation in verse 13, the final section of the psalm (vv. 14-16) takes

---

1. Marvin E. Tate, *Psalms 51–100,* WBC 20 (Dallas: Word, 1990), 382.

up the fervent tone of the petition from verses 1-7. Imperative verbs, pervasive in the opening section, resume here: "turn," "be gracious," "strengthen," "save" (v. 16), "show" (v. 17). The psalmist has portrayed himself throughout the psalm as Yahweh's loyal servant in great need. The enemies who threaten him are his antithesis: they are haughty and unwilling to submit to Yahweh's lordship (v. 14).

The psalmist situates her crisis in the history of Yahweh's saving activity, by employing ancient doxologies and recalling a heritage of faithfulness passed down from her mother. The psalmist invokes Yahweh as "a God merciful and gracious, / slow to anger and abounding in steadfast love and faithfulness" (v. 15 NRSV). This doxological formula conveys the community's fundamental claim about the character of Yahweh and appears in Exodus 34:6, with echoes in Numbers 14:18; Nehemiah 9:17; Psalms 103:8; 145:8; Jeremiah 32:18; Joel 2:13; and Jonah 4:2.[2] These formulas remind the psalmist that her suffering and hope of salvation, while personal, are not unique. Further, the psalmist claims a heritage of faithfulness through her mother, whom she identifies as Yahweh's maidservant (v. 16). The psalmist hopes that her legacy will further motivate Yahweh to listen and respond.

4. *God hears.* In the lectionary cycle, Psalm 86 appears along with the story of the expulsion of Hagar and Ishmael from Genesis 21:8-21. We read here of Sarah's forsaken maidservant (Gen 21:10, 13; cf. Ps 86:16) wandering in the wilderness. Out of water, she leaves her son under a bush, unable to watch him die. She sits down alone and weeps (Gen 21:16).

Several points of connection justify the binding of these texts for this Sunday's reading. Each passage describes a desperate situation: Hagar, scorned, alone, and starving in the wilderness; and the psalmist, beset by enemies who seek to kill him. Like the psalmist, Hagar can look back to an established relationship with Yahweh. An angel of the Lord had visited Hagar and promised that she, a maidservant, will be the mother of multitudes through Ishmael (Gen 16:7-15). The angel tells her, "Return to your mistress, and submit to her" (16:9). Hagar indeed returns, showing her faithfulness to Yahweh by remaining faithful to Sarai despite harsh treatment (16:6). The fact that Hagar was faithful to Yahweh makes her crisis in the wilderness even more devastating.

Both Genesis 21 and Psalm 86 vividly recount the desperate cries of

2. See Walter Brueggemann, *The Message of the Psalms: A Theological Commentary* (Minneapolis: Augsburg, 1984), 60.

Yahweh's servants. In the story of Hagar and Ishmael, God recognizes the voices of the faithful and responds to their cries. The surety of God's attention to Hagar's cries is confirmed in the very name of her son, Ishmael, which means "God hears" (Hebrew *yišmā' ['Jēl*). Indeed, *yišma' 'ēl* is the hope and certainty of the psalmist: that "God will hear" his servants and respond to their cries.

Joel M. LeMon

PSALM 89

Fourth Sunday of Advent, Year B
    First Lesson: 2 Samuel 7:1-11, 16
    (Luke 1:47-55 or **Psalm 89:1-4, 19-26**)
    Second Lesson: Romans 16:25-27
    Gospel Lesson: Luke 1:26-38

Ninth Sunday after Pentecost, Year B
    First Lesson: 2 Samuel 7:1-14a
    (Psalm 89:20-37)
    Second Lesson: Ephesians 2:11-22
    Gospel Lesson: Mark 6:30-34, 53-56

Psalm 89 is a *community lament* (see the introductory essay) that poses sharp questions to God. Yet this central aspect of this psalm is difficult to see from the lections selected for these two readings. The readings focus on the psalm's royal imagery: on the Davidic king (Pentecost) and God's reign as Sovereign of the Universe (Advent). These sections are confessional and powerful in their own right, but were placed in the context of a lament over God's silence to heighten the cry and pain that end this piece.

    The first thirty-seven verses of the psalm offer praise to God for God's faithful and steadfast love in two major sections, verses 1-18 and 19-37. The first section is lifted as praise to God in universal terms while the second focuses on the particularity of Israel and of David and his descendants.

    Verses 1-4 set the tone for all that follows. The one praying praises God for God's steadfast love (*ḥesed*) and faithfulness (*'ĕmûnâ;* vv. 1-2).

Next (vv. 3-4), the psalmist quotes God in a particular example of these attributes: the covenant with David (see the first lesson for both Sundays). Verses 5-8 call on the heavens to praise God; the imagery used is cosmic ("skies" v. 6; "sons of gods" [NRSV: "heavenly beings"], v. 6; "council of the holy ones," v. 7). Verses 9-12 declare God's rule over creation: the seas; the sea monster of chaos, Rahab; and heaven and earth and all in them. The section concludes with praise of God's power (v. 13, "mighty arm"), which is founded on God's righteousness and justice (v. 14), along with the characteristics of steadfast love and faithfulness that form a thematic *inclusio* with verses 1-2. These themes of control of the universe and creation are common in texts that proclaim God's kingship (see Pss 47; 93; 95-99).

The next section (vv. 19-37) is unusual in form. It is set as a long quotation of God's and contains a great number of parallels with the first lesson: verses 19-20 speak of God's selection of David (cf. 2 Sam 7:19-21); verses 21-25 speak of God's protection from enemies (cf. 2 Sam 7:9-11); verses 26-35 speak of the familial relationship between God and David (cf. 2 Sam 7:12-14); verses 35-37 speak of the enduring promise to David's line (cf. 2 Sam 7:16). This section provides the hearers with God's word, with God's promises, which are presented within the context of the first section. God's promises are as sure as God's control of the universe.

The two lessons are from these sections of the psalm and are a clear fit with the 2 Samuel reading. Indeed, both end with God's promises to David's kingdom. However, the psalm details a longer and darker reality in Israel's history because, within the context of the psalm, God's words in verses 19-37 become an indictment. The real message of the psalm begins in verse 38 with verses 1-37 being past history. The "problem" here is God and the feeling that God had indeed abandoned the promises to David, which were also promises to the people.

There are several possible historical backgrounds for this situation — the death of Josiah[1] or the exile[2] — but, as Richard Clifford notes, the "history" presented here is elusive and a specific context is not as important as the message of the psalm.[3] The heart and soul of the psalm is that it goes beyond the 2 Samuel text and tells of the tortured history of

---

1. See Hans-Joachim Kraus, *Psalms 60–150: A Continental Commentary* (Minneapolis: Fortress, 1993), 203.

2. See Marvin E. Tate, *Psalms 51–100*, WBC 20 (Dallas: Word, 1990), 416.

3. Richard Clifford, "Psalm 89: A Lament over the Davidic Ruler's Continued Failure," *HTR* 73 (1980): 35-47.

Israel and its kings. The message is one not often heard in contemporary churches, for it is a cry both *to* God and *against* God. The people want to know "How long will your wrath burn like fire?" (v. 46), and even more pointedly, because it directly addresses God's promises in verses 1-4 and 14:

> Lord, where is your steadfast love [*ḥesed*] of old,
>   which by your faithfulness [*ʾĕmûnâ*] you swore to David? (v. 49)

It seems to the people that God is gone and that God's promises are no more.

Walter Brueggemann argues that the purpose of preaching is to preach poetry to a prose world, proclaiming "shattering, evocative speech that breaks fixed conclusions and presses us always toward new, dangerous, and imaginative possibilities."[4] The words thrown to God at the end of this psalm do just that. The very word "Israel" means "to strive with God," and Israel does struggle and fight and kick and scream when its world collapses. This psalm speaks of powerful faith, faith that is strong enough to demand that God hear our pain and our cries and that (here is the dangerous part!) we can accuse God of not living up to God's promises when that is the way we truly feel. The psalm shatters the perfect world created in 2 Samuel. It shatters our ordinary life in the same way that the angel shatters Mary's belief in her life path. It shatters the way we often "do" church and says that pain and disillusionment are part of our lives and also a part of our relationship with God. It counters the "happy" Christmas that is part of the North American ethos, but is often not a part of the season's reality in our lives. It provides a way for our relationship with God to go on when the worst has happened and we feel that God has left us alone with broken promises. It is Good News that we are not flawed for wanting to be (and really being) angry at God. It is Good News that God wants an honest relationship with us.

Psalm 89 offers the radical chance to see God in a new way. For the ancient Israelites and for us, life does not always turn out as we wish; both Pentecost and Christmas have their darker side when the promises are hard to see and it is easy to lose faith. One way to sustain the faith proclaimed in the first two sections of the psalm is to voice the fear that

---

4. Walter Brueggemann, *Finally Comes the Poet: Daring Speech for Proclamation* (Minneapolis: Fortress, 1989), 6.

enters into our lives of faith. Even in the dark, we can continue to have a relationship with God, even if the story does not end happily ever after.

Beth LaNeel Tanner

PSALM 90

Twenty-third Sunday after Pentecost, Year A
    First Lesson: Deuteronomy 34:1-12
    (Psalm 90:1-6, 13-17)
    Second Lesson: 1 Thessalonians 2:1-8
    Gospel Lesson: Matthew 22:34-46

Psalm 90 is the only psalm in the Psalter attributed to Moses. The reason for this attribution is most likely connected with the sagacious tone of the psalm or to the fact that Moses prayed for God to "turn" (see Exod 32:12 and Ps 90:13). *Time* is the governing poetic motif of this ancient prayer, which probes the transient nature of human life from the perspective of one who lives in the shadow of the eternal God. The "wisdom" that comes from this perspective of eternity is perhaps best exemplified in the psalm's famous middle verses:

> The days of our life are seventy years,
>   or perhaps eighty, if we are strong. . . .
> So teach us to count our days
>   that we may gain a wise heart. (vv. 10a, 12)

(Abraham Lincoln's Gettysburg Address, which begins with "Fourscore and seven years ago," may contain an allusion at this point to the KJV of Psalm 90:10: "The days of our years *are* threescore years and ten; and if by reason of strength *they be* fourscore years.")

In form the psalm is a *prayer*. That is significant because it shows that the psalm is not simply a philosophical meditation on human frailty and transience. Rather, it is a genuine prayer that begs for *divine wisdom* that we might live today in light of eternity, *divine mercy* that God might redeem our days on earth so that we may know joy (cf. Eph 5:15-20), and *divine blessing* upon the work of our hands.

233

The poem starts out with the metaphor of God as the community's eternal "dwelling place." The term "dwelling place" can refer to God's abode in the temple or in heaven (in fact, the temple was seen in the ancient world as the earthly microcosm of God's heavenly abode). The image communicates God's presence, God's eternal nature, and also God's gracious intentions — God's presence in the Old Testament is usually a sign of God's favor. But as the psalm indicates in verse 3, God's presence is a two-edged sword. God pronounces judgment on us: "Turn back [√*šwb*], you mortals." This divine sentence, which echoes Genesis 2:17, names God as the source of human mortality. Thus, the poem sets up a tension between God's eternal presence as gracious blessing and God's eternal presence as judging decree.

The poem continues its prayerful lamentation about the transience of human existence with references to those normal measures of time — the watches of the night, the rising and setting of the sun, the growing of plants. Just as the life of desert grass, which blooms and fades in a single day, seems short to humans, so human life is short in the sight of God. The average life span in the ancient world was actually under fifty years. By citing the measure of life as seventy or eighty years, the psalmist is saying that even comparatively long lives are short in comparison with eternity. And more shockingly, the psalmist sees in all life signs of God's wrath. Even long life, often seen as a sign of God's favor in the Old Testament, is the locus of God's wrath — length of days is merely an opportunity for "toil and trouble" (v. 10) and affliction (v. 15).

And yet the psalm is not merely a pessimistic lamentation about human frailty and divine wrath. It is also an earnest prayer for divine mercy and grace. Just as God had decreed that humans "turn" (√*šwb*) back to dust, the psalmist cries out to God to "turn" (√*šwb*) and show compassion (v. 13). Apparently, "to gain a wise heart" is to seek grace and mercy from God. It is not enough merely to recognize one's condition; one must also seek deliverance from the Lord. And the psalmist trusts that God can redeem even evil times, blessing the years with joy and prospering the work of human hands and hearts. The word translated "prosper" (√*kwn*) has the basic sense of "establish." Normally this word implies both divine action (it is God and God alone who can establish) and permanence: that which God establishes *lasts;* it transcends the fleeting nature of human life. Thus the psalm comes to a close on a note of trust in the gracious and powerful nature of God. God is able to overcome for us what we cannot overcome for ourselves. God can establish us and rescue us from our condition.

In the lectionary the psalm is paired with Deuteronomy 34, the account of the death of Moses, the Lord's greatest servant. The two fit well together: Psalm 90 is attributed to Moses, Moses is reported to have lived to the age of 120 while still vigorous and healthy, and Moses died "at the Lord's command" (Deut 34:5; cf. Ps 90:3); the people at that time were homeless and landless, but God was their dwelling place. But perhaps the most poignant connection between the two texts comes from the agency of God to which both texts bear witness. It was God, after all, not Moses, who delivered the people out of Egypt, and it was God who *established* them in the Promised Land. There is a promise here for all generations of God's faithful people. Home, it has been said, is the place that, when you go there, they have to take you in. God is our home. God still abides with us in all places, redeeming our time, blessing our lives with joy, prospering the work of our hands. As Isaac Watts wrote in his beloved paraphrase of Psalm 90:

> O God, our help in ages past,
> Our hope for years to come,
> Be Thou our guard while troubles last,
> And our eternal home.

Rolf A. Jacobson

Psalm 91

First Sunday in Lent, Year C
First Lesson: Deuteronomy 26:1-11
(Psalm 91:1-2, 9-16)
Second Lesson: Romans 10:8b-13
Gospel Lesson: Luke 4:1-13

Nineteenth Sunday after Pentecost, Year C
First Lesson: Jeremiah 32:1-3a, 6-15
(Psalm 91:1-6, 14-16)
Second Lesson: 1 Timothy 6:6-19
Gospel Lesson: Luke 16:19-31

The history of Psalm 91 is somewhat checkered. The psalm is accused of making promises so remarkable that the unwary reader might be lured into superstition or foolish confidence. English clergyman Leslie D. Weatherhead goes so far as to conclude about the psalm, "it just is not true."[1] It is both striking and, perhaps, telling that amidst the division of the psalm between its two appointed Sundays in the lectionary, only verses 7-8, the two verses that make the most extreme promise and might cause the most theological trouble or discomfort, are excluded. Yes, Psalm 91 has had a checkered history, so much so that it has been discarded outright by some. But if it has its dangers (and what Scripture does not?), then it has riches as well. In Psalm 91's case, the riches are the riches of extravagant promise.

1. *The who and the where of the psalm.* The opening section of the psalm (vv. 1-4) is a powerful claim for the name of God, urging those who know the Lord to express their trust. In these verses the four chief appellations or titles for God are used: "the Most High" *(ʿelyôn),* "the Almighty" *(šadday),* "the LORD" *(yhwh),* and "my God" *(ʾĕlōhay).* In two short verses a name for God appears four times. And each name is different. This comprehensive "name-dropping" tells us something important about whom this psalm concerns, and, more pointedly, who speaks in the final four verses.

The statement is made, "In God I trust" (v. 2). Which God? Taken together, the appellations provide an answer: God the Almighty, who has promised blessing (Gen 49:25); God the Most High, who apportioned the nations (Deut 32:8); my God, who gives strength and safety (Ps 18:31); and most importantly, the God of the covenant name: Yahweh, "the LORD," the God of Abraham, the God of Isaac, and the God of Jacob (Exod 3:6). God is the central player in this psalm — it is God who acts, God who delivers, God in whom trust is rightly placed.

Psalm 91 has been placed between two chiastic psalms, the trio of which may be read as an introduction to the fourth book of the Psalter. The relationship of these three introductory psalms must not be overlooked. They share similar language and themes. Each psalm has the combination of night and day, which is a merismus, employing extremes to display the wide scope of God's attributes (90:4, 6; 91:5-6; 92:2); each promises the punishment of the wicked (90:7-8; 91:7-8; 92:7-9) and satisfaction in terms of years (90:10; 91:16; 92:14); and each describes the Lord

1. Leslie D. Weatherhead, *Key Next Door* (New York: Abingdon, 1960), 103.

as shelter (90:1; 91:1-2, 9-10; 92:[12-]13). These similarities are too many and too close to be accidental, and compel one to read and interpret the three in terms of their clear connections.

2. *"The way of an eagle in the sky": How Psalm 91 works.* The metaphor of verse 4 will be familiar to the average reader. The image is of a mother bird spreading out her wings to shade and shelter her young, which calls to mind the longing of Jesus in Luke 13. The psalmist describes God in terms of this potent theological metaphor.

Verses 5 and 6 are rich with poetic activity. Each verse contains a merismus — night and day, darkness and the noonday. The function of these two pairings is to accentuate the extent to which one is protected by God's wing. In and with these pairings is another poetic tool, the use of the abstract and the concrete. The abstraction "terror" is made concrete in "arrow."[2]

Psalm 91:11-12 is easily the most familiar part of the psalm. "In an infamous use of Scripture, Satan employed verses 11-12 in his attempt to corrupt Jesus."[3] This quotation by Satan is an example of how (cleverly? easily?) Scripture can be misappropriated. But more interesting and instructive is Jesus' response (Luke 4:12). He is quick to identify this ill use of God's word and responds appropriately. Even so, this exchange in the temptation narrative does press the issue of the psalm's interpretive history.

Clearly the promise of protection in Psalm 91 is not to be taken lightly. It is not a tool or standard by which one might evaluate the coinage of God's word. The slings and arrows of outrageous fortune remain potent. This promise is not permission to act the fool. Rather it is a promise of help *in trouble.* Thus, when we find ourselves, like a bird, trapped in a hunter's snare (cf. fig. 4), or teetering on the edge of a great precipice, even then we can count on this word of promise, this vow of deliverance — precisely when it is needed most.

The claim made regarding the promise of protection is stretched in verse 13 to include the wild world belonging to the king of the jungle. The question that leaps to mind is what is meant by this talk of lions and snakes? Franz Delitzsch has suggested that these two natural enemies of humankind are metaphorical of the dangers at large in the world: "they are kinds of destructive power belonging to nature . . . from

2. See Patrick D. Miller, *Interpreting the Psalms* (Philadelphia: Fortress, 1986), 40.
3. James L. Mays, *Psalms,* Interpretation (Louisville: John Knox, 1994), 297.

the side of their open power . . . and from [the side of their] . . . secret malice."[4] One can sketch an analogy — lions : serpents :: open power : secret malice. Again a merismus is employed to help us understand the vast protection under which we abide. The promise is familiar; we will be empowered to walk — to tread à la Genesis 3:15 — on such power and through such malice with unbruised heels!

A sudden change in voice occurs in verse 14. It is no longer the prayer who speaks, but the God to whom she speaks. This new voice begins with a reiteration of the thought of verses 1-2 and 9:

> Those who love me, I will deliver;
> I will protect those who know my name.

The connection between protection, deliverance, and the name of the Lord is intensified. And in these final three verses three synonyms for "deliverance" occur:

- I will *deliver* them (v. 14).
- I will *rescue* them (v. 15).
- I will . . . show them my *salvation* (v. 16).

This threefold promise of deliverance is carried in God's own words; and in the context of God's name we are confronted with pure promise.

This is the climax to which the psalm has risen in steady crescendo. These are the riches of extravagant promise that Psalm 91 presents. Extravagant promise that calls for an equally extravagant faith. For when Christians read these words, they are called to trust in the Lord, who has shown deliverance in the face of a tiny baby born in Bethlehem. Psalm 91 is bursting with a message for all who call upon the Lord as "my God." That message is of shade from the heat, of release from a snare, of freedom from fear, of protection from powers bold and powers subtle. It is the message of a refuge promised and of a refuge close at hand.

Karl N. Jacobson

4. Franz Delitzsch, *Biblical Commentary on the Psalms* (New York: Funk and Wagnalls, 1883), 64.

PSALM 92

Eighth Sunday after the Epiphany, Year C
　　First Lesson: Isaiah 55:10-13
　　(Psalm 92:1-4, 12-15)
　　Second Lesson: 1 Corinthians 15:51-58
　　Gospel Lesson: Luke 6:39-49

Psalm 92 holds the distinction of being the only psalm associated with a particular day, the Sabbath. Even if the reader overlooks this detail in the superscription — indeed, there is no evidence that the psalm was originally written for this day, and its themes overlap with other psalms not so designated — the psalm offers profound insights about the nature of God and humans. Reading through the lens of the Sabbath, though, one can find in these words unique perspectives on themes that appear elsewhere in the Psalter. And conversely, elements of this psalm, enhanced by other psalms sharing its themes, do much to illuminate the Sabbath, a day often described more in negative terms of what *not* to do and what happens when one does *not* keep it than in positive terms of what *to* do and what the Sabbath does to the one who *does* observe it.

At the heart of this psalm is the image of God as exalted or "Most High." Opening with praise and thanksgiving directed specifically to the divine name *'Elyôn* ("Most High," v. 1), the psalm explores and celebrates ramifications of that aspect of God's nature. The immediate impetus for such praise comes from joy and gladness the psalmist feels at God's "works" (*pō'al,* v. 4; *ma'ăśeh,* vv. 4-5). Elsewhere in the Psalms, these terms for divine activity refer to God's deliverance of people (see Pss 44:1; 77:14; 95:9; 96:3; 111:2, 3) as well as God's activity in creation (see Pss 8:3; 19:1; 103:22; 104:24; cf. Pss 33:4; 64:9; 90:16; 143:5). Certainly, both realms of activity give rise to praise, and not incidentally, both are associated with the Sabbath (see Gen 2:1-3; Exod 20:8-11; Deut 5:12-15). And in Psalm 92 itself, God's activity of lifting up and nourishing humans leads to deliverance (vv. 10-11) and draws on imagery from the natural world that can be linked to creation (vv. 10, 12-14).

Verse 5 celebrates a further, related dimension of divine activity by drawing a parallel between God's great "works" and God's deep "thoughts" (NRSV) or "designs" (NJPS), a term that points to the underlying structures and intentions of God's ways in the world. Namely, the Lord remains forever exalted ($\sqrt{rwm}$, v. 8) over evildoers and other enemies of God. Such designs in the world are "deep" *('mq)* in the sense of being great, drawing out the spatial imagery of God as "on high," but also deep in the sense of being hidden from obvious view. This is because evildoers and the wicked enjoy success on many fronts: they "sprout like grass" and flourish. Yet even in the midst of evil (emphasized literarily in the way God's opponents in vv. 7 and 9 surround God in v. 8), God's exalted status goes unchallenged since the wicked and evildoers "are doomed to destruction forever" (v. 7). Verse 9 offers further details of the fate of the wicked: they will perish and be scattered. Their destruction is "forever" *('ădê 'ād)*, just as God's position is on high "forever" *(lĕ'ōlām)*. Thus their *coming* devastation eclipses their *current* prosperity. To view the wicked in this way — and to view God's exalted status relative to them — requires an *eschatological perspective*.[1] Those without such a perspective, ignorant of the deepness of God's designs, the psalmist calls "dullards" *(√b'r)* or "stupid" *(√ksl; v. 6)*. Michael V. Fox, commenting on the use of these terms in Proverbs, points out that such characters do not necessarily lack moral qualities but lack "clarity of vision."[2] In this case, their focus on the apparent successes of the wicked keeps them from seeing the depth of God's designs and the height of God's exalted position.

Remarkably, *God's* exalted status reflects how the *worshiper* is exalted too. Using the same root that earlier described God as "on high" (v. 8), the psalmist declares that God "will exalt [*rwm*] my horn like that of the wild ox" (v. 10). Since there is no change between verb forms in verses 9 and 10, the verbs in verses 10-11 (as well as in vv. 12-14) likely have a future sense.[3] Thus the psalmist expresses trust that God will do such action at a future time. Still, the past sense of the NRSV and other translations may reflect the psalmist's understanding that, in an eschatological sense, the action already has occurred. Though the enemies and evildoers may still be flourishing (√*prḥ*, v. 7), already the psalmist's eyes can see their downfall and chaotic scattering (vv. 9, 11). Indeed, the psalmist has gained the clarity of eschatological vision that others lack (v. 6), realizing that, in fact, it is the *righteous* person who flourishes (√*prḥ*, vv. 12-13). Like palm trees and cedars — a vivid contrast to the wicked who "flourish" by sprouting like mere grass (v. 7) — their growth is abundant ("full of sap"),

1. J. Clinton McCann, Jr., "The Book of Psalms: Introduction, Commentary, and Reflections," in *NIB*, 4:1050, 1052.

2. Michael V. Fox, *Proverbs 1–9*, AB 19A (New York: Doubleday, 2000), 41.

3. McCann, "The Book of Psalms," 4:1051.

fresh, and enduring (v. 14). Even in old age they still (*'ôd*) bear fruit (v. 14; cf. the perpetual [*'ădê 'ād*] destruction of the wicked in v. 7). With steady, upward growth, the heights of the trees reflect the exalted position of the worshiper (v. 10), just as their freshness (√*r'n*) calls to mind the fresh oil anointing the worshiper (√*r'n*, v. 10). As with any plant, their growth results largely from their nourishing location — here it is the house of the Lord and the courts of God (v. 13). Such a location is no accident, as they have been *trans*planted there (√*štl;* cf. Ps 1:3; Ezek 17:7-10, 22-23; 19:10-13), that is, deliberately moved as partially grown shoots or branches from one site to another carefully chosen site where they may thrive.[4]

In this context, that protective, nurturing site for growth may be the very space of the Sabbath. Freed from obligations and burdens of work, one may still be like an unmoving, solidly grounded tree.[5] In the *temporal space* of the Sabbath,[6] the righteous also may gather in the *physical space* of "the house of the Lord and the courts of God" for worship of the kind described in the opening lines of the psalm (vv. 1-4). In this twenty-five-hour period, from morning to night (v. 2), one may receive divine nourishment by delighting in God's works (v. 4) and declaring — and experiencing for oneself — God's steadfast love and faithfulness (v. 2). Barbara Brown Taylor describes such sustenance received in her own Sabbath observance:

> By year three I had come to count on Sabbath the same way I count on food or breath. I could work like a demon the other six days of the week as long as I knew the seventh was coming. For the first time in my life, I could rest without leaving home. With sundown on the Sabbath, I stopped seeing the dust balls, the bills and the laundry. They were still there, but they had lost their power over me. One day each week I lived as if all my work were done. I lived as if the kingdom had come and when I did the kingdom came, for 25 hours at least. Now, when I know Sabbath is near, I can feel the anticipation bubbling up inside of me. Sabbath is no longer a good idea or even a spiritual disci-

4. See William P. Brown, *Seeing the Psalms: A Theology of Metaphor* (Louisville: Westminster John Knox, 2002), 77; and the essay on Ps 1 in the present volume.

5. Cf. Brown, *Seeing the Psalms,* 56, who points out the frequent contrast in the Psalms between the righteous and wicked in terms of *motion*, with the righteous having "an ability to stand still and reflect upon true things" as opposed to the frenetic activity of the wicked that leads them to oblivion.

6. Cf. Abraham J. Heschel, *The Sabbath* (New York: Farrar, Straus and Giroux, 2005).

pline for me. It is an experience of divine love that swamps both body and soul. It is the weekly practice of eternal life.[7]

Living "as if the kingdom had come" on the Sabbath, one participates in the eschatological vision that Psalm 92 describes and celebrates. *Already* one can experience exaltation over personal enemies, be they exhausting chores, oppressive work, pressures from a boss, or self-imposed stresses. In addition to the nurturing rest that allows a person to grow and flourish, this vision also encourages righteous living: one lives as if the world already has been made right. And in the end, the growth and flourishing of the righteous person testify to the righteousness of God (v. 15), the one who has rightly ordered the deep structures of the world. Once again in this psalm, then, humans reflect God: their righteousness testifies to God's righteousness just as their exalted status reflects God's nature as "Most High." Even the image of the righteous person as a still, unwavering tree, seen especially in the stillness of Sabbath rest, resembles the image of God as a solid, unmoving rock (v. 15). "To remember the Sabbath," Taylor writes, "is to remember what it means to be made in God's image,"[8] and this indeed is reason for praise.

Jennifer S. Green

PSALM 93

Ascension of the Lord, Years A, B
> First Lesson: Acts 1:1-11
> (Psalm 47 or **Psalm 93**)
> Second Lesson: Ephesians 1:15-23
> Gospel Lesson: Luke 24:44-53

"The LORD reigns!" With this acclamation, Psalm 93, often classified as an *enthronement psalm* (along with Pss 47; 96-99; see the introductory essay), proclaims God's indisputable kingship over all creation. Its lan-

---

7. Barbara Brown Taylor, "Sabbath Resistance," *Christian Century* 122, no. 9 (May 5, 2005): 42.

8. Taylor, "Sabbath Resistance," 42.

guage, mythical imagery, and poetic structure suggest that the psalm may be among the oldest poetic compositions in the Psalter. The precise cultic context in which this psalm was originally performed, whether as part of an annual "Enthronement Festival" or as part of the observance of the New Year or the Feast of Tabernacles, is unknown — and probably unknowable.[1] What is clear is that the psalm reflects Israel's regular communal celebration and reaffirmation of the Lord's eternal sovereignty displayed in creation and redemption.

The psalmist makes skillful use of a fivefold repetition of the divine name (vv. 1a, 1b, 3a, 4c, 5c) and of catchwords (√*lbš*, "to robe," vv. 1a, 1b; √*kwn*, "to establish," vv. 1c, 2a; √*nś*, "to lift up," vv. 3a, 3b, 3c; *něhārôt*, "floods," vv. 3a, 3b, 3c; *qwl*, "voice," vv. 3b, 4a; *'addîr*, "majestic," vv. 4b, 4c) to knit the various strands of the poem together. While the precise poetic structure of verses 1-2 is open to debate, the overall outline and movement of the psalm is clear and vigorous. "Using terse and powerful language, the hymn rushes along like the roaring water of which it speaks."[2]

Psalm 93's opening cry, "The LORD reigns," is also found in Psalms 96:10 (= 1 Chron 16:31), 97:1, and 99:1. The following lines of verse 1 depict Yahweh as a mighty warrior, robed in majesty (cf. Ps 104:1) and girded with might for battle (cf. Pss 18:39; 65:6). The magnitude of the Lord's power is evident in the work of creation. As the references to the sea and its waves in verse 3 make clear, the psalmist adopts here the ancient cosmogony in which the world is founded on pillars in the midst of the primeval deep (cf. Pss 18:15; 24:1-2; 75:3). Because of God's incomparable might, the earth is firmly established. It cannot be shaken (cf. Pss 96:10; 104:5), for the Lord's rule, symbolized by his heavenly throne, stands firm (v. 2a; cf. v. 4c). The shift to direct address in verse 2b draws attention to the ultimate ground of the enduring reign of Yahweh: "You are from everlasting" (NRSV).

Verse 3 abruptly shatters the mood of stability and peace established in verses 1-2. In three lines whose sound, rhythm, and repetitive lexical choice recall the relentless pounding of the waves of which they speak, the psalmist turns his attention to the constant threat to God's rule posed by the forces of chaos. In speaking of "floods" *(něhārôt)*, "mighty waters" *(mayim rabbîm)*, and "breakers of the sea" *(mišběrê yām)*, the poet

1. Marvin E. Tate, *Psalms 51–100*, WBC 20 (Dallas: Word, 1990), 474-75.
2. Artur Weiser, *The Psalms: A Commentary*, OTL (Philadelphia: Westminster, 1962), 618.

taps into a reservoir of images associated with the Canaanite myth of the battle of the sky god (Baal) with the primeval waters and his victorious establishment of the earth in the midst of the raging seas. The psalmist boldly appropriates this imagery to proclaim that Yahweh alone is the sovereign creator; Yahweh alone sustains the world in the face of constant threats to its order and stability (cf. Ps 46:1-3). The focus in verses 3-4 on the thundering, crushing might of the ocean's waves serves only to highlight the far greater might of the Lord, who sits enthroned on high above the chaotic floods (v. 4c; cf. Pss 29:10; 89:9), whether they are understood as representing the primeval waters or the enemies of God who oppress God's people (compare Ps 94:5, "they crush [*yĕdakkĕʾû*] your people," with 93:3, "their pounding [*dokyām*]"; see also Pss 65:7; 89:9; Jer 51:55; Zech 10:11).

The psalmist brings closure to verses 1-4 by returning in 4c to the vision of God enthroned on his lofty mountain (cf. Pss 7:7; 92:8; Isa 33:5; 57:15). But this is no distant sovereign who remains aloof and unapproachable. Verse 5, which may be a later addition to the psalm[3] but which now anchors Psalm 93 firmly within the larger context of Psalms 93-100,[4] proclaims that this holy, exalted king has condescended to dwell in the very heart of Israel ("your house," v. 5b = the temple), the people with whom God has made a firm, unchanging covenant ("your decrees," v. 5a; cf. Deut 6:17; Pss 25:10; 19:7; 119:14, 31, 36; etc.). And so the psalmist comes full circle: the stability of God's eternal rule over creation guarantees the enduring reliability of the Lord's gracious presence and trustworthy promises to God's people ("forevermore," v. 5c [*lĕ'ōrek yāmim*], echoes and extends into the future "from everlasting" [*mē'ôlām*] in v. 2b).

Read in canonical context, Psalm 93 resonates powerfully not only with various stories of creation, but also with Israel's memory of its redemption from Egypt to be Yahweh's own people. Much of the same vocabulary and imagery evoking the Lord's cosmogonic battle with chaos appears in the Song of the Sea (Exod 15:1-18), another piece of early Israelite poetry. In Israel's memory, creation and redemption are linked together and deeply rooted in the sovereign might and immutable faithfulness of God.

3. Frank-Lothar Hossfeld and Erich Zenger, *Psalms 2: A Commentary on Psalms 51–100*, ed. Klaus Baltzer, Hermeneia (Minneapolis: Fortress, 2005), 447.

4. See David M. Howard, Jr., *The Structure of Psalms 93–100*, Biblical and Judaic Studies 5 (Winona Lake, Ind.: Eisenbrauns, 1997), 105-19, 171; cf. Tate, *Psalms 51–100*, 475-78.

Later interpreters recognized these links between the creation of the world and the redemption of Israel and extended them into the future, seeing in Psalm 93 a pledge of eschatological redemption. The superscription to the psalm in some manuscripts of the LXX identifies this as a song "for the day before the Sabbath, when the land was settled." (The Mishnah similarly says the Levites sang Psalm 93 on the sixth day [*m. Tamid* 7:4].) This superscription may refer to the sixth day of creation (cf. the superscription to Ps 92, "A Song for the Sabbath Day"), to the original settlement of the land (cf. Josh 1:13), or to the return of Israel from exile. The latter interpretation would represent a continued fusion of the motifs of creation and redemption, with the return from exile understood as both "new creation" and "new exodus" (as often in Isa 40-55; cf. Hab 3:2-15). And, as the Mishnah attests, the Sabbath itself was understood as pointing forward to "the time that is to come, for the day that shall be all Sabbath and rest in the life everlasting" (*m. Tamid* 7:4).[5]

The use of Psalm 93 as a responsorial for the Feast of the Ascension further extends this long trajectory of interpretation grounding the hope of future redemption in the mighty acts of the Lord, who creates and sustains the world and who performs great deeds of deliverance on behalf of God's people (cf. Luke 24:44-47). On this day Christians celebrate the enthronement at God's right hand of Jesus, the one to whom all authority has been given (Eph 1:20-23), even over the crashing waves of the sea (Mark 4:35-41); the one through whom God has acted to redeem all the peoples of the world (Luke 24:46-47; Acts 1:8); the one who, though highly exalted, yet dwells intimately within and among us through the Spirit he has sent (Luke 24:49; Acts 1:4-5, 8); the one whose triumphant return we await with joyful anticipation and longing (Acts 1:11). On Ascension Day the church remembers all God's mighty deeds of creation and redemption and looks forward to that day when a multitude beyond counting, with a voice like "many waters" (cf. Ps 93:4), will celebrate the fullness of the reign of God with the ancient acclamation: "The Lord reigns!" (Rev 19:6).

J. Ross Wagner

---

5. Herbert Danby, trans., *The Mishnah: Translated from the Hebrew with Introduction and Explanatory Notes* (London: Oxford University Press, 1933); cf. Heb 4:1-11; Abraham J. Heschel, *The Sabbath* (New York: Farrar, Straus and Giroux, 2005).

PSALM 95

Third Sunday in Lent, Year A
   First Lesson: Exodus 17:1-7
   (Psalm 95)
   Second Lesson: Romans 5:1-11
   Gospel Lesson: John 4:5-42

Psalm 95 is one of the eight *enthronement psalms* found in the Psalter (Pss 29; 47; 93; 95–99; see the introductory essay). One would think that such a category would refer to the kings of Israel and their enthronement over God's people. In reality, however, this category of psalms has a much more elevated focus because these psalms celebrate the *divine king* of Israel and his enthronement over not only Israel but also all peoples, even over the cosmos itself. As such, the purpose of Psalm 95 is to provoke the people of God to worship Yahweh, "the great God, a great king over all gods!" (v. 3).

The idea of a divine monarch is a bit foreign to the modern believer. In fact, in most of the modern West the idea of a king of any sort is beyond the experience of the average person. This is why it is essential that preachers orient themselves and their listeners to the worldview of ancient Israel before going any further. In understanding Israel's *experience*, we will far better understand their *expression* of it.

For the ancient Israelite "the kingdom of God" was not an abstract concept. Rather, as a nation whose self-perception was that their political identity had been formed by divine fiat at Mount Sinai — when the Mosaic covenant was first offered to the offspring of Abraham — theocracy ("rule by God") was an everyday reality. According to Israel's political organizational chart, there were three human officers who served the government of the nation: the prophet, the priest, and the human king. But over all three of these political offices stood the *true* king of Israel: Yahweh himself. It was God who held the ultimate responsibility for defending his people and their territory from foreign oppression; it was he who authored and enforced their federal and civil law; and it was he whose responsibility it was to maintain civil and economic stability within the country. Certainly, the Lord's human officers assisted Yahweh in these tasks, but all these officers were expendable, replaceable, and subject to God's command.

Hence, for the ancient Israelite the "kingdom of God" was the nation of Israel, and their king was Yahweh, "enthroned above the cherubim" (see Ps 99, also fig. 9) within the inner sanctum of his palace, the temple upon Mount Zion. Yet Israel, like all nations, was faced regularly with the failure of its human leaders, who in their shortcomings did damage to the kingdom of God. The theological answer to this disconcerting reality is the thesis of the enthronement psalms: the eschatological message that even though human leaders will fail, the divine leader will not. The kingdom of God is coming in all its terrifying majesty, and all injustice and corruption will be obliterated at its arrival (compare Rev 11:15-17).

The truth of this thesis is further illustrated by the position of most enthronement psalms within the Psalter. Whereas the Psalter is collected into five books (see the introductory essay), and Books I-III (Pss 1–89) "document the failure of the Davidic covenant as experienced in the destruction of Jerusalem and exile in 587 B.C.E.," the enthronement psalms that occupy Book IV (Pss 90–106) offer a response: the proclamation of God's reign.[1] More than any of the other collections, Book IV recalls and celebrates Israel's premonarchic experience under Moses (Pss 90:1; 99:6; 103:7; 105:26; 106:16, 23, 32), "[p]erhaps [because] those who put the Psalter together wished to answer the problem of the failure of the Davidic king by reminding the people of that foundational period when Israel had no king except Yahweh."[2] So we see that in both *content* and *canonical shaping*, the enthronement psalms declare the truth that Yahweh is the true king of Israel, even the king of the cosmos, and with his reign humanity will at last know peace. Interestingly, the associations between Israel's response to divine kingship during the Moses era and the era yet to come seem to be particularly pertinent to Psalm 95.

The psalm opens with the exhortation to "come!" and "shout to the rock of our deliverance!" (v. 1). As will become clear as the psalm progresses, the rock that Israel is being called to celebrate is the rock of Exodus 17:6 — the rock that hid beneath its dry, crusty surface the waters of life that served to quench both the thirst and the grumbling of the Israelites in the wilderness.

The psalmist then calls the worshiper to approach Zion, the temple, the holy of holies and its royal resident. Many have theorized that the call to worship in verses 2-6 (and those like it elsewhere) is a liturgical re-

---

1. Richard N. Soulen and R. Kendall Soulen, *Handbook of Biblical Criticism,* 3rd ed. (Louisville: Westminster John Knox, 2001), 147.

2. Jerome F. D. Creech, *Psalms* (Louisville: Geneva, 1998), 54.

flection of some sort of ancient festival held at the celebration of the New Year in the fall, at which time the ark was marched up Zion's hill and Yahweh's cosmic reign was celebrated by the community.[3]

Although the gods of the ancient Near East were understood to be geographically limited, and therefore Yahweh could be nothing more than a minor deity of a minor region and a still more minor people group, the psalmist declares another truth:

> For a great god is Yahweh,
> and a great King above all gods! (v. 3)

On the basis of which attributes should the peoples of this world show the extreme expressions of obeisance commanded here? The psalmist shouts the answer: Yahweh is the master, the designer, the creator of all that is (vv. 4-6); he is worthy of worship. Moreover,

> He is our God,
> and we are the people of his pasture,
> even the flock of his hand. (v. 7a)

The application of the metaphor of a shepherd to human leaders is at least as old as writing in the ancient world. This is true in large part because the qualities of a good king are much the same as those of a good shepherd, and, of course, very few citizens of Israel's larger world had not seen both good and bad shepherds in action. Hence, the elevated position of Yahweh and the humble position of his citizens are effectively communicated through the image of the tender guardianship of the good shepherd: we are his, and he is ours, and the psalmist seeks to stir the heart of his audience with this truth.

At this juncture the psalm makes an abrupt shift (vv. 7b-9). Whereas up to this point the worshipers have been enjoined to celebrate with abandon the sovereignty of their creator, the message shifts abruptly to an admonition regarding future obedience — an admonition couched within the experiences of past failures. The "rock" of verse 1 makes a re-

---

3. See Hans-Joachim Kraus, *Psalms 1–59: A Continental Commentary* (Minneapolis: Fortress, 1993), 86-89; Frank Moore Cross, *Canaanite Myth and Hebrew Epic: Essays in the History of the Religion of Israel* (Cambridge: Harvard University Press, 1973), 173-80; and Jacob Klein, "Akitu," in *ABD,* 1:138-40.

appearance. C. H. Spurgeon speaks of this as a shift from "an invitation with reasons" to "an invitation with warnings."[4] This precipitous transition makes much more sense from the perspective of the enthronement psalms as a whole. They claim that Yahweh reigns, and when God's kingdom comes, this world will at last be what it was designed to be. The importance of the Mosaic era and the "pure" theocracy Israel experienced then for Book IV of the Psalter should also be recalled. Hence, the psalmist is here pulling back into view a time of great compromise on the part of the parents of her generation — that time in Exodus 17:1-7 (cf. Num 20:1-13) when Israel failed to believe that the God who had parted the Red Sea could also provide water in the wilderness. Moses was called to answer this insurrection by taking the selfsame staff that had struck the Nile and "strike the rock" so that life-giving water might flow out for the people of Israel. And although the disaster of dehydration and death was averted by Yahweh's miraculous act in the wilderness, Yahweh's wrath toward the people whose hearts never ceased to "wander" (a descriptor regularly applied to unruly sheep who endangered themselves by failing to heed their shepherds) produced far more dire results (vv. 10-11).

Why would these references to Israel's rebellion in the wilderness be found within a psalm celebrating the sovereignty of Yahweh? The psalmist here is calling upon the present generation to respond to the kingship of their God with a confidence and loyalty unknown in generations past. For as surely as Yahweh barred the children of Abraham from the Promised Land because of their failure to believe in the goodness of his rule, so too this generation will know his wrath if they fail to place their eternal trust and allegiance in the God who owns the sea, who formed the dry ground, the God who is willing to be known as the Shepherd of Israel. This is also the message of the author of the book of Hebrews. In chapters 3 and 4 of that book, there is a similar message for the people of God: "Take care, brethren, lest there should be in any one of you an evil, unbelieving heart, in falling away from the living God. . . . Today if you hear his voice, do not harden your hearts" (Heb 3:12; 4:7). These are powerful and necessary words for each generation of believers, and as the lectionary has placed them, these words are particularly appropriate for the season of Lent. But just in case this stern message stirs in the modern

4. C. H. Spurgeon, *The Treasury of David,* 7 vols. (New York: Funk and Wagnalls, 1892), 2:164.

believer only despair, the lectionary also offers us a word of hope from the book of Romans (see Rom 5:8-10).

Sandra L. Richter

PSALM 96

Christmas Day I, Years A, B, C
First Lesson: Isaiah 9:2-7
(Psalm 96)
Second Lesson: Titus 2:11-14
Gospel Lesson: Luke 2:1-14, (15-20)

Second Sunday after Pentecost, Year C
First Lesson: 1 Kings 18:20-21, (22-29), 30-39
(Psalm 96)
Second Lesson: Galatians 1:1-12
Gospel Lesson: Luke 7:1-10

Ninth Sunday after the Epiphany, Year C
First Lesson: 1 Kings 8:22-23, 41-43
(Psalm 96:1-9)
Second Lesson: Galatians 1:1-12
Gospel Lesson: Luke 7:1-10

Psalm 96 is part of a collection traditionally known as the *enthronement psalms* (Pss 93; 95-99; see also Pss 29; 47; and the introductory essay), since they either explicitly proclaim that God reigns or address God as "king" (Ps 96:10). An earlier generation of scholars connected these psalms to an annual New Year festival that celebrated God's reign, or perhaps even liturgically reenthroned God each fall for the coming year. While evidence for such a festival is minimal, it is certain that Israel and Judah recognized and celebrated God's reign regularly in worship. More recent scholarship has suggested the possibility that Psalms 93 and 95–99 proclaim God's reign in response to the crisis of exile articulated by Psalm 89 at the conclusion of Book III of the Psalter. Although there may no longer be an earthly monarch, the good news is that *God* still reigns! On canonical grounds, then, it is possible to conclude that the proclamation of God's reign is the central affirmation of the Psalter.[1]

Because Psalm 96 and the other enthronement psalms seem to offer a response to the exile and its aftermath, it is not surprising that there are numerous similarities between Psalm 96 and Isaiah 40-55 — for instance, the commitment to proclaiming the "good tidings" (Isa 40:9; 41:27; see the same Hebrew root translated "tell" in Ps 96:2) of God's reign (Isa 52:7; Ps 96:10), which means life or "salvation" for all (Isa 49:6; 52:7, 10; Ps 96:2), grounded in God's world-encompassing will for "justice" (Isa 42:1-2, 4; see Ps 96:10-13 where the two Hebrew roots translated "judge" would be better translated "establish justice"). Perhaps the most obvious connection between Psalm 96 and Isaiah 40-55 is the invitation to "sing to the LORD a new song" (Ps 96:1; Isa 42:10). In Isaiah the new song is to be sung in response to the "new things" (Isa 42:9; see 43:19) that God is doing — namely, the return from exile described as a new exodus (see Isa 43:18-21). Just as the people sang to celebrate the exodus from Egypt (see Exod 15:1-21, esp. v. 18, which affirms that God "will reign forever and ever"), so they will sing a *new song* to celebrate a *new divine deliverance*.

Historically and canonically, therefore, the opening invitation of Psalm 96 may be understood in relation to Isaiah 40-55 and the return from Babylonian exile; but its direction of meaning need not be so restricted. As Walter Brueggemann suggests, Psalm 96 itself may serve in any setting as a new song, because the psalm itself is "the evocation of an alternative reality that comes into play in the very moment of the liturgy."[2] In other words, liturgy is capable of creating and shaping reality away from the way we may find it and toward the way God intends the world to be.

So, what kind of reality does Psalm 96 imagine and evoke? Psalm 96 envisions a world claimed in its entirety — including the "families of the peoples" (v. 7), "the nations" (v. 10), and the whole creation (vv. 10-12) — by the sovereign God. The point is not superiority per se, neither the superiority of Israel's God nor of Israel itself. Rather, the point is *justice!* The critique of the gods (v. 5) should be heard in conversation with Psalm 82, where God condemns the gods to death precisely because of their injustice and unrighteousness in showing partiality to some people at the ex-

---

1. See James L. Mays, *The Lord Reigns: A Theological Handbook to the Psalms* (Louisville: Westminster John Knox, 1994).

2. Walter Brueggemann, *The Message of the Psalms: A Theological Commentary* (Minneapolis: Augsburg, 1984), 144.

pense of other people (Ps 82:1-4, 6-7). Such injustice threatens the world with chaos — "all the foundations of the earth are shaken" (Ps 82:5; see the essay on Ps 82). In contrast, the God of Israel is for all people; and God is coming precisely "to establish justice (on) earth. He will establish justice (in) the world with righteousness, and (among) the peoples with his faithfulness" (Ps 96:13, author's translation). And it is the pervasive establishment of justice and the setting of things right among all people that puts the world on a solid foundation — "it shall never be moved" (Ps 96:10; "moved" here is the same Hebrew verb as "shaken" in Ps 82:5). By the way, the establishment of world-encompassing stability and security is another point of contact with the book of Isaiah, the controlling vision of which is Isaiah 2:2-4, where "justice" is again the central concept (NRSV's "judge between" would be better translated "establish justice among" in Isa 2:4).

In a world still threatened with chaos, the vision evoked by Psalm 96 is indeed "good tidings" that beg to be proclaimed and embodied. As James L. Mays suggests, Psalm 96 "has a definite evangelical cast."[3] Indeed, Psalm 96 is perhaps more timely now than it ever has been, given the "global village" in which we now live. Although the phenomenon called "globalization" is operating at full force among us, its impact is not producing the kind of justice and righteousness that God wills. Rather, as one group of biblical scholars and theologians recently concluded, much of the world is mired in despair as a result of global economic arrangements.[4] Or, as Nobel Prize–winning economist Joseph E. Stiglitz recently put it, globalization is producing massive discontent among the vast majority of the world's people.[5] Given these sad and sobering realities, it is indeed good news to contemplate the world-encompassing claim of the God who wills justice and righteousness in "all the earth" (vv. 1, 9). This good news is desperately needed in a world of discontent and despair, and Theodore Mascarenhas aptly concludes that Psalm 96 "is missionary in character and that it imposes a missionary function upon Israel."[6] This "missionary function" has been inherited by the people of God in all times and places; that is, we are invited to

3. James L. Mays, *Psalms,* Interpretation (Louisville: John Knox, 1994), 308.

4. See Walter Brueggemann, ed., *Hope for the World: Mission in a Global Context* (Louisville: Westminster John Knox, 2001), especially 151-58.

5. Joseph E. Stiglitz, *Globalization and Its Discontents* (New York: Norton, 2002); see also the essay on Ps 36 in the present volume.

6. Theodore Mascarenhas, *The Missionary Function of Israel in Psalms 67, 96, and 117* (Lanham, Md.: University Press of America, 2005), 187.

Fig. 8. Psalm 96:2 speaks of blessing the Lord's name (see also Ps 145:1, 21); other psalms speak of "praising" the Lord's name (see, e.g., Pss 7:17; 9:2; 69:30; 74:21; 89:12; 99:3; 100:4; 113:1; 135:1; 145:2; 148:5, 13; 149:3), "singing" to it (Ps 135:3), or "giving thanks" to it (Ps 106:47). This image shows a worshiper revering the name of the pharaoh (written in hieroglyphic script within the cartouche) with uplifted hands, a standard Egyptian posture for praise.

"proclaim constantly the good news of God's life-giving will and work" (author's interpretive translation of v. 2b). In fact, this missionary function is certainly part of what it means to "bless" God's "name" (v. 2; see also fig. 8). The word "bless" seems originally to have had the connotation of kneeling in submission, so the invitation is to submit to God's claim on the world and to share this claim with "all the earth." This missionary function may be a particularly pertinent emphasis for the use of Psalm 96 during the season of Epiphany, and it accords well with Solomon's expansive prayer in 1 Kings 8.

Because the central affirmation of Psalm 96 is identical to Jesus' central message — "The kingdom of God has come near" (Mark 1:15) — it is appropriate that Psalm 96 is assigned for Christmas Day (see also Pss 97-98). The pairing with Isaiah 9:2-7 reinforces the crucial importance of justice and righteousness (see Isa 9:7). Just as God, the heavenly monarch, wills justice and righteousness, so the faithful earthly king or "anointed" (Hebrew *māšîaḥ;* Greek *christos*) will pursue justice and righteousness (see also Ps 72:1-7, 12-14). It is not necessary to conclude that Isaiah 9:2-7 is a prediction of Jesus. Rather, the mission of Jesus will not be fully understood apart from texts like Isaiah 9:2-7 and Psalm 96, including, and indeed especially, their communication of the crucial importance of God's will for justice, righteousness, and peace on nothing short of a world-encompassing scale. In a world weary of old patterns of injustice and unrighteousness, the best possible news is that God is still at work, creating new possibilities for life that are properly welcomed, celebrated, and facilitated by the singing of a "new song."

J. Clinton McCann, Jr.

PSALM 97

Christmas Day II, Years A, B, C
    First Lesson; Isaiah 62:6-12
    (Psalm 97)
    Second Lesson: Titus 3:4-7
    Gospel Lesson: Luke 2:(1-7), 8-20

Seventh Sunday of Easter, Year C
    First Lesson: Acts 16:16-34
    (Psalm 97)
    Second Lesson: Revelation 22:12-14, 16-17, 20-21
    Gospel Lesson: John 17:20-26

An *enthronement psalm* (see the introductory essay and the essays on Pss 93; 95-96), this hymn of praise is designed to declare to all that Yahweh reigns, that his authority extends beyond the heavens, that even the "mountains melt like wax because of his presence" (v. 5). As such, Psalm 97 arrests the reader with one of the most dramatic portrayals of

Yahweh's sovereign power to be found in the Psalter. At most a typical human king's (royal) "glory" might be described as filling his kingdom, or perhaps his conquered territories; but the glory of the divine king fills the cosmos. In other words, the imperial reach of Yahweh extends so far beyond all other monarchs that only a fool would consider trifling with his legal declarations or fail to offer him his due.

Three themes are discernible within this psalm. The first is *praise:* the psalmist revels in his proclamation of Yahweh's matchless position and unassailable authority. Verse 1 opens with a sweeping declaration of God's sovereignty:

> The LORD is king! Let the earth rejoice!
> Let the many coastlands be glad! (v. 1)

To the ancient Israelite a "coastland" (or "island") was any land that must be reached by ship. Thus, although Cyprus and the isles of Greece might be intended, so also is the coast of Italy, Spain, and beyond. In other words, this opening line communicates that in every place in which people are known to exist, those people ought to rejoice in the Lord!

As the psalm continues, God is portrayed in terms similar to human monarchs. But, unlike any human king, the Lord's throne room is depicted in cosmological terms, his arrival makes the earth itself tremble, he is armed with fire and lightning, his messengers are the heavens themselves, and his subjects are the inhabitants of the entire earth (vv. 1-6). Truly this is "the Lord of all the earth" (v. 5)! Moreover, as is typical of the enthronement psalms found in the fourth book of the Psalter, many of the images chosen by the psalmist originate at Sinai. Since it was at Sinai that Israel first felt the earth move under its feet, where the people first heard the thunder, saw the lightning, and experienced the "deep darkness" that attends the coming of the Almighty, these images are wholly appropriate here. Indeed,

> His bolts of lightning light up the world,
> the earth sees and writhes (in terror)! (v. 4, author's translation)

The second theme of this psalm grows from the first. Having declared God's imperial majesty, the psalmist celebrates by contrasting it to the "nothingness" of the gods of the other nations. Here we find that the poet communicates as much by choice of vocabulary as by discourse.

> All those who serve an idol [*pesel*] will be shamed,
> those who offer their praise to false gods [*ʾĕlîlîm*].
> All the gods have bowed themselves in worship to *Him!*
>
> (v. 7, author's translation)

The Hebrew word *pesel*, meaning "idol" or "god," is found throughout the Old Testament, but it has its highest profile in the Ten Commandments (Exod 20:4; Deut 5:8) and in Isaiah's diatribes regarding the folly of idol worship (see Isa 44:9, 15). This word is of interest because it is, as far as we know, a creation of the biblical writers. Whereas the verb *psl* is broadly known throughout the languages of Israel's neighbors, and generally has to do with carving or fashioning wood or stone,[1] the noun *pesel* (and its unusual plural *pěsîlîm*) has no cognates outside biblical Hebrew. Because of this, we must determine this noun's meaning by derivation, in which case it must mean something like "a thing fashioned." Hence, whenever a biblical writer addresses the audience regarding other "gods" and refers to them as *pesel/pěsîlîm*, the author is naming these "gods" as "things crafted." The derogatory message implied in this word choice is hard to miss. Simply by using the term *pesel*, the biblical writer is asking the question: What sort of fool worships a "god" of his or her own creation?

And what of *ʾĕlîlîm?* This word is also frequently used by the biblical writers to speak of gods other than Yahweh (cf. Ps 96:5; Lev 19:4; Isa 2:8), and it is also well known among the Semitic languages. It means something like "powerless, useless, weakness, vanity."[2] The disparaging message is again obvious: any who place their confidence in other deities are placing their lives in the hands of "weakness, vanity, uselessness" — in a word, they are fools. Our psalmist concludes by stating the ultimate irony — these other gods, who are supposedly deserving of humanity's worship, have already bowed themselves in worship to Yahweh (v. 7).

As is typical of several of the enthronement psalms (see especially Pss 95 and 99), the final theme of Psalm 97 has to do with *exhortation*. In the light of who the Lord is (both ontologically and in comparison with the other deities) and because of his "right to rule" (v. 8), how should the believer live? Verses 10-11 answer that question, enjoining the love of God

---

1. See *HALOT*, 2:949.
2. *HALOT*, 1:55.

and the hatred of evil, both of which lead to the protection of the righteous and upright.

Knowing that Yahweh will preserve his own, that even in the midst of an evil world he will defend them against injustice and reward them with light and joy (or, if Dahood is correct, with an eternal state filled with joy),[3] Yahweh's people are commanded to live with integrity. And so our psalm ends as it began — declaring that it is the Lord who reigns supreme, and when God's kingdom comes all evil will be annihilated and the righteous will know eternal joy. "Rejoice" (v. 12)!

The lectionary uses this psalm to celebrate both Christmas and Easter, and rightly so. Truly there are no events in human history that better declare the sovereignty of God celebrated in Psalm 97 than the incarnation of God the Son and his ultimate victory over death and the grave. The individual emphases within the Christmas readings (Isa 62:6-12; Titus 3:4-7; and Luke 2:[1-7] 8-20) include the ultimate deliverance of Jerusalem from all her enemies as a fulfillment of God's promised kingdom now here, the story of the Christ child, and the efficaciousness of the salvific effect of the Christ on behalf of fallen humanity (Titus 3:4-7). The emphases within the Easter readings are diverse and poignant. The first, John 17:20-26, recites Jesus' plea that the church would be one in order that both the church and the world might behold God's glory. The second reports the story of the slave girl whom Paul and Silas delivered from her soothsaying spirit. Ironically, although it was the demonic spirit that announced that Paul and Silas's message was "the way of salvation" (Acts 16:17), it was the girl's deliverance from this spirit that demonstrated the truth of this declaration: God does have power over other "gods"! The disciples are beaten and jailed in payment for their kindness, but when they declare the sovereignty of their God in jail, an earthquake shakes the building (cf. Ps 97:4), every prisoner is freed, and the Roman guard (i.e., a citizen of "the nations" who served the *'ĕlîlîm*) is converted. The last reading emphasizes the imminent return of Jesus Christ for those who have kept the faith in the midst of this fallen world (Rev 22:12-14, 16-17, 20-21). In each of these Easter readings God's cosmic sovereignty is declared: within the church, among the nations, and over all the world.

Sandra L. Richter

3. See Mitchell Dahood, *Psalms II: 51–100*, AB 17 (Garden City, N.Y.: Doubleday, 1968), 362; cf. Dahood, *Psalms I: 1–50*, AB 16 (Garden City, N.Y.: Doubleday, 1965), 222-23.

PSALM 98

Christmas Day III, Years A, B, C
    First Lesson: Isaiah 52:7-10
    (Psalm 98)
    Second Lesson: Hebrews 1:1-4, (5-12)
    Gospel Lesson: John 1:1-14

Sixth Sunday of Easter, Year B
    First Lesson: Acts 10:44-48
    (Psalm 98)
    Second Lesson: 1 John 5:1-6
    Gospel Lesson: John 15:9-17

Twenty-fifth Sunday after Pentecost, Year C
    First Lesson: Haggai 1:15b-2:9
    (Psalm 145:1-5, 17-21 or **Psalm 98**)
    Second Lesson: 2 Thessalonians 2:1-5, 13-17
    Gospel Lesson: Luke 20:27-38

The importance of Psalm 98 for the church is evident from its triple lectionary use on Christmas Day as well as in the Easter and Pentecost seasons. Its importance is also clear from the Psalter itself. Psalm 98 is a near double of Psalm 96. Both invite the reader to sing a new song and both conclude with the final reason for that new song. But the two psalms have subtly different emphases. Psalm 96 focuses on God's *glory,* with a rich palette of glory terms. Psalm 98 focuses on the natural human *response* to God's greatness and deeds: praise and music making, rich with musical instruments and terms of praise (vv. 4-6). What's more, the two psalms appear in the cluster of kingship psalms, which many scholars recognize as the theological heart of the Psalter.[1] Despite the disasters of sin and the terrors of history, the Lord alone is king, and he will make things right again.

The psalm falls naturally into three sections that expand in concentric circles: (1) Israel is invited to sing a new song, because of the Lord's deeds in the past (vv. 1-3). (2) All the earth (particularly the nations) is in-

---

1. Pss 93-99; see James L. Mays, *The Lord Reigns: A Theological Handbook to the Psalms* (Louisville: Westminster John Knox, 1994).

vited to praise God with all the instruments (products and symbols of human culture at its best) at its disposal (vv. 4-6). The grounds for this praise are not stated here (the expected motive clause is absent), but are implicit from the first part: "the ends of the earth" have seen the *salvation* accomplished by Israel's God (v. 3b). Thus the first two sections of the psalm focus on the Lord's deeds of salvation in the *past,* deeds done especially for his people Israel. (3) The third section (vv. 7-9) is a surprise for modern readers. Instead of imperatives directed principally at God's human subjects, the psalmist uses third-person jussives that invite creation and all within it to praise God. But this time the motive for praise (v. 9) is not deliverance done in the past, but is something *future:* God himself will come and judge the earth with "righteousness" and "equity." God's justice (his righting of all that's wrong and healing of all that's ruined) is something that creation itself longs for. Already now the creation breaks forth in anticipatory praise of the great day to come. When the Lord finally comes to earth, he will restore all creation to the way it *should* be. God's judgments are not opposed to his love but are the very instrument of that love. God's judgments restore all that is broken to the goodness that the Bible calls "righteous." This Old Testament perspective reappears when Paul writes that all creation eagerly awaits the redemption of the children of God (see Rom 8:18-24).

Psalm 98 is profoundly eschatological and cosmic. It begins with the circle of believers, expands to all humanity, and does not stop until all creation joins in the anticipatory praise that we call hope and eager expectation. This psalm flows over the neat divisions humans tend to make between believers and nonbelievers, and between humans and creation as a whole, precisely because God's glory is cosmic (cf. Isa 6:3). Remarkably, the praise of creation occurs because the world and its contents (Ps 98:7-8: wet sea and dry land, horizontal rivers and vertical mountains) do exactly what they were created to do (cf. Pss 19; 148; Rom 1:18-20). The activities of creation are not silent or meaningless — they are the praise of God. The sea and earth with all that's in them *roar* — the sound of creation at its most majestic. But when the rivers "clap their hands" and the mountains "shout for joy," we find human actions metaphorically ascribed to the creation, suggesting that all creatures are united in one purpose: the praise and adoration of the Creator and Redeemer who does justice to the ends of the earth (cf. Ps 96:11-12). That is the meaning and purpose of all that exists, including us.

The first lesson on Christmas (Isa 52:7-10), in language similar to our psalm, makes all this suddenly poignant for Israel and for Christians: Zion itself, where the Lord intended to dwell among his people, has been devastated. Jerusalem, the center from which praise and goodness should flow to all the earth, has itself fallen into ruins. Now, when all is lost, the preacher of good news appears to say that the Lord is coming again to Zion, and all nations, the ends of the earth, will see the salvation of Israel's God. For us, this is Christmas, cross, and resurrection — salvation in the *past.* But it is also the second coming, God's *future* salvation of all things.

The first lesson for Pentecost (Hag 1:15b-2:9) focuses on a dispirited governor, high priest, and people who, after returning from exile, find that God's promises have not been fulfilled as fully as they expected. They do not see God's glorious presence among them, and they themselves despise the small temple they have built as God's home among them. The older ones remember the glory of the former temple, built by Solomon (cf. Ezra 3:10-13), and the present temple seems a failure in comparison. God's answer to the people's small vision and discouragement is this: be strong, do not fear! God himself will keep his *word* of old, and his *Spirit* (of power and strength) is among them (Hag 2:5). God will shake up the world and its nations, *and the desire of all nations shall come* (2:7). Once again: our hope is eschatological, and the latter end of God's "house" (both cosmic and local) is more glorious than its beginning.

Raymond C. Van Leeuwen

PSALM 99

Twenty-second Sunday after Pentecost, Year A
>First Lesson: Exodus 33:12-23
>**(Psalm 99)**
>Second Lesson: 1 Thessalonians 1:1-10
>Gospel Lesson: Matthew 22:15-22

Last Sunday after the Epiphany, Transfiguration, Year A
>First Lesson: Exodus 24:12-18
>(Psalm 2 or **Psalm 99**)
>Second Lesson: 2 Peter 1:16-21
>Gospel Lesson: Matthew 17:1-9

  First Lesson: Exodus 34:29-35
  (Psalm 99)
  Second Lesson: 2 Corinthians 3:12–4:2
  Gospel Lesson: Luke 9:28-36, (37-43)

Psalm 99 is the last *enthronement psalm* of the Psalter (see the introductory essay and the entries on Pss 93; 95-98). As such, it concludes the cluster of psalms found in Book IV (Pss 90-106) that celebrate Yahweh's sovereignty and answer the problem of the failure of the Davidic kings, doing so, in large part, by recalling the story of Israel in the wilderness under Moses' leadership (see the essay on Ps 95). As in each of these psalms, the imagery of Yahweh's universal reign is couched in terms of regular human kingship. But his rule is described as so far beyond the reaches of "regular" kingship that the reader is swept up into an entirely new realm — God's kingdom-come glimpsed through the prophetic vision of the psalmist. Hence, the Lord is proclaimed as not merely the king of Israel, but as the king of all the nations and all their gods. It is important to recognize that this was a radical statement in Israel's world. For in the ancient world deities were regularly viewed as geographically constrained. They ruled only the lands controlled by the people who served them: Shamash ruled in Babylonia, Horus ruled in Egypt, Chemosh in Moab. Thus, the surrounding nations understood Yahweh to be regionally confined as well, ruling only in the hill country of Canaan (cf. 1 Kings 20:23-30). The message of the psalmist passionately contradicts this perspective. Although the nation of Israel did not rule the entire world, the God they served did (Ps 99:1-3).

The first refrain of the psalm is the thrice-repeated chorus "Holy is he!" (vv. 3, 5, 9). Three times the psalmist pauses in her recitation to make this declaration. The three stanzas that result speak to Yahweh's supreme and universal sovereignty; his just reign that has brought order and peace to Israel; and his past faithfulness to his servants. The larger anthem concludes with the final reiteration: "for the LORD our God is holy" (v. 9).

The title "the one enthroned upon the cherubim" (*yōšēb kĕrûbîm*, v. 1) was an appellation frequently assigned to God (see 1 Sam 4:4; 2 Sam 6:2; 2 Kings 19:15; Isa 37:16; Ps 80:1). The reference is, of course, to the golden cherubim that adorned the top of the ark. Housed first in the tabernacle, the ark was permanently relocated by David to Zion, which brought the divine king to the capital city. Yahweh claimed this spot as his throne and promised in Exodus 25:22 to meet with his people and to hear their petitions there. But what are cherubim? And what exactly does it mean to be "enthroned above" them?

Cherubim are first introduced in the garden of Eden where one is stationed to defend the garden against fallen humanity (Gen 3:24); they reappear among the decorations of the tabernacle (particularly the holy of holies; see Exod 25:18-22; 26:1, 31) and in Ezekiel's visions (Ezek 10:4, 7, 9, 14; 28:14, 16; 41:18). Unfortunately, the Hebrew language offers no further information to help us understand these creatures. Some help comes from the other Semitic languages, however, which attest cognates that signify "to bless; greet; worship; promise or offer sacrifice."[1] More helpful than the linguistic evidence is the visual imagery associated with the cherubim. It is clear from the tabernacle instructions that the Israelites knew exactly what these creatures were; no exhaustive description of their features was necessary.[2] Thus, we can conclude that cherubim were well known in Israel. We understand from Exodus that the cherubim are winged and have faces. Ezekiel describes them as a conglomeration of human, ox, lion, and eagle — typically understood as having the face of a human, wings of an eagle, and the bodies and feet of either lions or oxen. Genesis speaks of them as armed and dangerous (3:24). These descriptions help us identify these mysterious beasts because ancient Near Eastern art often portrays huge, intimidating, mythical creatures having human faces, eagles' wings, and bodies of either lions or oxen. In Egyptian art they are known as "sphinxes," in Assyria as "winged lions" or "winged bulls," and sometimes simply as "winged creatures." The function of these semidivine beings was to defend the throne room of the king and the temple of the deity.

A fairly famous image of such a creature, and one particularly relevant to Psalm 99, is found on the sarcophagus of King Ahiram of Byblos (see fig. 9). With this image(ry) in mind, the design of the ark and the title "enthroned on the cherubim" begin to make sense. The cherubim, "whose wings spread upward, covering the mercy seat" (Exod 25:20), form the seat of the Lord's throne (cf. 1 Kings 6:27). Like a human king, the di-

---

1. See *TDOT*, 7:308.

2. See 1 Kings 6:29; 7:32-37; 2 Chron 3:14; and Victor Hurowitz, "Inside Solomon's Temple," *BRev* 10, no. 2 (April 1994): 24-37, 50, for a discussion and drawings of these sacred spaces.

Fig. 9. The king in this image is seated on a throne. Flanking the throne are two creatures with human faces, eagles' wings, and leonine bodies and legs. These creatures are probably the equivalent of what the Old Testament calls cherubim; the throne thus demonstrates how the Lord might have been "enthroned upon the cherubim" (Pss 80:1; 99:1; 1 Sam 4:4; 2 Sam 6:2; 2 Kings 19:15; Isa 37:16).

---

vine king promises to hear the petitions of his people. Significantly, the cherubim show up only when God is near (e.g., the garden of Eden, the holy of holies, and the ark; cf. Ps 18:10-11, Ezek 1; 10:15, 20). Apparently, then, the cherubim of the Bible are fulfilling the same role as the "winged bulls" of Assyria: defending the throne room of the Great King and/or safeguarding the sanctity of the Almighty from all unholy advances. The message of the psalmist becomes clearer — the Lord is a great and terrible king, elevated upon his cherubim throne. Those who would approach him should tremble in fear at the danger they are engaging, and prostrate themselves on the floor before his footstool.

The emphasis of the second refrain (vv. 4-5) is the justice and resulting societal order that this Great King has brought to Israel. In the ancient Near East a human king's word was law, and the only hope the socially marginalized person had was an equitable king who took the time
to show compassion to people on the fringes. In their self-laudatory in-
scriptions, the ancient kings loved to portray themselves as defenders of
the weak. For example, Sennacherib describes himself as "the guardian
of the law, lover of justice, who lends support, who comes to the aid of
the needy" (Taylor Prism, col. I:i-ix). But we know that these sorts of declarations rarely expressed reality. In contrast, *Yahweh's* word was law in Israel (see Ps 99:4). Even so, the weak still depended upon the human king
to enforce that law. As a result, the Israelite kings are regularly praised or
condemned for their attention (or lack thereof) to Yahweh's law, particularly as regards the socially marginalized — the widow and the orphan.

The third stanza of this psalm shifts to a review of Yahweh's acts of
grace and kindness in the past, and various premonarchic heroes of the
faith that exemplify a right relationship with him (vv. 6-9). As should all
good preachers, the psalmist rehearses what Yahweh has done in the past
to give her current generation confidence that Yahweh will continue to
act similarly in the present. And, as with several of the other enthronement psalms, an emphasis on Moses and the wilderness era is visible
here.

The last few verses of this psalm are difficult. Although many translators render the final phrase of verse 8 "and the one avenging their
deeds," and take the verb from the root *nqm*, this is both an awkward
syntactical construction and an awkward complement to the preceding
line. To avenge *their* deeds communicates that it is Israel who has done
wrong and that Yahweh must right those wrongs.[3] Mitchell Dahood's
translation of this verse may be preferable. He understands the word in
question to mean "to exempt them from punishment."[4] This interpreta-

---

3. See Exod 20:5; 34:7; Num 35:19; Deut 32:40-43; Ps 79:10; P. King and L. Stager, *Life
in Biblical Israel* (Louisville: Westminster John Knox, 2001), 38-39; Roland de Vaux, *Ancient
Israel: Its Life and Institutions* (Grand Rapids: Eerdmans, 1997), 10-12, 21-22; Frank Moore
Cross, *From Epic to Canon: History and Literature in Ancient Israel* (Baltimore: Johns
Hopkins University Press, 1998), 3-22, for the kinship-based concept of blood vengeance
in Israel and Yahweh's role as Israel's divine patriarch and therefore blood redeemer
(gōʾēl).

4. Mitchell Dahood, *Psalms II: 51–100*, AB 17 (Garden City, N.Y.: Doubleday, 1968),
367; he reads the verb as √*nqh* with a pronominal suffix.

tion understands Yahweh to be one who "forgives" and "expiates" his people — a conceptually and poetically appropriate conclusion to the verse.

Thus, having recounted the Lord's faithfulness to Israel in the past, particularly in the era when they had no human king, the third stanza of this psalm concludes by exhorting Israel to prostrate themselves in acknowledgment of God's right to rule. "The mountain of his holiness" (v. 9) is of course Zion, the sacred space at the heart of the nation (even the heart of the world) where Yahweh chose to dwell among humanity. Although geographically Zion is not terribly impressive (the surrounding mountains are actually higher), because the Lord dwelt there, it was understood to be the center of the universe.[5] Moreover, for an ancient Israelite to speak of something as "holy" was to speak of it as set apart, unique, special; it was to define it as something (or someone) to which access must be mediated by purity and ritual. Zion's holy status issued from her royal resident. And it is this royal resident that the psalmist seeks to exalt before the world as she shouts for the last time: "for the LORD our God is holy!" (v. 9).

Sandra L. Richter

PSALM 100

Christ the King, Year A
> First Lesson: Ezekiel 34:11-16, 20-24
> **(Psalm 100)**
> Second Lesson: Ephesians 1:15-23
> Gospel Lesson: Matthew 25:31-46

Psalm 100 is a *hymn of praise* (see the introductory essay); in truth, it might be called *the* hymn of praise, because it is well known and loved and because it follows the form of the hymn of praise so precisely. It is familiar in English mostly due to the popularity of William Kethe's elegant metric paraphrase, "All People That on Earth Do Dwell." The basic form

---

5. See Jon D. Levenson, *Sinai and Zion: An Entry into the Jewish Bible* (San Francisco: HarperCollins, 1985), 111-76.

of the hymn of praise is a "call to praise" followed by "reasons for praise." Those elements are clearly visible in Psalm 100:

vv. 1-3a   Call to praise
   v. 3b   Reason for praise
v. 4   Call to praise
   v. 5   Reason for praise

In the final arrangement of the Psalter, the hymn crowns a series of *enthronement psalms* (i.e., those psalms that celebrate the reign of the Lord [Hebrew *yhwh mālak*])[1] with a final paean of praise. Whereas those psalms emphasize that the Lord reigns over all peoples, nations, and lands (see Pss 95:3-4; 96:1-3; 97:1; 98:4; 99:1; etc.), Psalm 100 calls on "all the earth" to praise the Lord of Israel.

As almost all commentators note, the hymn's distinguishing mark is a sequence of seven imperative verbs: "make-a-joyful-noise," "worship," "come," "know," "enter," "give thanks," and "bless." The verb "know" (Hebrew *yāda'*) is of special significance (see below).

The hymn begins with a threefold call for the nations to join in exuberant worship of the Lord. In three parallel phrases the hymn emphasizes the sheer joy and abandonment with which the nations are called to enter into the Lord's presence. Then follows what is perhaps the key verse in the psalm: "Know that the LORD is God" (v. 3). The Hebrew is more emphatic than this traditional rendering indicates. It includes the third masculine singular pronoun "he" *(hû')*, and it might be better rendered: "Know that the LORD *alone* is God." This is a call to universal acknowledgment of the Lord's universal reign. Some modern readers may misinterpret the call to "know" as an intellectual or mental activity (as compared with the physical activities implied by the other six verbs). Such an approach fails to understand that the Hebrew word "know" does not allow any wedge to be driven between thought and deed. As is evident from the way the word "knowledge" is used in Hosea 4:1 and 4:6, to know is to act. In the context of Psalm 100, the word calls us to "internalize fully" our worship of the Lord — to have it seep and soak into every cell of who we are.

---

1. See the introductory essay and the essays on Pss 93; 95-99 in this volume; further, James L. Mays, *The Lord Reigns: A Theological Handbook to the Psalms* (Louisville: Westminster John Knox, 1994).

The next clause suffers from a textual problem. It is alternatively translated "It is he who made us, and we are his" (so most modern versions, which follow the oral or read version of the Hebrew text [*Qere*] and the Aramaic Targum) or "It is he who made us, and not ourselves" (so KJV, following the written Hebrew text [*Kethib*] and the Septuagint). In spite of the better external witnesses favoring the latter option, the former translation is preferred because it fits the context better — because the assertion that "we made ourselves" is not characteristic of any ancient mind-set, and because "we are his" is better idiomatic Hebrew.[2] The important thing to note here is that the act of creation is the basis of the Lord's reign. The image of God as shepherd and the people as sheep is a traditional royal metaphor that reinforces the claim that the Lord *reigns* over all. Note that the image also implies the *ongoing* nature of God's care.

The psalm ends with another threefold call to worship the Lord and a second reason for doing so. This time the psalmist draws upon traditional liturgical language:

> For the LORD is good;
>> his steadfast love [*ḥesed*] endures forever,
>> and his faithfulness to all generations.

The traditional phrase confesses that the Lord is reliable, worthy of worship, and able to bear the burden of the faith we place in him.

In the lectionary cycle, the psalm is assigned for worship on Christ the King Sunday, traditionally the last Sunday of the Pentecost season, on which the universal and eternal reign of the triune God is celebrated. As should be clear, the psalm is a perfect choice for this setting, as both its content and its place in the Psalter indicate. The psalm confesses that the Lord reigns because of the once-upon-a-time act of creation and also because of the ongoing caring actions of the Lord.

Rolf A. Jacobson

---

2. Cf. Frank-Lothar Hossfeld and Erich Zenger, *Psalms 2: A Commentary on Psalms 51–100*, ed. Klaus Baltzer, Hermeneia (Minneapolis: Fortress, 2005), 492; Marvin E. Tate, *Psalms 51–100*, WBC 20 (Dallas: Word, 1990), 534; Richard J. Clifford; *Psalms 73–150*, Abingdon Old Testament Commentaries (Nashville: Abingdon, 2003), 134.

PSALM 103

Eighth Sunday after the Epiphany, Year B
First Lesson: Hosea 2:14-20
(Psalm 103:1-13, 22)
Second Lesson: 2 Corinthians 3:1-6
Gospel Lesson: Mark 2:13-22

The lectionary locates this beloved *hymn of praise* (see the introductory essay) on the Eighth Sunday after the Epiphany (Year B), deep in the days of ordinary time. Perhaps the hope is that the psalmist's self-summons to "bless the LORD" (vv. 1, 22) will remind us in the bustle of our everyday lives to do the same, to call ourselves to worship God with "all that is in us" because all of life finally rests in God. The psalmist's aspiration is clear: *to praise* God ("bless" is repeated six times in vv. 1-2, 20-22) and *to not forget* God's graciousness (v. 2b). This is "a liturgical 'not forgetting' of all the LORD's dealing; the body of the psalm is a recollecting, remembering, reminding."[1] Integral to this remembering is repetition. The psalmist repeats key words about the character of God, namely, "steadfast love" (*ḥesed,* vv. 4, 8, 11, 17), "compassion" (vv. 4, 8, 13), and "righteousness" (vv. 6, 17; cf. these attributes in Hos 2:19 [Hebrew v. 21], also assigned by the lectionary). These reverberate across the psalm, weaving God's goodness in the past with the present even as they cultivate hope for the future.

Painted in bold, broad brushstrokes across a huge canvas, the psalm is stunningly comprehensive. The frame, the self-summons to "bless the LORD" (vv. 1a, 22b; cf. 104:1a), surrounds twenty-two lines, the number of letters in the Hebrew alphabet. Within it the psalmist engages ever-widening circles: the self (vv. 1-2), other individuals ("you" in the singular, vv. 3-5), Israel (v. 7), those who "fear the LORD" (vv. 11-13), mortals (vv. 14-16), the angels and heavenly host (vv. 20-21), and finally the whole of creation (v. 22). She repeats the word "all" five times in the first six verses (vv. 1-3, 6) and four times in the last four (vv. 19, 21-22). And she evokes vast geographical distances — earth to heaven, east to west (vv. 11-12) — to convey the magnitude of divine graciousness. The effect is an ushering to praise that is at once personal and cosmic.

The psalmist offers reasons for this praise first with a series of participial phrases that highlight God's "benefits," that is, God's recompense,

---

1. James L. Mays, *Psalms,* Interpretation (Louisville: John Knox, 1994), 326.

for the individual (vv. 3-5). The participles — "forgives," "heals," "re-deems," "crowns," "satisfies" — outline a transformative process, a move-ment from sin, portrayed as a debilitating and ultimately deadly sickness (see, e.g., Isa 57:18-19; Jer 30:12-13), to restored health sustained by God's provision. The psalmist imagines this renewed vigor as a griffon-vulture (*nešer;* NRSV: "eagle"), a symbol of royalty and divinity in the ancient Near East. God's redemptive work, that is, moves each of us from frailty to majestic flight (cf. Isa 40:31).

The psalmist parallels rejuvenation of strength (vv. 3-5) with deliver-ance from slavery to freedom, God's work for all people as revealed in the history of Israel (vv. 6-10). Referring to Moses (v. 7) and echoing Exodus 34:6-7 (vv. 8-10), the psalmist recalls the episode of the golden calf (Exod 32). Although the Hebrews had witnessed firsthand God's provision — safe passage, dewy manna, bitter water made sweet, water from dry rock (Exod 14-17) — and although they had pledged "as one" to keep God's covenant (Exod 19:8), their faithfulness waned quickly in Moses' absence. Their conduct warranted God's wrath. But God proclaimed instead a di-vine disposition of compassion and graciousness (Exod 34:6-7). God's love prevails over God's anger, an attribute the psalms herald repeatedly (e.g., Pss 30:5; 78:38-39; 86:15; 99:8; 111:4; 145:8-9). As such, God's "benefits" (*gml* as a noun, v. 2) are startlingly generous; God does not "repay" (*gml* as a verb, v. 10) according to what we deserve.

Pointing to the horizon, the heavens, and the home, the psalmist elab-orates on the intensity of God's devotion (vv. 11-14). Each verse of this sub-unit begins with the Hebrew letter *k:* verses 11 and 14 with the particle *kî* ("for," "because") and verses 12 and 13 with the preposition *k–* ("as," "like"). The result of this assonance is both *explanation* and *comparison.* God's steadfast love is vast as all space (vv. 11-12), enduring as all time (cf. v. 17), and fierce as that of a parent (cf. Prov 3:11-12; Hos 11; Ps 68:5). The psalmist relates this love to the covenant. It is enjoyed by "those who fear the LORD" (vv. 11, 13; cf. v. 17), who revere God and obey God's commandments (e.g., Pss 25:12, 14; 31:19; 34:9; 85:9). The psalmist also associates it with divine memory (v. 14). Just as "not forgetting" God's benefits orients us toward God, God's knowledge (memory) of our origins (cf. Gen 2:7; 3:19; Ps 90:3-6) inspires God's ongoing compassion for us. And, for the Hebrews, such "divine remembrance ensures life; forgetfulness entails death."[2]

---

2. William P. Brown, *Seeing the Psalms: A Theology of Metaphor* (Louisville: Westmin-ster John Knox, 2002), 185; e.g., Pss 8:4; 9:12; 74:2; 83:4; 88:5.

Against this vibrant portrayal of God's graciousness, the psalmist picks up the motif of mortality ("we are dust," v. 14) and describes humanity anew, as flowers that flourish, fade, and are forgotten (vv. 15-18; cf. Ps 90). Worship of God, it seems, invites reconsideration of what it means to be human. The stark contrast between the two underscores God's generosity: although mortals are sinful (vv. 3, 10, 12), made of dust, and fleeting as chaff on the wind, God *nevertheless* honors the covenant, even with generations yet unborn. Awareness of our finitude inspires humility and more profound awe of God's fidelity.

God's steadfast love is ultimately for the psalmist an expression of God's sovereignty (vv. 19-22). The poet emphasizes that everything belongs to God by repeating third masculine singular suffixes (i.e., "[God's] throne . . . [God's] kingdom . . . [God's] angels . . . [God's] hosts . . . [God's] dominion") and summoning *all* of it to praise. The vision is of a cosmic chorus, the voices of angels and hosts who do God's will and obey God's word mingled harmoniously with those who do God's commandments on earth (v. 18). No one, not a thing, is silent, perhaps least of all the psalmist, who ends where she began: "Bless the LORD, O my soul."

Christine Roy Yoder

PSALM 104

Day of Pentecost, Year A
> First Lesson: Acts 2:1-21 or Numbers 11:24-30
> **(Psalm 104:24-34, 35b)**
> Second Lesson: 1 Corinthians 12:3b-13 or Acts 2:1-21
> Gospel Lesson: John 20:19-23 or John 7:37-39

Day of Pentecost, Year B
> First Lesson: Acts 2:1-21 or Ezekiel 37:1-14
> **(Psalm 104:24-34, 35b)**
> Second Lesson: Romans 8:22-27 or Acts 2:1-21
> Gospel Lesson: John 15:26-27; 16:4b-15

Twenty-second Sunday after Pentecost, Year B
First Lesson: Job 38:1-7, (34-41)
(Psalm 104:1-9, 24, 35c)
Second Lesson: Hebrews 5:1-10
Gospel Lesson: Mark 10:35-45

Day of Pentecost, Year C
First Lesson: Acts 2:1-21 or Genesis 11:1-9
(Psalm 104:24-34, 35b)
Second Lesson: Romans 8:14-17 or Acts 2:1-21
Gospel Lesson: John 14:8-17, (25-27)

One of the most extensive *hymns* (see the introductory essay) in the Psalter, Psalm 104 presents a grand tour of God's creation and maintenance of the cosmos. The psalm seamlessly moves from God's initial act of creation (vv. 2b-9) to God's providential care of the world and all therein (vv. 10-30). As a joy-filled "meditation" (v. 24), the psalm celebrates the plethora of God's works. Diversity is not a curse, the psalmist claims, but a gift, the product of God's unsurpassable wisdom (v. 24).

The journey of this psalm actually begins in Psalm 103, in which the opening command to "bless the LORD" is also found (see also the last three verses there). In this earlier psalm, God's gracious activity in the lives of human beings is the dominant focus (103:3-13, 17-19; see further on Ps 103 in this volume). Together, Psalms 103 and 104 form an essential theological pairing: the God of salvation and the God of creation are identified as one and the same (and woe to anyone who rends them asunder).

Psalm 104 opens with an exclamation of God's majesty cast in wonderful metaphorical guise: God is enwrapped with light "as with a garment." Here light is not so much an act of creation (cf. Gen 1:3) as an aspect of divine majesty. In the great Babylonian Epic of Creation, the gods wear "mantles of radiance" or effulgent "auras" as markers of their divinity (see *Enuma Elish* I 68, 138). Creation officially begins with the construction of God's abode in the heavens, established upon the supernal waters (cf. Gen 1:6-8). This "habitat for divinity" establishes an important theme that pervades much of the psalm, namely, that of *home*. God appoints a place for the waters (v. 8); the birds have their "habitation" (vv. 12, 16-17); mountains are the domain of the "wild goats" and rocks of the "coneys" or badgers (v. 18); the lions have their dens (v. 22); Leviathan has the sea (v. 26). By extension, every living thing has its place in the created order. Domicile and providence are inextricably linked.

Another related theme is *provision*. "God provides" could in fact be the motto of the psalm. God "gives drink to every wild animal" (v. 11), "waters the mountains" as well as the trees (vv. 13, 16), even provides the prey for the "young lions" (v. 21). God gives "them their food in due season" (v. 27). Verses 27-30 drive home creation's absolute dependence upon God. God either provides, thereby sustaining life, or withdraws, reducing life to the dust out of which it was created (cf. 103:13-14). God's "breath" or spirit is what animates all of life.

God's providential care, however, is devoted not just to sustaining life, but also to providing enjoyment, as John Calvin himself wisely noted.[1] Indeed, verse 15 was Calvin's favorite verse in the psalm: the delights of a good wine were for Calvin a sign of creation's abundance of joy (to be enjoyed, of course, in moderation). Both utility *and* enjoyment (Latin *uti* and *frui*) characterize God's providential care. God's "hand" is not clenched, but open and giving (v. 28b), and God finds pleasure in such giving. God is not duty-bound to creation, as in Genesis 9:14-16, but freely giving. The sustenance of creation is, according to the psalmist, a matter not so much of "remembering" covenant as of reveling in delight. The world according to the psalmist runs on God's gratuitous care, and the needle is never on empty! The myth of scarcity, along with its demand for the aggressive competition for resources, is undercut in this psalm.

On this panoramic tour the psalmist points out a few cosmic surprises. First is the diminished place of human beings. For the first thirteen verses human beings are nowhere to be found. Lacking, moreover, is any hint of human dominance in creation, in contrast to Psalm 8. Human beings are equally dependent upon God, as are the rock badgers and creepy crawlers. Indeed, all that distinguishes lions from humans is that the former take the "night shift" while the latter ply their trade during the day (v. 23). Far from endorsing a "dominance model" of creation, Psalm 104 adopts an "integration model" in which human beings act as interdependent partners with all the other creatures.[2]

1. John Calvin, *Commentary on the Book of Psalms* (Grand Rapids: Eerdmans, 1949), 155-58.

2. See James Limburg, "Down to Earth Theology: Psalm 104 and the Environment," *CurTM* 21 (1994): 340-46.

Another surprise comes from the shocking appearance of a creature considered an unwelcome guest by other biblical tradents, namely, Leviathan, the monstrous serpent of the sea. Contrary to NRSV and others, a preferable translation of verse 26 is the following:

> There go the ships,
>   as well as Leviathan, with which you fashioned to play *(lĕśaḥeq)*.

Traditionally, Leviathan serves as a symbol of chaos, an enemy of God and creation, as in Psalm 74:13-14 and Isaiah 27:1 (but see Job 41). In contrast to these traditions, no animosity is shared between God and Leviathan in Psalm 104. The psalmist pits these two powerful agents, God and monster, not as mortal enemies but as playmates, and in so doing has divested Leviathan of its dark side. The poet, in short, has *demythologized chaos.* Chaos is no longer associated with any mythical creature or the primordial waters. All creation is deemed good, even its furthest reaches. While still dangerous to those who do business on the sea (see the dangers of maritime commerce in Ps 107:23-27), Leviathan represents no cosmic hostility, much less duality, in relation to God and creation.

Another surprise is found at the conclusion of the psalm, and it has repulsed many a modern reader. The lectionary excludes verse 35a, and for good reason. The psalm's cosmic purview, which includes even the monstrous Leviathan within the orbit of God's providential care, has no room for the wicked. But for the ancient listener, this imprecation made perfect sense in a world that was otherwise perceived as harmoniously vibrant, despite the one human glitch. On the positive side, this grim conclusion rescues the psalm from taking a sentimental, rose-colored view of the world. Here is an authentic assessment of creation *as it stands,* a world in which the purveyors of chaos are not mythical beasts but genuinely *human* monsters. By taking chaos out of Leviathan and placing it squarely on the shoulders of human beings, the psalmist comes to a profound awareness of the "banality of evil." Hitler, too, was human.

But perhaps the greatest surprise comes from the neglected second half of verse 31, wherein the psalmist exhorts God to enjoy creation. The language of unabashed joy is rarely attributed to God in biblical tradition, and its implications are staggering. God's work in the world is not drudgery. Delighting, as God does in all of creation, counters all manner of treating the world solely in terms of utility. The psalmist makes, in effect, a startling ecological claim: ecology, at root, is an exercise of joy. To rejoice is to celebrate the abundance that God provides for the world and to resist the temptation to treat such abundance as a commodity.

God's active delight in sustaining creation paradoxically heightens human agency within creation. No guarantee is given that God's joy will last forever, hence the psalmist's urgent exhortation followed by an acknowledgment of God's destructive capabilities (v. 32). Thus, it is incumbent upon God's creatures to ensure that divine delight is sustained so that the world be sustained. The psalmist adds to this effort by poetically describing the world as God's playfield and offering this "meditation" in thanksgiving to God.

William P. Brown

PSALM 105

Tenth Sunday after Pentecost, Year A
First Lesson: Genesis 29:15-28
(Psalm 105:1-11, 45b)
Second Lesson: Romans 8:26-39
Gospel Lesson: Matthew 13:31-33, 44-52

Twelfth Sunday after Pentecost, Year A
First Lesson: Genesis 37:1-4, 12-28
(Psalm 105:1-6, 16-22, 45b)
Second Lesson: Romans 10:5-15
Gospel Lesson: Matthew 14:22-33

Fifteenth Sunday after Pentecost, Year A
First Lesson: Exodus 3:1-15
(Psalm 105:1-6, 23-26, 45b)
Second Lesson: Romans 12:9-21
Gospel Lesson: Matthew 16:21-28

Eighteenth Sunday after Pentecost, Year A
First Lesson: Exodus 16:2-15
(Psalm 105:1-6, 37-45)
Second Lesson: Philippians 1:21-30
Gospel Lesson: Matthew 20:1-16

One of the *historical psalms* (see Pss 78; 106; 135; 136; and the introductory essay), Psalm 105 is perhaps the most clearly chronological, following a familiar call to remember the action of God in Israel's past with a recollection of the covenant with the descendants of Abraham and Jacob (v. 6), and a recital of five primary stages in Israel's journey that runs from "few in number, of little account" (v. 12) to possessing "the lands of the nations . . . [and] the wealth of the peoples" (v. 44).

The function of the historical material in the psalm is twofold: (a) to proclaim God's "wonderful works" (vv. 1-2) to those who seek this Lord; and (b) to serve as a glad remembrance of those "wonderful works" (v. 5) that are the source of Israel's life and joy. History here is the realm in which God has worked, and in which God can be counted on to continue working.

Within the lectionary the division of the psalm into its major portions is followed, although not precisely, and not over consecutive Sundays. Each of the sections is paired either with the primary figure or with the definitive event of the first lesson. Although juggling the intervening Sundays may prove a challenge, one could certainly follow the lectionary walk with this psalm from the Tenth Sunday after Pentecost to the Eighteenth Sunday after Pentecost, retracing Israel's steps, remembering the Lord's mighty acts, and giving thanks to the Lord for the promise that the faith-descendants of Abraham now share. The exposition below follows the psalm as written, not as the lectionary has divided it.

As already noted, this psalm contains a series of five sections or stages of Israel's journey to nationhood, which follow an introduction that is a summons both to praise and to remembrance. Verses 7-15 are sometimes combined with verses 1-6 as one long introduction, perhaps following 1 Chronicles 16, which records the first fifteen verses of this psalm with portions of Psalms 96 and 106 as a summary of the praise of "Asaph and his kindred." But there is properly a division following Psalm 105:6, which shifts from a call to worship to a theological claim about the Lord "our God," and the covenant. Thus, the psalm proceeds as follows:

Introduction.	Call to worship/praise (vv. 1-6: "Remember . . .")	
I. Vv. 7-11	Remembering the covenant	
II. Vv. 12-15	Strangers among the nations: "When they were few in number . . ."	
III. Vv. 16-22	Famine in the land: "When God summoned famine . . ."	

> IV. Vv. 23-36   Israel in Egypt: "Then Israel came to Egypt . . ."
> V. Vv. 37-45   Israel in the wilderness: "Then he brought
>   Israel out . . ."
>
> Conclusion. Vv. 43-45

Divisions in the "poetic narrative" are nicely marked in the NRSV with "when" or "then." The psalm's movement selectively follows the history of Israel, dividing the journey from tribes to nationhood into five chapters, or, for the sake of paralleling the beginning of the Old Testament, perhaps five "books" that make up the foundational library of Israel's past.

After the introductory verses, the first "book" (vv. 7-11) of Israel's history fittingly begins with a remembrance of the covenant, which is named three times in this section of the psalm. Critical here is that the covenant is everlasting (v. 10), and that the Lord will be "mindful of his covenant forever" (v. 8). The promised remembrance of the Lord follows immediately after the call for the people to remember, in turn, the covenant that the Lord has wrought on their behalf. We who read and lay claim to this psalm are caught — or perhaps better, hemmed in — between these two acts of remembrance: our God's and our own.

The second section (vv. 12-15) centers on God's protection of the people as they wandered "from nation to nation." At every point, at every turn, the Lord is with this people. Striking here is the declaration of the Lord made in the face of those powers that might threaten the chosen ones. The function of this declaration is to parallel the statement that the Lord protects; the Lord "allowed no one to oppress," the Lord "rebuked kings." It is interesting that within this quotation the people are called "the anointed" and "prophets." These titles for the people may seem awkward or unusual, and are certainly unique to this psalm. But they seem to fit well within the stated goal of the psalm's introduction: to "make known" the Lord's deeds, and will among the peoples, which is one purpose of an anointed prophet.

In the third unit (vv. 16-22) we read of famine in the land. But "[w]hen he [the LORD] summoned famine against the land," Joseph was provided for. The action here is all initiated by God — the famine, the man God "sent ahead" to prepare a place for the people, the rise of Joseph to rule over Pharaoh's possessions, and the preparation of Egypt to face the coming famine (cf. v. 22, and further, Gen 41). It is God who is at work, the psalm declares and reminds the reader, God who is doing "wonderful works."

"Book" IV (vv. 23-36) finds Israel in Egypt. Here again the works the Lord performs are key, but in this case the works are terrible indeed. First, the hearts of the Egyptians are turned against the Israelites, and are now hardened and crafty (v. 25; see Exod 1:10). To redeem the difficulties of the people, the Lord sends Moses and Aaron (see Exod 3-4), whom the Lord has chosen to lead Israel out of Egypt. Ironically, the lectionary forgets the plagues, the prototypical "wonderful works" of the Lord. This is a shortcoming the preacher may well want to correct.

Finally, in the last section — Israel in the wilderness (vv. 37-42) — the emphasis is on God's provision for the people. The flight to the Red Sea and the death of the Egyptian armies are passed over. Indeed, the situation is summarized as follows:

Then [the Lord] brought Israel out with gold and silver. . . .
Egypt was glad when they departed. (vv. 37-38)

In the wilderness the Lord provides quails, "food from heaven," and water from the rock. But most striking is the reason given:

For he remembered his holy promise,
and Abraham, his servant.

The promise of verse 8 is reiterated. The Lord remembers, and so too must we.

Psalm 105 is an exercise in proclamation and remembering. The introduction in verses 1-6 is the key to understanding how the psalm functions, and it is no surprise that these verses are included in the reading of the psalm on each of its appointed Sundays. Those who read and hear this psalm are called to join in giving thanks, to make known the wonderful works of the Lord our God, and to remember how this God remembers us. This is the promise that the psalm offers and entrusts to us. So we, too, can conclude with the psalmist: "Praise the Lord!"

Karl N. Jacobson

PSALM 106

Twenty-first Sunday after Pentecost, Year A
First Lesson: Exodus 32:1-14
(Psalm 106:1-6, 19-23)
Second Lesson: Philippians 4:1-9
Gospel Lesson: Matthew 22:1-14

Another of the *historical psalms* (see Pss 78; 105; 135; 136; and the introductory essay), Psalm 106 employs historical material to provide the expected reasons for praise that are common to this genre of praise psalms. Moments from Israel's history are recalled to iterate and reiterate the steadfast love of the Lord for the people. As with Psalms 78 and 105, this psalm highlights the "mighty doings" of the Lord. In Psalm 106 God's deeds on behalf of the people are recalled in the form of a question:

> Who can utter the mighty doings of the LORD,
>   or declare all his praise? (v. 2)

Drawn into the psalm via this question, the reader is also given the answer: those who do not forget their God, "their Savior, who has done great things" (see vv. 7, 13, 21).

The historical memory in Psalm 106 functions in two ways: (a) drawing the individual reader/hearer directly into Israel's story — the individual Israelite and Israel are one and the same in this psalm; and (b) encouraging the present-day "people of Israel" to recognize their own standing before the Lord — they, too, forget as their ancestors did.

1. *Recalling the past deeds of the Lord: Who can utter . . . ?* The provocative question that follows the initial call to praise begs an answer. And while we do not then find an answering phrase like "The one who . . . ," the psalm offers itself as a tacit answer to the question. The historical events that are recalled, the "mighty doings" of the Lord, are to be remembered so that the sins of the nation's youth do not dominate all of its life.

Further, verse 3 implies that there is an ethical element involved in the utterance of the mighty deeds of the Lord:

> Happy are those who observe justice,
>   and who do righteousness.

A quick reading of the lection might leave one confused as to just what role this verse plays. But it seems clear that justice and righteousness are crucial in the remembrance of the down-and-dirty details of the relationship of Israel with her God. It may be something of a "chicken or the egg" dialectic — which comes first, the doing of justice or the remembering of the Lord's past actions? Will one produce the other? Regardless, the relationship between the two is clearly significant, precisely in the ordering of the psalm's statements. "Who can utter? Who can declare? Happy will be the one who observes justice." If unhappiness and trouble come from forgetting the Lord's past deeds on one's behalf, then there is surely a correlation between right relationship and right behavior.

Within the psalm is a recurring pattern of vignettes, which begin with the naming of a place/location during Israel's wilderness sojourn and a recounting of Israel's failures in that place. Included in this list are "the camp" (vv. 16-18), Horeb (vv. 19-23), "their tents" (vv. 24-27), Baal of Peor (vv. 28-31, which seems to be a Sinai parallel),[1] Meribah (vv. 32-33), and Canaan (vv. 34-39). The lectionary reading includes only one of these vignettes, the episode at Horeb. Central to this episode is the forgetting of God and the deeds that God has done. The people have forgotten their history — a misstep they seem doomed to repeat. This neglect is so serious that the Lord resolves to destroy the people, but Moses intercedes for them, "stepping into the breach" (see also vv. 28-30; cf. Ezek 22:30). This episode typifies the iniquity introduced in verse 6, and it is this memory of sin in the face of the Lord's goodness with which the psalm challenges the reader.

These memories of Israel's past failures and infidelity serve as a potent warning to all who would be in relationship with the Lord. Human sin, iniquity, and wickedness will always be a danger to that relationship (v. 6). More than this, however, there is something of promise in this remembrance. The ultimate end of the psalm is that the Lord, regardless of — or, perhaps better, flying in the face of — Israel's repeated failure and faithlessness, regards this people in their distress (v. 44). The Lord remembers the covenant even if the people do not, and shows both compassion and steadfast love (v. 45).

The one who remembers what the Lord has done, and how his ancestors have failed and how the Lord still heard their cry, will be less likely to

---

1. See Frank M. Cross, *From Epic to Canon: History and Literature in Ancient Israel* (Baltimore: Johns Hopkins University Press, 1998), 60.

fall into error. And even when such a one still sins, as his ancestors did, he will know that he can raise his voice in praise and prayer, and that the Lord will listen.

2. *The worldview of the psalm: From macro to micro.* One of the more striking elements of the psalm, and unique among the historical psalms, is the explicit equation of the individual with the nation that takes place in verses 4-5. The psalmist prays to the Lord for herself, but in terms of the nation:

> Remember *me* . . . when you show favor to your *people;*
>   help *me* when you deliver *them;*
> that *I* may see the prosperity of your *chosen ones,*
>   that *I* may rejoice in the gladness of your *nation.*

This move from the macrolevel of nation to the microlevel of the individual is significant in two ways: first, it brings the relationship with God to the personal, intimate level; second, it brings the question of doing justice and living righteously to bear on the individual. There is no shifting either of blessing or blame, of favor or responsibility at this point. The prayer of the individual echoes the reality of the people, claiming both the promise and the responsibility of this great and glorious heritage (v. 5) that the Lord has provided.[2]

3. *Psalm 106 and its lectionary companions.* Psalm 106, with the selection of the Horeb vignette, is a good match for the first reading from Exodus 32, the story of the golden calf, which Psalm 106 describes beautifully as an exchange of "the glory of God for the image of an ox that eats grass." Philippians 4:8 is another helpful and pointed connection, urging the reader to think about whatever is true, honorable, just, pure, and the like.

The psalm's answer to the question that moves the psalm, "Who can utter the mighty doings of the Lord, or declare all his praise?" is clear: the one who remembers the past — both human infidelity and divine steadfast love — and who seeks righteousness at all times.

Karl N. Jacobson

---

2. Cf. William P. Brown, *Seeing the Psalms: A Theology of Metaphor* (Louisville: Westminster John Knox, 2002), 46.

PSALM 107

Twenty-fourth Sunday after Pentecost, Year A
    First Lesson: Joshua 3:7-17
    (Psalm 107:1-7, 33-37)
    Second Lesson: 1 Thessalonians 2:9-13
    Gospel Lesson: Matthew 23:1-12

Fourth Sunday in Lent, Year B
    First Lesson: Numbers 21:4-9
    (Psalm 107:1-3, 17-22)
    Second Lesson: Ephesians 2:1-10
    Gospel Lesson: John 3:14-21

Eleventh Sunday after Pentecost, Year C
    First Lesson: Hosea 11:1-11
    (Psalm 107:1-9, 43)
    Second Lesson: Colossians 3:1-11
    Gospel Lesson: Luke 12:13-21

Psalm 107 was most likely a liturgy of thanks *(tôdâ)* offered by worshipers at a festival at the temple in Jerusalem. The first three verses introduce the content of the psalm with their words of celebration of the goodness of God, who has redeemed them from the hand of the oppressor and gathered them in "from the east and from the west, / from the north and from the south" (v. 3).

Four groups of people appear in the psalm, together representing, perhaps, the "redeemed of the LORD" mentioned in verse 2: (1) verses 4-9 tell of a group of wanderers, lost in the desert, who finally arrive at their destination; (2) verses 10-16 tell the story of prisoners who are set free; (3) verses 17-22 tell of "sick" persons who are healed; and (4) verses 23-32 are about a group of sailors who are saved from shipwreck.

Each vignette follows a pattern:

- a description of the distress (vv. 4-5, 10-12, 17-18, 23-27)
- a prayer to the Lord (vv. 6, 13, 19, 28)
- details of the delivery (vv. 7, 14, 19-20, 29)
- an expression of thanks (vv. 8-9, 15-16, 21-22, 30-32)

281

The first vignette (vv. 4-9) recounts the story of a group of wanderers who lose their way in the wilderness, a wasteland, a place where there is no city. East of Palestine lies a vast desert separating it from the eastern side of the Fertile Crescent, Mesopotamia. Few travelers in the ancient Near East dared to traverse this terrain. They followed the established trade routes: the "Way of the Sea," which led from Egypt to Mesopotamia north along the coast of Palestine, then east across the valley of Jezreel, and finally south along the Euphrates River; or the "King's Highway," which ran east of the Jordan River, north through Damascus into Syria, and then south along the Euphrates.

The wanderers described in verses 4-9 hunger and thirst; their inmost being is faint. In verse 6 the reader encounters the "prayer to the Lord" that is repeated in each of the four vignettes:

> Then they cried to the LORD in their trouble,
>   and he delivered them from their distress.

God then caused their path to be a straight path, leading them out of the wilderness to a city, an oasis, a place of habitation with wells of water and food to eat.

In verse 8, the expression of thanks that also occurs in the other four vignettes is first sounded:

> Let them thank the LORD for his steadfast love,
>   for his wonderful works to humankind.

This refrain echoes the opening words of the psalm (v. 1) and maintains the focus of the psalm — giving thanks to the God who has delivered the people and gathered them together from all the lands.

Following the refrain of verse 8, the psalmist gives the reason why those whom God steadfastly loves will give praise to the Lord. Verse 9 begins with the Hebrew word *kî* (translated "for" or "because"), a causal conjunction. God is worthy of thanks *because* God has satisfied the thirsting and hungering of the wanderers.

The second vignette (vv. 10-16) speaks of ones dwelling in darkness and the shadow of death. Following the four compass directions of verse 3, the west is the location of this second group of people. The west is the place where the sun sets, the deathly place of darkness in which the sun dies every night as it makes its journey over the earthly realm.

Psalm 19 references the daily journey of the sun through the heavens (see Ps 19:4b-6).

The ones dwelling in darkness will reemerge in the light with the coming of day, just as the sun reemerges from its deathly place of darkness each morning. They too can offer thanks (v. 15) because God has shattered the doors of bronze and broken into pieces the bars of iron.

The third vignette in Psalm 107 (vv. 17-22) speaks of ones who are "sick" because of their transgressions. The word translated "sick" (Hebrew *'wyl*) actually means "foolish." The people of the ancient Near East associated sickness with foolishness or sin and understood it as God's punishment for sin (see Pss 32:1-5; 38:3, 5). In the prophetic books, the north, the third direction mentioned in Psalm 107:3, was often depicted as the direction from which the punishment of God came. The prophet Jeremiah, for example, saw "a boiling pot, tilted away from the north," about which God said, "out of the north disaster shall break out on all the inhabitants of the land" (Jer 1:13-14). In Ezekiel 9 God summons the executioners of Jerusalem, and they "came from the direction of the upper gate, which faces north" (9:2; cf. also Jer 47:2; 50:41-42).

In the midst of their oppression, the ones who are "sick" cry out to the Lord, who sends comforting words and rescues them from the pits. But after the expression of thanks in verse 21, we find no *kî*, no "causal clause." Rather, the ones God rescues offer sacrifices of thanks *(tôdâ)* and recount God's deed with shouts of joy.[1] When thank offerings were sacrificed to God, the priests and the worshipers shared in a communal meal of gratitude for God's goodness. Thus those who had abhorred food and had arrived at the gates of death tasted again life-giving nourishment.

The last vignette of Psalm 107 (vv. 23-32) tells the story of ones going down to the sea in ships, doing business on the great waters. "The sea" is the fourth direction mentioned in verse 3 (see the text note in NRSV); it represented a real threat in the ancient Near East. Merchant ships sailing out of the Phoenician ports across the Mediterranean Sea often encountered difficulties in its unpredictable waters. Verses 25-29 depict God as the ruler of the sea, able to command its waters to do his bidding (see also Pss 29:3-4; 65:7; 89:9-10; 95:5). A storm on the waters (vv. 25-27) leads

---

1. Erhard Gerstenberger, *Psalms, Part 2, and Lamentations*, FOTL 15 (Grand Rapids: Eerdmans, 2001), 252, reminds us: "To offer a sacrifice of gratitude after being saved was an age-old religious obligation in the ancient Near East and other cultures"; see Pss 66 and 116.

the sailors to cry out to God (v. 28). God then calms the waters and gives the sailors rest in the haven of their pleasure (v. 30).

Verse 31 contains the expected expression of thanks that each group has offered in Psalm 107. As with the ones who were "sick," the rescued sailors do not state a reason for giving thanks to God (there is no *kî* here). Instead, they exalt God in the assembly of the people and glorify God in the dwelling place of the elders.

In each of the four vignettes, the "prayer to the LORD" (vv. 6, 13, 19, 28) and the "expression of thanks" (vv. 8, 15, 21, 31) are identical:

> Then they cried to the LORD in their trouble,
>   and he delivered them from their distress.

> Let them thank the LORD for his steadfast love,
>   for his wonderful works to humankind.

Such repetition provides further evidence that the psalm was used in a liturgical setting, in which groups of worshipers recited the words of Psalm 107 antiphonally with presiding priests.

Are the four vignettes actual accounts of deliverance by the Lord sung in celebration at a festival? Or is the psalm purely a literary composition, with the four groups representing, in the words of James L. Mays, "all those who have experienced the redemption of the Lord"?[2] We may never know.

In its original form, Psalm 107 most likely consisted only of verses 1-32 and was used at the temple in Jerusalem as a liturgy of thanksgiving for deliverance. Verses 33-42, which proclaim that the sovereign Lord can provide the people with all their needs, may have been a separate composition added to Psalm 107 at some point in its history. In these verses we read that the Lord makes it possible for the hungry to dwell safely in the land and establish a city; to sow fields, plant vineyards, and gather a harvest; to have children and increase their cattle (vv. 36-38). The Lord pours contempt on rulers who oppress the people (vv. 39-40). The future of the upright is secured, and the wicked are left speechless (v. 42). The psalm closes with the words:

> Let those who are wise give heed to these things,
>   and consider the steadfast love of the LORD.

2. James L. Mays, *Psalms,* Interpretation (Louisville: John Knox, 1994), 342.

Psalm 107 is a hymn of thanksgiving for a God who protects, delivers, and heals the people whom God had returned home from exile in Babylon. It is thus a fitting response to the first lessons in Years A, B, and C that record other saving acts of God that call for these words:

> O give thanks to the LORD, for he is good;
> for his steadfast love endures forever.
> Let the redeemed of the LORD say so,
> those he redeemed from trouble. (vv. 1-2)

Nancy L. deClaissé-Walford

PSALM 110

Ascension of the Lord, Year C
    First Lesson: Acts 1:1-11
    (Psalm 47 or **Psalm 110**)
    Second Lesson: Ephesians 1:15-23
    Gospel Lesson: Luke 24:44-53

A *royal psalm* with numerous affinities to Psalm 2 (see the introductory essay), Psalm 110 was probably associated in some way with the enthronement of the Davidic king in Zion.[1] In the context of the Psalter, where it appears as the third in a cluster of Davidic psalms (note *lĕdawīd* in the superscriptions to Pss 108; 109; 110), Psalm 110 may be understood as Yahweh's answer to the king's prayers for victory in battle (Ps 108) and for vindication and deliverance from his enemies (Ps 109). Although commentators continue to wrestle with "the extremely difficult and disputed state" of the Hebrew text,[2] the general outline of the psalm is clear. The speaker, who appears to be a cultic prophet or priest, solemnly utters two divine oracles installing David or his heir as king (v. 1) and priest (v. 4) in Zion. Each pronouncement is followed by a vivid description of Yahweh

---

1. H.-J. Kraus, *Psalms 60–150: A Continental Commentary* (Minneapolis: Fortress, 1993), 345, 346-47.

2. Kraus, *Psalms 60–150*, 345.

Fig. 10. In Psalm 110:1a, "The LORD says to my lord" (the king): "Sit at my right hand." This image shows the pharaoh sitting literally at the right hand of the god Horus. Note the god's right hand, which is behind and supportive of the king, while his left hand holds an ankh, the symbol of life.

as a mighty warrior who establishes the worldwide dominion of his chosen king (vv. 2-3, 5-7).

Verse 1 opens with the formula commonly used to introduce divine oracles *(nĕ'ûm yhwh)*. The word of Yahweh, addressed to the king, exalts him to the seat of honor at the right side of Yahweh's own throne (cf. 1 Kings 2:19; Pss 45:9; 80:17, where the king is called the "man of [Yahweh's] right hand"; see also fig. 10). Though embattled ("in the midst of your enemies," v. 2b), the king reigns secure while Yahweh subdues all

Fig. 11. In Psalm 110:1b, the psalmist states that the king is to sit at God's right hand "until I [the LORD] make your [the king's] enemies your footstool." In this image the pharaoh sits on the god's lap. His footstool is composed of subjugated enemies. Such imagery was common in the royal iconography of ancient Egypt (see also fig. 12).

nations under his feet (v. 1b; see figs. 11-12).[3] Because he shares in Yahweh's universal dominion, his sovereignty will extend outward from Zion (v. 2a) and ultimately encompass the whole world (*'al-'ereṣ rabbâ*, v. 6). In such a context, the command to "rule in the midst of your enemies" (v. 2b) carries the force of a divine promise whose fulfillment is certain.

3. For the imagery, see Josh 10:24 and the ancient Near Eastern parallels cited by Kraus, *Psalms 60–150*, 349.

While the precise meaning of verse 3 is disputed, its complex poetic imagery reinforces the conviction expressed in verses 1-2 that Yahweh alone is the source of the king's might.[4] In the Hebrew text (MT), verse 3a speaks of the eager willingness (*nĕdābôt;* cf. Judg 5:2; 1QM 7:5; 1QS 1:7, 11; 5:1) of the king's forces to follow him into battle. NRSV follows some later Hebrew manuscripts, Symmachus, and Jerome in reading "on the holy mountains" (*bĕharărê-qōdeš;* cf. Pss 2:6; 87:1), taking this phrase with verse 3a. In contrast, JPS and *The Revised Psalms of the New American Bible* (1991) translate the MT without emendation ("in majestic holiness," *bĕhadrê-qōdeš;* cf. Pss 29:2; 96:9; 2 Chron 20:21), and link the phrase to the following verse 3b. In the MT, verse 3b compares the abundance and power of the young men whom God has raised up to fight this holy war (*yaldūtekā,* "your youth," understood as a concrete, collective noun;[5] cf. NRSV) to the divine gift of the dew on the mountains (cf. Ps 133:3; see 2 Sam 17:12 for dew as an image of overwhelming military might). Another interpretation of verse 3b is possible, however. Some Hebrew manuscripts, Septuagint, and Peshitta vocalize the same consonants found in MT to read "I have begotten you" (*yĕlidtîkā*).[6] This notion of the divine origin/adoption of the Davidic king finds a parallel in Psalm 2:7. On either reading, verse 3b further grounds the reign of the king in the mighty deeds of Yahweh, who graciously elects and powerfully vindicates Israel's sovereign.

The second instance of divine speech, introduced in verse 4 as an irrevocable oath, invests the king with the office of priest "according to the order of Melchizedek," the ancient priest-king of Jerusalem (Gen 14:18-23) whose throne David and his heirs have now assumed (cf. Gen 14:19-20, 22, which identifies the "God Most High" whom Melchizedek serves as Yahweh). A number of Old Testament passages describe the Davidic kings carrying out priestly functions (1 Sam 13:9; 2 Sam 6:13, 14, 17, 18; 1 Kings 8:14, 56).[7]

As in the first oracle, so here the divine word is followed with a description, not of the king's activities, but of God's mighty deeds on the king's behalf. Verse 5 inverts the image of verse 1; now it is the Lord (*'ădōnāy;* cf. "my lord," *'ădōnî,* v. 1), Yahweh himself, who stands at the

---

4. For different evaluations of the text-critical and interpretive issues, too numerous and complex to discuss here, see Leslie C. Allen, *Psalms 101–150,* WBC 21 (Waco: Word, 1983), 79-82, and Kraus, *Psalms 60–150,* 344-53.

5. So Allen, *Psalms 101–150,* 81.

6. So Kraus, *Psalms 60–150,* 350; *The Revised Psalms of the New American Bible.*

7. See Kraus, *Psalms 60–150,* 351.

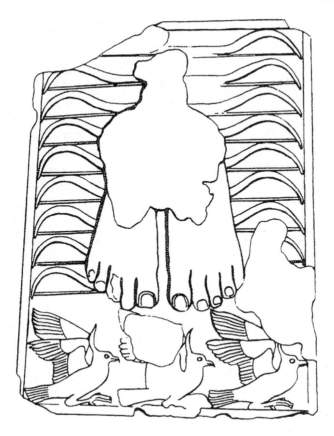

Fig. 12. The king's enemies in Psalm 110:1 might be thought of as human figures (see fig. 11) or as nations or regions. This image show the pharaoh's feet resting on "the nine bows" — an expression used in Egypt to designate the various regions of the country and, later, the countries hostile to Egypt. (The three birds with crossed wings — which prevents their escape — have the same connotation as the subjugated bows.) The king's footstool, then, is comprised of the entities he rules.

king's "right hand" (v. 5a; for this metaphor, see Pss 16:8; 121:5; Isa 45:1; 63:12). With chilling images the psalmist portrays YHWH as a warrior who crushes kings on the "day of his wrath" (v. 5b; cf. Ps 2:5; Isa 13:9; Zeph 2:3), judging among the nations, heaping up corpses, and crushing heads (or leaders) far and wide as he secures the universal dominion of his chosen ruler (v. 6).

In striking contrast to this scene of carnage and death, the final verse of the psalm depicts the king drawing continued refreshment and sustenance from Yahweh (cf. Pss 3:3; 27:6). In speaking of "the stream by the way," the psalmist may be referring to the Gihon spring, which seems to have been associated with enthronement rituals (1 Kings 1:38-40).[8] Alternatively, the image may be of a warrior halting in his pursuit of the enemy only long enough to refresh himself. In either case, the psalm closes with a picture of the complete and final victory of Yahweh and his king.

The use of Psalm 110 as a responsorial on Ascension Day follows a widespread early Christian interpretation of Psalm 110:1 as a divine oracle addressed to Jesus, the Son of David, whom God has raised from the dead and exalted to God's right hand. In fact, the New Testament writers quote or allude to Psalm 110:1 more frequently than any other Old Testament text (citations: Matt 22:44; Mark 12:36; Luke 20:42-43; Acts 2:34-35; 1 Cor 15:25; Heb 1:13; allusions: Matt 26:64; Mark 14:62; 16:19; Luke 22:69; Acts 2:33; 5:31; 7:55-56; Rom 8:34; Eph 1:20; Col 3:1; Heb 1:3; 8:1; 10:12-13; 12:2; 1 Pet 3:22). The author of the letter to the Hebrews extends this christological reading to the second oracle (Ps 110:4, cited in Heb 5:6; 7:17, 21; allusions in Heb 5:10; 6:20; 7:3, 11, 15; 8:1), constructing out of the fusion of the offices of priest and king in Psalm 110 a distinctive and powerful interpretation of Jesus as the perfected Son and high priest who "is able for all time to save those who approach God through him, since he always lives to make intercession for them" (Heb 7:25 NRSV).

In appropriating Psalm 110 to speak of the resurrection and exaltation of the crucified Messiah, the early Christian tradition significantly transforms the imagery of holy war. The Messiah's enemies, whose final defeat is certain, are not Gentile kingdoms, but the hostile principalities and powers of this world, including Death itself (Eph 1:20-23; 1 Cor 15:20-28). What is more, the worldwide dominion of Jesus, the exalted Son of David, now brings salvation not only to God's people Israel, but through the Spirit-empowered witness of Jesus' followers, even "to the ends of the earth" (Acts 1:8).

J. Ross Wagner

---

8. A. A. Anderson, *Psalms,* 2 vols., NCB (Grand Rapids: Eerdmans, 1981), 2:772.

PSALM III

Psalm 111 is the first of a sequence of three "hallelujah" psalms, each opening with "Hallelujah" (Hebrew *halĕlû yāh* = "Praise the LORD!"). Like its immediately following "twin," Psalm 112, it is a twenty-two-line acrostic poem in which each line begins with a successive letter of the Hebrew alphabet. Psalm 111 orchestrates praise of the righteousness of the Lord that issues in great deeds on behalf of Israel. Psalm 112 praises the righteousness of all those who "study" the works of the Lord by keeping the covenant and observing its precepts. Both psalms regard covenant and commandments as precious gifts. Despite the seeming simplicity of Psalm 111, it is rich and subtle, worthy of expressing a congregation's thanks to the Lord. The declaration "*I* will give thanks" (Ps 111:1) invites all members of the community to join the psalmist in giving praise; it is a *community hymn* (see the introductory essay).

Acrostic poems are given a framework by the successive letters of the alphabet that begin each line, but they usually proceed according to a logic of their own. The theme of Psalm 111 is the "works" of the Lord, which the psalm expresses in several different words: "work (sing.)," "deeds," "provides food," "covenant," "precepts," and "redemption." Note that "covenant" and "precepts" are counted among the great deeds; the psalm considers the covenant and its commandments benefits to Israel because they enable the people to do God's will and enjoy his favor. All the works and deeds celebrated in the poem appear to be aspects or consequences of one and the same event — the exodus. In the exodus Israel was liberated from Pharaoh's lordship and came under Yahweh's rule. The Lord formed them into his own people. The exodus is thus the central event of the Old Testament. It is not surprising that the psalmist relates the works of God in the psalm to that one event. Verses 5, 7b-8, 9b appear to speak of the liberation from Egypt, the feeding in the wilderness, and the covenant at Sinai; verse 6 speaks of the conquest of Canaan; and verse 9a speaks of the governance of the people in Canaan. Though the phrase "works of the LORD" can sometimes refer to divine acts of a general kind (Pss 104:24; 107:24), more frequently it refers to the founding of Israel in the exodus as in Exodus 34:10, Deuteronomy 11:7, and Joshua 24:31. The sequence of the "works of the LORD" in Psalm 111 — the people's liberation, their guidance in the wilderness, and their governance in the land — is the same in Psalms 105 and 106.

There is an ethical component to God's great acts for Israel. In the Bible, ethics generally flow from the surrounding narrative. Ethical reasoning is not deductive — from first principles — but often arises from one's response to the God who acted first. It is not surprising, therefore, that "I will give thanks to the LORD" in verse 1b is the singer's spontaneous reaction to God's action (e.g., Pss 7:17; 9:1; 109:30) and that the singer includes among those actions the covenant binding God and people (vv. 5, 9) and the precepts deriving from that covenantal bond. God's works invite not only wonder but also participation and response. The works of the Lord not only bring benefits and salvation to Israel; they also communicate God's love and will.

One verse requires comment. Verse 2b, "studied by all who delight in them" (NRSV), is a unique and puzzling phrase. NRSV and other translations adopt the traditional rendering. What does the verse mean? "Studied" is, literally, "sought" *(dāraš)* and can have the meaning "to seek with application, to study, to practice." Comparison with the similar Psalm 119:45 is helpful (words identical to Ps 111 are in italics):

> I shall walk at liberty,
> for I have *sought* [cf. Ps 111:2b] your *precepts* [cf. Ps 111:7b].

The parallel suggests that "studied" in Psalm 111:2b means prizing and responding to the precepts, which are mentioned in both psalms. Perhaps one can paraphrase Psalm 111:2b: "God's gracious self-communication in his works invites study and generous response."

Psalm 111 associates all God's gracious deeds with the one great deed of the exodus. The psalm allows one to incorporate one's thanks for a particular benefit into the thanks of all Israel for God's choosing of the people. The poem fits personal prayer into national prayer.

How might this psalm assist a modern congregation to respond to the lectionary readings? In the first reading, Deuteronomy describes God's promise to the people of a prophet like Moses who will help the people remain faithful in the land they are about to enter. Psalm 111 makes it clear that covenant and precepts should be considered as divine gifts no less than other saving acts. The reading from 1 Kings for the Thirteenth Sunday after Pentecost describes how Solomon asked God for wisdom to rule rather than those gifts a king might be expected to ask for, such as long life, riches, or the life of the king's enemies. Solomon is obviously one who has "studied the works of the LORD" (Ps 111:2b) in the sense of knowing their true inner meaning, and so asks to be able to recognize the works as the Lord's.

Richard J. Clifford

PSALM 112

Fifth Sunday after the Epiphany, Year A
> First Lesson: Isaiah 58:1-9a, (9b-12)
> **(Psalm 112:1-9, 10)**
> Second Lesson: 1 Corinthians 2:1-12, (13-16)
> Gospel Lesson: Matthew 5:13-20

Psalm 112 is the second psalm in a group of psalms in Book V (Pss 107–150) known as the "hallelujah" psalms (Pss 111–118; see the introductory essay). Psalm 111 opens with *halĕlû yāh* (the latter element a shortened form of the divine name Yahweh), as do Psalms 112 and 113. Psalm 113 closes with the same words, as do Psalms 115–118. Only Psalm 114 in this series does not contain the characteristic opening or closing, but some scholars suggest that the closing *halĕlû-yāh* of Psalm 113 (v. 9) may actually belong to the beginning of Psalm 114.

Psalms 111 and 112 are acrostics. Each of their twenty lines begins with a successive letter of the Hebrew alphabet. Psalm 111, classified as an *individual thanksgiving hymn,* consists of a mere seventy-two words. Psalm 112, classified as a *wisdom psalm,* consists of only seventy-nine words. The two psalms work together as a celebration of God's mighty deeds on behalf of the people and instruction for the proper response by the people. Klaus Seybold observes that Psalm 111 is "theology" while Psalm 112 is "anthropology."[1] Psalm 111:10 acts as a link between them:

> The fear of the LORD is the beginning of wisdom;
>> all those who practice it have a good understanding.

The acrostic body of Psalm 112 opens with the word *'ašrê* (content), rendered in most English translations as "happy" (so NRSV) or "blessed." The root *'šr* means "to go straight, to advance, to follow the track." "Content," coupled with two other words in the verse, "person" (*'îš*) and "delight" (*ḥāpēṣ*), recalls for the hearer the opening words of the Psalter, "Content is the person who does not walk . . . but who delights in the *tôrāh*" (Ps 1:1-2, author's translation).

Psalm 112:1 continues: "Content are those who fear the LORD." "Fear" is a very good translation of the Hebrew verb *yārē'*. In today's culture, however, the idea of fear is usually connected with the base instincts to run, defend, or retaliate. The Hebrew verb encompasses a larger meaning including "awe, reverent respect, honor." It appears in the Hebrew Bible as a synonym for "love" (see Deut 10:12), "cling to" (see Deut 10:20), and "serve" (see Deut 6:13; Josh 24:14). At its base, the word denotes obedience to the divine will.

Verses 2-3a outline the rewards for the one who "reverences the LORD" and "delights in the commandments." That person will have mighty, upright, and blessed descendants and a house full of riches and wealth. In many ways the words of these verses echo the promises given by God to Abram in Genesis 12, 13, and 15: descendants, land, house, and blessing.

Psalm 112:3-4 evinces strong parallels with Psalm 111:3-4. Yahweh is the subject of the latter's words of thanks:

> Full of honor and majesty is his work,
>> and his righteousness endures forever.
> He has gained renown by his wonderful deeds;
>> the LORD is gracious and merciful.

The righteous person is the subject of Psalm 112:3-4's words of wisdom:

---

1. Klaus Seybold, *Die Psalmen* (Tübingen: Mohr, 1996), 440.

Riches and wealth are in that person's house,
   and that one's righteousness endures for all time.
A light has shone forth in the darkness for the upright ones,
   gracious and merciful and righteous. (author's translation)

Just as the righteousness of God endures for all time, so does the righteousness of the "content" person of Psalm 112. Words derived from the Hebrew root *ṣdq,* translated as "righteous, righteousness, to be right," occur some 523 times in the Hebrew Bible. The basic meaning of the word includes the ideas of "a sense of right," "correct order," "being just," and "being true," and in Scripture has more to do with right actions than with right states of mind. A striking story of such righteousness is found in Genesis 38. Tamar, Judah's daughter-in-law, in an act of deception conceives twins by him to fulfill the levirate marriage requirements of the Torah (Deut 25:5-10). Though she deceived him, Judah declares at the end of the story, "She is more in the right than I" (Gen 38:26). Delighting in the commandments of the Lord renders the "content" person of Psalm 112 righteous.

In verse 4a the "content" person is promised light in the darkness. Even though the referent to "light" is unclear and verse 4b does not have a clear subject, the reader may be permitted to equate the light with Yahweh, who is described in Psalm 111:4b with the same words that describe the light in 112:4b — "gracious and merciful." "Upright" (*yāšār*), found at the end of verse 4a, is often used as a synonym for "righteous." The plural form here (*yěšārîm*) parallels the plural form of "wicked" (*rěšāʿîm*), which the hearer will encounter in verse 10.

Verses 5-9 describe the actions and demeanor of the "content" person of Psalm 112. In verse 5a the person is gracious (√*ḥnn*) and lends to others (√*lwh*). The Hebrew root *ḥnn* carries a basic meaning of "an aesthetically pleasing presentation or aspect of someone or something," "the pleasing impression made upon one individual by another."[2] The verb √*lwh* indicates a connectedness to others, such as what results when one lends to or borrows from another. In verse 5b, we read that the "content" person holds words in judgment, being slow to speak words of praise or condemnation.

Verse 6 acts as something of an interlude for this portion of the psalm. Here the reader learns that the person — now called "the righ-

2. *TDOT,* 5:22.

teous one" — with the character traits described in verse 5 (see further vv. 7-9a) will not stumble and will be for all time a memorial. The verse is strikingly parallel to Psalm 111:4, which states that Yahweh is a memorial because of his wondrous acts.

Verses 7-9a continue with a description of the "content/righteous" person. Despite potential danger from "a bad hearing" and oppressors, this one is not afraid, having a heart that is established and steady; in fact, here is one who reaches out a hand and gives to the needy (note the use of Ps 112:9 in 2 Cor 9:9). The final two cola of verse 9 offer a concluding refrain in praise of the "content/righteous" person. The words of verse 9b duplicate those of verse 3b, while verse 9c reiterates the promise of verse 2 concerning the person's might and strength.

Verse 10, in true "wisdom" fashion, contrasts the fate of the wicked one *(rāšā')* with the fate of the righteous one *(ṣaddîq)*. In verse 10c the singular "wicked one" is replaced by the plural "wicked ones" *(rěšā'îm)* to parallel the "upright ones" *(yěšārîm)* of verse 4. While a light will shine forth in the darkness for the upright ones (v. 4a), the desire of the wicked ones will perish (v. 10c).

Psalm 112 and Psalm 1 begin with the same word *('ăšrê,* "content") and end with the same word, "perish" *(√'bd).* Wisdom words weave their way through both psalms, words about how to live one's life according to the instructions of God.

Psalms 111 and 112 are a summary statement of what faith is all about, who God is, and what humans must do in response to God. In a rich intertwining of language and metaphor, the "content" person of Psalm 112 partners with the God of Psalm 111, working together to achieve righteousness — right living, correct order, truth — in this world.

In the first lesson, Isaiah 58, the prophet admonishes hearers to examine their attitudes and actions toward God and toward others. They ask God,

> Why do we fast, but you do not see?
> Why humble ourselves, but you do not notice? (v. 3)

God replies,

> Will you call this a fast,
> a day acceptable to the LORD? (v. 5b)

God questions whether their attitudes and actions are heartfelt and honest, or whether they are "in name only." Righteousness — again: right living, correct order, truth — is not achieved through empty outward action, but through a radically changed inward being that seeks in all things to bring God's "correct order" — God's righteousness — to this world.

Nancy L. deClaissé-Walford

PSALM 114

Seventeenth Sunday after Pentecost, Year A
    First Lesson: Exodus 14:19-31
    (Psalm 114)
    Second Lesson: Romans 14:1-12
    Gospel Lesson: Matthew 18:21-35

Psalm 114 is the second of the six "Egyptian Hallel" (Hebrew "to praise") psalms (Pss 113-118), which were sung at the end of the morning service at the three Jewish pilgrimage feasts. They are called "Egyptian" from the mention of Egypt in Psalm 114:1. Matthew 26:30 and Mark 14:26 suggest that Psalms 113-114 were sung before the Passover meal and Psalms 115-118 after it. The theme of Psalm 114 is the exodus, the defining event of the Old Testament. In genre, the psalm is closest to a *hymn* (see the introductory essay) in that it praises a divine act (the exodus), though it lacks the expected invitation to praise. Psalm 114 is abrupt, making it hard to imagine what its original context was. One sign of its abruptness is the absence of an antecedent of the third-person singular pronoun in verse 2.

Note the psalm's unusual perspective on the exodus from Egypt to Canaan. Instead of Israel passing from Egypt through the sea to the other side, there to begin its journey through the wilderness to Canaan, the people pass from Egypt through the sea directly to the land of Canaan. Psalm 114 shows no interest in the wilderness traditions, which occupy so much of the prose narrative of the Pentateuch and of such psalms as Psalms 78, 105, and 107. One should note that in Psalm 114:3 the poet puts "the sea" (the Red or Reed Sea) in poetic parallel to "the river" (river Jordan). Such a parallel was natural because "sea" // "river" was a common word pair in Israelite poetic tradition (see Pss 24:2; 66:6; 72:8; 89:25) and in comparable Ugaritic texts as well.

Modern readers may be confused by the battle scene and vivid personification of sea and mountains in verses 3-6. As the people effortlessly march through the sea to the other side, the speaker taunts the cosmic elements — sea and mountains — in the manner of a warrior in the *Iliad* or *Odyssey* taunting fallen enemies. Tremble, he demands, in obeisance to the Lord who can turn arid desert to well-watered arable land, i.e., can defeat chaos and impose order. In short, the Lord can "create" out of hostile waste a life-supporting cosmos. The psalm employs two different levels of language to describe one and the same event, the exodus. The "mythic" perspective gives depth and scope to the "historic," and the "historic" perspective nails down the universal to a particular place and time. The event has not happened in a secluded corner of the world, but has cosmic significance.

The psalm has two almost equal parts: the crossing and the reaction of the cosmic elements (vv. 1-4), and the speaker's taunt and warning to them (vv. 5-8). Some words and phrases require comment. Comparison of Psalm 114 with Exodus 15:17, another account of the exodus, helps one see the distinct perspective of the psalm:

> You brought them in and planted them on the mountain
> > of your own possession,
> > the place, O LORD, that you made your abode,
> > the sanctuary, O LORD, that your hands have established.

As noted above, verses 3-4 vividly personify the sea and the mountains as warriors fleeing in panic before the Lord as a warrior. Such personification is not unique in the Psalter. Psalm 104:6b-8 does the same thing: "Over the mountains the waters stood. At your rebuke they fled, at the sound of your thunder they rushed away. They went up the mountains, they went down the valleys, to the place you founded for them" (author's translation; cf. Ps 77:16). Likewise not unique is the view of mountains in Psalm 114. The mountains skip at the Lord's thundering in the sky, as in Psalm 29:5-6:

> The voice of the LORD breaks the cedars,
> > the LORD breaks the cedars of Lebanon.

> He makes Lebanon to skip like a calf,
> and Sirion like a young wild ox.

"Tremble" in verse 7 is holy war vocabulary: it refers to warriors reeling from overwhelming attacks (cf. Ps 96:9 and Deut 2:25). The sequence of actions — defeating the sea and then providing tamed and life-giving waters — is like Psalm 104, which begins with God defeating the waters (Ps 104:5-9) and then providing waters to all creatures (Ps 104:14-18, 24-26).

To Christians, the symbols associated with the exodus have also spoken of Easter: the waters through which one passes to freedom are the waters of baptism; the waters represent chaos and death; the resurrection of Jesus is victory over the forces of chaos.

How does Psalm 114 help a congregation respond to the reading from Exodus 14:19-31? As Exodus 14 takes a "historic" view of the exodus, Psalm 114 takes a mythic or cosmic view. Hence, reciting Psalm 114 can broaden a congregation's appreciation of the great deed of God in the exodus, and perhaps evoke its connection to Christ's resurrection.

Richard J. Clifford

PSALM 116

Third Sunday of Easter, Year A
> First Lesson: Acts 2:14a, 36-41
> **(Psalm 116:1-4, 12-19)**
> Second Lesson: 1 Peter 1:17-23
> Gospel Lesson: Luke 24:13-35

Fourth Sunday after Pentecost, Year A
> First Lesson: Genesis 18:1-15; (21:1-7)
> **(Psalm 116:1-2, 12-19)**
> Second Lesson: Romans 5:1-8
> Gospel Lesson: Matthew 9:35–10:8, (9-23)

The *song of thanksgiving* (see the introductory essay) in Psalm 116 is part of a liturgical response that testifies to God's steadfast love. It gives words to a public confession that the speaker's trust in God is well founded. "I love the LORD," the psalmist announces in the temple,

> because the LORD has heard
>> my voice and my supplications.
> The LORD has inclined his ear to me,
>> therefore I will call on the LORD as long as I live. (vv. 1-2)

This is the summary of the psalm, and other songs of thanksgiving, as it gives expression to the deepest concerns of every believer's heart: Does God hear me when I pray, and do my prayers move God to act on my behalf?

> Incline your ear, O LORD, and answer me,
>> for I am poor and needy.
> Preserve my life, for I am devoted to you;
>> save your servant who trusts in you.
> You are my God; be gracious to me, O Lord,
>> for to you do I cry all day long. (Ps 86:1-3)

Psalm 116 joyfully testifies to God's steadfast faithfulness and mercy and reassures those standing by that God does indeed hear and answer prayer.

The relationship between the psalmist and God in Psalm 116 is personal, engaging the senses. The one in distress calls out to be heard, God's ear is inclined, the petitioner's feet are kept from stumbling, and tears are wiped away. While God is tender and nurturing, the psalmist's former suffering is described in broad, expansive strokes:

> The snares of death encompassed me;
>> the pangs of Sheol laid hold on me;
>> I suffered distress and anguish. (v. 3)

The words "death" and "Sheol" are not necessarily confined to an illness or a mishap that leads to death; rather, in the Psalms, great distress is often the work of enemies and slanderers. "I was brought low," the psalmist testifies, and "I said in my consternation, 'everyone is a liar'" (vv. 6, 11). In the Psalms and the Prophets, "death" and "Sheol" are often metaphorical, describing a state of being, such as the trauma of unwarranted persecution, the slings and arrows of an enemy, or the distress of body and mind. Consider this example:

I call upon the LORD, who is worthy to be praised,
>   so I shall be saved from my enemies.
The cords of death encompassed me;
>   the torrents of perdition assailed me;
the cords of Sheol entangled me;
>   the snares of death confronted me. (Ps 18:3-5; 2 Sam 22:6)

Jonah's description of his underwater ordeal makes the same claim, but in the place of death and Sheol are the chaotic deeps and the entangling weeds:

The waters closed in over me;
>   the deep surrounded me;
weeds were wrapped around my head. (Jon 2:5)

Soul suffering is likened to being pulled down into chaotic waters where one is unable to break free, being hopelessly trapped in the darkness of the abyss.

Despite this powerful imagery, the psalmist is intentionally vague when speaking of his or her former distress. "The one speaking does not at all intend to speak of what actually happened to him, but to testify what God has done for him. For the congregation before whom he praised God with this confession the important thing was not the 'individual features' but the testimony of the witness. The one confessing in this manner did not intend to give a picture, but to call to them, 'O magnify the Lord with me, and let us exalt his name together!' (Ps. 34:3)."[1]

This thanksgiving may have been spoken by an ancient Israelite individual, but it has provided form and language for countless other individuals and communities whose cries to God have not gone unanswered. Psalm 116 is a part of the Hallel collection, which has been recited at the three major Jewish festivals, Passover, Pentecost, and Tabernacles, along with the feasts of Hanukkah and New Moon, from the first century of the common era until the present. The Hallel, which means "praise," refers to Psalms 113-118, which are considered a liturgical unit. At the Passover meal, traditionally celebrated at home with loved ones, Psalms 113-114 are recited just before the Seder meal and Psalms 115-118 afterward. Most probably, it is to Psalms 115-118 that Mark refers when he mentions

---

1. Claus Westermann, *Praise and Lament in the Psalms* (Atlanta: John Knox, 1985), 109.

that after the Passover meal, Jesus and the disciples "had sung the hymn [and] went out to the Mount of Olives" (Mark 14:26).[2]

The Christian church has selectively retained this usage of elements of the Hallel as it pertains to Psalms 114, 116, and 118. These are traditionally read during Holy Week and Easter. Psalm 115 is the only psalm from the Hallel that is not prescribed for reading in the Revised Common Lectionary, and Psalms 113 and 117 are read only during ordinary time. Psalm 116 is rich with liturgical language and cultic acts, and is assigned for reading in worship on Maundy Thursday, Years A, B, and C; on Easter III, Year A; and twice during ordinary time.

Psalm 116 is more than a spontaneous outburst of personal gratitude. In the Psalter praise is more than an inner experience or feeling; it is a public response that is practiced before others. The words of thanksgiving are spoken in the assembly of the redeemed and are a prelude to the sacrifice to follow (vv. 12-19). "What shall I return to the LORD for all God's bounty to me?" (v. 12), the leader asks. The psalmist responds:

> I will lift up the cup of salvation
>   and call on the name of the LORD.
> I will pay my vows to the LORD
>   in the presence of all God's people. (vv. 13-14)

The psalmist is a liturgist, calling on those assembled to celebrate their own experiences of rescue by God's hand. The vow is repeated:

> I will pay my vows to the LORD
>   in the presence of all God's people,
> in the courts of the house of the LORD,
>   in your midst, O Jerusalem. (vv. 17-19)

In the Psalms thanksgivings and praise are liturgical and communal events.

Kathryn L. Roberts

---

2. See William L. Holladay, *The Psalms through Three Thousand Years: Prayerbook of a Cloud of Witnesses* (Minneapolis: Fortress, 1993), 143.

PSALM 118

Easter, Year A
>First Lesson: Acts 10:34-43 or Jeremiah 31:1-6
>**(Psalm 118:1-2, 14-24)**
>Second Lesson: Colossians 3:1-4 or Acts 10:34-43
>Gospel Lesson: John 20:1-18 or Matthew 28:1-10

Easter, Year B
>First Lesson: Acts 10:34-43 or Isaiah 25:6-9
>**(Psalm 118:1-2, 14-24)**
>Second Lesson: 1 Corinthians 15:1-11 or Acts 10:34-43
>Gospel Lesson: John 20:1-18 or Mark 16:1-8

Easter, Year C
>First Lesson: Acts 10:34-43 or Isaiah 65:17-25
>**(Psalm 118:1-2, 14-24)**
>Second Lesson: 1 Corinthians 15:19-26 or Acts 10:34-43
>Gospel Lesson: John 20:1-18 or Luke 24:1-12

Palm/Passion Sunday, Year A
>First Lesson: Isaiah 50:4-9a
>**(Psalm 118:1-2, 19-29 [Palm]** or Psalm 31:9-16 [Passion])
>Second Lesson: Philippians 2:5-11
>Gospel Lesson: Matthew 21:1-11 (Palm); or Matthew 26:14–27:66 or
>   Matthew 27:11-54 (Passion)

Palm/Passion Sunday, Year B
>First Lesson: Isaiah 50:4-9a
>**(Psalm 118:1-2, 19-29 [Palm]** or Psalm 31:9-16 [Passion])
>Second Lesson: Philippians 2:5-11
>Gospel Lesson: Mark 11:1-11 or John 12:12-16 (Palm); or Mark 14:1–15:47
>   or Mark 15:1-39, (40-47) (Passion)

Palm/Passion Sunday, Year C
>First Lesson: Isaiah 50:4-9a
>**(Psalm 118:1-2, 19-29 [Palm]** or Psalm 31:9-16 [Passion])
>Second Lesson: Philippians 2:5-11
>Gospel Lesson: Luke 19:28-40 (Palm); or Luke 22:14–23:56 or Luke 23:1-
>   49 (Passion)

Second Sunday of Easter, Year C
First Lesson: Acts 5:27-32
(**Psalm 118:14-29** or Psalm 150)
Second Lesson: Revelation 1:4-8
Gospel Lesson: John 20:19-31

Psalm 118 is a liturgy of thanksgiving celebrating the king's deliverance from death and his victory in battle.[1] The psalm, which includes the voices of a number of different speakers, depicts a procession that leads to the gates of the temple (vv. 1-19) and concludes before the altar in the temple court (vv. 20-29).[2] A repeated call to the entire community (cf. Ps 115:9-11) to give thanks for Yahweh's goodness and unfailing covenant love (vv. 1-4, 29; cf. Pss 100:5; 106:1; 107:1; 136:1) frames the description of divine rescue (vv. 5-21) and the communal celebration of the king's deliverance (vv. 22-28).

In recounting his victory, the king gives all credit to the powerful help of the Lord (vv. 7, 13), whom he names six times as "Yah" (vv. 5a, 5b, 14, 17, 18, 19), a shortened form of Yahweh perhaps "inspired by the formula of Exod 15:2."[3] The echoes of the Song of the Sea in this psalm (compare Exod 15:2a//Ps 118:14; Exod 15:2b//Ps 118:28; Exod 15:6, 12//Ps 118:15-16) imply that Yahweh's faithfulness to save the king stems from the covenant relationship with Israel that Yahweh established by his foundational act of salvation in the exodus (cf. Exod 20:2). In two pairs of parallel lines, the king avows that it is reliance on the help of Yahweh, who is "on my side" (vv. 6-7), rather than trust in humans, however wealthy and powerful (vv. 8-9), that frees him from fear and gives him the assurance that he will prevail over his enemies. Despite the magnitude ("all nations," v. 10) and fierceness of their attack ("they surrounded me," four times in vv. 10-12; "like bees," v. 12; "they blazed like a fire of thorns," v. 12; "I was pushed hard, so that I was falling," v. 13 NRSV), the king has conquered completely and decisively ("I cut them off," *kî 'ămîlam*, with emphatic *kî*, three times in vv. 10-12) through Yahweh's mighty power ("in the name of Yahweh," three times in vv. 10-12; "Yahweh helped me," v. 13; "Yah is my strength . . . might . . . deliverance," v. 14).

In response, the king's victorious people joyfully attribute the tri-

---

1. See Mitchell Dahood, *Psalms III (101-150)*, AB 17A (Garden City, N.Y.: Doubleday, 1970), 155.
2. Leslie C. Allen, *Psalms 101-150*, WBC 21 (Waco: Word, 1983), 122-24.
3. Allen, *Psalms 101-150*, 120.

umph of their sovereign to Yahweh's valiant (v. 15a; cf. Num 24:18; 1 Sam 14:48; Pss 60:12; 108:13) and exalted right hand (vv. 15b-16; cf. Pss 18:35; 20:6; 44:3; 60:5; 98:1; 108:6; 138:7). And the king, knowing that God intended his sufferings for his good rather than for his destruction (v. 18; cf. Ps 89:30-33; Prov 3:11-12; Jer 10:24), confidently proclaims, "I shall not die, but I shall live," and vows to recount the Lord's mighty deeds of salvation (v. 17). He approaches the gates of the temple requesting admission to offer thanks (v. 19), where he is met by the priestly gatekeepers who invite the *ṣaddîqîm* to enter (v. 20; cf. v. 15). It is difficult to capture the sense of this Hebrew term adequately with a single English word, for the king's victory (*ṣaddîqîm* = "the victorious," NJPS; cf. v. 15) attests simultaneously to his right standing before God (*ṣaddîqîm* = "the righteous," NRSV; cf. Isa 26:2 and the entrance liturgies in Pss 15; 24).

Inside the temple courts the king for the first time addresses God directly, thanking Yahweh for answering his prayer (cf. v. 5b) and saving him from his enemies (cf. v. 14b). A chorus of worshipers now responds (vv. 22-24), likening the king to a stone that, though rejected by the builders, has now become the cornerstone or keystone of the whole edifice (of the temple? cf. Isa 28:16). Recognition of this marvelous deed of Yahweh (cf. *niplā'ôt*, Exod 3:20; Pss 78:4, 11, 32; 106:7, 21-22) evokes a call to celebrate the day of deliverance with glad rejoicing (v. 24). Moreover, the remembrance of Yahweh's covenant faithfulness (cf. vv. 1-4, 29) emboldens God's people to cry out for continued deliverance and prosperity (v. 25). In antiphonal call and response, the priests' blessing (v. 26; cf. Num 6:22-27) finds its answer in the worshipers' affirmation of faith:

> Yahweh is God,
>> and he has given us light. (v. 27a; cf. Num 6:25a)

This, in turn, is followed by the summons to continue the festal procession right up to the altar itself (v. 27b).[4] One last time the voice of the king (cf. v. 21) rises above the throng with a declaration of loyalty and trust ("you are my God," v. 28; cf. v. 27a) and a vow to praise. The psalm closes as it began, with an exhortation to the whole congregation to glorify Yahweh for his goodness and unfailing covenant love (v. 29).

According to the Mishnah, in the Second Temple period Psalm 118 (which together with Pss 111-117 makes up the "Egyptian Hallel") was re-

---

4. On the interpretive difficulties here, see Allen, *Psalms 101–150*, 122.

cited at the Feasts of Tabernacles (*m. Sukkah* 3:9; 4:1, 5) and Passover (*m. Pesahim* 5:7; 10:5-7). Both festivals looked back to the exodus not simply as the founding event that constituted Israel as God's own people, but also as the pattern for their future deliverance (cf. the echoes of Exod 15 in Ps 118, noted above). Not surprisingly, then, early Christian tradition associates Psalm 118 with Jesus' final Passover in Jerusalem. All four Gospels cite Psalm 118:25-26 in connection with Jesus' triumphal procession into the city that ends in the temple courts (Matt 21:9-12; Mark 11:9-11; Luke 19:37-45; John 12:12-13; cf. Luke 13:35; Matt 23:39). According to the synoptic evangelists, in his debates with the authorities in Jerusalem, Jesus appeals to Psalm 118:22 as the scriptural warrant for his parable of the tenants in the vineyard (Matt 21:42; Mark 12:10-11; Luke 20:17). Moreover, the mention by Mark and Matthew of the "hymn" sung by Jesus and his disciples after the supper (Matt 26:30; Mark 14:26), taken together with the rabbinic tradition that Psalm 118 was sung at the Passover meal (*m. Pesahim* 10:5-7), opens up the intriguing possibility of hearing the words of the king in Psalm 118 as Jesus' own affirmation of trust as he faces his impending trial and suffering:

> The Lord is on my side; I am not afraid.
>   What can mortals do to me? (Ps 118:6; cf. Heb 13:6; Rom 8:31)

> I shall not die, but I shall live,
>   and recount the deeds of the LORD. (Ps 118:17)

Whether or not they heard Jesus' own voice in Psalm 118, his first followers did find in this psalm a prophetic promise of Jesus' ultimate vindication by Israel's God, who raised him from the dead (Acts 4:10-12) and established him as the cornerstone of the new temple being built out of the "living stones" who trust in him (1 Pet 2:4-8; cf. Eph 2:19-22).

J. Ross Wagner

PSALM 119

Sixth Sunday after the Epiphany, Year A
First Lesson: Deuteronomy 30:15-20 or Sirach 15:15-20
(Psalm 119:1-8)
Second Lesson: 1 Corinthians 3:1-9
Gospel Lesson: Matthew 5:21-37

Seventh Sunday after the Epiphany, Year A
First Lesson: Leviticus 19:1-2, 9-18
(Psalm 119:33-40)
Second Lesson: 1 Corinthians 3:10-11, 16-23
Gospel Lesson: Matthew 5:38-48

Eighth Sunday after Pentecost, Year A
First Lesson: Genesis 25:19-34
(Psalm 119:105-112)
Second Lesson: Romans 8:12-25
Gospel Lesson: Matthew 13:24-30, 36-43

Fifth Sunday in Lent, Year B
First Lesson: Jeremiah 31:31-34
(Psalm 119:9-16)
Second Lesson: Hebrews 5:5-10
Gospel Lesson: John 12:20-33

Twenty-second Sunday after Pentecost, Year C
First Lesson: Jeremiah 31:27-34
(Psalm 119:97-104)
Second Lesson: 2 Timothy 3:14–4:5
Gospel Lesson: Luke 18:1-8

Psalm 119 is the longest psalm in the biblical canon and contains twenty-two eight-line strophes, one for each letter in the Hebrew alphabet. The biblical acrostics predate the Babylonian exile (see Nahum and Pss 9–10). Although there are parallels in Babylonian and Qumran literature, only six other biblical psalms have this acrostic structure (Pss 25; 34; 37; 111; 112; and 145).

Form critically, Psalm 119 is considered a *wisdom* or *torah psalm* (see the introductory essay) because of its themes. The acrostic structure further corroborates this designation. We should observe that three acrostic psalms have a twenty-two-line structure (Pss 33; 38; 103). But in Psalm 119, the lines of each eight-verse strophe begin with the same letter. The dominant theme of the psalm is the importance of the Torah.

1. On the Sixth Sunday after the Epiphany, the aleph strophe (Ps 119:1-8) is the responsorial psalm. A unique characteristic of this strophe is that it can both stand on its own and also frame the entire psalm. For instance, the first two lines begin with the term *'ašrê,* "happy is," reminiscent of Psalm 1:1, another torah psalm. Psalm 119 has common elements of a torah psalm. Three verbs dominate these first two lines: "walk," "keep watch," and "search." The psalmist chides the reader to be active.[1] The dominant nouns are *derek,* "way," and "torah." "Torah" occurs often in Psalm 119. Here "torah" means "the instruction of God," as well as referring to God's self-revelation.

The lectionary collateral texts provide important listening contexts for Psalm 119:1-8. Deuteronomy 30:15-20 sets the stage for the responsorial psalm by providing the listener with a covenantal choice. It shares with Psalm 119 the language of "path," *derek* (Deut 30:16). The juxtaposition of the two texts pushes Psalm 119:1-8 to reflect the wisdom dimension and play down the lament element. The passage from Deuteronomy about choosing the right path invites the listener to read Psalm 119:1-8 in the same manner. However, the Matthew passage is less about choice and more about the appropriate understanding of the torah, picking up on the main theme of Psalm 119.

2. For the Seventh Sunday after the Epiphany in Year A, the Hebrew letter he is central. The he strophe (vv. 33-40) contains seven hiphil imperatives. The hiphil conjugation conveys a causative sense. The imperative in the first section of the line prompts a first-person result in the last half of the line. For instance, in verse 33, "Teach me the path of your way" *(derek),* the Hebrew letter waw, which marks a result clause here, produces "then I will keep *(nāṣar).* . . ." The next line also begins with the hiphil imperative, "to cause to understand," followed by two first-person expressions. The first is the repetition of the verb "guard" *(nāṣar),* and the second is the more frequent term *šāmar,* "keep," "observe." These form a type of synonymous parallelism.

---

1. William P. Brown, *Seeing the Psalms: A Theology of Metaphor* (Louisville: Westminster John Knox, 2002), 34.

The path of the statutes in verse 33 parallels the way of the commandments in verse 35. Once again the imperative of the verb *dārak,* "cause me to tread," sets up the first-person verb "I delight." Verse 36 follows a different pattern. The imperative petition lifts up an unacceptable alternative. The language for violence used here occurs infrequently in the Bible, only fifteen times (Gen 37:26; Exod 18:21; Judg 5:19; Job 22:3; Pss 30:10; 119:36; Prov 1:19; 15:27; 28:16; Jer 6:13; 8:10; Lam 2:17; Ezek 22:27; Hab 2:9; Mal 3:14).

The other lections for this Sunday have little direct relationship to Psalm 119:33-40, which responds to Leviticus 19:1-2, 9-18, a collection of laws in the absolute or apodictic form. The conclusion of that pericope is Jesus' oft-quoted saying, "Love your neighbor as yourself. I am the LORD." The Gospel reading (Matt 5:38-48) plays on the love-of-neighbor theme. This makes an interesting background to the petition for discernment that dominates Psalm 119:33-40. A reflection on these texts could pursue the issues of love and torah prompted by the juxtaposition of these three texts.

3. The Eighth Sunday after Pentecost, Year A, brings us once again to Psalm 119. This time it is the nun strophe. The first line (Ps 119:105) of the passage is the famous saying:

> Your word is a lamp to my feet
> and a light to my path.

The genre of this section of the psalm is lament. The first-person expression of trust or faith in the second verse of the strophe has parallels in the Hebrew complaint (see Ps 13:6). The psalmist connects this movement of the lament to the initial affirmation through the repetition of the Hebrew word *dĕbārekā,* which means "your words."

Verses 106-107a use verbs of pious devotion. In 107b this description shifts to a clear petition, "give me life!" The next verse (108) puts the imperative verb of 107, "save my life," in synonymous parallelism to the requests in the imperative of verse 108, "accept my offerings . . . and teach me." This synonymous parallelism using syntactical parallelism indicates that the psalmist wants to accent the continuity between saving life and right ritual position. Thus verse 108 acts as a fulcrum. The next verse returns to an earlier theme of the poem, namely, the pious devotion of the psalmist amidst a sense of threat. As is often the case in laments, the wicked provide the sinister threat embodied in a trap. The pericope ends with a request that God incline the heart of the psalmist to fulfill the statutes. This seems quite reminiscent of "Create in me a clean heart" (Ps 51:10).

The first reading for this week, Genesis 25, recounts the birth of Esau and Jacob as well as the story of Esau's foolish selling of his birthright. This tale of family politics presents a different tone than the plea of the innocent psalmist. The temptation to contrast the morally flexible Jacob with the pious psalmist flattens the complex nature of both texts. The Gospel reading, Matthew 13:24-30, 36-43, brings us into the world of parable. First, verses 24-30 contain the parable of the wheat and the tares/weeds. The appendix to the lection is an invitation to consider parables. This is an interesting counterpoint to the Psalm 119 passage, for it invites the reader to provide a reading of torah that embodies interpretation. The juxtaposition of the Gospel and Psalm 119 invites the hearers to redefine what one means by the term "torah." Romans 8:12-25 portrays a theme of a spirit of adoption contrasted to a spirit of fear and slavery (vv. 12-17). A second theme in the Romans passage proclaims eschatological expectations. One might translate the word *dābār* as "promise."[2] Such a move reframes how one might hear the eschatological hope of Romans 8:18-27.

4. The Fifth Sunday in Lent, Year B, brings us to the bet strophe (Ps 119:9-16). The letter bet in Hebrew can connote several things, including the prepositions "in" and "with." The first three lines of the strophe use the preposition *b-* ("in"/"with") to introduce the line. Once again the motif of torah structures the piety of the wisdom psalms. Once again the psalmist uses first-person speech to emphasize the notion of reciprocal devotion between God and humanity. The fourth line (v. 12) begins with a confession of faith and loyalty. The same language is used in 1 Chronicles 29:10-19, in David's prayer of farewell. The phrase "bless the LORD" connects well with the plea language of this section. Verse 14 returns to the use of bet as a preposition. This rhetorical device revealed something about the psalmist in the early strophe — in verses 14-16 the preposition has a divine referent. While there is no explicit reference to torah, there are indirect references to the Lord's law, including several synonyms such as "commandments" (v. 10), "judgments" (see v. 13), "testimonies" (v. 14), "precepts" (v. 15), "statutes" and "words" (v. 16). The psalmist confesses an interior experience of these synonyms for torah. But there is also an inte-

2. Will Soll, *Psalm 119: Matrix, Form, and Setting,* CBQMS 23 (Washington, D.C.: Catholic Biblical Association, 1991), 38.

rior experience of the ethical space suggested in the metaphors of path (*derek*, vv. 9 and 14).

The Fifth Sunday in Lent picks up the theme of covenant renewal. Jeremiah 31:31-34 outlines a new covenant and Psalm 119 rehearses the instruction of God as the central element for covenant. A typological reading of Psalm 119 and Hebrews 5:5-10 lifts up Jesus as the one who embodies the sensibilities and allegiances of Psalm 119. While this is not the authorial intention, the reading has precedent in the church. John 12:20-33 describes Jesus breathing on the disciples and thereby bestowing on them the Holy Spirit. The Holy Spirit provides for the Gospel of John a mechanism similar to the way torah provides a mechanism for the psalmist. This analogy of theological epistemology might be a good way to put the Psalms and the Gospel text in conversation.

5. The Twenty-second Sunday after Pentecost, Year C, brings us to the mem strophe (vv. 97-104). The psalmist uses the syntactical properties of this letter as a rhetorical element in the strophe. The strophe begins with the use of mem as an interrogative ("what?") (v. 97), continues with the use of mem as comparative (the "more than" qualities of vv. 98-100), followed by the prepositional connotations of the term *min* ("from," vv. 101-102) and closing with a return to the interrogative (vv. 103-104). Like the bet strophe (v. 9), the mem strophe also begins with a question, "how?" (v. 97). The term "meditation" occurs both as a verb (Pss 55:3, 18; 64:2; 69:13; 77:4, 7, 13; 102:1; 104:34; 105:2; 119:15, 23, 27, 48, 78, 148; 142:3; 143:5; 145:5) and a feminine noun (Ps 119:97, 99). While the term can mean to complain (Ps 55:18) or muse (Ps 119:15; etc.), it consistently conveys a level of intensity. The semantic parallel is *hgh* (mediate) in Psalm 1:2.

Verse 98 emphasizes the comparative aspect of the mem. The following three lines are comparatives with statements of rationale. The psalmist is better than his/her enemies (v. 98), all the learned (v. 99), and the elders (v. 100). In each case the comparison is explained with the Hebrew term *kî* (for). The psalmist uses torah synonyms "commandments" (v. 98), "testimonies" (v. 99), and "precepts" (v. 100).

At the level of preposition, the words themselves keep the psalmist from the path of evil. The psalmist uses a binding strategy in verses 102 and 104 with the mem form as derivative. The modifiers are once again torah synonyms: "justice" (v. 102) and "precepts" (v. 104).

The first reading for this Sunday, Jeremiah 31:27-34, conveys themes of eschatological hope, transition, and covenantal renewal. This context invites the reader to understand the role of torah in such a renewal. The

Epistle (2 Tim 3:14–4:5) recounts the nature and function of Scripture. Here the text describes the connection between the psalmist's torah and the Christian writer's notion of Scripture. The Gospel lesson, Luke 18:1-8, provides a looser connection. One might imagine how the tenacity of the psalmist to torah compares to that of the widow in the parable.

Stephen Breck Reid

Psalm 121

Second Sunday in Lent, Year A
> First Lesson: Genesis 12:1-4a
> **(Psalm 121)**
> Second Lesson: Romans 4:1-5, 13-17
> Gospel Lesson: John 3:1-17 or Matthew 17:1-9

Psalm 121 seems especially appropriate as a text for Lenten proclamation if only because of its canonical location among the Psalms of Ascents (Pss 120–134; see the introductory essay) and the possibility that it was "used as a liturgy for travelers, with those going on a journey reciting vv 1-2 and those remaining at home speaking the words of encouragement and blessing in vv 3-8."[1] We may never be able to recover the original circumstances of the psalm's composition or its setting in Israel's life and worship, nor may we be able to know for certain if the various lines of the psalm were meant to be spoken antiphonally by different speakers.[2] Nevertheless, since the Christian tradition reflects upon the journey to the cross during Lent, Psalm 121 can help preachers show congregations the spiritual and theological resources inherent in this OT text that declares God's presence and protection for *all* journeys.

The eight verses of the psalm are nicely laid out with fairly consistent meter and an overall structural boundary using forms of the verb "to come" in verse 1 ("comes") and verse 8 ("coming"). The name Yahweh occurs five times in the psalm (vv. 2, 5 [twice], 7, 8), adding to the portrait of

1. James Limburg, "Book of Psalms," in *ABD*, 5:533.
2. For several interpretive options, see Leslie C. Allen, *Psalms 101–150*, rev. ed., WBC 21 (Nashville: Nelson, 2002), 152-53.

an ever-present, covenant God. The key verbal idea, repeated six times, is "keeping" (vv. 3, 4, 5, 7 [twice], 8; Hebrew *šāmar*). Many English versions use different terms to render these six instances of *šāmar*, lending some stylistic variety; but other translations maintain the same root word ("keep/keeper": RSV, NRSV; "guard/guardian": NAB, NEB, JPS) as a signal that one Hebrew root lies behind the concept that is central to the psalm. The word can be applied both to human and to divine watchfulness, with different shades of meaning depending on the immediate literary context,[3] but the notion of safekeeping seems to be close to the heart of this psalm's message. The synthetic or "stairlike" parallelism helps to build the portrait of Yahweh's keeping from one verse to the next.[4] With this in mind, the following themes are highlighted by the language and rhetoric of the psalm itself.

1. Yahweh the *creator of the universe:* the *source* of the keeping (vv. 1-2). These two verses are held together by the immediate repetition of "my help" as the last word of verse 1 and the first word of verse 2. This continues the thought of the psalmist's only use of a first-person verb (v. 1, "I lift"). The beginning of the psalm thus personalizes all that will be said about God's relationship with creation and the nation of Israel on the way to a conclusion that explicitly names the benefits of Yahweh's keeping for individuals.

The influence of the KJV in the English-speaking world means that many people of faith recognize its translation of verse 1 as a *statement:* "I will lift up mine eyes unto the hills, from whence cometh my help." This seems to imply that the hills are a source of protection on the journey. The Hebrew, of course, is not marked with any punctuation, but the grammar places "from where" first in the clause (v. 1b) and hence implies a *question.* Indeed, the majority of modern English versions render the sentence in this way; for example:

> I lift up my eyes to the hills —
> from where will my help come? (NRSV)

But this still leaves open the matter of whether the hills ("mountains" in NAB, TEV, JPS) are a help or a hindrance in the journey.

---

3. See Keith N. Schoville, "שׁמר," in *New International Dictionary of Old Testament Theology and Exegesis,* ed. W. VanGemeren (Grand Rapids: Zondervan, 1997), 4:182-84.

4. J. Clinton McCann, Jr., "The Book of Psalms: Introduction, Commentary, and Reflections," in *NIB,* 4:1180.

The natural image of the hills can indeed operate on more than one level. Pilgrims may sense the ambiguity inherent in the protection hills provide for them or for would-be attackers, but they may also contrast the spiritual differences between the many ceremonial "high places" and the one holy hill in Jerusalem.[5] Regardless of the emphasis placed on the *question's* different meanings, the psalmist provides an *answer* so that there is no doubt about the ultimate source of our keeping. Nature as a whole — even the highest hills — cannot provide complete protection, something found only in "Yahweh, the maker of heaven and earth." As Artur Weiser aptly put it, "Trust in God is the unassailable basis and presupposition of the comfort with which the speaker sets the traveller on his way."[6] This ancient affirmation also resonates with Christian creedal statements that open with almost identical language acknowledging the creator God.

2. Yahweh the *guardian of Israel:* the *character* of the keeping (vv. 3-4). Structurally these two verses are united by the shift to third-person speech and by the repetition of two forms of negative particles: *'al* (twice in v. 3, a more general negation; "Yahweh *does not* slumber") and *lō'* (twice in v. 4, a more specific and emphatic negation; "Yahweh *will not* slumber"). The particle *hinnēh* ("behold, look here"), the repetition of "slumber" (vv. 3, 4), and the addition of "sleep" (*yāšēn*, v. 4) all reinforce the certainty of Yahweh's watchfulness. Other gods may sleep when their followers call (note *yāšēn*, used of Baal, in 1 Kings 18:27), but Israel's God will not so much as doze off for a moment. Cain's age-old question — "Am I my brother's *keeper?*" (Gen 4:9) — revealed a lack of human integrity and love, but Yahweh will never fail to keep and guard Israel.

The experienced effect of Yahweh's keeping is contained in the promise of verse 3: that "he will not let your foot be moved." As with earlier phrases in the psalm, this too evokes different concepts, from the image of a shepherd guiding sheep along safe paths[7] to a pilgrim following the most level road,[8] or the spiritual picture of one who might slip when confronted by enemies.[9]

The close of verse 4 and the beginning of verse 5 mark the center of

5. McCann, "The Book of Psalms," 4:1180.

6. Artur Weiser, *The Psalms: A Commentary,* OTL (Philadelphia: Westminster, 1962), 747.

7. Weiser, *The Psalms,* 748.

8. McCann, "The Book of Psalms," 4:1180.

9. James L. Mays, *Psalms,* Interpretation (Louisville: John Knox, 1994), 391, points to Pss 38:16; 94:18 for this sense.

the psalm in terms of the word count in the Masoretic Text.[10] The two phrases provide a structure that in itself eloquently states the theme of the psalm: "the keeper of Israel" (v. 4a) and "Yahweh, the keeper of you" (v. 5a).

3. Yahweh the *protector of the individual:* the *scope* of the keeping (vv. 5-8). Three of the four verses here open with the emphatic use of the name Yahweh ("Yahweh is your keeper," vv. 5, 7; "Yahweh will keep," v. 8). These four verses also contain six second masculine singular suffixes and four contrasting pairs (sun/moon, day/night, coming in/going out, now/forever) so that the reader feels the personal nature and unlimited scope of divine protection. Some versions even translate the literal term "shade" (Hebrew *ṣēl*) as "defense" (NEB) or "protection" (JPS), which seems appropriate in the light of metaphorical uses elsewhere (Num 14:9; Ps 91:1). The richness of the metaphor is augmented by the fact that God's help at "the right hand" is surely closer than the hills at a distance, but the sense of "shade" raises an interpretive question about the "sun/moon" word pair. Scholars are divided over the precise scope of the dangers involved: literal heat, lunacy ("moonstruck"), or divine power (Hebrew *šemeš,* "sun," could allude to the Mesopotamian sun god of the same name). Leslie Allen thus refers to the pair of terms as "the blazing sun and the sinister moon" pointing to "fears both rational and irrational."[11]

Ultimately, the protection Yahweh provides is from "evil" (Hebrew *ra'*), though some English versions remove any moral overtones by translating it "harm" (NIV, JPS) or "danger" (TEV). The latter type of translation may strike us as a better rendering, since many specific dangers and harmful events come our way in this world, not all of which are "evil" in themselves. Even so, we must confess to not always being able to determine that for ourselves; nor can we say for sure where and how the Hebrews drew the line between "harm" and "evil." So, even though from our perspective not all of life's problems are evil in a strict moral sense, the psalmist may have wanted to imply as much or evoke as much and so we should not be too quick to dismiss moral overtones in this line.

Finally, while the verbal shift in verse 7 (to the imperfect) carries a future sense,[12] this should not be understood as meaning that the psalmist

10. McCann, "The Book of Psalms," 4:1181, says the syllable count also confirms this.

11. Allen, *Psalms 101-150,* 154.

12. Willem VanGemeren, "Psalms," in *The Expositor's Bible Commentary* (Grand Rapids: Zondervan, 1991), 5:774.

was promising false hope for an easy life. Allen is correct when he reminds us that the Israelites surely experienced the difficulties of life, but they still held a deep conviction that the whole of one's life was safe in God's keeping.[13] The total scope of the keeping is therefore affirmed in the strongest way possible in this concluding section: through *all* evil, in *all* places, and at *all* times, Yahweh guards the believer. Paul's language in Romans 8, with its word pairs (e.g., "neither death nor life"), provides a similar assurance, that *nothing* "will be able to separate us from the love of God in Christ Jesus our Lord" (Rom 8:39 NRSV).

James K. Mead

PSALM 122

First Sunday of Advent, Year A
    First Lesson: Isaiah 2:1-5
    (Psalm 122)
    Second Lesson: Romans 13:11-14
    Gospel Lesson: Matthew 24:36-44

The First Sunday of Advent presents a particular problem. It follows Christ the King Sunday, but it also introduces a season of waiting. The first collection of texts builds on the anticipation of the new day. Psalm 122 is recast by its location with this time and the other texts of the day.

Psalm 122 is the third in the collection of the Psalms of Ascents (Pss 120–134; see the introductory essay). Even though this collection has a background of pilgrimage, only Psalm 122 fits form-critically into the category of pilgrimage song. The psalm fits into an emerging plot of the collection from dispersion (Ps 120:5-7), to journey (Ps 121) to Jerusalem itself in Psalm 122.

Psalm 122, like the one that precedes it, begins with an oft-quoted line that has found its way into numerous liturgical resources.

> I was glad when they said to me,
>   "Let us go up to the house of the LORD."

13. Allen, *Psalms 101–150*, 154.

The phrase "I was glad" occurs only three times in the Old Testament (1 Sam 2:1; Pss 122:1; 137:6). On the other hand, there are some fifty-five occurrences of "glad." The psalmist utilizes this language to underscore the greatness of Israelite Jerusalem and nationhood during the Davidic reign.

The first verse is typically separated from the rest of the psalm because of the specific aspirations of the psalm. Psalm 122 knits together a pilgrimage song and a Zion song (other Zion songs include 46; 48; 76; 84; 87). Through the use of parallelism the psalmist connects the house of the Lord with Jerusalem. It therefore presents the same sort of interpretive challenges for Christians as the Zion songs. However, the psalmist does not accent the grandiose (see Pss 46; 48; 76), but rather underlines the warmth Jerusalem shares with pilgrims.[1] The language of "standing" has parallels in the beginning of the Psalter (Ps 1). Standing denotes social as well as physical location. The orienting verb, "glad," acts like a sustaining note in this song of Jerusalem. The opening verses thus bind together the house of the Lord and the house of David, namely, Jerusalem. However, the phrase "house of the LORD" frames the entire psalm (vv. 1 and 9). So one might think that "the house of the LORD" circumscribes not only Jerusalem but also all political entities.

With this tone established, the psalmist now addresses the nature of Jerusalem. Like Psalm 48, the city's architecture comes to the fore. The language of gates, thrones, ramparts, and citadels dominates the psalm. This may help us understand the phrase "Jerusalem is built as a city."

Even the architecture or structure of the psalm invites the reader in. It begins with the first-person "I was glad . . . ," then moves to Jerusalem (vv. 1-3 and 4-5), and then returns to first-person affirmations (vv. 7-8). The psalmist uses syntactical parallelism through the rubric "for the sake of" to connect the relatives of the psalmist with the "house of the LORD." Once again the psalmist knits together the human structures and the divine franchise. However, it is precisely this knitting that threatens to unravel the reading of this text. For the use of divine support for human institutions is a matter of some conflict today. The word translated "bound" or "compacted" (*ḥābar*, v. 3) generally refers to human compacts and alliances, and only here are there architectural elements present.[2] Jerusalem is a place of praise and justice, but the language of how Jerusalem is built in-

1. Leslie Allen, *Psalms 100–150*, WBC 21 (Waco: Word, 1983), 157.
2. J. Clinton McCann, Jr., "The Book of Psalms: Introduction, Commentary, and Reflections," in *NIB*, 4:1184.

dicates that it is also a place of refuge.[3] This is, after all, where the tribes of the Lord go up. The challenge for today's interpreter becomes to translate the tribal language of antiquity for a postmodern context. The tribes of antiquity were extended families. The recent work on families in antiquity might be helpful. How does today's reader in the light of Rwanda, Sudan, Bosnia, etc., reconfigure what we mean by the term "tribe"?

The interplay of Psalm 122, which has no emphasis on time, and the other texts for the day creates an almost dialogical tension. This psalm fits better into the prophetic tradition than many of the songs of Zion.[4] Isaiah 2 clearly introduces the eschatological times with the phrase "in the latter days." This invites the reader who places Psalm 122 in this context today to hear this pilgrimage song as an eschatological song about the coming prominence of Jerusalem. Psalm 122:1 parallels Isaiah 2:3:

> Come, let us go up to the mountain of the LORD,
>   to the house of the God of Jacob.

The Gospel reading, Matthew 24:36-44, emphasizes that no one knows the time. It challenges the reader to constant vigilance. Romans 13:11-14 continues the theme of eschatological time, but begins with the phrase "you know what time it is" (Rom 13:11a). One could explore the idea of knowing and not knowing in the midst of a pilgrimage. Moving in a different direction, one might consider how eschatological time reframes the tribal notions of Psalm 122.

Stephen Breck Reid

PSALM 123

Twenty-sixth Sunday after Pentecost, Year A
    First Lesson: Judges 4:1-7
    (Psalm 123)
    Second Lesson: 1 Thessalonians 5:1-11
    Gospel Lesson: Matthew 25:14-30

3. James Luther Mays, *Psalms,* Interpretation (Louisville: John Knox, 1994), 392-93.
4. Allen, *Psalms 100–150,* 157.

Psalm 121 begins with a reference to "eyes." There the psalmist says, "I lift up my eyes to the hills." Psalm 123 says, "To you I lift up my eyes." Indeed, in Psalm 123 we hear a lot about eyes. The link between the first three of the Psalms of Ascents invites the reader to understand the function of "eyes" as a metaphor for core relationships. The more oblique reference to God in the midst of the hills in Psalm 121 gives way to more explicit presence-of-God language in Psalm 123. One might say with regards to this passage, "The eyes have it."

We encounter the term "eyes" four times in the short course of two verses of the psalm. We all have heard the song, "Keep your eyes on the prize." There the "eyes" reference points to how we construe the eyes as windows not only to the soul but also to the intention. Psalm 123 has three movements. The first movement is the first-person declaration of the psalmist (v. 1). The second movement is the simile on "eyes" (v. 2). These first two movements develop the "eyes" motif. The second movement ends with a reference to mercy/grace. It is that reference that organizes the third movement (vv. 3-4).

The first movement gives witness to the sovereignty of God. The language "enthroned in heaven" carries this task effectively. Who were these people who understood the otherness of God? The first and the second movements use the image of eyes to demonstrate relationship. Each of us knows the power of eyes, though different cultures express it in distinctive ways. For instance, some cultures mandate eye contact while others forbid it as a manner of casual social interaction. Despite the different interpretations, both types of cultures pay attention to the power of eyes and eye contact. I remember as a young man the power of eyes. One day I looked into a pair of eyes and I knew I would marry the young woman who owned them. Eyes capture our attention. They let us know whether we have really found our place.

Eyes signal intention, but also approval. In Psalm 123 both things are in play. We can observe this through the eyes mentioned. A human being through socialization is trained how to read the eyes for the intention of the other, but also for the approval of the other. However, not everyone has the ability to see the eyes of another. For instance, if one is visually impaired, one might use other strategies. If one is hearing impaired, one might use other strategies. What are the clues we use to discern people's intention and approval, visual and otherwise?

In our communication we constantly need feedback. We use our eyes to seek it. We seek some indication of how our words or deeds are perceived. The psalmist uses this metaphor to express the way we eye our superiors. The psalmist uses only a particular set of examples: the way we eye our superiors. Sometimes eyes work together with our ears or other senses. Blind persons listen for feedback from their surroundings, listening for the traffic in much the way a sighted person looks with eyes. We look to the eyes of our superiors to receive approval and get instructions.

In the third movement (vv. 3-4) the psalmist describes us as we look to a superior in the way a plaintiff looks to the judge. In other words, we look with our eyes, expecting to get something. What we seek is mercy. The Hebrew verb *ḥānan* means "favor, grace, mercy." The challenge for the contemporary interpreter is to allow the English translation to carry the full semantic range here. The temptation is to settle on one rendering such as "mercy." While mercy clearly fits the semantic range of the term and the literary context, it also compels the contemporary reader to legal categories. On the other hand, if one were to translate the term "grace," the relationships of obligation noted in the first two movements become too diffuse. In other words, "mercy" is not sufficient to convey the wonderful promise of abundance that is grace. "Grace" is not sufficient to point to the abject vulnerability of the psalmist and us.

Our eyes focus on (or look to) the Lord our God until God shows us favor. Hebrew prepositions are almost always crucial in the interpretation of a text. Here too we find the preposition crucial. We look *with* expectation and patience — not the patience of unfeeling lifelessness, but rather the persistent patience of an expectant mother that keeps pushing during the pain of labor — until we encounter "grace" (*ḥānan*). But most often we meet "grace" (*ḥānan;* √*ḥnn*) as the fruit of God's mercy (√*rḥm*). Any "grace" we share is based on that prior reception. Grace comes unmerited and often unexpectedly. The prophetic texts remind us that the graciousness of God is inextricably bound to the graciousness we share with one another. But that is paid for with a high price. The other lections make clear that the task of Christian ministry, which we participate in as part of our baptism, is not easy. In fact, our graciousness is derivative of God. Often we find one another and ourselves as persons without hope of transformation. This happens in families and churches as well. We really don't think Sister Sarah will ever change and quit being such a pain in the neck. Then there is brother Harry. He has broken faith and has broken one of our commandments. How can we be gracious to these folks? By looking into the eyes of the God who has been so gracious to us.

The NRSV renders the term *rab* "much" or "more" and the verb for being satisfied *(śābaʿ)* "more than enough" in one place and "more than its fill" in another. The anguish of the psalmist calls for more colorful language here. The idea of a "bellyful" makes clear that this is over and above merely being satisfied. This is the bellyache of overconsumption.

The first reading for the Twenty-sixth Sunday after Pentecost, Year A, is Judges 4:1-7. We are introduced to Deborah, who seems to embody the trust that Psalm 123 presupposes. The Epistle reading, 1 Thessalonians 5:1-11, leads the reader into an eschatological world that does not easily connect with Psalm 123. The Gospel reading, Matthew 25:14-30, rehearses the parable of the talents in which the servants looked to the hand of their master.

Stephen Breck Reid

PSALM 124

Fourteenth Sunday after Pentecost, Year A
> First Lesson: Exodus 1:8–2:10
> **(Psalm 124)**
> Second Lesson: Romans 12:1-8
> Gospel Lesson: Matthew 16:13-20

Nineteenth Sunday after Pentecost, Year B
> First Lesson: Esther 7:1-6, 9-10; 9:20-22
> **(Psalm 124)**
> Second Lesson: James 5:13-20
> Gospel Lesson: Mark 9:38-50

Psalm 124 breaks into three stanzas. The first (vv. 1-5) begins with a strophe that contains two "if" clauses (vv. 1-2), followed by three "then" clauses (vv. 3-5). The second stanza expresses dependence on God's redemptive work in a different manner (vv. 6-7). The psalm concludes with a blessing and confession of trust (v. 8).

"If it had not been the LORD who was on our side . . ." (vv. 1-2). The language of contingency here is also the language of advocacy. We see a similar function in the story of Joseph (Gen 39:2-4). Psalm 94:17 carries the same contingency and dependence as Psalm 124. Isaiah 1:9 provides a sobering parallel:

> If the LORD of hosts
>   had not left us a few survivors. (NRSV)

This reminds us that the advocacy of God is not a blanket assurance of a life of ease. Here we find the language of advocacy. The Hebrew phrase "were it not" occurs more frequently in argument than thanksgiving. Psalm 119:92 is a personal expression of divine redemption. The vehicle for divine redemption was the torah. Consistently in Psalms 94 and 119 the phrase "if not" precedes a description of God's saving action that prevents some disaster. The idea of God on one side or another even if it is our side often offends sophisticated sensibilities. The advocacy of God calls into question human sovereignty in history. If God can take sides, then there is the chance that God will at some time not be on our side. The Enlightenment model of a God without advocacy trivializes the advocacy of God in the movement of history. The key interpretive challenge of Psalm 124 is to come to grips with the idea of God "for us." The NIV and the NRSV translate this as "on our side." How do the phrases "for us" and "on our side" share and diverge in their respective meanings?

The psalmist uses a makeshift chorus by including the phrase "Let Israel say . . ." The Hebrew verb *qwm* is translated "attacked" in both the NIV and the NRSV. However, the term is most often translated "rise." This will emphasize not only the military aspect but also the honor/shame aspect that occurs when one group rises above another. The psalmist here uses the subject *'ādām* (literally, "a man"; NRSV: "our enemies") to convey that the conflict has human and not divine origins.[1]

But the story does not end there. The "then" clauses recount what God prevents: the extermination of the people at the whim of others. The psalmist uses the language of "eaten alive" to accent the vicious nature of the extermination. The military victor sometimes disgraces a foe by literally consuming that foe. Such a practice of violence scandalizes the ethics of the Hebrew Bible (Prov 1:12). The process of committing it while the victim is still aware of the pain inflicts humiliation that increases disgrace. This extermination happens whenever the powerful become angry. Then we would have been swallowed alive. The film *Return of the Jedi* describes a beast that would eat people and digest them over the course of years as they watched themselves die. The term "swallow" is

---

1. James L. Mays, *Psalms,* Interpretation (Louisville: John Knox, 1994), 396.

also an apt metaphor to describe the trauma of the Babylonian exile. In fact, in Jeremiah 51:34 the same verb "swallow" *(bala')* describes the Babylonians' defeat of Zion.[2] The context of this swallowing is the burning of anger. The language here is sometimes thought to go back to the way the nose flares in anger (v. 36). The idea of kindling anger makes clear the connection between heat and anger.

The second "then" clause describes how the waters would have swept us away. One might think of this as hot and cold, dry and wet to describe the danger that God's protection averted. The innate fear of being swallowed alive is now joined to the fear of being drowned, swept over by waters (v. 4). The final "then" sentence continues with the chaos waters motif. The term rendered "raging" in both the NIV and the NRSV can also mean "boiling." Given the heat of the enemies' anger, one might think of being boiled alive by one's enemies.

The activity of God prevents the community from being washed away by waters, rivers, even torrential waters. The sense of being awash aptly catches the plight of the postexilic community as well as disenfranchised communities around us in North America. These people hear the psalm and know that they have been swallowed alive and swept over by rage.

The next section (vv. 6-7) shifts the nature of disaster from the natural, a flood, to the military realm. The psalmist uses hunting metaphors to uncover this danger. But before that the psalmist begins with blessings for what has not been done. God has refrained from giving the community as prey to "their teeth." The word "prey" is quite intriguing, for prey and food are synonymous. The psalmist uses the language of "their" teeth. While understood as "the enemies" in English, the use of the third person as the designated enemy is an effective tool. Listen to the sentence: "You do not want to be with them." The antecedent does not have to be clear. The psalm closes with a confession of trust and faith: *"Our help is in the name of the LORD."* The "name" as used especially in the book of Deuteronomy here becomes a metaphor for the presence of God.

This responsorial psalm is paired with Exodus 1 for the Fourteenth Sunday after Pentecost, Year A. As such, the psalm of thanksgiving frames this story of liberation. The Epistle reading, Romans 12:1-8, invites the reading of Psalm 124 as the thanksgiving before the rededication pre-

---

2. J. Clinton McCann, Jr., "The Book of Psalms: Introduction, Commentary, and Reflections," in *NIB,* 4:1190.

supposed in the Romans passage. The Gospel reading, Matthew 16:13-20, provides the connection through the reference to Jonah who was actually swallowed, even though the psalmist talks about that only as an unfulfilled and perhaps metaphorical danger.

For the Nineteenth Sunday after Pentecost, Year B, the responsorial psalm is paired with Esther 7:1-6, 9-10; 9:20-22. The story of Esther, Mordecai, and the persecuted Jews of the Persian period (539-333 B.C.E.) could not find a better response than the thanksgiving for divine advocacy found in Psalm 124. The Epistle reading, James 5:13-20, provides the waiting and prayer side of the advocacy reflections. The Gospel reading, Mark 9:38-50, seems to have less of a connection to the psalm.

Stephen Breck Reid

PSALM 125

Sixteenth Sunday after Pentecost, Year B
> First Lesson: Proverbs 22:1-2, 8-9, 22-23
> **(Psalm 125)**
> Second Lesson: James 2:1-10, (11-13), 14-17
> Gospel Lesson: Mark 7:24-37

Psalm 125 is the sixth of fifteen psalms in Book V (Pss 107-150) of the Psalter whose superscriptions identify them as "Songs of Ascents" (Pss 120-134; see the introductory essay). While scholars do not know the precise function of this collection of psalms, it seems likely that they were used by ancient Israelite pilgrims as they made their way to Jerusalem to celebrate certain festivals and holy days — Passover, Tabernacles, Weeks.

Jerusalem sits on a hill, so no matter where the pilgrims came from, they "went up" to Jerusalem. "Songs of Ascents" is thus an appropriate title for this special group of songs. We can imagine family groups setting out from their homes and villages and, as they travel along, joining with other family groups who are also headed for Jerusalem. These groups meet others, and soon large numbers of people are walking and riding together. And they sing the psalms as they travel along. During the period of the nation of Israel (from David until 586 B.C.E.), the pilgrims would have traveled to Jerusalem through land that they possessed, where the worship of Yahweh was the status quo. During the postexilic period, however, the Israelites lived on land ruled by Persians, Greeks, and then Romans. They were a minority people in a large empire, surrounded by those who did not worship Yahweh. Many scholars see this time as the setting for the assembly of the Songs of Ascents.

The first Song of Ascents, Psalm 120, is an individual lament, in which the psalm singer cries out,

> Too long I had my dwelling
> among those who hate peace. (v. 6)

Psalm 121's singer speaks words of encouragement:

> I lift up my eyes to the hills —
> from where will my help come? (v. 1)

In these ways the journey to Zion, the holy city of Jerusalem that sits on a hill, begins.

The opening words of Psalm 125 celebrate the constancy of Zion:

> Those who trust in the LORD are like Mount Zion,
> which cannot be moved, but abides forever. (v. 1)

Are we permitted to read Psalm 125 as a song the pilgrims sang after arriving in Jerusalem, the "safe place" of the Lord?

From this safe vantage point — surrounded by the Lord as the mountains surround Jerusalem (v. 2) — the pilgrims lament living among wickedness (v. 3) and "those who turn aside to their own crooked ways" (v. 5), but petition God to do good to the pilgrims themselves, those who are good and upright in heart (v. 5). The psalm closes with a statement of confidence:

> Those who turn aside to their own crooked ways
> the LORD will lead away with evildoers. (v. 5)

The words of Psalm 125 contrast those who trust in the Lord (v. 1), who are righteous (v. 3) and upright (v. 4), with wickedness (v. 3) and those who turn aside to crooked ways (v. 4), echoing the wisdom words with which the Psalter begins:

> For the LORD watches over the way of the righteous,
> but the way of the wicked will perish. (Ps 1:6)

The structure of Psalm 125 is three two-line strophes (vv. 1-2, v. 3, and vv. 4-5), with an interesting wordplay forming an *inclusio* at its "edges." In verse 1 we read that those who trust in the Lord are like Mount Zion, which cannot "be moved" but abides forever. The word translated "be moved" comes from the Hebrew root *mwṭ*, and has a range of meanings that include "to waver, to totter, and to quake." In verse 5 we are told the fate of "those who turn aside" to their own crooked ways. The word translated "those who turn aside" *(maṭṭîm)* comes from the Hebrew root *nṭh*, which means "to bend, to turn aside, to bow down." The two words and roots are similar in Hebrew — creating a wordplay that contrasts *the immovable righteous* with the wicked, who are *easily led astray.*

In Jerusalem, the city of Mount Zion, the righteous pilgrims pause for a moment and look out on the world. God's promises to them are sure; the wicked will not prevail. Thus the people can say with confidence, "Peace be upon Israel!" (v. 5).

In the first lesson the wisdom words from Proverbs remind the hearer that God does not favor the rich, those who sow injustice, or those who crush the afflicted. Rather, God seeks out those with a good name, those to whom injustice has been done, and those who have been robbed and afflicted.

The vast majority of pilgrims who made their way to Jerusalem for the festival seasons in the postexilic period were *not* rich; they *were* victims of injustice in their daily lives; they *most likely* felt crushed. As they gathered in Jerusalem, the holy city, and worshiped together at the temple, perhaps some measure of confidence was restored. God does do good to those who are good, to those who are upright in their hearts (Ps 125:4), despite the circumstances that surround them each day. And at the end of the appointed time, the pilgrims could return home with hope restored and with new energy for the days ahead. May we all find our Jerusalems — those places of gathering in which the upright in heart gain new strength for the days of our journeys.

Nancy L. deClaissé-Walford

PSALM 126

Third Sunday of Advent, Year B
First Lesson: Isaiah 61:1-4, 8-11
(Psalm 126)
Second Lesson: 1 Thessalonians 5:16-24
Gospel Lesson: John 1:6-8, 19-28

Fifth Sunday in Lent, Year C
First Lesson: Isaiah 43:16-21
(Psalm 126)
Second Lesson: Philippians 3:4b-14
Gospel Lesson: John 12:1-8

Psalm 126 is the seventh of the Songs of Ascents. In keeping with the directions of the preceding psalms in this collection, it not only recalls past deliverance (vv. 1-3; see Ps 124:1-7) but it also and simultaneously prays for help amid ongoing need (vv. 4-5; see Pss 122:6-7; 123:3-4; 125:4) and expresses confidence that God will indeed again deliver those in need (v. 6; see Pss 121:1-8; 123:1-2; 124:8; 125:1-2, 5). Some translations render the verb tenses in Psalm 126 so as to make the psalm consistently either a *prayer for help* (communal lament) or a *song of thanksgiving*, but the tension preserved by the NRSV between verses 1-3 and 4-6 is important and meaningful. In fact, it makes sense both historically and theologically.

The likely historical referent of verses 1-3 is the return from exile, especially since the phrase "restored the fortunes" elsewhere indicates this act of deliverance (see Deut 30:3; Jer 30:3, 18; 32:44; Ezek 39:25; and note also the pairing of Ps 126 with Jer 31:7-9 as alternate readings for the Twenty-third Sunday after Pentecost, Year B). This event would have been like a dream fulfilled (v. 1b), as well as a source of joy (v. 2ab) and a noteworthy international occurrence (v. 2cd). But the return from exile did not live up to the glorious expectations articulated, for instance, in Isaiah 40–55. As Isaiah 56–66 indicates, along with the books of Haggai, Zechariah, Ezra, and Nehemiah, there were ongoing problems and needs, which may have prompted the people to pray for what they had already experienced: "Restore our fortunes" (v. 4).

The probable historical referent of verses 1-3 need not exhaust the meaning of these verses, however. As Hans-Joachim Kraus concludes regarding the phrase "restored the fortunes," it can legitimately be construed as "an expression for a historical change to a new state of affairs for all things."[1] This interpretive direction significantly broadens the range of meaning. It suggests, for instance, that the people of God in all places and times live by both memory and hope. While we joyfully recall and celebrate the new things that God has done among us and for the world, we also continue to exist as finite and fallible human beings, who will always need to pray, "Restore our fortunes, O LORD." As James L. Mays concludes concerning what the people of God may learn from Psalm 13 and its juxtaposition of pain and praise, "The agony and the ecstasy belong together as the secret of our identity."[2] Or to put it in slightly different terms, the tears and the joy (see "shouts of joy" in Ps 126:2, 5, 6), the hurt and the hope, the suffering and the glory, perennially belong together in the life of faith. Or, in New Testament terms, we always live simultaneously as people of the cross and people of the resurrection.

This reality suggests the appropriateness of Psalm 126 for both Advent and Lent. Advent is not only preparation to celebrate Jesus' birth; it also directs our attention to the brokenness of our world and thus invites us to live hope-filled lives toward the new heaven and new earth that God has promised. During Lent we recall the painful circumstances of Jesus' suffering and death, but we dare to share in Jesus' suffering because we know we also share the hope of resurrection and renewal. Psalm 126 reminds us that memory and hope are inseparable.

Psalm 126 is also assigned for Thanksgiving Day, Year B, and is paired with Joel 2:21-27, a book that arose from the same postexilic circumstances as Psalm 126, according to Walter Beyerlin.[3] But even if Beyerlin is incorrect, both Joel and Psalm 126 articulate the grounds for genuine gratitude — that is, the trust that God will provide (see especially Ps 126:6). Psalm 126 may be especially valuable as a Thanksgiving text, because it both clearly attributes "great things" (vv. 2-3) to God and articulates an awareness of ongoing neediness. Without both of these directions, it is all too easy for alleged thanksgiving to become nothing more than the celebration of the status quo, or worse, mere self-congratulation.

More generally, the acknowledgment of neediness, tears, and weeping in Psalm 126 may help us to deal with something that our culture

---

1. Hans-Joachim Kraus, *Psalms 60–150: A Continental Commentary* (Minneapolis: Fortress, 1993), 450.

2. James L. Mays, "Psalm 13," *Int* 37 (1983): 282.

3. Walter Beyerlin, *We Are Like Dreamers,* trans. D. Livingston (Edinburgh: T. & T. Clark, 1982), 41-58.

routinely teaches us to deny or to try to avoid — that is, suffering. In their song and video "Everybody Hurts," the rock group REM includes written commentary at the bottom of the screen to accompany the song lyrics and visual images; at one point this commentary consists of the quotation of Psalm 126:6. The point of the video, as the title suggests, is that for finite, fallible human beings, suffering is part of life. Those of us who have been called "to take up [our] cross and follow" Jesus (Mark 8:34) should know this already. For us, not only will suffering be a normal part of human life that we cannot avoid, but also suffering for love's sake will be a mark of faithfulness (as opposed to suffering that results from or perpetuates injustice). But the church has not always conveyed this message very clearly, and our culture is often of no help in dealing with suffering constructively and faithfully. In any case, the juxtaposition in Psalm 126 of suffering and joy, hurt and hope, agony and ecstasy, pain and praise, may serve to open up a conversation that is desperately needed in contemporary North American church and culture.

J. Clinton McCann, Jr.

PSALM 127

Twenty-fifth Sunday after Pentecost, Year B
    First Lesson: Ruth 3:1-5; 4:13-17
    (Psalm 127)
    Second Lesson: Hebrews 9:24-28
    Gospel Lesson: Mark 12:38-44

Basic to Psalm 127 — a pilgrim "Psalm of Ascent" (Pss 120-134), and best read with 128 — is the idea of *double agency.* Modern folk tend to think of God and nature, God and humans in terms of an either/or, of one or the other. Something is either divine or natural, not both. This dichotomy is not biblical (cf. Phil 2:12-13). Rather, the creator of all things mysteriously works his providential purposes out in the patterns of creation and in the free, yet limited, agency of humans. Even wicked human purposes can end up fulfilling God's plan, as the amazing Joseph story twice insists (Gen 45:1-8; 50:15-20)! Most of God's work is not "miraculous" in the sense of "contrary to nature," but miraculous in that the Lord works in and through the wonderful world and human capacities he created.[1]

Also basic to this psalm is its wisdom aspects. Its superscription calls it a "Psalm of Solomon," the wisest of Israel's kings, who built his own great "house" and the Lord's "house" in Jerusalem. Wise house-building is something done by God in creation (Prov 3:19-20) and by humans made in God's image (see Prov 24:3-4; cf. also Exod 31:1-3; 1 Kings 7:13-14, which use the same Hebrew wisdom vocabulary).[2] To "build a house" or a city wisely was to shape one's immediate, material-social world according to the standards and purposes that God had placed in creation as a whole. What's more, "to build a house" in Hebrew also meant to make a family: "May the LORD make [Ruth] . . . like Rachel and Leah, who together built up the house of Israel" (Ruth 4:11 — which ties into the Old Testament lesson, for Ruth ultimately builds the royal "house of David," the "house" of the Messiah; see Luke 2:4). The two sections of Psalm 127 (vv. 1-2 and 3-5) play on this double sense of house building, also through puns on the verb *bnh* (to build) and the word *bn* ("son" — a product of "house building"!). In various ways ancient Israel organized their society and developed their entire culture in terms of the "house of the father."[3]

The background above makes this psalm rich and multireferential. The temple or "house of God" in the New Testament can refer to the people of God (1 Cor 3:9, 16-17; 6:19-20), to which we might add Augustine's phrase "city of God," taken up from Hebrews 11:10 and 12:22 and Revelation 3:12. Thus, one may apply the psalm to building up the people of God and protecting the church (as people) from its enemies within and without. But to stop at such an application would be to narrow the scope of the psalm far too much. This psalm, by implication, applies to *all* human cultural endeavors that are done in faithful service to God — with an implicit warning to those that are not. Metaphorically, the activities of Psalm 127 imply the full scope of life on planet earth. Building houses represents human use of the materials of created reality from wood and stone to wool and the sound waves that make music and speech. Its fur-

1. See Pss 7:14-16; 9:15-16, and G. von Rad, *Wisdom in Israel* (Nashville: Abingdon, 1972).

2. Cf. R. C. Van Leeuwen, "Building God's House: An Exploration in Wisdom," in *The Way of Wisdom: Essays in Honor of Bruce K. Waltke*, ed. J. I. Packer and Sven K. Soderlund (Grand Rapids: Zondervan, 2000), 204-11.

3. P. J. King and L. E. Stager, *Life in Biblical Israel* (Louisville: Westminster John Knox, 2000), 4-5.

niture, arts, crafts, and surrounding fields fill a house "with all sorts of pleasant and precious things" (Prov 24:3-4). A house or city embodies the organization of our world, and our relation to other humans. And it is in the house that we pass on wisdom and life from generation to generation. Guarding the city implies the political, social, and economic realms, with their dangers and opportunities, as well as all the cultural activities therein. Again, through the joyful, difficult, loving task of making babies and rearing them, culture and society continue, and God's purposes are accomplished through the generations, from Ruth to Solomon and Jesus, and to us who wait for a second coming.

This small psalm encompasses the entire world: cosmos and history alike. But it has one point. It is God who created all this and by his providential care makes it possible. He it is that blesses the family and makes it fruitful (vv. 3-5a; Gen 1:28). For humans, task and blessing are of one piece. Humans must work and watch. They must get up and go to work, and lose sleep to guard the city or feed the baby by night. And yet! Without the providential care of God, all this is simply "in vain." Israel may never say, "My power and the might of my hand have gotten me this wealth" (Deut 8:17). Israel may never forget that in all its labor and success, it is "God . . . who gives you power to get wealth, that he may confirm his covenant" (Deut 8:18). Throughout it all, Psalm 127 is joyful, even playful. (Adults may secretly delight in the warrior with his arrows in his "hand" [yād], which is sometimes a euphemism for the phallus.)

Raymond C. Van Leeuwen

PSALM 128

Tenth Sunday after Pentecost, Year A
   First Lesson: Genesis 29:15-28
   (Psalm 128)
   Second Lesson: Romans 8:26-39
   Gospel Lesson: Matthew 13:31-33, 44-52

Here we have a psalm of blessing. The psalmist uses two near synonyms, "happy" and "blessed." Psalm 128 begins with a word of blessing (*'ašrê*). The word "happy" can function as an interpretive node. It connects

Psalm 128 to Psalm 1:1-2, and an even closer parallel is the wisdom acrostic Psalm 112:1b, which explicitly connects happiness to the fear of the Lord. The fear of the Lord in Psalm 128 and Psalm 112 parallels the torah piety of Psalm 1.

The word "happy" also connects Psalm 128 to Psalm 127. So much so that one might think of them as companions.[1] Fear of the Lord includes ethical behavior conveyed in the phrase "walk in the paths." "Happy" repeats in verse 2. The synonym "bless" connects the next three verses (vv. 3-5).

What does fear of the Lord mean? The contemporary interpreter must address this. The theme occurs often in the Psalter (see Pss 2:11; 25:14; 31:19; 33:18; 34:9, 11; 60:4; 112:1; 115:11, 13; 118:4). It is clear that the notion includes recognition of divine sovereignty. However, the nuancing of this in a particular tradition and congregation remains the task for the "local authority," for "fear" prompts local translations — not all correct — of the phenomenon.

Three proposals concerning the structure of the psalm provide three different interpretive strategies. The NIV divides the psalm into two sections, with "fear" bracketing the first section (vv. 1-4), and then a conclusion (vv. 5-6). The NRSV structures the psalm in terms of areas of life: work-related happiness (vv. 1-2), family happiness (vv. 3-4), and happiness in God and Zion (vv. 5-6). Leslie Allen argues that we have two stanzas (vv. 1-3, 4-6). Both of them begin with the idea of fear of the Lord. Both begin with the language of happiness or blessing (*'ašrê* and *bērēk*). Both move from third to second person.[2]

The embodied world of wisdom has specifics for the blessing. The term for "labor/toil" occurs infrequently in the Hebrew Bible (Gen 31:42; Job 10:3; 20:6; Ps 128:2; Isa 8:8; 45:14; Jer 3:24; Hag 1:11; Zech 14:5). The more specific reference "toil/labor of the hands" occurs but two other times. The labor of the hands in Genesis 31 and Psalm 128 refers to the satisfaction of a worker with the yield. God saw the labor of Jacob's hand and rewarded it at Laban's expense (Gen 31:36-42). Similarly, Job 10:3 expresses the conventional wisdom that work, i.e., labor of the hands, redounds to one's benefit. The toil/labor of an agrarian culture relates to food, hence the benefit is the ability to eat. Hence the NRSV renders the term "toil/

---

1. J. Clinton McCann, Jr., "The Book of Psalms: Introduction, Commentary, and Reflections," in *NIB*, 4:1200.

2. Leslie Allen, *Psalms 100-150*, WBC 21 (Waco: Word, 1983), 184.

labor" as "fruit of the labor" to fit the verb "eat." The work that yields a benefit finds an interesting analogue in Isaiah 65:21. There those who build houses get the benefit of living in them and those who plant vineyards receive the profit of being able to drink the products of the vineyard. What is most interesting about this analogue is that it occurs in the midst of an eschatological or utopian vision, a new heaven and earth (Isa 65:17). The era of meaningful work accompanies an era of peace that reaches into the animal kingdom (Isa 65:25). The eschatological and utopian analogue renders the psalm passage a blessing, namely, a rhetorical expression of wishing for another the benefits of a utopian or eschatological world here and now.

If meaningful and productive work is the first specific of the blessing, familial fecundity is the second. The psalmist describes a wife who produces many children. The agrarian imagery continues. She is like a fruitful vine in one's house. Obviously there is a play on the term "house" as a residence, but also as a family. The productivity of the wife generates the image of children that resemble the numerous shoots out of a pruned olive tree. The shoots surround the nub much as children would surround a table.

The language of happiness is a node in the beginning of this psalm, and Zion (Pss 122:1-2, 6-9; 125:1-2; 126:1; 129:5; 132:15; 133:3; 134:3) and blessing (Pss 129:8; 132:15; 133:3; 134:3) are the nodes as the psalm concludes. Verse 5 locates the blessing as deriving from Zion. Two wishes follow. The Hebrew verb form is an imperative of the verb *rā'âh*, "to see." However, it has the force of a Greek optative, expressing a wish. The first wish addresses Jerusalem, a concern of the author of this psalm. "May you see the goodness of Jerusalem," the poet writes, the NRSV translating the Hebrew word *ṭôb* as "prosperity" instead of "goodness." The decision is wise but obscures the way prosperity and moral goodness were understood as two sides of the same coin in other uses of this word. In other words, if one were to see the prosperous Jerusalem, then it must be the morally good Jerusalem.

The second wish is that one will see one's children's children. While many in the affluent world realize this event, it remained a wish in an ancient world where much shorter life expectancy obtained. Even today in parts of Africa, South America, and elsewhere, a wish to see one's grandchildren is still a bold one.

During this season the lectionary readings are not strongly linked, as an examination of the collateral texts will demonstrate. The Tenth

Sunday after Pentecost, Year A, first reading, Genesis 29:15-28, the story of Jacob and Rachel, has little immediate connection to Psalm 128. The Epistle reading, Romans 8:26-39, contains the language of promise if not predestination. However, once again any connection to Psalm 128 is to be held lightly. The Gospel reading, Matthew 13:31-33, 44-52, provides a group of parables that shed no additional light on Psalm 128.

Stephen Breck Reid

PSALM 130

Fifth Sunday in Lent, Year A
    First Lesson: Ezekiel 37:1-14
    (Psalm 130)
    Second Lesson: Romans 8:6-11
    Gospel Lesson: John 11:1-45

Sixth Sunday after Pentecost, Year B
    First Lesson: 2 Samuel 1:1, 17-27
    (Psalm 130)
    Second Lesson: 2 Corinthians 8:7-15
    Gospel Lesson: Mark 5:21-43

Twelfth Sunday after Pentecost, Year B
    First Lesson: 2 Samuel 18:5-9, 15, 31-33
    (Psalm 130)
    Second Lesson: Ephesians 4:25–5:2
    Gospel Lesson: John 6:35, 41-51

Like Psalms 121 and 122, Psalm 130 begins with a famous phrase, "out of the depths." Sometimes the psalm is referred to simply by the Latin phrase *de profundis*.[1] For a generation Bernhard Anderson's introduction to the Psalms, *Out of the Depths,* has shaped the reading of this passage.[2]

---

1. J. Clinton McCann, Jr., "The Book of Psalms: Introduction, Commentary, and Reflections," in *NIB*, 4:1205.

2. See Bernhard Anderson, *Out of the Depths* (Philadelphia: Westminster, 1983), 97-98.

The term "depths" *(ma'ămaqqîm)* is a reference to chaotic forces that challenge human life. The metaphor of deep waters captures the closest parallel (see Ps 69:2, 14). From the midst of watery chaos the psalmist speaks. The NIV and NRSV translate the word *qārā'* as "cry out." Leslie Allen renders the term "invoke."[3] This better captures the power element from the powerless psalmist to the sovereign God. Whereas "cry out" better alludes to the plaintive utterance in anguish conveyed by the Hebrew term *ṣā'aq,* it is not used here. What does it mean to invoke God's name in the midst of the depths?

The genre of the psalm is not clear. Form critics have largely designated it a personal complaint or *individual lament* (see the introductory essay). The call to hear in verse 2 would support this view. The language of "supplication" *(taḥănûn)* in verse 2 is related to the Hebrew word for "grace" *(√ḥnn).* Likewise, the confession of guilt in verse 3 indicates a personal lament or complaint. One should note, however, that this is a qualified statement of innocence. It approximates the saying "nobody is perfect." As such it denigrates offenses while at the same time confessing them. This makes sense because, what is a supplication but a request for grace? However, a significant group of scholars label the psalm a *song of thanksgiving.* Verse 4 describes an attribute of God that would fit in either a personal complaint/lament or a song of thanksgiving. The form-critical indecision is not a problem. In fact, it provides a rich theological possibility for interpretation, namely, the intersection of thanksgiving and lament.

One issue that arises from the form-critical debate is how to render the Hebrew perfect verbs in verses 1b and 5.[4] Hebrew does not have tenses like English and many other languages but rather indicates whether the action is completed from the perspective of the author. Thus the Hebrew can be rendered into English as past tense, present tense, or future tense, depending on how one construes the perspective of the author. If one translates the verbs of 1b and 5 as past tense, then the psalm takes on the tone of thanksgiving. While the NIV and the NRSV translate the verb "wait" in verse 5 in the present tense, it can also be rendered in the future or past tense. Take a moment and notice how this changes the tone of the psalm.

From the early sixth century to the present, Psalm 130 has been desig-

---

3. Leslie Allen, *Psalms 100–150,* WBC 21 (Waco: Word, 1983), 191.
4. Allen, *Psalms 100–150,* 192.

nated one of the *penitential psalms* (see also Pss 6; 32; 38; 51; 102; and 143). The designation has taken hold in such a way as to persist despite form-critical waverings.[5] Psalm 130 functions at a form-critical level as a personal complaint/lament, a song of thanksgiving, and a penitential psalm.

The canonical context of the Songs of Ascents reveals a particular way of reading the psalm. Psalm 129 describes the persecution of the elect (Ps 129:1-2), but Psalm 130 makes the counterpoint of the moral fragility of the elect (see vv. 3 and 8). Psalm 130 with its penitential quality provides an apt segue into the profession of humility in Psalm 131.[6] When one looks at the canonical context, one recognizes the function of verses 7 and 8, which are the transition from the personal to a national voice.

When this psalm is read in the midst of Lent, the season of penitence, the interpreter is invited to listen for the penitential aspect of the psalm. The collateral text of Ezekiel 37:1-14 emphasizes the waiting of Israel (vv. 7-8). The national call for repentance now becomes a call for all believers. One should keep in mind that in the ancient church, Lent was the end of the preparation for baptism, which took place on Easter Sunday. The penitence is personal, national, and beyond. The Romans 8:6-11 passage contrasts the life in the flesh with the life in the Spirit, thereby echoing the theme of life in the Spirit from Ezekiel 37:1-14. The responsorial psalm embodies the piety of this life in the Spirit. The Gospel reading is the story of the raising of Lazarus (John 11:1-45). Aside from some oblique connection with "depths" and "the grave," this probably has a less apt connection to Psalm 130 than the other lections.

For the Sixth Sunday after Pentecost, Year B, Psalm 130 is a responsorial psalm to 2 Samuel 1:1, 17-27. The lament quality of 2 Samuel pulls the "blues" out of Psalm 130. When one adds to this mix the Epistle reading, 2 Corinthians 8:7-15, the theme of testing comes to the fore. Testing and lament as well as testing and waiting are often paired in the personal complaint process. Once again the Gospel reading, Mark 5:21-43, has little overt connection to Psalm 130. One might accent the theme of persistence, however, for embedded in the story of Jairus's daughter is the story of the woman who had suffered with a hemorrhage for twelve years before Jesus healed her.

Six Sundays later, on the Twelfth Sunday after Pentecost, Year B,

---

5. Harry Nasuti, *Defining the Sacred Song: Genre, Tradition, and the Post-Critical Interpretation of the Psalms*, JSOTSup 218 (Sheffield: Sheffield Academic, 1999), 30-33.

6. McCann, "The Book of Psalms," 4:1204.

Psalm 130 is the responsorial psalm again. The first reading, 2 Samuel 18:5-9, 15, 31-33, forms an almost Shakespearean *inclusio* to the sixth Sunday. The sixth Sunday relates the death of Saul and his household. The twelfth Sunday frames the death of David's own rebellious son, Absalom. Once again the "blues" elements of Psalm 130 provide the melodic accompaniment. The exhortation of the Epistle reading, Ephesians 4:25–5:2, has little obvious connection to the psalm. The Gospel reading, John 6:35, 41-51, likewise has no clear connection to the psalm.

Stephen Breck Reid

PSALM 131

Eighth Sunday after the Epiphany, Year A
    First Lesson: Isaiah 49:8-16a
    (Psalm 131)
    Second Lesson: 1 Corinthians 4:1-5
    Gospel Lesson: Matthew 6:24-34

Artur Weiser rightly says of this lovely gem set within the Psalms of Ascents, "It is the outpouring of a mature faith and deserves to be classed with the most beautiful psalms of the Psalter."[1] With a few deft strokes, the psalmist paints a deeply moving picture of the contentment, security, and peace that flow from humble, unreserved trust in Israel's God.

The psalmist begins by directly addressing Yahweh: "O LORD" (note the *inclusio* created by the reoccurrence of the name Yahweh in v. 3). In the first verse the speaker disavows all pride and selfish ambition. The references in verse 1a to a "proud heart" (see Prov 16:5; 18:12) and "haughty eyes" (see Ps 18:27; Prov 6:17; 21:4; 30:13) call to mind typical characteristics of those who exalt themselves above their fellow human beings and who, in so doing, unwittingly become adversaries of God (cf. Prov 3:34; James 4:6; 1 Pet 5:5). In contrast, the psalmist displays a sober self-awareness that eschews the pursuit of *gĕdōlôt*, "great things," and *niplā'ôt*, "things too marvelous/difficult for me." The pairing of *gĕdōlôt* and *niplā'ôt*, which so often refer to God's mighty deeds of creation and deliverance (see, e.g.,

---

1. Artur Weiser, *The Psalms*, OTL (Philadelphia: Westminster, 1962), 766.

Exod 3:20; Deut 10:21; Pss 71:19; 78:4, 11, 32; 106:7, 21, 22; 107:8, 15, 21, 24, 31; Job 5:9; 9:10; 37:5; 42:3; Jer 32:17, 27), suggests that the psalmist's humility is grounded ultimately not in self-deprecation but in a clear vision of the incomparable greatness of God, "who alone does great wonders" (Ps 136:4 NRSV). Renouncing an excessive ambition that refuses to be content with the vocation and abilities God has granted (cf. Jer 45:5), the psalmist also rejects the notion that religious performance determines one's standing with God, rather than God's gracious and marvelous acts of redemption.

The next verse offers a striking alternative to the lifestyle of the proud and ambitious. Deliberately, persistently, the psalmist takes herself in hand (cf. JPS, "I have taught myself to be contented"), settling (cf. Isa 28:25) and quieting her own soul (cf. Ps 62:1, 5; Lam 3:26, 28) as a mother soothes her child. The reference to a "weaned child" *(gāmūl)* with its mother evokes the image of a child who has passed through the stage of nursing and now rests contentedly in its mother's arms with no other need than the security and enjoyment of her strong and comforting presence. In likening the psalmist's soul to "the weaned child that is with me" (NRSV),[2] the last colon of the verse portrays the speaker as a mother (or perhaps father) who has come to the temple to worship with child in arms. If God's glory may be seen in great and marvelous deeds of redemption (v. 1b), it is also true that the quotidian activities of family life may mirror God's goodness and tender care for God's people (for God as a parent carrying Israel, see Deut 1:31; Isa 46:3-4; Hos 11:3).[3]

Having uttered this intimate personal prayer to YHWH before the congregation, the psalmist in verse 3 turns and exhorts God's people to imitate her example of humble trust:

> O Israel, hope in the LORD
> from this time on and forevermore. (NRSV)

The verb *yhl*, "hope" (NRSV) or "wait for" (JPS), appears frequently in the Psalter on the lips of speakers who resolve to relentlessly seek after God alone for deliverance (Pss 31:24; 33:18, 22; 38:15; 42:5, 11; 43:5; 69:3; 71:14; 119:43, 49, 74, 81, 114, 147; 130:5, 7; 147:11; cf. Lam 3:24). The intimate prayer of the psalmist thus becomes a pattern for imitation by all who would renounce any source of significance or security other than God.

2. Cf. Leslie C. Allen, *Psalms 101–150*, WBC 21 (Waco: Word, 1983), 197.
3. Allen, *Psalms 101–150*, 199.

The placement of this psalm among the Psalms of Ascents (see the introductory essay) creates a number of additional interpretive possibilities. The fact that Psalm 131:3 echoes and extends the call of Psalm 130:7 to "hope in Yahweh," taken together with other significant verbal links between the two psalms ("hope," 131:3/130:5, 7; "soul," 131:2/130:5, 6), suggests that the editors of the collection intended the two psalms to be read together. In that case, Psalm 130 may be understood as laying the theological foundation for the image of quiet, confident rest in God found in Psalm 131. Because with Israel's God there is forgiveness (130:4), steadfast love (130:7), and abundant redemption (130:7), God's people rightly respond not only with reverent fear (130:4) and hopeful longing (130:5-6) for a future redemption (130:8), but also with settled contentment in all that God is for them in the present (Ps 131).

In addition, the superscription "of David" *(lĕdāwīd)* and the placement of this psalm immediately before Psalm 132, which focuses on Yahweh's covenant with David and his descendants, open the way for finding in Psalm 131 the mind-set of the ideal Davidic king. Interestingly, the "proud heart" rejected by the psalmist is attributed by the Chronicler both to Uzziah, whose mad hubris drove him to attempt to offer incense in the temple (2 Chron 26:16), and to Hezekiah, who proudly refused to respond appropriately to God's goodness to him in healing him from his illness (2 Chron 32:25; note *kigmūl 'ālāw,* an intriguing verbal link with *kĕgāmūl 'ālê,* Ps 131:2).[4] While the ambition and pride of these two kings led to personal and eventually national disaster, a very different model of kingship is offered by the humble pray-er of Psalm 131 and the example of David's own devotion to Yahweh in Psalm 132 (cf. the Septuagint and Peshitta versions of Ps 132:1, which speak of David's "humility" [whereas MT reads "hardships"]).[5]

In the context of the lectionary, Psalm 131 follows the reading from Isaiah 49, which celebrates the great and marvelous deeds of God in leading his people out of captivity in Babylon. Surprisingly, Zion receives this good news of a "new exodus" with incredulity; she charges that Yahweh has abandoned and forgotten her (v. 14). Yahweh answers Zion's complaint in person, boldly comparing the divine compassion for Zion to the love of a woman for her nursing baby. Even if one could imagine a woman forgetting to show compassion to the child she has borne — un-

4. Allen, *Psalms 101–150,* 198.
5. See Allen, *Psalms 101–150,* 198.

thinkable! — even so, Yahweh will never forget Zion (vv. 15-16a). When Psalm 131 is sung in response to Yahweh's asseveration, the psalmist's declaration that she rests in God's presence as secure and contented as a child in its mother's arms becomes a resounding confession of faith and trust in the God whose maternal love for Israel is steadfast and unfailing.

The connections of Psalm 131 with the Gospel lection are no less profound. Jesus' words in Matthew 6:24-34 call for radical reliance on God as the one who will provide food and clothing and everything else necessary for life. The humble, trusting stance of the psalmist before God vividly illustrates the attitude that Jesus taught is required of those who would enter the kingdom of heaven (cf. Matt 18:1-4).

J. Ross Wagner

PSALM 132

Christ the King, Year B
> First Lesson: 2 Samuel 23:1-7
> **(Psalm 132:1-12, [13-18])**
> Second Lesson: Revelation 1:4b-8
> Gospel Lesson: John 18:33-37

Psalm 132 is a *royal psalm* (see the introductory essay) with a pronounced focus on Zion since it is one of the Songs of Ascent. It falls into two parts: a prayer that Yahweh remain faithful to his promises to David and his descendants (vv. 1-10), and in answer to this prayer, Yahweh's reaffirmation of his everlasting commitment to David and to Zion (vv. 11-18). Numerous verbal and structural parallels link the two halves of the psalm. Moreover, the psalm reaches its climax in verses 17-18, where the promise of Yahweh to uphold the Davidic king directly answers the double petition that frames the first half of the psalm (vv. 1, 10). For these reasons, the entire psalm should be read in the liturgy, not simply verses 1-12.

The first movement of the psalm, a prayer by, or on behalf of, the Davidic king, opens with a call to Yahweh to "remember" David for blessing (cf. 2 Chron 6:42; Pss 8:4; 89:50). It concludes with an appeal — "for the sake of your servant David" — not to reject David's heir ("your anointed," *měšîḥekā*, v. 10). In support of these petitions the psalmist portrays the king's tireless zeal for the glory of Yahweh and his temple (vv. 2-9), drawing on earlier traditions concerning David's transfer of the ark from Kiriath-jearim to Jerusalem (cf. 1 Sam 7:1-2; 2 Sam 6–7). Verses 2-5, framed by the use of the ancient appellation "the Mighty One of Jacob" (cf. Gen 49:24), recall David's sacrificial devotion to Yahweh (see 1 Chron 22:14; cf. Lev 23:27, 29), represented by his oath not to rest in his own dwelling before securing a proper dwelling for Yahweh's repose (note the parallel between "tent" [v. 3a], and "tabernacle" [v. 5b]; cf. 2 Sam 6:17; 7:6). Verses 6-9 recount David's search for the ark of God (for Ephrathah as a name for Bethlehem, David's home territory, see Ruth 4:11; Mic 5:2) and its discovery at Kiriath-jearim (here poetically termed "the fields of Jaar"; cf. 1 Sam 7:1-2). The festive procession of worshipers accompanying the ark on its journey (v. 8 recalls the cry at the setting forth of the ark in Num 10:35) culminates in the joyful worship of Yahweh in his new sanctuary (v. 7; cf. 5b; for the ark as God's "footstool," see 1 Chron 28:2; Ps 99:1, 5; for "footstool" as a metaphor for the temple in Zion, see Lam 2:1).

The second half of Psalm 132 systematically answers the petitions of verses 1-10. David's devotion to Yahweh is matched, and indeed far exceeded, by Yahweh's gracious covenant faithfulness to David and his descendants forever. Corresponding to David's oath (vv. 2-5), Yahweh swears an oath of his own: a faithful, irrevocable vow (cf. Ps 110:4) to establish David's descendants on his throne forever (vv. 11-12; note the repetition of "on your throne"). The conditional nature of this promise (v. 12) serves as an exhortation to David's heirs to follow their forebear's example of faithfulness (cf. 2 Chron 7:17-18). Ultimately, however, the permanence of the Davidic dynasty ("forever," v. 12) rests on Yahweh's own immutable election of Zion ("forever," v. 14) and his unfailing faithfulness to his anointed ruler (vv. 17-18; so also 2 Sam 7:11-16; Ps 89:3-4, 19-37).

Verses 13-16, which parallel verses 6-9, emphasize that David's transfer of the ark to Jerusalem depends on Yahweh's prior election of Zion as his place of repose (v. 14; cf. "resting place" in v. 8). David, for all his commendable zeal, is merely the agent of Yahweh's own sovereign, gracious choice to dwell forever in Israel's midst (note the repetition of "desire," vv. 13, 14). For this reason, the worshipers' prayer in verse 9 receives an immediate and unequivocal answer. Yahweh himself is emphatically resolved (*bārēk 'ăbārēk*, v. 15a) to bless, nourish, and rescue his people. And so God's people will *certainly* rejoice (*rannēn yĕrannēnû*, v. 16b) in Yahweh's unfailing presence and provision.

The final verses of the psalm constitute God's resounding "yes" to the petition that frames verses 1-10. For David (cf. v. 10, "for the sake of your servant David"), Yahweh vows to "cause a horn to sprout up" (v. 17). The "horn" connotes the power and prominence of the Davidic king (cf. 1 Sam 2:10; Pss 18:2; 89:17, 24; 92:10; 112:9; Dan 7:24), while the lamp metaphor that follows reaffirms Yahweh's promise that David's dynasty will never fail (vv. 11-12; cf. 2 Sam 21:17; 1 Kings 11:36). The imagery of light binds the final two verses together. David's enemies will be clothed with shame (v. 18, contrast vv. 9, 16), but the king's crown will sparkle with glory.

Psalm 132 occupies a unique place among the Psalms of Ascents, both because of its length and because it so closely links Yahweh's election of Zion to the covenant with David. Allen perceptively observes that this psalm amplifies the expression of national hope articulated in Psalm 130:7; 131:3 (cf. the possible link between Ps 131 and Ps 132:1, with its reference to David's "humility" [so LXX and the Peshitta]). Psalm 132 brings this hope to focus in "a longing for the messianic promises and Yahweh's Zion-centered purpose to come to fruition in the experience of God's people."[1]

As a response to today's reading from 2 Samuel 23:1-7, Psalm 132 takes up and further develops the main theme of David's oracular "last words": the "eternal covenant" established with David by Yahweh, who will be faithful to "cause all my salvation [cf. Ps 132:16] and my every desire to sprout [cf. Ps 132:17]" (2 Sam 23:5). The Chronicler, who cites Psalm 132:8-10 in 2 Chronicles 6:41-42, finds a preliminary fulfillment of these promises in the reign of Solomon, who completes and dedicates the temple begun by David; but as the Chronicler's narrative continues, it becomes clear that the full flowering of the promise is yet to come, on the other side of exile and return. In canonical context, the language and imagery of Psalm 132:17-18 continue to resonate with messianic overtones as prophets look ahead, past the unfaithfulness of David's house, to God's fulfillment of his promise. Compare Psalm 132:17, "I will cause to sprout" (√*ṣmḥ*), with images of a messianic ruler as a "sprout" or "branch" (*ṣemaḥ*) in Isaiah 4:2; Jeremiah 23:5; 33:15; Zechariah 3:8; 6:12 (note also the possible wordplay between *nēzer*, "crown" [Ps 132:18], and *nēṣer*, "sprout" [Isa 11:1], as well as between the two senses of *ṣwṣ* [Ps 132:18]: "to gleam" and "to bud, blossom"). The New Testament extends this trajectory of interpretation yet further, finding the ultimate realization of the Davidic covenant in Jesus, whom God has raised from the dead and exalted to God's right hand

1. Leslie C. Allen, *Psalms 101–150*, WBC 21 (Waco: Word, 1983), 209.

(Acts 2:32-33; cf. Ps 110:1 in Acts 2:34-35) as "the ruler of the kings of the earth," whose redemptive death has freed us and constitutes us as a community of worship: "priests (cf. Psalm 132:9, 16) serving his God and Father — to whom be glory and dominion forever" (Rev 1:5-6).

J. Ross Wagner

PSALM 133

Thirteenth Sunday after Pentecost, Year A
 First Lesson: Genesis 45:1-15
 (Psalm 133)
 Second Lesson: Romans 11:1-2a, 29-32
 Gospel Lesson: Matthew 15:(10-20), 21-28

Fifth Sunday after Pentecost, Year B
 First Lesson: 1 Samuel 17:(1a, 4-11, 19-23), 32-49
 (Psalm 9:9-20 or 1 Samuel 17:57–18:5, 10-16 or **Psalm 133**)
 Second Lesson: 2 Corinthians 6:1-13
 Gospel Lesson: Mark 4:35-41

Second Sunday of Easter, Year B
 First Lesson: Acts 4:32-35
 (Psalm 133)
 Second Lesson: 1 John 1:1–2:2
 Gospel Lesson: John 20:19-31

Psalm 133 is the fourteenth of the fifteen Songs of Ascents. Like several of the other psalms in this collection, Psalm 133 demonstrates an interest in family matters (see Pss 122:8; 127:3-5; 128:3, 6; 131:2), perhaps suggesting that the Songs of Ascents were used as a sort of hymnal as families made a pilgrimage to Jerusalem and returned home. In any case, Psalm 133, again like several other Songs of Ascents, invites attention to Jerusalem or Zion (see Pss 122:1-9; 125:1-2; 126:1; 128:5; 129:5; 132:13-17; 134:3), which would have been the goal and focal point of the pilgrimage.

The unique feature of Psalm 133 is that it establishes an intimate connection between these two frequent topics in the Songs of Ascents —

family and Zion. The focus in verse 1 is squarely upon the biological family. Several scholars suggest that this verse may have originated in family circles as a sort of folk proverb. The only other occurrence of the phrase "when kindred live together" is in Deuteronomy 25:5, where the context suggests contention and conflict. The likelihood, then and now, is that conflict will be the norm for family life, making it all the more "good and pleasant" when unity prevails!

But Psalm 133 is not finally about the dynamics of life in the biological, extended family. Rather, it is about the life of the gathered people of God, which is our true family. The broadening of focus on the family is begun by the two similes in verses 2-3, and it is completed by the mention of Zion and "there" in verse 3. The simile of anointing in verse 2 is linked to verse 1 by the repetition of "good" (NRSV "precious") to modify "oil." The image may communicate luxuriant hospitality in a general sense, but anointing also was a formal act to set apart kings and priests. The mention of Aaron, progenitor of one of Israel's primary priestly families, further encourages the reader to think in corporate terms. That the abundant "dew of Hermon," a mountain over a hundred miles north of Jerusalem, waters Mount Zion suggests that the resources from outlying areas will make their way to Jerusalem. This image of movement probably is meant to allude to all the pilgrims who have traveled to Jerusalem from outlying areas and are now gathered there. The "there" of verse 3 completes the shift of focus from biological family (v. 1) to faith family. Only as the gathered people of God in God's house — the temple on Mount Zion — do people experience the "blessing" (see Pss 128:4-5; 132:15; 134:3), the fullness of life that God intends. As James L. Mays puts it, "It is this abundant life, which Israel can receive only in its unity, and only from the Presence at this place that is the *summum bonum* ['greatest good'; see v. 1]. The life that the Lord gives his people in their unity is the supreme family value."[1]

The celebration of life as God's good gift makes Psalm 133 appropriate for the season of Easter. The pairing of Psalm 133 with Acts 4:32-35 for the Second Sunday of Easter, Year B, is particularly helpful, since this text portrays the early church in its unity, a "group . . . of one heart and soul, and no one claimed private ownership of any possessions, but everything they owned was held in common" (v. 32). Psalm 133 is also assigned for the Thirteenth Sunday after Pentecost, Year A, and it is an alternate reading for the Fifth Sunday after Pentecost, Year B. In the

1. James L. Mays, *Psalms,* Interpretation (Louisville: John Knox, 1994), 414.

former instance, the pairing with Genesis 45:1-15 invites attention to biological family unity — Joseph and his brothers; but the second lesson and the Gospel lesson actually capture better the spirit of Psalm 133 as they press toward a unity that transcends biological and racial-ethnic divisions. In the latter case, the pairing with 2 Corinthians 6:1-13 is helpful, because this text is a plea for unity between Paul and the Corinthians, based upon the reconciling work of God in Christ (see 2 Cor 5:16-21).

Beyond these liturgical settings, Psalm 133 offers the opportunity to attend to a perennial issue — family values. As Mays points out, Psalm 133 "is a witness that God was at work building a family that transcends all the given and instituted barriers that separate and diminish life."[2] As such a witness, Psalm 133 is a reminder that the contemporary discussion of family values, even in religious circles (and perhaps especially in religious circles), is often much too narrow. To be sure, the nuclear family is a vitally important social institution, but it can easily become a source of idolatry and even abuse, especially if it is not understood in the larger context of the family that God is gathering. Jesus called this family the realm of God; and when his biological family showed up to visit him, Jesus pointed to the crowd before him and said, "Here are my mother and my brothers! Whoever does the will of God is my brother and sister and mother" (Mark 3:34-35). These words capture precisely the spirit of Psalm 133.

In some Christian traditions, Psalm 133 is associated with the celebration of the Lord's Supper. At our best, we recognize and profess that because no one can deserve to come to the Lord's table, all are welcome. Like Jesus, this captures precisely the spirit of Psalm 133.

J. Clinton McCann, Jr.

PSALM 137

Twentieth Sunday after Pentecost, Year C
    First Lesson: Lamentations 1:1-6
    (Lamentations 3:19-26 or **Psalm 137**)
    Second Lesson: 2 Timothy 1:1-14
    Gospel Lesson: Luke 17:5-10

2. Mays, *Psalms,* 414.

Buried away in the last year of the three-year cycle of the lectionary, near the very end of Year C, tucked into a somewhat inauspicious Sunday and listed as a second, alternative (!), hymnic responsorial, lies Psalm 137. And why not? As C. S. Lewis wrote of *imprecatory psalms* (see the introductory essay) like this one: "the spirit of hatred [we find in them] which strikes us in the face is like the heat from a furnace mouth."[1] When it comes to the kitchen of Scripture, there are many who can't stand the heat — at least not heat like this — and quickly get out. And yet, Psalm 137's presence in the lectionary, despite its place on the calendar and its status as an alternative reading, is rather remarkable given the lectionary's tendency to censor many of the most difficult parts of Scripture. Psalm 137 is certainly among these difficult parts, and may well be president of the club.

For that very reason, however, it must be in the lectionary and it must be preached. Why? Because church people, or at least church critics (sometimes these are one and the same), know about Psalm 137 even if they cannot name or number it. They know the issue and are tempted to dodge it in simplistic — not to mention Marcionite — fashion with: "Well, that's just the *Old* Testament." Hence the need to preach Psalm 137. Not unlike difficult passages that the rabbis warned readers about, this psalm is rated "PG." We need "Pastoral Guidance" to know how to read, hear, and pray Psalm 137.

"The issue" mentioned above is of course the problem of violence, hatred, rage, wrath, and the like. Psalm 137 is certainly not alone in voicing such themes — indeed, after 136 psalms, the reader of the Psalter should be quite familiar with them. And so this is the first thing that should be stated: Psalm 137 is not alone. Other imprecatory psalms exist (see, e.g., Pss 5; 12; 41; 58; 79; 83; 94; 109; among others), and imprecations lurk in some of the most beautiful and beloved of psalms (see, e.g., Ps 139:19-24), such that it is hard to extricate the bad and gruesome from the beautiful and good. The unfortunate parts "may . . . be intertwined with the most exquisite things."[2] Moreover, the Bible — both Testaments, let it be stressed — contains passages that are difficult on these very same themes and for the very same reasons. Even so, given its brevity, power, and pathos, Psalm 137 must be a (if not the) parade example. What is one to do with it, if one is to do with it at all? The preacher must take into

---

1. C. S. Lewis, *Reflections on the Psalms* (San Diego: Harcourt, 1958), 20.
2. Lewis, *Reflections on the Psalms*, 22.

consideration a number of important aspects if the psalm is to be carefully and faithfully taken up.

1. First, the poem presupposes the exile. It may be that the psalm is exilic in date or even postexilic, looking back on the exile (scholars are divided on the point), but the psalm is clearly about the Babylonian exile and life there (note the repetition of "there" in vv. 1, 3; used four times in NRSV [vv. 1-3]). It is there, by the rivers of Babylon (v. 1), that the psalmist and company ("we") sat down and wept when they remembered Zion. What Zion did they remember? Verse 7 indicates that a destroyed Jerusalem haunts the psalmist's memory; the lectionary underscores the point by suggesting Psalm 137 as a response to Lamentations 1:1-6.

The memory of devastated Zion is not the only problem; life in Babylon is tormented by those responsible for Jerusalem's present state: Babylonian tormenters who mock the Judeans. "Sing us a song of Zion!" they scoff (v. 3). But the psychic trauma is too deep. It is not that the psalmist doesn't know a Zion song. Such songs are found in the Psalter itself (see, e.g., Pss 46; 48; 76; 84). Moreover, the psalmist's self-curse in verses 5-6 reveals that the poet has not yet forgotten Jerusalem even as that curse indicates the psalmist's resolve not to forget and, correlatively perhaps, the psalmist's worry that she might. If Zion/Jerusalem is forgotten, she prays, then may the tools of her craft (the hand that plays the harp [cf. v. 2] and the tongue that sings the song) fail (vv. 5-6). But, for all practical purposes, they already have, for the harps are hung (v. 2), not strung, in the face of the plaintive question:

How could we sing the LORD's song
　　in a foreign land? (v. 4)

The causal conjunction that begins verse 3, "for" (Hebrew *kî*), indicates that it is out of defiance that the harps are hung and the songs not sung. It is not that the psalmist does not know a Zion song or cannot remember one; the psalmist refuses to sing for those for whom such a song is merely an exercise in ridicule. For those Babylonian scoffers, such a song is just a "Zion song" (v. 3), but the psalmist knows better: this is the Lord's own song (v. 4).

The switch from "Zion song" to "the Lord's song" in verses 3-4, which corresponds to the shift from the Babylonian's perspective to the psalmist's perspective, offers insight into the importance of Jerusalem/Zion, which is a fulcrum point for the psalm and a key to right (and wrong) interpretation. It is easy, but cavalier, to say that the psalmist has a case of "misplaced faith": trusting in Zion rather than in the God of Zion. This hackneyed interpretation is undermined by the psalmist's shift in verses 3-4, which already indicates that these entities are inseparable: Zion's song *is* the Lord's song. Indeed, a look at the Zion psalms elsewhere in the Psalter reveals that they are as much about God as they are about Zion, and specifically about God's choice of Zion and presence within Jerusalem (see, e.g., Pss 46:1, 4-7; 48:1, 3, 8-14; 76:1-2, 6-9; 84:1-4, 8-9, 11-12). Not only that, but God's protection of Zion is celebrated in these songs, praised, made the subject of poetry. One psalm puts it like this:

> There is a river whose streams make glad the city of God,
> the holy habitation of the Most High.
> God is in the midst of the city; it shall not be moved;
> God will help it when the morning dawns.
>
> (Ps 46:4-5; cf. vv. 1-3, 6-9; Pss 48:3-8; 76:3-9; 84:7)

But Zion was moved . . . in 587 B.C. There was a morning when dawn did not witness God's help — 587 B.C. How true, then, the psalmist's question: How could we sing a song celebrating God's choice of Zion, God's protection of Zion, when Zion was devastated, God absent — perhaps due to wrath and judgment, but perhaps due to defeat? Despite these profound questions — profound theologically and existentially — the psalmist resolves to never forget Jerusalem and to set it above his highest joy, invoking a curse on himself if he does not (Ps 137:5-6). To summarize this point, the exilic context of the psalm must not be missed or neglected. In briefest terms, 587 B.C. was 9/11 on an even more massive scale. Those who would prejudge the pathos of the psalmist should first recall their own emotions in the face of that tragedy and the countless tragedies subsequent to it.

2. When considered in the exilic context, the cry for vengeance in this psalm must be seen as a cry for justice.[3] This does not lessen its violence, but it may make the sentiment more understandable if not more palatable because justice is among the highest values of Scripture and a quality of God's own character (see, e.g., Deut 16:20; 1 Kings 3:28; 10:9; 2 Chron 19:7; Ps 72:1; Isa 5:16; 30:18; Amos 5:15; Mic 6:8; Luke 7:29; 11:42; 18:7). The wrong that has been perpetrated against Zion is injustice; it must be set

---

3. See Erich Zenger, *A God of Vengeance? Understanding the Psalms of Divine Wrath* (Louisville: Westminster John Knox, 1996).

Fig. 13. Not unlike Psalm 137, this image depicts lyre players (perhaps even Judeans from Lachish or Jerusalem) being led off by an Assyrian soldier. The viewer gets a sense of the plaintive and oppressive situation faced by the psalmist in Psalm 137 (note, in particular, the soldier's weaponry).

right if God, who chose Zion, is truly its protector, and if the Lord will be proven worthy of the psalmic praise that Israel lavishes on God.

Attention to the poetic movement of the psalm underscores the cry for justice with particular force. Verses 7-8 turn to the objects of the psalmist's wrath: first Edom, which exulted in the destruction of Jerusalem (v. 7; cf. Obad 8-14; Ezek 25:12-14; 35:1-15; 36:5; Lam 4:21), and then Babylon, which is directly addressed here and called "the devastator" (v. 8, so NRSV; the Hebrew form is passive: "the devastated"; see below). Destroyed Zion is, therefore, still in the psalmist's mind. But then the poet invokes a blessing on the one (the Hebrew is singular) who pays Babylon back (√*šlm,* here with the meaning "to recompense, reward") the recompense *(gĕmûl)* that it did (√*gml*) to the exiles. The emphasis laid here that the punishment should meet the crime could not be more exact. It is a case of poetic *lex talionis:* eye for an eye, tooth for tooth — perfect retribution, no more, no less! (Contrary to popular understandings of *lex talionis,* this practice was a humanitarian one, ensuring that punishment was limited and kept from excess.) What is most striking is that it is precisely at this point that the psalmist hopes that Babylon's children be dashed (v. 9). Given the poetic movement and the desire that the payback fit the crime, it is tempting to suggest that the psalmist's own baby was dashed against a rock — and not just any rock for, somewhat oddly and unexpectedly, the poem specifies the rock with the definite article (*hsl'*, "the rock"): a very specific rock might be in mind. This too may not baptize the violence in the psalm, but it reads differently when read as a cry for justice on the part of a parent who saw her own little one killed by Babylonians who threw it against that rock that she cannot get out of her memory and that haunts her every dream. Whatever the case, Psalm 137, like all the imprecatory psalms, aligns the pray-er with the Lord. The pray-er's enemies are thus the Lord's enemies, and so it is God, not just the psalmist, who has a vested interest in punishing these enemies. It is a divine vendetta, not simply a personal one, because "Vengeance [√*nqm*] is mine, and recompense [√*šlm*]," says the Lord (Deut 32:35; cf. Rom 12:19; Heb 10:30).[4]

3. Psalm 137 is a poem. It is not ethical instruction — not law from Sinai, nor moral exhortation in an epistle. It is a poem, perhaps even a lyric (and liturgical) poem. Such poems are by definition episodic. The poet may write a very different poem tomorrow; indeed, such a possibility is quite likely because the poet wrote this poem today. Attention to genre is quite important, therefore. While violence in any literature is a cause for concern, the fact that this composition is a poem must not be forgotten. It is not enjoined on the faithful as a matter of practice. Indeed, it is crucial to observe that the final strike of the psalmist's rage is not addressed to the Lord directly, but to Babylon. It is somewhat removed, then, from the Lord's direct action and, indeed, speaks of the "blessed" avenger in vague, nondescript terms ("the one who pays you back . . . the one who takes . . . and dashes"). To miss the genre of Psalm 137 qua poetry could result in devastating consequences, for us and for others. We — and those to whom we speak — may very well need instructions for listening when hearing such a psalm.[5] There is explicit and volatile content in this psalm; it ought to be read and/or heard in this specific way. That way includes "as poetry."

---

4. Cf. Dietrich Bonhoeffer, *Psalms: The Prayer Book of the Bible* (Minneapolis: Augsburg Fortress, 1970), 57.

5. See Carol Antablin Miles, "'Singing the Songs of Zion' and Other Sermons from the Margins of the Canon," *Koinonia* 6 (1994): 151-73.

4. But Psalm 137 is not just a poem, it is also a prayer. Any instructions for listening/hearing must convey that this psalm is not only for hearing or reading, but also for praying. The best way this psalm (or any other imprecatory psalm) is to be read or heard is the way of prayer where the cry of rage is lifted, not in an angry fist against a human enemy, but in prayer to the God who claims sole proprietary rights to vengeance and payback. Perhaps this is because the psalm (and the psalmist) knows that our enemies — their bodies — cannot handle such rage. Someone will end up bleeding — or worse. But in prayer, God's body, as it were, absorbs such violence. So, to pray such a psalm is "at one and the same time to let it go and to hold it back" — to release it to the Lord but to keep it from going public: "It is not now a part of our dealing with our neighbor-enemy. It is a part of our life with God."[6] If so, then praying such a psalm may be letting God see to vengeance. If so, praying such a psalm could actually be prayer *for* our enemies — though certainly in a different way than we would normally expect. Ellen F. Davis's comments are insightful:

> No personal vendetta is authorized. . . . On the contrary, the validity of any punishing action that may occur depends entirely on its being God's action, not ours. And readers of the Bible recognize that this is in fact a severely limiting condition. For God's action is free, directed not only to our healing but to the healing of the whole moral order. Through these psalms we demand that our enemies be driven into God's hands. But who can say what will happen to them there? For God is manifest in judgment of our enemies but also, alas, in mercy toward them. Thus these vengeful psalms have a relationship with other forms of prayer for our enemies.[7]

5. Finally, a few thoughts on appropriating Psalm 137. First, remember that Psalm 137 is not alone. Not only are there other imprecatory psalms in the Psalter, or violent passages elsewhere in Scripture, there are also contemporary songs with sentiment very similar to Psalm 137. These songs, which are as available as today's musicians whose work appears on Top 40 radio (e.g., Garth Brooks's "Thunder Rolls," Martina McBride's

6. Patrick D. Miller, "The Hermeneutics of Imprecation," in Miller, *The Way of the Lord: Essays in Old Testament Theology* (Tübingen: Mohr Siebeck, 2004), 200.

7. Ellen F. Davis, *Getting Involved with God: Rediscovering the Old Testament* (Cambridge, Mass.: Cowley, 2001), 27; cf. Bonhoeffer, *Psalms,* 58-59.

"Independence Day," Jimmy Wayne's "The Rabbit," Bob Dylan's "Masters of War," Bruce Cockburn's "If I Had a Rocket Launcher," or Public Enemy's "Burn Hollywood Burn"), demonstrate that: (a) people still feel these feelings of rage and wrath; and (b) such songs often and typically arise out of experiences of great injustice, not violence for violence's sake. In the songs just listed the experiences include: abuse, infidelity, war, humanitarian crises, and mistreatment of ethnic minorities, among other things. These songs also demonstrate that while such powerful and volatile sentiments are more than some people can handle, they nevertheless make perfect sense to those who share the same social location.[8] But even those who do not share such a social (dis)location or who find these thoughts personally overwhelming, can still utilize songs like Psalm 137 as a window onto another's world. There are people who continue to feel such feelings and need to voice them in prayer. Those of us who do not feel such feelings need to be aware that such prayers also find a place in the worship of the Lord. These psalms, then, can "instruct our compassion"[9] even if we do not or have not felt the depths of their pain.

Second, following the lead of the early church and Scripture itself, perhaps we are permitted to revision the enemy. Scripture leads the way in this regard by revisioning Babylon in the book of Revelation.[10] There Babylon is "fallen" (Rev 14:8; 18:2, 21; cf. "devastated" in Ps 137:8 — is this verse eschatological?) and feels the force of God's fury (Rev 16:19). But there Babylon is not ancient Babylon but a symbol for all that stands opposed to God, God's ways, and God's people. Like the New Testament and some of the patristic authors, perhaps we too can redefine Babylon. It can become the cancer killing a loved one, the politics of oppression, the economics that keep the vast majority of the world in deathly poverty. Surely such things deserve God's damnation! And Babylon is still more: the sins that plague not only society, but even our souls. Note C. S. Lewis's revisioning of the enemies:

8. Cf. Leslie C. Allen, *Psalms 101–150*, rev. ed., WBC 21 (Nashville: Nelson, 2002), 309: "The citizen of a European country who has experienced its invasion and destruction or a victim of the Holocaust would be the best expositor of such a psalm"; similarly J. Clinton McCann, Jr., "The Book of Psalms: Introduction, Commentary, and Reflections," in *NIB*, 4:1229; Walter Brueggemann, *The Message of the Psalms: A Theological Commentary* (Minneapolis: Augsburg, 1984), 75, 77.

9. See Davis, *Getting Involved with God*, 20.

10. See Miles, "Singing the Songs," 151-73; cf. James L. Mays, *Psalms*, Interpretation (Louisville: John Knox, 1994), 423-24.

I know things in the inner world which are like babies; the infantile beginnings of small indulgences, small resentments, which may one day become dipsomania or settled hatred, but which woo us and wheedle us with special pleadings and seem so tiny, so helpless that in resisting them we feel we are being cruel to animals. They begin whimpering to us "I don't ask much, but," or "I had at least hoped," or "you owe yourself some consideration." Against all such pretty infants (the dears have such winning ways) the advice of the Psalm [137] is the best. Knock the little bastards' brains out. And "blessed" is he who can, for it's easier said than done.[11]

Third, and finally, we can, in the words of Davis, rotate the psalm 180 degrees so that it is no longer pointing at an unassuming enemy, but is pointing back at us.[12] Are there people in the community (or beyond) who would wish to pray such a psalm against us? That is a sobering thought, and the answer is probably more often affirmative than we would care to admit. Such a realization makes us pray differently and, still more to the point, act differently — act *better* — so there won't be occasion for anyone to pray such words against us. In this way the words of another imprecatory psalm, Psalm 58:11, cut to the heart of the matter:

People will say, "Surely there is a reward for the righteous;
    surely there is a God who judges on earth."

Those are words to know, to take to heart, whether one is righteous, a suffering pray-er, or someone guilty of perpetrating injustice. God has a vested interest in both persons and situations!

More could be said, but the above considerations suggest that "the issue" of violence in Psalm 137 or elsewhere in the Bible (and life) is not as simple as often thought. We would do well, then, to beware stereotyping the issue of the violence contained in Scripture; it may just be otherwise. All the psalms, even this one, can be good for the soul — for our souls and for the souls of those we serve.

Brent A. Strawn

11. Lewis, *Reflections on the Psalms*, 136.
12. Davis, *Getting Involved with God*, 28.

PSALM 138

Fifth Sunday after the Epiphany, Year C
First Lesson: Isaiah 6:1-8, (9-13)
(Psalm 138)
Second Lesson: 1 Corinthians 15:1-11
Gospel Lesson: Luke 5:1-11

Third Sunday after Pentecost, Year B
First Lesson: 1 Samuel 8:4-11 (12-15), 16-20; (11:14-15)
(Psalm 138)
Second Lesson: 2 Corinthians 4:13–5:1
Gospel Lesson: Mark 3:20-35

We may start with the three Epiphany readings. They each present an unworthy character — Isaiah, a man of "unclean lips"; Saul (later Paul), a zealous persecutor of the church; and the skeptical Peter. All three receive God's forgiving, healing grace, enabling them to fulfill the Lord's call to become his special agents to bring God's word to Israel and the world. And at Epiphany Christ appears to the representatives of the nations (Matt 2:1-12; cf. Ps 138:4-6).

Though it may well be postexilic, Psalm 138 begins a series of Davidic psalms (as indicated by the ancient superscriptions) that ends with Psalm 145, with which it shares key themes and vocabulary, especially about God's "name" and character as classically described in Exodus 34:6-7 (see Pss 138:2; 145:1, 2, 8, 21). Thus, in the context of the Psalter, the speaker of Psalm 138 is presented as a Davidic king or leader, who speaks to God on his own behalf, but also for the nation, the community he represents. As king, his work and actions, and his struggles against the enemies of Israel, are inevitably political in scope. As the life of David and his family so richly shows, the political is personal, and vice versa (note Absalom's revolt). Even kings or leaders like Ezra and Nehemiah speak as human beings who have been brought low, been in trouble (vv. 6-7), cried to God for help, and were answered (v. 3). This motif of calling and being heard represents the speaker as a faithful heir of David (cf. Ps 145:18-20), in contrast to Davidic kings who oppose God's ways of justice and righteousness, in a day when the people cry out against their self-chosen government but the Lord does not answer them (a point made by the lectionary reading for Pentecost, 1 Sam 8:18).

In its canonical context, then, Psalm 138 presents itself as a hymn of thanksgiving for prayers answered in a time of trouble, spoken by a faithful king of David's line; it is a declaration of confidence in God's name and his word of promise (v. 3) — with a final plea for future help: "Do not forsake the work of your hands" (v. 8; cf. 145:8-10).

In particular, the psalmist gives thanks to Yahweh, who revealed the meaning of his covenant *name* (v. 2) to Moses on Mount Sinai, in response to the spiritual adultery of Israel in the affair of the golden calf (Exod 32–34). There Yahweh's deepest character, as a God of love and faithfulness, a God of forgiveness and new beginnings, was revealed in the divine name itself: "a God merciful and compassionate, slow to anger, and abounding in *steadfast love* and *faithfulness*" (Exod 34:6; cf. Ps 145:8; and John's translation, "full of grace and truth," John 1:14). As in many psalms (e.g., Pss 25; 86; 103), the psalmist gives historical breadth and depth to his short prayer by picking up key elements of the Exodus name revelation. He highlights two attributes of the name, Yahweh's *steadfast love* and *faithfulness,* in conjunction with his *word* of promise (Ps 138:2). (The uncertain ending of this verse may be translated "You have exalted your name and your word above everything"; so NRSV.)

The psalm itself begins with declarations of thanksgiving "with my whole heart," that is, from the deepest center of the poet's being (vv. 1-2a; cf. Prov 4:23; Luke 6:45). Thereupon follow the fundamental grounds for the thanksgiving: the divine name and word (v. 2b) and its concrete manifestation in the life of the king and the nation: "I called, you answered me" and gave me strength to face my trouble (whatever that may have been, v. 3; see v. 7 for the probable reference).

To our modern minds, the sudden shift to "all the kings of the earth" in verses 4-5 may seem abrupt. But it is quite in keeping with the implied royal speaker. What is more, its eschatological claims — that the kings will praise Israel's God — tie in with the seemingly audacious Davidic claims of the entire Psalter, beginning with Psalm 2, that God in heaven has designated his anointed as ruler of the kings and nations of the earth.

Like the psalmist himself, the kings of the earth will praise (literally, *thank*) Israel's God, using his particular, covenant *name,* Yahweh, which the psalm celebrates. The reason for their thanks is that they too will have heard "the *words* of his mouth" (v. 4; cf. v. 2). Consequently, they will someday join Israel in the company of those who sing and celebrate the "ways of Yahweh" that Psalm 25:10 describes as "steadfast love and faithfulness." These are the ways that God revealed to Moses and showed to

Israel and the nations throughout its history (cf. Exod 18:1-10; Josh 2:8-11; 9:9-10; Pss 25; 47–48; 98:1-3; 105; Dan 4). Foreign kings will know the greatness of God's glory seen throughout cosmos and history (Num 14:20-23; Ps 97:6; Isa 6:3; 11:9; Hab 2:14), and see that he especially cares for the lowly of the earth, even though he himself is God most high (cf. Ps 145:13b-14; 1 Sam 2:3, 6-10; and especially Isa 57:15).

The last line of the psalm ("Do not forsake the work of your hands") reminds us that God's kingdom, and its righteous, saving rule, is "already and not-yet." We see it at work in Israel's history, and brought to this earth by the Messiah who was "full of grace and truth." Like the psalmist, we give thanks for it even as we earnestly pray for its full realization. As McCann notes, we pray both "Thine is the kingdom" and "Thy kingdom come."[1]

Raymond C. Van Leeuwen

PSALM 139

Ninth Sunday after Pentecost, Year A
    First Lesson: Genesis 28:10-19a
    (Psalm 139:1-12, 23-24)
    Second Lesson: Romans 8:12-25
    Gospel Lesson: Matthew 13:24-30, 36-43

Second Sunday after the Epiphany, Year B
    First Lesson: 1 Samuel 3:1-10, (11-20)
    (Psalm 139:1-6, 13-18)
    Second Lesson: 1 Corinthians 6:12-20
    Gospel Lesson: John 1:43-51

Second Sunday after Pentecost, Year B
    First Lesson: 1 Samuel 3:1-10, (11-20)
    (Psalm 139:1-6, 13-18)
    Second Lesson: 2 Corinthians 4:5-12
    Gospel Lesson: Mark 2:23–3:6

1. J. Clinton McCann, Jr., "The Book of Psalms: Introduction, Commentary, and Reflections," in *NIB*, 4:1233.

Sixteenth Sunday after Pentecost, Year C
  First Lesson: Jeremiah 18:1-11
  (Psalm 139:1-6, 13-18)
  Second Lesson: Philemon 1-21
  Gospel Lesson: Luke 14:25-33

Psalm 139 is one of the most familiar and beloved poems in the Psalter. Its soaring affirmations of God's incomparability, couched in the deeply affective and relational language of prayer, warrant its designation as both a doctrinal and a devotional "classic."[1]

The text of Psalm 139 resists categorization. Interpreters have classified it variously as a *hymn of praise,* a *prayer of contrition,* an *individual lament/complaint,* and a *wisdom psalm* (see the introductory essay). While the text contains elements of each of these forms, no one of them fully accounts for the content and structure of the psalm.

Perhaps the most promising proposal for the setting was given by Sigmund Mowinckel[2] and nuanced by later interpreters.[3] That suggestion is that Psalm 139 belongs to a subcategory of *prayers for vindication of the innocent* (cf. Pss 5; 7; and especially 17 and 26).

Although Psalm 139 differs structurally from others cited in this group and includes no explicit cry for vindication, it has additional features that support this proposal. For example, Psalm 139 contains several allusions to the book of Job (cf. Job 1:10; 3:3ff.; 7:17-19; etc.) that evoke the image of a righteous sufferer who seeks to be tried by God and found innocent. Similarly, its use of verbs such as "know" (*yd'*), "search" (*ḥqr*), "test" (*bḥn*), and "see" (*r'h*), with God as the subject, appeals to God's "providential role as judge," punishing the guilty and pardoning the innocent.[4]

While Psalm 139 is typically divided into four relatively equal strophes (vv. 1-6, 7-12, 13-18, and 19-24), the text breaks most decisively at the border between verses 18 and 19. The first three strophes function together to portray the extent to which the psalmist is known, and the psalmist's life encompassed, by God. The final strophe reveals the extent to which the psalmist self-identifies with God and longs to be found

---

1. Cf. James L. Mays, *Psalms,* Interpretation (Louisville: John Knox, 1994), 425.

2. Sigmund Mowinckel, *Psalmenstudien 5* (Oslo: Kristiana, 1924).

3. E.g., Bernhard W. Anderson, with Steven Bishop, *Out of the Depths: The Psalms Speak for Us Today,* 3rd ed. (Louisville: Westminster John Knox, 2000), 91-96.

4. Cf. Leslie C. Allen, *Psalms 101-150,* rev. ed., WBC 21 (Nashville: Nelson, 2002), 330-31.

righteous in God's sight. Verses 1 and 23-24 encompass the text and form an *inclusio* of sorts through the repetition of language.

The entire psalm is in the form of a prayer, which begins with direct address to God: "O LORD, you have searched me and known me" (v. 1). This affirmation is then unpacked with a string of poetic lines that build upon one another to express the extent of God's knowledge. Antitheses (e.g., "when I sit down . . . when I rise up," "behind and before") and modifiers such as "completely" and "all" function within these lines to convey a further sense of pervasiveness.

The first strophe, then, identifies God as one whose knowledge is not limited to the psalmist's comings and goings; rather, God is intimately acquainted with every moment and aspect of the psalmist's life — waking or sleeping, spoken or unspoken, conscious or unconscious. Nothing is hidden from God, and because God's knowledge exceeds even the psalmist's own self-understanding (by implication) God is uniquely positioned to assess the psalmist's guilt or innocence vis-à-vis any and all accusations. This realization elicits an ascription of praise that concludes the first strophe:

> Such knowledge is too wonderful for me;
>> it is so high that I cannot attain it. (v. 6)

The second strophe moves in a similar fashion, this time beginning not with an affirmation but with a question:

> Where can I go from your spirit?
>> Or where can I flee from your presence? (v. 7)

Here the psalmist appeals to creation language and its traditional antitheses (darkness/light, day/night) to explore the limits of God's presence (see vv. 8-10).

Once more, by stringing together image after image from the perimeter of the created order, the psalmist's answer is realized: there is no end to God's reach, no limit to God's sight (v. 12: "even the darkness is not dark to you; / the night is as bright as the day, / for darkness is as light to you"). There can be no escaping the presence of God because all of creation belongs to the realm of God. Even Sheol, which may not be within the sphere of God's blessing, remains within the sphere of God's sovereignty.[5]

5. Allen, *Psalms 101-150*, 328-29.

The third strophe carries the question of limits one step further — beyond the boundaries of life itself. Once again the psalmist draws on creation language and imagery to invoke a time prior to his own existence. Once again the psalmist discovers that God is already present even there (vv. 13-16).

By inviting us to imagine his experience in the womb in terms of God's ongoing creative activity, the psalmist shifts the figure and ground for us; suddenly we find ourselves no longer questioning the limits of God in our lives, but considering our own limits in the context of the life of God. In other words, like the psalmist, we discover that our very existence is encompassed within the reality of God. Once again, this recognition elicits an ascription of praise, and the third strophe ends in doxology:

> How weighty to me are your thoughts, O God!
> > How vast is the sum of them!
> I try to count them — they are more than the sand;
> > I come to the end — I am still with you. (vv. 17-18)

The translation of verse 18 is problematic. The Hebrew text reads literally, "I awoke." Many English translations (e.g., KJV, NIV, RSV, NASB) preserve this reading, which Christian interpreters have generally understood to be a reference to the resurrection. Other translations (e.g., NRSV, NJPS) follow a common emendation so as to read "I come to an end." If this latter option is correct, the interpretive question becomes: Of what, exactly, does the psalmist come to an end? Is it the process of counting the sum of God's thoughts (v. 17), or is it life itself (perhaps referring back to "all the days that were formed" for the psalmist and written in God's book [v. 16])?

The frequent use of antitheses in Psalm 139 leaves us searching for counterparts to the life/birth of the psalmist and to the time preceding the creation of the psalmist's being. For this reason, it is appropriate to assume that the end verse 18 refers to is the psalmist's death. The affirmation of the third strophe, therefore, is that God's presence extends — in both directions — beyond the boundaries of human life. As Patrick D. Miller explains:

> Here is faith affirming that in our death we are caught up in the memory of God, remembered by God, held forever in the hand and mind of God. . . . Those who pray with the speaker of this prayer know that

God has known them before they even came into being. In like manner
they claim in trust that God knows them after they go out of being, after they come to an end. . . . Most of us do not have any basic anxiety
about our prebirth nonbeing, but we tend to have that about our
postdeath nonbeing. The psalmist, however, calls us to look at both
states the same way.[6]

The literary dynamic we identified within each strophe is also at
work between them. The three strophes strung together have a com-
pounding effect that intensifies the meaning of the whole: nothing in
our lives can be hidden from God, nor can we escape the presence of
God — ever. Why? Because in life and in death we belong to God (cf.
Rom. 14:8).

At this point both the tone and the content of the prayer shift radically. The psalmist's cry in verse 19,

> O that you would kill the wicked, O God,
> and that the bloodthirsty would depart from me,

appears to be unrelated to anything in the text that has come before.
This, coupled with the offensive nature of the imprecations in verses 19-
22, is undoubtedly the reason the fourth strophe has been omitted from
the Revised Common Lectionary. If, however, we accept the suggestion
above that Psalm 139 is a prayer for vindication of the innocent, we must
understand that the psalmist's cry here is a cry for justice and, as such, is
integral to the psalm (see further the essay on Ps 137).

Reading the text as a prayer of vindication for the innocent makes
sense not only of the imprecations, but also of the psalmist's delight in
the notion that nothing can be hidden from God. Most people of faith
experience at least occasional moments when they would prefer to escape
the watchful eye of God — when they know that what they have done,
said, thought, or unconsciously wished for is not aligned with God's way
in the world. Perhaps this is why the psalmist concludes his prayer with
these lines:

> Search me, O God, and know my heart;
> test me and know my thoughts.

6. Patrick D. Miller, *Interpreting the Psalms* (Philadelphia: Fortress, 1986), 149.

See if there is any wicked way in me,
>   and lead me in the way everlasting. (vv. 23-24)

The psalmist, who has been examined by God in the past, seeks to be examined again in the present. It is possible that he has not assessed his guilt or innocence accurately. His course could be in need of correction without his even realizing it (cf. Pss 19:12-13; 51:6). In any case, the psalmist presents himself to God — who knows all things and will always be present with us — and allows God to be the judge.

Preachers of the gospel will find many points of entry into Psalm 139. At a time when technological innovations are making face-to-face human contact more unnecessary, and when the capacity for mobility is rendering communities more transient and people less available to one another, feelings of isolation and loneliness are widespread. In a recent poll reported on the local news, 94 percent of respondents agreed with the statement "Nobody really knows me." The affirmation of the psalmist that we are known by God, intimately and completely, is contemporary and compelling in such a context. Similarly, in a time of economic volatility, increasing threats of violence, and political instability in certain regions around the globe, more and more North Americans are feeling vulnerable and uncertain about the future. In times such as these it is possible that a sermon on Psalm 139 can make one of the most hopeful and credible claims that can be made in the Christian pulpit: in life and in death we belong to God.

Carol A. Miles

Psalm 145

Twenty-fifth Sunday after Pentecost, Year C
>   First Lesson: Haggai 1:15b–2:9
>   (**Psalm 145:1-5, 17-21** or Psalm 98)
>   Second Lesson: 2 Thessalonians 2:1-5, 13-17
>   Gospel Lesson: Luke 20:27-38

Psalm 145 is an *individual hymn of praise* (see the introductory essay), located at the end of Book V of the Psalter, just before the five-psalm doxological closing of the book (Pss 146–150). Its superscription, unique in the Hebrew Psalter, reads "Praise. Of David." Within its twenty-one-verse acrostic structure,[1] David, the former great king of Israel, leads the Israelites and all of creation in words of praise and thanksgiving to God as king. Perhaps the distinctive superscription is a clue to readers to give this psalm special attention.

Several years ago, this writer came across an old rabbinic saying. In reference to the daily reciting of Deuteronomy 6:4, the Shema, a rabbi commented, "Out of repetition, sometimes a little magic is forced to rise." What makes a biblical text worthy of repetition? Repetition is worthy when the content and message of a text speak truths to successive readers and to successive generations of the faithful. The text "speaks a world into being," to borrow a phrase from Walter Brueggemann.[2] And what world does the reader "speak into being" in Psalm 145?

The Babylonian Talmud tractate *Berakhot* 4b states that Psalm 145, like the Shema, is to be recited three times a day and everyone who does so "may be sure that he (or she) is a child of the world to come." Psalm 145 appears in the Jewish prayer book more than any of the other 149 psalms in the Psalter, and the great Psalms scroll 11QPs[a] from Qumran contains a version of Psalm 145 in which the refrain, "blessed is the LORD and blessed is his name forever and ever," is included after each verse, indicating some sort of liturgical use. All indications are that the words of this psalm were and are a vital part of the faith of the Jewish people.

The psalm begins, in verses 1 and 2, with the psalmist's individual words of praise and blessing for "my God the king." As readers make their way through the psalm, the significance of the opening words "my God the king" will become evident. In verses 3-7 the individual voice is mingled with the voices of the "generations" of the Israelites in celebration of God's greatness, mighty acts, glorious splendor, and abundant goodness. Verses 8-9 echo God's self-descriptive words recorded in Exodus 34:6-7: "The LORD is gracious and merciful, slow to anger and abounding in steadfast love" (Exod 34:6; Ps 145:8). In verses 10-12 the praise of the Israelites is blended with the praise of remembrance of "all God's works" (v. 10).

1. An acrostic is a Hebrew poetic form in which each verse or line begins with a successive letter of the Hebrew alphabet. In Psalm 145, each verse begins with a successive letter of the alphabet, with one missing line corresponding to the Hebrew letter nun.

2. Walter Brueggemann, *Abiding Astonishment: Psalms, Modernity, and the Making of History* (Louisville: Westminster John Knox, 1991).

The centerpiece of the acrostic structure of Psalm 145 occurs in verses 11-13. Verse 11 begins with the Hebrew letter kaph; verse 12 with lamed; and verse 13 with mem. The three Hebrew letters are the consonantal root of the word for "king," *melek*. Within verses 11-13 the word *malkût* (kingdom), derived from the same consonantal root, occurs four times, emphasizing the theme of the psalm, the kingship of God over Israel and all flesh.[3]

Descriptive words occur again in verses 14-20, which use active verbs to describe the care God the king gives to the people: upholding the ones who fall, giving food in due season, acting justly, hearing the cries for help and saving, and watching over those who love the Lord (see Pss 107:33-42; 72:1-14). The final words of Psalm 145 begin with the individual voice of the psalm singer and expand to encompass the voice of all flesh in the praise of God as king:

My mouth will speak the praise of the LORD,
and all flesh will bless his holy name forever and ever. (v. 21)

Psalm 145 is a masterful composition. It persuades the reader to move from one stage of the psalm to the next, as each successive element builds on the previous one. The individual worshiper declares the reasons for praising and blessing the name of God the king. The reasons take the form of a declaration of the greatness, goodness, and mercy of God. The individual worshiper persuades the generations of the Israelites to join in the act of blessing God. And together the individual worshiper and the generations describe the great and good and merciful acts of God the king. As a result, not only the individual worshiper but all flesh (including the generations of the Israelites) will praise and bless the name of the Lord for all time.

Might we read Psalm 145 as the summary statement of the theme of the Hebrew Psalter: *the Lord is king over all generations of the Israelites and over all flesh?* And might we hear David, the former earthly king of ancient Israel, leading the Israelites and all flesh in a joyous celebration of that confession? All indications are that the answer to these questions is a resounding yes. In the words of the psalm, a new world has been powerfully and decisively spoken into being.

3. The enthronement psalms (Pss 47; 93; 95-99) also celebrate the kingship of God, using much of the same language found in Ps 145.

Psalm 145 is included as a lectionary reading for the Twenty-fifth Sunday after Pentecost in Year C. The first lesson is from the prophetic book of Haggai. In Haggai 1:15b–2:9 the Lord admonishes Zerubbabel, the governor of Judah; Joshua, the high priest; and the people who had returned to Jerusalem after the Babylonian exile to get on with the task of rebuilding the temple of the Lord. God says to them, "Work, for I am with you . . . my spirit abides with you; do not fear" (2:4-5). No, life will not return to the way it was before Babylon conquered Jerusalem. No, the people will not have an earthly king like David. But the people must go on; they must continue to be faithful to the ways of their God, and God will abide with them and rule as king in their midst.

Nancy L. deClaissè-Walford

PSALM 146

Third Sunday of Advent, Year A
   First Lesson: Isaiah 35:1-10
   (**Psalm 146:5-10** or Luke 1:47-55)
   Second Lesson: James 5:7-10
   Gospel Lesson: Matthew 11:2-11

Twenty-fourth Sunday after Pentecost, Year B
   First Lesson: Ruth 1:1-18
   (**Psalm 146**)
   Second Lesson: Hebrews 9:11-14
   Gospel Lesson: Mark 12:28-34

Third Sunday after Pentecost, Year C
   First Lesson: 1 Kings 17:8-16, (17-24)
   (**Psalm 146**)
   Second Lesson: Galatians 1:11-24
   Gospel Lesson: Luke 7:11-17

Psalm 146 is the beginning of the Psalter's glorious end: the book and life itself reach their goal in five doxologies that form a continuous paean of praise to Yahweh. The five psalms begin and end with "Hallelujah," a plural, imperatival call to "Praise *Yah*" (a shortened form of Yahweh). This praise is never ending and cosmic in scope. It includes creation and all its creatures, from top to bottom (Ps 148). At the very end (Ps 150), dancing human bodies and all the instruments of human culture fill the air with music. The very air, which God created to give life to "everything that breathes," is revealed as an instrument of praise for all creatures (Ps 150:6).

Psalm 146 opens with a personal call to the psalmist's whole being and inner self (*nepeš* means both; see the parallel in Ps 103:1) to praise and sing to Yahweh her God. But with verses 3-4 we discover that the form of this praise will be instruction in wisdom for God's people (cf. v. 10). The instruction is first negative ("Do not put your trust in princes," vv. 3-4) and then positive, a statement of *blessing* for the one who instead finds her help and hope in the God of Jacob, Yahweh (vv. 5-9). This blessing echoes the blessing that begins and concludes the introduction to the Psalter formed by the first two psalms (1:1; 2:12). Also in its themes, Psalm 146 echoes the first two psalms.[1] Our psalm is *torah*, or *instruction*, like Psalm 1, and it raises personal and collective issues of allegiance and trust in the Lord alone, as opposed to the human powers that array themselves against God, his people, and his messianic king, an opposition found in both Psalm 1 (individually) and Psalm 2 (politically; cf. 33:12-22; Deut 17:16).

The instruction in Psalm 146 focuses not on its audience (as contemporary preaching too often does), but on the objects of their trust: either humans doomed to death — their present fearsome power and might notwithstanding — or the one true God who has made himself known to Israel. "The best-laid plans of mice and men come to naught," says the proverb, and Israel knew this well (Ps 146:4; cf. Prov 21:1, 30-31; 2 Sam 17:14; Pss 49; 73).[2]

Verse 5 begins a "beatitude" extending to verse 9. It describes the "blessed" or "happy" simply as one who finds his help and hope in the God of Jacob, Yahweh. The focus is not on trust or hope as a human virtue. Even the wicked trust and hope, and depend on the help of others whose power and resources appear greater than their own. For all their

---

1. See J. Clinton McCann, Jr., "The Book of Psalms: Introduction, Commentary, and Reflections," in *NIB*, 4:1262-63.

2. See the chapter "The Limits of Wisdom," in G. von Rad, *Wisdom in Israel* (Nashville: Abingdon, 1972).

achievements, humans are dependent creatures, en route to death. It is thus a form of self-deception to rely on humanity, whether oneself (Deut 8:17-20) or "princes." Humans are only secondary or tertiary agents in a cosmic drama of death and life, whose ultimate outcome lies solely in the hands of God. Reason declares that any other stance in life is false, and not true to the facts.

The true focus of the beatitude is thus on God. To stand our ground in the contested kingdom of creation, we need look not to ourselves (where we find false reasons for pride or grounds for despair) but solely to the Lord. The instruction of the beatitude is very simple: it describes Yahweh, the object of our hope, truly, and thus gives us the security and certainty we need to continue. The psalmist deploys a series of "hymnic participles" that describe both the character and deeds of Yahweh, the things that make him God. He is "the Maker of heaven and earth, the sea" (NIV), and all that's in them (v. 6). Because he is creator and ruler of all, he alone is God, for unless he rules creation he cannot save creation, including us humans. We, who destroy and ruin creation, including ourselves, through our rebellion against the gracious rule of creation's king and his life-giving word (Ps 119), are not adequate to save ourselves or our world.

As king of creation, Yahweh is able to save, and his help comes especially to those who find no help in humanity: the oppressed, the hungry, the prisoners, the blind, those bowed down, the righteous, the stranger, the widow and orphan (vv. 7-9). His salvation, his help is in each case appropriate to heal the damage done to his human creatures. The eyes of the blind see, the hungry are fed with creation's bounty, the widow and orphan find their support in him, and so forth. No Christian can read these words without thinking of the down-to-earth salvation that Jesus brought during his life down below. Here we see that the God of Israel, the Father, and the Son are one; the Creator and Redeemer are one. As king, Yahweh not only helps the helpless, but he also judges the ways of the wicked (v. 9), that is, he brings to an end the life and power of those who damage or neglect the little righteous ones whom he loves (v. 8).

The richness of this psalm warrants its triple use in the lectionary. Isaiah 35:1-10 points toward the ultimate Advent, when the Lord's promises will be fully realized, the desert and broken creation will blossom like a garden, and all the woes of humanity shall be changed to joy. For this salvation Israel hoped, and in it the church also hopes, knowing that he who came will come again (cf. Matt 11:2-11). The Pentecost Old Testament reading for Year B (Ruth 1) takes us into the world of the hungry, of widows and orphans who are strangers in a strange land. It tells the tale of an outsider who chooses to trust in the God of Jacob and so enters into the family of God, into the line of Judah and David from which the Messiah came (Ruth 4:18-22). The Pentecost readings for Year C (1 Kings and Luke 7) bring together the miracles of Elijah and Jesus, again with a focus on the little people whom God loves and saves in Psalm 146: the hungry, the widow, the orphan.

Raymond C. Van Leeuwen

PSALM 147

Fifth Sunday after the Epiphany, Year B
> First Lesson: Isaiah 40:21-31
> **(Psalm 147:1-11, 20c)**
> Second Lesson: 1 Corinthians 9:16-23
> Gospel Lesson: Mark 1:29-39

Second Sunday after Christmas, Years A, B, C
> First Lesson: Jeremiah 31:7-14
> **(Psalm 147:12-20)**
> Second Lesson: Ephesians 1:3-14
> Gospel Lesson: John 1:(1-9), 10-18

At its beginning, middle, and end (vv. 1, 12, 20), Psalm 147 resounds with the familiar call heard in all five of the psalms concluding the Psalter: "Praise Yah(weh)!" *(halĕlû yāh)*. Immediately, the first verse provides the motivation for that call, and its ambiguous wording in Hebrew points not just to one but to two reasons for praise. As the NRSV reads it, praise comes because *"he* (God) is gracious *(nā'îm)."* Bearing testimony to such graciousness, the psalm goes on to recount actions in history and creation done by God. Other translations instead read the adjective *nā'îm* in verse 1 as a praise of praise itself: "for *it* is pleasant" (NASB; cf. NJPS, NIV). Praise, in this perspective, has value not because it accomplishes something but because of its aesthetic qualities: it is intrinsically good and pleasant and beautiful. Ultimately, both God and praise fit the description of *nā'îm,* and the two merge together further in this psalm since the content of praise basically consists of a portrayal of God. The goodness of praise mirrors the goodness of the God it describes.[1]

Throughout the psalm God's praiseworthy character comes to light in several ways. A series of adjectives in verse 5 lists God's *attributes* as greatness, abundance in power, and immeasurable understanding. Verse 10 observes the *emotions* of the Lord, highlighting what brings God pleasure and delight. Primarily, though, it is divine *action* that reveals who God is and why God is to be praised. God builds, heals, binds, strengthens gates, hurls hail, scatters frost, makes declarations, lifts people up, and casts them down. Even God's word "runs swiftly" (v. 15). Almost every line of the psalm begins with a verb for divine activity. In contrast, the closest reference to human action is "the speed of a runner" (literally, "a man's legs," v. 10). And that receives mention only to point out its inability to please God and to stress what does instead: praising God, fearing God, and hoping in God's steadfast love (v. 11).

God's many actions occur within two realms. The *historical realm* receives emphasis in the first section of the psalm (vv. 2-6), which tells how God redeems those who are broken or oppressed. While those actions reflect a divine care for humanity in general, they also reveal God's care for a particular people, Israel, at a particular moment in history, most likely the exile. The psalm uses key terms that also appear in exilic and postexilic texts to describe God building up Jerusalem (v. 2; cf. Neh 12:27), gathering outcasts (v. 2; cf. Ezek 39:28; cf. Deut 30:4; Neh 1:9; Isa 11:12; 56:8; Ezek 34:13; Mic 4:6), healing the brokenhearted (v. 3; cf. Ps 107:20; Isa 57:18-19; 61:1; Jer 30:17), and binding the wounded (v. 3; cf. Isa 61:1; Ezek 34:16).[2]

Then, in the middle of this activity in history, attention shifts to the *cosmic realm.* Divine calculation of the number ($\sqrt{spr}$, v. 4) of the stars — uncountable to humans — shows how God's understanding exceeds human calculation or "numbering" ($\sqrt{spr}$, v. 5); the dual use of the Hebrew root *spr* emphasizes the vast gulf between human and divine knowledge. And even beyond knowing the number of the stars in the universe, God knows their very names. This important detail offers a glimpse into the

---

1. James L. Mays, *Psalms,* Interpretation (Louisville: John Knox, 1994), 442.

2. J. Clinton McCann, Jr., "The Book of Psalms: Introduction, Commentary, and Reflections," in *NIB,* 4:1267.

nature of God's power in the cosmos. Far from being a distant knowledge and power, it is intimate and personal. That is why the psalmist can in one breath speak of God's merciful interaction with humans and in the next speak of divine knowledge of the heavens. It all reflects the same divine nature. The One who knows the names of the stars also knows the situation of the countless outcasts of Israel (v. 2).

Just as God acts on behalf of humans in history, God's knowledge of the cosmos leads to action on its behalf, described in the next section (vv. 7-11). A pattern of interconnectedness emerges in the specific workings of God's activity, with each action laying a foundation for the next. God covers the heavens with clouds, which brings about rain for the earth, which causes grass to grow, which provides food for animals (vv. 8-9), and all this anticipates the sustenance God provides for humans in verse 14. In portraying God's provision of water for the earth and food for animals, the psalm focuses on baby ravens (v. 9). The condition of these fragile creatures, utterly dependent on something else to feed them, calls to mind the downtrodden people God nurtures and heals in the psalm's first lines (vv. 2-6). In the end, if people want a sign that God will provide for them, all they must do is look at God's nourishment of the cosmos. Importantly, the converse is true as well. God's provision for humans attests to God's care and provision for the cosmos, even the smallest elements of the natural world (v. 9). So also the natural world highlights another important facet of the human condition. The complete dependence and receptiveness of the tiny raven, standing in stark contrast to the strength of the horse mentioned in verse 10, is just the posture of total receptivity and trust in divine provision that brings delight to God. This stance epitomizes the fear of the Lord and hope in God's steadfastness (v. 11; cf. Luke 12:24).

As the celebration of God's power and provision in history and the cosmos continues in the final section of Psalm 147 (vv. 12-20), one can see noticeable development from earlier descriptions. Whereas earlier God binds the wounded and heals the brokenhearted (v. 3), here God goes even further and strengthens gates, blesses children, and grants *shalom* (vv. 13-14). God not only feeds creatures (v. 9), but also fills people with the finest of wheat (v. 14). In the cosmos, images of precipitation build from the rain that waters the earth (v. 8) to dramatic flashes of meteorological power including snow, frost, and hail (vv. 16-17), the force of which makes the psalmist declare, "Who can stand before his cold?" Indeed, nothing and no one can. But in the face of the destruction such forces might bring, God demonstrates mercy and provision yet again, melting the cold into life-giving waters (v. 18; cf. v. 8). The growing intensity of God's power in the cosmos corresponds to an increase in the intensity of divine provision for humanity and nature. Not only do divine acts in history and the cosmos reveal God's nature as sensitive to the needs of all creation, but also God's power in the cosmos testifies to the fact that God *can* act decisively on their behalf, even, for example, in the most desperate situations of suffering and destruction such as brought on by exile (cf. Isa 40:21-31, first lesson, Year B).

A further development in this last section is the revelation that it is God's *word* that brings about the melting of snow, frost, and hail (v. 18). Already in verse 15 God's word (√*dbr*) runs swiftly and the divine command, or word (√*'mr*), is sent out "to the earth." Situated as it is between references to divine actions in history (vv. 13-14) and the cosmos (vv. 16-17), mention of the "earth" may point to either the cosmic or the historical realm. Verse 18 confirms the role of God's word in the *cosmic realm*. Its language recalls the creation account of Genesis 1 in which God's word (√*'mr*) controls the waters (cf. Ps 33:6-9, esp. v. 7), and the reference to God's wind, or spirit, or breath (*rûaḥ*, v. 18) making the waters flow hearkens back to Genesis 1:2 where God's *rûaḥ* sweeps over the face of the waters (cf. Ps 33:6 where God's word and *rûaḥ* appear in parallel). At the same time, that reference also evokes the dramatic moment in Israel's history when God divided the waters of the sea by a wind *(rûaḥ)* and then caused the waters to return so that the Israelites could escape the Egyptians (Exod 14:21). The second line of verse 18 thus alludes to what verse 19 confirms: God's word also plays a decisive role in the *historical realm*. Specifically, God's word comes to Israel as "statutes and ordinances," that is, the law (*tôrâ*, v. 19). Not only does God's word as *tôrâ* sustain Israel's identity by setting it apart from the other nations (v. 20; cf. Deut 4:7-8), but it also sustains and gives life to Israel in a physical sense (cf. Ps 107:20). Since the statutes and ordinances *(mišpāṭîm)* given by God mandate justice *(mišpāṭ)*, they protect and ensure life in the community. The law promotes blessing (cf. v. 13) and peace (cf. v. 14), and it makes provisions for all members of the community to be filled with food (cf. v. 14), including the weakest and most helpless ones in the group (cf. v. 9). For those being saved from suffering and heartbreak (vv. 2-6), God's word then offers ongoing nourishment so that they may not only be rescued but may also grow and thrive (vv. 13-14; cf. Ps 1; Isa 55:10-11).

Focusing on the last section of Psalm 147 (vv. 12-20), the first and second lessons from the lectionary (Years A, B, C) draw out other aspects of God's life-bringing word. In Jeremiah 31:7-14 the word of the Lord comes through a prophet to sustain Israel with the promise of return to the land where they might walk "by brooks of water" (v. 9). Having been scattered, Israel now has hope of being gathered so that "their life shall become like a watered garden" (v. 12) and they will "be satisfied with my bounty" (v. 14). The nourishment that comes through God's word of hope gives rise to singing in the same manner as Psalm 147 (Jer 31:7, 12). Yet another understanding of God's word comes in John 1:1-18, where the Word reveals cosmic and historical dimensions, having been "in the beginning" and having become flesh and living among humanity in history (vv. 1-2, 14). For all these ways that humans may know and feed on God's word, Psalm 147 offers fitting words of praise and thanksgiving.

Jennifer S. Green

PSALM 148

First Sunday after Christmas, Year A
    First Lesson: Isaiah 63:7-9
    (Psalm 148)
    Second Lesson: Hebrews 2:10-18
    Gospel Lesson: Matthew 2:13-23

First Sunday after Christmas, Year B
    First Lesson: Isaiah 61:10–62:3
    (Psalm 148)
    Second Lesson: Galatians 4:4-7
    Gospel Lesson: Luke 2:22-40

First Sunday after Christmas, Year C
    First Lesson: 1 Samuel 2:18-20, 26
    (Psalm 148)
    Second Lesson: Colossians 3:12-17
    Gospel Lesson: Luke 2:41-52

Fifth Sunday of Easter, Year C
  First Lesson: Acts 11:1-18
  (Psalm 148)
  Second Lesson: Revelation 21:1-6
  Gospel Lesson: John 13:31-35

Although it is not based on Psalm 148, the title of Richard Smallwood's recent hymn captures the essence of the psalm — "Total Praise."[1] The central panel of a five-psalm Hallelujah collection (Pss 146–150; note that each of these psalms begins and ends with "Praise the LORD!") that concludes the Psalter, Psalm 148 invites praise from the totality of creation — "from the heavens" (v. 1) and the heavenly bodies, and "from the earth" (v. 7), including not only its range of creatures but also a full array of its features (note the repetition of "all" in vv. 2-3, 7, 9-11, 14). In fact, the praise invited is so total that it anticipates (and actually exceeds!) the climactic final verse of the Psalter, Psalm 150:6, which invites "everything that breathes" to praise God. In Psalm 148, having breath is not a requirement. Every creature and every thing are invited to praise God — total praise!

Such total praise has something crucially important to say about God's "name" (vv. 5, 13), or character. The numerous allusions to Genesis 1:1–2:4 reinforce what is explicit in verse 5, that is, God is to be praised as creator of the universe. As Daniel L. Migliore suggests, what creation reveals about God's "name" or character is that God is essentially *love:* "When we confess God as the creator, we are saying something about the character of God. . . . Creation fittingly expresses the true character of God, who is love."[2] Because God is love, and because God loves the whole world, it is necessary to gather nothing short of a universe-encompassing congregation of praise. Note the pairing of Psalm 148 with John 13:31-35 for the Fifth Sunday of Easter, Year C; the new commandment for the new creation present in Jesus — see John 1:1-18 — is love.

It is interesting to note that human beings are the last to enter this picture of total praise in Psalm 148. Perhaps the ordering of Psalm 148 is determined primarily by Genesis 1, where human beings are the culminat-

---

1. See the *African American Heritage Hymnal* (Chicago: GIA Publications, 2001), no. 113.

2. Daniel L. Migliore, *Faith Seeking Understanding: An Introduction to Christian Theology* (Grand Rapids: Eerdmans, 1991), 85.

ing act of God's creation; however, there is no "image of God" in Psalm 148 nor anything more than a hint of human superiority (see below). It seems that human beings form simply one section of a universal chorus. To be sure, the praise offered by humans will not be the same as that of a fruit tree. As for humans, praise will take the form of what Walter Brueggemann aptly calls "lyrical self-abandonment,"[3] the yielding of the self and its desires to God and God's purposes. Such praise-filled servanthood is the proper response to God's sovereign claim on all creation. The words "exalted" and "glory" in verse 13 regularly occur in contexts that proclaim God's sovereignty (see "exalted" in Isa 33:5 and "glory" in Pss 96:6; 145:5); and if God is master, then we are properly *servants*.

Such servanthood may provide a clue to the meaning of the phrase "praise for all his faithful" in verse 14 (which may be the only hint of human superiority, or at least vocation), as well as a clue to what praise may mean for a fruit tree or a snowflake. As Terence Fretheim suggests:

> God has made God's people strong, indeed has made them a praise in the earth, for the universal praise of God. . . . Just as the various other creatures show forth the praise of God by being what they are as God's creatures, so Israel having been made what it now is by God, shows forth God's praise by being who they are, the redeemed people of God. . . . God's people in every age are called upon to continue to show forth the praise of God because of what they have been made by God. In this way they will join with that vast chorus of God's non-human creatures in honor of God and in witness to God.[4]

In short, if there is something unique about the human creature, it is the responsibility to respect and protect the integrity of the whole created order, so that it may be able to "speak." The interrelatedness of all things, human and nonhuman, animate and inanimate, recalls not only Genesis 1:1-2:4 but also the original biblical covenant in Genesis 9:8-17, a relationship that involves God and humankind, as one would expect, but also "every living creature" (vv. 10, 12, 15, 16) and "the earth" (v. 13) itself. Again, for the creator of heaven and earth to be properly worshiped, the congre-

3. Walter Brueggemann, "Bounded by Praise and Obedience: The Psalms as Canon," *JSOT* 50 (1991): 67.

4. Terence Fretheim, "Nature's Praise of God in the Psalms," *Ex Auditu* 3 (1987): 29-30.

gation must be universe-encompassing. Needless to say, the ecological implications are profound and far-reaching! As Saint Francis of Assisi recognized in his "Canticle of the Sun" long before the age of environmental awareness, the sun, moon, wind, and waters are, in a real sense, our sisters and brothers.

Since the sovereign claim of God is implicit in Psalm 148, it is important to recognize that those psalms that explicitly proclaim God's reign also portray a creation-wide response (see Pss 29:1; 96:11-13; 97:1; 98:4, 7-9). The movement of one of these enthronement psalms, Psalm 29, is clearly present in Luke 2:13-14 as Luke narrates the birth of Jesus — that is, the heavenly proclamation of glory (Ps 29:1, 9; Luke 2:14a) is accompanied by the proclamation of earthly peace (Ps 29:11; Luke 2:14b). For Luke, the birth of Jesus is an enthronement proclamation, an event manifesting God's sovereign claim on the world. Appropriately, therefore, the enthronement Psalms 96–98 are the assigned psalms for Christmas Day; and Psalm 148 is a logical choice for the First Sunday after Christmas, Years A, B, and C. That Psalm 148 appears in both the seasons of Christmas and Easter is a fitting reminder that God's sovereignty is also exercised as suffering love, which, according to God's character and purposes, is true power.

J. Clinton McCann, Jr.

PSALM 149

Sixteenth Sunday after Pentecost, Year A
>   First Lesson: Exodus 12:1-14
>   **(Psalm 149)**
>   Second Lesson: Romans 13:8-14
>   Gospel Lesson: Matthew 18:15-20

Psalm 149 is fourth in the series of five hymns concluding the Psalter. Each psalm begins and ends with "Praise the LORD!" As will be shown below, placement in the Psalter can be an important clue to a psalm's meaning. On first reading, Psalm 149, especially verses 6-9, has a triumphalistic and violent tone that may make praying it difficult for people. After all, having the high praises of God in one's throat and a two-edged sword in one's hand, executing vengeance on the nations and binding kings with fetters (vv. 6-9), does not evoke the peace and quiet we expect in prayer. On the contrary, it seems to encourage violence in the name of religion. To top it all off, these acts are the "glory for all his faithful ones." These verses cry out for interpretation. Can one make them into prayer for the holy community?

The context of Psalm 149 in the Psalter provides some perspective. In the larger literary structure of the Psalter, Psalm 149 matches Psalm 2; each is next to the end, and their messages are remarkably similar. Psalm 2 tells how "the kings of the earth . . . and the rulers" conspired against "the LORD and his anointed, saying, / 'Let us burst their bonds asunder'" (Ps 2:2-3), and how "the decree of the LORD" (Ps 2:7) elevated the king and made him the Lord's "son" to subdue the nations with an iron rod that they might serve the Lord (Ps 2:9-11). In Psalm 2 the king is the instrument of divine rule over the nations. Divine rule also is the theme of Psalm 149, with one major difference. When Psalm 149 was written, the king was gone from public life and (according to some texts) his role of representing the Lord's kingship was transferred to the people (cf. Isa 55:3). Psalm 149 urges the people to embrace their role in promoting the Lord's reign in the world. To proclaim that the Lord is king is to unmask as false other kings' claims to absolute sovereignty. Such a proclamation in fact constitutes an act of war against kings who do not acknowledge the Lord as their divine sovereign. The military language in Psalm 149:6-9 (swords, binding in fetters, chains of iron) is therefore to be understood metaphorically. Israel's fidelity and public praise of the Lord are, as it were, weapons proclaiming the rule of the Lord (the kingdom of God).

Psalm 149 has two invitatory verses. Verses 1-3 and verse 5 invite hearers to give praise, using verbs in the imperative and jussive (exhortatory) mood. As in most hymns, the invitatory verses 1-3 are followed by the conjunction "for" (v. 4a), which provides the motive for singing praise. Here the motive for praise is the Lord's choosing of the people. The second invitatory in verse 5 has no "for"; it apparently appropriates the motive already expressed in verse 4. There are, then, two stanzas, verses 1-4 and verses 5-9. The first stanza invites praise for the Lord's victory. The second invites praise as well and goes on to equate it with weapons of war against the rebellious kings.

The "new song" (v. 1), which the people are invited to sing, is a response to God's great act of creating the world including Israel (Isa

42:10; Pss 33:3; 96:1; 98:1; 144:9). Here the great act is the creation of the world and of Israel. The phrase "on their couches" (v. 5b) has provoked much discussion. "Couch" (or bed) seems to symbolize private expression (as opposed to public expression) in Psalms 4:4, 6:6, 36:4, and Hosea 7:14. It seems to complement praise in "the assembly of the faithful" (v. 1c). To give praise publicly and privately is a merism to designate every moment. A merism is a literary figure in which two extremes on a spectrum are named to express the entire spectrum. Verse 6 requires one last look. The conjunction "and" ("*and* two-edged swords in their hands") turns the statements of colon A and colon B into a comparison: praising God is *like* wielding a sword. Such a use of the conjunction "and" is sometimes called the "comparative and." Examples can be found in Proverbs 17:3; 25:3; 26:3, 9. Verse 6 expresses a paradox. Israel's fidelity to the Lord and proclamation of his sovereignty further the Lord's reign as a military campaign furthers a king's reign. It is the honorable task of Israel ("glory for all his faithful ones," v. 9b) to embody the sovereignty of the Lord and make it visible and audible in the world. Israel's bold witness unmasks false kingdoms and invites the nations to join in their praise.

The warlike tone and exaltation of one nation over others might spoil the psalm for some. It should not. Divine kingship is active, and evil is powerful, entrenched, and embodied in individuals and institutions. Psalm 149 imagines a "worst-case scenario" — defiant and unjust kings — to dramatize the reality of the Lord's rule. Second, Israel is chosen for the sake of *all* the nations. They, more than any other nation, must recognize the Lord's total sovereignty. Israel's obedience and worship alert all the nations to that true sovereignty.

Richard J. Clifford

PSALM 150

Second Sunday of Easter, Year C
> First Lesson: Acts 5:27-32
> (Psalm 118:14-29 or **Psalm 150**)
> Second Lesson: Revelation 1:4-8
> Gospel Lesson: John 20:19-31

Psalm 150 is the fitting climax to the Psalter. Each of the preceding four books of the Psalms ends with a doxology (see Pss 41:13; 72:18-19; 89:52; 106:48). Psalm 150 does double duty: it serves as the concluding doxology to both Book V and the book as a whole. Indeed, Psalms 146-150, the so-called "hallelujah" psalms, bring the book of "Praises" (*těhillîm* in Hebrew) to an apt conclusion with their constant and insistent imperative, summoning any and all to praise: *halělû yāh*, "Hallelujah" — literally, "you (pl.) praise Yah(weh)!" (see, e.g., 146:1, 10; 147:1, 12, 20; 148:1-4, 7, 14; 149:1, 9). Psalm 150 is the grand finale to this overture of praise. Like its predecessors, it also begins and ends with the imperative to praise (vv. 1, 6). But, unlike them, Psalm 150 contains the *halělû* in *every* verse. It is a *hymn of praise* (see the introductory essay), perhaps *the* hymn of praise par excellence, replete with unrestrained and unmotivated praise.

The last point calls for some discussion. In the hymns of praise it is common for the psalmist to *motivate* the praise in some fashion. To cite just one example from Psalms 146-149, the psalmist enjoins Jerusalem/Zion to praise the Lord

> for [or: because; Hebrew *kî*] he strengthens the bars of your gates;
> he blesses your children within you.
>
> (147:13; see, similarly, 147:1; 148:5, 13; 149:4)

Even when the causal particle is absent, the psalmist often motivates praise by describing God's beneficent activity (see, e.g., 146:5-9; cf. 147:2-11, 14-20; 148:14). But in Psalm 150, *no reason or motivation* is offered — perhaps because, after 149 psalms, all the reasons have already been given! Instead of motivating the praise, the psalmist simply summons the community — indeed, *all of creation* (see below) — to join in the Lord's praise. The psalmist also provides instructions on *where* and *how* that praise ought to be rendered.

After the initial summons to praise (v. 1a), the psalmist commands that God be praised in God's "sanctuary" and in God's "mighty firmament" (v. 1b). The former seems to evoke the (earthly?) temple; the latter, God's heavenly precincts. Even the divine realms can be encouraged and called to give praise. In this regard, note Psalm 148, which commands the angels to praise (v. 2), and recall the near identical sentiment in the words to the familiar "Doxology":

> Praise him above, *ye heavenly host,*
> Praise Father, Son, and Holy Ghost.

Praise can and does unite the earthly and heavenly communities that serve the Lord.

The psalmist moves on from the temple and divine realms but continues to employ the same preposition used in verse 1: "praise him in [*bĕ-*] his mighty deeds" (150:2a). (NRSV's "*for* his mighty deeds" might mislead; the construction is not causal.) Psalm 150:2b reads similarly in some versions: "praise him *in* his surpassing greatness" (cf. 20:6; 54:1), but the NRSV correctly translates "*according to* [*kĕ-*] his surpassing greatness." The point here is not God's *activity* but God's *attributes*. God *is* mighty (√*gbr*; see 21:13; 65:6; 71:16; 103:11; 106:2; 117:2; 145:4, 11-12) and great (√*gdl*; see 35:27; 40:16; 70:4; 104:1). Hence, God is eminently "praise-able." While this is similar, at least to some degree, to praise motivations found elsewhere (see above), it is not exactly the same and is at best an echo or evocation of such. What is typically included in the hymns — *reasons* for praise — has instead been incorporated into the *summons* to praise.[1]

Those called to praise the praise-able God are, in turn, also able to praise, and in the rest of the poem the psalmist recounts how they might do so. The following verses offer a listing that is *comprehensive*. Virtually every instrument known to the ancient orchestra is included:[2] trumpet (literally, the *shofar*), lute, and lyre (v. 3); tambourine, strings, and pipe (v. 4); cymbals of all kinds and sounds (v. 5). Brass, strings, percussion! Some have argued that the different instruments reflect different musical groups: priests in verse 3a, Levites in verse 3b, and laypeople in verses 4-5.[3] But even if this is correct, it is not just the musicians and their score that resound God's praise — those who listen to the band can't help but *dance* in doxology (v. 4a).

The list is also *universal*. The first imperative summons all who hear

1. See Walter Brueggemann, *The Message of the Psalms: A Theological Commentary* (Minneapolis: Augsburg, 1984), 167; Leslie C. Allen, *Psalms 101–150*, rev. ed., WBC 21 (Nashville: Nelson, 2002), 402-3; Hans-Joachim Kraus, *Psalms 60–150: A Continental Commentary* (Minneapolis: Fortress, 1993), 570; contrast James L. Mays, *Psalms,* Interpretation (Louisville: John Knox, 1994), 449-50; J. Clinton McCann, Jr., "The Book of Psalms: Introduction, Commentary, and Reflections," in *NIB,* 4:1278.

2. See Joachim Braun, *Music in Ancient Israel/Palestine: Archaeological, Written, and Comparative Sources* (Grand Rapids: Eerdmans, 2002), esp. 1-45; cf. also Ps 98:5-6.

3. See Allen, *Psalms 101–150,* 404.

(or read!) to praise and proceeds, as already noted, straight to the temple, then to the heavens, and then to God's attributes so awesomely evident (vv. 1-2). The next section calls musicians and dancers to praise. The final verse, however, is staggeringly all-encompassing. "Let everything that breathes praise the LORD!" (v. 6a). The phrase "everything that breathes" is rather uncommon. Its use elsewhere in the Old Testament indicates that *the animal world* is also numbered among those "that breathe" (see especially Gen 7:22; cf. 2:7; also, in war contexts, Deut 20:16; Josh 10:40; 11:11, 14). Artifacts and images from the ancient Near East add further support to associations of animals with music: animal-shaped musical instruments have been recovered, along with fanciful depictions of "animal orchestras." Other psalms, too, also know of the nonhuman world giving praise to God (e.g., 19:1-6; 100:1; 145:21; 148:3-5, 7-10).

It is altogether appropriate, then, that this fitting conclusion to the Psalter calls *all of creation* — earth and heaven, musician and dancer, human *and* nonhuman — to praise their Creator (cf. fig. 14). If the world is truly "the theater of God's glory" (Calvin), then the theater company employs the entire universe. If "all the world's a stage,"[4] then the players are each and every created thing, not only "all the men and women." The world is therefore *both* the theater of God's glory — that is, where God's glory is manifested — *and* that which gives God the glory. The actors have one major part, one major line, even though it is refracted and retold in millions of ways. That line closes Psalm 150 even as it closes the entire Psalter. It echoes across time and space, down through all ages and throughout the far reaches of the universe. It is simply this: "Praise the LORD!" (v. 6b).

To conclude, it should be noted that the Psalter begins with Psalm 1, with an emphasis on *torah* and *torah* piety — i.e., obedience to the law of the Lord — and it ends, in Psalm 150, with unrestrained praise. There is, however, much more to life than just these two options of obedience and praise. There are, after all, 148 psalms between these two! Those psalms contain much more about life: more about *torah* and obedience and praise and doxology, to be sure, but also more about pain and lament, loss and suffering, candor and hope — as well as how all these are mixed up and mixed together in our life with God.[5] Some of the darker notes of

---

4. Shakespeare, *As You Like It*, act 2, scene 7.

5. See Walter Brueggemann, "Bounded by Obedience to Praise: The Psalms as Canon," in Brueggemann, *The Psalms and the Life of Faith*, ed. Patrick D. Miller (Minneapolis: Fortress, 1995), 189-213.

Fig. 14. This image nicely depicts the notion of the entirety of creation worship-ing the deity (in this case, the Egyptian god Ra-Horakhty). From bottom to top, the image shows the god being worshiped by the dead (represented by the two soul-birds); the gods Isis (on the right) and Nephthys (on the left); the animals (baboons); four kings (on the right); four common Egyptians (left); and finally, perhaps even lower-class Egyptians or foreigners. The image is of special signifi-cance for those places in the Psalms that invoke creation to join in the praise of the Lord (e.g., Ps 148:3-5, 7-10). Animals may also be included in the final sum-mons of the Psalter for "everything that has breath" to praise "the LORD" (Ps 150:6).

that life are also at work in the first lesson, Acts 5:27-32, where Peter and his fellow apostles face persecution and the threat of death (see 5:33), even though they end up testifying, like the psalmist, to the greatness of God (5:31-32). It is important to recognize, then, that Psalm 150 is an ending — *the* ending, if you will — but that there is much ground that must be traversed before the faithful reach it or say it with ease. Indeed, it may be that they never reach it or say it with ease, in this life, but are able to say it only as a testimony of hope, faith, and trust in the One worthy of praise, who was and is and is to come.

Let everything that has breath praise the LORD!
Praise the LORD!

Brent A. Strawn

ISAIAH 12

Twenty-sixth Sunday after Pentecost, Year C
First Lesson: Isaiah 65:17-25
(Isaiah 12)
Second Lesson: 2 Thessalonians 3:6-13
Gospel Lesson: Luke 21:5-19

Third Sunday of Advent, Year C
First Lesson: Zephaniah 3:14-20
(Isaiah 12:2-6)
Second Lesson: Philippians 4:4-7
Gospel Lesson: Luke 3:7-18

Isaiah 12 falls at a crucial juncture in the book of Isaiah. This song of thanksgiving caps off the opening section of the book, which has presented Isaiah's message as one of judgment and cleansing followed by eschatological deliverance and restoration (Isa 1-11), with a communal response of thanksgiving and praise. At the same time, the song anticipates the more extensive development of the theme of Zion's redemption and consolation throughout the second part of the book (especially Isa 40-55).

The song falls into two parts (vv. 1-3, 4-6), each introduced with the phrase "on that day you will say" (cf. Isa 25:9; 26:1). The temporal marker "on that day" links this hymn explicitly to the previous two chapters, where God promises "on that day" to judge Israel's foreign oppressor, Assyria, and to redeem his captive people through the messianic "root of Jesse" (Isa 10:20, 27; 11:10, 11; cf. 4:2). In verse 1 the speaker gives thanks that Yahweh's "anger," so long directed in judgment against his rebellious people through the agency of Assyria ("the rod of my anger," 10:5), has now "turned away" (contrast the ominous refrain, "for all this his anger has not turned away," in 5:25; 9:12, 17, 21; 10:4). Divine wrath has given way to divine "comfort" (cf. 40:1; 49:13; 51:3, 12; 52:9; 54:11; 61:2; 66:13).

Linked by a threefold reference to "salvation," verses 2-3 adopt the stance of dependence and trust that constitutes the proper human response to God (cf. 7:9b). The confession "God is my salvation" recalls the name of the prophet Isaiah (*yĕša'yāhû*, "The LORD is salvation"), who himself stood as a "sign" in Israel (8:18) during the Assyrian crisis by faithfully modeling patient, hopeful trust in God (8:17).[1] In Isaiah 12, that confident faith in the Lord now characterizes the entire community of the redeemed. Taking a line from the ancient Song of the Sea,

> Yah the LORD is my strength and might,
>> and he has become my salvation (Exod 15:2; cf. Ps 118:14),

verse 2 portrays God's mighty work of bringing Israel home from exile as nothing less than a new exodus. Despite the chronic unfaithfulness of his people (cf. Isa 1:2-4), the one who called Israel as his very own and covenanted with them to be their God has now displayed his faithfulness to that gracious promise once and for all. Now, because of God's forgiveness and restoration and comfort, instead of the terror of judgment (cf. 2:10, 19, 21), God's people are filled with genuine trust (cf. 10:27; 26:3-4; 50:10) and overflow with boundless joy. (For the "fountain/spring" imagery, compare the recollections of the exodus/wilderness journey in Isaiah 41:18 and Psalm 114:8 as well as the vision of the eschatological river of life in Joel 3:18; cf. Ezekiel 47:1-12.)

But the joy of salvation is not intended for Israel alone. The second stanza of the song, borrowing heavily from the language and imagery of

---

1. Cf. Christopher R. Seitz, *Isaiah 1–39*, Interpretation (Louisville: John Knox, 1993), 112-13.

the Psalms, calls Israel to make Yahweh's great deeds known among all the peoples of the earth (v. 4a; cf. Ps 105:1). Reference to the "glorious" work of the Lord (*gē'ût 'āśāh*, v. 5) further recalls the triumph of the exodus (*gā'ôh gā'āh*, Exod 15:1, 21) as the paradigmatic saving deed of the divine warrior who fights on Israel's behalf (cf. *'āśāh ḥayil*, Pss 60:12; 108:13; 118:15-16; Isa 26:18). As Isaiah's vision has already intimated, however (cf. Isa 2:1-5; 11:10), this new exodus, Israel's redemption from exile, now brings all the nations of the earth within the saving purpose of Israel's God. Through his mighty acts of judgment and salvation, Yahweh alone is exalted (v. 4b; cf. Ps 148:13; Isa 33:5), and all human pretensions are cast down (cf. Isa 2:11-12, 17).

The song closes with a summons to Zion to "shout aloud and sing for joy" (v. 6 NRSV). Indeed, celebration and joyful singing are recurrent themes in Isaiah's oracles of salvation (cf. Isa 24:14; 26:19; 35:2, 6; 42:11, 23; 49:13; 52:8, 9; 54:1; 65:14). And how could it be otherwise? For Isaiah's vision of salvation entails nothing less than the fulfillment of the end for which mortals have been created (cf. Isa 43:7), the satisfaction of the deepest desire of the human heart: the intimate fellowship of a life lived in God's very presence. "For great in your midst is the Holy One of Israel" (Isa 12:6 NRSV).

In the lectionary, Isaiah 12 provides the congregation with a fitting response to the proclamation of eschatological restoration and salvation, the "new heavens and new earth" (Isa 65:17), that brings the book of Isaiah to a close. In a similar way, in the lesson for the Third Sunday of Advent, Isaiah 12 gives voice to "daughter Zion," who is commanded to "sing aloud" (Zeph 3:14; cf. Isa 12:6). Isaiah's celebration of the Lord's presence in the midst of Zion resonates powerfully with Zephaniah's proclamation that "the king of Israel, the LORD, is in your midst" (Zeph 3:15) as a warrior who sings for joy over the people he has redeemed for himself (Zeph 3:17). In anticipation of "that day" (Isa 12:1, 4; Zeph 3:16), the congregation joins together with God's people throughout the ages in this bold confession of hope and trust:

> Surely God is my salvation;
>   I will trust, and will not be afraid. (Isa 12:2 NRSV; cf. Zeph 3:15-16)

J. Ross Wagner

LAMENTATIONS 3

Twentieth Sunday after Pentecost, Year C
    First Lesson: Lamentations 1:1-6
    (**Lamentations 3:19-26** or Psalm 137)
    Second Lesson: 2 Timothy 1:1-14
    Gospel Lesson: Luke 17:5-10

Lamentations lections are scarce in the Revised Common Lectionary. As the first lesson, it appears only once in the three-year cycle, on this Twentieth Sunday after Pentecost, Year C (Lam 1:1-6). Lamentations 3:1-9, 19-24 is designated once as an alternate to Job 14:1-14 (Holy Saturday, Years A, B, and C), and twice a selection from Lamentations 3 is offered as an alternate to a psalm. Preachers and planners for the Sunday under consideration here will need to choose between Psalm 137 and Lamentations 3:19-26 as a response to the first lesson.

The opening verses of the canticle (3:19-20) express the bitter experience of the destruction of the temple and the resulting desolation of Jerusalem in 586 B.C.E.:

> The thought of my affliction and my homelessness
>   is wormwood and gall!
> My soul continually thinks of it
>   and is bowed down within me.

These verses recount the devastating experience so graphically portrayed in the first lesson (1:1-6). The destruction of the temple and the forced exile to Babylon decimated the glory of Jerusalem. The vivid metaphors of the first lesson prepare the reader for the bitterness and despair expressed in Psalm 137 or Lamentations 3:19-20. Both responses give voice to themes common in our world, namely, that violence inflicts suffering and suffering can breed bitterness if unresolved.

But with verse 21 our canticle takes us in a different direction. It would be difficult to find a clearer contrast between a bitter lament (3:19-20) and a grateful song of praise (3:21-26). Properly understood, however, both responses are appropriate in the literary and historical contexts that gave them life. Despair turns to hope, bitterness to gratitude; therefore lament turns to praise. What happened to bring about this change? What intervened between the complaint with its accusation against God (chapters 1 and 2) and the burst of praise? The answer is *memory*; the speaker *remembered* something that changed everything:

> But this I call to mind,
>   and therefore I have hope:
> The steadfast love of the LORD never ceases,
>   his mercies never come to an end;
> they are new every morning;
>   great is your faithfulness. (vv. 21-23)

Remembering made the difference. Without the memory, praising God before the dust settled at Jerusalem's ground zero would have been like an obscene joke.

The memory reminds us that the early history of God's covenant people formed an ellipse around two foci: the slavery in Egypt followed by the exodus, and the exile in Babylon followed by the return home. When the speaker remembered something that refreshed his trust in the steadfast love and mercy of the Lord, he was remembering the character of God revealed in the exodus. Remembering the exodus was essential to the stories and songs that were rehearsed in the cult and practiced in the Passover. Even four hundred years of slavery in Egypt could not cancel God's steadfast love and unending mercies. God's great faithfulness is disclosed in the fulfillments of the promises to Abraham and Sarah.

Adele Berlin sees a relationship between the exile, Egypt, and the exodus: "The vassalage of Judah to Babylon is likened to the enslavement in Egypt in that it returned the people to their preexodus state. But unlike the Egyptian experience, the servitude to Babylon led not to freedom, but to exile. Later, the postexilic prophets will compare the return from exile to the exodus."[1] And F. W. Dobbs-Allsopp, noting the many allusions to the Egyptian captivity in Lamentations, concludes:

> By identifying the present post-destruction community with those mythopoetic "children of Israel" under the leadership of Moses, the poem is able to honor and to dignify associatively the present experience of suffering, and perhaps even to inculcate a small sliver of hope. That is, the Egyptian captivity is one of those "dangerous memories"

1. Adele Berlin, *Lamentations: A Commentary*, OTL (Louisville: Westminster John Knox, 2002), 51.

which ultimately testifies to the nonfinality of the powers of destruction and domination. The liberation and redemption of the Hebrew slaves from Egypt as remembered in the story of the exodus manifests the compassionate power of God in history and thereby holds out the prospect that God's compassion may yet be realized in the present as it was in the past, God's current silence and absence notwithstanding.[2]

Just as remembering the exodus nurtured hope, so remembering the resurrection sustains the faith and life of the Christian community. In the Epistle for today Timothy is reminded of the grace of God revealed in "our Savior, Jesus Christ, who abolished death and brought life and immortality to light through the gospel" (2 Tim 1:10).

Remembering the character of God disclosed in the exodus nourished hope in the present affliction for the speaker. "Speaker" here is singular in contrast to the poems of chapters 1, 2, 4, and 5, which are communal laments.[3] While the poems of chapters 1, 2, and 4 bear the most similarities as communal laments that are laced with elements of a dirge, the fifth poem (chapter 5) is similar enough to characterize it as such. Poem (chapter) 3 is also a lament, but in it an individual person plays a dominant role in contrast to the communal laments. The entire collection of poems, regardless of the nuances of difference among them, is characterized as lament, which Westermann describes as "the language of suffering. . . . When pain becomes verbalized, the cry becomes a lament."[4]

While lament may encounter resistance in the piety of many — if not most — North American Christians, "The lament is of fundamental importance when it comes to speaking of God in the Old Testament. If we regard the history of Israel as beginning with a mighty act of deliverance, we see how communal lamentation is a feature intrinsic to the account of that event. Regularly, throughout the narratives of the Old Testament, lamentation is a feature in the sequence of events leading from distress to deliverance."[5] And if Christians have difficulty bringing lament into the worship of the church, we have as our example the deepest lament of

---

2. F. W. Dobbs-Allsopp, *Lamentations,* Interpretation (Louisville: John Knox, 2002), 77.

3. See Claus Westermann, *Lamentations: Issues and Interpretation* (Minneapolis: Augsburg Fortress, 1994), 87-88, who describes Lamentations as a collection of five songs, the third of which is a personal lament.

4. Westermann, *Lamentations,* 89-90.

5. Westermann, *Lamentations,* 94.

all time in the words of our Lord Jesus Christ from the cross: "My God, my God, why have you forsaken me?" (Mark 15:34; Ps 22:1). Lament and praise both belong to the language of faith. In Lamentations 3 they belong to the same poem, perhaps even the same breath.

Remembering the character of God revealed in the exodus revived the speaker's hope. His language of hope is centered on "the LORD" (vv. 24-26). He issues no prescriptions regarding God's obligations to him; "the LORD is my portion" (v. 24) is sufficient. Just as the Lord was "the portion" for the priesthood of the house of Aaron (Num 18:20) in contrast to the "portion" of property assigned to the tribes in the Promised Land, so now hope in the Lord's steadfast love, mercy, and faithfulness is enough. "The LORD is my portion" is rooted in the Aaronic priesthood, echoed throughout the Psalms (16:5; 73:26; 142:5; etc.), confirmed here in the lament, and desperately needed in our consumer-driven culture.

The creed that emerges from the lament has the sound of *shalom* in it:

> The LORD is good to those who wait for him,
>> to those who seek him. (v. 25)

That creed has within it a call to a new lifestyle for people who have been through the hell and high water of Babylon, 9/11, tsunamis, hurricanes, and anything else life throws at them:

> It is good that one should wait quietly
>> for the salvation of the LORD. (v. 26)

If, as Westermann states, "lamentation is a feature in the sequence of events leading from distress to deliverance,"[6] lament may be the one — even the only — way toward increasing our praise.

Roger E. Van Harn

---

6. Westermann, *Lamentations*, 94.

LUKE 1

Third Sunday of Advent, Year A
First Lesson: Isaiah 35:1-10
(Luke 1:47-55 or Psalm 146:5-10)
Second Lesson: James 5:7-10
Gospel Lesson: Matthew 11:2-11

Third Sunday of Advent, Year B
First Lesson: Isaiah 61:1-4, 8-11
(Psalm 126 or **Luke 1:47-55)**
Second Lesson: 1 Thessalonians 5:16-24
Gospel Lesson: John 1:6-8, 19-28

Fourth Sunday of Advent, Year B
First Lesson: 2 Samuel 7:1-11, 16
(Luke 1:47-55 or Psalm 89:1-4, 19-26)
Second Lesson: Romans 16:25-27
Gospel Lesson: Luke 1:26-38

Fourth Sunday of Advent, Year C
First Lesson: Micah 5:2-5a
(Luke 1:47-55 or Psalm 80:1-7)
Second Lesson: Hebrews 10:5-10
Gospel Lesson: Luke 1:39-45, (46-55)

Second Sunday of Advent, Year C
First Lesson: Malachi 3:1-4
(Luke 1:68-79)
Second Lesson: Philippians 1:3-11
Gospel Lesson: Luke 3:1-6

Christ the King, Year C
First Lesson: Jeremiah 23:1-6
(Luke 1:68-79)
Second Lesson: Colossians 1:11-20
Gospel Lesson: Luke 23:33-43

Mary's song of praise (Luke 1:46-55), commonly known as the Magnificat, appears during Advent in each three-year cycle of the Revised Common Lectionary. It is traditionally thought to be modeled after Hannah's song (1 Sam 2:1-10; see the essay on this lection in the present volume). Zechariah's song (Luke 1:68-79) is found twice in Year C, once during Advent and once on Christ the King Sunday. The consistent presentation of these songs right at the start and end of the liturgical year suggests their framing importance for our identity as Christian worshipers. As those to whom God's involvement in salvation history is revealed, we are called — with Mary and Zechariah — to celebrate the coming of the kingdom, to rejoice in the faithfulness of God.

Mary begins her song with perfect clarity about where her praise is directed. "My soul magnifies the Lord," she says, "and my spirit rejoices in God my Savior" (vv. 46-47). Mary recognizes that God's glory is becoming manifest in an unlikely place — in her very body, the body of a peasant woman. The lessons preceding the reading of Mary's song similarly name surprising places and ways in which God's glory is revealed: "the wilderness and dry land will rejoice and blossom" (Isa 35:1; Third Sunday of Advent, Year A); the "prisoners" will be "released" (Isa 61:1; Third Sunday of Advent, Year B); the tent, not the tabernacle, is the locus from which God speaks (2 Sam 7:1; Fourth Sunday of Advent, Year B); and "one of the little clans of Judah" will bring forth the "ruler of Israel" (Mic 5:2). Mary speaks for all who see the hand of God where it might not be expected. She leads us in responding, with joy, to the concrete manifestations of our salvation that are evident in our lives.

Mary's recognition of where and how God is acting has both a personal and a corporate dimension. "From now on all generations will call me blessed," she notes, marveling that the "Mighty One has done great things for me" (vv. 48-49) that will benefit the "generations" who receive God's mercy (vv. 48, 50). The "lowly" have been "lifted up" (v. 52); the "hungry" have been "fed" (v. 53); the nation of Israel has, as promised, been "helped" (v. 54). It cannot go unnoticed, of course, that these things have been accomplished as reversals of the normal pattern of affairs. For the lowly to be lifted, the powerful are brought down (v. 52). While the hungry are fed, the rich are "sent . . . away empty" (v. 53). The inbreaking of God on a corporate level, then, entails a judgment of systemic, as well as personal, sin. The coming of God's kingdom means radical reversals of the power structures that define our lives in this world. Liberation theologians and Roman Catholic moral theologians are among those who argue that, in this sense, God exercises a "preferential option for the poor." The posture of the Christian believer, then, as reflected in Mary's song, is not only to recognize that God works in unexpected ways, it is also to see that the unexpected ways in which God works consistently denounce oppressive uses of power and favor the marginalized who "fear" and serve God (vv. 50, 54).

Traditionally, Christian theology understands Mary to be the model Christian believer, the representative of the church. Along these same lines, the Magnificat itself may be read as a paradigmatic response of believing persons who (like Mary) are faithfully embracing their vocation, giving all credit to God even while recognizing their integral place in salvation history.

Zechariah's song (Luke 1:67-79), often called the Benedictus (because it is framed as a blessing of God, v. 68), shares many of the same themes as the Magnificat. Having been struck dumb by God for the duration of Elizabeth's pregnancy due to his lack of faith (see Luke 1:18-19), Zechariah confirms that his newborn son will be called "John," as God has instructed. Zechariah, filled with the Holy Spirit, is then enabled by God to prophesy in detail about the work of both Mary's child and John, "the prophet of the Most High" (v. 76). While Zechariah's response to the work of God does not, as does Mary's, highlight the reversals wrought by the inbreaking of the kingdom, it does share the same emphases on God's faithfulness to the people of Israel and salvation's coming to fruition. God has kept God's promises to the ancestors, rescuing God's people from their enemies (vv. 71-73). The people of God may now "serve God without fear" (v. 74), guided by "the light . . . from on high . . . into the way of peace" (vv. 78-79).

Zechariah's song elaborates on the specific roles of both the coming Savior and his son John, supporting the place of each in salvation history through reference to prophecy. John Calvin[1] notes the allusion, in verse 69, to Psalm 132:17, where the psalmist anticipates the "budding" of the "horn of David." He also points out that the song reflects knowledge of both Malachi and Isaiah, where the prophets look forward to the "dawn from on high" that will "break upon us" (v. 78; cf. Mal 4:2) and the "light" that will be given to "those who sit in darkness" (v. 79; cf. Isa 9:2).

As Jonathan Knight points out, Zechariah's Benedictus reflects a "high evaluation" of John as well as of the coming Savior: "'What then will this child become?' the neighbors of Elizabeth and Zechariah ask in

---

1. John Calvin, *Commentary on a Harmony of the Evangelists, Matthew, Mark, and Luke,* trans. William Pringle (Grand Rapids: Eerdmans, 1949), on Luke 1:76-80.

verse 66. The answer is clear in Zechariah's response: John is the one who ushers in the 'age of salvation.' The *Benedictus* [thus] makes the point that, although the full realization of the eschatological hope still lies in the future, 'knowledge of salvation' (1.77) is present already."[2] In this way the Benedictus resembles the inference made in verse 48 of the Magnificat, where Mary speaks of what will be true "from now on." Joseph A. Fitzmyer notes that Mary's phrase, typical of Luke, "refers to the coming inauguration of a new age of salvation."[3]

In Year C, when Zechariah's song is used as a response both to the question, "who can endure the day of his coming?" (Mal 3:1-4; Second Sunday of Advent), and to the promise that God will "raise up shepherds" to care for the flock (Jer 23:1-6; Christ the King), it will be especially fruitful for worship leaders to remind the people that our salvation is at once both ever-on-the-way and ever-present, both ever-challenging and ever-reassuring. As disciples of the Word who both *has become* and *will become* flesh, we are called to be ever-watchful for the coming of Christ even as we simultaneously live with the confidence that he is surely with us "always, to the end of the age" (Matt 28:20). With Zechariah and Mary, we are called to engage in expressions of faith even as we seek to discern where and how God is entering our world.

Cynthia L. Rigby

---

2. Jonathan Knight, *Luke's Gospel* (London: Routledge, 1998), 75.

3. Joseph A. Fitzmyer, *The Gospel according to Luke: Introduction, Translation, and Notes*, 2 vols., AB 28-28A (New York: Doubleday, 1981-85), 1:367.

PART II

WORSHIP WITH THE PSALMS

This section of the volume appears in a slightly expanded form in a previous publication, *The Biblical Psalms in Christian Worship: A Brief Introduction and Guide to Resources* (Grand Rapids: Eerdmans, 2007).

An Introduction and Guide to Resources

JOHN D. WITVLIET

The two parts of this book are designed to be mutually interactive. Preaching from the Psalms will increase the likelihood of using the Psalms in worship, and worship with the Psalms is likely to increase the hunger to hear preaching and teaching from the Psalms. That hope arises in the context of three observations.

First, the Psalms are a font of inspiration, encouragement, and instruction in the life of both public and private prayer. From Basil to Bonhoeffer to Bono, the enthusiasm that emanates from wise Christian writers of every historical period points to the Psalms as one of the richest sources of wisdom for the practice of worship and to the indispensability of the thoughtful use of the Psalms in the practice of worship.

Second, there is relatively tepid enthusiasm for the Psalms in worship throughout vast stretches of North American Christianity. This is the bad news. One can often find great enthusiasm for a particular musical or dramatic setting of a psalm, but relatively little interest in promoting a sustained program of publicly praying the Psalms (though there are notable exceptions). Many churches do use lectionary-based psalms each week, but often they are rendered without enthusiasm or understanding.

Most often, those who dismiss the Psalms associate them with music they don't like, usually by mistakenly assuming that psalmody necessarily entails either overly sumptuous Victorian choral harmonies, dirgelike chorales, sentimental folk music, or inaccessible chant. The good news is that in addition to the exegetical essays on the Psalms and hymnic lections in part I, the present volume, in part II, catalogues hundreds of worship resources in many spoken, musical, and visual idioms —

so much so that nearly everyone will find resources here they will both love and hate. The last thirty years have witnessed an outpouring of creativity! The problem is that these resources are not often used in a consistent way that encourages deep participation in worship. We live in a time of both need and opportunity in the practice of worship in general, but particularly with respect to the role of the Psalms in worship.

Third, we have unprecedented access to vast amounts of information about the Psalms, as well as copious resources for using them in worship. Taking into account all commentaries, introductions, devotionals, musical settings, and historical studies, there are now over three thousand volumes on the Psalms in print, in addition to thousands of Web sites. One goal of part II is to provide an orientation to this material. The quality of a good deal of this material is heartening. The challenge is putting this material to good use for the sake of the church.

Aims and Audiences

In the light of these observations, this section of the book is designed to be a catalyst for a renewed engagement with the Psalms in the context of public worship. The goal here is to both promote and discipline the creativity we bring to praying the Psalms in community. With this goal in mind, I do not aim to provide a summary of all possible themes related to the Psalms, but rather to highlight those themes that bear especially on their use in worship. Specifically, I gather up insights from and provide some orientation to four bodies of literature that are often disconnected from each other:

- biblical scholarship on the Old Testament and Hebrew Bible;
- writings on the history, theology, and pastoral practice of worship, liturgy, and preaching;
- writings on the history and practice of church music; and
- currently available liturgical and musical resources.

Given the complexity of each body of material, I am very aware of how difficult it is to present a fair and balanced account of each, especially in a relatively short space. Each of these four bodies of literature draws different kinds of readers and audiences. For these reasons, and others, I have tried to write with an awareness of a very broad ecumenical range of practices, including: lectionary-based psalmody in Roman Catholic, Anglican, Lutheran, Methodist, and Presbyterian sources; Presbyterian and Reformed metrical psalmody; and the growing use of the Psalter in evangelical, Pentecostal, charismatic, and emerging worship traditions.

I begin with a vivid awareness of what radically different practices come to mind when readers across this spectrum of Christianity think about the Psalms in worship. Some readers will come from churches whose liturgy and music are quite fixed, liturgical, and well established.

Other readers will come from congregations that pour enormous resources into creative worship expressions, generating new songs, dramatic scripts, video clips, and other elements of worship on a regular basis. Perhaps the majority of readers will come from congregations with limited resources for worship, in terms of preparation time, musical or artistic talent, and collaborative planning processes.

Whatever the case, it has occurred to me that nearly every reader will find some of what follows to be a bit perplexing! Preachers who do not use, or are not aware of, the lectionary may not realize its value. Lectionary users may not realize how much of the Psalms they are missing in worship. Congregations that chant psalms do not often read material about praise choruses. Congregations in the emerging-church movement may not be aware of the outpouring of recent music in multiple musical styles for responsorial psalmody. Congregations with quite formal worship may not have considered using a speech choir alongside an "anthem choir." Congregations with informal worship may not have considered the value of careful study of the texts for public reading or singing. All of this means that readers will use this material in remarkably different ways, depending on where they find themselves on the broad Christian landscape.

The breadth of the intended audience has led me to a different approach than some volumes on this topic. In contrast to earlier volumes, a more topical approach seemed a wiser route, with historical examples interspersed occasionally throughout.

There are also inevitable limitations to the ecumenical scope of any volume. For example, this volume does not address in detail the role of psalmody in Orthodox worship, in monastic worship, or in worship in the global South and East. Further, this book focuses primarily on a congregation's weekly assembly for worship. I acknowledge and celebrate the tradition of daily public prayer that has provided the most regular setting for psalmody in many Christian traditions. I am eager to promote the recovery of public daily prayer, with copious psalm singing.[1] But for the majority of congregations in North America, the primary focus for worship renewal remains the weekly (usually Sunday) assembly of the church.

This ecumenical approach has some downsides. The space here does not allow me to speak to the specifics of the liturgical use of the Psalms in any particular tradition or permit me to speak in a sustained way about inclusive language translations, and so on and so forth. But an ecumenical approach also has some decided advantages. The Psalms encompass both sides of some of the most striking divisions within Christian communities today. They speak of both social justice and personal transformation; they embody hand-clapping exuberance and profound introspection; they express the prayers of the exalted and the lowly; they are fully alive in the present but always point to the future; they highlight the extravagance of grace and the joy of faithful obedience; they express a restless yearning for change and a profound gratitude for the inheritance of faith; they protest ritualism but embody the richest expression of ritual prayer. It is little wonder then that any journey into literature on the Psalms will quite quickly lead us to materials produced by many different people of many different persuasions and emphases.

A temptation that results from this situation is that we all have a bit of the Psalms to latch on to, regardless of our confessional identity or personal idiosyncrasies, and that we leave the rest aside. But the psalms in their richness offer each community and each believer — regardless of stance — an opportunity to work their weak sides, to develop habits and modes of prayer that do not come naturally.

The Psalms and the Basic Grammar of Christian Worship

Learning to talk is one of life's greatest miracles. But even for toddlers, healthy speech habits don't come naturally. "I love you." "I'm sorry." "Thank you." "Help." Words and phrases like these are the building

---

1. See, for example, Dorothy C. Bass, *Receiving the Day: Christian Practices for Opening the Gift of Time* (San Francisco: Jossey-Bass, 2000), 22-24, and Arthur Paul Boers, *The Rhythm of God's Grace: Uncovering Morning and Evening Hours of Prayer* (Brewster, Mass.: Paraclete, 2003).

blocks of healthy relationships. Every close relationship depends on them. When they are left unpracticed, marriages fail and friendships disintegrate. Faithful speech is also central to the Christian life. One of the most provocative and inspiring word pictures in all of Scripture is that God is related to the church like a marriage partner. The God of the Bible is not just interested in being contemplated or appeased. This God is interested in the give-and-take of faithful life together, with good communication right at the center of it. Ample evidence for this claim is the Bible's songbook, the 150 psalms, each of which expresses at least one essential communication habit for a people in a covenant relationship with God.

One of the ways we learn good communication habits with God is by participating in public worship. When we gather for worship, the church invites us to join together to say to God, "We love you. We're sorry. Come again — we're listening. Help. Thank you. I will serve you." In fact, some orders of worship pretty much follow this pattern, ensuring a healthy, balanced diet of faithful speech. To use a phrase from Thomas G. Long's recent book *Testimony,* worship is God's "language school." As Long explains:

> The way we talk in worship affects the way we talk in the rest of our lives, and vice versa. . . . The words of worship are like stones thrown into the pond; they ripple outward in countless concentric circles, finding ever fresh expression in new places in our lives. . . . Worship is a key element in the church's "language school" for life. . . . It's a provocative idea — worship as a soundtrack for the rest of life, the words and music and actions of worship inside the sanctuary playing the background as we live our lives outside, in the world.[2]

As with toddlers, these speech habits take practice. But the discipline is worth it, forming us over time to express our deepest fears, hopes, and joys in profound ways.

The challenge is that on any given Sunday, each of us comes to church with something different to say. To put it another way, some of us

2. Thomas G. Long, *Testimony: Talking Ourselves into Being Christian* (San Francisco: Jossey-Bass, 2004), 47-48. Long also suggests: "When a congregation every single Sunday of the year sings the psalms, they acquire a vocabulary that touches the raw nerve of every possible human emotion but always comes unfailingly around to praise. In doing so, they are worshiping, but they are also in training to know how to speak when out in the world: candidly and honestly, but never cynically or despairingly" (33).

come ready to sing Psalm 100 ("thank you"), others Psalm 13 ("why?"), and all us, if we're honest, need to speak Psalm 51 ("I'm sorry"). Good worship services make room for these essential words. They help each of us express our particular experience, but they also help us practice forms of speech we're still growing into. This is one reason public worship is so important — it challenges us to practice forms of faithful speech to God that we are not likely to try on our own. Authentic worship expresses who we are and forms what we are becoming.

The biblical psalms are the foundational mentor and guide in this vocabulary and grammar for worship. In a provocative and inspiring book, Eugene Peterson speaks of the Psalms as the tools God has given us to form in us a vibrant and well-grounded faith: "the Psalms are necessary because they are the prayer masters. . . . We apprentice ourselves to these masters, acquiring facility in using the tools, by which we become more and more ourselves. If we are willfully ignorant of the Psalms, we are not thereby excluded from praying, but we will have to hack our way through formidable country by trial and error and with inferior tools."[3]

Indeed, the Psalter of the Hebrew Scriptures is the foundational and paradigmatic prayer book of the Christian church. Time and time again, worshiping communities have returned to the Psalter for inspiration and instruction in the life of both personal and public prayer. Some of the most auspicious liturgical reform movements in church history — including those of sixth-century monastic communities, the sixteenth-century Lutherans and Calvinists, and the twentieth-century liturgical movement — have called for a renewed appreciation for the liturgical possibilities of the Psalter.[4] Early African American expressions of Christian worship were known for "a kind of extatic Delight in Psalmody,"[5] and the Psalms are also pervasive in the context of recent black gospel mu-

---

3. Eugene Peterson, *Answering God: The Psalms as Tools for Prayer* (San Francisco: Harper and Row, 1989), 4.

4. For a fascinating history on the use of the Psalter, see William Holladay, *The Psalms through Three Thousand Years* (Minneapolis: Fortress, 1993).

5. Rev. Samual Davies, letter of 1755, in Eileen Southern, ed., *Readings in Black American Music* (New York: Norton, 1983), 27-28. For further discussion, see Melva Wilson Costen, *In Spirit and in Truth: The Music of African American Worship* (Louisville: Westminster John Knox, 2004), 34, 48, 141; Christopher Small, *Music of the Common Tongue: Survival and Celebration in African American Music* (Hanover, N.H.: Wesleyan University Press, 1987), chap. 3; and several references indexed in Eileen Southern, *The Music of Black Americans: A History,* 3rd ed. (New York: Norton, 1997).

sic.[6] If we want to better understand the DNA of the Christian faith and to deepen our worship, there are few better places to begin than with careful and prayerful engagement with the Psalms.

At root, this conviction arises from the place of the Psalms within the canon of Scripture. The Psalms, like all Scripture, are "inspired by God and [are] useful for teaching, for reproof, for correction, and for training in righteousness, so that everyone who belongs to God may be proficient, equipped for every good work" (2 Tim 3:16-17). The words of the Psalter are reliable and trustworthy, though, to be sure, they are challenging and even perplexing. For several commentators throughout the history of the church, this conviction suggested that praying the Psalms was one of the best ways to pray "in the Spirit" (Eph 6:18; Jude 20). Indeed, when we pray these texts we are, in a profound if elusive sense, praying the words the Spirit has given us. In the words of Thomas Merton, "Nowhere can we be more certain that we are praying with the Holy Spirit than when we pray the Psalms."[7] In John Calvin's words, when the Psalms are sung, "we are certain that God has put the words in our mouths as if they themselves sang in us to exalt his glory."[8]

Yet the church has not always been a good steward of the Psalms as liturgical prayer. For one, we are often guilty of speaking the strange words of a lament or enthronement psalm without serious attempts to help worshipers understand what they are saying. Here we might be helped by John Cassian's ancient advice that it might be "better to sing ten verses with a modicum of comprehension than to pour out the whole psalm with a distracted mind."[9] For another, we often render the Psalms in remarkably unimaginative ways. Over three generations ago, Earle Bennet Cross contended: "it is deplorable to waste the art and beauty of the Psalms on the desert air of systems of responsive readings which bore so many congregations to somnolence."[10] This critique is as relevant today as then.

Thoughtful, prayerful use of the Psalms in both public worship and personal devotion requires theological poise, pastoral perception, and ar-

---

6. Glenn Hinson, *Fire in My Bones: Transcendence and the Holy Spirit in African American Gospel* (Philadelphia: University of Pennsylvania Press, 2000), 46-48.

7. Thomas Merton, *Praying the Psalms* (Collegeville, Minn.: Liturgical Press, 1956), 18.

8. See Ford Lewis Battles, "John Calvin: The Form of Prayers and Songs of the Church," *CTJ* 15 (1980): 160-65.

9. John Cassian, *The Institutes*, trans. Boniface Ramsey, ACW 58 (New York: Newman Press, 2000), 44 (II.XI).

10. Earle Bennet Cross, *Modern Worship and the Psalter* (New York: Macmillan, 1932).

tistic imagination — all grounded in the texts themselves. So before studying practical options for reading, singing, and praying the Psalms in worship, it is valuable to pause and consider the way the Psalms form us for prayer. The Psalms teach us what faith-filled prayer looks like. They provide what might be called the deep grammar or the paradigmatic structure for Christian prayer.[11]

In what follows, I outline seven lessons the Psalms teach us about prayer. In each case, I briefly describe the lesson and then point to examples of how that lesson is reflected in Christian worship practices. Indeed, the Psalms reflect an ancient, biblical way of praying that continues to shape Christian worship, even when the Psalms themselves are not used. Understanding the nature of that formation will help us both deepen our practice of worship generally and be better stewards of the Psalms themselves.

Lesson One:
Personal Address and Dialogic Structure

First, the biblical psalms teach us that prayer and worship are not monologues. Rather, in the memorable words of Augustine, Benedict, Cassian, and Calvin, prayer is a "conversation with God."[12] The Psalms themselves are often scripts of conversations. Often they express prayer, words *to* God. At other times they depict proclamation, words *from* God. In a few psalms petitions seem to alternate with oracles.[13] Psalm 12, for example, begins with the plea: "Help, O LORD, for there is no longer anyone who is godly." This plea is interrupted by what many think is an oracle: "Because the poor are despoiled, . . . I will rise up, says the LORD." This alter-

11. This is roughly similar to the point made by Thomas F. Torrance, that the "basic patterns of worship which we find set out in the ancient liturgy or in the Psalms" are one of the "permanent structures of thought and speech" about God mediated first to Israel (*The Mediation of Christ* [Grand Rapids: Eerdmans, 1983], 28).

12. See John Calvin, *Institutes of the Christian Religion,* ed. John T. McNeill, trans. Ford Lewis Battles, LCC 20-21 (Philadelphia: Westminster, 1960), 3.20.4, and the accompanying note. See also Patrick D. Miller, *They Cried to the Lord: The Form and Theology of Biblical Prayer* (Minneapolis: Fortress, 1994), 33; Samuel E. Balentine, *Prayer in the Hebrew Bible,* OBT (Minneapolis: Fortress, 1993), 261-64; Luis Alonso Schökel, *A Manual of Hebrew Poetics* (Rome: Editrice Pontificio Istituto Biblico, 1988), 170-79.

13. Though this has been debated. See the introduction to part I in the present volume.

nation of speakers depicts what Raymond Jacques Tournay has called the "prophetic liturgy of the temple."[14] The Psalms teach us, to use Walter Brueggemann's phrase, that "biblical faith is uncompromisingly and unembarrassedly dialogical."[15] This, in turn, reflects the larger pattern of covenant reciprocity that undergirds large portions of both Old and New Testaments. There is nothing impersonal about biblical faith, and nothing impersonal about biblical worship. Worship is more than mere contemplation of timeless truth, it is a personal encounter between God and the gathered congregation. We can think of it as the exchange of messages between God and the community of faith.

This understanding of worship as interpersonal encounter is a frequently used metaphor for Christian liturgy across traditions. Orthodox, Catholic, and Protestant liturgical theologians have all been known to speak of liturgy as dialogue, as the mutual exchange between God and the community of believers, mediated through the forms of human speech, visual arts, and music. In worship, we speak to God through prayers, including sung prayers, and in our offerings. In worship, God also speaks to us, through the reading and preaching of Scripture, including the readings of Scripture that function as calls to worship, words of assurance, and benedictions. God also works to assure and challenge us through songs and artworks, testimonies and greetings. In worship, God speaks to us and we speak to God.

Lesson Two:
Identifying God's Character through
Metaphor and Historical Recitation

Second, Hebrew prayer is addressed to a specific and known God rather than an amorphous divine being. As Brueggemann points out, "Israel's prayer consists in the utterance of 'you,' addressed to a named, known, addressable, reachable You."[16] This is a particular God, Yahweh, whom Christians identify further as the God of Jesus Christ.

The Psalms specify God's character in at least two ways. First, they

14. Raymond Jacques Tournay, *Seeing and Hearing God with the Psalms: The Prophetic Liturgy of the Second Temple in Jerusalem* (Sheffield: JSOT Press, 1991).

15. Walter Brueggemann, "From Hurt to Joy, from Death to Life," in Brueggemann, *The Psalms and the Life of Faith*, ed. Patrick D. Miller (Minneapolis: Fortress, 1995), 68.

16. Walter Brueggemann, "The Psalms as Prayer," in *The Psalms and the Life of Faith*, 37.

draw on a large range of metaphors to speak about God. In the words of William P. Brown, "a storehouse of metaphors both target the deity and tease the reader. In the judicial area, God is judge, advocate, scribe, and bounty hunter, as well as attacker. From a more personal poignant standpoint, God is guide and partner, as well as sun, weaver, and procreator. . . . Yet for all the iconic characteristics ascribed to the divine, the Psalmist . . . never loses sight of God's unattainable transcendence."[17]

By definition metaphors "both lie and tell the truth." By comparison they illuminate at least one aspect of divine character. But not every aspect of each metaphor is significant or illuminating. For example, calling God "a rock" implies that God is steadfast and faithful, but not lifeless. Naming God as almighty speaks of divine capacity for action, but does not entail that God is ruthless in the exercise of power.[18]

One salient feature of these metaphors is their sheer number and range. The Psalms speak of God as the king, the Lord of Hosts, mighty one, but also as shepherd, refuge, "my light," and portion. These metaphors complement and correct each other to depict a God with vast power, but a God who often deploys this power in surprisingly tender ways.

A Sampling of Names for God in the Psalms

(Several of these forms of address are used multiple times in Scripture, but only one Scripture reference has been listed for each.)

O God of my right (Ps 4:1)
My king and my God (Ps 5:2)
O Lord my God (Ps 7:1)
O righteous God (Ps 7:9)
Lord, the Most High (Ps 7:17)

---

17. William P. Brown, *Seeing the Psalms: A Theology of Metaphor* (Louisville: Westminster John Knox, 2002), 212. See also Leland Ryken, "Metaphor in the Psalms," *ChrLit* 31 (1982): 9-30, and Barbara P. Green, O.P., *Like a Tree Planted: An Exploration of Psalms and Parables through Metaphor* (Collegeville, Minn.: Liturgical Press, 1997).

18. For more on metaphor, see Mark Searle, "Liturgy as Metaphor," in "Language and Metaphor," a theme issue of *Liturgy: Journal of the Liturgical Conference* 4, no. 4 (1985); Gail Ramshaw, *Christ in Sacred Speech* (Philadelphia: Fortress, 1986); Ramshaw, *Liturgical Language: Keeping It Metaphoric, Making It Inclusive* (Collegeville, Minn.: Liturgical Press, 1996); Janet Soskice, *Metaphor and Religious Language* (Oxford: Clarendon, 1965); and John D. Witvliet, "Metaphor in Liturgical Studies: Lessons from Philosophical and Theological Theories of Language," *Liturgy Digest* 4 (1997): 7-45.

O LORD, our Sovereign (Ps 8:1)
My rock (Ps 28:1)
God of Israel (Ps 41:13)
LORD God of hosts (Ps 59:5)
God of our salvation (Ps 65:5)
O Holy One of Israel (Ps 71:22)
O Shepherd of Israel (Ps 80:1)
God of vengeance (Ps 94:1)
Judge of the earth (Ps 94:2)
Mighty King (Ps 99:4)
Lover of justice (Ps 99:4)
A shield around me (Ps 3:3)
My glory (Ps 3:3)
A righteous judge (Ps 7:11)
King (Ps 10:16)
Rock (Ps 18:2)
Fortress (Ps 18:2)
Deliverer (Ps 18:2)
Horn of my salvation (Ps 18:2)
Stronghold (Ps 18:2)
Redeemer (Ps 19:14)
Shepherd (Ps 23:1)
God of Jacob (Ps 24:6)
King of glory (Ps 24:7-10)
God of glory (Ps 29:3)
LORD of hosts (Ps 24:10)
God of my salvation (Ps 25:5)
My light (Ps 27:1)
My salvation (Ps 27:1)
My strength/strength of his people (Ps 28:7-8)
Saving refuge of his anointed (Ps 28:8)
Help in trouble (Ps 46:1)
Helper (Ps 54:4)
Mighty one (Ps 50:1)
Upholder of my life (Ps 54:4)
Refuge (Ps 62:8)
God of Sinai (Ps 68:8)
Almighty (Ps 68:14)
Mighty one of Jacob (Ps 132:2)

Hope (Ps 71:5)
Trust (Ps 71:5)
Portion (Ps 73:26)
Merciful and gracious (Ps 86:15)
Father (Ps 89:26)
Great God (Ps 95:3)
Great King above all gods (Ps 95:3)
Maker (Ps 95:6)
Lord of all the earth (Ps 97:5)
Keeper (Ps 121:5)
Shade at your right hand (Ps 121:5)
God of gods (Ps 136:2)
Lord of lords (Ps 136:3)
God of heaven (Ps 136:26)

Second, the Psalms specify the divine character by rehearsing God's deeds in history. Large portions of Hebrew prayer are devoted to telling God what God already knows, what God has done in history. This act of remembrance has the function of more than merely telling a story. It also gives identity and specificity to the God who is addressed in prayer, and, correspondingly, to the people who pray.[19] The historical psalms, such as Psalm 105, are certainly paradigmatic examples of this. Yet this specificity of address and recital of God's deeds can be observed widely in other texts as well.[20] Both psalms of lament and psalms of praise rehearse the acts of God in history. In lament, the psalmist recites history to petition God to be faithful to that same history (see Pss 85 and 89). In praise, particularly declarative praise, the psalmist names the specific acts of God that elicit thankfulness (see Pss 66; 116; 118; and 138). Especially important is the preposition "for" (Hebrew *kî*), which signals the listing of specific acts of God (Pss 30:2; 116:2; 138:2). God's saving work in the exodus is particularly significant, especially in Psalms 77, 78, 105, 106, and 114. Psalmic praise teaches us to render praise *for* something in particular to a God who has acted in particular, historical ways.

This literary feature corresponds with a central theological theme in many definitions of Christian worship. A chorus of voices gives testimony

19. This is a much discussed concept among liturgical scholars. See also Brevard Childs, *Memory and Tradition in Israel,* SBT (London: SCM, 1962).
20. Robert Alter, *The Art of Biblical Poetry* (New York: Basic Books, 1985), 39.

to this central theme. Roman Catholic systematic theologian Catherine Mowry LaCugna argues, for example, that "The trinitarian character of Christian liturgy is to be sought and located in the fact that liturgy, by definition, is the ritual celebration of the events of the economy of redemption and as such is the celebration of the mystery of God."[21] John Burkhart posits that "true worship celebrates the most definite God of the covenant in Moses and Jesus, the God of Abraham, Isaac, and Jacob, of Sarah, Rebekah, and Rachel, and of countless others. Fundamentally, worship is the celebrative response to what God has done, is doing, and promises to do."[22] Nicholas Wolterstorff concurs: "A striking feature of the Christian liturgy is that it is focused not just on God's nature but on God's actions; and more specifically, on actions which took place in historical time."[23] The rehearsal of God's actions in history is commonly accepted as a fundamental component of Christian liturgy.

This point can be cast in boldest relief by contrasting narrative worship with some alternatives. Worship oriented to God's actions in history stands in contrast with ahistorical mystical introspection that seeks an experience of God apart from historical time, and often posits a God beyond the divine economy. Commenting on mysticism in the interpretation of Paul, Lewis Smedes argues that "oriental mysticism could not tolerate dependence on specific historical events or concrete historical personalities. The one thing people need is to escape the concrete things of history and to be immersed into the divine life. . . . Mysticism and history were incompatible as foundations of religion."[24] Donald Bloesch distinguishes ahistorical mysticism from acts of meditation that are "centered on the works and acts of God not only in creation but also and

21. Catherine Mowry LaCugna, "Trinity and Liturgy," in *The New Dictionary of Sacramental Worship,* ed. Peter E. Fink (Collegeville, Minn.: Liturgical Press, 1990), 1293-96; and also "Making the Most of Trinity Sunday," *Worship* 60 (1986): 211.

22. John E. Burkhart, *Worship* (Philadelphia: Westminster, 1982), 17, 31-33.

23. Nicholas Wolterstorff, "The Remembrance of Things (Not) Past: Philosophical Reflections on Christian Liturgy," in *Christian Philosophy,* ed. Thomas P. Flint (Notre Dame, Ind.: University of Notre Dame Press, 1990), 128. Wolterstorff suggests that the absence of commemoration-memorializing in Christian liturgy likely signals the influence of "immediately experiential, or abstractly theological or ethical, approaches to God" (142). He points out that Immanuel Kant believed both that God could not act in history and that traditional liturgy would fade away because it was so bound up with remembrance of God acting in history.

24. Lewis Smedes, *Union with Christ: A Biblical View of New Life in Christ* (Grand Rapids: Eerdmans, 1983), 28.

preeminently in Jesus Christ."[25] Any time you hear advice about how prayer "helps us live into the present and escape the past," know that you are leaving the world of psalmic prayer.

This historical emphasis also stands in contrast with worship practices that merely celebrate nature and nature's annual cycles. Adrio König stresses that ancient Israel changed its calendar of feasts from one "linked with nature, into one which was tied to history," and thus transformed what had been celebrations of natural cycles into celebrations of historical events. König argues that this shift in cultic practice corresponded to the theological commitment to conceive of God on the basis of God's action in history.[26] Christians have inherited this historically oriented pattern of liturgy. Christian worship is rooted in history: it is offered to a God who is conceived and named as an agent involved in particular historical events.

In Christian liturgy the act of remembrance by a recital of God's specific deeds is nowhere more clear than in the emerging eucharistic prayers of the second and third centuries. In Justin Martyr's description of early Eucharist, we are told that "the president . . . sends up prayers and thanksgivings to the best of his ability."[27] A key element in the desired charism was the ability to adequately recite the full range of God's deeds in history. Soon, in formalized and prescribed liturgical texts, the prayer of thanksgiving at Eucharist consisted largely of an extended recital of God's deeds.

This historical precedent has encouraged modern-day liturgists to renew appreciation for the structures that accent the narrative recital of God's deeds in history: the Christian year as narrative portrayal of salvation history, baptismal and eucharistic prayers that resemble the narrative prayers of the early church, and narrative hymns that recount and extol specific acts of God in creation, redemption, and sanctification.[28]

25. Donald Bloesch, *The Struggle of Prayer* (San Francisco: Harper and Row, 1980), 21.

26. Adrio König, *Here Am I: A Christian Reflection on God* (Grand Rapids: Eerdmans, 1982), 124, 171.

27. See Leslie William Barnard, *St. Justin Martyr: The First and Second Apologies*, ACW 56 (New York: Paulist, 1997), 71 (par. 67). See also Allan Bouley, O.S.B., *From Freedom to Formula: The Evolution of the Eucharistic Prayer from Oral Improvisation to Written Texts* (Washington, D.C.: Catholic University of America Press, 1981).

28. The recovery of a full anamnesis in the baptismal and eucharistic prayers has been a central feature in recent liturgical reform. See, for example, *The Book of Common Worship* (Louisville: Westminster John Knox, 1993), 39, 42-43, 69-70, 410.

In each of these ways Christian liturgy extends a particular pattern of prayer prominent in the Psalter. Whether we lament or praise, we specify the God to whom our prayers are directed by offering biblically grounded names and metaphors for God and naming particular historical deeds our God has enacted. We identify God, we might say, by both nouns and verbs, and thus point to God of both presence and action.

Lesson Three:
The Ebb, Flow, and Fittingness of
Praise and Petition, Gratitude and Lament

Third, psalmic prayer teaches us how to link our praise and petition in fitting ways. Patrick D. Miller makes the theological point as follows: "prayer is consistent with the will of God as it seeks something that is consistent with divine nature."[29] Thus, the cry for mercy in Psalm 130:1 ("Out of the depths I cry to you, O LORD") is dependent upon the assertion "but with you there is forgiveness" in verse 4. Psalm 68's urgent plea for God to "summon your might" (v. 28) follows the praise of God for similar actions in the past. Psalm 68:28, in fact, is a key to unlock the logic of vast portions of the Psalter: "show us your strength, O God, *as you have done before*." Petition is always grounded in praise. Prayers for God's future work begin with a look into the past.

This has served as a reliable pattern for Christian liturgical prayer as well. Petitions or laments are right and fitting if they can be placed in the context of praise that addresses corresponding characteristics of God. Just as Israel, in Brueggemann's words, "prays God's character back to God, insists that Yahweh be who Yahweh asserted God's own self to be, and reminds Yahweh that Yahweh can be 'no other God,'"[30] so too Christian liturgical prayer looks for ways, in Miller's words, to "ground the petition in the character of God."[31] A clear example of this can be found in the Collect prayer form.[32]

29. Miller, *They Cried*, 321.

30. Brueggemann, "The Psalms as Prayer," 47.

31. Miller, *They Cried*, 381 n. 44. Jean-Jacques von Allmen makes the same point: "it is part of the theological meaning of common prayer that it should be controlled by what we know of God's will revealed in Jesus Christ" ("The Theological Meaning of Common Prayer," *Studia Liturgica* 10 [1974-76]: 129).

32. For an excellent introduction to the history of this prayer form, see A. Corrêa,

A simple Collect has four distinct parts to it. First, we *address* God and sometimes *embellish* our calling upon God. For example, a simple address would be "O God"; an address with an embellishment might be "O living and loving God." Second, we say something about God; in prayer language this is called an "attribute." For example, at Christmas dinner we might say, "O living and loving God, you sent your only Son to become one like us." Third, we tell God our needs and ask for God's action, usually expressing a desired result; for example, at Christmas dinner we might say, "Bless this food so that we might be strengthened to bring the light of your Son Jesus to all we meet." Finally, we Christians always pray to the Father through Christ, so we always add this or a similar statement called the statement of *mediation:* "We ask this (or: Grant this) through Christ our Lord," and finally conclude the prayer with "Amen."

The Collect form itself, so intimately tied to the poetic qualities of the Latin language, may not be the form of choice for all English-speaking Christians. But neither should it be set aside as a source of instruction. Indeed, the basic pattern of the Collect is even part of colloquial speech. A sentence like "Ron, you're good at handling technology, would you scan and e-mail this document to someone, so that we can prepare for our meeting successfully?" contains most of the key parts of Collect prayer.[33]

So, the lesson of fittingness ought to remain. Like the prayers of the Psalms, the crucial and defining aspect of a given prayer involves both the particular petition that is offered and the way in which God is blessed. The crucial relative clause in the Collect that follows the opening address, just like the psalmic participial phrases that specify God's character, serves to ground petition in praise.

At the same time, none of this should be buttoned down too tightly. The fit between praise and petition does not mean that there is always symmetry between them. Rather, in the Psalms, as in daily life, our prayers ebb and flow between praise and lament, gratitude and intercession. Steven Chase speaks of this dynamic in his extended study on prayer:

The Durham Collectar, Henry Bradshaw Society 107 (London, 1991), and *The Collect in Anglican Liturgy: Texts and Sources, 1549-1989* (Collegeville, Minn.: Liturgical Press, 1994). See also Louis Weil, *Gathered to Pray: Understanding Liturgical Prayer* (Cambridge: Cowley, 1986), 27-58.

33. Thanks to Clay Schmit and Ron Rienstra for this example.

Conversation in prayer expands, taking on new meaning and dimension, when we realize, for instance, that adoration implies confession of who we are in relation to God and who God is in relation to the world. In a similar way, praise enters conversation with intercession as we begin to see that what we praise God for can become what we ask for on behalf of others. A petitionary prayer becomes a prayer of thanksgiving as we give thanks in faith, believing that what we ask for will be granted. A thanksgiving prayer becomes a petition as our awareness expands to understand that God's gifts are precisely in line with our needs. As modeled in the Psalms, adoration and praise seem to be intimate partners of lament. And as lament makes its painful arc back to adoration, we begin to see verbal prayer not only as rhythmic but also as a continuum on the circle of conversation.[34]

As we ponder the Psalms, then, as well as our own public worship life, one dynamic to attend to is the movement among these modes of prayer, and the profound ways that each mode of prayer shapes the others.

Lesson Four:
Individual and Communal Speech

The Psalms teach us the simultaneous distinction and integration of corporate and individual prayer. The balanced life of prayer is not only "I pray" or "we pray"; it is both. The Psalter has both personal and communal laments, both personal vows of praise and communal hymns of praise. The two distinct genres of individual and communal prayer remind us that no need is too personal nor is any reason for praise too expansive to be gathered up in prayer.

More profoundly still, the Psalms teach us that even prayers offered in the first-person singular are not always soliloquies. "I psalms" often express the sentiments not of an isolated poet, but rather of the entire nation of Israel (e.g., 25:22; 130). They are expressions of a corporate personality that is a hallmark of the faith of Israel and a challenge to any culture marked by individualism.

Likewise, Christian prayer is both personal and communal, each

---

34. Steven Chase, *The Tree of Life: Models of Christian Prayer* (Grand Rapids: Baker Academic, 2005), 95.

with its own characteristics. Liturgical prayer is not individual prayer offered in a public space. It is qualitatively different.[35] Public prayer emphasizes the communal nature — the corporate personality — of the congregation. Like individual prayer, public prayer specifically names the particular pleas of individuals but accents the corporate dimensions of those concerns.[36] Public prayer challenges individual Christians to think of ways to pray vicariously, on behalf of and in the words of another. Then also, public prayer always views the world through a wide-angle lens. Ideally, the needs and hopes and fears of all sorts of people, and races, and cultures are gathered together in corporate prayer.[37]

Part of this expansive vision comes through the use of the Psalms themselves. The ancient cadences of this language challenge us when we use them as contemporary prayer, precisely because of their ancient, almost timeless feel. The Psalter is like a cathedral in words. Praying the Psalms challenges us to stretch our internal horizons to sense our solidarity with those who prayed these words over three thousand years ago.

Theologian David Ford has developed this theme in a particularly compelling way:

> [T]he Psalmist's "I" accommodates a vast congregation of individuals and groups down the centuries around the world today. They are all somehow embraced in this "I." A vast array of stories, situations, sufferings, blessings, joys and deaths have been read and prayed into the Psalms by those who have identified with their first person. It amounts to an extraordinarily capacious and hospitable "I." . . . It is a feature of good liturgical texts that they allow large numbers of diverse people to identify themselves through them. The liturgical "I" suggests a conception of selfhood, in line with earlier chapters, which

35. See Paul F. Bradshaw, *Two Ways of Praying* (Nashville: Abingdon, 1995), 18, 40-41; Weil, *Gathered to Pray*, 2-20.

36. For example, the individual prayer of a recently divorced Christian and the communal prayers in that person's congregation may both name the same concern. But the former would likely focus on the personal pain of the experience, while the latter might focus on the ways the experience wounded the community's experience of *shalom*.

37. Public prayer ought to be much more than simply an amplified version of the minister's private prayers. See William Willimon, *Preaching and Leading Worship* (Philadelphia: Westminster, 1984), 39-50.

does not simply see itself as separate from all the other selves and groups worshipping through the same liturgy or the Psalms. Seeing oneself as one among the many who indwell the Psalms by singing them encourages one to consider how the others might be related to oneself. To see (in the flesh or in imagination) the faces of the others who receive and perform their identity through singing the Psalms can lead along the path I have followed through a hospitable self, rejecting idolatries, to a worshipping self for whom the orientation to the face of God and the face of other people is primary.[38]

Ford works this theme into an expansive and joyful vision of divine redemption in musical terms, in which he depicts the redeemed as the "singing self." Ford's work once more illustrates how the Psalms become part of the DNA of Christian worship, doctrine, and life. Some three thousand years after most of them were written, they are still inspiring significant constructive theological work.

Lesson Five:
Specificity and Generality in Prayer

Fifth, the Psalms present us with general, open, and metaphoric speech that can be applied to varied circumstances, as well as event-specific language that may be most pertinent on only one occasion. In Claus Westermann's terms, there are both "declarative" and "descriptive" praise, both event-oriented songs of celebration and expansive paeans of praise.[39] In Psalm 30 we find both — general, descriptive praise ("Sing praises to the LORD," v. 4) and specific declarative praise (e.g., "you have drawn me up"; see vv. 1-3, 11-12). We also find both in Psalm 83, a communal lament, where the psalmist prays, generally, "see how your enemies are astir," and specifically, "with one mind they plot together . . . the tents of Edom and the Ishmaelites, of Moab and the Hagrites, Philistia, with the people of Tyre." Such general language — perfect for repeated use in all circumstances — teaches us the value of familiar and trustworthy

---

38. David F. Ford, *Self and Salvation: Being Transformed* (New York: Cambridge University Press, 1999), 127.

39. See Claus Westermann, *Praise and Lament in the Psalms* (Atlanta: John Knox, 1981).

words and phrases that can rescue us from endless innovation in liturgical prayer. Specific language teaches us how brutally honest and particular our speech to God can be. As Brueggemann phrases it: "Israel's prayer — even though stylized and therefore in some ways predictable — is rarely safe, seldom conventional, and never routine. It is characteristically daring, outrageous, and adventuresome. Israel's prayer is indeed limit-language that pushes to the edge of social possibility, of cultural permit, of religious acceptability, and of imaginative experimentation."[40] Reliable patterns of general language become the basis for daring liturgical improvisations that respond to specific circumstances.

Likewise, well-celebrated Christian worship features a judicious balance of general and specific speech. We use tried and true phrases that imprint themselves on our hearts and burrow into our spiritual bones: "Lift up your heart to the LORD"; "Come, let us worship and bow down"; "Open our lips, that our mouths may show forth your praise"; "Our help is in the name of the LORD, maker of heaven and earth"; "We bring a sacrifice of praise." We also use language that is specific. Prayers of intercession name the joys and concerns of particular people and events. Sermons conclude with specific applications for the Christian life.

Our worship suffers when it lacks either type of language. Without common words and phrases, we are cut off from the biblical and historical roots of our faith. Without specific, event-oriented language, we are left with liturgy removed from our particular time and place.[41]

This penchant for specificity is also what makes liturgical prayer such an indelibly political act. In the Psalms and in Christian liturgy, the fullness of life in the world is not properly left at the door when we enter for worship. No, liturgy must be fully integrated with life in this world. Liturgy and justice are not exclusive concerns.[42] Our praise and thanks-

40. Brueggemann, "The Psalms as Prayer," 50.

41. One of the most diagnosable liturgical diseases throughout the history of the church has been the excessive use of cliché-laden, generalized speech. As Claus Westermann has pointed out, the hymns of the Enlightenment period are almost entirely descriptive, while those of Luther are more declarative (*Praise of God* [Richmond: John Knox, 1965], 32-33 n. 20). The difference, in part, lies in the immediacy of Luther's prose. It also lies in the eagerness to specify that praise is directed to the God of Abraham, Isaac, Jacob, the Abba of Jesus, our Lord. Christian worship ought to resound with specific reference to the works of God in creation, in the life of Jesus, and in the ongoing presence of the Spirit.

42. Nicholas Wolterstorff, "Justice as a Condition of Authentic Liturgy," *ThTo* 48 (1991): 6-21.

giving rightly name God's goodness to the oppressed (Ps 146). Our petitions to God specifically call for justice to be promoted and injustice squelched.[43] Walter Brueggemann has suggested that because of their political ramifications, psalms like Psalms 2 and 149 may "be too dangerous to sing in our more bourgeois liturgies." This warning comes as prophetic critique to those of us who lead benign worship services that are content with the status quo or are comfortable leaving our hurts and fears at the sanctuary door.

Lesson Six:
Emotional Engagement and Range

The Psalms convey the whole range of human emotion, from despondent sorrow (Ps 88) to ecstatic joy (Ps 47 or 48), from ravaging guilt (Ps 51) to profound gratitude (Ps 136). In John Calvin's famous phrase, the Psalms are "the anatomy of the soul."[44] They teach us that with the God of the covenant, no human emotion is out of place in prayer.

This emotional range in the Psalms is permission giving in worship. As Ellen F. Davis notes, the Psalms "enable us to bring into our conversation with God feelings and thoughts that most of us think we need to get rid of before God will be interested in hearing from us."[45] The Psalms model not only humble gratitude but also profound doubt and frustration.

To be sure, the emotional range of the Psalms also can create internal dissonance. The Psalms convey sentiments that not every worshiping community has experienced. Yet even when we are not feeling the profound ecstasy or the deep sorrow of a given psalm, the psalm is forming us nevertheless. It is allowing us to practice certain moves in our relationship with God. As Davis conveys it, "the Psalms instruct our feelings

43. See the perceptive comments of C. S. Lewis in *Reflections on the Psalms* (New York: Harcourt Brace Jovanovich, 1958), 9-12. In Lewis's turn of phrase, "Christians cry to God for mercy instead of justice; they [the psalmists] cried to God for justice instead of injustice" (12).

44. John Calvin, *Commentary on the Book of Psalms*, vol. 1 (Grand Rapids: Eerdmans, 1948-49), xxxvii. See also Howard Wallace, *Words to God, Word from God: The Psalms in the Prayer and Preaching of the Church* (Burlington, Vt.: Ashgate, 2005), 37.

45. Ellen F. Davis, *Getting Involved with God: Rediscovering the Old Testament* (Cambridge: Cowley, 2001), 5.

without negating them. They draw upon our particular experience of God as at the same time they expand it exponentially."[46]

For two thousand years this psalmic emotional range has challenged and inspired Christian hymn writers, prayer book editors, and worship leaders to develop liturgical language, including language for prayer, that explores the full range of human emotion before God. There are several historical examples of prayers written directly in response to prayers from the Psalms.[47]

Recent years have witnessed a recovery of prayers of lament, generally thought to be a neglected mode of prayer.[48] Popular Christian songwriter Michael Card reflects: "Through [David's] psalms of lament, as perhaps nowhere else in scripture, David reveals a God who uses and utilizes everything, especially pain. All true songs of worship are born in the wilderness of suffering." Card goes on to call for the recovery of lament: "If it is true that we must be conformed to [Jesus'] image, then perhaps we must also learn to speak Jesus' lost language. If we must learn to never let go of God, then the best means, provided by the language of lament, must become ours as well."[49]

As Card (echoing the work of Walter Brueggemann and others) ex-

46. Ellen F. Davis, *Wondrous Depth: Preaching the Old Testament* (Louisville: Westminster John Knox, 2005), 21. Likewise, Rolf Jacobson suggests that the "cognitive dissonance" we experience when praying the Psalms might be precisely the means through which we grow in the life of prayer ("Burning Our Lamps with Borrowed Oil: The Liturgical Use of the Psalms and the Life of Faith," in *Psalms and Practice: Worship, Virtue, and Authority,* ed. Stephen Breck Reid [Collegeville, Minn.: Liturgical Press, 2001], 90-98).

47. For example, see See I. D. MacFarlane, "Religious Verse in French Neo-Latin Poetry," in *Humanism and Reform: The Church in Europe, England, and Scotland, 1400-1643,* ed. James Kirk (Oxford: Blackwell, 1991), and Rikvah Zim, *English Metrical Psalms: Poetry as Praise and Prayer, 1535-1601* (Cambridge: Cambridge University Press, 1987).

48. Of the large and growing bibliography on this theme, see especially Kathleen D. Billman and Daniel L. Migliore, *Rachel's Cry: Prayer of Lament and Rebirth of Hope* (Cleveland: United Church Press, 1999); Sally A. Brown and Patrick D. Miller, eds., *Lament: Reclaiming Practices in Pulpit, Pew, and Public Square* (Louisville: Westminster John Knox, 2005); Michael Jinkins, *In the House of the Lord: Inhabiting the Psalms of Lament* (Collegeville, Minn.: Liturgical Press, 1998); J. Frank Henderson, *Liturgies of Lament* (Chicago: Liturgy Training Publications, 1994); Carl Bosma, "A Close Reading of Psalm 13: Daring to Ask the Hard Questions," in *Reading and Hearing the Word: From Text to Sermon,* ed. Arie C. Leder (Grand Rapids: CRC Publications, 1998), 125-60; and chap. 2 of John D. Witvliet, *Worship Seeking Understanding* (Grand Rapids: Baker Academic, 2003).

49. Michael Card, *A Sacred Sorrow: Reaching Out to God in the Lost Language of Lament* (Colorado Springs: NavPress, 2005), 63, 138.

plains, when practiced as an act of faith, lament can be a powerfully healing experience. But even more, the very structure of a lament psalm forms us in a pattern of God-filled Christian living. Laments, to be sure, begin with a cry against the deplorable human condition, a cry against the painfulness of individual tragedy, a cry against the injustices of society. But laments almost never stay there. Having voiced our pain and struggle, laments then recite God's mighty deeds on our behalf. Remembering these deeds — even in the face of pain and struggle — brings us to praise and thanksgiving for God's fidelity and compassion. Laments give voice to our pain but lead us out of that pain by God's strength. Laments are our great prayers of hope, for they remind us that we belong to God and that God's care will sustain us and protect us. This is the very pattern of our everyday living: from struggle to praise, from pain to remembering God's faithful goodness, from injustice to awe and wonder at the divine majesty.

Lesson Seven:
Image and Poetry in Christian Speech

Seventh, liturgical prayer is an act of vital imagination. "The church speaks in large, metaphorical phrasings that are evocative, generative, suggestive, and ultimately constitutive but resist every closed meaning," says Brueggemann. "Praise is opposed to memo, even as sacrament opposes technique. Memos reduce, minimize, routinize, and seek to control; this sung poetry leaves things open in respect, awe, and astonishment."[50] Praying the Psalms requires vivid, playful imagination, which makes praying the Psalms liturgically in North America a stubborn countercultural act.

The Psalms give us a whole gallery of images for use in prayer and preaching. Their expressions rely on evocative use of natural symbols, including chaotic waters, illuminating light, faithful movement of heavenly bodies. Through vivid poetic speech, the Psalms inspire an abandon in the praise of God. They ring with sheer delight in praise of God.[51] They depict a world in which trees clap their hands, in which whales and

50. Walter Brueggemann, "Praise and the Psalms: A Politics of Glad Abandonment," in *Psalms and the Life of Faith,* 125, see also 113, 119-21. On metaphors and images in the Psalms, see especially Brown, *Seeing the Psalms.*

51. For a joyful account discovering delight in the Psalter's praise, see Lewis, *Reflections on the Psalms,* 45-52, 83, 95-97.

hippos sing praise, in which all creation is caught up in a symphony of *shalom* to God. The Psalms, in the words of Gail Ramshaw, are "not only a primer, but something of an encyclopedia of biblical imagery."[52]

On the basis of these precedents, Christian worshipers too have felt freedom to explore a rich variety of ways to express praise to God. Joyful abandon is expressed in exuberant ringing shouts of nineteenth-century African American worshipers and in the final hallelujahs of Handelian choral anthems. Vivid stained glass windows in vast Gothic cathedrals and colorful weavings at remote Mexican pilgrimage sites celebrate the variety and wonder of God's creative power. Congregational offertory dances by Kenyan Catholics and solemn processions in large Presbyterian churches depict in movement the broad sweep of committed faith and worship. After the model of the Psalms themselves, Christian liturgical prayer is called to be imaginative, vivid, passionate, immediate, and intense, as it embodies the praise and petition of God.

Conclusion

In at least these seven paradigmatic ways, the patterns of prayer found in the Psalms have shaped and continue to shape Christian praise and lament. Consider then seven basic questions to ask of each psalm:

1. Who is speaking in the psalm? To whom? Does the speaker change during the course of the psalm?
2. How does the psalm identify God? Which metaphors and names does it use? What actions are attributed to divine initiative?
3. What actions does the psalm convey (praise, thanksgiving, petition, lament)? How are those actions related or linked?
4. Is the psalm expressing an individual or communal prayer?
5. Does the psalm employ specific or general language?
6. What emotions does the psalm express?
7. What poetic qualities are particularly compelling and challenging in the psalm?

And because the Psalms ground so much of the practice of worship, these questions can also be turned into helpful criteria for assessing the

---

52. Gail Ramshaw, *Treasures Old and New: Images in the Lectionary* (Minneapolis: Fortress, 2002). See also Brown, *Seeing the Psalms*.

practice of worship in any Christian community. Consider asking these questions in a worship committee meeting in your congregation:

1. Does our worship include both our words to God and God's words to us? Do worshipers experience them as such?
2. Do we speak about God with the beauty and range of imagery and actions that the Psalms use?
3. Do we link praise and petition, lament and gratitude in ways that are responsive to our life situation and bear testimony to God's faithfulness?
4. Do we use language in worship that is deeply personal and yet also profoundly communal, linking worshipers within the congregation with believers in every time and place?
5. Do we use both specific and concrete language in worship and also language that is applicable in every time and place?
6. Do we express the full range of human emotions before God's face?
7. Is our worship poetic and beautiful?

Paying attention to these features suggests how the Psalms can continue to be mentors for liturgical prayer. And when the Psalms themselves do function in worship, we should present them in ways that do not obscure these basic features.

Praying the Psalms in Christian Worship

At their best, the biblical psalms are meant not only to be studied and preached but also to be read, sung, and prayed. They not only teach us about God, they also help us enact our relationship with God. As Davis phrases it, the Psalms are "packaged ready to be put directly into our mouths. . . . Using their words brings us into direct encounter: through them we find ourselves talking to the living God, sometimes in language we would never have imagined would come from our lips into God's ear."[53]

Preachers and worship leaders need not choose between using the Psalms for preaching and using them for prayer and praise. Ideally, they should be regularly sung in worship, and frequently preached. Even when the Psalms are not preached, there are rich practices of praying the

53. Davis, *Getting Involved with God*, 9.

Psalms that complement sermons on other biblical texts and themes. When they are preached, the sustained attention given to the text opens up several possibilities for both presenting and praying a psalm in creative ways that can break open the significance of the text for worshipers.

Fortunately, using the Psalms in worship does not have to be complicated. In some congregations the matter is as simple as looking to the lectionary to choose which psalm to sing in a given week and looking to a hymnal or readily available collection of responsorial psalms to find a musical setting of that psalm. In others, it is as simple as looking in one of the many resources described later in this essay to identify a musical style and particular psalm text that match the pastoral needs of a congregation on a given week. Regular reading, singing, and praying from the Psalms is one of the simplest and most effective ways to keep worship grounded in Scripture and to help connect worship with the vast range of personal experience that worshipers bring with them. If we want "authentic" worship, we do not need to search further than the Psalms.

For congregations that already practice regular lectionary-based use of the Psalms in a set liturgy, the following analysis is designed to help make explicit what is already happening implicitly. These congregations have the benefit of working with established patterns that harvest generations of wisdom about which psalms to use at what time and in what way. The danger these congregations face is that this wisdom is not always accessible. Sometimes historic practices persist, but without any sense of what makes them significant. My hope is that reflection on these themes helps uncover a part of this wisdom. The paragraphs that follow may help you look at your cherished practices in new ways, or assist you in exploring other methods of speaking, singing, or depicting the Psalms. Indeed, there are many creative and well-grounded possibilities for use of the Psalms in worship that the lectionary and other set patterns of worship leave unexplored.

For congregations that read, sing, or pray the Psalms only sporadically in worship, or do not follow a set liturgy or use the lectionary, the following analysis is designed to suggest ways of becoming more intentional about using this remarkable biblical book in worship. These congregations have the freedom to draw on the Psalms in interesting, creative, and pastorally responsive ways that prayer-book congregations may not. The challenge here is that this creativity and responsiveness require uncommon insight and energy, not to mention careful coordination between the preacher and those who will lead music or other aspects of worship.

The following resources and perspectives focus on using either extended portions of psalms or entire psalms, rather than merely a single verse or short portion of a selected psalm. The evolution of the medieval mass witnessed the attrition of the Psalter from the use of entire psalms to the use of mere versicles, often sung during the processions at the Introit and the Communion.[54] The same process of attrition has occurred in some expressions of recent Protestant congregational song, in which preference is given to singing one scriptural verse several times rather than extended portions of the text. Single verses from the Psalms certainly have their place in worship. They are significant as the texts for simple songs of praise (whether in Scripture choruses or Handelian arias) and for liturgical leaders looking for a good spoken transition. But for too long many traditions have been content to limit the use of psalm material to a favorite or convenient versicle for liturgical use, totally ignoring the structures and contexts by which these verses gain meaning.[55]

The bulk of recent scholarly analysis of the Psalms has focused on identifying basic literary structures or patterns in the Psalms and discerning how individual texts improvise within a given structure. One consistent theme throughout this work is that most psalms convey much of their meaning through movement, by taking us somewhere. They offer more than simply beautiful epigrams or metaphors. As Brown summarizes, the meaning and metaphors of the Psalms forge a theological vision that is "wrought in movement . . . by fits and starts, the pray-er of Psalms is taken from trench to temple, from lament to praise, from 'pathway' to 'refuge.'"[56] This insight suggests the significant value of using larger rather than smaller portions of Scripture.

Readers may well be surprised by the stylistic breadth of the resources included in this section. They include musical suggestions in classical, jazz, folk, and popular styles, in multiple languages, and textual suggestions in both authorized translations and free paraphrases. The Psalms can make a significant contribution to every worshiping community. Whatever our congregational type, we all have much to learn from the Psalms. Indeed, even though they may be three millennia old, the

---

54. Josef A. Jungmann, *Mass of the Roman Rite: Its Origins and Development* (New York: Benziger Brothers, 1995), 34 n. 5.

55. My hope, then, is not to displace the use of single verses or images from the Psalms, but to add to them the reading or singing of longer literary units.

56. Brown, *Seeing the Psalms*, 215.

Psalms are still out ahead of us. We are still growing into them. They are cutting-edge material for effective contextual ministry.

The following suggestions briefly consider each step in the process of preparing to pray or sing the Psalms in worship:

- choosing a psalm,
- choosing a psalm's liturgical placement or function,
- studying the text of the psalm, and
- choosing how to render the psalm in speech, song, or visual depiction.

Note carefully: the extensive analysis that follows is not meant to suggest that psalmody needs to be inordinately complicated! I realize that such a detailed process of selecting and preparing psalms cannot be followed every week in the vast majority of congregations. Still, pausing to reflect on the assumptions built into each step of the process can enhance and discipline the pastoral work of worship leadership over time. Consider giving extended attention to one aspect of the process each week as a way of developing new capacities for effective leadership.

One final note: this material is written out of my own great enthusiasm for a renewed appreciation for and use of the biblical psalms. That enthusiasm comes from experiencing the robust and gritty significance of the Psalms in both worship and personal study and from a vivid awareness of how little the Psalms, especially in longer literary units, are used in worship today in many traditions. I also am aware of some of the possible unintended consequences of this enthusiasm. It is easy to romanticize the significance of the Psalms in earlier periods of church history or to give the impression that their pervasive use is absolutely necessary for vital and faithful worship.[57]

Choosing a Psalm

Choosing an appropriate psalm for worship is a challenging and significant task.[58] When we choose a psalm (or any other prayer or song), we are

---

57. Thus I am grateful for Paul Bradshaw's work on de-romanticizing our view of psalmody in the early church. See his *Two Ways of Praying*, 73-87.

58. For historical perspectives on this, see J. A. Lamb, *The Psalms in Christian Worship* (London: Faith Press, 1962); Massey H. Shepherd, Jr., *The Psalms in Christian Worship:*

placing words on the lips of the congregation that shape their experience of relating to God. This means that our choice of text always needs to take into account not only the text but also our theology and our awareness of the experience that people bring with them to worship. Consider three broad types of rationales that inform the choice of a psalm: liturgical, homiletical, and pastoral.

Liturgical Criteria

In many contexts the obvious way to choose a psalm is simply to find one that says what we want to say. If we want to praise, we sing Psalm 98. If we want to repent, we pray Psalm 51. If we want to lament, we use Psalm 13. So when we have firmly in mind what we want a psalm to accomplish in worship, we set off on a search. We thumb through our Bibles until we come upon a text that more or less fits our purposes. Task accomplished.

While this may be effective for planning a particular service, the results of using this method exclusively over time are not altogether promising. Often this method results in a severely restricted use of the Psalms. Certain favorite psalms are used a great deal to the virtual exclusion of others.

Another danger of this ad hoc approach is the tendency to choose texts that are only generally applicable. Worship leaders in a wide spectrum of congregations tend to choose the psalm texts that feature the most general language, such as "Sing to the LORD a new song," "The LORD is my shepherd," or "Create in me a clean heart." These are certainly significant, paradigmatic texts, worthy of repeated and sustained use. But if those are the only kinds of texts chosen, after a while all the psalms sound alike. If we don't choose a text for a very specific reason (and communicate that reason), then these prized poetic expressions, with their profound parallelisms and vivid images, can become a sea of clichés in our worship. If, after years and years of eager and well-intentioned participation in public worship, veteran Christians have only a vague memory of using small parts of Psalm 103 and maybe, on a deep day, Psalm 51, then something is seriously wrong with their congregation's liturgical diet.

Further, this approach can, without care, perpetuate the impression

---

A Practical Guide (Minneapolis: Augsburg, 1966); and Aimé-Georges Martimort, "Fonction de la Psalmodie dans la liturgie de la Parole," in *Mirabile Laudis Canticum* (Rome: Edizioni Liturgiche, 1991), 75-96.

that worship, and the liturgical use of biblical materials, relies on language that expresses only the praise, petition, and lament — especially the first! — we have previously felt, forgetting that worship also needs to teach us to say things that do not come naturally to us. Worship, that is, not only should express our prayer, but also should form us to pray more deeply.[59] If this is to happen, we must learn to pray the psalms that we otherwise might not so readily choose.

And even if we never end up using a particular psalm to express "authentically" our own internal emotional states, it is of benefit for us to pray the Psalms in solidarity with others in the body of Christ. At any given moment, no one person or group of persons are feeling and experiencing all the emotions represented in the Psalter, but at any given moment, some people are experiencing this or that facet of the Psalms (and eventually we all will have these experiences somewhere along the way). The Psalms are varied so as to give voice to life's many seasons.[60]

All this suggests the value of some regular regimen of praying the Psalter, some way of ensuring that we will use a larger portion of the Psalms. Indeed, there is precedent for a regular pattern of psalm selection in most worship traditions. In the Middle Ages, Benedictine monks prayed the Psalms each week in a particular order. In Calvin's Geneva, despite the rejection of the Roman lectionary for Scripture readings and sermon texts, the Psalms were sung in public worship according to a regular regimen printed in the back of the published Psalters (indeed, it was a lectionary for singing!).[61] Long before the day of thematic worship planning, Reformed worshipers sang whatever psalm came next in the regular order, rather than psalms chosen to correspond with the sermon or because they were a favorite of members of the congregation. In twentieth-century liturgical renewal, the Psalms have again been featured as a vital part of the lectionary, which disciplines the use of Scripture in many worshiping communities. This discipline results in exposure to a far greater number and range of psalms than usually results

59. Such is the advice of countless wise veterans of Christian prayer, such as Dietrich Bonhoeffer: "We also ought not to select Psalms at our own discretion, thinking that we know better what we ought to pray than does God himself" (*Psalms: Prayerbook of the Bible* [Minneapolis: Augsburg, 1970], 26).

60. I am grateful to Scott Hoezee for helping me express this point. For seasons of life, see Walter Brueggemann, "Psalms and the Life of Faith: A Suggested Typology of Function," in *Psalms and the Life of Faith*.

61. Pierre Pidoux, *Le Psautier huguenot du XVIe siècle* (Basel, 1962), 2:45, 63, 135.

when psalms are chosen for occasional use at the discretion of a given pastor or worship leader. Such discipline has much to commend it.

There are several possible regimens for choosing psalms.

Canonical Order One obvious method would simply be to pray the Psalms, both privately and communally, in canonical order. This is the least common regimen evidenced in the history of worship (though it has been practiced in some monastic communities). Yet, given the remarkable scholarly energy in the past generation that has uncovered the genius of the organization and editing of the Psalter as a complete book,[62] the practice of reading or praying the Psalms in canonical order would be an appropriate spiritual discipline for individuals or a congregation. Just as reading Romans from beginning to end helps us sense the logic of its overall structure (from sin to grace to service) and offers a framework for interpreting specific texts, so, too, praying the Psalter from beginning to end helps us sense its ebbs and flows. Doing this would help us feel the crescendo of the Psalter as it moves from a relatively high percentage of lament psalms (Books I-III) to nearly exclusively psalms of praise (Book V), and from a relatively high percentage of individual expressions to many more communal exclamations.

The Lectionary and the Christian Year Many of the readers of this volume are likely regular lectionary users. Each of the major lectionaries published in the last forty years, including the Revised Common Lectionary, includes a selection from the Psalms as one of the assigned texts for each week. The psalms in the Revised Common Lectionary are chosen primarily to function as a response to the designated reading from the Old Testament, rather than to serve primarily as the best psalmic counterpart to the New Testament Gospel readings (though often there is natural correspondence between the psalm and the New Testament or Gospel reading).[63] Several lectionary choices also reflect his-

---

62. See, e.g., Gerald H. Wilson, *The Editing of the Hebrew Psalter* (Chico, Calif.: Scholars, 1985); Wilson, "The Shape of the Book of Psalms," *Int* 46 (1992): 138-39; Nancy L. deClaissé-Walford, *Reading from the Beginning: The Shaping of the Hebrew Psalter* (Macon, Ga.: Mercer University Press, 1997); deClaissé-Walford, *Introduction to the Psalms: A Song from Ancient Israel* (St. Louis: Chalice, 2004); and J. Clinton McCann, Jr., ed., *The Shape and Shaping of the Psalter* (Sheffield: Sheffield Academic, 1993).

63. Horace T. Allen, Jr., "The Psalter in the Revised Common Lectionary (1992)," *Reformed Liturgy and Music* 26 (1992): 84-85. For more background on the logic of the lectionary, see Fritz West, *Scripture and Memory: The Ecumenical Hermeneutic of the Three-*

torically significant psalms for a given day in the Christian year (Ps 22, for example, has been a psalm of choice for Good Friday all the way back to the extant lectionaries of the early church).

For congregations that do follow the lectionary, the Psalms can be approached as much more than a response to the Old Testament reading. As Paul Westermeyer suggests, "The singing of a psalm between the OT and Epistle functions to call to mind the whole story, the whole *Heilsgeschichte,* the whole panorama of salvation history. The Psalms allow us to sing the church's ballad, structured with a telos of Gospel. The lessons and the sermon are laser-like shafts of light that illumine the whole Psalmic story and our places in it; but the paradoxical reverse is also true: the Psalmic story itself provides context and makes it possible for the laser-like shafts to shine at all."[64] The Psalms also often introduce the language of personal or communal prayer into the set of Scripture selections for the day. The juxtaposition of psalmic poems with the Old Testament texts, Gospel narrative, and epistolary exposition creates a fertile mix of rhetoric to shape the congregation's prayer.

For congregations that do not follow it, the lectionary is still a source of significant wisdom. First, whenever the sermon is based on an Old Testament text included in the lectionary, then the lectionary will usually suggest a psalm that is especially appropriate as a response (or adjunct, corollary, or complement) to the text. Any preacher preparing a sermon on an Old Testament text is wise to consult the lectionary to see which psalm it suggests.

Second, the Revised Common Lectionary is a good source for locating which psalms have been traditionally associated with particular events in the life of Christ or season of the church year.[65] It reminds us of the appropriateness of, for example:

> Advent   Psalm 24 ("Lift up your heads . . . that the King of glory may come in") and Psalm 80 ("Awaken your might, come and save us")

Year Lectionaries (Collegeville, Minn.: Liturgical Press, 1997); Normand Bonneau, *The Sunday Lectionary: Ritual Word, Paschal Shape* (Collegeville, Minn.: Liturgical Press, 1998); and especially Irene Nowell, *Sing a New Song: The Psalms in the Sunday Lectionary* (Collegeville, Minn.: Liturgical Press, 1993).

64. Paul Westermeyer, personal correspondence, June 1, 2006.

65. See *The Worship Sourcebook* (Grand Rapids: Faith Alive/Baker, 2005), for extensive psalm materials for each element of worship and the season of the church year.

Christmas	Psalms 96, 97, 98 ("the LORD has made his salvation known") [note: Isaac Watts's famous carol, "Joy to the World," is based on Psalm 98]
Epiphany	Psalm 72 ("All nations will be blessed by him")
Ash Wednesday and Lent	Psalm 51 ("Create in me a clean heart, O God")
Palm Sunday	Psalm 118 ("Hosanna in the highest")
Maundy Thursday	One or more of the Hallel Psalms (Psalms 113–118), the psalms that may have been sung in the traditional Passover celebration
Good Friday	Psalm 22 ("My God, my God, why have you forsaken me?")
Easter	Psalm 118 ("The stone the builders rejected has become the capstone") and Psalm 16 ("You will not let your Holy One see decay")
Pentecost	Psalm 104 (with its prayer for the Spirit to "renew the face of the earth")

Suppose a nonlectionary congregation chose to feature a given psalm during a season of the year, reading or singing that psalm weekly over time (this may also be a wise idea for congregations that *do* follow the lectionary!). In that case the lectionary would be one of the best sources to consult to identify seasonally-appropriate psalmody. It would, for example, suggest seasonally-appropriate psalms for Advent (Pss 25; 72; 80), Lent (Pss 32; 51; 126; 130), and Eastertide (Pss 16; 23; 30; 47; 93).

Liturgical Elements and Types of Services One unintended effect of lectionary use in some traditions and congregations is to limit the use of the Psalms to one moment in worship (typically, between the Old and New Testament readings). Yet there are beautiful and appropriate psalm texts for nearly every element in worship:

- Psalms 95 and 98 (and many more) function beautifully as calls to worship. The Roman Catholic Sacramentary, for example, has Introit psalm verses assigned for every Mass.

- Psalms 32 and 51 (or any of the penitential psalms) function as prayers of confession.
- Psalms 34, 103, and 116 have a long association with use at the Lord's Supper.[66] Note also that the Roman Catholic Church has an assigned communion antiphon for every Mass drawn from the Psalms.
- Psalm 67 is a beautiful, all-encompassing benediction as worship concludes.
- Historically, Psalms 23 and 42 have been most commonly sung at baptisms. Baptism may also be aptly complemented by a psalm of covenant faithfulness (e.g., Pss 89 and 105).
- Historically, Psalm 128 has been associated with marriage rites.
- Historically, Psalm 130 has been associated with funeral services.
- Psalm 84 is a natural choice for the dedication of a worship space or church building.
- Psalms 117, 132, and 134 are appropriate for ordination services.
- Psalms 3 and 13 are especially appropriate for morning prayer.
- Psalms 4 and 141 are especially appropriate for evening prayer.

In each case these choices can be either read or sung. In congregations with a fixed liturgy (perhaps governed by a prayer book), the best way to incorporate psalmody may be by singing metrical psalms in place of a hymn (indeed, most worshipers may not be able, at first, to discern a difference between a hymn and a metrical psalm).

Homiletical Criteria

Choosing a psalm for liturgical use can also be driven by the process of preparing for preaching. Psalms not only help worshipers pray, they also help preachers preach.[67]

---

66. Ideally, these psalms become closely associated with particular liturgical acts: Dutch Calvinists have traditionally used Ps 103 after the Lord's Supper, while some Scottish Presbyterians used Ps 24 before it. See A. C. Honders, "Remarks on the Postcommunio in Some Reformed Liturgies," in *The Sacrifice of Praise*, ed. Bryan D. Spinks (Rome: Edizioni Liturgiche, 1981); Leigh Eric Schmidt, *Holy Fairs: Scottish Communions and American Revivals in the Early Modern Period* (Princeton: Princeton University Press, 1989), 98-99; and Millar Patrick, *Four Centuries of Scottish Psalmody* (London: Oxford University Press, 1949).

67. See especially J. Clinton McCann, Jr., and James C. Howell, *Preaching the Psalms* (Nashville: Abingdon, 2001). See also Sidney Greidanus, *Preaching Christ from the Old Testament: A Contemporary Hermeneutic Method* (Grand Rapids: Eerdmans, 1999); Thomas G.

Effective use of the Psalms homiletically often involves the pairing of psalm texts with other portions of Scripture. Davis makes this point from the perspective of preaching a psalm: "the Psalms have nearly inexhaustible potential for making connections with the larger story."[68] She invites preachers, once a psalm has been chosen as a preaching text, to imagine that psalm contextualized in a variety of narrative contexts — both in Scripture and in present-day life. A psalm of deliverance (Ps 30, for example) might be juxtaposed both with an Old Testament healing narrative and with a contemporary situation. Preaching on the Psalms often drives the preacher to other parts of Scripture.

The reverse is also true. In working with preaching texts *not* from the Psalms, it is often instructive to ask and imagine what psalms could be fruitfully juxtaposed with the chosen text. Having the freedom to explore choices far beyond the lectionary creates many interesting possibilities.

For sermons on Old Testament texts, the possibilities are endless. Consider first the evocative superscriptions that appear before some psalms. However we feel about when those labels were written and by whom, some very ancient source perceived a degree of fittingness between the psalm and the particular event or personage mentioned in the superscription. It is not unreasonable for us to at least explore the same.[69] A sermon on David and Bathsheba can be immeasurably enriched by the liturgical use of Psalm 51. A sermon on David and Absalom may suggest the use of Psalm 3. Singing or reading these psalms in conjunction with the primary Scripture text for the sermon allows the worshiper to live into the drama of a particular biblical narrative, and provides the preacher with additional material for the development of the sermon.[70]

Long, *Preaching and the Literary Forms of the Bible* (Philadelphia: Fortress, 1993), chap. 3; and Elizabeth Achtemeier, "Preaching the Praises and Laments," *CTJ* 36 (2001): 103-14.

68. Davis, *Wondrous Depth,* 28.

69. Erik Haglund, *Historical Motifs in the Psalms* (Stockholm: Liber Tryck, 1984). Concerning superscriptions, Miller comments, "While they may not be read to justify the precise situation in which the prayer was first composed, they indicate how the community of faith and those responsible for the transmission of these prayers associated them with varying human predicaments, primarily in the life of David" (*They Cried,* 83). Miller also suggests that we may reasonably assume that the types of laments that we know were offered by Hannah and Tamar, for example, likely correspond to the Psalms (85). It is on this same basis that I am proposing the choice of psalms for liturgical use.

70. For imaginative and suggestive development of contemporary superscriptions, see Marchiene Rienstra, *Swallow's Nest: A Feminine Reading of the Psalms* (Grand Rapids: Eerdmans, 1992).

At times the thematic content of the psalm, rather than the super-scription, might suggest the pairing of a psalm with a particular Old Testament event: Psalm 20 is a prayer prior to battle, Psalm 21 is a prayer after victory, Psalm 44 is a cry for help after defeat. Together they provide an option for any sermonic treatment of the texts related to conquest or deliverance. Psalms 105, 106, and 107 are obvious correlates for any sermon on the exodus, the desert wanderings, and the conquest of the land of Israel. A sermon on Israel's exile and return calls for the use of Psalm 126 or 137.

A connection, though less tight, can also be made between psalms and Old Testament prayer reports. Throughout the Old Testament we find accounts of various persons praying to the Lord without indication of the words they used. We are told at various points that Tamar, Hannah, and Jonah, among others, "cried to the Lord." As Miller asserts, we may imagine "without much fear of contradiction" that such prayers for help resemble those recorded in the Psalms.[71] Choosing fitting psalms in conjunction with these biblical texts allows the worshiper not just to hear about but also to imagine more fruitfully the experience of these biblical characters.

Psalms can also be paired with specific Old Testament texts through obvious theological correspondence. A sermon on the covenant theology of Deuteronomy is aptly complemented by a salvation history psalm (e.g., Ps 136) or one of the torah psalms (Pss 1; 19; 119).[72] A sermon on the eschatological longings of the prophets is well complemented by Psalms of Zion (Pss 46; 48; 76; 87) or psalms of the future reign of God (Pss 96; 97). A sermon on Proverbs or Ecclesiastes is well complemented by wisdom psalms (Pss 1; 37; 49). There are easy choices for sermons on creation (Pss 8; 29; 104), sin (Pss 32; 51), and redemption (Pss 78; 105; 106). In sum, nearly every Old Testament text suggests specific points of correspondence with one or more psalms.

For sermons on New Testament texts, the possibilities are equally numerous. An obvious connection exists in the many New Testament texts that quote Psalms. A sermon on Hebrews 1 would be well complemented by singing any of the psalms quoted in that chapter. Singing the entire psalm that is quoted allows the congregation to experience the continuity between the Testaments and to sense the particular way in

---

71. See Miller, *They Cried,* 84-85.
72. See Miller, *They Cried,* 114.

which the ancient text was adapted for the New Testament's use (provided that some explanation is offered in the sermon itself or in some other forum).

In addition, there is the long tradition of reading much of the Psalter christologically, especially in patristic interpretations on the Psalms. The New Testament itself treats Psalms 2, 22, 69, 72, and 110 as key texts for understanding the person and work of Jesus (see Luke 24:44).[73] Other texts provide theological correlates with aspects of New Testament theology. Westermann, for example, sees the theme of divine accommodation recorded in Psalms 113 and 138 as the context by which the New Testament explores the theological significance of the incarnation.[74] And Bonhoeffer went so far as to conclude that "If we want to read and to pray the prayers of the Bible and especially the Psalms, therefore, we must not ask first what they have to do with us, but what they have to do with Jesus Christ. . . . The Psalms are given to us to this end, that we may learn to pray them in the name of Jesus Christ."[75] Much of modern biblical scholarship has backed off from christological interpretations, noting the strained christological links sometimes imagined by interpreters, but this need not discourage more sober and carefully drawn connections.

Then also, there are psalms that, together with New Testament counterparts, create evocative symbolic portraits that depict the mystery of God's grace. Consider choosing a psalm because its central images or metaphorical world (e.g., military, medical, cultic) corresponds

---

73. See Jean Danielou, S.J., *The Bible and the Liturgy* (Notre Dame, Ind.: University of Notre Dame Press, 1956), 177-90, 311-47, with copious references to messianic interpretation of the Psalms in patristic literature and liturgical practice. See also Brian McNeil, *Christ in the Psalms* (New York: Paulist, 1980); Hans-Joachim Kraus, "The Psalms in the New Testament," in Kraus, *Theology of the Psalms*, trans. Keith Crim (Minneapolis: Augsburg, 1986), 177-203; and T. Ernest Wilson, *The Messianic Psalms* (Neptune, N.J.: Loizeaux Brothers, 1978).

74. See Westermann, *The Living Psalms* (Grand Rapids: Eerdmans, 1989), 297-98.

75. Bonhoeffer, *Psalms,* 14-15. A similar view is expressed memorably in a sermon of Jonathan Edwards on Ps 89:6: "This book of Psalms has such an exalted devotion, and such a spirit of evangelical grace every[where] breathed forth in it! Here are such exalted expressions of the gloriousness of God, and even of the excellency of Christ and his kingdom; there is so much of the gospel doctrine, grace, and spirit, breaking out and shining in it, that it seems to be carried clear above and beyond the strain and pitch of the Old Testament, and almost brought up to the New. Almost the whole book of Psalms has either a direct or indirect respect to Christ and the gospel publish" (*Sermons and Discourses, 1720-1723,* ed. Wilson H. Kimnach [New Haven: Yale University Press, 1992], 415).

with the chosen preaching text or a particular situation in the life of a given congregation.

Consider, for example, the symbolic use of water. Psalms 42:7, 69:1, and 124:3 all depict the waters of chaos that provide the symbolic matrix for the New Testament image of "drowning" (dying with Christ) in baptism. In contrast, Psalms 36:8-9, 46:4, and 87:7, along with Ezekiel 47:1-2 and Revelation 22:1-2, describe the waters that flow in Zion, the "streams which make glad the city of God." In biblical cosmology, the transformation of God's new creation is depicted in part as the transformation of the waters of chaos (Gen 1:2) into the "sea of crystal" (Rev 4:6). In worship, these images ought not merely to be explained, but experienced. Creative uses of psalms and hymns ought to stimulate our imaginations with visions of the primeval chaos, joyful dancing streams, pillars of fire, clouds of mercy, and the multitude of other natural phenomena that are used as literary pictures to portray the vastness of God's mighty works of creation and re-creation.[76]

Given all the ways that preachers can find correspondences between preaching texts and the Psalms, imagine a preacher or congregation who would choose to accept the discipline of ending each sermon with the reading or singing of an appropriate psalm. Or preachers might consider identifying the "key" phrase in a psalm and using it as a repeated refrain in the composition of a sermon. A sermon that included the psalmic refrain "How excellent is your name in all the earth" or "why have you forsaken me?" would deepen the reading of that entire psalm.[77] In this case, rather than merely serving as a response to the first lectionary reading, the psalm would function as a response to the entire section of the service devoted to Scripture readings and sermon. This practice could relatively easily be adopted across the whole spectrum of congregations — from traditional to contemporary, "liturgical" to so-called nonliturgical. It would work to nurture the habit of linking preaching with the life of prayer, all shaped by the biblical text.

Pastoral Criteria

Psalms can also be chosen for use in worship for pastoral reasons. The Psalms are one of the richest resources in all of Scripture for pastoral

---

76. It is for this reason that we might juxtapose Ps 29 ("the voice of the LORD thunders") with the narrative of Jesus' baptism, for example.

77. I am grateful to Debra Rienstra for this suggestion.

care. What is significant for worship here is the opportunity to link the use of the Psalms in pastoral care and liturgy. Imagine a congregation marking the one-year anniversary of the death of one of its members by reading or singing a portion of the psalm used at the funeral. Or imagine the leaders of a congregation's pastoral care ministry identifying five or six psalms as key texts for a season for use in pastoral counseling sessions, hospital and prison visits, and then using those same psalms regularly in worship (congregations that follow the lectionary might choose psalms from upcoming lessons). This practice would connect a congregation's worship life and pastoral care ministry. And when a given psalm is used in a home, hospital room, nursing home, or prison, the text gains a certain resonance that makes its use in worship even more pastorally significant.

One pastor I am aware of distributed various psalm texts printed on index cards to people in hospitals and nursing homes, leaving the cards at their bedsides for others also to read. In this way, over time, people get exposed to lots of psalms and can talk to the pastor about their favorites. When these loved ones die, these texts can be incorporated in their funerals and in a congregation's public worship, thus enriching the pastoral care of these people even as the deceased person is allowed to "speak" vicariously through the psalms he or she flagged as particularly meaningful.[78]

The same kind of linkage is desirable with just about every other aspect of congregational life, including ministries of education, social justice, and evangelism. Consider having each ministry of your congregation identify a particular psalm as central to its mission. Imagine compiling the selected psalms into a small collection that represents your congregation's ministries. Think of this as a kind of expanded mission statement — though in the form of scriptural poetry rather than corporate memo. Whenever the language of liturgy can echo in the resonance chamber of day-to-day congregational life, the congregation's life in ministry is enriched and worship gains depth and force.

These examples demonstrate only some of the nearly endless possibilities for the creative juxtaposition of specific psalms with other biblical texts. When psalms are well chosen, their liturgical use has the great

---

78. I am grateful to Scott Hoezee for alerting me to this practice. For more on this theme, see John D. Witvliet, "How Common Worship Forms Us for Our Encounter with Death," in Witvliet, *Worship Seeking Understanding*, 291-308.

potential to stimulate the imaginative reception of the Scripture for worshipers in every worship tradition. For every service, there is a perfect psalm waiting to be chosen. The goal for thoughtful worship leaders is to find it. When Egeria reported on her fourth-century pilgrimage to Jerusalem, she commented on the use of the Psalter in daily prayer at Jerusalem: "What I found most impressive about all this was that the Psalms and antiphons they use are always appropriate. . . . Everything is suitable, appropriate, and relevant to what is being done."[79] May Egeria's plaudit be a goal for all worship leaders today!

Choosing a Translation

Most pastors and worship leaders may not give weekly attention to the version or translation of Bible used in worship. They simply use either an officially authorized version or the most readily available translation. There is good wisdom in using authorized translations in worship.

But especially given the nuance and intensity of the poetry of Psalms, much can be gained if leaders are students of several translations (attempts to render the original Hebrew text in modern vernacular) and paraphrases (free compositions more or less based on the original Hebrew text). Indeed, the English language strains to capture the gritty poetic beauty of the Hebrew original — note that Hebrew is not only another language, but it also comes from an entirely different family of languages.[80] We need more lyrical sensibility, both in our reading of the Psalms and in our prayer more generally.

In other translations or paraphrases, preachers and songwriters may find a word, phrase, or image to unsettle their thoughts about a given psalm, and suggest new angles for helping modern listeners engage the text. Composers may find the cadences and rhythms of a given version more suitable for singing. Prayer leaders may choose to use a paraphrase of Scripture as a basis for a liturgical prayer, even when an authorized translation is used for the formal reading of the text.

Consider the following translations and paraphrases of Psalm 42:1-2:

79. Egeria, *Pilgrimage of Egeria* 25, trans. John Wilkinson, *Egeria's Travels* (London: SPCK, 1971), 126.

80. I am grateful to Nathan Bierma for his sensibilities on this point.

As a deer longs for flowing streams,
  so my soul longs for you, O God.
My soul thirsts for God,
  for the living God.
When shall I come and behold
  the face of God? (NRSV)

As a deer stretches itself out toward the deepest, clearest spot
  of the flowing water,
that is how I stretch out myself toward you, O God —
I am thirsty for God! the living God. . . .
When shall I go in and see God face to face?[81]

Like a hind crying for water,
  my soul cries for You, O God;
  my soul thirsts for God, the living God;
  O when will I come to appear before God! (Tanakh/NJPS)

As a deer craves running water,
I thirst for you, my God;
I thirst for God,
the living God.
When will I see your face?[82]

Just as the doe longs for the springs of water,
  so my soul longs for you, O God.
My soul thirsted for the living God.
  When shall I come and appear to the face of God?[83]

A white-tailed deer drinks
  from the creek;
I want to drink God,
  deep draughts of God.
I'm thirsty for God-alive.

---

81. Calvin Seerveld, *Voicing God's Psalms* (Grand Rapids: Eerdmans, 2005), 73.
82. *The Psalter,* ed. Gabe Huck (Chicago: Liturgy Training Publications, 1995).
83. Albert Pietersma, *A New English Translation of the Septuagint: The Psalms* (Oxford: Oxford University Press, 2000), 40.

I wonder, "Will I ever make it —
    arrive and drink in God's presence?"[84]

My soul thirsts for you, O God, just like a doe thirsts
      for a bubbling spring.
My soul is parched with desire for God, so vibrantly alive.
How long before I can feast my eyes on Almighty God?[85]

As a long-distance swimmer struggles towards land,
I struggle towards you, Lord.
I am in danger of drowning.
My feet long to rest on solid ground again.[86]

It is certainly true that some paraphrases of Scripture take great liberties with the Hebrew text, some in ways that genuinely help modern readers encounter the nuance of the Hebrew text, but some in ways that work directly against the central literary and theological force of the psalm. Any innovation, in word choice or sentence structure, should ultimately be tested against the original Hebrew text, a task made much easier for non-Hebrew readers through the use of any of several fine published commentaries (see the bibliography in part I). In general, one should avoid two extremes: capricious use of various paraphrases that we "raid" to make the text say what we want to say, and reluctance to consult anything but the authorized version for our tradition. In worship itself, one way to achieve a balance is to use an authorized version for the formal reading or singing of the psalm, and to draw on paraphrases for use in shaping prayers, sermons, or spoken transitions.

TRANSLATIONS AND PARAPHRASES OF THE PSALMS
In addition to the standard Bible translations, see the following translations:

Arackal, Joseph J., V.C. *The Psalms in Inclusive Language.* Collegeville, Minn.: Liturgical Press, 1993.

---

84. Eugene Peterson, *The Message* (Colorado Springs: NavPress, 1993), 964.

85. Juanita Colón, *The Manhattan Psalter: The Lectio Divina of Sister Juanita Colón* (Collegeville, Minn.: Liturgical Press, 2002), 67.

86. James Taylor, *Everyday Psalms* (Winfield, B.C., Canada: Wood Lake Books, 1995), 59.

The Grail Psalter. A translation that aspires to evoke the "musical" quality of the Hebrew text, by regularizing the number of accentuated syllables in each poetic line.

The New Jerusalem Bible. A translation, prominent in Roman Catholic usage, that gives special attention to the literary quality of the English.

Pietersma, Albert. *A New English Translation of the Septuagint: The Psalms.* Oxford: Oxford University Press, 2000.

The Psalter. Edited by Gabe Huck. Chicago: Liturgy Training Publications, 1995. The lengthy subtitle of this work suggests its value: "a faithful and inclusive rendering from the Hebrew into contemporary English poetry intended primarily for communal song and recitation."

Psalter for Christian People: An Inclusive-Language Revision of the Psalter of the Book of Common Prayer. Edited by Gordon Lathrop and Gail Ramshaw. Collegeville, Minn.: Liturgical Press, 1993. This Psalter is a particularly interesting example of a translation alert to the cadence of the English poetry.

Seerveld, Calvin. *Voicing God's Psalms.* Grand Rapids: Eerdmans, 2005. Offers rugged and gritty translations that recapture the force and energy of the original Hebrew texts in compelling ways.

For paraphrases or adaptations of the Psalms, see, for example:

Brandt, Leslie F. *Psalms Now.* 3rd ed. St. Louis: Concordia, 2004.

Colón, Juanita. *The Manhattan Psalter: The Lectio Divina of Sister Juanita Colón.* Collegeville, Minn.: Liturgical Press, 2002.

Mitchell, Stephen. *A Book of Psalms.* San Francisco: Harper Collins, 1993.

Peterson, Eugene. *The Message.* Colorado Springs: NavPress, 1993.

Rienstra, Marchiene Vroon. *Swallow's Nest: A Feminine Reading of the Psalms.* Grand Rapids: Eerdmans, 1992.

The Saint Helena Psalter: A New Version of the Psalms in Expansive Language. New York: Church Publishing, 2004.

Taylor, James. *Everyday Psalms.* Winfield, B.C., Canada: Wood Lake Books, 1995.

Among the many discussions that evaluate translations and paraphrases of the Psalter, see Alastair G. Hunter, *Psalms: Old Testament Readings* (New York: Routledge, 1999), 15-32.

The Liturgical Placement of a Psalm

Liturgical Congregations

For congregations with established liturgies based on historic liturgical patterns, the position of the psalm is usually fixed. Most often in a Service of Word and Sacrament, a psalm is sung or read after an Old Testament reading and before a New Testament reading. Short phrases from the Psalter may be used in other parts of the service, but the use of an extended passage or entire psalm as a larger literary unit is reserved for this part of the service. In a service of Morning or Evening Prayer, one or more psalms are read or sung near the beginning of the service.

These practices have much to commend them. They offer a regular place for psalmody in worship, and give worshipers regular exposure to a range of psalm texts over time. These practices also convey the sense that Scripture includes not only didactic readings, but also doxological poetry. There is something altogether fitting about singing at least one of the assigned scriptural selections for the day.

In liturgies of Word and Sacrament, the use of a psalm between Old and New Testament readings can create some ambiguity (sometimes helpful, sometimes not) as to whether the psalm is functioning as a response to the first reading or as a presentation of Scripture in and of itself or even as an introduction to what follows. As noted above, the psalms in the Revised Common Lectionary primarily serve as responses to the Old Testament text. Yet if the psalm is to serve as the primary preaching text, it should ideally be experienced in liturgy as something that is significant in and of itself — not only as it stands in relationship to the prior reading. At minimum, a spoken or written note could explain its function as the preaching text.

Congregations that follow the patterns of traditional liturgy may often neglect other natural opportunities for using the Psalms in worship. For example, a metrical setting of a psalm might be sung in place of a processional or recessional hymn (unless told, most congregations may not realize the difference). Additional psalmody may be incorporated in a sequence of songs sung during the distribution of the Lord's Supper.

Other Congregations

Congregations that do not follow a fixed liturgy have limitless possibilities for using the Psalms in worship. Some of the more typical possibilities include the following:

1. If a sermon is based on a psalm, the psalm (like any other sermon text) could be read or sung just prior to the sermon.
2. If a sermon includes significant references to a psalm in addition to another primary text (as suggested above), then the psalm could be read or sung as the second Scripture lesson prior to the sermon, or read or sung as the conclusion to the sermon.
3. Psalms of praise and thanksgiving can be incorporated into a sequence of praise songs as a service begins.
4. Psalms of lament, confession, or thanksgiving can be read or sung as the introduction to one of the prayers during worship.
5. A benediction psalm (such as Ps 67) could be read or sung as the closing blessing to worship.

Framing the Congregation's Mode of Engagement

A neglected aspect of the use of the Psalms in worship is how congregations are asked to engage the text. In both formal and informal, liturgical and nonliturgical services, it is not uncommon for congregations to experience a psalm as a jumble of odd phrases and ancient geography. Outside of monastic communities, most worshipers are not psalm-literate. We are not familiar with their nuance and typical patterns of expression.

Being intentional about introducing the meaning(s) and purpose(s) of a specific text can significantly deepen the congregation's level of engagement with a psalm. A simple explanatory sentence or a brief notice in a printed or projected order of worship can accomplish a great deal unobtrusively. A more extensive introduction might be especially valuable if the congregation is not accustomed to using the Psalms. For example, Methodist pastor James Howell offered significant printed introductions during a summer sermon series on the Psalms. In a service that focused on Psalm 73, the following text appeared in the congregation's bulletin:

Psalm 73 is one of the most eloquent, and moving, of all the Psalms. It was Martin Buber's favorite; he asked that verses 23 and 24 be inscribed on his tombstone. And the last of Charles Wesley's 6,500 hymns was written on his deathbed, and it was inspired by Psalm 73. It begins with a little motto, one of those familiar religious sayings everyone knows and loves: "Surely God is good to the pure in heart."

But this Psalmist has a few questions, and they are intensely personal. Verses 1-12 are an outburst, a cry against the unfairness of life. The Psalmist, in some ways like Job, has been faithful to God — but has enjoyed no great "good" from God. Instead he has faced constant sickness and poverty — all made worse by the fact that he has to look upon wicked people who are all health and prosperity. Aren't there rewards for goodness? and punishments for wickedness? Why does it seem reversed so often? Verses 13-17 form a turning point, as the Psalmist manages not to jettison his faith in God. Somehow, going to the sanctuary of God changes everything. Verses 18-28 then form one of the most beautiful expressions of faith in God, love for God, intimacy with God, in all the Bible.[87]

Even better, at the beginning of each season print a schedule of the psalms that will be used each week in worship, with an invitation for worshipers to study or pray them prior to their use in worship.

Psalm Types

One of the most helpful single pieces of information for a congregation to know as it encounters a psalm for the first time is what type of psalm it is.[88] Psalm scholars use a variety of terms to name particular genres of psalms, but most groupings of the Psalms feature a list of genres like this:[89]

- *Salvation History Psalms* (such as Pss 78; 105; 136). These are psalms of thanksgiving for God's actions. They read like condensed history lessons about God's saving work with the people of Israel.

---

87. James C. Howell, "The Psalms in Worship and Preaching: A Report," in *Psalms and Practice*, 132-33.

88. See also the introduction to part I.

89. Introductory texts on the Psalms typically include schemes for organizing psalm types that are dependent upon the work of Hermann Gunkel (again, see the introduction to part I). More recently, some Psalms scholars have contested these categories.

- *Lament Psalms.* These are texts that begin with laments to God about the brokenness and pain of life. Most laments move from expressions of anger to expressions of trust or praise (with Ps 88 as the notable exception). Scholars often divide these texts into groups of "community laments" (such as Pss 80; 85; 137) and "individual laments" (such as Pss 13; 22; 42).
- *Thanksgiving Psalms.* Scholars often divide these texts into groups of "community thanksgivings" (such as Ps 124) and "individual thanksgivings" (such as Ps 116).
- *Hymns of Praise.* These are texts that focus on the praise of God — usually with reference to God's being and character (in contrast to God's actions in history).
- *Wisdom Psalms* (such as Pss 37; 49; 133). These psalms are like parts of the book of Proverbs, featuring wise statements about faithful living.
- *Torah Psalms* (such as Pss 1; 19; 119). These psalms both extol the virtues of God's law and summarize part of the law.
- *Songs of Trust* (such as Pss 11; 23; 27). These psalms express trust as their main motif.
- *Covenant Renewal Liturgies* (such as Pss 50 and 81). These psalms model and teach the importance of faithful covenant (or promise-based) prayer.
- *Royal Psalms* (such as Pss 2; 72; 110). These psalms feature references to the kings of Israel and are usually interpreted by Christians in a messianic way as referring to Jesus.
- *Zion Psalms* (such as Pss 46; 84; 122). These psalms extol the virtues of Mount Zion, the location of the temple in Jerusalem, and thus focus on the beauty of the presence of God.
- *Enthronement Psalms* (such as Pss 24; 47; 95-99). These psalms are directed to a king or are about a king. They highlight the image of God as the ruler of creation.
- *Psalms of Ascents or Pilgrim Psalms* (Pss 120-134). These psalms were sung by the people on their pilgrimages to Jerusalem.

Even a simple note in a printed order of service or spoken by a Scripture reader (e.g., "Hear Psalm 50 — a text for covenant renewal between God and the people") can help the congregation enter into its meaning more quickly. To be sure, the reading or singing of the Psalms in worship should not be a didactic experience with long explanations that overwhelm the beauty and power of the text. But brief introductory words can effectively highlight for worshipers the significance and central meaning of the text in unobtrusive ways.

Contemplation or Prayer

When Scripture is read in worship, the congregation is most often invited to contemplate the text. A narrative from 1 or 2 Kings, for example, invites the congregation to remember a certain historical episode and contemplate its meaning. A treatise from Paul invites the congregation to ask particular questions about the mystery of the gospel or to analyze its own level of commitment and obedience. But the texts of the Psalms are more intimate. When the Psalms are read or sung — particularly if the congregation participates in reading responsively or singing the text — we are often placing words of prayer on the lips of the people. We are inviting the congregation to make the prayers of the Psalms their own. The Psalms thus often engage us more personally and more intimately than other forms of biblical literature.

This raises the larger question. Are all the Psalms prayer, our speech to God? Or are they primarily Scripture, God's speech to us?[90] We can approach these questions by considering momentarily Scripture as a whole. Scripture has a variety of functions in Christian worship and in the life of prayer: it is the basis for proclamation, a sourcebook for meditation, a handbook for instruction, as well as a prayer book for liturgical praise and petition. The book of Philippians, for example, contains various types of texts that might be used in a variety of ways in worship: its opening greeting (Phil 1:2) might function as a liturgical greeting, its great christological hymn (2:5-11) might serve as a text for Christian praise, its testimony about life in Christ (3:2-11) might serve as a text for expository preaching, its call to persistent prayer (4:6) might be read as a biblical warrant for liturgical intercession. The same is true for the Psalms: some are typically used as prayers (e.g., Ps 51), some as mentors for meditation (e.g., Ps 119), some as oracles for proclamation (e.g., Ps 50).

90. See Davis, *Wondrous Depth*, 18; and Wallace, *Words to God*, chap. 1. Christoph F. Barth argued that although "there is no doubt that it [the Psalter] is meant to be frequently read and prayed . . . the Psalter is intended just as much, if not more, to be listened to." In part this is to "make clear the whole strangeness and harshness, the indelibly 'Israelite' element in the Psalms" ("The Psalms in the Worship of the Church," in Barth, *Introduction to the Psalms* [New York: Charles Scribner's Sons, 1966], 74).

Many psalms function in more than one way depending on their content and their liturgical context. Consider Psalm 72, for example, which Robert Alter notes "manages at once to be prayer, prophecy, portrait, and benediction."[91] This is why James Luther Mays speaks of the functions of praise, prayer, *and* instruction for the Psalter in the life of faith.[92] Just as in theology and in the living of the Christian life, the texts of the Psalms fulfill more than one function in Christian liturgy.[93]

Consider, then, a spectrum of possibilities in which a congregation might be asked to engage with a psalm.

$$\longleftarrow \hspace{8cm} \longrightarrow$$

| *Praying* | *Meditating* | *Wrestling* |

On one end of the spectrum, there are (frequent) times we invite worshipers to actually pray the psalm, to make the words of the text their own. This is the most intimate form of engagement. Congregational singing is an especially appropriate way to invite intimate engagement with the text.

On the other end of the spectrum there are psalms we do not dare pray on first reading — particularly the imprecatory psalms. These are the psalms we struggle with. This form of engagement might be cultivated by reading the psalm and leaving time for silent reflection. Alternatively, a worship leader might suggest what kinds of people (both within and beyond the congregation) might quite naturally pray a psalm like

91. Alter, *Art of Biblical Poetry*, 131.

92. James Luther Mays, *The Lord Reigns: A Theological Handbook to the Psalms* (Louisville: Westminster John Knox, 1994), 20-22. The varied functions of psalmody in early Christian worship are described by Paul F. Bradshaw, "From Word to Action: The Changing Role of Psalmody in Early Christianity," in *Like a Two-Edged Sword: The Word of God in Liturgy and History; Volumes in Honour of Canon Donald Gray*, ed. Martin R. Dudley (Norwich: Canterbury, 1995), 21-38.

93. See the discussion in Bradshaw, *Two Ways of Praying*, 89-96. I believe that it is this point that provides the correct angle to address the difficult question regarding the use of the imprecatory psalms in public worship. The imprecations cannot be used as liturgical prayer without a great deal of explanation. Yet they might function poignantly in liturgy as a source for meditation or exposition. For example, consider the striking juxtaposition of psalmic imprecations against the enemies of God with a New Testament reading concerning the "powers and principalities." Or consider reading the imprecations in stark juxtaposition with Jesus' command to pray *for* our enemies. In both cases, the imprecations have profound liturgical possibilities, if handled with care.

the one in question, and invite the congregation to offer the text in solidarity with them.

In between these two modes of engagement are texts that we meditate on, that we ponder, savor, and delight in. Here we want the congregation to engage and appropriate the text, but also have time to allow the text to sink in. Responsorial psalmody (described below) is one way of rendering the Psalms that allows for this kind of engagement, with its alternation between a congregational refrain and verses sung by a soloist or cantor.

Finally, it could be very appropriate for a given service to allow worshipers to engage a psalm text in more than one way. For example, in a service in which the psalm is the basis for preaching, the sermon might aim to help a congregation move from puzzling over a psalm to actually praying it. In this case the psalm could be read by a solo reader or choral reading group prior to the sermon and sung by the now-more-knowledgeable congregation after the sermon.

Christological Framings of Psalm Texts

Each psalm conveys different meanings in the light of the person of Jesus and the teaching of the New Testament. This is especially true for messianic psalms like Psalms 24, 72, and 110, and psalms that Jesus quoted, such as Psalm 22. Thoughtful worship leaders have the opportunity to either highlight or downplay the christological significance of psalms like these, sometimes with something as simple as a one-phrase spoken introduction.

If Psalm 22 is introduced (either verbally or in a printed service folder) with the phrase "the psalm Jesus quoted from the cross," or if Psalm 72 is introduced with the phrase "a psalm to extol the virtues of the king, true enough for King Solomon, even more fitting for Jesus, the Christ," the christological frame becomes very explicit. The same effect is achieved through the use of an explicitly christological spoken or sung refrain (see under "Responsorial Psalmody" below).

Some congregations never practice such framing, leaving more to the imagination. Others always practice such framing, sometimes with elaborate teaching comments prior to the reading of any scriptural text. Perhaps a wise rule of thumb is to suggest that any introductory comments or framing like this should match the liturgical context. That is, when a psalm is chosen for christological reasons, that can helpfully be made clear. When that is not primary, then any christological framing notes will likely distract worshipers.

In either case, there is great value in moderation, offering enough information to evoke deeper understanding by worshipers but not so much that the entire meaning of the text is pinned down before the text is read. Like all effective poetry, the texts of the Psalms, with their own powerful imagery and cadences, command a power all their own.

Canonical Context

Such framing of a psalm through a spoken or written introduction, musical refrain, or other liturgical action can also be helpful in engaging other kinds of psalm texts. We hear explicit psalmic prayers against the enemy quite differently in the light of Christ's command to pray *for* our enemies. One historical liturgical practice that arose, in part, out of this sense of discontinuity was the use of a brief psalm prayer following the liturgical recitation of a psalm. These prayers interpreted the Psalms in the light of New Testament experience.[94] Thus, Psalm 104, with its intriguing reference to the cosmic work of the spirit of God, could be followed by this Collect: "God of majesty, we are constantly surrounded by your gifts and touched by your grace; our words of praise do not approach the wonders of your love. Send forth your Holy Spirit, which came in fullness at Pentecost, that our lives may be refreshed and the whole world may be renewed, in Jesus Christ our Lord. Amen."

What was implicit in the psalm (the work of the Holy Spirit) is made explicit in the psalm prayer. A similar effect is achieved by concluding a psalm with the Gloria Patri or by following the reading of a given psalm with a Christian hymn based on the same text. For example, follow Psalm 72 with Watts's "Jesus Shall Reign Where'er the Sun," Psalm 98 with Watts's "Joy to the World," or Psalm 46 with Luther's "A Mighty Fortress Is Our God." These three familiar hymns are all based on specific psalms — but each not only reflects, but also interprets, the psalm on which it is based.

---

94. See texts of ancient psalm-collects in A. Wilmart and L. Brou, *The Psalter Collects from V-VI Century Sources,* Henry Bradshaw Society 83 (London: Henry Bradshaw Society, 1949). For recent texts, see *The Book of Common Worship* (Louisville: Westminster John Knox, 1993), 611-783. Psalm prayers were introduced to the Reformed tradition in some early metrical Psalters in both Geneva and Scotland. See J. A. Lamb, *The Psalms in Christian Worship* (London: Faith Press, 1962), 153.

Each of these liturgical practices has subtle ways of helping worshipers sense at once both the continuity and discontinuity between the Testaments. These practices are also wonderful topics for church education sessions. Many of the best church education sessions not only teach biblical literacy, but also help congregations better understand the use of the Bible in personal and communal worship.

Studying the Psalm

Once a psalm is chosen and placed in worship, how should it be brought to life?[95] How can we lift it off the printed page in a way that does justice to the power and poetry of the text?

Every rendering of a psalm, whether spoken or sung, is an act of interpretation. As J. P. Fokkelman argues, "Whether they realize it or not, readers, when engaged in the act of reading, are extremely involved: they infuse a text with meaning."[96]

Sometimes our renderings of the text fit beautifully with the text itself: imagine a reader reading Psalm 22 with quiet, somber longing, until a transition to a brighter, even exuberant, rendering of its final doxological verses.

Sometimes, however, reading — especially of the uninspired sort — can undermine the text. Reading Psalm 2 on "automatic pilot" — with the same tone of voice for "let us break their chains" (v. 3) and "today I have begotten you" (v. 7) — dulls the force of the contrasting rhetoric of the psalm. Indeed, reading on automatic pilot usually induces congregations to listen on automatic pilot.

Often, out of sheer necessity, a psalm will be read in worship with only a few moments of prior rehearsal. Or a musical setting of a psalm will be chosen in which a composer has already made key decisions about how the rhetoric of the psalm (its pace, structure, script, and poetic cadence) will be rendered.

Yet one of the most rewarding disciplines for any public reader of Scripture and for any liturgical musician is that of careful study of the

95. See also David Held, "The Psalms," and Paul G. Bunjes, "The Musical Carriage for the Psalms," in *Lutheran Worship: History and Practice*, ed. Fred L. Precht (St. Louis: Concordia, 1993), 471-77.

96. J. P. Fokkelman, *Reading Biblical Poetry* (Louisville: Westminster John Knox, 2001), 49.

psalm — to notice how its particular words and images convey meaning. Careful literary and theological analysis of psalm texts can lead to profound devotional encounters with the text, and lead to liturgical use of the texts in ways that help worshipers pray the psalms more meaningfully.

As with most poetry, the best place to begin in encountering the text is simply to read it (out loud). As one poetry scholar put it, "A poem may turn out to be a deep and complex experience, but the experience begins by responding to the language of poetry in front of you, not by detective work that puts that response aside."[97] Reading the text out loud once a day for a week, each time trying to simply make clear what is there, generates the kinds of questions that help us encounter the text more meaningfully.

Pace

First, the Psalms require a sense of *pace* suitable to their content. Psalms 96, 98, 121, and 149, among others, cry out to be spoken or sung with a sense of *anticipation*. Their crisp imperatives and tight parallelisms — salient attributes of the Hebrew poetry that most often (but not always) come through in translation — call for use of a bright pace. One acclamation of praise propels us into the next. In contrast, Psalm 51 and 73 require deliberate solemnity. They invite worshipers to pause for moments of silent reflection.

In general, in early-twenty-first-century North America, our liturgical reading and music are often (arguably) too fast. One of the key characteristics of poetry is its *density*, the way it compresses significant meaning into a modest number of lines. In general, the best kind of exposure to poetry — even in translation — is to *give it more time*.

Structure

Second, praying the Psalms can be enriched by sensitivity to their *structure*. Consider the following examples:

1. The genius of Psalm 19 lies in its stark juxtaposition of creation (vv. 1-6) and law (vv. 7-13) motifs. Even the hastiest examination of the psalm reveals its bipartite structure. How can we make this structure

97. Kenneth Koch, *Making Your Own Days: The Pleasure of Reading and Writing Poetry* (New York: Touchstone, 1998), 111.

447

and its redolent meaning come to life through its liturgical use? Consider rendering the psalm with two readers or cantors, each speaking one half of the psalm (vv. 1-6, 7-13), allowing the congregation to join in the final prayer of dedication (v. 14). Or, in a congregation that does not follow a strict liturgy, allow the psalm to inform the structure of the first two parts of a worship service, where the service might begin with the singing or reading of the first half of the psalm along with acts of praise for creation, and then continue with the second half of the psalm as a spur to confession and a guide for gratitude.

2. Similarly, Psalms 34 and 92 both begin with the praise of God and continue with instruction in the wisdom of God. In so doing, they cohere with the structure of most Sunday services of the Word. They might be used in two parts: one, at the beginning of worship, with its typical focus on praise; two, preceding the Scripture readings and sermon. Alternatively, they might be used in their entirety to pivot from the "praise" section to the "proclamation" section of worship.

3. Psalm 90 is a psalm in three stanzas, each of which features a very different perspective on time.[98] Consider using three readers or cantors to heighten the contrast between these three sections.

4. The ultimate significance of Psalm 13, and many other psalms of lament, depends on the arresting adversative "but" (v. 5) that pivots into the final vow of praise. Something — whether a musical accent, a change in readers, cantors, gestures, tone of voice — should highlight this key structural element.

5. Psalm 103's genius lies, in part, in the way wise instruction is embedded in praise. Its meaning, in part, lies in its structure. Consider introducing Psalm 103 by saying that it is like "an entire worship service wrapped up in a poem: it begins with a call to worship, continues with a medley of praise, leads up to a sermonlike proverb, and concludes with an extended doxology."

In sum, consider the structure of a psalm as a guide for bringing the psalm to life in liturgy. Preachers are accustomed to outlining both their text and their sermons. Some homileticians have argued that the outlines of the text and the sermon should look alike most of the time. I am suggesting that we begin to apply the same skills to liturgical practice —

98. Alter, *Art of Biblical Poetry,* 129.

both for the rendering of psalm texts in worship and for planning how the various elements of worship might be combined.

Script

Third, praying the Psalms requires sensitivity to their implicit or explicit *script.* We need to be like playwrights both as we study the Psalms and as we use them liturgically. Before singing or reading a psalm in worship, imagine scripting it for a choral reading group of four or forty people. Who should say what line — and why? Many psalms feature a complex juxtaposition of acclamations, petitions, oracles, and proverbs. Yet upon first reading (which is often the *only* reading for a congregation), these variations are not altogether clear.

One suggestion is that when psalms are sung and read, worship leaders should acknowledge their script and — when possible — assign roles in the assembly that call attention to dramatic shifts in voice. Oracles of salvation should be read by a single worship leader in response to the common prayer of the congregation. The shift in voice between verses 7 and 8 of Psalm 32 suggests a shift in the script for how the psalm is sung or read. Likewise, the oracle of Psalm 12:5 or Psalm 50:5, 7-15, 16b-23 might best be read or sung by a different voice than the one that begins the psalm. The same strategy might work well with proverblike wisdom sayings that are interspersed in the Psalms (e.g., Ps 103:15-19).[99]

More challenging are psalms of lament in which a salvation oracle, whether explicit or implicit, may function as a hinge that transforms a lament into an anticipation of thanksgiving. Thunderous silence cries out between the lines of Psalm 6:7-8. It is quite possible, in the ancient temple liturgy, that words of assurance or an oracle of salvation was spoken at this point.[100] In our use of the Psalter, the very least we might do is to interpose a brief time of silence if speaking the psalm or a brief musical interlude if singing it.

99. See Robert Davidson, *Wisdom and Worship* (Philadelphia: Trinity, 1990), 31-46; also Joyce Zimmerman, *Pray without Ceasing: Prayer for Morning and Evening* (Collegeville, Minn.: Liturgical Press, 1993), which features the voicing of several psalms for use in the context of daily prayer services, as well as helpful explanation in the introduction. One should be clear that the voicing is not certain.

100. See Joachim Begrich, "Das priesterliche Heilsorakel," *ZAW* 52 (1934): 81-92, and Miller, *They Cried,* 141-47, for more on salvation oracles. Note also the introduction to part I in the present volume.

Not only do the implied speakers sometimes change in a psalm, but so also does the implied audience. Psalm 30 begins with an address to God (vv. 1-3), and shifts to an address to the gathered congregation (vv. 4-5), only to return to a direct address to God (vv. 6-12). A shift in readers, or in tone of voice, or in posture or gesture can reflect this change. At times psalmic speech is "interior dialogue," the speech of the psalmist directed to the self (e.g., "Bless the LORD, O my soul").[101] Such phrases could be read by a single voice, with the complementary calls to praise directed to the whole cosmos read by the entire congregation. Psalm 4 may well be directed to two groups of people, the first a hostile group of enemies (vv. 2-3), the second a group of dispirited friends (vv. 4-5).[102] Again, the pacing and tone of a liturgical rendering of this psalm might well reflect this subtle change. No psalm has a more complex script than Psalm 2, with separate lines spoken by the kings of the nations (v. 3), the Lord (v. 6), and the one anointed by the Lord (vv. 7-9).[103] In sum, creative liturgical usage, even to the point of scripting the psalm, may do more for our understanding of and participation in a psalm than many expository sermons. Many congregations, even small congregations, are blessed with those skilled in dramatic arts, including junior high drama teachers, and high school students who participate in school plays. Often these are people with talents waiting to be used to bring the Psalms to life.

Poetic Lines

Fourth, praying the Psalms is enriched by sensitivity to their poetic qualities. At the most basic level, careful study of the text begins by simply observing where each poetic line ends. Poetic lines are more important than the verse markings found in the modern biblical text.

Indeed, responsive readings spoken directly from a printed Bible often manage to split poetic lines in ways that make even amateur poets cringe (see Ps 19:4-5 for one example where the verse markings do not match the natural divisions of the poetry). Instead of responsive readings, consider a choral reading of the psalm that allows variance in pace and sensitivity to parallel structures. This strategy allows readers to express the particular nuances of their assigned lines. It also involves the

---

101. The term "interior dialogue" is from Schökel, *Manual of Hebrew Poetics,* 178.
102. Schökel, *Manual of Hebrew Poetics,* 197.
103. See below for an example of Ps 2 for choral reading.

congregation enough to sustain interest, without overwhelming them with so much text to speak that it is impossible to follow the meaning.

Parallelism

Parallelism is the most common and significant Hebraic poetic device.[104] A huge portion of the Psalms features verses that seem at first glance to say the same thing twice (such as Ps 3:1: "O LORD, how many are my foes! / How many rise up against me!"). An effective reader is almost instinctively aware of this, using the pacing and tone of the reading to convey the relationship between the two (and sometimes three) related lines.

It is important to realize, however, that parallelism is not merely an archaic poetry form resulting from the felt need to say things twice. Rather, each slight alteration of the text helps us see a given reality in a new way — just as looking at an object with two eyes rather than one eye helps us perceive nuances and depth in the object.[105] In the words of Celestin Charlier, parallelism in Hebrew poety is "not only to enrich the primary statement by giving it precision, but also to create a gradual and insistent rhythm. The result can be compared to a succession of waves, ebbing and flowing over a rock, or to a series of concentric circles rising in a spiral around an axis."[106]

Even when an idea is presented twice in a single verse, the restatement usually contains subtle variation that adds nuance and depth. Psalm 100:3, for example, testifies that "it is God who made us, and we are his," and then restates the point, "we are his people, the sheep of his pasture." The restatement of the theme conveys the same basic point but adds an evocative sheep-pasture metaphor. An effective reading of the text could, through subtle changes in the tone of voice and in pacing, convey that those two statements are intimately related, but also that the second line introduces something new and lovely to reinforce the point.

These examples are a form of parallelism known as "synonymous parallelism." But there are other forms of parallelism, too. Some verses present "antithetical" lines (such as Ps 27:10: "Though my father and mother forsake me, / the LORD will receive me"). Still other verses develop

---

104. See also the introduction to part I.

105. Fokkelman, *Reading Biblical Poetry*, 78.

106. Celestin Charlier, *The Christian Approach to the Bible* (New York: Paulist, 1967), 138.

a comparison over the course of two lines, such that either line would be incomplete without the other (such as Ps 103:11: "For as high as the heavens are above the earth, / so great is his love for those who fear him").

To reiterate a point made above, it is extremely tempting for readers of the Psalms to read on "automatic pilot." That is, it is tempting to develop a regular, predictable cadence in which every verse is read in virtually the exact same way, with the same falling of vocal pitch near the end of every line. Yet the nuances of the biblical text resist this. Some verses present lines that are essentially synonymous; others introduce subtle metaphors in their second lines; others present stark contrasts. Learning to recognize and cherish these subtle moves is one well-tested way to come to love (and read!) the Psalms more deeply. And in each case, these poetic nuances suggest ways of reading or singing the psalm more imaginatively. After pondering the inner workings of each psalm, it is difficult to read the text out loud in the same way again.

In these sorts of ways, the close study of the psalm texts teaches us not only how to exegete for homiletical purposes, but also how to realize the psalm in liturgy. Such close study calls liturgical leaders to function like twentieth-century apprentices of German baroque composer Heinrich Schütz, whose brilliant settings of the Psalms evidence remarkable attention to many of these same poetic nuances.

To be sure, most worshipers are not interested in which verses of a given psalm feature antithetical parallelism. But, it is equally true that worshipers *will* come to value highly the thoughtful and poignant reading or singing of a psalm by a worship leader who cared enough to study the text in this way.

BIBLIOGRAPHY

On Reading Poetry

Hirsch, Edward. *How to Read a Poem and Fall in Love with Poetry.* New York: Harvest Books, 1999.

Koch, Kenneth. *Making Your Own Days: The Pleasure of Reading and Writing Poetry.* New York: Touchstone, 1998.

Hebrew Poetics

Alter, Robert. *The Art of Biblical Poetry.* New York: Basic Books, 1985.

Berlin, Adele. *The Dynamics of Biblical Parallelism.* Bloomington: Indiana University Press, 1985.

Fokkelman, J. P. *Reading Biblical Poetry: An Introductory Guide.* Louisville: Westminster John Knox, 2001.

Kugel, James K. *The Idea of Biblical Poetry: Parallelism and Its History.* New Haven: Yale University Press, 1981.

Muilenburg, James. "A Study in Hebrew Rhetoric: Repetition and Style." *VT,* supplement 1 (1953): 97-111.

Schökel, Luis Alonso. *A Manual of Hebrew Poetics.* Rome: Pontificio Istituto Biblico, 1988.

Watson, Wilfred G. E. *Classical Hebrew Poetry: A Guide to Its Techniques.* Sheffield: JSOT Press, 1984.

————. *Traditional Techniques in Classical Hebrew Verse.* Sheffield: Sheffield Academic, 1994.

Stek, John H. "The Stylistics of Hebrew Poetry." *CTJ* 9 (1974): 15-30.

Realizing the Psalms: Options for Singing or Speaking

Before proceeding any further, it is helpful to pause for a moment. Once preachers have selected a psalm for preaching, it is useful to consider the following questions. Discussing these kinds of questions would be especially valuable in a meeting of a worship team, worship planning team, worship committee, or other church leadership group. Together, these questions constitute a kind of worship planning checklist for preachers using the Psalms:

1. How will the psalm be presented? How might it be presented differently after the sermon versus before it?
2. What information will your congregation need to know before they hear or sing the psalm for the first time?
3. Can part of the psalm be incorporated into one of the spoken prayers in the service? Alternatively, can the Psalms be the pattern for an extemporaneous prayer?
4. Can the psalm be sung at some point in the service? What kind of music will best capture the spirit of the psalm?
5. Can portions of the psalm be used as a call to worship or a benediction?
6. For leaders in congregations with a flexible structure of the service, can the service itself follow (at least in part) the structure of the psalm?

7. What similar psalms can you recommend to your congregation for their personal prayers?

Having at least preliminary answers to these questions in mind will prove instructive as we navigate the various options for realizing the psalms presented below.

Throughout Christian history the Psalms have been presented or "performed" in liturgy in many ways, both spoken (solo voice, choral reading, or congregational responsive reading) and sung (in one of several forms of chant, in responsorial settings, metrical settings, solo or choral anthems), though the vast majority of practices in history push beyond speaking to some form of song. In recent years the Psalms have also been sung to new settings in popular, folk, or contemporary styles of music, and depicted visually. The following paragraphs briefly describe this range of options, offer brief commentary on their strengths and weaknesses, and provide an annotated guide to publications and recordings of each mode of presentation.[107]

Solo Reading

The simplest form of rendering a psalm is having it read by a single reader or lector, just as with any other Scripture reading. While appropriate for all psalms, the use of a single reader is particularly fitting for the Psalter's most intimate texts, its personal prayers of lament and trust. In fact, congregations that practice regular corporate singing or recitation of the Psalms may benefit from occasionally diverging from this practice for certain intimate psalms (perhaps Pss 88 and 139).

While a solo reading is relatively simple compared with some of the more elaborate forms for reading or singing, it is by no means an easy alternative. Reading poetry is a challenging assignment. The best readings are those that are alert to a psalm's pace, form, script, and other poetic devices that contribute to its meaning (see the previous section for more details).

107. For other categorizations of ways to render the Psalms, see Kenneth E. Williams, "Ways to Sing the Psalms," *Reformed Liturgy and Music* 18 (1984): 12-16; *Pilot Study on a Liturgical Psalter* (Washington, D.C.: International Commission on English in the Liturgy, 1982); Erik Routley, *Musical Leadership in the Church* (Nashville: Abingdon, 1967), 78; and Routley, "On Using the Psalms in Worship," in *Exploring the Psalms* (Philadelphia: Westminster, 1975).

BIBLIOGRAPHY

Printed Resources

Seerveld, Calvin. *Voicing God's Psalms*. Grand Rapids: Eerdmans, 2005. The volume includes a recording of the author's effective and moving readings of his own translations.

Workbook for Lectors and Gospel Readers. Liturgy Training Publications. Published annually for lectionary texts. Scripture readings are printed with helps for effective interpretation.

For general guidance in the public reading of Scripture, see:

Bartow, Charles L. *Effective Speech Communication in Leading Worship*. Nashville: Abingdon, 1988.

Brack, Harold A. *Effective Oral Interpretation for Religious Leaders*. Englewood Cliffs, N.J.: Prentice-Hall, 1964.

Childers, Jana. *Performing the Word: Preaching as Theater*. Nashville: Abingdon, 1998.

Jacks, G. Robert. *Getting the Word Across: Speech Communication for Pastors and Lay Leaders*. Grand Rapids: Eerdmans, 1995.

Rang, Jack C. *How to Read the Bible Aloud: Oral Interpretation of Scripture*. New York: Paulist, 1994.

Schmit, Clayton J. *Public Reading of Scripture: A Handbook*. Nashville: Abingdon, 2002.

Choral Reading

Choral readings of psalm texts offer rich possibilities for presenting the Psalms in creative and accessible ways in many congregations. The advantages are many: multiple readers convey the communal nature of many psalm texts; rehearsed reading promises to capture more of the poetic nuance than unrehearsed congregational reading; and the interplay among readers is useful for capturing the dialogic nature of many psalms.

The danger of this practice may be the temptation toward overly complicated renderings of a psalm that call more attention to the innovation of the performance than the text — though this danger is no different from dangers that face any preacher or musician in almost any part of the service.

455

The best choral readings of psalm texts are those developed with careful attention to the text and structure of the psalm itself — rather than through an arbitrary assignment of parts to particular voices. Consider the following examples from Calvin Seerveld, *Voicing God's Psalms* (Grand Rapids: Eerdmans, 2005).

Psalm 8

[Chorus begins]

1 Lord, our Lord! How wonderful is your name in all the earth!
  Lord, our Lord! How wonderful is your name in all the earth!
2 You who have set your glory in the heavens
  so that your adversaries, obstinate and vindictive enemies,
      may be stilled,
  you may now find that glory praised in the mouths of us
      babes and sucklings.

[Solo voice addresses God]

3 When I look at the night sky, the work of your finger,
  When I look at the moon and the stars, held there by your hand,
4 What are we mortal humans that you remember a man or a
      woman and pay them attention?

[Chorus thunders in answer]

5 You have made us humans almost like gods,
  crowning humanity with glory, a lordliness,
6 making us rule over the work of your hands,
  with everything put under our feet:
7 sheep and cows, wild animals of the fields,
8 birds of the heavens, fish in the waters
  and whatever other creatures prowl the deep paths of the sea —
9 O Lord, our Lord! How wonderful is your name in all the earth!
  Lord, our Lord, how wonderful is your name in all the earth!

This setting of Psalm 8 would work well with a group of almost any size. Only one solo reader is needed. The switch from the group to a solo reading and back nicely complements the text's switch from first-person plural to singular to plural. And the congregation might be invited to express the last line.

Psalm 2

The wise cantor:

1 Why do the peoples of the world rage about like madmen?
   Why in the world do the different nations keep on thinking up
        stupid schemes?
2 Earth kings get together "for a consultation" —
   important rulers hold conferences all together
   against the LORD God and against God's anointed one *(mashiach)*.
   These earthly rulers say:
3 "Let us smash the chains of this God that hold us down!
   Let us throw off the reins of God's 'anointed one'!"

Another liturgete, perhaps a priest:

4 The One who sits enthroned in heaven begins to laugh,
   my LORD mimics their foolish bluster;
5 and then God turns to them in holy anger,
   stops the upstarts short with God's fierce outrage:
6 "It was I! it is I who have set up my anointed king
   on Zion, my set-apart mountain."

Princely ruler taking official part in the liturgy:

7 Yes, I will recite the decisive appointment by the LORD God.
   God said to me:
   "You are my son. Today is the day I have borne you.
8 Ask it of me and I will give you peoples of the world
        for your heritage;
   the most distant nations of the earth will be yours to tend.
9 You may have to break them with a rod of iron.
   You may have to smash them for remolding
   as a sculpting potter reshapes her clay dish — "

[The congregation stands]

Wise cantor again:

10 So now, you small-time little rulers, you had better wise up!
  You who only judge on the earth,
   hadn't you better get the point?
11 Serve the LORD God with an attentive awe —
   Take joy *in your task only* with trembling —
   Give homage to this *adopted* son *of God too* —
   lest he also get worked up, and you obliterate any way
      for you to walk,
   for God's anger can flash up like lightning. . . .

Congregated chorus:

12 Blessèd are all those who have run
   to take shelter with the anointed one.
   Blessèd are all those who have run
   to take shelter with the anointed one.
   Blessèd are all those who have run
   to take shelter with the anointed one.

This example involves a bit more interpretive work, suggesting multiple readers and the dramatic element of the congregation standing. Any sermon on this text would benefit greatly from a reading like this that helped the congregation sense the interior drama, the shifts in voice, and the dramatic contrasts the text paints between the rulers and God's anointed.

Examples of choral readings of the Psalms can be found in:

Griggs, Donald L. *Praying and Teaching the Psalms.* Nashville: Abingdon, 1984.
Parker, John, and Audra Parker. *Psalms for Worship.* Shawnee Press/Harold Flammer Music.
Perry, Michael. *The Dramatized Old Testament.* Grand Rapids: Baker, 1994. Suggested choral readings for most psalms.
Seerveld, Calvin. *Voicing God's Psalms.* Grand Rapids: Eerdmans, 2005.

Responsive or Antiphonal Readings

Psalms may also be read responsively with a single leader alternating with the full assembly, or with the assembly divided into two or more groups — either by gender or by seating arrangement.[108]

Antiphonal readings are a staple of some monastic renderings of the Psalter during their cycle of daily prayer (though other monastic communities sing the majority of psalms). Responsive readings also became a prominent way of increasing congregational participation in worship among twentieth-century Protestants. A large number of twentieth-century hymnals included a section of responsive readings of the Psalms. This mode of rendering the Psalms has the advantage of being relatively easy to do with little rehearsal or preparation.

This practice is, however, very difficult to do well. And many musicians lament the lost opportunities in having congregations read, rather than sing, a psalm. Indeed, it is this practice that Earle Bennet Cross labeled "deplorable." There are at least three barriers to overcome to make this practice work well.

The first barrier is the verse markings of modern Bibles, which often are the basis for marking off who reads what text. In many psalms, verse markings do not correspond with the form or flow of the poetry (and were added long after each psalm was originally composed). This can easily be remedied by reprinting the psalm with markers for readers that correspond to the poetic structure rather than the verse markings.

Another barrier to effective responsive readings is the low-pitched tone in which most congregations habitually read together. This is, no doubt, a difficult habit to break. But leaders could consider adding instructional cues to the reading (e.g., "read with quiet intensity" or "with urgency"), much like the composer's cues in a musical anthem. Even subtle invitations to read with interpretive sensitivity can make quite a difference in congregational reading.

Still another issue is the pace of congregational readings. Many monastic communities over time develop a beautiful contemplative pace for reading the text, with ample silence between verses or half-verses. In some monastic communities all psalms are read at the same measured,

108. Some sources make a distinction between "responsive" or "responsorial" readings (alternation between a single reader or small group of readers and the congregation) and "antiphonal" readings (alternation between two or more groups within the congregation).

contemplative pace, regardless of genre. This has the value of encouraging a disciplined, contemplative approach to all texts, though it does risk missing some of the exuberance of the more celebratory psalms. Other communities intentionally develop variation in their approach to group reading, rendering psalms of praise and thanksgiving with more exuberance and rendering psalms of lament or intimate trust with more reflection. For congregations that use responsive reading infrequently, it can be enormously helpful to have a choir or other leadership group rehearse the reading of the psalm ahead of time and lead the congregation in speaking their parts.

BIBLIOGRAPHY

Readings with Musical Refrains

The following hymnals include several psalms set for responsive reading, with boldface print to indicate the congregation's part. Each of the sources alternates parts between leader and people in ways that follow the poetic structure of the psalm rather than verse divisions. Each text also includes a musical refrain (see "Responsorial Psalmody" below).

> *Chalice Hymnal.* St. Louis: Chalice, 1995. Pp. 726-68.
>
> *Come, Let Us Worship: The Korean-English Presbyterian Hymnal and Service Book.* Louisville: Geneva Press, 2001. Pp. 393-537. In both Korean and English.
>
> *The Covenant Hymnal: A Worshipbook.* Chicago: Covenant Publications, 1996. Pp. 779-861.
>
> *Sing! A New Creation.* Grand Rapids: Faith Alive, 2002. A publication of the Reformed Church of America, the Christian Reformed Church, and the Calvin Institute of Christian Worship.
>
> *Voices United.* Etobicoke, Ont., Canada: United Church Publishing House, 1996. The denominational hymnal of the United Church of Canada. See pp. 724-875, which also include a few metrical psalm settings.
>
> *United Methodist Hymnal.* Nashville: United Methodist Publishing House, 1989. Pp. 736-862. The official denominational hymnal of the United Methodist Church includes 100 responsorial selections, including one for each psalm appointed by the 1983 Common Lectionary.

Readings Only

Hymnal: A Worshipbook. Brethren Press, Faith and Life Press, Mennonite Publishing House, 1992. See nos. 811-825. A hymnal for the Church of the Brethren, the General Conference Mennonite Church, and the Mennonite Church in North America.

Trinity Hymnal. Atlanta: Great Commission Publications, 1990. Pp. 785-841. The hymnal of the Presbyterian Church of America and Orthodox Presbyterian Church. Responsive readings for portions of most psalms.

Voices in Worship: Hymns of the Christian Life. Christian Publications, 2003. Pp. 674-734. A hymnal for Christian and Missionary Alliance congregations. Includes over sixty responsive readings based on representative examples of each type of psalm.

Classification Challenges

Any classification system for types of psalm singing will be inadequate to convey the multiple possibilities that composers and songwriters have at their disposal. I have chosen to present this material in four basic categories: chant, responsorial settings, metrical psalmody, and Scripture choruses.

The challenge is that some chant involves responses by the congregation, some responsorial settings use verses that are metrical, and some metrical psalms are done in a popular music style and thus are known as Scripture choruses. Indeed, strictly speaking, the term "chant" refers, in practice, to a melodic style, "responsorial" refers to a type of leadership, "metrical" to a type of textual adaptation, and "chorus" (often) to a style of music.

Still, these four categories seem to me to map the territory most efficiently, reflecting the basic primary musical literatures used in the majority of North American congregations.

Chant

While reading psalms is accessible and open to several creative variations, the vast majority of resources for rendering the Psalms in worship involve singing. The Psalms cry out to be sung.

And indeed, the Psalms have been sung for three thousand years, in innumerable musical idioms and styles. The most ancient traditions for psalm singing — and indeed, some of the most vital living traditions — involve some form of chant. Rendering a psalm by means of chant has two main advantages. First, it invites the participation of the community (either a choir or the entire congregation), a fitting mode of expression for corporate prayer. Second, in contrast to metrical psalmody (see below), it allows for singing the unadapted text of the psalm.

For congregations new to chanting, the process of learning to chant together in a manageable unison may seem daunting. However, the practice is very learnable, provided there is a confident and patient musical leader. In fact, Erik Routley once referred to chant as "the only really simple way of singing [the Psalms] congregationally."[109] Over the past decade I have been gratefully surprised to hear numerous testimonies of pastors, musicians, and worshipers in a variety of traditions who have said, in effect, "chanting psalmody seemed daunting, but wasn't. Once we started, it grew and developed quite naturally, and now seems as natural as breathing." Typically, the most successful chanting happens in communities with a small group or choir that rehearses it first in order to unify the pace and strengthen the basic cadences of the chant.

There are several vibrant living traditions for chanting the Psalms. Each of the following forms of chant can be rendered in several ways:

- Having the whole congregation sing the entirety of the psalm text.
- Having a cantor (or small ensemble) sing a verse, with the entire congregation answering with the subsequent verse. This may be known as the "responsorial" form of chant (though the term "responsorial" can mean different things in the context of psalmody).
- Having the congregation divide into two equal groups and sing each verse or half-verse in alternation. This is often called "antiphonal chant."

Note: some psalm traditions suggest alternating between a cantor and the assembly at the half-verse, with the congregation essentially completing the thought of the cantor. While this is technically possible, it also can break up the psalm into too many tiny parts. It also can make it difficult to interpret the nuance of the poetic parallelism contained within the verse (see the discussion on parallelism above).

In every form, what distinguishes chant from other musical forms is

109. Routley, *Musical Leadership,* 67.

the closeness of the music to human speech. Chant is a form of heightened speech. Erik Routley once advised thinking of chant as "reading-plus" rather than "music-minus." Here are several forms of chant.

Psalm Tones and Pointed Text The simplest form involves the use of an eight-note psalm tone, with "pointing" marks included in the printed text.

1. *Music.* The eight notes outline a simple melodic pattern that can be applied to any text, regardless of its length. Typically, the eight notes are divided into two four-note sequences, the second of which feels like a satisfying musical completion of the first. (Or, to use slightly more technical terminology: the first is an antecedent phrase; the second is a consequent phrase.)

In each of these four-note sequences, the first pitch (called the "reciting tone") is the pitch on which the first several words of each half-verse are sung. The final three notes create musical movement near the end of the phrase. Several liturgical resources offer double tones with four (rather than two) four-note clusters. These provide music for two rather than one psalm verse.

2. *Pointed text.* Printing marks included within the psalm text itself guide singers in mapping these musical phrases appropriately onto texts — no matter how short or how long a given verse might be. Each verse is divided into two parts, typically marked by an asterisk (*), with the first half of the verse sung to the first part of the psalm tone, and the second half sung to the second part of the psalm tone. A simple mark, usually a dot, is placed above the syllable at which the singer switches from the reciting tone to the remaining pitches.

Singers would recite the first syllables of a line on the first pitch of the psalm tone, and then sing the last three syllables on the last three notes of the tone. The point, then, tells the singer when to change pitch. The point is usually placed above an accented syllable, and at a point in the phrase that guarantees that an accented syllable is sung on the final pitch.

The most effective chant is usually very much like speech. The pace for chanting a text is similar to that of reading it out loud. Accented syllables are stressed in singing, just as they quite naturally are in speaking.

Fortunately, most congregations can learn this form of chanting without any technical knowledge of textual accent, antecedent and consequent phrases, and text points. They simply hear it done, and follow the lead.

BIBLIOGRAPHY

See the following resources for this form of psalmody.

Hymns and Psalms. London: Methodist Publishing House, 1983. This project of the British Methodist Conference includes the melody line only for several chant settings of the Psalms.

Libro de Liturgia Cántico. Minneapolis: Augsburg Fortress, 1998. A Spanish-language hymnal of the Evangelical Lutheran Church in America. Includes pointed text for several psalms in Spanish and multiple psalm tones. Pp. 151-79.

Lutheran Book of Worship. Minneapolis: Augsburg, 1978. The official hymnal of the Evangelical Lutheran Church in America. Includes pointed text for the entire Psalter (pp. 215-89) and ten psalm tones (p. 291). See also D. Rotermund, *Intonations and Alternative Accompaniments for LBW Psalm Tones.* St. Louis: Concordia.

Lutheran Worship. St. Louis: Concordia, 1982. Pp. 313-68. The official hymnal of the Lutheran Church–Missouri Synod. Includes the pointed text for the entire Psalter, ten psalm tones, and instructions on chanting psalmody. See also D. Rotermund, *Intonations and Alternative Accompaniments for LW Psalm Tones.* St. Louis: Concordia.

A New Hymnal for Churches and Schools. Edited by Jeffery Rowthorn and Russell Schulz-Widmar. New Haven: Yale University Press, 1992. Five psalm tones and eight antiphons, along with the pointed printing of a majority of psalm texts (also includes thirteen metrical psalms and twenty-four hymns based on psalms).

Anglican Chant   Anglican chant uses psalm tones and a pointed text, just as the previous example, but features psalm tones with four-part harmony. The use of this harmony, often with organ accompaniment, has created a very expressive and beautiful form of psalmody.

The best examples of Anglican chant feature the sensitive adaptation of a given psalm tone to the meaning of each verse of text. For Psalm 23, for example, expressive organists can use soft and subtle sounds to accompany the words "The Lord is my shepherd," dark and brooding sounds to accompany "the valley of the shadow of death," and triumphant sounds to accompany "I will dwell in the house of the Lord forever." Expressive choir directors may, for example, ask singers to sing Psalm 24 with both quiet intensity (for phrases like "who shall ascend the hill of the Lord") and majestic breadth (for phrases like "The Lord, mighty in battle, is the king of glory"). The combination of a repeated harmonized melody, with dramatic possibilities for choir and organ, makes this form of psalmody one of the most expressive. I should also note that some congregations have explored how this same approach to psalmody might work with jazz chords in a very different musical idiom than the choirs and organs of English cathedrals.

BIBLIOGRAPHY

Music

Hymnal 1982: Service Music. Accompaniment Edition. Vol. I. Church Publishing, 1982. Nos. S 408-445.
The RSCM Chant Book. Croydon, England: Royal School of Church Music, n.d.
Wyton, Alec, ed. *The Anglican Chant Psalter.* New York: Church Publishing, 1987.

Recordings

The beauty and popularity of Anglican chant are signaled by the significant number of available recordings.

Psalms. 2 vols. Virgin Classics. Westminster Abbey Choir. Martin Neary, director.
Psalms from St. Paul's. 11 vols. Hyperion.
The Psalms of David. 10 vols. Priory.
The Psalms of David from King's Choir of King's College. 3 vols. EMI Records, Ltd.

In general, this form of chant is best for choirs and organists with ample rehearsal time. As Erik Routley once said of it: "Never was there such exquisite Psalm singing as one can count on in the cathedrals: but the congregation at large has to some extent lost this."[110] This form of chant is also very valuable for devotional use made possible by modern recordings.

Gelineau Psalmody Eager to promote a form of chanted psalmody appropriate for congregational use, in the early 1950s Roman Catholic li-

110. Erik Routley, *Twentieth Century Church Music* (New York: Oxford University Press, 1964), 108.

turgical reformer Joseph P. Gelineau developed a form of chant in which a regular pulse is maintained and accented syllables in the text are sung to correspond with the recurring pulse. Thus, the basic idea behind Gelineau chant is that the presence of a regular pulse makes it easier for a congregation to sing together. This form of psalmody is especially associated with the Grail Psalter, a translation that gives particular attention to the pattern of syllabic stress in the English text.

When well led, this form of chant can be effective for encouraging participation. When poorly led, it can risk artificial imposition of a rhythm on a text that may be too complex to fit it. Published settings of Gelineau psalms also feature antiphons that recur throughout the psalm.

Note: most often Gelineau chants are sung with a congregational refrain — and thus could well have been included below in the section on responsorial psalmody. I have included them here because of their unique approach to chanting the text.

BIBLIOGRAPHY

Printed Resources

Caroll, J. Robert. *A Guide to Gelineau Psalmody.* Chicago: GIA Publications. A how-to guide for singing psalms in this style.

Lectionary Psalms: Grail/Gelineau. Chicago: GIA Publications. The complete Psalter in Gelineau-style settings. GIA also publishes several smaller volumes of Gelineau settings, and a few individual psalms. These individual settings would be useful for a choir that might experiment with this style of chanting for a particular service.

Recording

Joseph Gelineau: Psalms of David. Chicago: GIA Publications, 1995. With the Cathedral Singers, Richard Proulx, conductor.

Plainchant Many plainchant settings are essentially variations on the psalm tones and pointed texts described above, but with a more extensive pattern of notes to end each psalm tone sequence. More complex patterns of chant involve use of a unique chantlike melody for each psalm verse. Published and recording examples offer historic melodies that date back into the medieval period, from both Western and Eastern liturgical rites. The most complex forms of chant, in which the cantor improvises a melody in the style of a given chant, are often called "cantillation."

BIBLIOGRAPHY

Printed Resources

By Flowing Waters: Chant for the Liturgy. A Collection of Unaccompanied Song for Assemblies, Cantors, and Choirs. Edited by Paul F. Ford. Includes 102 psalms. Liturgical Press.

Hymnal 1982: Service Music. Accompaniment Edition. Vol. 1. Church Publishing, 1982. No. S 446.

The Plainchant Psalter. Edited by James Litton. New York: Church Hymnal Corporation, 1988. Includes substantial introduction on the practice of chanting the psalms, and plainchant psalm tones, with pointed text, for all 150 psalms.

Psalterium monasticum. Available from GIA Publications. Includes Gregorian settings of the Psalms in the Liturgy of the Hours based on the Vatican-approved *Thesaurus liturgiae horarum monasticae.*

Responsorial Psalmody (or Psalmody with Congregational Refrains or Antiphons)

The term "responsorial psalmody" refers to any rendering of psalms in a back-and-forth, call-and-response format between a leader or small group of singers and the congregation.

Often, however, the term has come to be associated with the use of a refrain or antiphon sung by the congregation in conjunction with either the reading or singing of the entire psalm by a single voice (reader or cantor) or choir.

As they frame the psalm text, these refrains play a significant interpretive role, signaling to the congregation a key theme or image in the text. Often a key phrase or central verse of the psalm is chosen as the antiphon or refrain.[111] Some published settings choose refrains or antiphons that are not directly from the psalm, but rather come from

---

111. For a variety of recent examples of responsorial psalmody, see John Holbert, S. T. Kimbrough, Jr., and Carlton R. Young, *Psalms for Praise and Worship: A Complete Liturgical Psalter* (Nashville: Abingdon, 1992); *The Psalter: Psalms and Canticles for Singing* (Louisville: John Knox, 1993); and Betty Pulkingham and Kevin Hackett, *Celebration Psalter* (Pacific, Mo.: Cathedral Music Press, Mel Bay Publications, 1991).

the season of the year or place in the service in which the psalm might be sung. (Note: in some contexts the term "refrain" refers to the use of an actual line from the psalm, while the term "antiphon" refers to a paraphrase or summary of the meaning of the psalm.)

This form of psalmody works especially well for psalms that themselves have refrains, as do Psalms 42, 46, 59, 80, and 107, for example. It is especially effective in psalms where a refrain may not be noticed upon first reading, as in the acclamation "God is holy" in Psalm 99:3, 5, 9.

This method of psalm singing is also useful because it can be particularly responsive to local needs and cultural contexts. Refrains could presumably be drawn from *any* musical style. Published refrains are currently available in classical, jazz, folk, folk-rock, gospel, and other musical idioms.

This method of psalm singing has also achieved an impressive ecumenical reach in the past two generations. Several mainline Protestant, liturgical Protestant, Roman Catholic, and even some evangelical publishers have issued extensive publications of responsorial psalmody. Evangelical and charismatic churches may well be drawn to this tradition because of the recent publication of volumes of responsorial psalmody in a variety of folk music styles. In fact, several praise choruses (which are often based on a single psalm verse) may be used as a congregational refrain before, during, and after the reading of a psalm.

Responsorial psalmody has the advantage of using the actual biblical text, not a poetic reworking of it (though some responsorial psalm settings feature reworkings of the psalm text for solo singers or cantors). In the hands of skilled composers and cantors, responsorial psalmody calls attention to the poetic features of the Psalter that are so carefully studied by biblical scholars. It is also quite possible for local musicians to compose psalm refrains in ways that are attentive to local needs — making this one of the most contextual forms of psalmody.

BIBLIOGRAPHY

Printed Resources

The Basilica Psalter: Responsorial Psalms for the Parish Church. Edited by Jay Hunstiger. Collegeville, Minn.: Liturgical Press, 1990.

Book of Psalms. Presbyterian Church in Canada, 1995. Responsorial settings with at least two different refrain options and psalm tones for each of the 150 psalms.

Daw, Carl P., Jr., and Kevin Hackett. *A Hymn Tune Psalter.* New York: Church Publishing, 1998. Responsorial psalms with psalm tones and antiphons derived from familiar hymn tunes.

Holbert, John C., S. T. Kimbrough, Jr., and Carlton R. Young, eds. *Psalms for Praise and Worship.* Nashville: Abingdon, 1992. Pointed printing of all 150 psalms, along with 127 musical antiphons and several psalm tones.

Lead Me, Guide Me: The African American Catholic Hymnal. Chicago: GIA Publications, 1987. Includes over 20 responsorial psalms, with music in African American gospel style (nos. 499-545), plus 20 psalm tones (nos. 546-565).

Lift Every Voice and Sing II: An African American Hymnal. New York: Church Hymnal Corporation, 1993. Includes 8 responsorial psalms, with music in African American gospel style. Pp. 273-80.

Mil Voces Para Celebrar: Himnario Metodista. Nashville: United Methodist Publishing House, 1996. Includes responsorial settings for the majority of psalms in Spanish. Pp. 87-140.

The New Century Psalter. Cleveland: Pilgrim Press, 1999. Responsorial settings for all 150 psalms.

Psalms and Ritual Music. 3 vols. Years A, B, C, in multiple editions. World Library Publications.

Psalms for the Church Year. 10 vols. Chicago: GIA Publications. Responsorial psalms for cantor and congregation in a folk liturgical style.

The Psalter: Psalms and Canticles for Singing. Louisville: Westminster John Knox, 1993. An extensive collection of responsorial psalms and psalm tones in a variety of formats and styles.

Psalter for Worship. 3 vols. Cycles A, B, C. Minneapolis: Augsburg Fortress.

Singing the Psalms. 5 vols. Portland: Oregon Catholic Press.

This Far by Faith: An African American Resource for Worship. Minneapolis: Augsburg Fortress, 1996. Nos. 1-36. Responsorial psalms and psalm tones, with music in African American gospel style.

United Methodist Hymnal. Nashville: United Methodist Publishing House, 1989. The denominational hymnal of the United Methodist Church. Includes 100 responsorial selections for each psalm that is appointed by the 1983 Common Lectionary. Pp. 736-862.

Jazz Settings

Carter, Bill, ed. *Swing a New Song to the Lord: Resources for Jazz Worship.* Presbybob Music (visit www.presbybop.com). Includes 9 psalm settings.

Jazz Psalms — Sheet Music. Grand Rapids: Calvin College, 2004. A recording is also available from Calvin College.

Single Authors

Alonso, Tony, Michael Mahler, and Lori True. *As Morning Breaks and Evening Sets: Psalms, Canticles, and Hymns for the Liturgy of the Hours.* Winona, Minn.: St. Mary's Press, 2004. Includes 10 responsorial psalm settings for cantor and congregation in a folk liturgical style. A recording of music from this collection is also available from GIA Publications.

Bolduc, Ed. *A Collection of Songs and Psalms.* World Library Publications.

Burkhardt, Michael. *Psalms for the Church Year.* MorningStar Music Publishers.

Consiglio, Cyprian, O.S.B. *Lord, Open My Lips: Music for the Hours.* Portland: Oregon Catholic Press. Includes 9 psalm settings. A recording of music from these collections is also available from the publisher.

Cooney, Rory. *Cries of the Spirit.* 2 vols. Portland: Oregon Catholic Press. Includes responsorial psalm settings for cantor and congregation in a folk liturgical style. A recording of music from this collection is also available from the publisher.

Cotter, Jeanne. *We Are God's People: Psalms for the Family of God.* GIA Publications. Includes 10 responsorial psalm settings for cantor and congregation in a folk liturgical style. A recording of music from this collection is also available from GIA Publications.

Guimont, Michael. *Lectionary Psalms* and *Psalms for the Revised Common Lectionary.* GIA Publications. A recording of music from these collections is also available from GIA Publications.

Hass, David. *Light and Peace: Morning Praise and Evensong.* GIA Publications. Includes 4 responsorial psalm settings for cantor and congregation in a folk liturgical style. A recording of music from this collection is also available from GIA Publications.

Hawthorne, Robert A. *Portland Psalter: Book One; Liturgical Years ABC.* Church Publishing. Settings for all psalms appointed for the Sunday Eucharist according to the Book of Common Prayer lectionary and the Revised Common Lectionary. *Book Two* will contain the balance of psalm settings as well as a CD-ROM with printable versions of the congregational refrains.

Hopson, Hal. *18 Psalms for the Church Year.* Hope Publishing Company. See also his *Psalm Refrains and Tones* and *10 More Psalms* (also Hope Publishing).

Hurd, Bob, Eleazar Cortés, Jaime Cortez, Mary Frances Reza, and Donna Peña. *Cantaré Eternamente / For Ever I Will Sing Bilingual Psalms for the Liturgical Year.* 2 vols. Portland: Oregon Catholic Press. Includes 46 bilingual psalms. A recording of music from these collections is also available from the publisher.

Kelly, Columba, O.S.B. *Lectionary Psalms for Lent and Easter* and *Lectionary Psalms for Advent and Christmas.* For cantor, assembly, and keyboard.

Kreutz, Robert. *Psalms.* Portland: Oregon Catholic Press.

Gerike, Henry V. *Psallite: Psalms Settings for the Church Year.* St. Louis: Concordia. 23 psalm settings.

Hruby, Dolores. *Seasonal Psalms for Children.* World Library Publications.

Psalm Songs. Edited by David Ogden and Alan Smith. 3 vols. London: Cassell, 1998. Also published by Augsburg Fortress, 1998. Responsorial psalms for cantor and congregation in a folk liturgical style. Also available in a one-volume *Psalm Songs: Complete Set.*

Rosas, Carlos. *¡Grita de Alegría! Salmos para el año litúrgico.* Portland: Oregon Catholic Press.

Schiavone, John. *A Lectionary Psalter.* Psalms and Gospel acclamations for Sundays, solemnities, and feasts for the three-year lectionary cycle.

Talbot, John Michael. *Chant from the Hermitage.* Portland: Oregon Catholic Press. A recording of music from these collections is also available from the publisher.

Waddell, Chrysogonus. *Psalms for the Advent Season.* World Library Publications.

Willicock, Christopher. *Psalms for the Journey.* Collegeville, Minn.: Liturgical Press, 1991. Twelve responsorial psalms for cantor or choir and congregation.

Most responsorial settings use a refrain sung by a congregation, or antiphon, interspersed with the singing of the *literal* psalm text by a cantor or choir. Some, however, use a refrain sung by a congregation interspersed with an *adapted* psalm text sung by a cantor or choir. This form has become particularly popular in recent years, with hundreds of folklike psalm settings emerging from Roman Catholic congregations, following the Second Vatican Council. Roman Catholic publishers, such as GIA Publications, Oregon Catholic Press, and World Library Publications, offered hundreds of published psalm settings for cantor and congregation. Their published hymnals also include substantial sections of psalmody, most often with a simple, folklike refrain or antiphon for congregation, with adapted psalm text set for soloist (and guitar, keyboard, or small instrumental ensemble).

BIBLIOGRAPHY

Catholic Community Hymnal. Chicago: GIA Publications, 1999. See nos. 19-48.

The Collegeville Hymnal. Collegeville, Minn.: Liturgical Press, 1990. Nos. 104-160.

Flor y canto. Portland: Oregon Catholic Press, 1989. Pp. 494-579 (musical refrains only).

Gather Comprehensive. Chicago: GIA Publications, 1994. Nos. 18-152.

Glory and Praise. Portland: Oregon Catholic Press, 1997. Pp. 167-285.

One Faith, Una Voz. Portland: Oregon Catholic Press. Includes extensive bilingual responsorial psalms.

Ritual Song. Chicago: GIA Publications, 1996. Nos. 28-200.

Worship: A Hymnal and Service Book for Roman Catholics. 3rd ed. Chicago: GIA Publications, 1998. See nos. 24-100 for settings of the majority of psalms, with an antiphon, psalm tone, and Gelineau-style tone.

Musicians need access to the music leader's editions of these hymnals for complete musical accompaniments.

Recorded Examples

Haugen, Marty. *Come, Let Us Sing for Joy.* Chicago: GIA Publications, 2000. Includes eleven responsorial psalms for cantor and congregation in a folk liturgical style.

Sing Out! A Children's Psalter CD. World Library Publications.

For suggestions about effective leadership of responsorial psalmody, see Kathleen Harmon, *The Ministry of Cantors* (Collegeville, Minn.: Liturgical Press, 2004).

Metrical Psalmody

Metrical psalms feature poetic reworkings of the biblical text that provide regular patterns of stressed and unstressed syllables so that the Psalms can be sung to hymn tunes. Some metrical psalms also feature rhyme.

The advantage of metrical psalmody is the accessibility of musical settings, an advantage that was central to the sixteenth-century Protestant Reformers. Metrical psalmody was promoted by Martin Luther "so that the Word of God even by means of song might live among the people."[112] John Calvin, who restricted church music to metrical psalmody for the congregation, contended that "the Psalms can stimulate us to raise our hearts to God and arouse us to an ardor in invoking as well as exalting with praises the glory of his name."[113] As Emily Brink concludes, "the great strength of metrical song is the accessibility and memorable quality of patterned texts and tunes to a large gathering of untrained singers."[114]

Metrical psalmody was the exclusive form of church music for early Reformed and Presbyterian congregations, with distinct traditions of Genevan and Scottish psalmody. The Puritans sang psalms as they founded new communities in what became the United States, taking with them the *Ainsworth Psalter* from Europe and publishing *The Bay Psalter* as one of the most prominent early American publications. Isaac Watts began his work as a text writer by writing numerous metrical psalm settings. Later, he expanded these to include explicitly christological references. "Jesus Shall Reign Where'er the Sun," for example, is his metrical setting of Psalm 72, but with explicit naming of Jesus as the king referenced in the psalm. Watts's psalmody influenced nearly every subsequent English-language hymnal, and was particularly significant in shaping the musical repertoire of many African American denominations in the United States.[115]

---

112. *D. Martin Luthers Werke: Kritische Gesamtausgabe,* Weimarer Ausgabe: Briefe, 8:220; for an English translation see *Luther's Works: American Edition,* ed. J. Pelikan and H. T. Lehmann (St. Louis and Philadelphia, 1955-1986), 53:221.

113. "1537 Articles for the Organization of the Church," in *Joannis Calvini Opera Selecta,* ed. Peter Barth, Wilhelm Niesel, and Dora Scheuner, 5 vols. (Munich: Chr. Kaiser, 1926-1952), 1:375; for an English translation see *Calvin: Theological Treatises,* trans. J. K. S. Reid, LCC 22 (Philadelphia: Westminster, 1954), 53.

114. Emily R. Brink, "Metrical Psalmody: A Tale of Two Traditions," *Reformed Liturgy and Music* 23, no. 1 (1989): 3. For an orientation to the tunes and text of historical metrical psalms, see Paul Westermeyer, *Let the People Sing: Hymn Tunes in Perspective* (Chicago: GIA Publications, 2005), 83-122; Erik Routley, *A Panorama of Christian Hymnody,* ed. Paul A. Richardson (Chicago: GIA Publications, 2005), 13-38; and John D. Witvliet, "The Spirituality of the Psalter in Calvin's Geneva," in *Worship Seeking Understanding,* 203-30.

115. Gilbert I. Bond, "Psalms in a Contemporary African American Church," in *Psalms in Community: Jewish and Christian Textual, Liturgical, and Artistic Traditions,* ed. Harold W. Attridge and Margot E. Fassler (Atlanta: Society of Biblical Literature, 2003), 313-23.

Metrical psalmody has also been practiced by several other Christian traditions. In the late nineteenth century C. P. Jones, an early African American Pentecostal Holiness bishop, produced several metrical psalms for use by his congregation in Jackson, Mississippi. In the 1970s, several renewal groups began to produce metrical psalms that could be sung to a variety of musical idioms shaped by more popular music. The Iona community has produced a particularly influential collection of metrical psalms. Recent work has called for new inclusion of metrical psalmody as a form of congregational participation in Roman Catholic worship.[116]

Metrical psalms vary widely in how closely they correspond with and parallel the biblical text.[117] Some closely follow the logic, script, imagery, and even the parallelism of the psalm text, while others exercise great freedom in rearranging the basic ideas of a given text. Some (especially settings of longer psalms) omit several ideas, images, or petitions from a psalm, while others "pad" the psalm text with additional images or insights to fill out the desired meter.

The choice of meter is especially important when setting a psalm. The meter of a text can change the entire feel of the text, with some meters conveying strength and vigor (especially those that begin each line with an accented syllable) and others conveying a more introspective or narrative feel.[118] In contrast with the English and Scottish traditions of psalmody, in which nearly all psalms were set in a ballad-like Common Meter (8/6/8/6), the Genevan Psalter used 110 different meters to set 150 psalms!

Some well-known hymns are clearly inspired by specific psalms, but are sufficiently independent of the psalm so that they are usually categorized not as metrical psalms but as hymns:

- "A Mighty Fortress Is Our God" (Martin Luther's hymn based on Ps 46)
- "O God, Our Help in Ages Past" (Isaac Watts's hymn based on Ps 90)
- "Praise, My Soul, the King of Heaven" (based on Ps 103)
- "O Worship the King" (based on Ps 104)

116. See Christoph Tietze, *Hymn Introits for the Liturgical Year: The Origin and Development of the Latin Texts* (Chicago: Hillenbrand Books, 2005), 100-119.

117. Henrietta Ten Harmsel, "Versifying the Psalms for Singing," *Reformed Worship* 4 (June 1987): 14-15.

118. Austin C. Lovelace, *The Anatomy of Hymnody* (Chicago: GIA Publications, 1965), 63. Lovelace also adds brief instructive comments on less common accent patterns and various rhyme schemes.

Congregations (and hymnal editors) would do well to clearly identify the connection between the hymn and the biblical psalm.

Metrical psalmody continues to be the exclusive form of church music for some Presbyterian denominations (e.g., the Reformed Presbyterian Church), remains prominent in the church music of others (e.g., Orthodox Presbyterian), and has witnessed renewed attention in several others (e.g., Presbyterian Church, USA). Numerous recent publications signal a modest resurgence of published metrical psalmody. Many recently published texts and tunes may well prove to be among the most accessible and creative ever produced, though their influence depends on the intentionality of congregations.[119]

One disadvantage of metrical psalmody is that worshipers are singing an adaptation of the text (some of which depart rather significantly from the text), rather than the psalm itself.

BIBLIOGRAPHY

Denominational Hymnals

Book of Praise. Quebec: Presbyterian Church of Canada, 1997. The denominational hymnal of the Presbyterian Church of Canada. Includes 108 metrical psalm settings.

Book of Praise: Anglo-Genevan Psalter. Winnipeg: Premier Printing, 1984. The denominational Psalter of the Canadian Reformed Church. English-language metrical settings of all 150 psalms for use with Genevan tunes.

The Book of Psalms for Singing. Pittsburgh: Board of Education and Publication, Reformed Presbyterian Church of North America, 1973. The denominational Psalter of the Reformed Presbyterian Church of North America.

Praise! Psalms, Hymns, and Songs for Christian Worship. Praise Trust, 2000. Includes metrical settings of each psalm, with multiple settings of select psalms.

119. See Darryl G. Hart, "In the Shadow of Calvin and Watts: Twentieth-Century American Presbyterians and Their Hymnals," in *Singing the Lord's Song in a Strange Land: Hymnody in the History of North American Protestantism,* ed. Edith L. Blumhofer and Mark A. Noll (Tuscaloosa: University of Alabama Press, 2004), 92-121; Emily R. Brink and John D. Witvliet, "Contemporary Developments in Music in Reformed Churches Worldwide," in *Christian Worship in Reformed Churches Past and Present,* ed. Lukas Vischer (Grand Rapids: Eerdmans, 2003), 324-47. This article includes a brief list of metrical Psalters currently in use in the Netherlands, Hungary, Switzerland, Scotland, and Japan.

Presbyterian Hymnal. Louisville: Westminster John Knox, 1990. The denominational hymnal of the Presbyterian Church, USA. Selections 158-258 feature settings of psalms in multiple formats (metrical, chant, responsorial), but with a predominance of metrical. The same volume is published for ecumenical use under the title *Hymns, Psalms, and Spiritual Songs* (Westminster John Knox, 1990).

Psalter Hymnal. Grand Rapids: CRC Publications, 1987. The denominational hymnal of the Christian Reformed Church in North America. The collection begins with metrical settings of all 150 psalms, and includes several dozen additional metrical psalms scattered throughout the thematic sections of the book.

Rejoice in the Lord. Grand Rapids: Eerdmans, 1985. A denominational hymnal for the Reformed Church of America. Selections 81-143 include metrical settings of roughly one-third of the biblical psalms.

Trinity Hymnal. Atlanta: Great Commission Publications, 1990. The hymnal of the Presbyterian Church of America and Orthodox Presbyterian Church. Includes several metrical psalm settings scattered throughout the thematically organized sections of the hymnal.

Trinity Psalter. Presbyterian Church in America, 1994. Words-only metrical settings of all 150 psalms, with suggestions for use with familiar hymn tunes. Both a text-only edition and a music edition are available from Crown and Covenant Publications.

Crown and Covenant Publications also distributes the Psalters from the Reformed Presbyterian Church in Japan, the Free Church of Scotland, the Presbyterian Church of Eastern Australia, and the Irish Reformed Church.

Single-Author Collections

Anderson, Fred R. *Singing Psalms of Joy and Praise.* Philadelphia: Westminster, 1986. Includes 53 metrical psalms, along with suggested tunes, and brief prayers that correspond with each psalm.

Bell, John. *Psalms of David and Songs of Mary.* Chicago: GIA Publications, 1993. Includes settings of 7 psalms. A recording of music from this collection is also available from GIA Publications.

———. *Psalms of Patience, Protest, and Praise.* Chicago: GIA Publications, 1993. A recording of music from this collection is also available from GIA Publications.

Bringle, Mary Louise. *Joy and Wonder, Love and Longing.* Chicago: GIA Publications, 2002. Includes metrical settings of Psalm 42.

Daw, Carl P., Jr. *New Psalms, Hymns, and Spiritual Songs*. Carol Stream, Ill.: Hope Publishing, 1996.

Duck, Ruth C. *Circles of Care*. Cleveland: Pilgrim Press, 1998. See pp. 1-4 for settings of Psalms 8, 23, 40, and 90.

Dudley-Smith, Timothy. *A House of Praise: Collected Hymns, 1961-2001*. New York: Oxford University Press; Carol Stream, Ill.: Hope Publishing, 2003. Includes 45 metrical psalms (pp. 131-76).

Edwards, Rusty. *As Sunshine to a Garden*. Minneapolis: Augsburg Fortress, 1999. Includes paraphrases of Psalms 23, 27, 30, 43, 47, 51, 62, 65, 66, 121, 122, 139, and 149.

Grindal, Gracia. *We Are One in Christ*. Kingston, N.Y.: Selah Publishing, 1996. Includes a section of 12 psalms.

Idle, Christopher. *Light upon the River*. London: St. Matthias Press, 1998. Includes over 60 metrical psalms (pp. 201-64).

Kaan, Fred. *The Only Earth We Know: Hymn Texts by Fred Kaan*. Carol Stream, Ill.: Stainer and Bell, 1999. See pp. 86-90 for settings of Psalms 8, 23, 92, and 130.

Leach, Richard. *Memory, Take the Hand of Hope*. Kingston, N.Y.: Selah Publishing, 2000. Includes a short section of psalm paraphrases.

―――. *Over the Waves of Words*. Kingston, N.Y.: Selah Publishing, 1996. Includes a short section with paraphrases of Psalms 1, 8, 137, and 150.

Morgan, Michael. *Psalter for Christian Worship*. Louisville: Columbia Theological Seminary, Witherspoon Press, and the Office of Theology and Worship, Presbyterian Church, USA, 1999.

Perry, Michael. *Singing to God*. Carol Stream, Ill.: Hope Publishing, 1995. Includes approximately 60 psalm paraphrases.

Quinn, James. *Praise for All Seasons: The Hymns of James Quinn, S.J.* Kingston, N.Y.: Selah Publishing, 1994.

Stuempfle, Herman, Jr. *Redeeming the Time*. Chicago: GIA Publications, 1997. Includes paraphrases of 5 psalms: 31, 130, 138, 139, and 144.

Vajda, Jaroslav J. *Sing Peace, Sing Gift of Peace*. Saint Louis: Concordia, 2003. Includes paraphrases of Psalms 23, 46, 93, 111, 130, and 133.

Webber, Christopher L. *A New Metrical Psalter*. New York: Church Hymnal Corporation, 1986.

Historical

Kimbrough, S. T., Jr., and Oliver A. Beckerlegge, eds. *The Unpublished Poetry of Charles Wesley*. Vol. 2, *The Hymns and Poems on Holy Scripture*. Nashville: Kingswood Books, 1990. See pp. 441-51 for psalm-based examples.

> *The Songs and Hymns of Isaac Watts.* Reprinted by Soli Deo Gloria Publications, 1997.

See also the Hymn Society in the United States and Canada for facsimile editions of *The Bay Psalm Book* (1640) and Henry Ainsworth's *Psalter* (used in the Plymouth Colony).

Recorded Examples

> *Korean Psalter and CD Set.* Twenty CDs from the Korean *Book of Psalms for Singing.* Available through Crown and Covenant Publications.
>
> *Music of the Genevan Psalter.* H. Henry Meeter Center for Calvin Studies at Calvin College and Calvin Theological Seminary. Available at www.calvin.edu/worship/psalms.
>
> *Psalms.* Music of the Genevan Psalter recorded by the Japan Bach Collegium, Masaakoi Susuki, conductor. Available at www.calvin.edu/worship/psalms.
>
> *Psalms of the Trinity Psalter.* 2 vols. Savannah, Ga.: IPC Press, 1999. Scottish Festival Singers, Ian McCrorie, director. Available through Gothic Records.
>
> *Scottish Metrical Psalms.* Northern Presbytery Choir, Reformed Presbyterian Church of Ireland, conducted by Kathleen R. Wright. 5 CDs. Available through Crown and Covenant Publications.

Crown and Covenant Publications also lists over a dozen other recordings of metrical psalms by individual choirs and artists.

Psalm-Based Solo and Choral Anthems

There are literally thousands of choral and solo anthems on texts from the Psalms, including famous examples from George Frideric Handel's *Messiah* ("Lift Up Your Heads," based on Ps 24) and Johannes Brahms's *A German Requiem* ("How Lovely Are Your Dwellings," based on Ps 84). The catalogue of nearly every publisher of sacred and liturgical music includes many selections based on particular psalms, with dozens of new psalm settings published every year.

Many psalm settings for solo voice or choir are written in what musicians call a "through-composed" form. That means that unique music is written for every phrase in the entire psalm, without the repetition of a melody as in a hymn or responsorial setting of the psalm. Through-composed settings are almost impossible for effective congregational singing, because congregational singing relies on the use of repeated melodies (as in the repetition of melodies in each stanza of a hymn) or refrains (as in responsorial psalmody). But they are very effective for soloists or choirs, given their capacity to rehearse the nuances of more complex music.

BIBLIOGRAPHY

Printed Resources

To locate solo and choral works based on individual psalms, consult:

> Laster, James. *Catalogue of Choral Music Arranged in Biblical Order.* 2nd ed. Vol. 1, plus supplement. Lanham, Md.: Scarecrow Press, 1996.
> ———. *Catalogue of Vocal Solos and Duets Arranged in Biblical Order.* Lanham, Md.: Scarecrow Press, 1984.

Several publishers also offer online scriptural indices for their music.

Recordings

Several choral and vocal solo recordings include psalm-based selections. For a sampling of recordings devoted exclusively to musical settings of the Psalms, see:

> *Goostly Psalmes: Anglo-American Psalmody from 1550-1800.* Paul Hillier, conductor. Harmonia Mundi, 1996.
> *Make a Joyful Noise: American Psalmody.* Ron Jeffers, conductor. New World Records, 1996.
> *Psalms.* Turtle Creek Chorale. 1999.

The Psalms in Contemporary and Emerging Worship, Psalm-Based Scripture Songs, and the Psalms in Popular Music Idioms

The majority of published resources for using the Psalms in worship were developed for what many now think of as "traditional" or "liturgical" worship — though some of them use a folk or jazz musical idiom that is associated with "contemporary" worship. They present a rich repository of pastoral, homiletical, and artistic wisdom, and continue to be used by millions of Christians each week.

Yet many congregations in contemporary or emerging worship traditions may not perceive the potential of this material for their own learning or use. As hundreds of congregations have embraced a variety of newer approaches to worship, many have set aside any psalm-based music or liturgical texts. When they replaced the organ with the praise team and the hymnal with the media projector, they also set aside the use of the Psalms.

Yet, the Psalms remain one of the richest sources for inspiration, instruction, and use in worship. In fact, the three largest streams of influence behind various approaches to contemporary or emerging worship each have significant reasons to embrace psalmody.

- Seeker-sensitive worship, eager to make worship relevant to a particular cultural context for the purpose of evangelism, can find in the Psalter a map of the whole range of human experience. The Psalms can be a powerful way of identifying with the experience of all kinds of people who do not (yet) love God, attend worship, or bother with church.
- Charismatic worship, eager to experience intimacy with God in prayer and worship, can find in the Psalter not only psalm verses that make good praise choruses, but also entire texts that demonstrate God's faithfulness.
- Emerging-church worship, eager to recover a sense of mystery in worship and personal authenticity and intimacy in community, can hardly find anywhere else such evocative and challenging images and metaphors.

Many of these possibilities have been recently explored in writings on the Psalms in *Worship Leader* magazine and other recent publications.[120] In contemporary and emerging congregations, the easiest way to incorporate a psalm might simply be for a worship leader to read the text, perhaps over a simple musical accompaniment by a guitar or band. But once the pastoral and creative possibilities of the Psalter are discovered, there is no end to the creative potential for the use of psalms in worship. In fact, each type of use described in this volume — from choral

120. See articles by Mark Roberts, who is also the author of *No Holds Barred: Wrestling with God in Prayer* (Colorado Springs: Waterbrook Press, 2005), which is closely based on the Psalms. Mark's work has been commended and cited by a wide range of influential songwriters and contemporary worship leaders, including Matt Redman and Andy Park.

reading to responsorial psalmody, from metrical psalmody to chanting — has very possible analogues in contemporary and emerging idioms.

The best place to begin is with the already extant body of Scripture songs based on the Psalms. Over the past thirty years the biblical psalms have significantly shaped the development of a variety of contemporary song forms, including the "praise and worship" chorus and other worship songs based on various forms of popular music in rock, folk, country, and jazz musical idioms.[121] In fact, the CCLI licensing company has administered the copyright to over 3,500 songs based on the Psalms. A significant percentage of these songs are based directly on single verses or memorable images from the Psalms (e.g., "As the Deer," "We Bow Down," and "Shout to the Lord"). These songs have done much to make selected verses of the Psalms well known and loved.

A desideratum for future composition would be setting larger portions of psalm texts for reasons described above. The use of psalms versicles in contemporary Scripture songs finds its closest historical precedent in the versicles used at transition points in the medieval mass. This is not bad in itself. It is only incomplete unless complemented by musical settings of larger portions of the Psalms, if not the entire poems themselves. As the growing size of the following recording list suggests, new energy is being given to revitalizing the inclusion of whole psalm texts in the repertoire of contemporary and emerging worship.

One of the simplest ways to achieve this is to pair short choruses based on a single verse of a psalm with the reading of the entire psalm (which results in another type of responsorial psalmody, as described above). For example, Darlene Zschech's "Shout to the Lord" might be paired with a reading of Psalm 65.[122] Or Martin Nystrom's "As the Deer" might be paired with a reading of Psalm 42, the source of its primary imagery. As these songs move from being considered "contemporary" to more traditional, no doubt new compositions will emerge, also based on verses or images from particular psalm texts.

Other contemporary and popular songwriters have begun to write rhapsody-like songs that mirror the structure of specific psalms or to adapt metrical psalms to music of a contemporary idiom. The leading ex-

121. For more on this theme, see Greg Scheer, "Singing the Psalms in Modern Worship," www.calvin.edu/worship, and Ron Rienstra, "Singing, Saying, Preaching, Praying: Using the Psalms in Contemporary Worship," *Reformed Worship* 60 (June 2001): 42-43 — available at www.reformedworship.org.

122. *Sing! A New Creation* (Grand Rapids: Faith Alive, 2002), hymn 222.

ample of an individual text is likely U2's setting of Psalm 40, entitled "40" (see the recording "Under the Blood Red Sky"). Bono, in fact, is a leading spokesperson for the value of the Psalms in contemporary culture.[123]

A number of new recordings in "contemporary" rock or folk-rock style have been produced in the last few years, many by individual congregations or local recording companies.

BIBLIOGRAPHY

Barnard, Shane, and Shane Everett. *Psalms.* Franklin, Tenn.: Inpop Records, 2002. www.inpop.com and www.waitingroomministries.com.

Becker, Margaret, and David Edwards. *Psalms: Faithfully Yours.* West Monroe, La.: Select Artist Group/Here to Him Music, 2004.

Brenner, Scott. *King of Glory: Worship from the Book of Psalms.* Franklin, Tenn.: MMV Scott Brenner Music. www.scottbrenner.org.

Celtic Psalms: Featuring the Praise and Worship of Eden's Bridge. Brentwood, Tenn.: StraightWay Music (a division of EMI Christian Music Group), 1997.

Field, Paul. *Make a Joyful Noise: Psalms for a New Generation.* Eastbourne, England: ICC Studios, 2003. www.iccrecords.com (2 CD set).

Graham Kendrick Psalm Collection, The. Croydon, England: Make Way Music, 2002. www.makewaymusic.com.

Moss, Brian. *Prayerbook No. 1: New Songs Inspired by the Psalms.* 150 Records, 2005.

Psalms: Series with Kent Henry. 2 vols. Chesterfield, Mo.: Kent Henry Ministries, 2000-2001. www.kenthenry.com.

Psalms and Hymns: Praying the Bible with Wesley Campbell. Vol. 1. Produced by Stephen Mullin for YB4 Productions. Kelowna, B.C., Canada: Revival Now! Resources Inc. www.revivalnow.com.

Sing unto the Lord: The Psalms of David for Daily Living. Brentwood, Tenn.: MMV Martingate Music, LLC. www.martingalemusic.com. Distributed by CBD. A collaboration of twelve songwriters.

Sojourner, *These Things I Remember.* Produced by Mike Cosper, coproduced by Eddy Morris. Louisville: Sojourn Community, 2005. www.sojourn community.com.

Sword of the Spirit: The Psalm Series. Chesterfield, Mo.: Kent Henry, 1999. www.kenthenrymin.org.

123. See Bono, introduction to *The Book of Psalms* (New York: Grove, 1999), and discussion in Steve Stockman, *Walk On: The Spiritual Journey of U2,* rev. ed. (Lake Mary, Fla.: Relevant Books, 2005), 130-32, 169-70.

Talbot, John Michael. *Songs for Worship.* Vols. 1-2. Navarre Corporation, 1992. Several other of John Michael Talbot's recordings also include songs based on the Psalms.

New publications and recordings in these genres appear almost weekly.

Basis for Improvised Prayer

The Psalms can also be well used as the basis for newly prepared or extemporaneous prayers.[124] This can happen in any number of ways:

- the use of a psalm paraphrase that is itself a prayer (see list of psalm paraphrases above)
- the adaptation of a psalm into a prayer
- the use of a key verse from the psalm of the week[125]
- the intentional of pervasively scriptural language in prayers[126]

The following example is based on Psalm 121:

No matter where we are, where we are going, or what we are doing,
we know that we find our help in you, our Lord.
You are the creator and sustainer of all
that has been made and will be made.
And yet, the immensity of creation does not distract you
from caring personally for every person in it.
We know that is true of your care for us too!
You do not daydream or become weary in that care.
We thank you that you not only watch over us with diligence
but that you will guide us so that we will not fall —
so that we won't even stumble.
Whether we are awake or asleep, you are there,

---

124. For a historical example of this, see Peter Martyr Vermigli, *Sacred Prayers,* trans. and ed. John Patrick Donnelly, S.J. (Kirksville, Mo.: Sixteenth Century Journal Publishers, 1996).

125. Wallace, *Words to God,* 128; *The Worship Sourcebook* (Grand Rapids: Faith Alive/ Baker Books, 2004).

126. H. O. Old models prayers based on psalm adaptations. See "The Psalms as Prayer," in *Leading in Prayer: A Workbook for Worship* (Grand Rapids: Eerdmans, 1995), and "Praying the Psalms," in *Praying with the Bible* (Louisville: Geneva Press, 1984).

sheltering and protecting us from all that would hurt us.
We know that you watch over all our living —
you have in the past, and we know you are now.
Your promise holds for the future and for eternity,
and we praise and thank you for that. Amen.[127]

It is also possible that the structural analysis of a psalm (see analysis above) might suggest ways of using the Psalms as a guide to structure extemporaneous prayer. Just as the Song of Mary (Luke 1) improvises on the Song of Hannah (1 Sam 2), so too worshipers today can use the Psalms as the basis for improvising our own prayers (see further suggestions below). Consider using Psalm 51, for example, as the basis for improvising a prayer of confession, as follows.

Leader 1:	Psalm 51:1-6: "Have mercy on me . . ."
Leader 2:	Extemporaneous Prayer of Confession
Leader 1:	Psalm 51:7-12: "Cleanse me . . . create in me a pure heart . . ."
Leader 2:	Extemporaneous Prayer for Renewal
Leader 1:	Psalm 51:13-19: "Then I will teach transgressors your ways."
Leader 2:	Extemporaneous Prayer of Dedication

Or, consider taking an entire worship service, perhaps a midweek prayer service or Thanksgiving Day service, to "pray through" Psalm 33.[128]

BIBLIOGRAPHY

Resources for Adapting the Psalms for Prayer

Dunnam, Maxie, and John David Walt, Jr. *Praying the Story: Learning Prayer from the Psalms.* Nashville: Abingdon, 2005. See pp. 89-100 for complete prayers based on adaptations of particular psalms, plus several psalm excerpts for use during prayer.

127. *The Worship Sourcebook* (Grand Rapids: Faith Alive/Baker Books, 2004), 204. Used by permission. See also Wallace, *Words to God,* 120-21.
128. See, for example, Leroy Christoffels, "In the Pit . . . Waiting: A Service Based on Psalm 40," *Reformed Worship* 34 (December 1994): 9-11. I have also benefited from sample services by Wayne Brouwer, Leroy Christoffels, Norma de waal Malefyt, and Howard Vanderwell. Several of these are available at www.reformedworship.org (search for "Psalms"), and at www.calvin.edu/worship/psalms.

Griggs, Donald L. *Praying and Teaching the Psalms*. Nashville: Abingdon, 1984.

Moore, T. M. *The Psalms for Prayer*. Grand Rapids: Baker, 2002. The complete Psalter, with psalms interspersed with suggested topics for prayers. The introduction also describes several ways of praying the Psalms: verbatim praying, paraphrase praying, guided praying, and responsive praying. This volume is particularly useful for connecting the materials in the volume in your hands with other resources in what has broadly been called the "prayer movement" among evangelical Christians.

Patterson, Ward. *Under His Wings: Psalms 1–50* and *Into His Love: Psalms 101–150*. Denver: Accent Books. A series of prayers based on individual psalms.

Stradling, Leslie E. *Praying the Psalms*. Philadelphia: Fortress, 1977. Meditations on over twenty psalms that prompt ways of praying in the light of the text.

Thompson, Marjorie. *Soul Feast: An Invitation to the Christian Spiritual Life*. Louisville: Westminster John Knox, 2005. See pp. 45-46 for suggestions for preparing prayers based on particular psalms.

In addition to complete psalm paraphrases, single verses or small portions of a given psalm can be used as refrains during prayer, such as the familiar refrain from Psalm 136 (and several other Old Testament canticles):

Give thanks to the LORD, for he is good.
God's love endures forever.

Short sections of a psalm can also be used to begin or end an otherwise extemporaneous prayer, such as:

We pray to you, O LORD;
you hear our voice in the morning;
at sunrise we offer our prayers
and wait for your answer. (from Ps 5:2-3)

Or,

May the words of our mouths
and the meditations of our hearts,

be acceptable in your sight,
O LORD, our Rock and our Redeemer. (from Ps 19:14)

Visual Imagery, Children's Books, Calligraphy

Worship leaders and planners might also look for ways that visual artists
might work to convey the meaning and significance of particular psalms.
Psalm-based images, whether gleaned from professionally printed materials or commissioned from local artists (or children), could be either
projected in some form or printed on worship folders or bulletins. As
with liturgical music, the use of published artwork requires securing
copyright permission. See especially:

> Kaai, Anneke. *The Psalms: An Artist's Impression.* Downers Grove, Ill.:
> InterVarsity, 1999. She offers abstract settings of individual psalms,
> containing over twenty four-color renderings.
> *Psalms.* Donald Jackson, artistic director and illuminator. Collegeville,
> Minn.: Liturgical Press, 2006. The second in a seven-volume series of
> full-color, page-by-page reproductions from the Saint John's Bible.

Several psalms are depicted evocatively in books suitable for children
(but instructive and inspiring for people of all ages). These books might
also suggest new possibilities for children's sermons (simply reading
these books in worship would engage children around the straightforward words of the biblical text). See the following children's books:

> Anderson, Joel. *God Knows Me!* (Psalm 139). Golden Books, 1999.
> Bluedorn, Johannah. *Bless the Lord: The 103rd Psalm* and *The Lord Builds the
> House: The 127th Psalm.* Trivium Pursuit, 2005.
> Chocheli, Niko. *The Praises: Psalm 148.* Crestwood, N.Y.: St. Vladimir's
> Seminary Press, 2000.
> *Illustrated Psalms of Praise/Salmos De Alabanza Ilustrados.* Illustrated by
> Amy Ribordy Reese. Liturgy Training Publications, 2005.
> Ladwig, Tim. *Psalm 23.* Grand Rapids: Eerdmans, 1997.
> Le Tord, Bijou. *Sing a New Song: A Book of Psalms.* Grand Rapids: Eerd-
> mans, 1997.
> Papademetriou, Dorrie. *Celebrate the Earth: Psalm 104.* Crestwood, N.Y.: St.
> Vladimir's Seminary Press, 2000.
> Webber, Christopher L., and Preston McDaniels (illustrator). *Psalms for*

Children Series. Morehouse Publishing: *Shout for Joy and Sing!: Psalm 65 for Children; Praise the Lord, My Soul: Psalm 104 for Children; The Lord Is My Shepherd: Psalm 23 for Children.*

Calligraphy is also a means of rendering the text of the Psalms memorable, instructive, and inspiring. See, for example, Timothy Botts, *The Holy Bible: Botts Illustrated Edition* (Tyndale House, 2000), or *The Book of Psalms* (Tyndale House, 1987).

Composite Collections of Psalmody

The following volumes include selections of psalms in multiple styles and formats:

El Himnario. New York: Church Publishing, 1998. A Spanish-language hymnal developed by the Episcopal Church, the United Church of Christ, and the Presbyterian Church, USA. See nos. 405-441 for several Spanish-language psalm settings in both metrical and responsorial formats.

Journeysongs. 2nd ed. Portland: Oregon Catholic Press.

Leach, Richard, and David Schaap, eds. *The Selah Psalter.* Kingston, N.Y.: Selah Publishing, 2001. See also selected examples in David Schaap, ed., *New Songs of Rejoicing* (Kingston, N.Y.: Selah Publishing, 1994).

Perry, Michael, and David Iliff, eds. *Psalms for Today.* London: Hodder and Stoughton, 1990.

Perry, Michael, David Peacock, Christopher Norton, and Chris Rolinson, eds. *Songs from the Psalms.* London: Hodder and Stoughton, 1990.

Psalm Praise. London: Falcon, 1973. Chant and metrical settings for all 150 psalms.

The Psalms in Worship: Arrangements from the Psalter for Performance and Liturgy. By Jeff Allan Wyatt and Paul M. Miller. Kansas City, Mo.: Lillenas, 1995.

Sing! a New Creation. Grand Rapids: Faith Alive, 2003. Includes over 70 psalm settings in both metrical and responsorial forms.

Tam, Angela, ed. *Hymns of Universal Praise.* Chinese Christian Literature Council, 2002. Includes 30 psalms in multiple formats, in Chinese and English.

The following recordings include settings of the Psalms in multiple styles and formats.

The Jerusalem Psalter. Hänssler, 2000. Four CDs, with psalmody from the city of Jerusalem by Catholic, Protestant, and Orthodox congregations.

Psalms for the Soul. Naxos, 2000. With the Choir of St. John's, Elora, Ontario, Noel Editon, director.

Refuge and Strength: Selections from the Psalter of the Book of Common Prayer. New York: Church Publishing. With the choir of the Church of St. Luke in the Fields, conducted by David Shuler.

Spirituality of the Psalms. The Schola Cantorum of St. Peter the Apostle; J. Michael Thompson, director. Collegeville, Minn.: Liturgical Press.

Children, Youth, and Intergenerational Worship

It also must be stressed that there is nothing about psalmody that should limit its use to adults. The Psalms offer the kind of honesty and authenticity that adolescents long for. They offer to young children a language for worship that is at once vivid, formative, and surprisingly accessible (witness the list of children's books above based on the Psalms).

Children and youth need appropriate instruction to help them engage the text more meaningfully. Importantly, this instruction is often equally needed by adults! One value of engaging children and youth in praying the Psalms is that it often gently forces congregations to offer better instruction to the whole community.

Several available resources on psalmody are specifically geared toward children, youth, or intergenerational audiences.

BIBLIOGRAPHY

Brown, Carolyn C. *Forbid Them Not: Involving Children in Sunday Worship.* 3 vols. Nashville: Abingdon, 1991. Offers suggestions for each Sunday, based on the Revised Common Lectionary, many of which involve the psalm readings.

Hawn, C. Michael. *Halle, Halle: We Sing the World Round, Songs from the World Church for Children, Youth, and Congregation.* Garland, Tex.: Choristers Guild, 1999. Includes several psalm refrains that could be used by adult, as well as children's, choirs.

Witvliet, John D. *A Child Shall Lead: Children in Worship.* Garland, Tex.: Choristers Guild, 1999.

Over 200 anthems for children's and youth choirs based on the Psalms are available from Choristers Guild (see www.choristersguild.org/catalog/).

Selecting from among These Methods

The Psalms are so varied in style, voice, and tone. It is unfortunate that most congregations and most traditions are familiar with only one form of rendering the Psalms. Ideally, a congregation would have the flexibility to move among various forms — choral reading, metrical psalmody, and simple chant, perhaps — in order to choose the form best suited to a particular text. Some texts call for exuberance, others for introspection. Some are conventional, others defy convention. In each congregation, in each cultural context, the musical or dramatic form that best suits a given psalm will vary.

This flexibility (and this volume) could encourage greater experimentation in worship. This is potentially either a very good thing or a very bad thing. Some communities suffer from years of drought when it comes to creativity. Others suffer from endless innovation. Ministry with pastoral poise requires a judicious mix of repetition and innovation, form and freedom, creativity and accountability. While creativity is a subject for an entire book in itself, let me say briefly that innovation is typically best when it is:

- piloted in a small group outside a congregation's normal worship services (perhaps with a choir or education class — and especially with the children in a congregation),
- explained (best in an educational session, but also through a congregational newsletter or worship bulletin announcement),
- modeled first (perhaps by a soloist or small vocal ensemble), then done with full participation,
- done more than once (it typically takes a while for a new form of participation to become natural), and
- limited to one innovation at a time (it is difficult for most congregations to absorb changes in too many directions at the same time).

Wise, winsome leadership is a key to helping congregations both sense the value of the Psalms and pray them with open hearts and minds.

Finding Sources

The majority of hymn and psalm collections mentioned in this survey are available from the Hymn Society in the United States and Canada

(1-800-THE-HYMN), from the Web sites of individual publishers, and through Web sites such as www.amazon.com. Most Christian resource stores or outlets carry only a small portion of these resources.

Pastoral Postscript

Though the practice of psalmody in worship can be simple and accessible, there is no denying that any call to promoting the Psalms in worship seems daunting. This is particularly true because we live in a period of biblical illiteracy. In such a time, it is tempting to restrict, rather than expand, our use of the Psalter liturgically. As one pastoral leader noted: "Only in a climate where the Bible is well-known and made a part of the community consciousness can the Psalms be used in a way that allows the faithful to integrate them fully into their spiritual life. For the Psalter is, in a manner, a summary of the Old Testament. It presupposes a knowledge of the law, of the history of Israel, of the prophets and the wisdom literature. Moreover, the Psalter occupies a central place in the understanding of the New Testament and of the person of Jesus and his function in the history of salvation."[129]

Students of this lectionary commentary will sense the same point. Studying the Psalms in the lectionary forces us to ask questions about the meaning of both the psalm texts before us and the other parts of Scripture to which they lead us.

Yet while the Psalms do require biblical literacy for rich, nuanced use, they also *promote* biblical literacy. Rather than wait for biblical literacy to return before resuscitating psalm singing, it can be pastorally wise to revitalize psalm singing in local congregations, and to do whatever education is necessary to make it successful. Patient, winsome promotion of psalm singing in contextually appropriate ways remains one of the most expedient ways to promote worship that is at once vital and faithful, both relevant and profound.

Another way to explore this theme is to admit frankly that praying the Psalms is difficult, but it is extremely rewarding. As Dietrich Bonhoeffer testified:

---

129. John Eudes Bamberber, foreword to *The Abbey Psalter: The Book of Psalms Used by the Trappist Monks of Genesee Abbey* (New York: Paulist, 1981).

In many churches the Psalms are read or sung every Sunday, or even daily, in succession. These churches have preserved a priceless treasure, for only with daily use does one appropriate this divine prayer book. When read only occasionally, these prayers are too overwhelming in design and power and tend to turn us back to more palatable fare. But whoever has begun to pray the Psalter seriously and regularly will soon give a vacation to other little devotional prayers and say: "Ah, there is not the juice, the strength, the passion, the fire which I find in the Psalter. It tastes too cold and too hard" (Luther). . . . Whenever the Psalter is abandoned, an incomparable treasure vanishes from the Christian church. With its recovery will come unsuspected power.[130]

Praying the Psalms is not easy, but — like many of life's richest experiences — the practice is well worth the effort.

One of the most fruitful ways to approach the challenge of worship leadership is to see it in terms of the rich practice of Christian hospitality.[131] The practice of hospitality is central to the Christian life and the practice of public worship. Among other practices, faithful Christian living is fundamentally about looking for ways to offer the peace of Christ to all fellow pilgrims, to embrace the stranger and the orphan, to minister to the deepest needs of each other's souls. Faithful Christian worship is, at its core, a practice of hospitality. This practice is first of all God's practice, as God welcomes us to the waters of baptism, the feast of the Lord's Supper, the nourishment of the Word, and the encouragement of the assembly. And then hospitality becomes our practice, as we greet each other in Jesus' name, pray for each other, respond together to the Word, and extend the feasting of the table into lives of joyful and obedient Christian service.

Hospitality is a practice that involves profound sensitivity to the needs of the guest, the seeker, the weak and the strong. However, the best

---

130. Bonhoeffer, *Psalms*, 25-26.

131. For more on this theme, see Reinhard Hütter, "Hospitality and Truth: The Disclosure of Practices in Worship and Doctrine," in *Practicing Theology: Beliefs and Practices in the Christian Life*, ed. Miroslav Volf and Dorothy C. Bass (Grand Rapids: Eerdmans, 2002), 220-22; Christine Pohl, *Making Room: Recovering Hospitality as a Christian Tradition* (Grand Rapids: Eerdmans, 1999), 182-83; and John Ferguson, "Hospitable Leadership of Songs for Worship," in Cornelius Plantinga, Jr., and Sue A. Rozeboom, *Discerning the Spirits: A Guide to Thinking about Christian Worship Today* (Grand Rapids: Eerdmans, 2003), 117-19.

hospitality practices attention beyond our *felt* needs to our *ultimate* needs. The exemplary host offers both water and living Water, both a warm welcome and practices that will sustain us in difficult days. And that is where the Psalms are especially crucial. The Psalms address fundamental human needs. They give voice to the whole range of human experience. They invite us in to the shared experience of believers in every time and place. The Psalms themselves are an invitation to a spiritual feast.

An ancient fourth-century church order, the *Apostolic Constitutions,* gives good instructions for all leaders of public worship: "Be a builder up, a converter, apt to teach, forbearing of evil, of a gentle mind, meek, long-suffering, ready to exhort, ready to comfort, as one of God." Only then does this ancient church order go on to speak of skill: "When you call together an assembly of the Church, it is as if you were the commander of a great ship. Set up the enterprise to be accomplished with all possible skill, charging the deacons as mariners to prepare places for the congregation as for passengers, with all due care and decency."[132]

These instructions point to hospitality as one of the key virtues of a thoughtful worship leader. Serving as a worship leader is like serving as a host for a voyage or a feast. The goal is to guide worshipers through the feast of worship — to help them feed on God's Word, to feel connected as a community, to help them participate fully in every aspect of the service, all for the glory of God. We need our most disciplined, creative, and earnest poets, pastors, preachers, educators, musicians, and artists to take up their priestly role in the Christian community and bring the Psalms to life in ways that form us for faithful and obedient service.

May God's Spirit strengthen all of us who lead God's people, and help us all to grow in grace and in our desire to worship the Lord in spirit and truth.

General Bibliography

Extensive bibliographies have been suggested earlier in the book. The following is a supplemental list of significant general sources in the history, theology, and practice of the Psalms.

132. *Ante-Nicene Fathers,* vol. 7 (Grand Rapids: Eerdmans, 1979), 421.

The Psalms in Worship

The History of Psalms in Worship

There are several hundred available volumes that probe the history of the Psalms in worship. These resources are among the most available sources, and their bibliographies will provide easy access to the vast majority of significant resources.

HISTORICAL OVERVIEWS

Attridge, Harold W., and Margot E. Fassler. *Psalms in Community: Jewish and Christian Textual, Liturgical, and Artistic Traditions.* Atlanta: Society of Biblical Literature, 2003.

Cambridge History of the Bible. 3 vols. Cambridge: Cambridge University Press, 1963, 1969, 1970.

Holladay, William. *The Psalms through Three Thousand Years.* Minneapolis: Fortress, 1993.

Lamb, J. H. *The Psalms in Christian Worship.* London: Faith Press, 1962.

Old, Hughes Oliphant. *The Reading and Preaching of the Scriptures in the Worship of the Christian Church.* 6 vols. Grand Rapids: Eerdmans, 1997-2007. Following the "Psalms" entries in Old's indices offers a close-up view of specific ways the Psalms have been preached in the history of worship.

Sheperd, Massey H. *The Psalms in Christian Worship: A Practical Guide.* Minneapolis: Augsburg, 1976.

Westermeyer, Paul. *Te Deum: The Church and Music.* Minneapolis: Fortress, 1998. See the index for references to Psalms and Psalters.

EARLY AND MEDIEVAL CHURCH

Heffernan, Thomas J., and E. Ann Matter. *The Liturgy of the Medieval Church.* Kalamazoo, Mich.: Medieval Institute Publications, 2001.

Hiley, David. *Western Plainchant: A Handbook.* Oxford: Clarendon, 1993.

McKinnon, James. *Music in Early Christian Literature.* Cambridge: Cambridge University Press, 1987. See the extensive list of references for psalmody in the index.

Stapert, Calvin R. *A New Song for an Old World: A Volume on Musical Thought in the Early Church.* Grand Rapids: Eerdmans, 2007. See especially chapter 10.

———. "Singing Psalms from Bible Times to the Protestant Reformation." In *Psalter Hymnal Handbook,* edited by Emily R. Brink and Bert Polman. Grand Rapids: CRC Publications, 1998.

REFORMATION TRADITIONS

Brink, Emily R. "Metrical Psalmody: A Tale of Two Traditions." *Reformed Liturgy and Music* 23 (Winter 1989): 3-8.

Brink, Emily R., and John D. Witvliet. "Contemporary Developments in Music in Reformed Churches Worldwide." In *Christian Worship in Reformed Churches Past and Present,* edited by Lukas Vischer, 324-47. Grand Rapids: Eerdmans, 2003.

Davies, Horton. *The Worship of the American Puritans.* Morgan, Pa.: Soli Deo Gloria Publications, 1999. See especially chapter 5.

———. *The Worship of the English Puritans.* Morgan, Pa.: Soli Deo Gloria Publications, 1997. See especially chapter 10.

Leaver, Robin A. *"Goostly Psalmes and Spirituall Songes": English and Dutch Metrical Psalms from Coverdale to Utenhove, 1535-1566.* Oxford: Clarendon, 1991. The most comprehensive scholarly study of metrical psalmody in the sixteenth century.

Patrick, Millar. *Four Centuries of Scottish Psalmody.* London: Oxford University Press, 1949.

Stackhouse, Rochele. *The Language of the Psalms in Worship.* Lanham, Md.: Scarecrow Press, 1997.

Temperley, Nicholas. *The Music of the English Parish Church.* 2 vols. Cambridge: Cambridge University Press, 1979, 2005.

Wilson, Ruth M. *Anglican Chant and Chanting in England, Scotland, and America, 1660 to 1820.* Oxford: Oxford University Press, 1997.

Theological, Literary, and Devotional Guides to the Psalms in Worship

Of the many volumes that introduce the Psalms in general, the following pay particular attention to the role and function of the Psalms in worship.

Brueggemann, Walter. *Praying the Psalms.* Winona, Minn.: Saint Mary's Press, 1982.

———. *The Psalms and the Life of Faith.* Minneapolis: Fortress, 1995.

Costen, Melva Wilson. "Liturgy: Praising God." In *Ordo: Bath, Word, Prayer, Table,* edited by Dirk G. Lange and Dwight W. Vogel. Akron, Ohio: OSL Publications, 2005.

Human, Dirk J., and Cas J. A. Vos, eds. *Psalms and Liturgy*. London: T. & T. Clark, 2004.

Jinkins, Michael. *In the House of the Lord: Inhabiting the Psalms of Lament*. Collegeville, Minn.: Liturgical Press, 1998.

Kidd, Reggie M. *With One Voice: Discovering Christ's Song in Our Worship*. Grand Rapids: Baker, 2005. See especially chapters 2-4.

Merton, Thomas. *Bread in the Wilderness*. New York: New Directions, 1953.

Peterson, Eugene. *A Long Obedience in the Same Direction: Discipleship in an Instant Society*. Downers Grove, Ill.: InterVarsity, 2000.

————. *Answering God: The Psalms as Tools for Prayer*. San Francisco: Harper and Row, 1989.

Stuhlmueller, Carroll. *The Spirituality of the Psalms*. Collegeville, Minn.: Liturgical Press, 2002.

Vos, Cas J. A. "Psalms in Liturgy." In *Theopoetry of the Psalms*. London: T. & T. Clark, 2005.

Wallace, Howard Neil. *Words to God, Word from God: The Psalms in the Prayer and Preaching of the Church*. Burlington, Vt.: Ashgate, 2005.

Ward, Rowland S. *The Psalms in Christian Worship: A Doctrinal, Historical, and Expository Guide*. Melbourne: Presbyterian Church of Eastern Australia, 1992.

Resources on the Practice of Psalmody in Worship

The following books and articles are concerned primarily with how to render the Psalms in worship.

Bourgeault, Cynthia. *Chanting the Psalms: A Practical Guide with Instructional CD*. New Seeds, 2006.

————. *Singing the Psalms: How to Chant in the Christian Contemplative Tradition*. Sounds True, 1998.

Box, Reginald, S.S.F. *Make Music to Our God: How We Sing the Psalms in Worship*. London: SPCK, 1996.

Coddaire, Louis, and Louis Weil. "The Use of the Psalter in Worship." *Worship* 52 (1978): 342-48.

Duba, Arlo. "Liberating the Psalter." *Reformed Liturgy and Music* 14, no. 4 (1980): 27.

Eaton, J. H. *The Psalms Come Alive: An Introduction to the Psalm through the Arts*. London: Mowbray, 1984.

Frost, David L. *Making the Liturgical Psalter.* Bramcote, England: Grove Books, 1981.

Hotstetter, David B. *Psalms and Prayers for Congregational Participation.* Lima, Ohio: C. S. S. Publishing, 1982.

The Hymn 33, no. 2 (April 1982). Theme issue on psalmody, with articles by Paul Westermeyer, Virginia Folkerts, Carl Schalk, Oliver C. Rupprecht, Mark Bangert, and Leslie Brandt.

Johnson, Terry L. "Restoring Psalm Singing to Our Worship." In *Give Praise to God: A Vision for Reforming Worship,* edited by Philip Graham Ryken, Derek W. H. Thomas, and L. Ligon Duncan III, 257-86. Phillipsburg, N.J.: Presbyterian and Reformed, 2003.

Lamb, J. H. "The Liturgical Use of the Psalter." *Studia Liturgica* 3 (1964): 65-77.

————. *The Psalms in Christian Worship.* London: Faith Press, 1962.

Leaver, Robin, David Mann, and David Parkes. *Ways of Singing the Psalms.* London: Collins Liturgical Publications, 1984.

Old, Hughes Oliphant. "Praying the Psalms." In *Praying with the Bible.* Louisville: Geneva Press, 1984.

————. "The Psalms as Prayer." In *Leading in Prayer: A Workbook for Worship.* Grand Rapids: Eerdmans, 1995.

————. *Worship: Reformed according to Scripture.* Louisville: Westminster John Knox, 2002. See several references to the Psalms in the index.

Pilot Study on a Liturgical Psalter. International Commission on English in the Liturgy. Washington, D.C., 1982.

Polman, Bert. "Singing the Psalms Anew." *Sing! A New Creation.* Leader's edition. Grand Rapids: Faith Alive, 2002.

The Psalter: Psalms and Canticles for Singing. Louisville: Westminster John Knox, 1993. See the introduction.

Reformed Liturgy and Music 23, no. 1 (1989). Theme issue on psalmody.

Reid, Stephen Breck. *Psalms and Practice: Worship, Virtue, and Authority.* Collegeville, Minn.: Liturgical Press, 2001. See especially part II for seven volumes on the function of the Psalms in worship.

Routley, Erik. *Musical Leadership in the Church.* Nashville: Abingdon, 1967. See especially pages 67-86.

————. "The Psalms in Today's Church." *Reformed Liturgy and Music* 14 (1980): 20-26.

Sheperd, Massey H. *The Psalms in Christian Worship: A Practical Guide.* Minneapolis: Augsburg, 1976.

"Singing the Psalms and Canticles in Corporate Worship." In *The New Century Psalter.* Cleveland: Pilgrim Press, 1999.

Williams, Kenneth E. "Ways to Sing the Psalms." *Reformed Liturgy and Music* 18, no. 1 (1984): 12-16.

Witvliet, John D. "Lament." In *Worship Seeking Understanding.* Grand Rapids: Baker Academic, 2003.

The Psalms in Eastern Orthodoxy and Eastern and Western Monasticism

These volumes often access the rich tradition of worship and use of the Psalms in both Eastern Orthodoxy and Western monasticism (note: these are two distinct topics, but the literature about them often analyzes them together).

Bradshaw, Paul. *Two Ways of Praying.* Nashville: Abingdon, 1995.

Dyer, Joseph. "The Psalms in Monastic Prayer." In *The Place of the Psalms in the Intellectual Culture of the Middle Ages,* edited by Nancy Van Deusen. Albany: State University of New York Press, 1999.

Fassler, Margot E., and Rebecca A. Baltzer. *The Divine Office in the Middle Ages: Methodology and Source Studies, Regional Developments, Hagiography.* Oxford: Oxford University Press, 2000.

Guiver, George. *Company of Voices: Daily Prayer and the People of God.* New York: Pueblo, 1988.

Lingas, Alexander. "Tradition and Renewal in Contemporary Greek Orthodox Psalmody." In *Psalms in Community: Jewish and Christian Textual, Liturgical, and Artistic Traditions,* edited by Harold W. Attridge and Margot E. Fassler. Atlanta: Society of Biblical Literature, 2003.

Manley, Johanna. *Grace for Grace: The Psalter and the Holy Fathers.* Menlo Park, Calif.: Monastery Books, 1992. See page 703 for a liturgical concordance regarding the use of the Psalms in Orthodox, Catholic, and Episcopalian liturgies.

McKinnon, James W. "The Book of Psalms, Monasticism, and the Western Liturgy." In *The Place of the Psalms in the Intellectual Culture of the Middle Ages,* edited by Nancy Van Deusen. Albany: State University of New York Press, 1999.

Reardon, Patrick Henry. *Christ in the Psalms.* Ben Lomond, Calif.: Conciliar Press, 2000.

Rouguet, A. M. *The Liturgy of the Hours.* Collegeville, Minn.: Liturgical Press, 1971.

Taft, Robert. "Christian Liturgical Psalmody: Origins, Development, Decomposition, Collapse." In *Psalms in Community: Jewish and Christian Textual, Liturgical, and Artistic Traditions,* edited by Harold W. Attridge and Margot E. Fassler. Atlanta: Society of Biblical Literature, 2003.

————. *The Liturgy of the Hours in East and West: The Origins of the Hours in East and West.* Collegeville, Minn.: Liturgical Press, 1986.

Uspensky, Nicholas. *Evening Worship in the Orthodox Church.* Translated and edited by Paul Lazor. Crestwood, N.Y.: St. Vladimir's Seminary Press, 1985.

Woolfenden, Gregory W. *Daily Liturgical Prayer: Origins and Theology.* Burlington, Vt.: Ashgate, 2004.

The Case for Exclusive Psalmody

Some denominations and congregations in the Reformed and Presbyterian traditions have maintained the practice of Calvin's Geneva, Scottish Presbyterianism, and the English and New England Puritans of singing exclusively from the Psalms. A significant number of volumes have been produced throughout the last four centuries to defend this practice. The following books offer an entry point into this literature — see their bibliographies for additional sources.

Bushell, Michael. *The Songs of Zion: A Contemporary Case for Exclusive Psalmody.* Pittsburgh: Crown and Covenant Publications, 1993.

McNaughter, John. *The Psalms in Worship.* Pittsburgh: United Presbyterian Board of Publications, 1902, 1992. Available from Still Waters Publications.

Stewart, Bruce C. *Psalm Singing Revisited: The Case for Exclusive Psalmody.* Pittsburgh: Crown and Covenant Publications, 1999.

Williamson, G. I. *The Singing of Psalms in the Worship of God.* Phillipsburg, N.J.: Presbyterian and Reformed.

General Bibliography on the Psalms

Introductions to the Psalms

These volumes provide an overall orientation to the Psalms, analyze challenges in interpreting the texts, and describe various psalm types. These volumes typically assume no scholarly background in the study of the Psalms, but they do introduce readers to the scholarly literature and themes.

Anderson, Bernard. *Out of the Depths*. 3rd ed. Louisville: Westminster John Knox, 2000.

Crenshaw, James. *The Psalms: An Introduction*. Grand Rapids: Eerdmans, 2001.

DeClaissé-Walford, Nancy L. *Introduction to the Psalms: A Song from Ancient Israel*. St. Louis: Chalice, 2004.

Hopkins, Denise Dombkowski. *Journey through the Psalms*. St. Louis: Chalice, 2002.

Interpretation. April 1992. This is a theme issue on the Psalms.

Longman, Tremper, III. *How to Read the Psalms*. Downers Grove, Ill.: InterVarsity, 1999.

Mays, James Luther. *The Lord Reigns: A Theological Handbook to the Psalms*. Louisville: Westminster John Knox, 1994.

McCann, J. Clinton, Jr. *A Theological Introduction to the Book of Psalms: The Psalms as Torah*. Nashville: Abingdon, 1993.

Miller, Patrick D. *Interpreting the Psalms*. Philadelphia: Fortress, 1986.

Murphy, Roland E. *The Psalms Are Yours*. Mahwah, N.J.: Paulist, 1993.

Pleins, J. David. *The Psalms: Songs of Tragedy, Hope, and Justice*. Maryknoll, N.Y.: Orbis, 1993.

Reid, Stephen Breck. *Listening In: A Multicultural Reading of the Psalms*. Nashville: Abingdon, 1997.

Commentaries on the Psalms

Brueggemann, Walter. *The Message of the Psalms: A Theological Commentary*. Minneapolis: Augsburg, 1984.

Davidson, Robert. *The Vitality of Worship: A Commentary on the Book of Psalms*. Grand Rapids: Eerdmans, 1998.

Kraus, H. J. *Psalms 1–59*. Minneapolis: Augsburg, 1988.

———. *Psalms 60–150*. Minneapolis: Augsburg, 1993.

Limburg, James. *Psalms*. Louisville: Westminster John Knox, 2000.

Mays, James Luther. *Psalms*. Interpretation. Louisville: Westminster John Knox, 1994.

McCann, J. Clinton, Jr. *1 and 2 Maccabees, Job, Psalms: New Interpreter's Bible*. Edited by Leander Keck. Vol. 4. Nashville: Abingdon, 1996.

NIV Study Bible. Grand Rapids: Zondervan, 2002. With notes by John Stek.

Psalms. WBC 19-21. Waco: Word, 1983. Volumes by Peter C. Craigie, Marvin E. Tate, and Leslie C. Allen.

Terrien, Samuel. *The Psalms: Strophic Structure and Theological Commentary*. Grand Rapids: Eerdmans, 2003.

Bible Study Curriculum for Congregational and Small Group Use

Here is a modest sampling of the hundreds of available curriculum materials for general education purposes within congregations. These volumes assume no scholarly background.

Futato, Mark D. *Joy Comes in the Morning: Psalms for All Seasons*. Phillipsburg, N.J.: Presbyterian and Reformed, 2004.

———. *Transformed by Praise: The Purpose and Message of the Psalms*. Phillipsburg, N.J.: Presbyterian and Reformed, 2002.

Griggs, Donald L. *Passion, Promise, and Praise: Discovering the Psalms*. The Kerygma Program, 1993.

Kaiser, Walter. *Psalms: Heart to Heart with God*. Grand Rapids: Zondervan, 1995.

Peterson, Eugene. *A Long Obedience in the Same Direction*. Downers Grove, Ill.: InterVarsity, 1996.

Rudie, Carol Veldman. *Discover God in the Psalms*. Grand Rapids: CRC Publications, 2000.

Smith, Harvey A. *Psalms: Speaking Honestly with God*. 2 vols. Grand Rapids: CRC Publications, 2002.

Vander Ark, Daniel. *Honest to God: A Study of the Psalms*. Grand Rapids: Bible Crossroads/CRC Publications, 1988.

Appendix: Some Creative Thinking about Worship Renewal

In our work at the Calvin Institute of Christian Worship, we have been privileged for the last seven years to administer a Worship Renewal Grants Program, which has awarded over 300 grants to congregations in a wide variety of denominations. As grant recipients prepare their proposals, we invite them to consider the following statement:

Worship renewal cannot be reduced to a formula or generated by a set of techniques. We invite you to prayerful consideration of the dynamics or hallmarks of worship renewal, which we continue to learn about from congregations:

- Worship renewal is not something that human ingenuity or creativity can produce or engineer, but is a gift of God's Spirit. Renewal is a gift for which we pray, rather than an accomplishment we achieve.
- Worship renewal mines the riches of Scripture and leads worshipers to deeper encounters with the message of the gospel.
- Worship renewal arises out of and leads to the full, conscious, and active participation of all worshipers — young and old, the powerless and powerful, newcomers and lifelong worshipers.
- Worship renewal leads a congregation beyond itself, to give itself away to minister to the needs of the local community and the world.
- Worship renewal happens best in healthy congregations, which are marked by honesty, integrity, unity, and pastoral concern for each worshiper.

Pastoral worship leaders who yearn for renewal begin by asking thoughtful questions about the purpose and meaning of worship before addressing the style or mechanics of worship. A worship committee, a board, pastoral staff, or worship team might begin by asking questions such as:

- How can we help our congregation to pray more honestly and deeply through the words we speak and the music that we sing together?
- How can we proclaim the gospel message more meaningfully through preaching, music, and the arts?
- How can we practice Christian hospitality in worship more intentionally?
- How can we celebrate baptism and the Lord's Supper in more profound and significant ways?
- What practices will form our congregation more richly in the contours of the Christian faith?
- How can we improve patterns of communication among worship leaders and between our leaders and all members of the congregation?

These questions will eventually lead to suggestions regarding worship practices and style, but they begin by probing deeper issues about worship.

A collaborative effort to lead a community in praying the Psalms more intentionally would speak to nearly every one of these basic questions. In working through this volume, it occurred to me that over the past seven years we have not yet received a proposal (from among over 1,500 submitted) that approached worship renewal by attempting to promote praying the Psalms. But what a good idea that could be — with or without grant funding!

Suppose, for example, that a congregation's leadership:

- chose a balanced diet of fifteen (or thirty!) psalms,
- looked for contextually appropriate musical settings for each,
- agreed to use one psalm in worship each week for six months or a year,
- featured the Psalms in sermons and educational settings, with people of all ages,
- provided resources for praying those psalms in personal and family settings,
- prayed those psalms in pastoral care settings,
- created resources for spiritual seekers that could demonstrate the power of these texts to speak to and from their situation in life,
- engaged local artists, dramatists, and songwriters in preparing creative and thoughtful ways of engaging these texts, and
- used them in any number of other ways that the congregation's leadership could come up with.

An approach to praying the Psalms need not be complicated or inaccessible. It simply needs to be intentional and pastoral.

So often, worship renewal is approached in North America in terms of programming. We add new worship services, purchase new equipment, and look for more engaging modes of preaching, technology, or singing. These efforts have their place. Yet, if history has anything to teach us, it could be much more fruitful to put our energies into forming congregations through some of the most robust scriptural resources available to us.

Contributors

Nancy R. Bowen
Associate Professor of Old Testament
Earlham School of Religion
Richmond, IN

William P. Brown
Professor of Old Testament
Columbia Theological Seminary
Decatur, GA

Walter Brueggemann
William Marcellus McPheeters Professor of Old Testament, Emeritus
Columbia Theological Seminary
Decatur, GA

Richard J. Clifford, S.J.
Dean and Professor of Old Testament
Boston College School of Theology and Ministry
Boston, MA

Nancy L. deClaissé-Walford
Professor of Old Testament and Biblical Languages
McAfee School of Theology — Mercer University
Atlanta, GA

JENNIFER S. GREEN
Adjunct Instructor in Old Testament
Columbia Theological Seminary
Decatur, GA

KARL N. JACOBSON
Assistant Professor of Religion
Augsburg College
Minneapolis, MN

ROLF A. JACOBSON
Associate Professor of Old Testament
Luther Seminary
St. Paul, MN

MELODY D. KNOWLES
Associate Professor of Hebrew Scriptures
McCormick Theological Seminary
Chicago, IL

EUNNY P. LEE
Assistant Professor of Old Testament
Princeton Theological Seminary
Princeton, NJ

JOEL M. LEMON
Assistant Professor of Old Testament
Candler School of Theology
Emory University
Atlanta, GA

JAMES LIMBURG
Professor of Old Testament, Emeritus
Luther Seminary
St. Paul, MN

J. CLINTON McCANN
Evangelical Professor of Biblical Interpretation
Eden Theological Seminary
St. Louis, MO

JAMES K. MEAD
Associate Professor of Religion
Northwestern College
Orange City, IA

CAROL A. MILES
Associate Professor of Preaching
Luther Seminary
St. Paul, MN

LUKE A. POWERY
Perry and Georgia Engle Assistant Professor of Homiletics
Princeton Theological Seminary
Princeton, NJ

STEPHEN BRECK REID
Professor of Christian Scriptures
George W. Truett Theological Seminary
Baylor University
Waco, TX

SANDRA L. RICHTER
Associate Professor of Old Testament
Asbury Theological Seminary
Wilmore, KY

CYNTHIA L. RIGBY
W. C. Brown Professor of Theology
Austin Presbyterian Theological Seminary
Austin, TX

KATHRYN L. ROBERTS
Grand Haven, MI

BRENT A. STRAWN
Associate Professor of Old Testament
Candler School of Theology
Emory University
Atlanta, GA

Contributors

BETH LANEEL TANNER
Associate Professor of Old Testament
New Brunswick Theological Seminary
New Brunswick, NJ

ROGER E. VAN HARN
Associate Pastor
Grace Christian Reformed Church
Grand Rapids, MI

RAYMOND C. VAN LEEUWEN
Professor of Biblical Studies
Eastern University
St. Davids, PA

J. ROSS WAGNER
Associate Professor of New Testament
Princeton Theological Seminary
Princeton, NJ

†GERALD H. WILSON (DECEASED 11/11/05)
Professor of Old Testament and Biblical Hebrew
Azusa Pacific University
Azusa, CA

JOHN WITVLIET
Director of the Calvin Institute of Christian Worship
Professor of Music and Worship
Calvin College and Calvin Theological Seminary
Grand Rapids, MI

CHRISTINE ROY YODER
Associate Professor of Old Testament Language, Literature, and Exegesis
Columbia Theological Seminary
Decatur, GA